Historical Roots of the Wondertale

HISTORICAL ROOTS OF THE WONDERTALE

VLADIMIR YAKOVLEVICH PROPP

Translated by Miriam Shrager, Sibelan Forrester,
and Russell Scott Valentino
Afterword by Sergei Nekliudov

INDIANA UNIVERSITY PRESS

This book is a publication of

Indiana University Press
Office of Scholarly Publishing
Herman B Wells Library
1320 East 10th Street
Bloomington, Indiana 47405 USA

https://iupress.org

First Printing 2025

Cataloging information is available
from the Library of Congress.

ISBN 978-0-253-07402-7 (hardback)
ISBN 978-0-253-07403-4 (paperback)
ISBN 978-0-253-07405-8 (ePub)
ISBN 978-0-253-07404-1 (pdf)

CONTENTS

Acknowledgments

We wish to thank Jordan Hussey-Andersen, Bethany Romashov, Chana Toth-Sewell, and Polina Vlasenko for their invaluable assistance with the extensive editing and bibliographic research that went into this volume. Sincere thanks are also due to Dan Ben-Amos, who provided much-needed encouragement; to the Andrew W. Mellon Foundation Endowment; to Indiana University's Robert F. Byrnes Russian and East European Institute; to anonymous readers for Wayne State University Press and Indiana University Press; to our remarkable editors at Indiana University Press; and to the Office of the Provost and Dean of the Faculty at Swarthmore College. This book would not have been possible without their generous support. Any infelicities (or outright errors) are, of course, our own.

Translators' Introduction

Miriam Shrager, Sibelan Forrester, and Russell Scott Valentino

The works of the renowned Soviet folklorist Vladimir Propp have helped to shape not only folklore studies but also scholarship on formulaic literature in general. Propp had a particular interest in the structure of the wondertale, or what English speakers refer to colloquially as the fairy tale: folktales that begin "Once upon a time" and often end "happily ever after." The present volume is meant for readers and scholars of folktales, for teachers of courses on folklore, and for anyone curious about the application of approaches developed by linguists and anthropologists to traditional plots in hopes of tracing them back to their origins in material and religious culture—to their historical roots.

Our translation of *Historical Roots of the Wondertale* is based on the third version of the Russian text, which was published in 1998 in Propp's *Collected Works*, in a single volume together with his earlier book *Morphology of the Folktale.*[1] This was the first instance in which *Historical Roots* functioned as a de facto second part of *Morphology.*

By publishing the two works as a single volume, the editors of this third published version were in fact fulfilling the author's wishes and original intent. As Propp states in his 1966 response to Claude Lévi-Strauss's critical review of the French translation of *Morphology*, "*Morphology* and *Historical Roots* represent, so to speak, two parts, or two volumes, of a single work—the second proceeds directly from the first, the first is the premise of the second."[2] Propp explains, moreover, that the original title of his *Morphology* was supposed to be *Morfologia skazki*—that is, *Morphology of the Tale*—but the editor replaced *tale* with *folktale* and by doing so led readers to believe that the book was concerned with general laws of the folktale rather than with the particular genre of wondertales (on which see below); he even expressed regret that he had used the word *morphology* at all and considered that he should have employed the more explicit title *Composition of the Folk Wondertale* [*narodnaia volshebnaia skazka*].[3] As the editors of the third (1998) edition rightfully point out, the original title also indirectly emphasizes the dialogic character of the work as a whole. Since *Morphology* already exists in a widely used English version (on which see below), only *Historical Roots* was still in need of translation into English. However, interested readers should keep in mind that the book was initially planned as the second part of *Morphology*.

Morphology of the Folktale, one of the world's most influential scholarly books on folklore, was first published in 1928. The book's approach to the study of folktale narrative was revolutionary for its time. Following a structural analytic framework, *Morphology* reveals the stable structure of the wondertale through its invariant functions—that is, the characters' acts and experiences as significant in the arc of the tale's action. Propp identified thirty-one invariant functions of the wondertale narrative. These need not all be present and, in fact, are almost never all present in each tale, but they always occur in the same sequence, and any of the functions may occur in any wondertale. Combined with various connective elements and a typical cast of characters (Propp also distinguishes eight basic character types, reflecting their roles in the tale), and following the invariable sequence, these functions make up the composite structure of the wondertale. Thus, the *abstraction* revealed in *Morphology* represents, according to Propp, the deep structure of the wondertale as a whole.

The method was deliberately modeled on methods routinely employed in the sciences, but here it was applied to folktale narrative for the first time. As Propp writes, "The highest goal of every science is to discover laws. Where the naive empiricist sees only disjointed facts, the empiricist-philosopher recognizes a law. I noticed a law in a small and narrow area—one type of folktale, but it occurred to me even then that the discovery of this law could also be of some general importance."[4] *Morphology*'s importance began to grow in the West after its first translation in 1958, in a publication of the Research Center in Anthropology, Folklore, and Linguistics at Indiana University.[5] The translation by Lawrence Scott and introduction by Svatava Pirkova-Jakobson were subsequently used in a second edition, revised and edited by Louis A. Wagner, with a new introduction by Alan Dundes.[6] This edition, which is still in print in English over sixty years after its first appearance, has offered scholars new ways to approach all kinds of formulaic literary and oral texts, from detective and romance novels to folk epics.

When it appeared in French translation in 1960, however, *Morphology* was criticized by scholars such as Claude Lévi-Strauss for its abstraction, formalism, and lack of distinction between form and content, which, according to Lévi-Strauss, in effect reduced all folktales to a single schema.[7] Few scholars outside the USSR knew at the time that

Morphology was only the first part of Propp's analysis of the wonder-tale. In fact, *Morphology*, which was based on Propp's dissertation, had excluded the final chapter; an expanded version of this chapter was published in 1946 as *Istoricheskie korni volshebnoi skazki,* or *The Historical Roots of the Wondertale.* In this work, Propp addresses the main task he had proposed in the introduction to *Morphology,* which was the central aim of his research: to discover the origins of the wondertale.

In *Morphology,* Propp does not engage in purely theoretical abstraction. He employs formal methods of structural analysis as preparation for turning to a historical-comparative analysis, a procedural approach he makes explicit: "Meanwhile the study of the tale [*skazka*] has been pursued for the most part only genetically, and, to a great extent, without attempts at preliminary, systematic description. We shall not speak at present about the historical study of the tale, but shall speak only about the description of it, for to discuss genetics, without special elucidation of the problem of description as it is usually treated, is completely useless. Before throwing light upon the question of the tale's origin, one must first answer the question of what the tale itself represents."[8] Propp's response to Lévi-Strauss was first published in 1966, during the Thaw period and twenty years after the publication of *Historical Roots.*[9] He responded forcefully to the criticism that he was "merely" a formalist and clarifies Lévi-Strauss's misunderstanding of his *Morphology.*

> [Lévi-Strauss's] main charge is that my work [in *Morphology*] is of a formalistic stamp and for that reason alone cannot be of any epistemological value. Lévi-Strauss has not provided a precise definition of what he means by formalism; he merely limits himself to some characteristics that he points out in passing. One of these is that the formalists study their data without reference to history. Lévi-Strauss attributed such a formalistic, ahistorical method to me too, but then, in a seeming attempt to mitigate his harsh judgment somewhat, informed the readers that I had renounced formalism and morphological analysis after I wrote my *Morphology* and devoted myself to the historical and comparative study of the relationships between oral literature (as he calls folklore) and myths, rites, and institutions. . . . When he says that I am torn between the "formalist vision" and the "obsession with historical explanations," he is simply wrong. Using the most rigorously consistent means possible, I went from the scientific description of the phenomena and facts to an explanation of their historical roots.[10]

Propp's work was an organic whole and, he emphasizes, available for anyone to see.

> If [Lévi-Strauss] had taken a look at [*Historical Roots*], he would have realized that it begins with an exposition of the theses developed in

Morphology. There the wondertale is defined not through the plot, but through composition. In fact, once the unity of the composition of the wondertale was established, I could do no less than ask myself the cause of this unity. It was clear to me from the beginning that the cause would not be found in immanent laws of form and that it should be sought in early history, or prehistory, that is, in the stage of human society studied by ethnology and ethnography. Lévi-Strauss is perfectly right when he says that morphology is sterile if it is not bound directly or indirectly to data from ethnology. For this very reason I did not abandon morphological analysis but set myself the task of searching for the historical foundations and historical roots of the system revealed by a comparative study of wondertale plots. *Morphology* and *Historical Roots* represent, so to speak, two parts, or two volumes, of a single work—the second proceeds directly from the first, the first is the premise of the second.[11]

Propp's response emphasizes his use of formal methods to find historical origins, especially where he notes, "It is inadmissible to separate formal inquiry from the historical approach and juxtapose them. On the contrary, formal analysis, that is, a careful systematic description of the material, is the first condition, the prerequisite, and the first step of historical research."[12] This approach gives his work a special kinship to historical linguistics, where linguistic analysis and comparison are always intertwined with the search for possible common origins, and where historical comparison and study can only ever be undertaken on the basis of careful structural analysis.

Indeed, *Historical Roots* continues where *Morphology* leaves off, turning from structural analysis to the question of origins: "The current work is a genetic study. Genetic research is, by its very nature, always historical, but it is nonetheless not the same thing as historical research. The designated goal of genetics is to study the origin of phenomena, while the goal of history is to study the development of these phenomena."[13] In *Morphology*, Propp approaches the folktale synchronically. He uses a structural analysis and identifies the wondertale's minimal units and "deep structure." In *Historical Roots* he moves on to use tools like those of historical linguistics and comparative ethnography. He compares the wondertale's structure to the rituals and customs of early human societies from across the world. It could be considered an overly bold move to compare the structure and elements of mostly European wondertales to elements of rituals in societies far removed from them geographically and often historically. However, thanks to his rigorous and careful methodology, which incorporates the work of ethnographers, cultural historians, and scholars of myth, religion, and more, this approach reveals important commonalities.

For Propp's comparisons, the essential aspect is the stage of social development of a given people, not necessarily the historical date. His assumptions clearly reflect the stadial model of societal development found in the work of anthropologists like Edward Burnett Tylor or syncretists like James George Frazer. He moves freely across time, geographical distance, and cultures in search of analogous structural and compositional elements in ritual and myth, to compare them with structural and compositional elements of the wondertale. Finally, Propp examines the similarities of patterns in relation not to isolated plots but to the whole structure of the wondertale.

Through structural and historical-comparative methods, Propp posits that the wondertale originated in rituals from earlier stages of societal development, during what naturalist Michael McCarthy aptly calls "the fifty thousand generations" of early humans. Patterns from these rituals were then repurposed, by the "five hundred generations" of agriculturists who followed, as myths and tales when the dimly remembered rituals were themselves no longer practiced.[14] In the process, Propp makes a series of remarkable discoveries, among which the parallel between the wondertale structure and hunter-gatherer initiation rites becomes central to his study. In both, the young hero leaves his home and travels to the "other world." There he meets a supernatural figure or a magical helper who aids him in acquiring a magical object or wisdom by testing him. After adventures, tests, and trials, the hero returns home with what he has acquired and is ready for marriage. This quick outline is just the tip of the iceberg, though. Indeed, Propp's detailed analysis and comparisons offer compelling solutions to the long unanswered question of the wondertale's origins while suggesting plausible explanations for the origins of the rituals themselves.

Historical Roots is, thus, a multifaceted work: it seeks the origins not only of wondertales but also of myths, religious practices, and common human beliefs around the world. It thereby connects the study of folklore to such disciplines as anthropology, ethnography, and the history of religion.

Some readers will disagree with the very premises of Propp's work. As a scholarly study, it relies on assumptions about what can be proved. It is also concerned with a historical-materialistic explanation of the emergence of deities in human cultures, which ignores or at least minimizes spiritual and philosophical explanations. Whether readers agree or disagree with Propp's methods or conclusions, his work is essential for anyone interested in the history of human culture. His rigorous methodology and extensive use of primary sources offer many intellectual challenges. For professional folklorists, this book is one of the fundamental works in the field, and we hope that this translation will at last enable wider access to its many treasures.

Notes on This Translation

As noted above, this translation fills an important lacuna in the study of folklore and helps to provide a more complete picture of Vladimir Propp's revolutionary contribution to the methodological analysis and understanding of folktales as a cultural production. As such, it necessarily relies upon, and in some cases diverges from, earlier translations of Propp's work into English.

Translations are always characterized by interpretive choices, and this one is no exception. Among the first issues we faced was Propp's use of the term *skazka*. As the author makes clear in his opening remarks, the subject of analysis for this study is the *volshebnaia skazka*, or wondertale. However, in his exposition, he often uses *skazka* without any attribute. This term is a possible shorthand for *narodnaia skazka*, or folktale, fairy tale, or simply tale in English. Propp, moreover, sometimes uses it in reference to origin stories in aboriginal cultures, episodes from the Egyptian *Book of the Dead*, and scenes from the *Rig Veda*. How to approach this plethora of uses for a single term is complicated by the fact that Propp's best-known work, which bears the Russian title *Morfologiia skazki*, was translated into English as *Morphology of the Folktale*, is regularly cited in that form, and as such has come to occupy a central place in global folklore studies. This title, however, rests on an interpretive move that is not often remarked upon, an assumption about what the author intended without noting it explicitly—namely, that the word *skazka* was an abbreviated version of *narodnaia skazka*, "folktale," which is not the case.

As the second part of his earlier study, *Historical Roots of the Wondertale* is explicit where *Morphology* was less so. In his introductory chapter, moreover, Propp makes clear the connection to the earlier book: "By 'wondertale' [*volshebnaia skazka*] I shall mean those tales whose structure I examined in *The Morphology of the Folktale* [*Morfologiia skazki*], a book that sets out the genre of the wondertale [*volshebnaia skazka*] with adequate precision." This fact was noted by Louis A. Wagner in his preface to the revised second edition of *Morphology*:

> The expression *narodnaja skazka* has been rendered as "folktale," *volšebnaja skazka* as "fairy tale," and the words *skazka* (noun), *skazočnyj* (adjective) simply as "tale." The chief departure from this practice is in regard to the title itself *(Morfologija skazki)*, since *a change here might have led to undue confusion.* The morphology presented by the author is, of course, a morphology of the fairy tale specifically and he is careful to make note of this fact in the Foreword and in Chapter II. *Thus the title of the work is, unfortunately, somewhat unclear.* It is evident from the text that the unqualified word *skazka* is used by Propp both in the sense of tale in general and in the sense of fairy tale, depending upon context. The reader must infer the appropriate meaning in each instance.[15]

In other words, *Morphology of the Folktale* perhaps should have been called *Morphology of the Fairy Tale* in its first English translation since that was its subject, and indeed the first edition's introduction, by Svatava Pirkova-Jakobson, opened with the clear declaration, "The subject of this study, the Russian fairy tale."[16]

Why the first edition chose to specify "folktale" in the title when everyone seems to have known that the book's subject was actually narrower and more specific is unclear. The opposite tack was taken in the 1984 translation—by Ariadna Y. Martin and Richard P. Martin—of a brief excerpt from *Historical Roots* published as part of the book *Theory and History of Folklore*. Here the translators chose to render every instance of *skazka* in the original as "wondertale" despite Propp's sometimes more expansive use of the term, noted above. Actually, Propp uses the full "wondertale" [*volshebnaia skazka*] relatively infrequently in his book—many times in the first chapter, then not at all from chapters 2 to 9, then again a few more times in chapter 10—which means that the interpretive challenge in effect multiplies in the middle. However, this also suggests that Propp's use of the term, while definitional, tends to be less important for his analysis beyond setting out its general parameters. We hope our choices about where to specify the kind of tale Propp appears to have in mind and where his use of the term is intentionally general will be clear. As recent folklore research has tended to favor *wondertale* over *fairy tale*, we have used the former term in this translation.

We reached another interpretive impasse regarding the Russian term *zmei*, which can refer to a serpent, a dragon, or an ambiguous conflation of the two. It is, of course, possible to specify the being intended in Russian, and Propp occasionally places the word *drakon* in brackets after *zmei* or combines the two words, but it is also possible to let the term *zmei* loosely cover both. As with the term *skazka*, Propp tends to do the latter. For instance, when he notes (in chap. 7, I.5) that this figure's functions are not limited to devouring or carrying away a maiden, the word appears to more closely approximate "dragon" in English usage, but when he adds, in the same sentence, "or entering her body in the form of an evil spirit and tormenting her," it seems to be more of a serpent. Then he shifts back to a dragon, which "arrives with threats, besieges the city, and demands a woman as tribute." As it is not possible to shift back and forth continually between the two in the text, we point out this ambiguity here and have included a note in chapter 7, where the concept of the serpent/dragon is the focus. Otherwise, we use the term *dragon* throughout where the text points to a composite mythological figure and *serpent* where it indicates a snakelike animal that creeps and crawls.

The Russian *tsar'* refers to a Russian monarch while *korol'* is used for Western monarchs. Often translators of Russian folktales use *tsar* in English rather than translating it as "king," to offer a more authentic sense of local context. In the current translation we use *tsar* when Propp quotes Russian tales and where the context denotes specifically a Russian monarch. However, when Propp is referring to a ruler in general or to foreign kings, we translate it as "king." Similarly, we translate *tsaritsa* as "queen"; *tsarevich*, the son of the tsar, as "prince"; and *tsarevna*, the daughter of the tsar, as "princess" so as not to overwhelm the reader with too many unfamiliar Russian monarchical terms that are not essential for Propp's project.

Translating the quotations from regional Russian tales occasionally added challenges of dialectal forms, which are often incomprehensible even to today's native speakers of Russian. For this, we relied on the capacious *Dictionary of Russian Dialects* and on the expertise and occasional intuition of historical linguists, in particular those with dialectal fieldwork experience in Russian rural areas and villages.[17]

Additional instances of terminological ambiguity are indicated in textual notes where they occur. The Library of Congress standard has been used for all words, untranslated titles, names, and toponyms except for those in common English usage.

For large canonical collections, Propp frequently references tale numbers rather than page numbers. In such cases, we have provided the abbreviation No. to avoid confusion. Thus, references to the *Narodnye russkie skazki* of A. N. Afanas'ev are indicated as "Afanas'ev, No. 123." In addition, we have provided the corresponding tale numbers—most though not all of which are identical—to the English translation by Jack V. Haney immediately following each reference to Afanas'ev, each of which is designated by the letter *H* followed by the tale number in the English edition—for example, "Afanas'ev No. 177; H177." References to the Grimm tales are noted as "Grimm, No. 123." All other references to tale collections include the date of compilation—for example, "Smirnov 1917: No. 35."

Authors introduced by Propp are presented on first appearance in the English text with their first and last names.

Finally, we must also note here the numerous citations and quotations of communist authorities that reflect the Soviet Party line (e.g., Marx, Engels, and Lenin). These quotes appear especially often in the author's introduction and sometimes in other chapters as well. They will perhaps seem strange and out of place to readers unfamiliar with the Soviet context in which Propp worked.[18] Without being able to comment on Propp's personal beliefs, we must note that in the USSR, especially in 1946 at the height of Stalinism, when *Historical Roots* was first published, it was accepted practice to insert quotes and references from the "fathers of the Party." Without these protective references, such a work would likely never have seen the light of day. Propp, moreover, was a man of his time: his heroes are always *he*, unless the subject is explicitly female. His use of the term *primitive* for aboriginal and indigenous cultures slots into Marxist theory of historical development but also echoes the attitudes of early Western anthropologists, who saw their own cultures as most advanced, indeed the vanguards of the world.

The same situation explains the book's apparent attitude toward Western ("bourgeois") scholarship. Soviet scholars were expected to criticize Western scholarship in any field, but especially in works concerned with history. Propp's work is conventional in this regard. For example, in chapter 9, section 21, Propp writes, "But [Frazer] was a bourgeois scholar, and even where he gropes toward the right path, he still cannot go beyond the thinking and beliefs of his class." Many Soviet readers would have automatically brushed off this statement as an obvious and empty nod toward the party line. In fact, Propp relies heavily on Western scholars in his work—not only Frazer but many German, British, American, and other collectors and theorists. Statements like the one above should be filtered, therefore, through an appropriate historical lens. They serve as a reminder of the perils of ideological pressure on the work of scholars in authoritarian regimes.

Author's Preface

As the work presented here is equipped with an introductory chapter, this preface is limited to a few observations of a technical nature.

This book frequently refers to tales or excerpts from tales. These excerpts should be viewed as illustrations, not as proofs. Each example points toward a more or less widespread phenomenon. All available cases should be cited for proper analysis of the phenomena, not just one or two illustrations. This, however, would require an index thicker than the book itself. The difficulty might be avoided by citing existing indexes of plot types or motifs, but the classification of folktales by plot type, and plot types by motif, utilized in such indexes is often exceedingly tentative; this book, moreover, cites tales hundreds of times, which would require hundreds of index references. All this has forced me to neglect the tradition of citing the tale type number for every plot. Readers will understand that the materials cited should be taken as examples

The same concern affects examples from the realm of tradition, rituals, religious cults, and so on. The facts cited are simply illustrations whose number could be increased or decreased at will, and the referenced illustrations could be replaced by others. In this way, the book conveys no new facts: the only new aspect is the linkage established between the facts cited, and this comprises the book's gravitational center.

I must convey one more reservation concerning the manner of exposition. Tale motifs are so tightly interconnected that as a rule no single motif can be taken in isolation. The exposition, however, must be undertaken in parts, and so the beginning of the book often refers to points that are yet to be developed while the latter half refers to what was laid out before.

The book represents a single whole and cannot be read from the middle for information about individual motifs.

Readers will find no analysis of many motifs that they have every right to expect in a work of this kind. Many things could not fit into it. The book emphasizes analysis of the fundamental and most important images and motifs of the wondertale [*volshebnaia skazka*]. One part of the project was published earlier and is not repeated here while yet another portion will perhaps appear in the future in the form of separate essays.

This work emerged within the walls of Leningrad State University, recipient of the Order of Lenin. Many of my colleagues have supported me, generously sharing their knowledge and experience. I owe a particular debt to Professor Ivan Ivanovich Tolstoi, Corresponding Member of the Academy of Sciences, who gave me invaluable suggestions with regard both to the Classical materials I have employed and to the work's general questions. I would like to express to him my deepest and most sincere gratitude

V. Ya. Propp

Historical
Roots of the
Wondertale

1

PREMISES

1. The Fundamental Question

What does it mean, concretely, to study the wondertale—how does one begin? If we limit ourselves to comparing tales with one another, we remain within a comparative framework. We wish to broaden the scope of study and find the historical basis that brought forth the wondertale. Such is the aim of this investigation of the wondertale's historical roots, which for the moment has been formulated only in the task's most general outlines.

At first glance, there might seem to be nothing new in this undertaking. There have been attempts at the historical study of folklore long before today. Russian folklore studies have an entire historical school, led by Vsevolod Miller. For example, Mikhail Speranskii notes in his work on Russian oral literature, "When we study the *bylina*, we strive to guess the historical fact that lies at its roots and, proceeding from this assumption, we demonstrate the *bylina* plot's resemblance to some known event, or set of events."[1]

Here we shall be neither *guessing* at historical facts nor demonstrating their *equivalence* with folklore. Our question is different in principle. We wish to investigate which phenomena (rather than events) in the historical past bear relations to Russian wondertales and to what degree they in fact affect and produce those tales. In other words, our goal is to find the wondertale's sources in historical reality. Studying a phenomenon's genesis is not yet studying that phenomenon's history. The study of its history cannot be carried out all at once; it is the work of many years and more than one individual—it is the work of generations and of the Marxist folklore studies taking shape in our country. Studying this genesis is the first step in such a direction and constitutes the fundamental question posed in this work.

2. The Significance of Premises

All researchers proceed from some kind of premise that precedes the beginning of their work.

As long ago as 1873, Aleksandr Veselovskii indicated the vital need to clarify one's positions first and foremost to oneself, to approach one's own method critically.[2] Taking Angelo de Gubernatis's book *Zoological Mythology* as his example, Veselovskii showed how the absence of self-scrutiny had led to false conclusions, despite all the erudition and synthesizing talent of the work's author.

It would be customary to provide here a critical sketch of the history of folktale studies. We shall not do so. The history of folktale studies has been laid out more than once, and we see no need to recapitulate the literature. If, however, we ask why to date there have been no entirely solid results that everyone accepts, we see that this is often the case precisely because authors proceed from false premises.

The so-called Mythological School began with the premise that the external similarity of two phenomena and their external analogue were evidence of a historical connection. Thus, if a hero grew not by the day but by the hour, then his rapid growth supposedly reflected the rapid growth of the sun as it rose above the horizon.[3] However, in the first place, the rising sun does not seem to grow larger to the human eye but smaller, and in the second, an analogy is not the same thing as a historical link.

One premise of the so-called Finnish school was the supposition that the forms encountered most frequently must be present in a plot's original form. Aside from the fact that the theory of plot archetypes is itself in need of proof, we shall often have occasion to notice that the most archaic forms appear in fact quite rarely and that they are often crowded out by new forms that become widely disseminated.[4]

One may point to a great many such examples, and in most cases it is not difficult to show that the premises are erroneous. One might wonder why the authors themselves did not see their mistakes, which are so clear to us. We shall not blame them for such errors—the errors were made by great scholars. In fact, it was not possible for the authors to think otherwise: their thoughts were conditioned by the period in which they lived and the class to which they belonged. In most cases they did not even pose the question of premises, and the brilliant Veselovskii, who reexamined his own premises on multiple occasions and came to new conclusions, remained a voice crying out in the wilderness.

This leads us to the conclusion that one must painstakingly verify one's premises before beginning one's research.

3. Defining the Category of the Wondertale

We wish to investigate and uncover the historical roots of the wondertale. What we mean by *historical roots* will be laid out below. Before this we must make one proviso concerning the term *wondertale*. Folktales are so rich and various that it is impossible to study the phenomenon as a whole in all its breadth and among all nations. The material addressed must be delimited, therefore, and I shall restrict it here to wondertales. This means I hold the premise that there are certain distinctive folktales that may be termed wondertales. By *wondertale* I mean those folktales whose structure I examined in *Morphology of the Folktale*, a book that sets out the genre of the wondertale with due precision.[5] The genre of tales to be studied here begins with some kind of damage or harm (a kidnapping, exile, and so on) or with a desire to acquire something (e.g., the ruler sends his son to bring back the firebird), then unfolds through the hero's departure from home and his meeting with a donor who gives him a magical device or with a magical helper who helps him find the object of his quest. After this, the wondertale features a battle with an opponent (fighting a dragon is the most important form), return, and pursuit. The composition often yields complications. As the hero is on his way home, his brothers throw him into an abyss. After he gets back home, he is subjected to trial by difficult tasks, is crowned sovereign, and marries, either in his own kingdom or in that of his father-in-law. This brief schematic exposition of the compositional spine underlies a great many plots of all kinds. The tales that reflect this schema are what we will term wondertales here, and they constitute the subject of our study.

Thus, the first premise states: there is a distinct category of folktales customarily called wondertales. These may be distinguished from other tales and studied independently. The very fact of setting them apart may prompt doubt. Does this compromise a principle of connectedness according to which the phenomenon should be studied? In the end, all the world's phenomena are connected with one another, but science always isolates the phenomena that it subjects to study. The entire point in this case is where and how the boundaries are drawn.

Although wondertales constitute a part of folklore, they are nevertheless separable from the whole. They are not the same as an arm with respect to the body or a leaf with respect to a tree. While constituting a part, they simultaneously make up something whole, and they are taken here as a whole.

Study of the wondertale's structure indicates the close interrelationship of such tales, which is so intimate that no one plot can be precisely distinguished from another. This leads to two more especially important premises. *First, no wondertale plot can be studied in isolation from others, and second, no wondertale motif can be studied outside its relationship to the whole.* In this way, the present work sets out on a fundamentally new path.[6]

Until now, studies have usually proceeded as follows: one plot or motif of some kind was selected, all possible recorded variants were collected, and then conclusions were drawn through comparison and contrast of these materials. For example, Jiří Polívka studied the formula "It smells of Russian spirit" (*russkim dukhom pakhnet*); Ludwig Radermacher the motif of being swallowed and spat out by a whale; and Walter Baumgartner the motif of selling someone to the devil ("Give me what you do not know in your home"); and so on.[7] The authors reach no conclusions—indeed, they refuse to do so.

Individual plots have been studied in the same way. Thus, Lutz Mackensen has studied the tale of the singing bone, Sven Liljeblad that of the grateful dead man, and so on.[8] There is a fair number of such studies; they have greatly advanced our knowledge of the dissemination and lives of individual plots, but they do not resolve questions of origin. Therefore, for the time being, we shall turn away completely from study of the folktale according to plot type. For us, the wondertale is something whole, and all of its plots are interlinked and mutually conditioned. This is why it is also impossible to study a motif in isolation. If Polívka had not only collected all variants of the formula "it smells of Russian spirit" but asked himself who was making this exclamation, in which settings it was uttered, to whom it was uttered, and so forth—that is, if he had studied it *in connection with the whole*—then quite possibly he would have reached a reliable conclusion. The motif can be studied only within the plot system, and plots can be studied only in their mutual interconnections with one another.

4. The Wondertale as a Superstructural Phenomenon

Such are the premises gleaned from preliminary study of the wondertale's structure. But the matter does not end here.

We stated above that authors usually proceed from premises produced by the age in which they live.

We live in the age of socialism, which has developed its own premises too, and these are the basis of our study of phenomena of spiritual culture. Unlike the premises of other ages, however, which lead the humanities to a standstill, ours has generated premises that set the humanities on the sole correct path.

The premise in question is a general one, required for studying historical phenomena: "The mode of production of material life conditions the social, political, and intellectual life process in general."[9] From this it follows quite clearly that we must find the means of production that conditioned wondertales in the past.

What, then, were these means of production? Even a cursory acquaintance allows us to conclude that capitalism, for example, is not what conditions the wondertale. This, of course, does not mean that capitalist means of production are not reflected in it. On the contrary, we find characters such as the cruel factory owner, the greedy priest, the officer-flogger (*sekun maior*), the master-oppressor, the runaway soldier, and the impoverished, drunken, and ravaged peasantry.[10] Here it must be emphasized that we are talking about wondertales, not about novelistic tales. The authentic wondertale, with winged horses, fire-breathing dragons, magical princes and princesses, and so on, is clearly not a product of capitalism. It is certainly more ancient. Without wasting time on additional remarks, we can say that the wondertale is also more ancient than feudalism. This last point will become apparent over the full course of the present study.

Here, however, we face a conundrum. It appears that the wondertale does not correspond to the means of production in which it was most widespread and lasting. The explanation for this discrepancy can also be found in Marx: "With the change of the economic foundation the entire immense superstructure is more or less rapidly transformed."[11] The words "more or less rapidly" are very important. A change in ideology does not always occur immediately after changes in the economic base. This creates a discrepancy that is extremely interesting and valuable for researchers. The discrepancy indicates that the wondertale was created on the foundations of precapitalist forms of production and social life. The nature of these forms is precisely the subject under investigation.

We should recall that it was just such a discrepancy that helped Engels shed light on the origin of the family. Quoting Lewis H. Morgan and citing Marx, in "The Origin of the Family" Engels writes, "The family, according to Morgan, is an active source. It never remains unchanged; it transitions from a lower to a higher form, from a lower stage to a higher as society develops. The systems of kinship, on the other hand, are passive. It takes them long periods of time to register the progress the family has accomplished during this time; they undergo radical changes only when the family has already been radically changed."[12] "And," Marx adds, "the exact same thing is true of political, legal, religious, and philosophical systems in general."[13] Let us add that this is likewise true of the wondertale.

Thus, the wondertale's emergence does not correspond to the material foundations of the time when it began to be recorded, at the beginning of the nineteenth century. This brings us to the following premise, formulated for now only in very general terms: the wondertale should be held up against the historical reality of the past, and only there may one uncover its roots.

This premise involves the obscure concept of *the historical past.* If we shared Vsevolod Miller's understanding of the historical past, then quite possibly we would arrive at conclusions identical to his, claiming, for example, that Dobrynia Nikitich's battle with the dragon was based in the historical reality of the baptism of Novgorod.

Therefore, we need to decipher this concept of the historical past. We must determine what exactly in this past can contribute to our explanation of the wondertale.

5. The Wondertale and Social Institutions of the Past

If we regard the wondertale as a product that arises atop a certain substructure of production, then clearly we must consider what forms of production it reflects.

Processes of production appear directly in wondertales only rarely and scantily. Agriculture plays a minor role, while hunting is reflected more extensively. We usually find plowing and sowing only at the beginning of a story. A tale's beginning is the part that most readily submits to change. Later, however, figures like archers and hunters, sometimes belonging to the tsar and sometimes free, play an important role, as do all kinds of forest animals.

However, studying the forms of production in the tale from the standpoint of its subject matter or technical features alone does not get us very far in understanding its sources. The important thing is not the technical aspects of production per se but rather the corresponding social structure. We thus arrive at an initial refinement of the concept of the historical past in relation to the wondertale. The entire exploration boils down to determining what social system allowed the creation of individual motifs of the wondertale and the wondertale as a whole.

A *social system,* however, is a very general concept. We must consider concrete manifestations of this system—its institutions, for example. Thus, we cannot compare the wondertale to a tribal system itself, but we can compare certain of its motifs with a tribal system's institutions, since these are reflected in the tale or perhaps even condition it. From this premise, we can determine that tales should be compared to social institutions of the past and that this is where we should search for their roots. This, in turn, clarifies the concept of the historical past where we must seek the origins of wondertales. For example, we see that tales contain marital customs different from those practiced today. The hero searches for a bride far from his home. This may reflect the phenomenon of exogamy: evidently, for some reason, the bride cannot come from the hero's own environment. Therefore, marital customs reflected in the wondertale should be analyzed in order to find the particular social arrangement, the phase or stage of social development, in which these marriage practices actually occurred. Furthermore, we see that the hero frequently ascends to the throne. Whose throne does the hero take? As it turns out, he does not come to occupy the throne of his father but of his father-in-law, whom he has in many cases killed. This rouses our curiosity about the forms of succession reflected in the wondertale. In other words, we proceed from the premise that wondertales have retained vestiges of now-extinct social arrangements, that these remnants must be studied, and that such study will unearth the sources of many of their motifs.

But this is not all, of course. Certainly many motifs can be explained by their reflections of past institutions, but there are also motifs that lack direct links to any institutions. Consequently, there is not enough material in this domain for comparison. Not everything can be explained by the presence of this or that institution.

6. Wondertales and Ritual

It has long been observed that the wondertale has some connection with cults and religion. Strictly speaking, a cult or religion may be considered an institution as well. However, just as the social system manifests itself in various institutions, the institution of religion also manifests itself in certain ritual activities. One cannot call every action of this sort an institution, and the connection to religion may be treated as a separate question, arising from the wondertale's connection to social institutions. Engels formulated the essence of religion very precisely in his 1878 *Anti-Dühring*:

> All religion, however, is nothing but the phantastic [*sic*] reflection in men's minds of those external forces which control their daily life, a reflection in which the terrestrial forces assume the form of supernatural forces. In the beginnings of history it was the forces of Nature which were at first so reflected. . . . But it is not long before, side by side with the forces of Nature, social forces begin to be active; forces which present themselves to man as equally extraneous and at first equally inexplicable. . . . The phantastic [*sic*] personifications, which at first only reflected the mysterious forces of Nature, at this point acquire social attributes, become representatives of the forces of history.[14]

Just as it is wrong, however, to compare tales with any social system in general, so too is it wrong to compare them with religion in general; tales should be compared against specific manifestations of religion. According to to Engels, religion reflects the forces of nature and society. This reflection can be double: it can be cognitive, represented in dogmas or doctrines and manifested in ways of explaining the universe; or it can be volitional and represented in acts and deeds that aim to influence nature and subdue it. We will refer to actions of this type as rituals and customs.

Ritual and custom are not the same thing. For example, if burial involves burning, this is a custom, not a ritual. Custom, however, is filled with ritual, and it would therefore be methodologically incorrect to separate them.

Wondertales have preserved the traces of a great many rituals and customs: the origins of numerous motifs can be explained only through comparison to rituals. For example, one tale recounts how a girl buries the bones of a cow in her garden and waters them.[15] Such a custom or ritual existed in fact. For some reason, the bones of animals were not eaten or destroyed but buried.[16] If we could show the connection of certain motifs to corresponding rituals, the origin of such motifs could be explained to some extent. We need systematic study of the connection between tales and rituals.

Such comparison can prove to be much more difficult than it seems at first glance. Tales are not chronicles. There are various forms of relationships between tales and rituals as well as various forms of connections. Let us briefly review these forms.

7. Direct Correlation between Wondertales and Ritual

The simplest case is when ritual and custom completely correlate with a tale. This is rare. Thus, bones are buried in the tale, and exactly the same thing was done in historical reality. Or: a tale relates how a king's children are locked up in an underground dungeon, kept in darkness, and fed so that no one sees, and again, in historical reality the same thing was done. Discovering such parallels is extremely important for folklorists. These correlations must necessarily be worked out, and it often turns out that a given motif derives from a particular ritual or custom, and thus its origin can be explained.

8. Resignification of Ritual through the Wondertale

As noted above, however, such a direct correlation between wondertales and ritual is not common. More frequently, we find a different relationship, a different phenomenon—one that can be termed the resignification of ritual. Here we shall use the term *resignification* (*pereosmyslenie*) when the tale replaces an element (or several elements) of a ritual that has become superfluous or incomprehensible over time with another, more comprehensible element. Resignification is thus usually connected to deformation, to formal change. Most commonly what has changed is the motivation behind the ritual, though other components may undergo change as well. For example, a tale relates how the hero sews himself into the skin of a cow or horse in order to climb out of a pit or reach the Thrice-Tenth Kingdom. Then a bird picks up the skin with the hero inside and takes it to a mountain or across a sea where he would not otherwise be able to go. How can this motif's origin be explained? The custom of sewing a dead person inside an animal's skin is well known. Does the given motif originate from this custom? A systematic study demonstrates an unquestionable connection between the two: there is complete correlation not only in external form but also in internal content, in the significance of the motif in the story's action and in the significance of the ritual in the historical past (see below, chap. 6, sec. 3), but with one exception—in wondertales, the person who sews himself inside the skin is *alive*, while in the ritual, the person sewn up is *dead*. This discrepancy demonstrates a very simple case of resignification. Sewing the dead in an animal skin was a custom that provided the deceased with the means to enter the kingdom of the dead. In wondertales it gives the hero the means to get to the Thrice-Tenth Kingdom.

The term *resignification* is convenient in that it points to the process of changes that occurred. The fact of resignifying demonstrates that certain changes have occurred in the life of the people, and these changes, in turn, led to changes in the motif. Such changes must be shown and explained on a case-by-case basis.

Here we have provided a very clear and simple case of resignification. In many cases, however, the initial source is so obscure that it may be impossible to discover it.

9. Conversion of Ritual

We should consider as a special case of resignification the preservation of all forms of a particular rite within a tale while giving it an opposite sense or meaning—a reverse treatment. Such cases in the current work will be called *conversion* (*obrashchenie*). Let us illustrate our observation with examples. There was once a custom of killing the elderly. Yet in one tale an old man identified as someone who ought to be killed is instead saved. When this custom existed, a person who spared an old man would have been ridiculed, perhaps insulted, or even punished. In the tale, however, the person who does this is treated as a hero who acted wisely. There also used to be a custom of taking a young girl as a sacrifice to the river, which guaranteed fertility. This ritual was performed at the beginning of sowing to promote crop growth. However, wondertales recount how the hero appears and rescues the maiden from a monster to whom she was brought to be eaten. In reality, in the era in which this ritual was observed, such a liberator would have been literally torn asunder as a terrible reprobate who was endangering the welfare of the people and threatening their crops. These facts demonstrate that a plot is sometimes created out of a negative attitude toward former historical reality. This last plot (or motif) could not have been created given a way of life that required sacrificing maidens. But as this manner of living fell away, a custom that was once considered holy and whose hero was the young victim marching, sometimes voluntarily, to her death became unnecessary and disgusting, and the reprobate who prevented this sacrifice now became a hero. This is a very important principle to establish, as it demonstrates that the story is created not in an evolutionary manner, as a direct reflection of reality, but by denying this reality. The story correlates to reality in an oppositional manner. This confirms the words of V. I. Lenin, who opposed the concept of evolutionary development with the concept of development as a unity of opposites: "The second [conception] *alone* furnishes the key to the 'self-movement' of everything existing; it alone furnished the key to the 'leaps,' to the 'break in continuity,' to the 'transformation into the opposite,' to the 'destruction of the old and emergence of the new.'"[17]

All these considerations and preliminary observations prompt us to advance another premise: the wondertale should be compared to rituals and customs in order to determine what motifs reach back to various rituals and what type of relationship exists between tales and rituals.

This raises a difficult point since a ritual that originally emerged as a way of battling against nature later, when rational ways of dealing with nature and its impact emerged, did not die but was instead resignified. Thus, it may happen that, after connecting the motif back to a ritual, the folklorist might find that the motif reaches back to a resignified ritual and then must explain the ritual as well. There may be cases where a ritual's original foundation is so obscured that it requires its own study. This, however, is the realm not of folklore but of ethnography. Having established the link between a tale and a ritual, folklorists are at times justified in abandoning additional study of the ritual in question, as this would take them too far afield.

Sometimes another difficulty arises. Like ceremonial life, folklore is composed of literally thousands of different details. Do we need to look for economic reasons for each one? On this score, Engels writes, "The low economic development of the prehistoric period is supplemented and also partially conditioned and even caused by false conceptions about nature. And even though economic necessity was the main driving force of the progressive knowledge of nature and becomes ever more so, it would surely be pedantic to try and find economic causes for all this primitive nonsense."[18] These words are clear enough. On this occasion, we must nevertheless add the following: if in this work we examine one and the same motif from the stage of tribal society, the stage of slavery (e.g., in ancient Egypt), antiquity, and so on (and we very often do have to conduct such comparisons), and what is more, if we establish the evolution of the motif, then we do not consider it necessary to stress every time that the motif has changed not due to evolution from within but because it entered a new historical condition. We shall try to avoid the risk not only of *pedantry* but also of *schematism*.

But let us return to ritual. As a rule, if a link between a ritual and a tale has been established, the ritual provides an explanation for the corresponding motif in the tale. In a narrow schematic approach this should always be true. In fact, however, sometimes precisely the opposite occurs. Sometimes it happens that although a tale harkens back to a ritual, the ritual is completely unclear while the tale preserves the past so fully and faithfully that the ritual or other phenomenon of the past is in fact illuminated only through the tale. In other words, there may be instances in which a tale, instead of being the *explained* phenomenon, upon closer study becomes the *explanatory* phenomenon; it can then be a source for study of the ritual. Dmitrii Zelenin writes, "The folk legends of mingled Siberian peoples served as perhaps the most important source for the reconstruction of ancient totemic beliefs."[19] Ethnographers often refer to folktales but do not always know them. This is especially true of the work of James Frazer. The grandiose construction of his *Golden Bough* relies on premises taken from tales, though from misunderstood and understudied tales. A careful study of wondertales will allow us to add a number of amendments to Frazer's work and even shake its foundations.

10. Wondertales and Myth

If, however, we consider ritual as one manifestation of religion, we cannot ignore its other manifestation—namely, myth. There is a vast amount of literature on the relationship between folktales and myth that we are completely bypassing. Our goal is not directly polemical. In most cases, the distinction is made in a purely formal way. At the starting point of our study, we still do not know what the relation of a tale to a myth is. At this point we simply propose to study the matter and incorporate myth as one possible source of tales.

The variety of existing interpretations and understandings of myth forces us here to specify this concept explicitly. In the current work a myth is understood as a story about gods or godly beings in whose reality people believe. Faith is understood here not as a psychological factor but as a historical one. Stories of Heracles closely resemble our wondertales, but Heracles was a god to whom a cult was dedicated. Our hero, on the other hand, who, like Heracles, goes to fetch golden apples, is the hero of a work of fiction. The myth and the wondertale differ in their social functions as opposed to their forms.[20] The social function of a myth is not always the same either, and it depends on a people's cultural development. Myths of nations that did not reach statehood in the course of their development are one phenomenon; myths of ancient cultures that we know—through the literature of their people—reached statehood are an entirely different one. Myth cannot be formally differentiated from tales. Tales and myths (especially the myths of primitive societies) may occasionally coincide so completely with one another that, in ethnography and folklore, such myths are often called folktales. There even used to be a certain fashion for "tales of primitive peoples" [*skazki pervobytnykh*], and many such collections appeared, both scholarly and popular. However, if we not only examine these texts but also explore their social function, we discover that most are not folktales but myths. Contemporary bourgeois folklore studies often do not take into account the great importance of these myths. They are collected but hardly studied by folklorists. For example, in Bolte and Polívka's index (1913–32), "folktales of primitive people" occupy a very modest place. Yet these myths are not just "variants of folktales" but creations of earlier stages of economic development that have not yet lost their connection with their productive base. Elements that have been resignified in modern European folktales are frequently found in these tales in their original form. In this way myths often provide the key to understanding wondertales.

Of course, some researchers do perceive this significance and discuss it, but everything stops at the level of declaration. The fundamental importance of these myths is not understood precisely because researchers adhere to a formal rather than a historical point of view. The myths are ignored as a historical phenomenon while many instances of inverse relations are observed and studied, in particular those where the folklore of "primitive" people is influenced by "civilized" people. The idea of myth's social significance has only very recently emerged in bourgeois scholarship, where a close relationship has now been acknowledged between the word, the myths, and the sacred stories of the tribe on the one hand and the social organizations and ritual, moral, and even practical actions on the other. However, there is usually no suggestion that this proviso applies to European folktales as well, as such an idea is considered too bold.

Unfortunately, however, in most cases the records of such myths are not very satisfactory, as only texts are provided and nothing more. Often researchers do not even inform the reader whether they know the language and whether they recorded directly or through an interpreter. Even in the records of such a major researcher as Franz Boas, we find texts that are undoubtedly retellings, but this is not mentioned anywhere. Yet for us the smallest details, particulars, and nuances are important; often even the tone of the story is important. An even worse scenario occurs when the natives narrate their myths in English. That is how Alfred Kroeber sometimes used to record. His collection *Gros Ventre Myths and Tales* contains fifty texts, forty-eight of which were narrated in English—something we learn only in the middle of the book in a footnote, as if it were a completely secondary and unimportant fact.[21]

As noted above, the myth has a social value. But this value is not the same in every place. The difference between the myths of antiquity and Polynesian myths is obvious to everyone. But even among people in pre-class societies, the fact and degree of this value are not the same; they cannot be thrown into one pot. In this respect, we can speak of the differences among the myths of individual countries and peoples with reference to their stages of cultural development.

The most valuable and important materials for our study have turned out to be not European and Asian, as one would have expected given their territorial proximity to Russia, but American, African, and to some extent Oceanic. Asian peoples on the whole stood at a higher cultural stage than the peoples of America and Oceania when they came into contact with Europeans who began to collect ethnographic and folklore materials among them. Furthermore, Asia is home to the most ancient cultures, a cauldron in which streams of populations moved about, mixed, and forced each other out. This continent has samples of all the cultural stages, from the almost primeval Ainu to the Chinese, who have reached the highest pinnacles of culture, and now also the socialist culture of the USSR. Therefore, Asian materials exhibit a mixing that poses a significant challenge for research. For example, the Yakuts tell a story about Ilya Muromets alongside their own most likely native Yakut myths. Vogul folklore mentions horses, which were unknown to the Voguls.[22] These examples show how easy it is to make a mistake and take something from another culture, something alien, as aboriginal. Thus, this is where the greatest danger for the folklorist lies, for it is important to study not only the phenomenon itself—that is, the text—but also the myth's relationship to the foundation from which it arose. For example, a folklorist might mistake a phenomenon that came from India for an indigenous phenomenon among primitive hunters, given that it was recorded among these hunters.

To a lesser extent this is the case in Africa. It is true that we also find there people at a very early level of development, such as the Bushmen;[23] livestock-raising people such as the Zulu; farming peoples; and people who already practice blacksmithing. Yet mutual cultural influences are less strong than in Asia. Unfortunately, African materials have sometimes been recorded not much better than American materials. Americans, in fact, live in the immediate vicinity of Native Americans whereas Africa is studied by outsiders, colonizers, and missionaries—the French, British, Dutch, and Germans—who make minimal efforts to learn the language, and if they do, it is not for the purpose of recording folklore. One of the greatest explorers of Africa, Leo Frobenius, did not know any African languages, but this did not prevent him from publishing masses of African materials without specifying how he acquired them; this fact, of course, makes us treat his data with caution.

America too is not completely free from extraneous influences, but nevertheless, American material has provided us with what is frequently lacking in materials from other continents.

Such is the significance of the myths of primitive peoples for the study of wondertales, and such are the difficulties encountered when studying them.

The myths of Greco-Roman antiquity, Babylon, Egypt, India to some extent, and China are a completely different phenomenon. We know the myths of these people not directly from their creators, the common people, but through the prism of written texts. We know them through the poems of Homer, the tragedies of Sophocles, through Virgil, Ovid, and so on. Ulrich von Wilamowitz-Moellendorff tried to deny the connection of Greek literature to folk tradition.[24] According to him, Greek literature is not suitable for the study of folk plots just as the Nibelungen works by Hebbel, Wagner, and Geibel are not suitable for studying the real Nibelungs. This view, which denies the classical myth's folk character, paves the way for reactionary theories and attitudes. For our purposes, we shall accept the genuine folk character of these myths. However, we must keep in mind that they do not appear in their pure form and thus cannot be equated with recordings of folklore directly from the people. This is more or less the case with the myths of Egypt. We do not know them firsthand either. Egyptian ideas are known to us through tombstone inscriptions, through the *Book of the Dead*, and so on. For the most part, we know only the official religion, which was cultivated by priests for political purposes and approved by the court or the nobility. But the common people may have had different ideas, different plots, so to speak, than the official cult; we know very little of the notions of these common people. Nevertheless, the myths of the peoples of ancient civilizations should be included in the research corpus. Sources of this kind, however, are *indirect* whereas the myths of pre-class societies present direct sources. The former undoubtedly *reflect* the ideas of the people but do not always *represent* them in the direct sense of the word. It is ultimately possible that Russian wondertales may provide us with more archaic material than Greek myths.

Thus, we distinguish myths that were created in pre-class societies, which we consider primary sources, and myths transmitted to us by the ruling classes of ancient civilizations, which can serve only as circumstantial proof of the existence of a certain worldview among their respective peoples.

From this premise, it follows that we must compare tales both with the myths of primitive pre-class peoples and with those of the civilizations of antiquity.

This is our last clarification of the concept of "the historical past," which has been introduced here for the comparison and study of wondertales. It should go without saying that we are not interested in particular events of this historical past—that is, what is usually meant by "history" and what the so-called historical school intended by "history."[25]

11. Wondertales and Primitive Thought

From everything above, it is clear that we are looking for roots of wondertale images and plots in the reality of the past. There are, however, images and situations in tales that clearly do not refer back to any existing reality. Among such images are, for example, the winged dragon and winged horse, the hut on chicken legs, Koshchei the Deathless, and so on.

It would be a serious error if we took up the position of pure empiricism and considered tales as a kind of chronicle. Such a mistake occurs, for instance, when scholars look for real winged dragons in prehistory and claim that wondertales have preserved a memory of them. Neither winged dragons nor huts on chicken legs ever existed. Nevertheless, they too are historical, not in and of themselves but rather in their emergence, and this is what needs to be explained.

It is clear that ritual and myth are conditioned by economic interests. If, for example, people dance to summon rain, this act obviously arises from a desire to influence nature. What is not clear is why they dance for this purpose (sometimes even with live snakes) instead of doing something else.[26] We might understand better if they poured water for this purpose (as is frequently done), since this would be an instance of sympathetic magic and nothing more. This example shows that the action does not come *directly* from economic interests but from a certain manner of *thinking* that is ultimately conditioned by the same factors as the action itself. The ritual, like the myth, is the product of a particular manner of thought. Explaining and defining these forms of thought can sometimes be quite difficult. Folklorists, moreover, must not only take this into consideration but also discover what ideas underlie certain motifs. Primitive thinking knows no abstractions; it manifests itself in actions, forms of social organization, folklore, and language. Sometimes a motif cannot be explained by any of the premises mentioned. For example, conceptions of space, time, and number, unlike those we are accustomed to, lie at the heart of some motifs. Hence, we conclude that primitive forms of thought must also be considered in order to explain the genesis of the wondertale. For now, we can only highlight this immensely complex issue, but it will form another premise for our work. We need not begin a discussion here of the existing views on primitive thought. For our purposes, thought is first and foremost a category that can also be defined historically. This frees us from the need to "interpret" myths, rites, and wondertales. The goal is not to interpret them but to find their historical sources. Myth undoubtedly has its own semantics, but there is no absolute, permanent semantics that is separate from history. In this situation, we face a great danger. It is easy to mistake *mental* reality for *objective* reality and vice versa. For example, if Baba Yaga threatens to eat the hero, this surely does not demonstrate absolute evidence of past cannibalism. The image of Yaga the people-eater might have arisen from a different source as the reflection of certain mental (and therefore also historical) but not real-life images.

12. Genetics and History

This study is a project in genetics. Genetic research, by its very nature, is always historical, but this is not the same thing as historical research. The stipulated goal of genetics is to study the origins of phenomena whereas the goal of history is to study the development of such phenomena. Genetics precedes history and paves the way for it. Nevertheless, here too we are not dealing with fixed phenomena but with processes—that is, with movement. We consider each phenomenon related to the wondertale a process. For example, when a connection is established between certain motifs and notions of death, we view death not as an abstract concept but as a process of ideas about death that is expressed in its development. Readers might therefore easily get the impression that the present work recounts the history or prehistory of individual motifs. While we sometimes analyze a process in a more or less detailed manner, this nevertheless is still not history. It also happens that a phenomenon related to a particular tale is quite clear on its own but difficult to explain as a process. Such is the case with some very early forms of social life that the wondertale preserves remarkably well (e.g., the rite of initiation). Phenomena such as these require special historical and ethnographic study, which folklorists do not always dare undertake. One obstacle may be that ethnographic analysis of such phenomena is not sufficiently developed. Therefore, historical analysis is likewise not always sufficiently deep and broad. Often it is possible only to identify an existing connection, nothing more. A degree of unevenness in historical analysis also arises from paying disproportionate attention to certain motifs. More important motifs, the "classic" cases, are considered in great detail while other less important ones are analyzed in only a cursory and schematic manner.

13. Methods and Materials

The principles outlined here seem quite simple. In practice, however, their implementation presents a considerable challenge. The difficulty lies primarily in mastering the material. Researchers have often made the mistake of limiting themselves to one plot or one culture alone, or to other arbitrarily conceived boundaries. For us, these boundaries do not exist. Such a mistake was made, for instance, by Hermann Usener, who studied the story or myth of the Deluge using materials from antiquity.[27] This does not mean it is impossible to study these topics within defined limits. But it is wrong to study their genesis only within the boundaries of a single people, as Usener does, and then offer general conclusions. Folklore is an international phenomenon. Given this fact, folklorists are in a quite disadvantageous position vis-à-vis narrower specialists in, for instance, Indology, classics, Egyptology, and so on. The latter are complete masters of these specialized areas; folklorists, by contrast, only glance into them like wandering passersby, in order to observe something for their own purposes, and move on. It is impossible to have comprehensive knowledge of all such material. Nevertheless, it is absolutely necessary to broaden the scope of folklore studies. We must risk errors, therefore, unfortunate misunderstandings, inaccuracies, and so on. All this is dangerous, but it is less dangerous than the immaculate mastery of limited material that rests upon methodologically unsound foundations. Such broadening is necessary for specialized studies as well: these must be reexamined through the lens of comparative data. There are so many preliminary works on the individual cultures of different peoples that the time has come to begin actively using this material, even if it turns out to be impossible to master it in all its breadth.

Thus, I assume from the start the standpoint that it is possible to begin research even if the material has not been completely exhausted—this too is a premise of the present study. I take this position not out of sad necessity but because I find it possible in principle, and this is where I part ways with the scholarly majority. My rationale is based on the observation of repetitions and consistent patterns in folklore material. This work studies the *recurring* elements of the wondertale. It is immaterial for us whether all two hundred, three hundred, or five thousand variants and versions of each element and each particle of the investigated material have been taken into account. The same applies to rituals, myths, and so on. As Engels writes, "If one should wait until the material for a law was in *a pure form*, it would mean suspending the process of thought in an investigation until then and, if only for this reason, the law would never come into be-ing."[28] All material under study either requires explanation—for us, this is first of all the wondertale—or provides it. Everything else is *control material*. Laws emerge gradually and are not necessarily explained by one set of selected material rather than another. Folklorists, therefore, surely are not required to take into account the whole sea of available facts, and if a law is valid, it will be so for any material, not merely for what has been selected.

The principle put forward here is the opposite of the one underlying other studies in folklore. In such works the main research goal is usually to assemble an exhaustive amount of data. But we see that questions are still in fact solved incorrectly in cases where the available material has been truly exhausted, because the task was formulated incorrectly. In the present study, by contrast, we proceed from a different standpoint: first of all, the task must be properly set, and then the correct method will lead to the right solution.

14. The Wondertale and Later Formations

From everything expressed above, it should be clear that I consider the rituals, myths, primitive forms of thinking, and certain social institu-tions to be formations that predate the wondertale and make it possible to explain it.

But folklore is not confined to the wondertale. There is also the heroic epic, which is related to the wondertale in plot and motif, and a vast array of all sorts of stories, legends, and so on. There are the *Mahabharata*, the *Iliad* and the *Odyssey*, the *Edda*, the Russian *byliny*, the *Nibelungenlied*, and so on. All such compositions, as a rule, we leave to one side. They can be explained by the wondertale and often harken back to it. Sometimes, however, the opposite occurs. Epics have preserved details and features that are absent in the wondertale and other sources as well. For example, in the *Nibelungenlied* Siegfried, having killed the dragon, bathes in its blood and becomes invulnerable. This detail is important for studying the dragon in that it explains something about the dragon's image; however, it is not found in the wondertale. In such cases, where other sources are lacking, we may make use of the heroic epic as well.

15. Prospects

The premises from which we begin have now been clarified, as has our primary task. A question arises: what prospects open to us through this comparison? Suppose we find that children in a wondertale are thrown into an underground dungeon and that this was also done in historical reality. Or perhaps we find that a maiden preserves the bones of a slaughtered cow, and this too was performed in reality. Is it possible to conclude that in such cases the motif entered the folktale from historical reality? Certainly. But would not the picture then be extraordinarily fragmented? This we do not know, and it is precisely the question that should be examined. To date, it has been believed that the folktale absorbed elements of primitive social and cultural lives. We shall see that the wondertale is in fact composed of them. As a result, we will arrive at a picture of the wondertale's sources.

Resolving this question will advance our understanding of the wondertale, but it will not resolve other not yet answered questions, such as why these stories were recounted or how they came to take form as a narrative genre. This latter question arises of itself when we set forth our task. Therefore, alongside the question of where individual motifs derive as integral parts of a story, we must also answer the question of where this storytelling comes from—where the wondertale itself comes from.

I shall try to answer this last question in the final chapter, but its resolution faces a certain difficulty. The present study examines only wondertales, but the act of recounting wondertales is inseparable from the act of recounting folktales in other genres, such as animal tales. Therefore, until other genres are historically examined, the answer to this question can be only preliminary, hypothetical, and it may or may not be tenable.

In essence, this kind of work can never be considered complete, and the present study serves as an introduction to examining the genesis of the wondertale rather than pretending to provide a solution.

In this way, it can be compared to an exploratory expedition into a yet unknown land. We note mineral deposits and sketch rudimentary maps, but thorough investigation of each of the deposits will await future research. A detailed elaboration of individual motifs and plots in reference to the whole might be a next step. At this stage of our research, however, it is more important to study the connection between phenomena than to elaborate on each phenomenon separately.

Finally, one additional proviso regarding the material under analysis. The present study is based on Russian wondertales, with special consideration given to those of the north. We have already pointed out that the folktale is international, and its motifs are predominantly international. Russian folklore is distinguished by its considerable diversity, richness, exceptional artistry, and well-preserved status. Therefore, it is quite natural for the Soviet scholar to look, first of all, at our native folklore rather than at foreign folklore. The present study takes into account all the main types of wondertale. These types are represented in the global repertoire of both Russian and foreign materials. For a comparative study, it is irrelevant which samples of a given type are employed. Where Russian material has proven insufficient, we have drawn upon the foreign corpus. But I wish to emphasize that this work is not merely a study of the Russian wondertale (such a task might be undertaken separately after the general issues of genesis were resolved; it would require a special study). This is a work of comparative historical folklore that takes Russian material as its point of departure.

2

BEGINNINGS

I. Children in the Dungeon

1. Absence

From the wondertale's first words—"In a certain kingdom, in a certain land"—the listener is immediately engulfed by a particular mood, the epic mood of tranquility. But this mood is deceptive. Soon events of the greatest intensity and passion will unfold before the listener. The calm is only an artistic wrapping that contrasts the inner dynamics, passionate and tragic or sometimes comical and realistic. Then follows this: "there lived a man with his three sons," or "there lived a king with his daughter," or "there lived three brothers"; in short, the tale introduces a family. Strictly speaking, we should begin by examining this wondertale family. But the elements are so closely related to one another that the nature of the family at its start may only be revealed gradually, as events unfold. Let us say simply that the family is living happily and calmly and could do so for some time to come if some very small, unnoticeable events did not occur and quite unexpectedly erupt into a disaster. The events sometimes begin with someone from the older generation temporarily leaving the house: "Dear daughter! Now we shall go to work";[1] "[The prince] needed to go on a long journey, leaving his wife in the care of others";[2] "On one occasion [the merchant] was leaving for faraway lands."[3] The merchant goes to trade, the prince to hunt, the king to war, and so on; the children or the wife, who is sometimes pregnant, remain behind alone, unprotected. This sets the stage for trouble. An enhanced form of absence might involve the death of the parents. Many tales begin with parents either leaving the house or dying. The same situation can be created by the departure of the younger members of the household rather than the older. They go into the forest for berries, or a girl goes to the field to bring breakfast to her brothers, or a princess goes for a walk in the garden, and so on.

2. Interdictions Connected with Absence

The older people somehow know that some kind of danger threatens the children. The very air around them is troubled by a thousand unknown perils. The father or husband, leaving himself or allowing his child to do so, accompanies the leave taking with an interdiction—which is, of course, violated, and this brings about some terrible misfortune, sometimes in a flash of surprise. Disobedient princesses who venture into the garden to walk are carried off by dragons; disobedient children who go to the pond are enchanted by a witch, and suddenly they are swimming in the form of white ducks. The disaster promotes our interest as events begin to develop.

Let us concentrate on one such interdiction for the time being: the prohibition against leaving the house. "The prince pleaded with her and commanded her not to leave the *terem*."[4] Or, "Whenever this miller went out hunting, he commanded: 'You, girl, do not go anywhere.'"[5] "Dearest daughter! Be a good girl and take care of your brother. Don't leave the yard."[6] In "The Snot-Nosed Billy Goat," the daughters have a bad dream: "The father grew frightened and refused to let his favorite daughter even out onto the porch." In these cases, as indicated, disobedience leads to misfortune: "But no, she did not listen, and out she went! And instantly the billy goat snatched her up on his high horns and carried her over steep banks."[7] Here one might think of parents' usual solicitousness for their children. Even today, when parents leave the house, they forbid their children from going out alone. But this is not the case. Something else is concealed here. When the father urges his daughter not to go "even onto the porch," "not to leave the tower," and so on, what we see is not merely concern but some deeper fear, a fear so great that the parents do not merely forbid children from going out, they sometimes even lock them up. And they do so in a way that is not ordinary. They place them in a tall tower, "in a pillar"; they lock them inside an underground dungeon and completely smooth over the earth that covers it. "They dug a very deep pit, cleaned it up, decorated it like a chamber, brought there all kind of supplies, so there was plenty to eat and drink; after that they put their children inside, and on top they made a ceiling, scattered earth over everything and smoothed it out so it was very flat."[8]

Here the wondertale has preserved the memory of measures that really were taken in connection with the offspring of kings and has done so with remarkable completeness and accuracy.

3. *James Frazer on the Isolation of Kings*

James George Frazer's *Golden Bough* reveals the complex system of taboos that once surrounded kings or high priests and their children. Their every movement was regulated by an entire code, which was extremely burdensome to fulfill. One of the rules of this code was never to leave the palace. This rule was observed in Japan and China up until the nineteenth century. In many places, the king was a mysterious being, never seen by anyone. We shall soon see why this was so, but for now let us examine some other prohibitions surrounding the king, choosing the most typical, which characterize all varieties of this custom. Among these prohibitions, Frazer points to the following: the king should not show his face to the sun, so he lives in constant darkness. Furthermore, the king must not *touch the ground*. Therefore, his dwelling is raised off the ground: he lives in a tower. His face must not be seen by a single person; therefore, he exists in *complete solitude*, conversing with his subjects and people close to him through a curtain. *Eating* is surrounded by a system of the strictest taboos. A number of products are totally prohibited, and meals are served through a small window.

It must be said that Frazer makes no attempt to arrange or explain his material historically. He begins with examples from the Japanese Mikado, then moves on to Africa and America, then to the Irish kings, and from there jumps to Rome.[9] But his examples make clear that the phenomenon is relatively *recent*. In North America it was observed in ancient Mexico, and in Africa wherever small monarchies had already formed. In short, it is a phenomenon of early statehood. The chief or king is credited with magical power over nature, the sky, rain, people, and livestock, and the people's well-being depends on the king's well-being. Therefore, carefully guarding the king means magically guarding the welfare of the entire nation. "The fetish king of Benin, who was worshipped as a deity by his subjects, might not quit his palace." "The king of Loango is confined to his palace, which he may not leave."[10] "The kings of Ethiopia were worshipped as gods, but were mostly kept shut up in their palaces," and so on.[11] If such monarchs tried to leave, they were stoned to death. There is no need to cite all the examples Frazer supplies and all the details on the isolation of kings. Let us turn to the wondertale and see what picture contemporary folklore provides.

4. *Isolation of the Royal Children in the Wondertale*

The simplest cases have isolation alone: "He ordered that a tall pillar be built, placed Ivan Tsarevich and Elena the Beautiful on top of it, and left them provisions for five years."[12] "She watched over him very carefully, without letting him out of the room."[13] Elsewhere: "The king watched over them like the apple of his eye, set up underground chambers and placed them there, like birds in a cage, so that no violent winds blew on them, nor did the fair sun scorch them with its rays."[14] This example already hints at a prohibition against sunlight. The parallel examples make clear that we have here not just a natural desire for protection from the sun but a fear of a different character. The royal children are kept in total darkness. "They built her a dark dungeon."[15] "Only the father and the mother did not allow [their two sons] to be shown any light for seven years."[16] "And the king ordered a room built in the ground, for her to live there, day and night with only a fire, and for her not to see any male."[17] The prohibition on light here is quite clear. In Georgian and Mingrelian folktales the princess is referred to as *mzeθunagav*. This term may have two meanings: "she who is not seen by the sun" and "she who has not seen the sun."[18] The prohibition against sunlight is also found in German folktales, but the sun's light is resignified as the light of a candle. The maiden here has become the wife of a lion; she is happy with him but asks him to go with her to visit her parents. "But the lion said it was too dangerous for him, since if a ray of light touched him there, he would turn into a dove and have to fly with the doves for seven years." He goes with her after all, but the girl "ordered a room constructed with such thick, strong walls that not a single beam of light could penetrate it, and in it he had to stay."[19]

The injunction against light is closely connected to the ban against seeing others. The detainees must not see anyone, nor should anyone be able to see their faces. Aleksei Smirnov offers an extremely interesting example in the tale "How a Soldier Made a Portrait of the Queen." "The king there has a beautiful wife. It would be good to make her portrait, but she always walks around in a mask."[20] A king comes to see the imprisoned hero: "When he came in, the prince said to him: 'Do not come near' as he turned away from the king and sighed."[21] Here we see the same beliefs that lead to fear of the evil eye. A priest has his wife placed in an underground dungeon: "Someone might jinx my wife."[22] A tale from the Vyatka region preserves the consequences that may follow if someone looks at the detainees: "She lived in the basement. If any of the young men looked at her, those people got very sick."[23] Another tale from the Vyatka region has preserved the ban on mentioning the detainees: "And he's in a dungeon. . . . You mustn't speak about him, or you'll be taken away!"[24]

Let us consider another striking example from a Russian wonder-tale where we have several types of prohibitions at once. The hero finds himself in a different kingdom, and the following conversation unfolds between him and a stranger:

> "Kind host, sir, what sort of place is this you have here that is so spacious? And why was this tower built without a single window and without any light? What is it for?"
>
> "Oh, my friend, the king's daughter is locked in this tower. She was taken there immediately upon birth, and she is never shown the outside world. Whenever the cook or the nurse brings her food, they just slip it through to her there and don't go inside. That's how she lives. She knows nothing of the people who live hereabouts."
>
> "Kind host, sir, do people really not know what she's like? Whether she's comely, clean, or unclean?"
>
> "God only knows whether she's comely, plain, clean, or unclean. The people know not what she's like, and she knows not what the people are like. She never comes out and never appears before them"[25]

This curious example includes one more detail: the way food is served. "They just slip it through to her there and don't go inside." We have seen above that the sovereign's children are supplied with provisions for five years at a time.[26] Of course, this is only a fantastic distortion. Wondertales have also preserved more accurate information about how food was served: "His father ordered him to build a stone pillar, with only a bed-bench for him and a little window, and he ordered that the bars should be strong, and that they should leave a small opening to slip the food through."[27] The same is related concerning a girl: "It was ordered that she be placed inside a stone pillar. . . . They left a small window for serving her a glass of water and a piece of rusk every day."[28]

An Abkhazian tale has preserved two other prohibitions quite well: the prohibition against touching the ground and the ban on regular food. Royal children are fed a diet suited to their magical qualities: "They kept their sister in a high tower. They raised her in such a way that her foot touched neither the ground nor the soft grass. They fed her only the brains of animals."[29]

In Russian wondertales the ban on touching the ground is not expressed explicitly, but it follows from living in the tower.

Thus, we see that the wondertale has preserved all kinds of taboos that once surrounded the royal family: the prohibition on light, the ban on being seen by others, food taboos, the prohibition against touching the ground, and the injunction against interacting with people. The correlation between the wondertale and the historical past on this issue is so complete that we may say that here the tale reflects historical reality.

However, this conclusion is not entirely satisfactory. Thus far, we have considered only forms of confinement and prohibitions connected with them, irrespective of who is being confined. If we compare the materials compiled by Frazer with those provided in wondertales, we can see that Frazer refers to kings and chieftains while the wondertale sometimes speaks of royal *children*. We must note, however, that in wondertales, the king himself sometimes finds himself with the children in the dungeon: "The king built himself a huge basement and hid in it, and they buried the king inside."[30] Second, in historic reality as well, the prohibitions were obligatory not only for kings but also for their heirs. We find in Frazer, "The Indians of Granada, in South America, 'kept those who were to be rulers or commanders, whether men or women, locked up for several years when they were children, some of them seven years, and this so close that they were not to see the sun, for if they should happen to see it they forfeited their lordship.'"[31]

But we have not yet cited all the examples. The wondertale has preserved another kind of prohibition, not attested in this context but in a slightly different one. This is the prohibition against cutting hair. Hair was regarded as a seat of the soul or a source of magical power. Losing one's hair meant losing power. We will come upon this subsequently many times. Here it suffices to recall the story of Samson and Delilah. "She never left the women's quarters; the princess did not breathe the free air; she had many colorful dresses and precious stones, but the princess was bored: she felt stifled in the towers, her bedcovers weighed her down! Her hair was thick, golden-silk, uncovered, plaited in a braid, and it reached her heels; and therefore they started calling the princess Vasilisa the Golden Braid, the veil-less beauty."[32] We shall address the golden color of her hair later in this work; for our present purposes the length of her hair is what is important. The motif of the confined princess's long hair is particularly clear in German tales.[33] "When the girl turned twelve years old, the sorceress locked her in a tower in the woods that had neither stairs nor door. . . . She had long, beautiful hair, fine as golden cloth. When she heard the sorceress's voice, she would take down her braids, wrap them around the hook of the window, where they would fall twenty cubits, and the sorceress would climb them." The imprisoned princess's long hair is a feature frequently encountered. In the Georgian tale "Iadon and the Nightingale," a beauty lives in a high tower from which she lets down her golden hair. To win over this beauty, the hero must tightly wind her hair around his arm.[34]

The prohibition against cutting hair is not expressed *directly* anywhere in wondertales. Nevertheless, the detained princess's long hair is a frequent element. This hair endows the princess with a special attraction.

The prohibition against cutting hair is also not mentioned in the description of the confinement of kings, royal children, or priests, although it is quite possible that it existed. Yet the prohibition against cutting hair is known in a completely different context—namely, the custom of isolating menstruating girls. It is well known that menstruating girls were subject to confinement. Frazer also notes that these girls were forbidden to cut or comb their hair.

There is an indubitable link between the custom of isolating kings and royal children and the custom of isolating girls. Both customs are based on the same beliefs, the same fears. The wondertale reflects both forms of isolation. The figure of the detained girl has already been compared to the isolation of girls, which used to occur long ago during monthly purifications. To confirm this idea, Frazer cites the myth of Danaë.[35] Friedrich Von der Leyen expresses the same notion in his book on the folktale, and it is also repeated in the publication of Afanas'ev's folktales edited by Azadovskii, Andreev, and Sokolov.[36] Indeed, Rapunzel is subject to confinement when she turns twelve years old—that is, at the beginning of puberty; she is detained in the forest. And indeed, pubescent girls were taken away to the forest. In addition, they sometimes wore helmets and concealed their faces. Here one recalls the princess who wore a mask.

There is another consideration in favor of this apposition: the girl's confinement is usually followed by her marriage, as we see in wondertales. Often the deity or the serpent does not kidnap the girl but visits her in the dungeon. This is the case in the myth of Danaë, and it sometimes happens in Russian wondertales that a girl might become pregnant from the wind. "He was afraid that she would start fooling around with boys, and he put her in a high tower. The masons blocked the door. There was a little hole in one spot between the bricks—in a word, a crack. And once the princess stood just beside this fissure, and the wind inflated her belly."[37] Sitting in the tower is clearly preparation for marriage, moreover for marriage not with an ordinary creature but with a creature of a divine nature, from which a divine son will be born. In the wondertale this is Ivan the Wind, and in Greek myth it is Perseus. More often, however, it is not the hero's *mother* who is imprisoned but the hero's future *wife*. In general, the analogy here between the custom and the wondertale is much weaker than the analogy between the motif of confining kings and royal children. In the wondertale, girls and boys, brothers and sisters, are all subject to identical confinement.

Comparing these facts, we must ask ourselves how the two forms of confinement are connected with each other and with the wondertale. The confinement of girls is more ancient than the confinement of kings. It is found among the most primitive, the most primordial peoples— for example, in Australia. The wondertale has preserved both types of confinement. These two forms are derived from each other, superimposed one upon the other, and assimilated to each other; moreover, the isolation of girls has been preserved in forms whose features have faded. The isolation of royal heirs is of more recent origin; here a number of historically attested details have been preserved.

6. *The Motives for Confinement*

Our analysis would not be complete without lingering on one additional detail—namely, the question of what causes this confinement and how it is motivated. In historical reality the confinement of kings was motivated by the fact that "the king or priest is often thought to be endowed with supernatural powers or to be an incarnation of a deity, and consistently with this belief the course of nature is supposed to be more or less under his control, and he is held responsible for bad weather, failure of the crops, and similar calamities."[38] Precisely this fact led to special care of the king, to protecting him from any danger. Frazer accepts this fact, but he does not attempt to explain why the effects of light, being seen, or contact with the ground were considered pernicious.

The wondertale has not preserved motivations of this nature for us. In such tales, the lives of the people surrounding the detainees do not depend on them. Only in one case do we find that a breach of the ban causes many to "grow very sick."[39] In wondertales the only issue is the personal safety of the prince or princess. But the concern for protection of the king is based on a more ancient notion that Frazer did not elaborate on—namely, that the air was filled with dangers, with forces that could fall upon a person at any instant. We shall not elaborate on this proposition here. It has already been pointed out by Martin Nilsson: everything is filled by the unknown, by the fearsome. A taboo emerges from fear that physical contact may cause something like a short circuit.[40] According to Daniel Brinton, "To the Maya, the woods, the air, and the darkness are filled with mysterious beings who are ever ready to do him injury or service, but generally injury, as the greater number of these creations of his fancy are malevolent sprites."[41]

It is safe to say that ethnographers like Brinton and Nilsson are mistaken in only one thing: the powers and spirits that surround a person appear "unidentified" only to ethnographers, not to the peoples themselves. They know these spirits very well, picture them for themselves quite concretely, and call them by their names. It is true that fear in wondertales is often undefined, but just as often it is defined and precise: it is the fear of creatures that can kidnap the royal children.

This religious fear generates anxiety over the royal children and produces the artistic motivation of misfortune, which follows the violation of the prohibition. It is enough for the princess to leave her imprisonment for a walk in the garden and a breath of fresh air to have a dragon appear "suddenly out of nowhere" and carry her away. In short, the children are being protected from abduction. This kind of motivation appears quite early; we read in a Zulu tale, "They lived without going outside. Their mother forbade them, saying that if they went out, they would be carried away by the crows and killed!"[42] We see the same, though at a much later stage, in an Egyptian mythological tale. As he is leaving, Bata says to his wife, "Do not go out (of the house), so you will not be carried away by the sea."[43] And in a tale from a more recent age we read, "The king ordered nannies to guard the princess and not let her go outside lest Raven Ravenson carry her away."[44]

Of all the kinds of bans people employed to protect themselves from demons, which appear in wondertales as dragons, ravens, goats, devils, spirits, whirlwinds, Koshchei, and Yaga, who kidnap women, girls, and children, the best-reflected in the wondertale is the injunction against leaving the house. The remaining types of catharsis (e.g., fasting, darkness, bans against seeing and touching, etc.) are reflected more weakly. However, not all is clear yet regarding this issue. Thus, through certain indirect features, it is possible to see that remaining underground, in the dark, or in a tower contributed to the accumulation of magical powers, not by virtue of the prohibitions but simply on their own. For example, in the legend of the Zuñi tribe of North America, "the father, being a great priest, dedicated his daughter to the sacred ministry (to sacred things) and *therefore* always kept her in the house away from the sight of all the men and adolescents." But sunlight gets into her room, and a child is born. That child is secretly sent away from home to the woods, where he is raised by a deer.[45] These cases must be kept in mind by researchers of the Danaë myth. We know that in ancient Peru, "sun maidens" were kept locked up. People never saw them. They were considered the wives of the sun, but in fact they served as the wives of the sun god's priests—that is, the Inca.[46] The sun generally appears at a later stage, and in those cases, as we shall see below, it reflects concepts of agrarian life. The wondertale, as already indicated, almost never knows the sun in that role; it is more archaic than such examples.

7. Conclusions

All the materials presented above give us the right to make the following conclusion: the most ancient religious substratum of our motif is the fear of invisible forces surrounding human beings. The reasons for this phenomenon have not yet been sufficiently studied by historians and ethnographers and are not within the purview of folklore. This fear leads to subjecting menstruating women to confinement so as to protect them from such dangers. In the wondertale, this phenomenon is reflected in the image of a girl's confinement in the forest, where her hair incidentally grows long. With the advent of the ruler-king's or priest's power, these concerns appear in the same forms but now for the king and his entire family. The details of the confinement of a king and of the prohibitions accompanying this confinement correspond precisely to the details available in wondertales. In particular, the tales reflect the injunction against light and the prohibitions related to meals and food, against revealing the face, and against touching the ground. The wondertale contains only isolated traces of the belief that the king's well-being is related to the well-being of the nation. In wondertales, we see an aspiration toward the personal safety of the royal children. They use the motif of confinement and its violation as an artistic introduction and motivation for the abduction of royal children by serpents and other creatures that suddenly appear out of nowhere. Confinement itself is never motivated in the wondertale. The motivation provided by a father's anger, and so on, which is sporadic but not typical of wondertales, provides a transition to the novelistic genre.[47] This motif of confinement indeed entered novelistic literature, folk literature, and hagiographic literature, but there it is often obscured and deformed. In wondertales with novelistic content, after the wedding the husband "built a palace for his wife and left only a window, no door," and so on.[48] Later it turns out that this was done to test the wife's fidelity. Sometimes such imprisonment is a way to persecute wives: "And the poor, innocent woman was put there for no reason. The landlord built a tower for her in his yard, a column of bricks, and locked her inside. . . . They left for her a tiny window: through it they fed her a dry crust of bread and water."[49] The motif of imprisoned girls and women is widely used in novelistic literature. This device is used by jealous husbands while the imprisoned women, by contrast, are presented as holy martyrs; thus does this motif pass into hagiographic literature.[50]

II. Misfortune and Counteraction

8. The Misfortune

We can follow the development of events in the wondertale further. The commandment "not to leave the *terem*" is always violated. Neither locks, bolts, towers, nor basements can help. Misfortune immediately ensues. We must add only that placing the children inside a pillar is not a mandatory element and that the misfortune sometimes occurs at the tale's opening.

A misfortune of some sort—this is the basic form of the beginning. And from the misfortune and the responses to it arises the plot. The forms of misfortune are terribly varied, so much so that it is impossible to examine them together. This chapter cannot explicate these forms. Confinement in a pillar or a dungeon is usually followed by abduction. To analyze this abduction we shall have to study the figure of the abductor. The principal abductor of girls is the dragon. But the dragon shows up in the wondertale twice. It appears first in a flash, then carries off the girl and disappears. The hero sets out in pursuit and meets it, and they battle. The dragon's nature can be clarified only through the analysis of the episode of battling it. Only here can one obtain a clear picture of the dragon and explain the abduction of girls. In other words, for the naive listener the course of action and the ending proceed from the beginning of the action. For scholars, this order may be reversed: the beginning is a product of the middle or the end. While the beginning of a wondertale is varied, the middle and end are much more uniform and constant. The beginning, therefore, can often be explained only from the middle or even from the end. The same applies to other types of wondertale beginnings. For example, sometimes a tale begins when unwanted children are driven from home. This is the type, for example, of "Jack Frost," "Baba Yaga," and others. We shall be able to explain what kind of expulsion this is only after analyzing the environment in which the children find themselves upon their expulsion. Another kind of beginning involves no misfortune. The tale opens with the king making a nationwide proclamation, promising the hand of his daughter to the man who can reach her window by leaping on a flying horse. This is one of the types of difficult tasks. The task can be explained only in connection with study of the magical helper and the figure of the old king, but the helper is usually acquired in the middle of the tale. Here too, then, the middle can explain the beginning for us.

Analysis of the elements in the middle will also allow us to clarify the question of why a tale so often begins with a misfortune and of what kind. Usually by the tale's end the misfortune has turned into something good. The kidnapped princess returns unharmed with her fiancé; the banished stepdaughter returns with handsome gifts and often gets married just afterward. The study of the forms of this marriage will show what sort the suitor is and how the marriage comes about.

Thus, in our study, must we skip over one part of the action and begin the analysis from the middle.

Already at this point, however, we can raise the question of whether a certain unity lies behind this diversity. The middle elements of the tale are stable. Whether a princess is kidnapped, a stepdaughter banished, or a hero sent off to fetch the apples of youth, in all cases the hero eventually reaches Baba Yaga. This uniformity of the middle elements forces us to assume that the initial elements, despite all their diversity, are united by some uniformity. We shall see below whether this is true.

9. Equipping the Hero for the Journey

In the previous section we examined several types of wondertale beginnings. These are unified by one common feature: the occurrence of some sort of misfortune. The course of action requires that the hero somehow find out about this misfortune. Indeed, this point in the story may take very different forms—for example, a kingdom-wide proclamation from the sovereign, a narration from a mother or from randomly encountered individuals, and so on. We shall not dwell on this point. It is not essential for us how the hero learns about the misfortune. It suffices to establish that he learns about it and that he sets out on a journey.

At first glance the hero's departure contains nothing at all interesting. "The bowman set off on a long journey," "The son mounted his horse and set off for a distant realm," "The brave bowman mounted his heroic steed and rode to distant lands"—such is the usual formula of this departure. Indeed, these words contain nothing problematic. The important thing, however, is not the words themselves but the fact of the hero's *departure on a journey*. In other words, the tale's composition is structured around the hero's spatial displacement. This type of composition is not limited to the wondertale alone but also occurs in epics (the *Odyssey*) and in novels—for example, *Don Quixote* is composed in this way. On his journey the hero can be met by a variety of adventures. Indeed, the adventures of Don Quixote are quite varied and numerous, as are the adventures of the heroes of other earlier half-folk chivalric romances (*Wigalois* and others). But unlike these literary or half-folk romances, a true folktale knows no such diversity. The adventures could have been quite varied, but they always resemble one another; they are subject to some very strict, consistent pattern. This is the first observation.

The second is that such tales skip over the time of movement. Movement is never outlined in detail; it is always described by only two or three words. The first stage of the journey from home to the forest hut is expressed in the following words: "He rode for a long or a short time, near or far. . . ." This formula refuses to describe the journey. The journey is present only in the composition, not in the texture. The journey's second stage extends from the forest hut to the faraway realm. This realm is separated by an immense space, but the space is traversed in an instant. The hero flies across it. The hat that flies off his head is already thousands of miles away by the time he realizes it is gone. What we see here is again, in essence, a rejection of the epic development of this motif.

This shows that space plays a dual role in the tale. On the one hand, it is present—it is an indispensable element of the composition. On the other, it is practically nonexistent in it. All development occurs in stops, and these are elaborated in abundant detail.

For us there is no doubt that the *Odyssey*, for example, is a later phenomenon than the wondertale. In it the journey and its space are elaborated in the style of epic. We conclude from this that the static elements, the stops of the wondertale, are older than its spatial composition. Space has intruded into something that already existed before. The fundamental elements were created prior to the appearance of spatial representations. We shall see this in greater detail below. All the elements of the stops already existed as ritual. Spatial representations separated into long distances things that were in fact the phases of ritual.

Where, then, does the hero go when he departs? Looking closer, we find that sometimes he is not simply going away: before his departure he asks to be supplied with certain items, and this detail requires our attention.

The objects supplied to the hero are quite varied: they might be rusks, money, a ship with a drunken crew, a tent, a horse. They all usually end up being unnecessary and are requested only as a diversionary move. For example, analysis shows that a horse taken from the father's house is no good and is exchanged for another. But there is one among these objects that is worth special attention: the club. It is a club of iron, usually requested before the hero's departure: "Forge me, good fellows, a club of twenty pounds."[51] What sort of a club is this? As a test, the hero throws it into the air (up to three times). Based on this we might conclude that it is a mace, a weapon. But this is not the case. First of all, the hero never uses the club as a mace. The storyteller later simply forgets about it. Second, comparative study shows that the hero takes an iron mace, iron altar biscuits, and iron boots along with him. "Ivanushka went to a blacksmith, forged three crutches, baked three altar biscuits, and set off to look for his dear Masha."[52] When Finist the Falcon flies away, he tells the maiden, "If you decide to search for me, search in faraway lands, in a realm beyond the seas. You will have to wear out three pairs of iron shoes, break three cast-iron staffs, and consume three stone altar biscuits before you find me."[53] The frog wife says the same: "Well, Prince Ivan, search for me in the seventh kingdom; wear out a pair of iron boots and consume three iron altar biscuits."[54]

From the combination of staff + bread + boots, one or even two elements can be easily discarded. We often have only bread ("Bake him three pounds of bread"[55]) or only the shoes ("Tell him to sew twenty-seven pairs of different kinds of shoes"[56]) or, finally, only the staff. Often the bread develops in effect into rusks, provisions, and so on, and the staff into a stick or a club, which is resignified as a weapon, though it never functions as a weapon. This is easy to establish based on examples such as the following: "The slippers are frayed by the sand, the hat worn down by the rain, and the staff worn thin in his hand";[57] here the staff does not serve as a weapon but preserves its original function. Or, "If he wants, let him forge three bronze hats, and then proceed. When he uses up the spears and wears out the hats, then will he find me."[58] Here the staff turns into a spear, but this spear is used as a stick for walking, not as a weapon. It is interesting to learn that this triple element is best preserved in women's tales ("Finist," etc.). This is because a woman's image is not associated with weapons, and the staff here consistently preserves its original form.

It is possible to establish that the shoes, staff, and bread were the items that had once been supplied to the dead for their journey to the other world. Later these items were described as made of iron so as to symbolize the length of the journey.

Nikolai Kharuzin writes, "The kinds of things that are put into the grave or burned with the dead depend on the conceptualization of the journey to the underworld. It is quite natural that if a dead man has to cross a stretch of water to reach the world of shadows, a boat should be put into his grave. If a long journey on foot awaits him, then they must adorn him with very sturdy shoes."[59]

This concept was present among the indigenous peoples of North America. In a legend recorded by Boas, the hero wants to find his deceased wife, and it is noted, "He asked his father for five bear skins and cut from them a hundred pairs of shoes for himself."[60] Thus, to travel to the realm of the dead, one must have sturdy shoes. In California, the Indians were always buried in moccasins.[61] "The aborigines of California provided their deceased with shoes because the way to the place of the eternal hunt is long and difficult."[62] In Bengal, the deceased were "supplied with equipment as if a long journey were awaiting them."[63] The Egyptians supplied their deceased with strong staves and sandals.[64] One variant of chapter 125 of the *Book of the Dead* notes the following: "This chapter shall be said [by the deceased] after he hath been cleaned and purified, and when he is arrayed in apparel and is shod with white leather sandals."[65] The hieratic papyrus of Astarte says, when Astarte is in the underworld, "Where are you going, daughter of Ptah, fierce and terrible goddess? Have not the sandals upon your feet been worn out? Have not the garments upon you been torn by your coming and going in the sky and on the earth?"[66] These actual sandals, though sturdy, are gradually replaced by symbolic ones. Clay shoes were often found in the tombs of ancient Greece, sometimes even two pairs.[67] The concept lived on into the Middle Ages and survives in the modern era. In Alemannic graves, candles, fruits, staffs, and footwear were found.[68] In some parts of Lorraine the deceased is shod with boots, and a stick is placed in his hand for the upcoming journey to the other world.[69] In Scandinavia, "at the burial they used to put a special kind of footwear for the dead in the coffin; with its help the deceased could freely pass over the rocky and thorny path leading to the other world."[70] According to Anuchin, "When the path there goes by land, they take care to facilitate its passage by putting boots on the deceased, and by placing a stick with him, etc."[71]

This material is sufficient to establish that a hundred pairs of shoes or two pairs, clay shoes, or special shoes, as they appear in our examples, as well as a special staff have become iron shoes and an iron spike in the wondertale, and because of a misunderstanding of this motif's meaning, the staff has become a mace, a weapon.

These materials—there is an especially large collection of them in Samter 1911—suggest that iron shoes are a sign of the hero's departure to the other world.

Another question that may arise in this regard concerns the hero's character. Who is he? Is he a living person who goes to the realm of the dead, or is he deceased, representing the idea of the wanderings of the soul? In the first case the hero could be compared to a shaman who follows the departing soul of the dead or the sick. When a hero casts out an evil spirit that has possessed the princess, he acts just like a shaman. If this were the case, the composition would be clear: the princess is carried away by a serpent, the king calls for a powerful shaman who is also a magician, a wizard, and an ancestor, and he sets off after her. However, although this statement has some truth in it, further analysis will show that it is too simplistic and that there are other more complex concepts also present here.

Thus, the resolution of one issue entails the emergence of others. We expect these to be resolved upon analysis of the middle elements of the wondertale. First, we must discover where the hero finds himself while on his journey.

3

THE MYSTERIOUS FOREST

1. Further Composition of the Wondertale. Obtaining the Magical Agent

As mentioned previously, the plot's starting point usually contains some misfortune and sends the character away from home. Sometimes the separation from home itself is the misfortune, as, for example, when a stepdaughter is driven out of the house. The misfortune must be overcome, and usually it happens that some magical agent winds up in the hands of the hero. This, in fact, predetermines the outcome. However, this is only a colorless, dry outline; the story is clothed in rich garments of various extremely colorful details and accessories. The richness of the tale lies not in its composition but in the diverse ways the same compositional element is realized. Specifically, here we must pose the question: how does the magical agent come into the hands of the hero?

The wondertale repertoire offers many ways of delivering this agent to the hero. As a rule, a new character is introduced for this purpose, and with this the course of action enters a new phase. This character is the donor.

The donor represents a defined category of the wondertale canon. The classical form of the donor is Baba Yaga. We must stipulate that researchers should not always trust the way tales name their characters.

Often characters from completely different categories, such as a stepmother, are called Yaga.[1] On the other hand, a typical Yaga may be called merely an old woman, the old woman who lives "around here," and so on. Sometimes animals (a bear), an old man, or others assume Yaga's function.

2. Types of Yaga

It is quite difficult to analyze the Yaga character. Her image is composed of an array of details. These details, compiled from various tales, sometimes do not correspond to one another, do not fit together, and do not combine in a unified image. The wondertale on the whole knows three forms of Yaga. There is Yaga the donor whom the hero visits. She usually interrogates the hero, and either he or the heroine receives a horse, rich gifts, and the like from her. Another type is Yaga the abductor, who kidnaps children and plans to cook them; flight and escape ensue. Finally, the wondertale uses Yaga the warrior, who comes flying into a hero's hut, carves a strip of skin off his back, and so on. Each type has its own specific features, but there are also features common to all of them. This poses immense difficulties for research.

We find the solution to the problem not in describing all three types in detail. It is possible to resolve the problem differently: the whole course of a tale's development, especially the beginning—sending the hero to the realm of the dead—shows that Yaga may have some connection to this realm. Let us first distinguish which of her features confirm this assumption in light of historical data. Here it must be noted that this will illuminate only one side of Yaga's image, but this side must be examined because both the wondertale's artistic logic and its historical material point to it.

3. The Rite of Passage

The question that emerges from our material can therefore be formulated in the following manner: what is the connection between the image of Yaga and the conception of death? In this form, however, the question does not address our material exhaustively. We shall see that Yaga is indeed closely linked with notions of this sort. For now, let us assume that such a linkage will be established. Another question immediately arises: why does the hero end up at death's gates? It is true that this is motivated by the course of the action; the beginning of the tale, as we saw previously, emerges from concepts regarding death. But this does not resolve the issue, only moves it elsewhere: why does the tale reflect mainly notions of death rather than any others? Why did precisely such notions turn out to be so tenacious and susceptible to artistic treatment?

An answer may be found by analyzing a certain phenomenon drawn not from the domain of worldviews but from concrete social life. The wondertale has preserved not only traces of concepts regarding death but also traces of a once widespread rite closely connected with such ideas. These are adolescent initiation rites upon reaching puberty (*initiation*,[2] *rites de passage, Pubertätsweihe, Reifezeremonien*).

These rites are so closely linked with the concept of death that one cannot be considered without the other. We shall therefore compare the wondertale not only with material about beliefs but also with relevant social institutions.

With this we touch on a new and extremely important issue. The rites' characterization will be provided later; for now, in view of the extreme importance of this issue, a brief review of the history of their study is required.

It has been noted already that the wondertale reflects rites of passage, but the issue has never been systematically studied. Frazer raises it in *The Golden Bough*. However, the wondertale as such does not interest Frazer. He uses folktales only as an argument in favor of his theory that, during the initiation, the initiate's soul is removed and transferred to an animal totem. But since the ethnographic materials do not support such an assertion, Frazer refers to the folkloric character Koshchei. It is true that Koshchei's soul is kept outside his body, but Frazer does not demonstrate a link with rites of passage.

The French researcher Pierre Saintyves looks at this issue from a different perspective. He proceeds directly from the tales themselves.[3] According to him, some tales ("Tom Thumb," "Bluebeard," "Puss in Boots," "Ricky with the Tuft") originate in initiation rites. But how can this be proven? For each of these types he provides a number of variants and then informs his readers that the tale goes back to a rite of initiation. In this manner, after recounting several European and non-European tales such as "Tom Thumb," the author notes, "It is remarkable that this form of our tale reminds us of initiation. The difficult tasks can be explained quite naturally by the testing at initiation."[4] He offers no proof for this hypothesis, only the statement that it is so. Other types are analyzed in the same manner. Only "Bluebeard" is worked out in more detail, but even there the ethnographic material is provided extremely sparingly and not always successfully. This method cannot be called research, and Saintyves's book is interesting only because it spells out the issue.

This idea has also been expressed in Soviet scholarship. For example, B. V. Kazanskii finishes his work on Tristan and Isolde by pointing out that the Tristan and Isolde complex goes back to rites "of initiation into puberty."[5] This idea is proven with schematic features of initiation rites, but, once again, the connection with Tristan is not elaborated, only stated. We see that researchers approach the issue intuitively, sensing some connection, but they cannot or do not want to plunge into the depth of the material and establish the connection in its essence.

This reproach is less true of S. Ia. Lur'e's work, *The House in the Forest*.[6] The author relies mainly on the work of Heinrich Schurtz, which cannot be considered sufficient. Nevertheless, a number of wondertale phenomena are explained indisputably and, moreover, independently of the works of other researchers. For the first time, we see work that has been performed not as speculation or superficial analogies but as genuine scholarly research. Unfortunately, however, the author sets out from the traditional premises of tale types. Only two or three types are addressed (mainly "Sleeping Beauty" and the Grimms' "Twelve Brothers") while the rest of the material is left on the sidelines. As a result, the whole breadth of this phenomenon remains unclear to the author. The connection is much broader and deeper than what the given work demonstrates.

All the cited works consider the phenomenon we are exploring in a purely descriptive way, without regard to the social order on whose basis it was created.

We see that the question is quite new and unclear. Here one must not limit oneself to a rough outline. It is necessary to look into the matter more closely.

One must compare the material of the wondertale with that of the rite of passage, and to do so one must first describe this rite.

Here a serious difficulty arises. We should provide not just a description of this rite but also its history; however, we are unable to do so here. The problem is purely ethnographic, and in ethnography the question is always presented only descriptively. We have a great number of individual testimonies, observations, and records. We have several studies where these testimonies are systematized and reduced to some artificial arithmetic average.[7] There are monographs within territorial boundaries.[8] But all this cannot satisfy the folklorist. The main question of this rite is not posed; details extraordinarily important to folklorists are not illuminated. Each researcher emphasizes one side while neglecting others. Due to this, we too must limit ourselves at first to a schematic representation of this ritual. The historical perspectives, the range of problems, and particular details will come to light gradually.

What is initiation? It is one of the institutions peculiar to tribal systems. This rite took place at the onset of puberty. With this rite, the young person was inducted into the tribal association, became a member with full rights, and acquired the right to marry. Such is its social function. Its forms vary, and we shall examine them in connection with the material of the wondertale. These forms are determined by the rite's conceptual foundation. It was assumed that during the ceremony the boy died and then was resurrected, now as a new man. This is a so-called temporary death. The death and resurrection were caused by actions that depict absorption, the devouring of the boy by monstrous animals. It was as if the boy were swallowed by these animals and, after spending a certain amount of time in the stomach of the monsters, came back—that is, he was spat out or regurgitated. Sometimes special houses or huts were built to carry out this ritual; they were shaped like animals, and their doors took the form of jaws. Circumcision was performed there as well. The rite always occurred in the depths of the forest or bushes in strict secrecy. It was accompanied by physical torture and injuries (cutting off a finger, knocking out some teeth, and others). Another form of temporary death is expressed in the way the boy was symbolically burned, boiled, fried, cut into pieces, and resurrected anew. The resurrected boy would receive a new name; his skin was marked with brands and other signs of the rite he had passed through. The boy underwent a more or less prolonged and strict training. He learned methods of hunting; he was told secrets of a religious nature, historical information, the rules and requirements of everyday life, and so on. He had to learn to be a hunter and a member of the community; he learns dances, songs, and all the things that seem necessary in life.

This is a schematic presentation of the rite's main features. Its details will unfold before us gradually. Here we should note only in particular that the initiate appeared to go to his death and was quite convinced that he had died and risen again. Study of the details will gradually also reveal to us the meaning of this custom as well as its aim. We shall see that it was motivated by relations of production. Let us return to the wondertale. To this point we have proceeded from the tales themselves and adduced the historical material after outlining the tale material. Now, for the purposes of easier and more convenient presentation, we shall proceed inversely. We will not change our method of argumentation, only occasionally the order of presentation.

4. The Forest

Walking aimlessly, the hero or heroine winds up in a dark, dense forest. The forest is a constant feature in episodes with Yaga. Moreover, even in wondertales without Yaga (like "The Armless Maiden"), the hero or heroine is still sure to wind up in the forest. The hero, whether prince, exiled stepdaughter, or fugitive soldier, invariably winds up there. It is where his adventures begin. This forest is not described in any greater detail than being dense, dark, mysterious, somewhat provisional, and not entirely realistic.

Here researchers are confronted with an ocean of material connected to perceptions of the forest and its inhabitants. In order not to be distracted, we must adhere strictly to only those ideas that are associated with the wondertale. For instance, forest spirits, the Russian *leshii* and *rusalka*, are almost never reflected in wondertales.[9] In Afanas'ev's entire three-volume collection, a rusalka turns up just once, and this is only in an introduction. The leshii is in essence always a Yaga by another name.

This gives the wondertale forest a stronger link to the forest in rites of passage. Such rites invariably take place in the woods. They have this constant, indispensable trait all over the world. In places where there is no forest, children would at least be taken away into bushes.

The link of initiation with the woods is so strong and constant that it holds in reverse order as well. Every time a hero winds up in the woods, we must question the connection of the particular plot with the cycle of initiation events. When we read in a modern tale, "His father took him to the forest to a special cabin, and he prayed to God for twelve years,"[10] or "Let's go to the woods, there is a house for us there,"[11] and so on, the connection is still sufficiently transparent and can easily be worked out. It must nonetheless be said that there are no other signs as yet of the forest in the wondertale that indicate a direct connection. This changes, however, when we consider the forest's functional role, which is generally as a barrier that holds the hero back. The forest the hero enters is impenetrable. It is a kind of net that captures visitors. This function of the forest is clear in another motif: throwing down a hair comb, which turns into dense woods and delays a pursuer. Here, however, the forest detains not the pursuer but the visitor, the outsider. It is impossible to pass through. We shall see that the hero gets a horse from Yaga, and on it he flies across the forest. The horse is said to fly "above the towering forest."

It appears that this issue has been insufficiently studied by ethnographers. Why is the rite of passage always performed, anywhere in the whole world, in a forest or in bushes? We can make any number of conjectures—for example, we can say that the forest makes it possible to perform the rite in secret, that it conceals the mystery. But it is more correct to adhere to the data, and the data show that the forest surrounds a different kind of realm, that the road to another world leads through the forest. American mythology includes a story about a man who goes to look for his dead wife. He enters the forest and discovers that he is in the country of the dead.[12] In the myths of Micronesia, the country of the sun is located beyond the forest.[13] More recent material, for which the ritual has long been extinct along with the systems that created it, shows that the forest surrounds *a different kind of realm*, that the road to another world passes through the forest.

This is clear already in classical materials, and it was noticed long ago. "Most entrances to the underworld were surrounded by impenetrable virgin forest. This forest has been a permanent fixture in the ideal representation of the entrance to Hades."[14] Ovid refers to this in books IV and VII of his *Metamorphoses* while in the sixth book of the *Aeneid* Aeneas's descent into Hades is described: "a deep cave there was / With huge gape monstrous, jaggèd, and hemmed in / By the dark mere and forest's gloom."[15]

Like Ovid, Virgil provides a *literary* reflection of such concepts, but these reflections demonstrate that the concepts indeed existed.

These materials make it possible to make the following—for now purely preliminary—conclusion: the wondertale forest reflects a memory, on the one hand, of the forest as a place where the rite was performed and, on the other, as the entrance to the realm of the dead. The two concepts are tightly interconnected.

This linkage has not yet been established. Let us now see what happens to the hero further on.

5. The Hut on Chicken Legs

The forest as a separate isolated element does not yet prove anything. But the fact that this forest is not an entirely ordinary one is clear both from its inhabitants and from the hut that the hero, Ivan, suddenly comes across. Walking along "aimlessly" and casually looking up, he sees an unusual sight: a hut on chicken legs. It seems that this hut has been familiar to Ivan for a long time: "We need to get inside you, to eat bread and salt," he says. He is not at all surprised by it and knows how to behave.

Sometimes this hut is turning around—that is, it rotates on its own axis. "She saw before her a hut on chicken legs, constantly turning."[16] "It stands and turns around."[17] Such an interpretation arose from a misunderstanding of the words *turning around*. Some tales clarify that it turns around when it needs to. However, it does not turn by itself. The hero must make it do so, and for this he needs to know and pronounce a word. Once again we see that the hero is not at all surprised. He does not need to search for the right word; he knows what to say. "According to the old saying, according to my mama's telling: 'Little hut, little hut,' said Ivan, blowing on it, 'turn your back to the forest and your front to me.' And the hut turned to Ivan, and a gray-haired old woman was looking out its window."[18] "Little hut, little hut, turn so your eyes face the forest, and the gates face me: I didn't come to stay forever. I'll just spend one night. Let the passerby come in."[19]

What is happening here? Why is it necessary to turn the hut around? Why is it impossible to enter in the usual way? Often Ivan finds a blank wall before him, "without windows, without doors," and the entrance on the opposite side. "This hut has no windows, no doors, and nothing at all."[20] But why not go around the house and enter from the other side? Apparently, this is not possible. The hut stands on some kind of visible or invisible border that Ivan can get across only by passing through the hut, and the hut must be turned around "so that I can go in and get out."[21]

It is interesting to look here at one detail of an American myth. The hero wants to pass a tree. But it sways and will not let him by. "Then he tried to go around. It was impossible. He had to pass by the tree." The hero tries to go under the tree, but it lowers itself. Then the hero runs right at the tree, and it breaks apart while the hero turns at once into a light feather that flies through the air.[22] We shall see that our hero Ivan too does not walk out of the hut but rather flies, either on horseback or on an eagle, or he himself is turned into an eagle. The hut's open side faces the Thrice-Tenth Kingdom while its closed side faces the kingdom that is accessible to Ivan. This is why Ivan cannot go around it and turns it around instead.

The hut is an outpost. Ivan will not get across the border before being subjected to interrogation and trial, which will show whether he can continue his journey. Actually, he has already passed the first test. Ivan knew the spell and managed to blow on the hut and make it turn. "The hut turned its front side toward them. The doors opened wide by themselves. The windows opened."[23] "The little hut stood still and the door opened."[24] The hut's liminal position is sometimes emphasized: "Beyond the steppe was a thick forest, and right by the forest stood a little hut."[25] "And at last he flew to the edge of the earth. And there stood a little hut, and there was no place else to go. It was just an unending darkness; you could see nothing!"[26] Sometimes the hut stands on the shore of a sea, sometimes next to a ditch, which one must jump over. The further development of the tale shows that sometimes Yaga is put there to guard the border by masters who are above her, who scold her for letting Ivan pass. "How did you dare let such a scoundrel into my realm?"[27] or "What good does it do to have you posted there?"[28] The Tsar-Maiden asks, "Did anyone pass this way?" Yaga replies, "What do you mean? We don't let even a fly pass."

This example suggests that the donor of the magical agent is guarding the entrance to the kingdom of death. Earlier materials show this more clearly: "After he had wandered for some time, he saw smoke far away, and when he came closer, he saw a house on the prairie. A pelican lived there. It asked him: 'Where are you going?' He replied: 'I am looking for my dead wife.' 'This is a difficult task, my grandson,' said the pelican. 'Only the dead can find the path easily. The living can reach the land of the dead only with great danger.' It gave him a magical object to help him in his endeavor and taught him how to use it."[29]

Here too we find an interrogation. Let us note that the donor is in the shape of an animal. This observation will come in handy later in this study. There are other examples that belong to the same category. A Dolgan tale reads, "In one place they [the shaman-geese] had to fly through a hole in the sky. An old woman was seated near this hole, lying in wait for the flying geese." This old woman turns out to be the mistress of the universe. "Let no shaman fly through this way. The mistress of the universe objects to it."[30]

We note also that in all such cases, the hero is not a dead person but a living person or shaman who wants to penetrate the realm of the dead.

In such cases, however, there is no rotating hut. To explain the image of the rotating hut, we may recall that in ancient Scandinavia, doors were never made to face north. This direction was considered unlucky. On the contrary, the residence of death in the *Edda* (*Naströnd*) has a door on the north side. The unusual arrangement of the doors in our hut is another indicator that this hut is an entrance to another realm. The residence of death has its entrance in the direction of death.

In tales with a female protagonist, the hut has particular features. Before she goes to Yaga, the heroine visits her aunt, who warns her about the things she will see in the hut and tells her how to behave there. This aunt is obviously a character introduced later in history. We saw previously that the hero always knows how to behave and what to do in the hut. This knowledge is not motivated from outside; it is motivated, as we shall see, from within. An artistic instinct makes the tale-teller bring forth this knowledge by introducing an aunt as adviser. This aunt says the following: "There, my niece, a birch will poke you in the eye. Tie it up with a ribbon. Then the gate will creak and slam. Pour a little oil beneath the hinges. Then dogs will rush at you. Throw them a bit of bread. Then the cat will scratch at your eyes. Give it a bit of ham."[31]

Let us first consider the girl's actions. When she pours oil under the gate, we see in this a remnant of aspersion. It can be seen more clearly in another text: "She sprinkled the door with water."[32] We have already seen that the hero also blows on the hut. If the heroine gives the animals who are guarding the entrance to the hut meat, bread, and butter, these products point to the later agricultural origin of this feature. We shall discuss the propitiatory sacrifices given to animals guarding the entrance to Hades (such as Cerberus and others) in another chapter. Finally, if the tree is tied with a ribbon, there too it is easy to see a remnant of widespread cult performances. And if the girl performs these actions while she is leaving rather than entering the hut, then here again one can see signs of a later treatment.

In order to explain all these phenomena, we must refer to the myths and rites of peoples that stand at an earlier stage of development. There we find no aspersion, bread, butter, or ribbons on the trees. On the other hand, we see something else that explains a great deal in the image of the hut. In the rite, the hut, which stands on the border of two worlds, takes the form of an animal; in myth there is often no cabin at all—there is only an animal or a hut that has pronounced zoomorphic features. This explains the "chicken legs" and many other details.

We see in American hunting myths that in order to get into the hut, one must know the names of its parts. There too the hut retains more vivid traces of zoomorphic characteristics; sometimes we find an animal instead of a hut. Here is the way a North American legend describes building the house: The hero comes down to earth from the sun. He is the son of the sun. He marries a woman of the earth and builds a house. The front and the rear pillars in his house are men. The text gives us their quite complicated names (Speaker, Braggart, etc.). The two front pillars directly hold the long beams, representing a snake, while the rear pillars are covered with a crossbeam, which represents either a snake or a wolf. The door of the house hangs on hinges from the top, and it kills anyone who does not run out fast enough. "When he finished building the house, he made a great feast and all the pillars and beams came to life. The snakes started flicking their tongues, and the men who stood in the back of the house (i.e., the pillars) would tell him when a wicked man entered the house. The snakes would kill the wicked man immediately."[33]

How is this material important, and what does it reveal about the history of our hut's formation? There are two important features: the first is that some parts of the house are animals, and the second is that some parts of the house have their own names.

Let us first consider the names. In order to get inside, the hero must know a certain word. Some materials show that he needs to know a *name*. Let us merely recall the tale of Ali Baba and the Forty Thieves, where it is also necessary to know a name to open doors.

This verbal magic turns out to be more ancient than sacrificial magic. Therefore, the formula "Stand with your back to the forest," the formula that opens the doors to a stranger, should be considered older than "she gave the cat some butter." This magic of words or names is preserved in the Egyptian cult of the dead with particular clarity. "Magic was a means on the path of the dead, which opened for him the doors to otherworldly dwellings and provided his afterlife existence," notes Boris Turaev.[34] Chapter 127 of the *Book of the Dead* states, "'We will not let thee enter in through us,' say the bolts of this door, 'unless thou tellest [us] our names.'" "'I will not let thee enter in by me,' saith the [right] lintel of this door, 'unless thou tellest [me] my name.'" The left abutment says the same. The dead person says the name of each part of the door, although sometimes the names are quite intricate. "'I will not let thee pass over me,' saith the threshold of this door, 'unless thou tellest [me] my name.'" "'I will not open unto thee,' saith the fastening of this door, 'unless thou tellest [me] my name.'" The same is said by the hinges, jambs, and floor. And finally, "Thou knowest us, [they say,] pass on, therefore, by us."[35] We see how the recounting of all the parts of the door is detailed so as not to miss a single part. It is clear that special importance was ascribed to this ritual, a naming ritual—that is, opening the door.

It is well known that sacrifice and aspersion were already widely practiced at the same time in agricultural Egypt.

All these materials show that at an earlier stage the hut guarded the entrance to the realm of the dead and that the hero either uttered the magic word that opened the entrance to the other world for him or else performed sacrifices.

The second issue is the hut's animal nature. In order to understand it, we need to look a little more closely at the rite. A cabin, a hut, or a shack is as stable a feature of the rite as the forest. This hut was located in the depths of the forest, in a remote and secret place. Sometimes it was specially built for this purpose; often this was done by the neophytes themselves. In addition to its location in the forest, we can note a few more of its typical features: Often it took the shape of an animal. It was most often the doors that took animal form. Furthermore, it was surrounded by a fence. Occasionally these fences were adorned with skulls. And finally, sometimes a path leading to the hut is mentioned.

Here are several examples: "The youths here, during initiation, go to a hut in the woods, where they are supposed to consort with ghosts."[36] "The place where the cabin is located is surrounded by a high and thick fence, within which only certain persons are allowed."[37] "In the Kwat cult of Banks Island an enclosure in a retired place is made by a fence of reeds, the two ends of which overlap to form an entrance. This is called the shark's mouth. In Ceram and New Guinea the candidate is said to be swallowed by the monster."[38] There, the entrance is called "crocodile mouth, and the youths at the time of initiation are supposed to be devoured by this animal."[39] "The 'pal na bata' was actually located in the forest, in seclusion, 100 meters from the dancing place. This is the only building of its kind I have ever seen. . . . It was surrounded on all sides by dense thickets, and there was a narrow path through them, so narrow that one could get through it only while bending over."[40] The structure mentioned here stood on carved pillars. The topic of skulls was specially studied by Frobenius, and there is no need to write out his materials here. The examples above not only give a description of the house but also show one of its functions. There the hero is supposed to be swallowed, to be eaten. At this point we shall not enter into the interpretation of this rite; this will be provided elsewhere (see chap. 7). But Yaga also appears as a man-eater both through her house and through her words: "Near that house was a thick forest, and in a glade of that forest there stood a hut, and in the hut lived Baba Yaga. She never allowed anyone to come near her and ate human beings as if they were chickens."[41] "The fence around the hut was made of human bones, and on the spikes were human skulls with staring eyes; the doors had human legs for doorposts, human hands for bolts, and a mouth with sharp teeth in place of a lock."[42] We have seen above that the door of the hut bites—that is, it represents a mouth or jaws. Thus, we see that this type of hut corresponds to the hut in which circumcision and initiation are carried out. This beast-hut gradually loses its animal appearance. The doors prove to be the most resistant to change; they retain the form of jaws for the longest time: "the door to the room of Koma-Koa closed and opened like jaws." Or there is an eagle standing in front of the house: "Beware! Whenever the eagle opens its beak, jump inside quickly one by one!" Or, "First you'll have to get past a bunch of rats, and then past the snakes. The rats would like to tear you apart; the snakes will threaten to swallow you. If you manage to pass through them, then the door will bite you."[43] These instances strongly remind us of the admonitions of the aunt in our wondertale. It seems that bird legs are also no more than a remainder of the zoomorphic pillars on which structures of this kind once stood. This also explains the animals guarding the entrance to the hut. We have here the same phenomenon that occurs in the process of anthropomorphization of animal gods. What once played the role of the god later becomes an attribute of the god (the eagle of Zeus, etc.). Here we find the same: what was once the hut itself (an animal) becomes an incorporated attribute of the hut—for example, as its entrance.

In this presentation of the motif in question, we have proceeded from more recent (i.e., wondertale) material to materials of a transitional nature and ended up pointing to the rite of passage. This conclusion could be reached in the reverse order. We cannot say that everything is now clear, finite, and completely resolved. But it is already possible to find certain links.

The hut's arrangement in animal form during the initiation rite can be considered the oldest substrate. During this rite it was as if the initiate was descending to the realm of death through this small hut. This is why the hut has the character of a passage into another realm. The myths lose the hut's zoomorphic character, but the door and the columns in the Russian wondertale retain their zoomorphic appearance. This rite was established by tribal societies, and it reflects the interests and views of hunting. With the emergence of states such as Egypt, the traces of initiation disappear. There is a door, which is the entrance to another kingdom, and the dead must be able to conjure the door. At this stage emerge aspersion and sacrifice, which are also preserved in the wondertale. The forest, originally an indispensable condition of the rite, is subsequently also transferred into the other world. The wondertale becomes the last link in this chain of development.

<h1 align="center">6. Foo, Foo, Foo[44]</h1>

Let us continue following the actions of the hero. The hut has turned around, and the hero enters. He sees nothing yet, but he hears, "Foo, Foo, Foo! Before you never sensed or saw a Russian spirit. Nowadays, a Russian spirit sits down on my spoon and rolls right into my mouth!"[45] "A Russian spirit has come to the woods to visit me!"[46] Or, in a shorter form, "Bah, it stinks of a Russian bone!"[47] We must linger on this detail; it is very important.

The motif we wish to examine has been studied before. Polívka dedicated a special work to this topic. In it, the author collected all the known instances of such exclamations. The number of examples is quite high, yet the author comes to no conclusion. Of course, there could be none since Polívka limited his examples to Slavic materials alone.[48]

However, as soon as we turn to relatively earlier stages, we immediately find the key to our motif. This material shows that Afanas'ev was not mistaken when he argued that Ivan smells of a *human being*, not of a specifically Russian man. But his statement may be further clarified. Ivan smells not just like a person but like a living person. The dead, the disembodied, do not smell. The living do, and the dead recognize living people by their smell. This can be seen very clearly in North American legends. For example, a man sets off to seek his deceased wife. In the underworld, he comes upon a house. The master of the house wants to swallow him but says, "He smells terrible! He's not dead!"[49] Many more such cases may be found, as explored—for example—in A. H. Gayton's "The Orpheus Myth in America."[50] In these stories, the hero is recognized as a living being by his smell. In this kind of myth we find the following: "His wife was on the other side with a lot of other people." His wife has already died, and after some searching he finds her. She is dancing a special dance with the other deceased. The newcomer is noticed by his smell. "Everyone spoke of the newcomer's unpleasant smell because he was alive." This is a constant feature of this myth.[51] But this feature is not unique to this myth and is not unique to America. In an African legend a girl's mother dies, but the dead mother comes to help her daughter dig in the garden. People recognize her, and she goes away, taking her daughter with her. Here is how Friedrich Fülleborn continues the story: "Down there the mother hides her daughter in an enclosed space inside the hut and forbids her to speak. After some time guests arrive, relatives and friends, all shadows. But as soon as they sit down in the hut they ask, wrinkling their noses: 'What's in the hut? What is this smell? It smells so strongly of life here. What have you got hidden here?'"[52] The Zulus have this: "They say that if a man died here on earth, he went to the dead, and they say, at first, do not come to us, you still smell of the fireplace. They say, stay away from us, until you cool down from the hearth."[53]

This smell of living beings is repugnant in the highest degree to the dead. Apparently, here the attitude of the world of living beings is transferred onto the world of the dead but in the opposite direction. The smell of living beings is as disgusting and terrible to the dead as the smell of the dead to the living. As Frazer notes, the living insult the dead with the very fact that they are alive.[54] Accordingly, in Dolgan folklore, "They put that man to death because he came to her with the habits and the words of his world."[55] Therefore, heroes who want to enter the other world sometimes undergo a pre-cleansing of their odor: "Two brothers went to the forest and stayed hidden there for months. Every day they bathed in the lake and washed with pine branches until they were completely clean and did not spread a human smell. Then they climbed Kulen Mountain and found the house of the thunder god."[56]

All this shows that Ivan's smell is the smell of a living person who tries to enter the realm of the dead. If this smell is disgusting for Baba Yaga, it is because the dead in general are horrified by and scared of the living. No living being should cross the sacred threshold. In an American myth, the dead are so frightened upon seeing a live person in their kingdom that they shout, "There he is!" and hide under each other, forming a tall pile.[57] Some data indicate that during the initiation rite neophytes were made to bathe in order to get rid of "a feminine odor" (attested in former British New Guinea).[58] In the myths of the Kwakiutl tribe, which, as Boas has shown, is closely linked to the rite, during his journey the hero very often washes or rubs himself with strongly fragrant plants (such as hemlock) to kill the smell.[59]

There is a great deal more material on this issue that we could provide, but what has been given so far is sufficient for understanding the motif's significance.

7. She Gave Food and Drink

The laws of the wondertale require that, after shouting "Foo Foo Foo" and so forth, an interrogation should follow about the purpose of the journey: "Are you trying for deeds or flying from them?" We expect that the hero will now speak about the goal of his travels. However, the answer he gives must be recognized as a complete surprise and not as one that ensues from the threats of Yaga. He demands, first of all, to eat. "Well, old thing, what are you shouting about? First you must feed us and give us drink, then lead us to the bath house, and after that ask us for our news."[60] And the most surprising thing is that Baba Yaga is completely pacified by this answer: "Baba Yaga fed them, gave them drink, led them to the bathhouse."[61] "She climbed down and bowed down low to him."[62]

Food and refreshments are unfailingly mentioned in encounters not only with Yaga but also with many characters equivalent to her. In cases where the prince enters the hut and Yaga is not yet there, he finds a set table and sits down to eat without her. Sometimes the tale-teller describes the hut itself so that it fulfills this function: it is "propped up with a pie" or "it is roofed with a pancake," which corresponds to the gingerbread house in Western children's tales. Sometimes this house already reveals by its very appearance that it is a house of food.

We must note that this is a constant and typical feature of Yaga. She feeds and hosts the hero. We also note that he refuses to talk until he is fed. Yaga herself says, "Oh, silly me! I started asking questions while he is still hungry and cold."[63] What is this? Why does the hero never eat, for example, before he leaves his house, but only at the hut of Baba Yaga? This detail is neither novelistic nor neorealistic; it has its own specific history. The food here has a special meaning. As early as the stage of development of North American Indians, we see that a person who wants to enter the realm of the dead is offered a special kind of food. For example, in one North American legend, the master of the water brings young people to where he lives. "But an old woman, a mouse, warned the young people not to eat the food that Komokoa would give them, otherwise they would never return to the upper world."[64] According to Maori beliefs, "even if a soul has crossed that sombre stream, he may still return to the land of the living, if only he refuses to partake of the food set before him by the ghosts; but should he taste of it, he cannot come back."[65]

These cases show quite clearly that, having partaken of the food meant for the dead, the traveler permanently joins the world of the dead. This is why the living have a ban on touching this food. The dead not only are not disgusted by this food but must partake of it because it gives them explicit magical power, which is as necessary to the dead as their own food is necessary to the physical strength and vigor of the living.

By demanding this food, the hero shows that he is not afraid of it, that he is entitled to it, that he is genuine. This is why Yaga is humbled by his demand to give him food. In another American legend, sometimes the hero only pretends to eat it and actually throws this dangerous food on the ground. The wondertale hero does not do this; he is not afraid of the food. In places where the cult of the dead has already been fully developed, the traveler's need for food on his way is expressed clearly and preserved with details. In this regard Egypt provides a particularly striking example. Egyptian material explains why it is necessary first to eat, and only then is it possible to talk. The food opens the mouth of the deceased. Only after partaking of this food is the deceased able to speak.

In the Egyptian mortuary cult, food and drink were offered to the deceased—that is, to his mummy—before anything else was delivered to

the crypt. This was the so-called table of proposals. According to Wallis
Budge's description of the ceremony,

> The food was brought in upon a table, and two 'royal tables of offer-
> ings' were also set forth in the *usekht* hall, or chamber, of the tomb.
> The statue could not, of course, sit down to eat at the table, but it seems
> that someone, perhaps a priest, sat down to partake vicariously of the
> food on the table. The repast consisted of a few different kinds of bread
> and cakes, beer, *tchesert* drink, &c., and when it was ended the mouth
> of the statue was 'opened,' and the deceased whom it represented was
> believed to have become a *khu*, or spirit, and to possess all the faculties
> of the spirits in the Other World.[66]

This text clearly shows that the food "opens the mouth" and turns the
deceased into a spirit, a substitute of the transformation into an animal
that had been there in former times. The opening of the mouth was one
of the cult's most important ceremonies. In funerary texts, a special
book is dedicated to this, entitled *The Book of Opening the Mouth*. But
it is possible to find examples in the *Book of the Dead* as well. Here is
an excerpt from chapter 122 of the *Book of the Dead*: "'Open unto me.'
'Who then art thou? Whither goest thou? What is thy name?' 'I am one
of you, Assembler of Souls is the name of my boat. . . . Let there be given
unto me vessels of milk, together with cakes, and loaves of bread . . . and
pieces of meat. . . . Grant thou me [these things] wholly. . . . Let it be so
done unto me that I may enter in . . . like the *Bennu* bird.'"[67]

This excerpt contains two wishes: "let me eat" and "let me become
a bird." But in essence, it is one wish that in our language would be expressed this way: *let me eat in order to become a bird.* In chapter 106
of the *Book of the Dead* this is expressed more clearly: "Grant ye unto
me bread, grant ye unto me ale, and let me cleanse myself by means of
the haunch and by the offerings of cakes."[68] This means that the food
cleanses and purifies earthly things and transforms a man into a heavenly,
flying, lightweight being—into a bird. J. H. Breasted notes, "Finally this
strangely potent bread and beer which the priest offers the dead, not only
makes him a 'soul' and makes him 'prepared', but it also gives him 'power'
or makes him a mighty one." "Without this power . . . the Egyptians
believed the dead to be helpless. This 'power' was also intended to give
the dead ability to confront successfully the uncanny adversaries who
awaited him in the beyond."[69] As Budge's study shows, this ceremony was
considered very important and was applied to everyone, even the poor-
est, which is to say that it had a nationwide character and could easily be
preserved in folklore.

We find something similar in Babylon as well. In the second table of
the *Epic of Gilgamesh*, Eabani recounts a dream about how he descended
or was carried into the underworld: "Come down with me, go down with

me to the house of darkness, to the abode of Irkalla, to a dwelling from which, upon entering, nobody returns . . . to the place whose inhabitants do not know the answers." Like birds, they are clad in "plumage." Next there is an unclear passage, followed by a feast: "Apu and Ellil offer him roasted meat (perhaps broth). They offer bread, give him a cold drink, water from the wineskins."[70] Here too we see that, having stepped across the threshold of this world, the hero must first eat and drink. Here, likewise, we note first the consumption of magical food and afterward an interrogation at the home of the host.

In the ancient Iranian religion, "the soul, which has arrived in the sky, is showered with questions of how it got there. But Ahura Mazda prohibits asking about the terrible and horrible path by which it came, and orders that it be given some heavenly food."[71] Thus, here too (with an obvious rationalization), we see a ban on asking questions and the priority of offering heavenly food.

We find the same idea in antiquity. "Calypso wants Odysseus to take some nectar and ambrosia from her: only the one who has eaten the food and drunk the drink of the Elba inhabitants will forever remain in their power"; "Just as Persephone belongs to Hades, having eaten a pomegranate"; "It is also possible to recall lotus eating. Whoever among the Greeks ate this sweet food forgot his homeland and remained in the country of the lotus-eaters."[72] Similarly, Erwin Rohde writes, "*Wer von der Speise der Unterirdischen geniesst, ist ihnen verfallen*" (Whoever ate the food of the subterranean inhabitants was added to their assembly forever).[73]

All the materials and the analysis laid out here lead us to conclude that the motif of Baba Yaga feeding the hero on his way to the Thrice-Tenth Kingdom was formed on the basis of the notion of magical food consumed by the deceased on his way to the underworld.

8. Bony Leg

These are the first actions of Yaga when the hero appears at her hut.

We now turn to the analysis of Yaga herself. Her image is composed of a number of particular details. We shall first examine each of these individually, then analyze her figure as a whole. We see Yaga's appearance in two forms: either she is lying in the hut when Ivan enters, or she flies in.

Yaga the donor is in her hut when Ivan arrives. In the first instance, she is lying down. She lies on the stove, on a bench, or on the floor. Furthermore, her body takes up the whole hut. "Her head was out in front, one leg in a corner, and the other in another corner."[74] "On the stove lay Baba Yaga, she of the bony leg, from corner to corner, her nose in the ceiling."[75] But how shall we understand the details that her "nose was grown into the ceiling"? And why does Yaga's body take up the whole hut? After all, she is nowhere described or referred to as a giant. Therefore, it is not that she is big but that her hut is small. Yaga resembles a corpse in a narrow coffin or a special cubicle either for burial or for leaving someone to die. She is dead. Other researchers have also seen her as a dead character, a corpse. For example, Hermann Güntert, who studied the image of Yaga based on the ancient Calypso, claims, "If Hel (the northern goddess of the underground country of the dead) has the color of a corpse, it means nothing but the fact that she, the goddess of death, is herself a corpse."[76]

The Russian Yaga does not exhibit any other signs of being a corpse. But Yaga as an international phenomenon possesses such attributes to a great extent. "Such figures always contain an inherent attribute of decomposition: a hollow back, softened meat, brittle bones, the back eaten through by worms."[77]

If this observation is true, it will help us understand a constant trait in Yaga: her bony leg.

In order to understand this feature, we must bear in mind that "the perception of a corpse" is a very late phenomenon. In the materials from America mentioned above, which reflect an earlier stage of development, the guardian of the kingdom of the dead is always an animal or a blind old woman with no signs of being a corpse. The analysis of Yaga as the mistress of the forest kingdom and its animals will show us that her animalistic image is her oldest form. She also sometimes appears this way in Russian tales. In a tale from the Vyatka region compiled by D. K. Zelenin, which is in general replete with extremely archaic features, the role of Yaga in the hut is played by a he-goat. "The he-goat is lying on the bunk, his feet in the garden-beds," and so forth.[78] In other cases, a bear, a magpie, and others correspond to Yaga.[79] But the animal never possesses a bony leg, neither in the Russian material (which could be explained as a language feature, since *Yaga* rhymes with the Russian *noga*, or leg) nor in the international material. Therefore, the bony leg is somehow connected to Yaga's human image; it is associated with the process of Yaga's anthropomorphization. A transitional stage from animal to human is a human with an animal leg. But Yaga never has that kind of leg, the sort that is possessed by Pan, fauns, and a colorful array of various evil spirits. All kinds of elves, dwarfs, demons, and devils have animal legs. They preserve their animal legs the same way the hut has preserved them. But at the same time Yaga is so strongly associated with the image of death that the animal leg is replaced by the bony leg—that is, by the leg of a corpse or a skeleton. The bony-leg feature is connected to the fact that Yaga never walks. She either flies or lies down; in other words, even on the outside, she looks like a corpse. Perhaps this historical substitution explains why Empusa, who stands guard at the threshold of Hades, has a shifting appearance, looking at one time like a "great beast" and at others like a bull, a donkey, or a woman. As a woman, she has one iron leg and one leg made of donkey dung. When turning into a woman, she retains some features of her donkey nature. This leg is boneless. The decomposing leg can be viewed as another form of a dead leg. This form is not alien to Russian tales either: "One leg is full of sh . . . t, and the other's above the earth."[80]

It must be noted, however, that the explanation put forward here is still somewhat problematic, though it is more plausible than the theory proposed by Güntert. According to him, animal legs developed from the bony leg. He claims:

> There is a strange belief manifest in the widespread superstition that dwarfs, elves, and demons have animal feet, especially goose and duck feet. . . . It is natural first of all to assume a transformation into animals in order to explain this strange feature of many legends, but I do not think that the real reason lies here. We know that demons are thought of as decomposing skeletons, so, therefore, the ugly look of the feet can be explained in the following manner: the footprint of the skeleton was seen as the footprint of a duck or a goose, and when this connection was no longer felt, the legend of a demon foot arose.[81]

This explanation suffers from forced interpretations, and moreover it is historically inaccurate. The explanation that the bony leg evolved from the footprint of a skeleton is incorrect because such traces cannot be observed in nature. This trace plays a role in folk beliefs (the German *Drudenfuß*),[82] but this belief itself requires an explanation. The assertion that the bony leg is primary and the animal leg secondary is not supported by the materials recorded in their developmental stages: the animalistic image of death is older than the bony or skeletal image.

9. Yaga's Blindness

Yaga gradually assumes a clear shape before us as a guardian of the entrance to the Thrice-Tenth Kingdom and, at the same time, as a creature associated with the animal world and the world of the dead. She recognizes the hero as a living being and does not want to let him in, warns him of dangers, and so on. She shows him the path only after he has eaten. She recognizes Ivan as a live being by his smell. But there is another reason why Yaga perceives Ivan this way. Although it is never stated in Russian folktales, it is nevertheless possible to establish that she is blind and cannot see Ivan but instead recognizes him by his smell. Incidentally, this blindness is already assumed by Alexander Potebnia. He explains it as follows: "Yaga, among other things, seems to be blind. One can guess that Baba Yaga's blindness means ugliness. The notions of darkness, blindness, and ugliness are akin and can replace one another."

Potebnia demonstrates this through an analysis of the root *lep* in Slavic languages.[83] This conclusion is incorrect because Yaga appears blind not only on Russian or Slavic soil. The blindness of creatures like Yaga is an international phenomenon. If we decide to take the approach of studying the etymology of the name or word that denotes a phenomenon (which is always very dangerous and often incorrect in essence, for meanings change while the word remains), then we would have to do a comparative study of designations of blindness in different languages. None of them will lead to the name Yaga. But such an analysis could show that *blindness* means not just a lack of vision. For example, the Latin *caecus* means not only an active blindness (sightlessness) but also, so to speak, passive blindness (lack of visibility—e.g., *caeca nox*, "blind" night). The same thing can be derived with respect to the German *ein blindes Fenster* (the "blind pane" of a window).

Thus, analysis of the concept of blindness could lead to the notion of invisibility—of a person who is not blind himself but in relation to something else. The sense of a certain mutual invisibility may lie behind this blindness. With regard to Yaga, this could lead to the transfer of relationships from the world of the living to the world of the dead: the living do not see the dead just as the dead do not see the living. However, one could argue that then the hero would also have to be presented as blind. And indeed, this is how it should have been, and this is how it really is. We shall see that the hero becomes blind after coming to Yaga.

But is Yaga really blind? This is not directly apparent, but it can be inferred based on some circumstantial evidence. In "Baba Yaga and Zhikhar," Yaga wants to kidnap Zhikhar, so she flies in when his friends and housemates, a cat and a sparrow, have gone out to collect firewood.[84] She begins to count the spoons: "'This is tomcat's spoon, this is sparrow's spoon, and the third is Zhikhar's.' Zhikhar could not stand it anymore and shouted out, 'Don't touch my spoon, Baba-Yaga!' Yaga grabbed Zhikhar and dragged him off."[85] Thus, in order to find Zhikhar, Yaga has to hear his voice. She does not look for him; she listens, the same way she sniffs to recognize her visitors.

In other tales someone blinds Yaga: "As soon as she fell asleep, the girl filled her eyes with pitch, packed them with cotton. Then she picked up the child and ran away with him."[86] Polyphemus (who is very closely related to Yaga) is blinded by Odysseus exactly the same way; in the Russian versions of this story the eye is not pricked out but has something poured into it.[87] For these kinds of creatures, having only one eye can be interpreted as a type of blindness. In German tales, the witch has swollen eyelids and red eyes—that is, she has no actual eyeballs but red eyeholes without eyes.[88]

All these arguments speak to Yaga's possible but not factual blindness. On the other hand, we have the real, true blindness of creatures analogous to Yaga in the stories of hunting peoples where such creatures are more alive, not yet relic phenomena. In these stories old women of this type are always (or almost always) truly blind: "He came to a tent that stood alone: one blind woman was in it."[89] This old woman is met by the miraculously born hero after he leaves his house. She questions him regarding his journey. In other examples, the hero goes to the bottom of the sea, and there he sees three women eating: "He saw that they were blind." They show him the way.[90]

If it is true that Yaga guards the Thrice-Tenth Kingdom from the living, and if the visitor blinds her as he is returning, then this means that Yaga does not see the one who has gone to the realm of the living, the one who has returned from her kingdom. Similarly, in Nikolai Gogol's "Viy" the devils do not see the Cossack. The devils who are able to see the living are like shamans among them, similar to living shamans who are able to see the dead, something ordinary mortals cannot do. The devils call to this kind of shaman, and this is Viy.[91]

But the problem is not yet solved.

It was previously stated that Yaga has some connection to the rite of initiation. This connection will gradually become clear to us. The initiate was taken into the forest, led into a hut, and there stood before a monstrous creature, the master of death and the ruler of the animal kingdom. He descended to the realm of death in order to come back again to the upper world. We know that he underwent a symbolic blinding in precisely the same ways that Yaga and Polyphemus are blinded in tales: his eyes were plastered. Frobenius describes this as follows: "The neophyte is led to the hut blindfolded. In the pit, they prepare a thick porridge-like mixture, a type of mortar. Someone among those already initiated grasps the neophyte and rubs this mixture, to which pepper was added, into his eyes. A horrible cry is heard, while those standing outside the hut clap their hands and sing praises to the spirit."[92] This is not an isolated case. Hans Nevermann reports from Oceania, "After a few days of rest, the neophytes are covered with a lime mixture, so that they look completely white and cannot open their eyes."[93] The meaning of these actions becomes clear when understanding the meaning of the whole rite. White is the color of death and invisibility. Temporary blindness is also a sign of departure for the realm of death. Afterward the lime is washed away, with simultaneous recovery of sight, which symbolizes the acquisition of new vision just like the initiate's acquisition of a new name. This is the last stage of the ceremony; afterward the neophyte returns home. Along with the opening of the mouth discussed above, we have here an opening of the eyes. We also know that at the same time a circumcision was performed, not preserved by the tale, and a knocking out of the front teeth, also not preserved. Comparison of all these actions helps to explain circumcision as another type of magical opening, preceded by abstinence, like the opening of the eyes that is preceded by artificial blindness and the opening of the mouth that was preceded by muteness: there is evidence of a prohibition of expression in these cases. After this, the young man gains the right to marry. However, since these phenomena are not reflected in the wondertale, we shall not discuss them here.

The actions performed on the boys remind us of actions that the hero carries out on Baba Yaga or on Polyphemus. However, there is one fundamental difference between the rite and the tale. In the rite it is the boy's eyes that are plastered whereas in the tale it is the eyes of the witch or the corresponding character. In other words, the myth or tale shows a precise reverse transformation of the rite. What is the reason for this reversal?

For children and mothers this rite was scary and horrible, but it was considered necessary because the initiated gain something, what we would call a magical power over animals—that is, the rite correlates to the methods of primitive hunting. But with the improvement of tools, with the transition to agriculture, and with the advent of new social systems the old cruel rites were perceived as unnecessary and cursed, and their sharp end was turned against the ones who carried them out. If during the rite the boy is blinded in the forest by a creature who torments him and threatens to devour him, then the myth, by now detached from the ritual, begins to serve as a kind of protest. We shall see a similar case in the analysis of the motive of combustion: in the rite the children are "burned" while in the tale the children burn the witch.

But apart from these cases of inverse transformation, the tale retains some traces of the hero's blindness in particular. In Yaga's hut the hero sometimes complains of pain in his eyes. The causes of this pain are diverse. "First give me water to wash out my eyes, give me drink, feed me, and then question me."[94] "My eyes swelled up from the wind," he complains in another tale.[95] One could argue that this is a purely rational motif. But in light of the material summarized above, the situation looks different. In one Zulu tale a girl who has returned after initiation says, "I can't see anything."[96] Perhaps a separate study of blindness will show why prophets and seers (Tiresias), liberators of peoples (Samson), patriarchs (Jacob, Isaac), and prophetic poets (Homer) are often depicted as blind.

10. The Mistress of the Forest

Another feature of Yaga's image is her pointedly emphasized female physiology. Her gender attributes are exaggerated; she is depicted as a woman with huge breasts, "her tits hanging over the ridge"[97]; "Yaga

Yagishna, Ovdot'ia Kuzminishna, her nose up in the ceiling, her tits over the threshold, her snot through the flower bed, she rakes the soot with her tongue."[98] Or, "On the ninth brick of the stove lies Baba Yaga the bony leg, her nose rooted in the ceiling, her snot hanging over the threshold, her tits wrapped around a hook, while she herself sharpens her teeth." Or, even more bluntly, "Baba Yaga the bony leg jumped out of the hut, her a . . . ropey, her c . . . soapy."[99]

Yaga is thus equipped with all the attributes of maternity. But at the same time, she knows nothing of married life. She is always an old woman, moreover an old woman without a husband. Yaga is not a mother of humans; she is the mother and mistress of the animals, specifically of forest beasts. She represents the stage when fertility was imagined as involving a woman without a man's participation. The hypertrophy of Yaga's maternal organs does not correspond to any matrimonial functions. Perhaps this is why she is always an old woman. Although she is a representative of her sex, she does not live the life of her sex. She is solely a mother, not a wife in either the present or the past. It is true that she is never called the mother of animals in folktales, but she has unlimited power over them. Here is an example of how she summons the animals in a northern tale: "Gray wolves, wherever you are, all of you run and roll into one place and into one circle; choose among yourselves the biggest and the strongest to pursue Ivan Tsarevich."[100] In a tale about Koshchei, the youngest Yaga sends the hero to the elder Yaga: "On the road ahead lives my elder sister, —perhaps she knows; she has answer-givers. Her first answer-givers are the beasts of the forest, second are the birds of the air, third are the fish and creatures of the sea. Whatever is in the whole world obeys her."[101] Or, "The old woman went out onto the porch and shouted in a loud voice, and suddenly—out of nowhere—all kinds of animals came running, all kinds of birds flew up."[102] Sometimes the winds are also subordinated to Yaga: "The old woman went out onto the porch. She shouted in a loud voice and whistled a hero's whistle. Suddenly wild winds arose and blew from all directions. They shook the hut."[103] Elsewhere she is called the mother of winds.[104] She keeps the keys of the sun.[105] The male equivalent of Yaga is Jack Frost (*Morozko*), the master of frost; in German folktales, the equivalent is Frau Holle, who calls forth the snow. The Eskimo equivalent is the mistress of sea animals.[106] The equivalent in Dolgan folklore is the mistress of the sea.[107]

But we ask ourselves, where is maternity in this? We must acknowledge here the traces of extremely ancient social relations. A mother is at the same time a sovereign. With the fall of matriarchy women are deprived of their power, and motherhood remains merely as one of women's social functions. But in myth it is different for woman, the mother-mistress: her motherhood is lost; only *attributes* of her motherhood and her *power* over the animals remain. Additionally, since the hunter's whole life depends on animals, she also retains power over the life and death of humans.

The detail that she rules over animals, and specifically over forest animals, is connected to the fact that humans at that stage of development depended on forest and game animals, to which they attributed their own clan structure. In other words, Yaga represents a phenomenon known in ethnography as *the master.*

The question of the master is extremely complex and far from being well studied. As Zelenin writes, "How did the idea of 'the master' evolve? A special study must be undertaken to understand this complex and large issue."[108]

What does *the mistress* mean? Lev Shternberg demonstrates on the basis of many examples that the cult of animals was originally a cult of the animal in general. Later the cult was transferred to certain representatives of these species, which remained sacred (the bear, the Egyptian Apis, and so on). Eventually an anthropomorphized image of the master of these species evolves; it may already have a human, mixed, or intermittent form. All individuals of these species are subordinate to this master. Animals are not the only ones who have a master. There are masters of the forces of nature such as thunder, the sun, mountains, winds, and so on. Tribal relations are projected onto animals, and subsequently masters of this kind evolve into individual gods.

Let us now examine what Yaga was at earlier cultural stages and ask what she corresponded to in these cases. We have seen that Yaga is presented as an old woman in these stages as well. We have also seen that she is often an old woman and at the same time an animal ("This woman was a duck"). Cases in which the Russian Yaga corresponds to an animal are of particular interest to us. In a Native American myth, parents take their children into the forest and abandon them there, tying them to a tree. A wolf (it is stressed that the wolf is old) and a coyote appear. The old wolf cries, "Come everyone from all directions." It continues, "The wolves and coyotes came from all parts of the earth." The old wolf commands those gathered to untie the children. By winter the children have built a cabin. The sister receives from the wolves the gift of fulfilling wishes. At her wish the tent is surrounded by herds of deer, buffalo, and other game animals. One look from the girl can kill them. It is enough for her to say a word, and the skins sew themselves together and become a teepee. Patterns of drawings appear by themselves on the bedcovers, the same patterns that the tribe has used to the present day. She gives her brother helpers—a panther and a bear.[109]

This example is extraordinarily revealing. The master is an animal (the old wolf). But he not only has power over the wolves yet also bestows the power over all the animals needed by the hunter. He transmits this power to the sister, not the brother. She provides her brother with helpers. This example reveals the basis of these stories in the economy of hunting. It also shows the connection with totemism: this girl gives the tribe its sacred patterns.

There are many more examples of this kind. We are concerned, however, not with the number of examples but with the essence of the phenomenon.

Before we continue our study of Yaga the mistress, we must address another issue. Until now Yaga has appeared to us as guardian of the entrance to the realm of the dead. Now she appears as mistress of the animals. Is there a connection? What do we have here—two lines, two traditions, in a single image or a single image with a causal link between Yaga the mistress and Yaga the guardian of the entrance? Why is it specifically the master of nature who guards the entrance to the other world? We can answer these questions by examining the materials themselves. We already know that at some stage death was conceived of as a transformation into animals. Given this fact, it is precisely the master of the animals who guards the entrance to the realm of death (i.e., the animal kingdom) and who bestows the power to change into an animal and power over animals; in a later interpretation the master bestows a magical animal as a gift. For example, in a very interesting tale in Boas's collection, the hero comes to the wolves. All the wolves, bears, and otters are summoned, and every kind of honor is bestowed upon the stranger. "Then the wolf suddenly brought in a corpse. They wrapped it up in a wolf's skin, put it by the fire, and began to dance around it and beat time. Then the dead man got up and started to stagger. But the more they sang, the more confidently he began to move, and finally he started running exactly like a wolf. And the leader of the wolves said, 'Now you see what happens to the dead, we turn them into wolves.' These wolves teach him the dance of the wolves. 'When you return home, teach the people our dance.'" They give him a magic arrow whose mere aim is enough to kill the game without firing a shot.[110] This example, among other things, provides an explanation of Yaga's magical gifts.

This myth also explains the ritual. We now understand the purpose of leaving for the realm of the dead to see the totemic ancestor-master.

We will not examine now the image of Yaga as a woman but will do so later, while examining transvestism. It is important for us to establish that the image of Yaga goes back to a totemic ancestor of the female line. Later the role of progenitor along with its power is transferred to a male. It is specifically as an ancestor that Yaga is linked to the hearth. She "rakes coals with her hands"[111]; "on the stove lay Baba

Yaga"[112]; "she rakes the soot with her tongue."[113] "She herself is lying on the bench, while her teeth are on the stove."[114] The *hearth* appears historically alongside the cult of the male ancestor. The hearth, in fact, is not tied to Yaga as a woman but to the clan's female progenitor. The hearth as a clan (male) attribute of progeny is transferred to the image of Yaga. This is why she is ascribed all sorts of female attributes linked not so much with the hearth as with the kitchen: a poker, a broom, and a hearth-broom; hence too the connection with other kitchen accessories such as the pestle, the mortar, and so on.

At this point it is possible to describe the further evolution of creatures of this kind. There is a direct link from the deer-giving wolf, through animal women, to goddesses such as Cybele with her exaggerated organs of fertility; Artemis the eternal virgin, who is accompanied by animals and resides in the woods; and others. The hunting origin of Cybele is shown both by Shternberg's lectures on the evolution of religious beliefs and by Frazer in *The Golden Bough.*

Subsequently, as the guardian begins to lose her connection with the animal world during the advance of agriculture, she still remains the guardian of the entrance and a helper who points the way to the other world. This is the case in the Egyptian mortuary cult: "He has come from these his two mothers, the two vultures with long hair and hanging breasts, who are on the mountain of Sehseh. They draw their breasts over the mouth of king Pepi."

The deceased Pepi must pronounce these words in order to get into the kingdom of the blessed.[115] Thus, the woman-animal who guards the entrance to the other world is found not only in myths and folktales but also directly in the later stage's mortuary cult.

11. Yaga's Tasks

It is widely believed that the Yaga character typically assigns difficult tasks. This is true only when the main hero is a woman, and even then it can be shown that these tasks are mainly of recent origin. Men are given tasks much less often, on the whole rarely, and the tasks are quite few in number. Usually the reward follows immediately after a dialogue. "You'll hardly make it there! Shall I help you?" said the old woman, and then she gave him her horse.[116] "She fed him, gave him a drink, and gave him the Young Mare Zolotitsa."[117] We could cite a great many examples here; this is the typical form.

The question is, what has the hero done to receive the award from Yaga? The award itself has no external or artistic motivation. But in light of the materials discussed above, we can say that the hero has already passed a series of tests. He knew the magic to open the door.

He knew the spell that turned and opened the hut and knew the magic of gestures: he sprinkled the door with water. He brought a propitiatory offering to the beasts that guard the entrance. Finally, and most importantly, he was not afraid of Yaga's food, demanded it himself, and by doing so attached himself forever to the host of otherworldly beings. The tests are followed by inquiries and the inquiries by a reward. This also explains the confidence with which the hero carries himself. He sees nothing surprising in the things he encounters here; on the contrary, it is as if all this is long familiar to him and just what he expects. He feels confident because he is armed with magic. This knowledge has no actual motivation in the tales themselves. We only occasionally encounter characters such as the aunt who instructs the maiden on how to behave at Yaga's house. The hero knows all this because he is the hero. His heroism consists specifically in his knowledge of magic and of its power.

The entire testing procedure reflects the ancient idea that just as you can summon forth rain or make animals come to the hunter by magic, so can magic force an entry into the other world. The important thing is not virtue or purity but power. As technology developed, however, so did social life. Certain standards of legal and other relations evolved; these were introduced into the cult and began to be called virtues. Therefore, already at a very early stage, new concepts of verifying the virtue of the deceased began to appear along with checking the magical power of "the deceased." Both the earliest and the more recent concepts are reflected in the Egyptian *Book of the Dead*. An example of a later concept is "weighing the heart" of the dead on a scale—a concept that, as we shall see below, is also reflected in wondertales. It is notable that a feather, symbol of the goddess Maat and a symbol of law and truth, serves as the counterweight.

These notions of verifying virtue also entered the wondertale and were preserved in it, from relatively early concepts about virtues associated with the cult of ancestors to the most recent domestic virtues such as the ability to beat a featherbed well or wash clothes. Checking the magical power of the deceased and granting the hero a helper for the further journey in the kingdom of the dead turned into a test of virtue and a reward for it. This is how the function of assigning tasks arose. The tasks themselves are sometimes transferred from another motif, from the tasks assigned by a princess. There they are really appropriate and canonical. Such, for example, is the task of choosing one among twelve identical maidens or keeping together a herd of cattle. Still, some of the tasks set by Yaga reach back to great antiquity. Such tasks or requirements include, for example, the requirement of not falling asleep—that is, the prohibition against sleep.

12. The Trial by Sleeping

Yaga's demand that a hero or heroine not fall asleep is very often associated with the quest for magical *gusli* that can play by itself.[118] "Perhaps I'll give you one [gusli], but with a single condition: No one must sleep when I start tuning it up!"[119] "Now, you sit and do not doze, otherwise you will not get the self-playing gusli."[120]

The above examples may make it seem that the prohibition against sleep is consistently associated with the motif of the gusli. But that link is not stable and is only a tendency evident in the Russian material. This association, nevertheless, does in fact occur quite often. The hero's wife gives him a flower as he leaves. "'Plug your ears,' she says, 'with this flower, and do not be afraid of anything!' And the Fool did it. The tinker began to play his harp, and the Fool sat there and sleep did not overtake him."[121] Here we inevitably recall Odysseus, who similarly plugged his ears against the sirens. Perhaps this analogy sheds light on the image of the sirens, who lure the hero with their singing and kill him. Falling asleep in Yaga's hut immediately results in death. "'Mind you,' wolf the people-gobbler says to him, 'don't dare sleep! If you fall asleep, I'll swallow you straight off.'"[122] The prohibition against sleep occurs without being associated with the gusli even in Russian materials. The forest itself is magical and causes an irresistible drowsiness. "They walked and walked till they came to a deep forest. As soon as they entered it, they were overwhelmed by drowsiness."[123] Among other peoples, the motif of sleep is not connected to the motif of the gusli, but it is always associated with the motif of the witch. In Dolgan folklore we find a very detailed elaboration of this prohibition. Here the hero is playing cards with the witch, and suddenly an irresistible drowsiness attacks him. He deceives her twice, saying that he is not falling asleep but sinking into a reverie. But the third time he admits that he fell asleep, and the witch wants to eat him up.[124]

We shall begin the explanation of this motif by pointing to American material. Gayton's aforementioned work on the story of a husband who goes in search of his deceased wife shows that the visitor must not yawn and must not sleep, as this will give away the fact that he is a living being. Sleep here has the same significance as smell. The living are recognizable because they give off a scent and they yawn, sleep, and laugh. The dead do none of these things. It is natural, therefore, that the keeper who guards the kingdom of the dead from the living should try to learn the nature of the visitor by his smell, laughter, and sleeping and thereby determine his right to continue the journey. For example, here is how Gayton retells one recording of this story: The hero goes to look for his dead wife, comes to the leader of another world, and, after a meal, expresses his wish. "Tipiknits said he did not think that the man could get his wife as he would have to stay awake all night. He told the man that he could not take his wife back if he dozed off for one instant."[125]

The fact that the test by sleeping is not an accidental phenomenon is evident also in the epic of Gilgamesh. There the hero is looking for Ut-Napishtim in order to receive immortality from him (which is similar to the water of life in Russian folktales). Ut-Napishtim is the same sort of tester and donor we find in wondertales. He suggests that the hero not sleep for six days and seven nights. But Gilgamesh, tired from the long journey, dozes off. However, Ut-Napishtim's wife feels sorry for him and wakes him just as he is falling asleep.[126] Hugo Gressmann adds, "Then her husband asks her to bake bread for Gilgamesh, probably for his journey. Quite a mysterious scene of bread-baking follows, with the bread, it seems, credited with some magic power."[127] We know by now the power attributed to the food eaten at the entrance to the realm of the dead. In general, these cases show that the prohibition against sleep fits perfectly with the image of Yaga and her role.

In works devoted to a rite of passage, there is no specific mention of the prohibition on sleep. However, isolated examples of such a ban have been recorded. Among the southeastern African nations, where boys undergo circumcision at the age of fourteen, initiates are not allowed to sleep until the wound heals. Among the Jews the night before circumcision is called "night of vigil," as on this night one should not sleep lest Shedim, the evil spirits, try to seize the boy before circumcision.[128] In general, the rite of initiation is poorly known. We know that it is perceived as a death and resurrection or rebirth. Samter collected a great deal of material on the prohibition against sleep during birth, death, and marriage. For us, these materials are important because they indirectly confirm the sleep prohibition's connection to the sphere of death and birth—that is, to the sphere that was the basis of the initiation rite.

13. Children Banished and Taken to the Forest

Up to this point, we have examined the image of Yaga that is mainly associated with her role as a guardian of the path to the Thrice-Tenth Kingdom. In passing, we might note that this image reflects not only the abstract concept of death but also concrete rituals associated with this concept. Traces of these rituals exist, but so far they have been sporadic and hardly noticeable. We must now directly approach comparison of the ritual with the wondertale. Even those somewhat hypothetical cases of correspondence that we have found force us to examine the material more closely and to carry out a more accurate and in-depth comparison.

In presenting the material so far, we have proceeded from the tales. Based on the hero's journey, we have examined the things that he sees as he proceeds. Now we shall begin with the rite as our basis and examine the material in the order the rite dictated. Let us trace its entire course from beginning to end and compare it with the material the tale provides. This will allow us to shed light on some initial elements of the tale that have so far been left on the periphery.

The age at which children were subject to the rite of passage varied, but there was a tendency to carry it out just before the onset of puberty. Recall that it is always children who come to the house of Yaga in her hypostasis of devourer.

When the decisive moment arrived, children one way or another left for the forest to see a creature that was terrible and mysterious to them. The forms of this departure vary. Three forms are of interest for the folklorist: when children are taken to the forest by their parents, a staged abduction of children into the woods, and, finally, sending a boy into the forest on his own with no parental involvement.

If children were taken away, it was always done by the father or a brother. The mother could not do it because the place where the rite was performed was forbidden to women. Failure to comply with the ban could lead to the woman's immediate execution. "At nightfall, the novices, each accompanied by his father or male guardian, are led into the depths of the forest and brought before *Kovave*." This is how Hutton Webster describes the children's abduction in Papua New Guinea.[129] We must imagine that the children were not always brought to the sacred place; they might be left alone to find the hut themselves. We know that in the wondertale, children who are lost or abandoned in the woods climb a tree and look for a spark of light. In these cases, they do not find a human dwelling but wind up in a forest hut of the type under study here.

The initiate boy was seen off with a ceremony as if he were being sent to his death. The initiate was decorated, painted, and clothed in a special way. "When the women first gaze upon the lad thus ornamented, they all begin to cry, and so do his immediate relatives, his father and mother's brothers, who further smear themselves over with grease and ashes to express their grief"—which is to say we have a typical picture of primordial mourning.[130]

We can see from such a description that this forced departure was experienced as a disaster by part of the population, first and foremost by the boys themselves. They did not yet know what great benefits awaited them. But while the forced departure seemed to be a hostile act, it was necessary because public opinion demanded it. The initiate gained great benefits. The father was the initiator of the departure. But later, when the rite started to die out, public opinion had to change. The benefits obtained by the act of initiation became unintelligible, and public opinion shifted and began to condemn this terrible practice. This is precisely the moment when the plot emerges. As long as it was a living rite, there could be no tales about it.

In the wondertale, taking children into the forest is always a hostile act, although later on things turn out well for the person expelled or abducted. Let us see how the child is sent to the woods in the tale. The family is initially afflicted with a certain ambivalence. On the one hand, they desire and are awaiting a baby, and when it arrives, they care for it in a touching way: "And in place of the block of wood there began to grow in the swaddling clothes a little son, Tereshechka, a real little jewel."[131] On the other hand, the family experiences muted or open hostility. The usual formula is, "How can it be destroyed?" These words may be said by any family members with respect to each other, but with one exception: they are never uttered by a character of the younger generation with respect to their elders—that is, sons or daughters never say it of their father or mother. It is only the older ones who want to destroy the younger. This desire to destroy is associated with one dominant form: the unwanted boy or girl, or brother and sister, is expelled, taken, or sent to the forest: "He became furious, took his sister, and drove her off into the dense forest."[132] "Come along, children, let's go to the woods. I'll chop wood, and you'll pick berries."[133] Often, a hut is already there at the outset. "He took his daughter to the forest and left her there in the hut."[134] "I'll take every son of mine to the forest, and I'll find out what they're capable of."[135] In this case, it is clear from the very beginning that the son will exhibit or acquire certain skills in the forest. "Once they asked their mother to let little brother Ivan go out hunting with them. They led him into a dark forest and left him there."[136] "If that's the case, get ready to go to the woods. They came into the forest. They took the clothes off him and told him to sit down in the hollow of an oak tree, and left him there, naked and barefoot."[137] We could write out several pages of examples like these. One can create an entire classification system and study which stories have a departure by taking the boy or expelling him and which do not; it is possible to study the motivation of this expulsion or to ask who is taken away (a son, a daughter, at what age, etc.). For our purposes, this is not essential. We shall concentrate on only one feature, the question of who takes the children to the forest.

We have seen that the expulsion is motivated by some ad hoc animosity. Historically the initiator of the removal was the father or, in the absence of a father, an older brother, the mother's brother, and so on. But a father's enmity to his son is something alien and incomprehensible for storytellers; it does not conform to their family ideals. In order to justify this enmity, the wondertale proceeds along two lines. On the one hand, it blackens and demeans the son: he deserves to be expelled from home. This son is a sluggard ("He did no work at all"[138]) and mischief maker;

people complain about him; he is hapless, a fool. But these examples are relatively rare. More often than not this hostility is made to fit the conditions of a family feud, known to the Russian village from real life. The feud appears with the entry of a new member into the family, the bearer of this hostility; these are second wives or second husbands with children from the first marriage. This is how the stepmother enters the wondertale, and her historical role is to take on the animosity that once belonged to the father. She is the main initiator of driving the children into the forest, to Yaga, and so on.

Examples of hatred from the parents themselves are quite rare. "When the son was born, at the beginning the mother loved him very much, felt compassion for him and caressed him, bringing him up as well as possible. The father even more so. It was when he began to grow, learned his letters, and had turned thirteen years old that she began to dislike him."[139] The same occurs when a brother and a sister live peacefully, but a sister-in-law appears on the horizon. The sister-in-law becomes the enemy of the sister, and her brother takes her into the woods. Thus, parents themselves do not destroy their children directly. I will not cite here examples of the enmity of the stepmother and her stepdaughter, which are well known. But it is still the father who takes the daughter off into the woods after all, and he plays a most wretched role there. "Our peasant thought and thought, and took his daughter off into the woods."[140] "The old man felt sorry for the eldest daughter. He loved her . . . and didn't know how to assuage his grief. The old man was weak, the old woman crabby."[141] "The old man began to grieve and lament; but still he put his daughter on a sledge."[142] The question arises: why can't the stepmother get rid of the stepdaughter or stepson herself? Why, vicious and ferocious as she is, does she not take the children into the forest with her authoritative hand? Logically she can well do it, but historically she cannot because the children were always taken to the forest only by a father, a brother, or an uncle, never by a woman. Only a man could do it, and the man in this role is not entirely supplanted in the tale.

14. Kidnapped Children

Another form of sending the boy away in the rite was a real or staged kidnapping. "It often happens that the boy is seized by the so-called devil and Gri-Gri takes him into the woods. Notably, no one knows about it, but it is conjectured."[143] In such cases, they would tell the mother that the children had been carried away by a spirit. Use of the words *devil* and *spirit* prove either that we are dealing with a later phenomenon or that there is a flaw in the recording. The creatures that appeared from the woods were masked like animals or birds, depicted these animals, and imitated them. The sound of rattles was heard in the forest, and everyone fled in terror. After they had taken away the uncircumcised boys, people said that Marsaba had swallowed the boys and would not bring them back until people had made abundant offerings of pigs and taro.[144] Fear of these creatures and the mysterious ceremonies associated with them was so great that it lasted long after the introduction of Christianity and the termination of these rites.[145] The fear of these creatures served as an educational tool. "Instead of corporal punishment, a Navajo mother substitutes the threat of the vengeance of these masked characters, should her children be disobedient."[146] This fear and this threat have survived the centuries and come down to our days. Such threats were present in antiquity. The lamia was a creature that kidnapped children. Lamia was the common name while *Mormo*, *Gello*, *Carco*, and *Empusa* were particular types of lamia.[147] The belief in such creatures in Europe was studied by Wilhelm Mannhardt, and there is no need to provide a résumé of his materials here and prove the connection of these creatures with the Russian Yaga who abducts children.

15. Advance Sale

Besides taking the boy away directly or with a staged kidnapping, there was another form of sending him to the woods, but in order to understand this form we must make a clarification in our account of the rite and its significance. To this point it has been presented in such a way that the boy who had undergone the initiation rite would return home, marry, and so on. It should be noted that the initiated members constitute something of an organization, usually called a male association or, in English terminology, a secret alliance. The word *secret* here is not entirely appropriate since the association's existence was not a secret. The secret (for the uninitiated) was its internal organization and inner life. The associations played a huge and quite diverse role in the life of the tribe. They often held political power. There could be several associations that differed from one another in rank. The initiation rite was simultaneously a rite of admission to the association. Following initiation into the association's secrets came not just entry but also transition from its lowest to its highest rank. A formal (but not actual) entry into the association took place immediately at birth and perhaps even before birth. At the baby's birth he was, as we might say today, assigned to an association. In other words, it was as if the baby were sold in advance. The father thereupon paid a certain fee to the association and, when the time came, gave the boy away to the association, and the boy was subjected to the initiation rite. "Boys are admitted to the association in their childhood, even though they learn the appropriate dances and take part in them only later."[148] Schurtz expresses this more precisely: "And the children may be sold in advance (*eingekauft*), but they learn the dances only upon reaching the appropriate age." The same thing happens when joining the famous "Duk-Duk" association.[149] Boys could be sold in advance immediately upon birth, but their induction did not take place before they were sixteen years old. In exact correspondence to this, the Russian folktale says, "When your son or daughter is born, they will be yours until the age of sixteen, and after sixteen, prescribe them to me."[150]

In other words, this parallel sheds light on the motif "give me what you have at home that you do not know." This can be called the motif of advance sale. Its general pattern is as follows: A man far from home gets into some unexpected trouble. For example, his ships suddenly stop their sailing journey at sea, or he bends over to take a drink and a monster pops out of the water and grabs him by the beard, or he is lost in the woods, or he picks a flower in a strange magic garden for his daughter, and so on. There are many types of motivations, but for our purposes examining them here is unimportant.

The second part of this motif is when a sea king, or an old man in the pond, or the owner of the garden, the devil, and so on, requires that the man in trouble "give me what is at your home that you do not know." Not knowing what he is doing, he promises the monster his baby and, having bought his way out of trouble, leaves for home; at home, he discovers that in fact he has a newborn son. This motif was specifically studied by Baumgartner, who was forced to conclude that the "essence and roots of this motif are not sufficiently clear."[151] However, if one looks closely at what is happening in the tale, the following becomes clear: a deal is struck upon the birth of a baby, after which the child is put at the disposal of a mysterious forest or water creature.

Let us examine this deal a little more closely. It is surrounded by the deepest secrecy. Things are not called by their names. The baby in this case is never explicitly named. "What is at your home that you do not know" is a euphemistic expression. In the system of the secret association, which is surrounded by a number of the strictest taboos, this euphemism is probably a historical fact. The second feature to note is the water or forest character of one of the parties to the contract. The nature of this mysterious old man cannot yet be explained; it will become clearer when we see where the boy ends up. Finally, for us the third and most important aspect of the deal is its time frame. After the deal, the boy still remains with his father up to a certain age and leaves only after the "right time has come." What is this right time? What are the benefits for the old man in claiming the boy for himself, and why does he not take him right away? Everything becomes clear if we assume that "the right time" is the onset of puberty. "You will have a son born but with one condition—you must give him to me when he is seventeen years old."[152] Sometimes the storyteller himself is puzzled at such a postponement and understands it in his own way: "Let me raise my son until he is twelve years old. At least I will have the chance to feast my eyes on him"[153]—that is, the storyteller sees some leniency in this unclear postponement. A son leaves with these words, for example: "'Farewell, Papa! Send me where you have promised to send me! Give me your blessing, the time has come.' His father and mother were crying, not letting him go. At last, however, they released him, and he left."[154] "'Daddy dear, farewell now, I'm not yours anymore!' 'But, son, where will you go?' The son said, 'Now I will set off to the forest monster to be devoured.'"[155]

Sometimes the boy leaves to see his godfather. This is a very interesting variation that is quite justified since the rite of baptism and the rite of initiation are historically connected. The godfather replaces the teacher and the mentor of more ancient times. "And he ordered that his goddaughter be sent to him when she grew up."[156] In these cases the godfather sometimes tries to eat his goddaughter.

Advance sale is very similar to a simple sale, or giving the son away, to some mysterious or suddenly appearing sorcerer, craftsman, devil, or other figure. We will learn the nature of this teacher below. A woman has a son who is a fool. An old man comes. "'Come on, give him to me,' he says, 'I will teach him.' So she gave him away."[157] "'Well, give him to me,' the man said. 'For three years I'll teach him everything clever he needs to know.'"[158] The *Oh* creature that appears (sometimes out of the grave) when a person says "oh!" also belongs among these mysterious teachers. Paul Kretschmer sees in it a messenger or embodiment of death, which is quite consistent with the range of phenomena discussed here.[159] "'Old man, where are you going? Where are you taking your son?' 'To the forest, to leave him there: we have nothing to eat any more.' 'Give your son to me. I will teach him for three years.'"[160] Thus does the hero, upon leaving home, often end up in a "place of teaching." Let us see what kind of teaching this is.

16. She Beat and Beat

So what happened to the boys who came across the terrible spirit in the forest that was supposed to eat them? As stated above, the focal point of the initiation rite in every land was circumcision. But circumcision is only a small part of the actions performed on the boys. There in the forest, they were subjected to the most terrible tortures and torments. Many travelers describe with horror the cries that resound in that hut.[161] We shall see that the children were subjected to fire. Another method of torture was peeling their skin, inflicting deep wounds with the aim of causing scarring. Both Schurtz and Webster talk about making incisions in the back from the neck down. "The visible symbol of such initiation consists of deep scarring from the back of the neck downward."[162] Sometimes belts were run under the skin of the back and chest, from which the boys were hung.[163] These ceremonies were especially cruel in South America. There, pepper was rubbed into the boys' wounds, similar to what appears in the wondertale.[164] These actions were accompanied by beatings. Heroes in wondertales are tortured in the exact same way, likewise in a hut, and similarly by a forest creature. Yaga "grabbed her pestle and began beating Usynia.[165] She beat and beat him, beat him down under the bench, cut a strip from his back, ate everything up, and rode off."[166] "Up came the old man riding in a mortar with a pestle to prop it up. . . . He took him with a hook and into the mortar—bang bang—and he stripped the skin off his back to his shoulders, rubbed it clean with chaff, and threw it under the house."[167]

To account for the meaning of these atrocities, researchers have noted that they were meant to train young people in absolute obedience to their elders, that future warriors were tempered in this way, and so on. The natives themselves have sometimes explained them as a desire to reduce the population, because a certain percentage of children would perish as a result of these "dedications." None of these explanations seem convincing. Apparently, these atrocities were supposed to "paralyze the brain," so to speak. Their long duration (sometimes weeks) and the hunger, thirst, darkness, and horror that accompanied them were together supposed to call forth a state the initiate would consider death. They cause temporary insanity (facilitated by consumption of various poisonous drinks) so that the initiate forgot everything in the world. He suffered such memory loss that after his return he did not remember his name, did not recognize his parents, and so on; and perhaps he really believed it when he was told that he had died and come back as a new, different person.

We shall analyze the phenomenon of temporary death and temporary insanity below; their forms are very diverse. Let us examine another curious detail. "The Fingernail-sized man seized Usynia the hero and started to thrash him; he completely did him in and shoved him under the bench; and he fouled their food, and left only trash behind."[168] Schurtz and other authors say that there is a desire to make the boys feel disgusted. They had to drink their teacher's urine and so on.[169] They were placed in a pit with manure and water; they were sprinkled with animal feces.[170] Without going into the particulars, Schurtz notes that "along with enduring pain, it was often required to overcome repulsion." The feature noted in the phrase "she kicked him under the bench" may correspond to a loss of consciousness, a collapse into the dark, a sense of death and darkness.

17. Madness

Let us very briefly touch upon the issue of insanity, an essential phenomenon in these cases. It is almost not reflected in wondertales but still important for the overall context, and it explains something about the general phenomena of folklore. The neophyte was plunged into a state of frenzied madness in every possible way: either by being battered or through hunger, pain, torment, or poisonous or narcotic drinks. Schurtz believes that the moment of madness was when the spirit entered—that is, the moment of acquiring the relevant skills. Frobenius perceives it in exactly the same way. "It seems that we have here one of those cases that are more common in South Guinea than in New Guinea, and which should be understood as possession. The implementation of such states is still unclear. It is as if these people are being endowed with unusual powers; they are, for example, able to pull up trees."[171] "In some cases, it seems that it is really believed that the newly circumcised is possessed by the spirit and goes insane."[172] We have the same phenomenon in shamanism (whose connection to our ceremony could be the subject of a separate study). "Buryat shamans need to bring themselves, and often do bring themselves, to the point of hallucinations and epileptic seizures. Precisely these types of shamans are especially respected and honored by the Buryat people."[173] Finally, Greco-Roman antiquity had a wide range of manifestations of this type of ecstasy. We shall see below that the madness of Orestes bears a strong association with the complex discussed in the present work. But there are also other cases of sacred μανία that may be placed in this connection.

We find cases of madness in wondertales, but they are very rare. It is associated with the spectacle of chopped-up bodies. When we consider the motif of bodily hewing, we shall see that there is a historically attested link between the hewing itself and madness in the rite. In these cases, wondertales say, "And she herself became like a crazy person."[174] Or "She felt a harrowing agony and went mad."[175] The motif of madness is developed more strongly in a folktale from the Vyatka region that states, "And if you listen to them for three hours and do not lose your mind, you will receive the gift of a magical gusli that plays by itself; if you lose your mind, your head will be cut off. . . . The soldier listened for only a quarter of an hour and lost his mind: that is, he went mad."[176] In all these cases the madness occurs in the environment of a house in the forest, whether the house belongs to a robber or to a mysterious creature that provides the gusli whose sound causes the madness. For now, we can limit ourselves to these brief references. The question could be the subject of a further specialized study, but for us it is important to point to this phenomenon as it will aid in understanding other phenomena of the wondertale that have not yet been analyzed.

18. The Severed Finger

Wondertales preserve one type of body mutilation with extreme integrity: severing a finger. They do not preserve any other forms of mutilation (such as knocking out the teeth). Severing a finger was performed after circumcision. Webster puts it as follows: "After a partial recovery, they presented themselves before a masked man who, with one blow of his ax, cut off the little finger of the left hand. Sometimes, we are told, the candidates would offer as an additional sacrifice the forefinger of the same hand."[177] In wondertales, the hero very often loses a finger in the cabin, and it is the little finger of his left hand. The loss of a finger is often found in the following situations: (1) At the home of Yaga or similar creatures, the finger is chopped off to see whether the boy has been fed well enough; (2) At the home of the one-eyed Likho (Polyphemus), the fleeing hero gets his finger stuck in a certain object—Likho is about to overtake him, so he chops off his finger and saves his life at the price of the severed finger; (3) In the house of robbers, the victim's finger is chopped off because of a ring. There are a number of different cases besides these. In general, it can be noted that the hero sometimes returns from his exploits minus a finger. Sometimes cutting off a finger marks a false hero. At the price of a finger or a toe and for a strip of skin from his back, he buys from the hero the rare and sought-after object and passes it off as his own, and then he is exposed based on the severed finger or toe.

In a tale from the Vyatka region, a he-goat tells the children, "'Each of you cut off a finger, and I'll taste you.' He throws the fingers on the stove, but they do not fry. 'No, they still aren't fat enough; they aren't ready to be fried yet.'"[178] In a German folktale, the finger is only felt but not chopped off. In Russian folktales the finger is chopped off. "The she-bear roars . . . 'my dear daughters, my comely daughters, cut off his finger, the little finger.'" The finger is severed. "'No, Mama, he's not plump.'"[179]

Another situation in which the hero loses a finger is when staying with Polyphemus and the like. This detail makes it possible to compare Yaga with Polyphemus. The Russian Polyphemus lives in the forest, in a paddock behind a fence. His having only one eye can be compared to Yaga's blindness. When the hero, before fleeing, pours liquid tin into his eyes, this can be compared to a maiden plugging up Yaga's eyes with batter. Finally, Polyphemus, like Yaga, is the master of animals, but in contrast to Yaga, who commands the forest animals, Polyphemus breeds sheep, cows, or goats. In one version, Likho throws the hero over a fence together with a bull, which the hero grabs onto. In order to keep the hero, Likho (in the folktale entitled "Need") throws a golden ax after him and a gold chain (recall that Polyphemus throws a stone after Odysseus). The hero, a blacksmith, is tempted. "The smith grew envious and wanted to steal the chain; but he was afraid and touched it with one finger, and that finger stuck to the chain. The smith saw that the situation was bad, pulled out a knife, cut off his finger, and went home."[180] Similarly, "He didn't pity his own hand. He cut it off and went away."[181]

Seeing that instead of a finger the whole hand is severed in the woods, we can assume that "Kosoruchka" (or "The Armless Maiden") also has its origin here. It is the motif of a girl whose brother chops off her hand or both hands in the forest. These hands then miraculously grow back.

A finger is also severed from the hands of girls who have been dragged to the forest house by robbers. "The robbers pricked out one girl's eye with a fork and stripped off her skin; and they cut off the other girl's finger, which had a golden ring on it."[182] In other cases, it is the other way around: the groom-robbers themselves lack fingers or hands. "They finished the preparation and sat down to feast. But the groom didn't have hands there, so he put on black gloves and stuffed them with sand." When he is asked about this, he replies, "It's nothing. My hands hurt a little."[183] Also, a finger often drops off after it has been dipped into a forbidden vessel or boiler.[184]

Here too Orestes comes to mind. In Messina, there was a temple of the goddesses called Maniai a mile from Megalopolis. There Orestes, having killed his mother, fell into madness and bit off his finger in a fit. Near the temple was an elevation with a stone finger on its top. This elevation was called δακτύλου μνῆμα (*Daktulou Mnema*, the Finger of Memory).[185]

19. Signs of Death

An inevitable question arises at this point regarding the meaning of this rite. Apparently, here it is not only a matter of the scar as a sign of the accomplished initiation. In wondertales, a finger or a hand is sometimes severed instead of chopping up the whole person. Sometimes a girl is really cut into pieces, and in addition her finger is chopped off. "They took her, stripped her naked, put her on the block and stabbed her to death, and then began to take off the rings from her hands." One ring does not come off. "He took an ax and chopped off her finger with such a blow that the ring flew away."[186] More often, however, the hewing of the whole body does not occur and is replaced by severing a finger. This replacement is especially frequent in "The Armless Maiden." "Lay your head on a stump, I'm going to hack it off." "If I hacked up your child, then . . . cut off my hands to the elbow."[187] In another version, the wife commands her husband to kill his sister. "Go fetch firewood," she tells him, "and kill your sister." His sister pleads, "Chop off both my hands and take them to her." The brother does this, and his wife is satisfied: "Good! That means you have killed your sister!"[188]

But if this is so, then it throws light on the motif of the hero or heroine sent into the woods to die. There is a demand for evidence that the death indeed occurs: bloodied clothes, gouged out eyes, a heart, a liver, blood-stained weapons, and so on. "Headsman, here is my son for you. Take my son to the field, chop him into small pieces and bring me back the sword dipped in his blood!" "Headsman, don't cut me! Cut off the little finger of my left hand and smear the blood on the sword."[189] Sometimes a bloody dress is displayed. "He killed a dog, dipped the dress in its blood and let her (i.e., the girl—V.P.) go."[190]

We know by now that it was as if the initiates were killed. In such cases, the relatives were shown signs of their death. Schurtz reports that a bloody spear was stuck out through the roof of the hut—that is, bloodied weapons, like the bloodied sword in tales. In this way, the people present knew that the mysteries had taken place. Sometimes bloody clothes were displayed. "The next day the women are shown bloody garments and told that the youths are dead and will not return."[191]

20. Temporary Death

These materials make us focus on a phenomenon mentioned above but whose meaning is not yet clear. This is the phenomenon of temporary death.

The forms of this death were quite varied; for now we shall concentrate not on the form but on the fact itself. Here are a few testimonials. "Almost universally initiation rites include a mimic representation of the death and resurrection of the novice."[192] "The main part of the ceremony was the killing and resurrection of the initiate, who thus acquired magical powers."[193] "With the onset of the appointed day a rural magician shakes a rattle at the young men, who fall down as if dead. They are dressed in funeral clothes and carried into a fenced place outside the village, called Vela. It is assumed that these 'dead' are decaying, and that the magician-wizard collects their bones and brings the young men back to life."[194] Such testimonials are abundant; they can be systematized and studied, but this should concern the ethnographer, not the folklorist. We can only point to the fact without going into its explanation. The fact is that the acquisition of magical qualities was attributed to this death and resurrection.

But while we cannot examine the phenomenon's essence in depth, we can do something else: we can examine the forms of killing and resurrection because they are reflected by the wondertale. We will see that these forms are very diverse and that wondertales preserve them quite fully and accurately.

We must also point out that this death took the form of a spatial translocation, and we see the same here. It is said of the initiate that "he is dead and has gone to the spirit-world."[195] "During this time he is believed to be in the underworld," or "he goes to heaven."[196] Here we shall find a clue to the hero's travels.

There are many materials regarding temporary death. However, we cannot express any speculations without first thoroughly investigating. Let us proceed by examining some specific examples.

21. Chopped into Pieces and Brought Back to Life

One form of temporary death was cutting a man open or chopping him into pieces. We know that there were rites of a kind that involve bodily dissection or hewing, but information about them is very scarce. For example, among the Warramunga tribe of Australia, a boy falls asleep, and the priests "during his sleep kill him, dissect his corpse, change out his organs (*changent ses organes*), and put inside him a small snake that embodies magical powers."[197] Another example is from the Arunta tribe. Here the initiation is performed in a cave. The initiate falls asleep in front of the cave. Then the priest "pierces him with an invisible spear that comes out his back through the nape of his neck, passes through his tongue, leaving a large opening in it, and then exits again through his mouth." (The tongue remains damaged forever, and this serves as evidence of his link with the spirits.) With a second blow, the spear is taken through the ears. After this, the sleeping boy is carried to the cave. There those carrying out the initiation "sort out all his insides and add new ones. . . . Some magical crystals are put in the open body. Then they revive him, but he is deprived of reason." Afterward, he comes to his senses and is recognized as a shaman.[198]

If we look closely at these examples, we see that the tongue perforation with a spear was real. However, dissection of the body and sorting out of the viscera was performed while the neophyte was unconscious—that is, it was probably not performed in reality; only the impression of it was created. How was this impression achieved? We do not know exactly. Later examples exhibit a substitutionary killing and hewing not of the initiate but of another person or an animal. There is some evidence that it was a prisoner or slave who was actually killed. In some cases, cutting off the head was performed over images. Here are some examples: "A slave was killed by members of the secret association. . . . He was chopped up and eaten by them."[199] In this case, a real person was actually killed. In the Kwakiutl tribe "the head of the dancer is cut off, and the person who cuts it off shows a carved human head bearing the expression of death, which he holds by its hair. These heads are as nearly portraits of the dancer as the art of the carver will permit."[200]

There is evidence that the initiates were shown dead, hacked-up bodies and that these bodies were put on top of the boy or that he crawled under or stepped over them. Apparently, this symbolized the killing of the initiate himself: "They had to step over a man who was spattered with blood, on whose naked body pig guts were laid, as if their own guts were protruding from the body. The rest were lying down as if they were also dead; and one of the 'Vere' rebuked the initiates for being guilty of their deaths."[201] The initiate boy is not killed, but someone else is killed fictitiously in his place. It is possible that this substitute killing was preceded by the real killing of one of the boys, who in such a case was eaten.

There is not the slightest doubt that cannibalism exists in this ritual. All the researchers of this rite confirm it, although for obvious reasons none of them has ever observed it directly.

The chopping and tearing apart of the human body play a huge role in many religions and myths; they also play a big role in wondertales. Here we can touch on only some examples in which hewing and recovery are a source of strength or the condition for deification.

N. P. Dyrenkova's work "Reception of the Shamanic Gift According to the Views of the Turkish Tribes" provides excerpts from a vast body of material showing that the experience of chopping and slicing up the body and sorting the insides is a necessary condition of shamanism, and it precedes the moment when a person becomes a shaman.[202] Among the Turkic tribes of Siberia, the procedure of hewing the body was exactly the same: it is performed in a state of hallucination. Here are a few excerpts from such materials. The Yakut shaman Gerasimov told the ethnographer A. A. Popov how he became a shaman. Suddenly (while searching for a lost deer) he saw three ravens in the sky; he felt a blow on his back and lost consciousness. Then "spirits" came to him and began to torture him. "He was beaten with ropes and straps; reptiles dug into his body. He was dipped in blood clots, he choked on blood, he had to suck the breast of a terrible old woman, his eyes were poked out [see above on blindness], his ears were drilled into, his body was cut into pieces and placed in an iron cradle," and so on.[203] According to the records of many researchers and observers, the future shaman of the Yakuts "experiences all the tortures of having his head cut off and his body sliced up and cooked."[204] The Teleut shaman Koyon (rabbit) began her shamanic practice after having a vision. "Several people were cutting her body into pieces at the joints and putting these pieces in a pot to cook. Then two more people arrived. They again cut her flesh, gutted her body, and cooked it."[205] This is a typical picture of the shaman's visions prior to taking up his shamanistic functions. One may ask why all the shamans hallucinate in the same way and why the images of these visions sometimes correspond in the smallest detail (being cooked in a pot, etc.) to the practice of the rite in America,

Africa, Polynesia, and Australia on the one hand and to the material found in wondertales on the other. In the ritual, we have a more ancient form, strongly associated with the economic foundation and social organization of these peoples. Turkic peoples reflect a later stage of economic, social, and religious culture. The wondertale, however, contains the same material on the level of a relic in a completely new and altered social environment. It can be pointed out that, at the stage of the states of classical antiquity and the ancient Near East, this motif is found in religion but in a different form: it is not the shaman who is torn to pieces but a god or a hero. The most famous example is Orpheus. But chopping the body into pieces happens also to Osiris in Egypt, to Adonis in Syria, to Dionysus Zagreus in Thrace, to Pentheus, and to others. They all "die prematurely in a violent death, but they do not quite die: they rise from the dead and become the subject of a cult."[206] In these examples from antiquity it is possible to establish decapitation, tattoos, insanity, dancing, the preservation of musical instruments in a sanctuary, and the connection of a supposed corpse to a tree, about which more comments will follow.

As Adolf Jacoby has noted, Buddha too cut his own body into pieces and put them back together again; this version is given by Aśvaghoṣa.[207] The motivation here is clearly of late origin, indicating a misunderstanding: he does it to convert his father.

The motif of hewing and rejuvenation is also quite popular in the wondertale. We can establish several types of this motif depending on the plot and a large number of individual cases that have no integral connection to the plot.

One of the plots where we find hewing the body into pieces is the tale of a bride at a robber's house in the forest, a subtype of which is "Bluebeard." We shall learn more about the robber's house below, but for now suffice it to note that in tales such as "Bluebeard" a girl sees Bluebeard's hacked-up wives in a forbidden storeroom. We find in the Grimms, "But what did she see when she went in? A great bloody basin stood in the middle of the room, and therein lay human beings, dead and hewn to pieces, and hard by was a block of wood, and a gleaming ax lay upon it."[208] When the wizard detected that the girl had been in the forbidden storeroom, "He threw her down, dragged her thither by her hair, cut her head off on the block, and chopped her into pieces so that her blood ran on the ground."[209] In a northern tale a girl and a boy get to the house of some robbers. She is invited inside: "'Come in to dine.' They went in, and [somebody] poured them cabbage soup and brought them some white bread; then they brought them beef—cooked human arms and legs."[210] When the robbers came, "they ran into the strange room [i.e., the room of the strangers], dragging the boy by his arm into the kitchen. The stove was burning and the iron pot boiled.

They shoved the boy into the iron pot and cooked him for dinner. The boy started screaming badly, but he didn't cry for long. Then he died. They brought out the boy on a plate and sat down to eat: they ate their fill and settled down to sleep."[211]

In cases like this it is important to note that the hewing takes place in a house in the forest. In a Yakut tale, two maidens wind up in the iron tent of a terrible old woman with one leg and one arm. The girls hear her cutting human flesh in the next room; she cuts off the arms and legs, which she feeds to the girls. One girl's head is cut off and hung on a tree. The head is not dead; it is crying.[212] It is interesting to note that the girls eat the meat of the chopped-up humans. In wondertales this kind of food is usually rejected. On the other hand, in the Russian tales the person who has been chopped up and has come back to life gives the hero human blood to drink.[213] This blood is a source of enormous strength. "'Give him some strength!' He squeezed a bottleful of blood from his ribs, gave it to him, and said, 'If you feel a lot of strength inside, leave some for me—don't drink all of it.' Vanya drank the bottle and felt an immeasurable strength. (He left nothing for the warrior)."[214] Severing the head is found in folktales such as "The Self-Playing Gusli." "'Are the twelve merchants with you?' 'Yes, they are.' He ordered them brought into the dungeon and said, 'Now you just sit and do not doze. Otherwise you will not get the magical gusli.' The merchant's son sits and sees how the merchants with whom he arrived are taken past him one by one; their heads are cut off, their corpses thrown into the dungeon, and there they come back to life."[215]

And thus does the hewing of a person take place in the forest hut, in different types of wondertales.

Another type of hewing, closely associated with a particular plot, occurs in the folktale of "failed doctoring." This is a popular tale with several variants. An old man goes to a forge, or he meets Nikola, who chops him into pieces, brings him back to life, and rejuvenates him.[216] "'Old man, lie down in the trough!' said the stranger. The old man lay dawn, and the stranger took an ax and chopped him into small pieces. A priest brought some water. The wanderer sprinkled the cut up body with it, and foam appeared; he sprinkled a second time, and a dead body was formed; he sprinkled a third time, and he became a young man."[217] Here the meaning of the rite is clear: the chopping into pieces creates a new man.

But this is only one aspect of the matter. Above we saw that during the initiation a snake is placed in the body of the neophyte. It is placed directly in his intestines. The benefit and necessity of this procedure must have soon become incomprehensible and were reinterpreted: the body is cut in order to remove the snakes and the reptiles, which are causing a disease. This folktale or this motif within the given plot has been studied by Professor I. I. Tolstoi, who collected all the Russian material and pointed to some ancient parallels corresponding to it.[218]

The third form is hewing the body of an enchanted princess whom the hero marries. This hewing is not associated in a consistent way with any particular plot. "He took an ax and began to cut Maria the Beautiful into pieces. . . . Then he commanded that fire be brought, and he threw pieces of Maria the Beautiful into it. Then all sorts of vermin started crawling out of her: snakes, frogs, lizards, mice."[219]

Besides the three main forms (at the robber's house, in the tale of failed doctoring, and the hewing of a princess) there are many individual cases in which hewing is episodic. Even the brief characterization that we have managed to provide here shows a link between wondertale and ritual. This is supported not only by facts; setting and some details also point to it. The frequent connection of this motif with the hut points to it as well. Another feature of this motif, the introduction or removal of snakes to or from the body can also be traced back to the rite. Finally, the fact that the chopped-up person always comes back to life points to a type of temporary death, and the rejuvenation of the old man indicates a person's revival or rebirth, which is the real essence of the rite. A different question would be how these varieties came to be. Snakes or demons are never extracted from anyone in Yaga's hut or the robbers' house. This question cannot be resolved by a general comparative study of wondertales. It must be explored through the further study of each plot separately.

22. Yaga's Stove

We have noticed that in these cases, the chopped-up bodies are often cooked. The fire is as rejuvenating as the hewing.

We know that in initiation rites, the neophytes were exposed to fire in various forms. Here we could trace these forms, contrasting them with one another; trace the dependence or independence of one from another; and consider their development and the emergence of substituted, mitigated, and symbolized forms. Parallel to this, consideration should be given to the exceedingly rich, nearly inexhaustible material of myths and religious beliefs, to track resemblance of the forms of burning in the myths with the forms in rites and to establish why, how, and where the phenomenon is transformed into its opposite and manifested in the transfer of the burning object: burned children are replaced by the would-be burners getting burned themselves. This is material for an extensive social and historical study. Here again we can only establish the main landmarks and indicate some of the linkages.

The burning, roasting, and boiling of initiates has been traced already in the earliest stages of the initiation rite known to us. Baldwin Spencer and Francis Gillen recorded these rituals among the Australians.[220] The rite they recorded lasted for many days and represented something like a play. In one of its episodes a long groove was dug in the ground, big enough to accommodate a man's body. This was the "oven." One of the performers was laid in the groove; another knelt at his feet and a third at his head. The latter two represented Arunta men who were roasting the first in an earthen oven. Each of these two pretended with a boomerang to water the roasting body and cover it with coals; at the same time, they imitated surprisingly well the hissing and popping sounds of roasting meat. Then out of the darkness appeared the fourth actor, who represented a man of the totem frog of Alcheringa times (i.e., of great antiquity). He walked with an uncertain gait, constantly drawing in the air as if smelling the roasting meat, but apparently, he could not find out where the smell came from.

Such is the account of Spencer and Gillen. The last performer arrived at the very end of the performance. By that time the initiate had burned up. There was no remaining trace of the old mortal human nature, which is reflected in the fact that after the burning nothing could be detected by the sense of smell.

In this example, the rite was performed symbolically. It could have been carried out in a crueler way. The initiates were held in the fire for four to five minutes. In Upper Guinea initiates "were killed, roasted and totally changed."[221] The rite in Victoria is described as follows: "The strong fire lit the night before had already burned down, so that it contained only ashes and glowing embers. An opossum skin is held above the fire, and coals and ashes are poured onto it with shovels. The boys pass under the skin and are showered with embers and ashes." The people who shovel the coals have a special name.[222] Crawling beneath the skin is obviously a later form of crawling through the animal. In Melanesia the initiate crawled through a long, narrow building while boiling water was poured over him.[223]

We know that at the initiation the initiate boy supposedly received a new soul and became a new person. Here we see the belief that the power of fire is cleansing and rejuvenating, a belief that later extends to Christian purgatory.

In Oceania, the evening before, they "make a huge fire. The men order the neophytes to sit near it, while they themselves sit down behind the boys in a few tight rows. Suddenly they grab the unsuspecting boys and hold them close to the fire until all their body hair is burned, and many boys even get burns. Screaming does not help."[224] Many different examples of substitution combustion can be found in the work of Boas on the social organization of the Kwakiutl tribe.

In all cases, the consumption by fire, scorching, and roasting leads to a supreme blessing to which the entire rite leads in general—acquisition of the abilities that a full-fledged member of a clan society needs.

We know that the whole rite represented a descent into hell. Whatever happened to the initiates also happened to the deceased. In the Society Islands, it was assumed that "the soul was cooked whole in an earth-oven, as pigs are baked on earth, and was then placed in a basket of coconut leaves before being served up to the god whom the deceased had worshipped in life. 'By this cannibal divinity he was now eaten up; after which, through some inexplicable process, the dead and devoured man emanated from the body of the god, and became immortal.'"[225]

We will not linger at the stage of primitive myths represented by vast material but will move on directly to the wondertale, with an initial look at burning as a blessing. In a Novgorod folktale a boy is taken to a "forest grand-dad" to acquire knowledge. The old man's daughters heat the furnace. "Then the old man threw the boy into the stove, where he turned about in all directions. The old man took him out of the stove and asked, 'What do you know?' 'I don't know anything'" (three times; the oven became red hot). "'Well, now? Have you learned anything?' 'I know more than you, gramps,' said the boy. The learning was complete, and the forest grand-dad summoned the boy's father to come for his son." It is clear from what follows that the boy has learned to transform into animals.[226]

In a Vyatka tale, a boy also makes his way to a forest master. His father comes for him. "'No. I won't give him back to you yet. I still need to cook him in a cauldron.' He made a fire, placed the pot in it, grabbed the boy, and threw him in the pot. He jumped out without any harm done to him. He threw him in another time, and again he got out un-harmed. 'Is that enough?' 'No, one more time. . . . Now you know more than I do, so that will be enough.'"[227] In this example, the boy learns to understand the calls of birds. In both cases, the original hunting base is preserved: the boy who undergoes the initiation acquires the character-istics of animals. It is possible to find other examples in the materials of Bolte-Polívka, where the burnt person turns into an animal.[228] The same idea is expressed in legends about the blacksmith, Christ, and the devil, who reforge old people to make them become young, since they acquire youth upon burning.

However, along with this idea of burning as a blessing, very early there was another view that is the opposite. For now, let us simply estab-lish the fact. We shall explain it after examining the materials.

We find such a negative attitude, for example, in the Cook Islands. It was believed there that the soul, after some adventures, gets caught in the net of a terrible creature called Miru. Frazer writes,

At last the net was pulled up with the ghost in it, who, half-drowned, was now ushered trembling into the presence of the grim hag Miru, generally known as 'the Ruddy,' because her face reflected the glowing heat of the ever-burning oven in which she cooked her ghostly victims. At first, however, she fed, and perhaps fattened, them on a diet of black beetles, red earth-worms, crabs, and small blackbirds. Thus refreshed, they had next to drain bowls of strong *kava* brewed by the fair hands of the hag's four lovely daughters. Reduced to a state of insensibility by the intoxicating beverage, the ghosts were then borne off without a struggle to the oven and cooked.[229]

Who would fail to recognize here the children who wound up in the witch's house and were fattened by her to be eaten?

It is interesting that in this example, there is no struggle against the burning. What is very striking is the total inevitability of what is happening, the way the souls are doomed. This material was recorded in the Cook Islands, and the material that was mentioned before, in which burning leads to deification, was recorded not too far from there—in the Society Islands. Consequently, we have diametrically opposed views in the same territory. The reason, therefore, lies not in the territorial principle but in something else: the fate of the soul depends on the social status of the deceased. Burning is fatal for women, children, and all those who die a natural death. They fall into the nets of the Red Miru, and this means definitive death, being destroyed forever. Those, however, who are killed in battle, and in general all warriors and leaders, die differently: their souls travel through a forge into the celestial world for eternal life.

Thus, this duality appears with the beginning of social differentiation.

We know that myths are actually sacred stories that have become taboo. We shall see this in more detail in the final chapter. But the greater the profanation of the story, which is related to the improvement of tools and the abandonment of magic and, consequently, with social stratification, the more dominant the profane version—that is, the version that denies the blessing of combustion (burning) and turns the burning against the burner, who is thrown into the oven. But along with this an archaic version, which grew out of the rite, continues to be recounted for the social elites: leaders, heroes, demigods, and later gods.

It is interesting to study the material of antiquity from this perspective. The actors there are gods and heroes. In the Homeric hymn to Demeter, the goddess of earth, fertility, and the underworld is wandering in search of her daughter and enters the house of Kehl. She lives there unrecognized and is accepted as a nurse of baby Demophon. "She gathered him to her fragrant breast / with her immortal hands. And the mother rejoiced."[230] Thus Demeter raises Demophon, and the child grows up like a god. He does not take the breast and does not eat bread. But Demeter rubs him daily with nectar (ambrosia), as if he were indeed the offspring of the gods; she gently breathes on him, holding him in her arms; at night, however, when she is alone with the child, she secretly hides him as a piece of firewood in the power of fire, for her heart is inclined to the child, and she would gladly give him immortality.

This is what the Homeric hymn recounts. As indicated here, combustion does not occur in this case. One night the child's mother watches Demeter; she sees her child in the fire and screams in horror. The goddess, in anger at the unreasonable mother, pulls him out of the fire and, by doing so, deprives him of immortality. The subject of this myth is not so much the burning itself as the resistance to it.

We see exactly the same in the myth of Peleus and Thetis. Thetis, Achilles's mother, puts her son in the fire every night in order to eliminate from him, to burn away, the mortal nature of his father, Peleus, and to grant him divinity and immortality. But Peleus sees this and grabs his son from her.[231] Thus did combustion cease taking place in antiquity, where the motif was already on the wane. Thereupon it moved to the sphere of afterlife representations, and these are very close to the wondertale. Even though the main characters of the myth are gods and demigods, those figures who are supposed to turn into gods do not do so because of the lack of understanding of ordinary people. Here the historical process of resignification is quite clear.

In precisely the same way, the wondertale, while preserving archaic forms of combustion that result in the acquisition of skills relevant to the hunter and the leader, also preserves the opposite view of combustion as something horrible and happily avoided. We will not provide any examples as they are too well known.

23. A Tricky Science

If our observations on the link between wondertales and the initiation rite are correct, then they shed light on yet another folktale—namely, "A Tricky Science" and the entire complex of tales in which the boy expelled or exiled from home comes back with some extraordinary skill, knowledge, or ability.[232] The parents in "A Tricky Science," sometimes of their own choice and sometimes out of necessity, send their son away for training. This would seem to be quite a realistic element. And indeed, the hero sometimes (especially in German folktales) returns as a deft master craftsman. However, more often, neither the figure of the teacher nor the atmosphere, teaching methods, or acquired knowledge look like the historical reality of the nineteenth century but resemble rather the historical reality of a very distant past.

The teacher to whom the boy comes is a very old man, a sorcerer, a wood demon, or a sage. He lives overseas. "Beyond the sea there is a teacher who teaches various sciences."[233] He is "across the sea," "beyond the river"—that is, somewhere in another realm or sometimes another city. "Beyond the Volga, in a city there was a craftsman who taught different languages and different crafts, and he [could] turn into all sorts of things. He trained young people: he took children from their mothers and fathers for three years."[234] Sometimes he appears from out of a grave if you say "oh."[235] He appears if you sit down on a stump. This is the "Grandpa of the Woods."[236] These examples show that the teacher appears from the woods; he lives in a different realm; he takes children from their parents and brings them into the woods for three years (or for one year or seven years).

So what does the hero learn? He learns to turn into an animal, or he learns the language of the birds. "They sent him off to this wise man to learn the various languages, perhaps to become a knowledgeable person, too, who would know all sorts of things: what a bird was singing, or a horse neighing, or a sheep bleating. Well, in a word, so that he'd know everything!"[237] He learns sorcery: "Lend the boy to me to do magic."[238] "I'll send him to learn the language of the birds."[239] When the training comes to an end, it is said of him, "Your son has learned well, and he has a mighty strength."[240] "And he had a great magical power and cunning; he knew such power not only regarding what had already happened—he knew also what was going to happen."[241]

The method of instruction is almost never reported. In one example mentioned above the hero is cooked in a cauldron, and that is how he gets his prophetic knowledge.[242] The teacher's house is also almost never described. Only in one case do we find out that it is a "house in the garden" that is home to twelve young men.[243] In another case, we hear about a "broad school courtyard."[244]

All these particulars—the forest nature of the teacher, the departure of children from their parents, the magical character of the learning, the ability to turn into animals or understand the language of birds, and so on—force us to ascribe this group of motifs to the same phenomenon, to which the previous motifs referred.

The rite of passage was a kind of school—learning in the truest sense of the word. During their initiation, the boys were introduced to all the mythical beliefs, rites, rituals, and practices of the tribe. Researchers speculate that a certain secret science was introduced to them there—that is, that they acquired a certain kind of knowledge. Indeed, they were told the myths of the tribe. One witness reports, "the young men sat still and learnt from the old men [; as my informant said,] 'It was like a school.'"[245] But all the same, this is not the core point. It is not knowledge that is important but ability; the point is not to understand the imaginary world of nature but to influence it. This aspect of the matter is what is well reflected in "A Tricky Science," where, as noted above, the hero learns to transform into animals; he acquires an ability rather than knowledge.

This education or training is an essential feature of initiation all over the world. In Australia (New South Wales), elders taught youngsters "to play the native games, to sing the songs of the tribe, and to dance certain corroborees which neither the gins nor the uninitiated are permitted to learn. They were also instructed in the sacred traditions and lore of the tribe."[246] Again, we can establish that the moment of the story recedes into the background before the moment of action. "The rites . . . constitute a rude but often very effective dramatization of the myths and legends. . . . The actors, masked or costumed, represent animals or divine beings whose history the myths recount."[247] This statement holds the premise that myths are more primary than the dramatic actions, that the myth is being dramatized. In our opinion it happened the other way around. First was the dramatic action, and the myth developed later. In this regard, Australia offers especially convincing evidence. We find there very complex and lengthy dramatic performances wherein the myths are short, very inconsistent, amorphous, and often incomprehensible to Europeans.[248] These performances and dances are not spectacles. They are magical methods of impacting nature. The initiated boy studies all the dancing and singing painstakingly and for a long time. The slightest mistake can be fatal and can ruin the whole ceremony. Incidentally, let us mention that the bear of the Belarus tale releases the stepdaughter only after she dances for him. Boas's collection includes cases where the hero goes to "another kingdom" and brings a dance back with him, which he then teaches to his tribe.

A young man learns the dances and ceremonies that are part of the autumn, spring, and winter rites, which aim to increase the game, bring forth rain, increase the crops, ward off disease, and so on.[249]

The heroes of Russian tales do not bring dances from the forest teacher: they bring magical abilities. But the dances were also expressions or instruments of using these abilities. The wondertale has lost the dancing: only the forest, the teacher, and the magic skills remain. But it is possible to find some traces of dancing in tales of different types. The dancing was accompanied by music, and the musical instruments were considered sacred and taboo. The house in which the initiation took place and in which the initiates sometimes lived for a while was sometimes called "the house of flutes."[250] The sound of these flutes was considered to be the voice of the spirit. If we keep this in mind, it becomes clear why the hero in the forest hut so often finds there self-playing gusli, pipes, violins, and so on. When the gusli plays, everyone must dance. The hero acquires power over dancing. The nature of this dancing, of course, has completely changed. "They went to the side, and there stood a hut. They entered the hut. . . . He looked everywhere and saw a pipe under the crossbar. He began to play the pipe."[251] At the sound, a goblin the height of an elbow appears.[252] The sound of the pipe summons the spirit.

In one version of "The Self-Playing Gusli" the gusli is strung with human tendons. "The craftsman took them to his workroom, immediately placed one person into the machine, cut him in half, and began to pull out his tendons."[253] The fact that sacred instruments are made of human bones is well known. But the dancing is also preserved somewhat in wondertales. "Then Nikita began to examine the cabin. He saw on the window a small whistle, placed it to his lips and began to whistle. He looks—what a wonder! His blind brother is dancing, the cabin is dancing, the table, the dishes are dancing, everything dancing."[254] At the sound of this, Baba Yaga appears. "Merry-man went with his violin, and he stood near a pine tree [he has settled with his brothers in the forest] Baba Yaga approached Merry-man: 'Merry-man, what are you doing?' 'I'm playing the violin.' [Baba Yaga] put down her buckets . . . and began dancing."[255] In a Vyatka tale a soldier who has served his term stays overnight in the little chamber of an orphan.[256] The house is large and decorated (on the house, see below). The soldier spends the night in the house. "Then the demons began presenting all the comedies. Now the demons have exhausted all the comedies. 'Come on, soldier, now you perform: we have exhausted them all.'" Calling the forest dancing "the demons' comedy performance" is very curious and revealing. It is also important that now it is the hero's turn, that he too is forced to make some mimic actions.

In a Permian tale three girls are in the forbidden storeroom of a large house. Vanya gives them back their dresses. "They put on their dresses, took him by the arm, and started waltzing around."[257] As mentioned above, girls' dresses and wings could represent totemic masks and costumes. Finally, as indicated by Zelenin, religious rites often turn into games.[258] Perhaps the game of hide-and-seek with the bear in the forest hut is a reflection of the dances learned in the woods.

Here too the comparative characteristics of wondertale material and ethnographic material demonstrate a close relationship.

24. The Magical Gift

We have seen that the wondertale places some magical gift into the hero's hands and that he reaches his goal by means of this gift. The gift is either an object (a ring, a small towel, a little ball, and so on) or an animal, usually a horse. We have also seen how closely the image of Yaga is connected to rites of initiation. Is there something in these rites that corresponds to receiving a gift?

We shall set aside the question of the helper for a special chapter. At this point we are interested only in the moment when the helper is given to the hero in connection with study of the rite. It turns out that in rites of initiation, this kind of moment not only existed but occupied a central place, a climax point for the whole ritual. The magical abilities of the hero depend on acquisition of a helper that English-speaking ethnographers have not very successfully named the guardian spirit. Webster writes in this regard, "Everywhere the belief is general among the women and uninitiated children that the elders, the directors of the puberty institution, are in possession of certain mysterious and magical objects, the revelation of which to the novices forms the central and most impressive feature of initiation."[259] And elsewhere, "A fundamental doctrine was the belief in a personal guardian spirit (*nagual*) into which by various rites of a phallic character the members of a society were supposed to be metamorphosed."[260] Schurtz notes that the whole boys' initiation rite "amounts to acquisition of a guardian spirit, to acquisition of the magic powers of Manitou."[261] A more detailed examination of this question will be given in the next chapter. We shall gain understanding of the rings, the sticks, the little balls, and other objects as well as the hero's relationship with his helpers, the animals. Here it suffices to mention that the helping guardian is associated with the totem of the tribe.

25. Yaga the Mother-in-Law

However, not all is clear yet in the image of Yaga. From everything said above, it is apparent that we connect Yaga with the person or mask that performs the rite of passage. But a certain discrepancy emerges at this point. Yaga can be either a woman or an animal. Her animal appearance fits perfectly well with all that we know about this rite. The great teacher and ancestor who performed the rite often appeared as an animal and wore its mask. If we talk about his human form, although in the ethnographic material it is not specified, it still seems that it was a man, not a woman. Let us examine both Yaga and the rites a bit more closely.

One of the purposes of the rite was to prepare the young man for marriage. It turns out that a rite of passage in societies practicing exogamy was performed not by representatives of the tribal association to which the young man belongs but by another group—namely, the one with which this group was endogamous, from which the initiate would take a wife. This is an Australian feature, and it can be assumed to be a most ancient form of initiation.[262] Before they give the young woman to a young man from another group, the wife's group subjects the boy to circumcision and initiation.

Mathews notes yet another thing in Victoria: "The helper (acquired by the boy) should not be one of the initiate's relatives; he is chosen among those tribes that came (to the celebration), which the boy will later enter through marriage."[263] As we shall see in the chapter on helpers, this helper is passed on as an inheritance. Here we see that the helper is inherited through the female line.

The wondertale has preserved this aspect as well. We can observe the following: if Yaga or another female donor or female inhabitant of the hut is a relative of one of the characters, then she is always a relative of the hero's wife or mother, never of the hero himself or his father. In a Vyatka tale Yaga says, "Oh, you dear child! You are my own nephew; your mama is a sister to me!"[264] The word *sister* here should not be understood literally. In different forms of kinship systems, this word can mean that his mother belongs to the same tribal alliance as Yaga. This can be seen more vividly when the hero is already married. In this case it is stated, "Here, my son-in-law has come"—that is, Yaga is the mother or sister of his wife or a relative of his wife or belongs to the same association as his wife. "Here, my son-in-law has come."[265] "This old woman is your mother-in-law."[266] "She says: 'Oh, you are my nephew.'"[267] "Oh, my brother-in-law has come."[268] "She (the princess) is my own niece," and others.[269]

There is a very interesting example in a Permian tale.[270] Here the hero in search of his vanished wife finds his way to Yaga. "'Dear friend, where have you lived?' 'I resided at an old man's place for six years as his student. He married me off to his young daughter.' 'What a fool! For you lived with my brother and married my niece.'" Here the great teacher is called Yaga's brother. The hero is the husband not of the sister but of Yaga's niece. Of course, all these are only indirect pieces of evidence. It is very strange for the hero never to have heard of or to know nothing of his mother-in-law who lives in the woods, if the words *mother-in-law, aunt, sister,* and so on mean what they mean now to us. But if we assume that mother-in-law, sister, and so on have replaced other forms of kinship and that the protagonist entering the hut meets the "family" of his wife on the totem line rather than the family kinship line, then this is not surprising; moreover, it becomes clear, in light of Webster's observations, why he meets his wife's relatives in the woods and not his own.

All these materials explain the forms of the hero's kinship with Yaga, but they still do not fully explain why Yaga is a woman. They do show, however, that the explanation must be sought in the matriarchal relations of the past. We have just seen that the initiation occurred through the family line of the wife. Some materials indicate that the initiation went not only through the wife's family line but literally through a woman: the initiate temporarily turned into a woman. On the other hand, the guiding spirit also could be thought of as a woman. Let us now examine this issue.

26. Transvestism

There is a discrepancy in the materials that have been compared here. Through the course of the comparison it becomes clear that Yaga, based on the sum of her features and functions in a wondertale, should correspond to the figure or the mask to which the initiate comes. However, the materials presented here do not show that the person who conducts the rites was considered or actually was a woman. Yaga and the forest teacher present a mutual correspondence: they both burn or boil children in a cauldron. But when Yaga tries to do it or does it unsuccessfully, a desperate struggle ensues. If the forest teacher does it, then the student acquires omniscience. But Yaga is also a beneficent creature. We shall become acquainted with her gifts later. There is an affinity in the wondertale between the image of Yaga and the image of the forest sorcerer.

Are there any historical reasons for this affinity? Wondertales suggest that a woman is also present in the rite.

In most cases the travelers or researchers who recorded or described this rite say nothing about women as its administrators. But in some cases we see that the men performing the rites were dressed as women. Based on other testimonies, all the members of the associations had a common mother, an old woman. Let us consider some relevant examples. Nevermann describes the beginning of the rite in former Dutch New Guinea among the Marind tribe: "Men dressed as old women with women's aprons, brightly colored and with fangs over their mouths, which signal that they are not allowed to speak, approached Mayo-anim (i.e., the initiates). The initiates put their arms around the necks of the 'foremothers,' who began to drag them to the hiding place. There they were dropped to the ground and pretended to be asleep."[271] Here we have nothing but a mimic representation of abduction to the woods by an old crone, a woman. The myths correspond to this as well: the benefactor, the donor, is a woman. Dorsey has recorded the following story: a person has a dream urging him to put clay on his head, to depart for a hill, and to stand there for days and nights. He stands there in this way for four days. On the fifth he is surrounded by eagles. One big red eagle says, "I am a *woman* who stays up in the heavens, goes to the people in the night, and gives them dreams. I am going to send someone to you and you must place my feathers upon a stick, which shall be a wand for you." A buffalo approaches and delivers further teachings to him: "The eagle which you lately saw is the bird which controls all animals." After returning home, he founds the "Buffalo-Dancers Association" and teaches his tribe the dances and songs of the buffalo.[272]

In this myth, which reflects the acquisition of shamanism, it is interesting that the animal who appears to the neophyte is a woman.

In the feminine nature of these creatures, as in the feminine nature of Yaga, one can see a reflection of matriarchal relations. These relations come into conflict with the historically evolving rule of men. How is this conflict resolved? This process must come to an end while the initiation rite still exists, the rite being the condition for admission to the male association. The conflict is resolved in different ways: the administrator of the rite dresses as a woman. He is a man-woman. This connects directly to gods and heroes who are disguised as women (Heracles, Achilles) and to the hermaphroditism of many gods and heroes. Sometimes it is resolved differently: the rite is performed by men, but somewhere in the mysterious distance there is a woman present—the mother of the members of the association. This form seems to be more prevalent than others. Here are a few examples. "All the masks of the (New Britain) tribe have a common mother. She supposedly lives on the site of gatherings of the mask carriers' association, and the uninitiated can never see her. . . . She is described as being ill, as having abscesses, and that is the reason why she cannot walk."[273] The lameness of this mysterious mother corresponds to the walking disability of Yaga. In the Duk-Duk association, the most important spirit is called Tubuan. "He is considered to be a woman and the mother of all the masks of Duk-Duk (i.e., of all those who wear the masks). Originally, he probably was a spirit-bird, but this has almost disappeared from the minds of the natives."[274] Nevermann also reports that strange figures used to appear for the festival that "possessed both breasts and phallus simultaneously and looked like hermaphrodites to the naive observer. But the natives strongly reject this interpretation and point out that they are only ever presented as men." Finally, sometimes it is the initiate himself who seems to turn into a woman. His secret name is sometimes feminine.[275] The highest degree of initiation includes the ability to turn into a woman.[276] Many examples of transvestism are given by Indian narrative literature. But here too we find that the transformation into a woman takes place in the forest. This forest is cursed: there men turn into women, and this is why men avoid walking in it. This is an obvious relic of the forbidden forest.[277]

These materials are enough to establish that O. M. Freidenberg's interpretation that "female-male transvestism is a metaphor for a sexual fusion: a woman becomes a man, a man becomes a woman" is fundamentally wrong.[278] Transvestism as such is not important for us; it is important, however, as a factor explaining Yaga's female nature and the presence of her male equivalent in the wondertale. The forest teacher is a historical figure; the woman, the crone, the mother, the hostess, and the female giver of magical properties are prehistoric figures and extremely archaic, but they can be traced through rudiments of the materials on ritual. Yaga is a woman for the same reason that the Siberian shaman is often represented as a woman, a hermaphrodite, or a male with female attributes in his costume. For us, it is important to establish a link here, which is possible even from the few materials selectively enumerated above.

27. Conclusion

This completes the analysis of Yaga. She was broken down in our study to an array of particular features and individual trajectories. Now we must bring them together again.

It turns out, however, that it is impossible to do so. Yaga the abductor, who seeks to cook or roast the children, and Yaga the donor, who interrogates and rewards the hero, cannot be combined into one whole image. At the same time, they do not appear to be two very different figures united only by their name.

In general it has been found that Yaga the abductor is related to the initiation complex; acquiring the helper is connected with this as well. But the attributes of Yaga and some of her actions and exclamations are associated with the concepts of a person's arrival in the kingdom of death. These two complexes, however, do not exclude each other. On the contrary, historically they are closely related.

The departure of children for the forest is a departure toward death. This is why the forest appears both as the house of Yaga who abducts children and as the entrance to Hades. There is no particular difference between actions that take place in the forest and a real death. But the rite died out while the death remained. Whatever was once attached to the rite, whatever happened to the initiate, later happened only to the deceased. This explains not only the fact of the forest in both cases but also the fact that the dead were boiled and fried from very early times, as was done to initiates, and that the initiate was tested for smell; subsequently, the visitor to the other world was also tested for smell.

But this is not all. With the advent of agriculture and agricultural religion, the whole forest religion is transformed into a total perversion. The great magician turns into an evil sorcerer and the mother and mistress of animals into a witch, who carries away children for totally nonsymbolic devouring. The way of life that destroys the rite also destroys its creators and bearers: the witch who burns the children is burned herself by the storyteller, who is the carrier of an epic folktale tradition. This motif does not exist anywhere in rites or beliefs. But it appears as soon as the story starts to circulate independently of the rite, showing that the plot is not created during the way of life that creates the ritual but rather during the way of life that replaces it and that turns the sacred and terrible into half-heroic and half-comic grotesque.

4

THE BIG HOUSE

I. Forest Brotherhood

1. The House in the Woods

Yaga is far from being the only donor in the wondertale. We should now consider other forms of the donor. However, since we have touched on the rite of passage, we will first look through everything that refers to this rite and then examine other donors.

Up to this point, we have considered only the act of the rite. But the act itself was only one of the rite's phases. It had one more phase, which was associated with the neophyte's return home.

After completion of the act of initiation, three different forms of the continuation or termination of the initiation stage have been observed among different peoples and in different places: (1) upon his wounds being healed, the initiate immediately returned home or goes to where he was to be married; (2) he remained living in the forest hut, lodge, or tent for a longer period, amounting to several months or even years; (3) he moved from the forest hut to a "men's house" for several years.

It is impossible to draw a precise border between the period of initiation and subsequent life in the forest or in the men's house. These phenomena constituted a whole complex. Nonetheless, two points can be distinguished in the absence of an immediate return home: the actual time of initiation and the period following it, which lasted until marriage. This period, as well as the circumstances surrounding the return of the hero, will concern us now.

But first of all, we must explain the term *men's house*. Men's houses were a special kind of institution peculiar to the tribal system. They ceased to exist with the rise of the slave-owning state. Their emergence was connected to hunting as the main form of production of material life and to totemism as the ideological reflection of this life. This institution still existed in places where agriculture was beginning to develop, but there it had already begun to degenerate and sometimes had taken on hideous forms. The functions of men's houses were diverse and unstable. At any rate, it is possible to establish that sometimes part of the male population—namely, the young men—no longer lived at their parents' houses from the moment of puberty until they married. They went to live in large, specially built houses that were commonly called *houses of men, men's houses*, or *bachelor houses*. They lived there in a special kind of commune.

Usually all the initiated men were united in an alliance that had a specific name, specific masks, and so forth. The association's functions were very broad and diverse. Often it held actual power over the whole tribe. Men's houses functioned as the center of the association's gatherings. Dances and ceremonies were performed there, and sometimes masks and the tribe's other holy items were stored there. Sometimes there were two houses on the same site—a small one (where circumcision takes place) and a large one. Married men usually did not live in a men's house.

A detailed account of the organization of male unions, or, in English terminology, secret societies, is given in the works of Frobenius, Boas, Schurtz, Webster, Loeb, van Gennep, Nevermann, and others (see chap. 2, sec. 4).

Wondertales have preserved very clear traces of the institution of men's houses. Often the hero, after leaving his home, suddenly sees before him in a clearing or in the forest a special type of structure, usually just called *a house*.

Examination of this house shows that in all its features, it resembles the abovementioned men's house. Let us examine all the specific features of this house in the wondertale.

The hero is impressed by this house in many ways, especially by its size: "They drove and drove, entered the woods and got lost. Suddenly in the distance they saw a fire. They got there and saw a house, and it was huge."[1] "Then he [the hero] came out into a large clearing and saw a house standing there, and the house was tremendously big. He had never seen its like before."[2] "The house was huge, big."[3] "They were walking in the forest. A winter storm began. It started raining and hailing. They needed to run. They ran and ran. An enormous house stood in front of them. The time was toward evening. An old man came out. . . . 'Are you taking your son for training? . . . Give him to me for training, I will teach him everything.'"[4] In another version, this old man is five hundred years old.[5] Such examples are numerous. The strangeness of the combination of a huge house in a forest wilderness never holds the storyteller back, just as it has never caught the attention of researchers. Of course, the huge dimensions of the house prove nothing in themselves. However, we should note that men's houses were sometimes distinguished precisely by their striking dimensions. These were huge buildings equipped for the communal living of all the young bachelors of the village. James Cook saw a house two hundred feet long in Tahiti. After life in one's parents' pitiful shack, this house would have made quite a striking impression.

Another feature of the house is that it is surrounded by a fence: "There is an iron trellis all around the palace."[6] "The palace is surrounded by a high iron fence. Nobody can either walk or ride into the courtyard."[7] "And a very tall fence is placed around it; neither a pedestrian nor a horseman can get in."[8] Indeed, Schurtz also points out that the men's house was surrounded by a fence.[9] In the house, the relics of the tribe were stored, and access to it was forbidden to women and the uninitiated on penalty of death. Skulls were often stored in this house, and these skulls could be carried out and put on the fence:[10] "Around the palace there is a high palisade stretching for a whole ten miles, and a head is fixed on each spike."[11] The fence protected the house from the eyes of any curious outsiders, for whom approaching would mean death on the spot. In some versions of the tale, the house is surrounded by a live railing: "When festivities take place, members of the Duk-Duk protect themselves from outsiders even more than usual and set around Tarayu (the place of celebration) a high wall, which they cover with hanging mats. Sometimes a hedge is grown inside the fence."[12] The hedge has not been preserved in Russian tales, but where it does occur, such a fence typically grows around a beautiful maiden who is sleeping but not dead. The taboo of entering this site is also preserved in these types of tales: "And there was a garden, enclosed by an iron fence, locked, and the doors locked. This garden was forbidden; a father and his son lived in it."[13]

Wondertales have even preserved vague recollections of the pagan religious functions of these houses: "And there are no icons at all, only fir cones are sticking up."[14]

All the other specific characteristics of this house can be explained by the desire to isolate oneself from the world. It stands on pillars: "They walked and walked, and saw a high house standing on poles, an enormous house."[15] Men's houses were often built on poles. The men lived and slept upstairs. In various tales, the house is often presented as multistory, but the original form can be easily discerned behind these high-rise versions: "He approached the palace and immediately stepped into the top floor."[16] "He started to look for the path and came out into a meadow, looked around, and saw a large stone house three stories high standing in the meadow: the gates were locked, the shutters closed. Only one window was open, and a ladder leaned against it."[17] Thus, the entrance is actually through the upper floor by means of an exterior ladder. "When he approached the palace, he looked but saw no doors or windows, nothing. He felt around and found a button, and when he pressed on it the door immediately opened, and he went up into the palace."[18] The hero goes in through the top floor, bypassing the lower levels. An even clearer example: "He walked all around the palace—there was no gate, no doors, nor any entrance. What was he to do? Suddenly he saw a long pole lying there. He picked it up, leaned it against the balcony and started climbing along it."[19] "In the middle of the forest there was a huge house, surrounded by planks. . . . The house was not that amazing, but there was a wonderfully built garden house. It was wonderful because it was so high up and painted colorfully. . . . A ladder led to the top."[20] The rudiments of the pillars are found in such examples as "The boy walked several times around the house and did not find any doors or gates and was about to go back. Then . . . he noticed hardly visible little doors in the pillar. He opened them and went in."[21] These examples show the various ways to get into the house and emphasize the thoroughness with which all the openings are covered and camouflaged.

Here is a description of a men's house on Anoes Island as conveyed by Schurtz: "The house stands on pillars. Some pillars there have been carved in the form of male and female figures. The log they climbed to the front door presented the figure of a man with a huge phallus. The entrance passages were curtained, so that not a single woman could look inside . . . and would not be subjected, consequently, to death."[22] The house in the Ladrones Islands is described as follows: "A huge closed space rests on the poles. Through it an opening led into the upper apartments, which consisted of four rooms: for food, for sleep, for supplies, and for work."[23]

This last case shows us the house's interior. Its peculiarity is that it consists of separate sections or rooms. We see that this specific construction is preserved in the wondertale: "No one was there. He walked around through the rooms," and so on.[24] This is a typical feature. The hero goes through the halls and the rooms. We shall soon see why there is nobody in the house. The fact that the tale usually mentions the rooms demonstrates that something unusual and extraordinary lies in this circumstance for the hero.

As pointed out by Schurtz, these houses often served as a refuge for male newcomers. Sometimes we read in the tales about "a strange upper room" in the house—that is, a room for strangers.[25] Another example: "He was wandering in the Urals and saw a huge house. There was nobody in the house. He walked through the rooms. He . . . entered a special room and lay down on the sofa to rest."[26]

These houses sometimes look magnificent, are decorated with carvings, and are colorfully painted. It is no wonder that they are turned into "marble palaces."

The wondertale house is quite frequently guarded by animals, most often snakes or lions. We shall not examine this feature here, as it will come up again in the description of the Thrice-Tenth Kingdom.

Schurtz has brought together material on men's houses. The appearance of such houses could vary quite a bit, but they had some typical common features, and these have been preserved in the wondertales. We can summarize them by reference to the following features as reflected in the tales: (1) the house is located in a hiding place in the forest; (2) it is distinguished by its large size; (3) it is surrounded by a fence, sometimes with skulls; (4) it stands on pillars; (5) it is entered by climbing a ladder or a pole; (6) the entrance as well as other openings are curtained and covered; and (7) it has several internal compartments.

Among these points, only the first gives rise to doubts. The men's house does not or does not always stand in the depths of the forest. A certain shift has occurred here, and I shall now turn to this feature.

2. Big House and Small Hut

In wondertales, we find not only the "big house" in the woods but also a small hut, such as the hut of Yaga and its various versions. As mentioned above, initiation sometimes took place in a forest hut or cabin, after which the initiated either returned to his family, stayed to live in the hut, or moved into the big men's house. Schurtz calls these latter two types of buildings the "circumcision house" (*Beschneidungshaus*) and the "men's house" (*Männerhaus*). All three types of structures can be found in various wondertales. The tale may include a direct return home from a forest hut. But in this case, it is always either children or young women who return. A second type of tale, which involves staying in the forest for a long time until marriage, is also found. The hero does not always meet the "big house" on his way, but he often builds (or comes across) a cabin and stays to live there with his comrades. We shall look at this type of story in greater detail. The correlation here is very precise. Building the house with one's own hands in the forest occurs, for example, in the famous Egyptian tale about two brothers. The hero, Bata, goes to "the valley of the cedars." There is an extensive literature about this "valley of the cedars," but no one yet has compared it to the "forest" of our wondertales in the sense explored here. "And so, after many days, he had built with his own hands a tower in the valley of the cedars. The tower was full of all sorts of good things that he had made to fill up the house."[27] Later in this tale, one can see a temporary death and resurrection, transvestism, and marriage.

The situation is somewhat different regarding the move from the small house to the big one. These houses were often located on the same site.[28] The same external layout appears sometimes in the wondertale: "So one day he is walking in the forest and sees a large and beautiful house and a simple hut nearby."[29] There are also examples where the hero first lives in a small hut and then in a big house. In a tale from the region of Perm, parents send the hero off to an old bathhouse in the forest because of his laziness: "Vanyukha got sent out to the bath house. He began going to the forest to cut wood; he would sell firewood and buy bread. He found a house in a meadow far away in the forest: the windows were shut and the gates too."[30] If this were the only example, one could argue that the bathhouse is a purely domestic element. But similar examples exist in other collections.[31] The same is found in Afanas'ev: the hero lives in a bathhouse. "The Fool began to go into the forest to work, and that's what they lived on." Then one day, he loses his way, sees a large stone house with three stories, and so forth.[32] A maiden first lives in a hut in the ravine and then in a large robbers' house.[33] However, such examples are still rare. It would be more accurate to say that the wondertale in general does not offer a transition from the small house to the large one. It features either a small house or a large one. These two types of buildings do not have sharp functional differences in the wondertale. It has transferred the men's house, usually located in the village or nearby, to the forest and does not distinguish it from the small hut. We shall examine the life of the house in the forest, regardless of whether it is localized in the big or small house, but, as noted, we shall now turn to elements that follow the initiation, not the act of initiation itself. One characteristic feature of this life is when several warrior-heroes live together in the forest.

3. The Set Table

Let us now look closely at the inhabitants of this house. The hero finds a set table there: "In one room a table was set, there were twelve table settings, twelve loaves of bread, and the same number of bottles of wine."[34] There, the hero encounters a different way of serving the food, not the one to which he is accustomed. Everyone has his own portion, and the portions are equal. The visitor does not yet have his own portion, so he eats a little bit of each portion. In other words, the eating is done here in a communal way. We shall see that at this place, they not only eat in a communal way but also live as a commune. In a Baloch tale, two ways of eating are very clearly juxtaposed, though in a somewhat different situation. "When you get into the royal house, first you will be greeted, and then they will bring you seven different dishes: bread, apples, meat, and things like that. But you do not behave according to your former shepherd's custom of eating a whole plate from each dish. Instead, eat a small piece from every dish."[35] Among the families in the villages where the boy lived to this point, people would eat exactly "a whole plate." There is a motif in African materials where the father eats secretly from his children and eats more than they do: "He ate up the sour milk by himself, while the children and their mother were asleep."[36] Here, by contrast, this is not possible. Here, everyone lives in a tight-knit fashion; they live as brothers.

4. Brothers

Contrary to the wondertale tradition of repeating every action and avoiding simultaneous actions, the brothers always come home together, all at once.

The number of these brothers varies. There could be two to twelve of them in tales, but sometimes there are twenty-five and even thirty.[37] Isn't a small number incompatible with a large house? Is there not an inconsistency here? There could be more in these men's houses. Men lived there for several years; after a year (or other lengths of time), there was an influx of new members while those who had reached marriageable age departed. But first, as indicated above, brothers lived not only in the big house but also in a small one. Second, within this communal group, there were more closely related fraternities. There are peoples where boys who are circumcised or dedicated at the same time are regarded as particularly closely connected to one another, almost like a family. In Australia, there is even a special name for this kind of relationship. Webster too talks of how peers form special and tight-knit groups: "The members of these brotherhoods are supposed never to give evidence against one another, and it is a great offence for any of them to eat food alone if their comrades are near. In fact, the friendship is greater than is that between men in England who go up to the University together."[38] All the members of this union call one another brothers.[39] Schurtz notes that within these groups even smaller groups can be formed, where two people are obliged to protect each other in battle. Thus, we can assume that the wondertale does not reflect the entire life of the house but the life of one group within it.

5. Hunters

When the hero comes to the house, it is usually empty. The hero is met sometimes by an old woman, sometimes by a young woman. We shall discuss young women later; the old women actually could have access to the men's houses since they were no longer considered women.[40] The brothers refer to the old women as mothers.

The following dialogue between a hero and an old woman explains why the house is empty. "Who lives here?" "Certain people, twelve of them, robbers." "Where are they?" "They've gone out hunting, they'll come back soon."[41] The young men went hunting as a group and return home only at night. Often the men's house served mainly as a place to spend the night, while during the day it was empty.[42] Since the brothers did everything together, as a group, we can assume they go hunting as a group too. This assumption does not contradict the forms of primitive hunting.

In the wondertale, the brothers begin to hunt as soon as they settle in the forest (it doesn't matter whether they are in a large house or a small one): "The warriors started to live in the forest and hunt migratory birds."[43] "They stopped there to live and made themselves a yurt. Then they began to kill all kinds of bird and all kinds of animals, and they piled up feathers and fur."[44] The men's commune lived exclusively by hunting. The food of the young men was exclusively meat; agricultural products were sometimes banned for them. Schurtz connects this with the fact that agriculture was in the hands of women. Sometimes a kind of monopoly on hunting developed. Only those who had been initiated into the union had the right to hunt.[45] In the Grimms' "The Twelve Hunters," we see this kind of team of hunters, supplying game to the table of the leader-king. We see the same in a Russian folktale: "In a certain kingdom there lived a single, unmarried king, and he had a whole company of archers: the archers went hunting, shooting migratory birds, and supplied the king's table with game."[46]

6. Brigands

But often, in tales, this commune lives by a different profession. These brothers are brigands. We can think of this as simply a common deformation of an old motif that has shifted to accommodate a later way of life—in this case, the more recent and comprehensible phenomenon of brigandage. This is how it is viewed by, for example, Lur'e. However, the brigandage of the forest brothers also has its historical past. The newly dedicated were often granted the right to robbery either of a neighboring tribe or, more often, of their own tribe. "The boys are no longer under the influence of the usual rules and laws but have the right to excesses and violence, especially theft and extortion of food supplies. In 'Fouta Djallou' the newly circumcised may for a month steal and eat whatever they want. In 'Dar Fui' they roam the neighboring villages and steal poultry." This is not an isolated phenomenon but a typical one. "The power of the neophytes extends so far that they can appropriate any object belonging to the uninitiated."[47] The meaning of this permission is evidently that as a warrior and hunter, the boy needs to develop an opposition to his former home, to women, and to agriculture. Robbery was the prerogative of the newly dedicated young men, and our young hero is one of them.

Might the forest robbers of the wondertale be compared to criminals of the recent past? Even what would seem to be the most realistically reworked motifs are sometimes interspersed with extremely archaic features. "He walks along in the city, sees a two-story house and stops. But a gang of robbers lives in this house. He enters the house. They are sitting at the table, sharing a bottle of vodka," and so on. The hero asks to be admitted to the gang. "If you don't believe me, look at my hands: they even have brands on them."[48] We mentioned above that branding is a characteristic feature of initiation rites. This is nothing other than a tattoo. The topic of branding and marking was specifically studied by Loeb. But there is another feature that testifies to the connection of this motif with the rite of passage: the human flesh that is usually eaten by the robber brothers. We see the remnants of ritual cannibalism in such details as the human bones found in the soup; in arms, legs, and heads that are torn off and chopped off; in corpses, which are put on the table in robbers' house to be eaten; and so forth.[49]

7. The Division of Duties

This brotherhood has its own very primitive organization. It has a senior figure who is chosen from among the brothers. Tales sometimes call him the "big brother." Sometimes the brothers go outside and throw a ball or shoot arrows, and the one whose arrow flies the farthest is selected as the head. In the following example, we see the attitude toward the forest house more clearly: "So the four warriors set off. And they came across a stone wall, encircling a kingdom, and an iron fence. 'Whoever breaks off this gate will be the big brother.'"[50] In Khudiakov, the boy who is given to the cook to be fried winds up as the apprentice of a blacksmith. He becomes a head of a band: "Over there in the river frogs are croaking; whoever makes them stop croaking will be tsar."[51] In a Permian tale: "Shout: 'River, come back!'" (cf., "Forest, bend down to the damp earth!" "Forest creatures, be still!"). Apparently, the most dexterous and strong is selected, the one who possesses magical power over nature. Namely, this is one of the aspects of initiation: a hunter would allegedly acquire power over nature, over the "creatures of the forest" in particular. Schurtz also mentions the selection of a head in the circumstances indicated.[52]

This commune had a well-known division of responsibilities. While the brothers were hunting, one of them prepared the food. In the tale the brothers always take turns. "They settled in. They left Dubynets at home to cook breakfast," and so on. "'Which one of you cooked the porridge?' asks the newcomer to the brigands' house."[53] The tale has not preserved the historical situation where the whole group of the newly admitted had to cook for the entire home and keep it in order.[54] In America, newly admitted men had to bear service like slaves for two years. In some areas of Asia the lowest rank of the newly admitted was called "carriers of fire wood," and they performed these duties for three years.[55] In Russian and German tales, the soldier who has come to the devil (this motif is equivalent to staying in the woods with the forest spirit, etc.) is supposed to stoke the boilers with wood for a number of years. This connection is also pointed out by Lur'e, who cites, among others, the example of a Swiss folktale in which "the primary responsibility of the boys who entered the forest hut was to make sure the fire in the hearth was not extinguished."[56]

8. "Little Sister"

Everything we have said thus far has the quality of accessories, furnishings, that are static rather than dynamic, not actions. The dynamism begins when a woman appears in this fraternity.

We will not concentrate here on the question of how a girl gets to the forest house in wondertales. She can be driven out by her stepmother, invited to the house by the robbers, kidnapped, and so forth. Out of all the possible ways the girl might end up there, we shall focus only on her abduction. In an Afanas'ev tale two warriors live in the forest: "One is blind; the other has no legs. They grow bored and come up with the idea of stealing a girl somewhere from her father and her mother."[57] The position of the abducted girl is quite honorable: "The warriors brought the merchant's daughter to their forest hut and said to her, 'Be like a sister to us, live with us, and keep house; otherwise we have no one to cook dinner or wash our shirts, crippled as we are. And God will not forsake you for it!' The merchant's daughter stayed with them. The warriors loved and respected her and saw her as their own sister. They were always off hunting, their so-called sister always stayed at home, managed the household, cooked the meals, washed their clothes."[58] This one example is enough to establish the following characteristics of this "little sister": She is abducted or, in other versions, comes by herself voluntarily or accidentally. She manages the brothers' household and is revered by them. She lives with the brothers as their sister. Of these three points, the third one does not correspond to historical reality, and I will discuss it below; the first two reflect historical reality quite faithfully, even in their details.

On the one hand, life in the men's house aimed to separate the young men from women. The whole house, and everything that happened there, was forbidden to women. Such animosity has been preserved, for example, in one of Grimm's fairy tales: "We vow: wherever we find a girl, we'll shed her red blood."[59] This example is a clear reflection of bans on women. But the example also makes clear that it refers to women outside the house.

The men's house was prohibited to women as a rule, but the inverse is not true: women were not in all cases prohibited in the men's house. This means that women (one or more) who served the brothers as their wives were always present in men's houses. This feature is so typical for this system that Schurtz directly talks about the presence of three groups of male population: the uninitiated, the young men in the men's house living in open marital relationships, and married men who live in regulated marital relations.[60] Many examples of this can be found in the works of Webster and Schurtz. "Girls who entered the *'maisons des celibataires'* suffered no disgrace; parents would even urge their children to enter them. . . . In these houses there are usually one or more unmarried girls, who are often the temporary property of the young men."[61] According to Schurtz, "Among the Bororo, the sexual needs of young men are satisfied in such a way that individual girls are forcibly taken away to the men's house, where they simultaneously serve as lovers to several men and receive gifts from them."[62]

Besides abduction by force or the desire of parents, there could be other reasons that compelled girls and women to go to the men's house. Sometimes they were running away from their husbands, a case that is also reflected in the folktale. In a tale from Perm, the priest's daughter beats her husband on their wedding night with a belt and says, "'I have a lover, Khark Kharkovich, Solon Solonych; he has such a face that one can only dry leggings on it, but even he is better than you!' (The groom was hideous!) Then she gave him one with a silk belt and got away from him. In the morning the groomsmen got up and saw that the bride was not there." Her husband goes to look for her, and he finds out "she's at Khark Kharkovich's, Solon Solonych's. There's a fence around the house, and a human skull stuck on each spike."[63] In a tale from Samara, a wife flees from her husband to the forest and becomes a robber chieftain, but seven years later she repents and goes back home to her husband.[64]

The respected position enjoyed by the "little sister," as well as her household duties, is entirely attested to in history. Frazer reports the following about the girls who live in the men's houses on the islands of Palau: during the period of her service a girl has to keep the house clean and watch over the fire. The men treat her well and do not force her to bestow on them her favors.[65] The girl lives in special quarters by the house. They treat her with knightly courtesy. None of the young men would dare to enter her quarters. She is abundantly supplied with food, and the young men take the trouble to bring her luxuries such as betel nuts and tobacco.

Here I would like to draw attention to one additional detail that will turn out to be very significant in explaining tales of the "Cupid and Psyche" type—namely, food is served to her in such a way that she sees no one. It is given to her in a special room. We shall be obliged to elaborate on this more below. Women reside in these houses only temporarily, and afterward they get married. If a woman chose to stay there for her whole life, she would not have been respected.

It can be seen from all these materials that a girl who lived in a men's house was not at all a little sister for these brothers. Before analyzing the forms in which one or more women might have a marriage relationship with a group of men, let us see whether a sister in a wondertale is always only a sister.

First, the wondertale sharply denies the existence of a marital relationship, and this already should make us suspicious. In "The Magic Mirror" we read, "After they had a good look at her, each of them wanted to marry her, but as they could not agree, they took her to live with them as their sister and respected her very much."[66] In another version, "If any one of us dares to encroach on our sister, then without sparing him, we should slash him with this very saber."[67] Here the wondertale has somewhat shifted the borders of marriage and brotherly relations. This can be confirmed by reference to a tale from Vyatka in which a stepdaughter is driven out and ends up in the forest house of two robbers. They go away. "And they left her all manner of food dishes and clothing: everything is here for you, eat and drink, and dress yourself in the best clothes! . . . And she had already begot from them a little baby girl."[68] It says "from them" rather than from one of them. We shall discuss the baby later. We read in a Belarusian tale, "There was a king and queen. They had a very good daughter. Twelve suitors wooed her, and those suitors were all robbers."[69] Here one girl is wooed by twelve suitors at once rather than by one suitor. It is true that these are separate details and single cases, but they demonstrate the feasibility of such a shift of boundaries under the influence of later forms of marriage, which exclude and punish polyandry. Our case is expressed more clearly in places where couple marriage is not the law. In a Mongolian tale seven princes go to a grove (a rudimentary forest) "to dispel their boredom." There they meet a girl of extraordinary beauty. "Listen to what we'll suggest to you. We are seven brothers, princes, and we still have no wives. Be our spouse! The girl agreed, and they began to live together."[70]

We must point out in passing that not only were there men's houses but there could be women's houses as well. It is impossible here to go into the issue of women's houses; we can only point out the fact itself. Schurtz considers them a later phenomenon and an imitation of men's houses. In a tale from the Perm region, three sworn brothers travel around the world. Just like the girl who winds up in a men's house, the heroes here come to a house inhabited by women. "Out of the blue they see a good house. They stop into the house, open the gate, and enter the palace. . . . They find white bread there and all sorts of cooked food." Three maidens fly home and find out the following: "There has been an intrusion in our house today. Three young men came in, and one of the three was very handsome." The maidens interrogate these heroes and tell them, "Call us wives, and we will call you husbands. You will sleep with us but not talk to us in a bad way! If you speak to us in a bad way, then we will not keep you here but will kick you out!"[71]

Thus we see that marital relations are not completely crowded out by brotherly ones in the folktale.

So what were the forms of marital relations in men's houses like? There is very little material on this topic. In any case, we can say that these relationships were not always the same and varied from place to place. Women could belong to all the men, to several, or to only one, either by their own choice or by the choice of one of the brothers. They were "often the temporary property of the young men."[72] They were rewarded for their services, first with rings or other things for themselves or with arrows to give to the other brothers; later on, they were paid. This collective marriage tended to end with an individual marriage. "She chooses a companion or lover, whose mistress she is nominally, and who is responsible for the payment of her wages; but she is free to consort with other men on certain conditions." In this case, the initiative came from the woman. But it could also proceed from the man. "A man may, and often does, offer to marry a girl during her term of service, and if his offer is accepted, he pays a sum to the brotherhood for his wife. More commonly, however, it would seem, the girls marry after their period of service is over and they have returned to their own village."[73]

The wondertale does not reflect all these options. The girl belongs either to no one or to all of them. However, in some relatively rare cases we can establish that she belongs to one of the brothers. In Khudiakov she is given as a wife to the young man who just arrived. Here the hero comes to the robbers' house. "Timonya, why go home? Stay with us, and we'll marry you off; we'll give you our sister."[74] In other cases it is possible to establish that she belongs to the head of the gang. He exchanges crosses with her.

Russian tales do not reflect gifts that she receives, but such examples may be gathered from international materials.[75]

They do, however, reflect another phenomenon: the tendency of this marriage to turn into an individual one and the role of children in this tendency.

9. *The Birth of a Child*

Obviously children were born as a result of such cohabitation. The attitudes toward these children varied. "Children that were born from such unions were nearly always killed."[76] We can assume that this happened in cases where the woman belonged to all of the men together. But when, against the background of promiscuity, a new union of two people was created and when paternity was known, the treatment might be different. "In many cases, the child was not considered undesirable but became the reason for transforming the love affair into a solid marriage."[77]

It is possible to see in the tale traces of complications caused by the birth of a baby. In a tale from Perm, the hero walks along the forest path and gets to the house ("there stood a house"). A woman warrior lives there. The hero says, "I got lost. Won't you accept me to live with you as your husband?" She agrees, and in a year they have a baby boy. The wife says, "'Now, Fedor Burmakin, live with me in the right way and be a family man, as the child is both mine and yours.'" But Fedor prepares an escape. His wife goes to battle, and he escapes from her on a raft. "Then the baby started crying and the forest began to crack. When she heard the baby crying, she immediately hurried home. She came running, grabbed the baby, and came running to the sea. She stepped on one foot [of the baby], grabbed the other, and tore him in half. She threw this half to him [Fedor], and his raft began to sink. Somehow he managed to push this half off the raft and went on ahead; and she ate the other half."[78] The elements are clear: the forest house, cohabitation in it, the birth of a child, the woman's desire to turn the marriage into a permanent one, the man's reluctance regarding such a marriage, destroying (eating) the baby, using the corpse as a way to keep the husband, and the husband's departure. In this example, the husband successfully escapes from his wife.

We have a similar example in a northern tale. Twins are born, after which the hero runs away. After some adventures, he comes home and finds his wife there. In this example, the wife follows her forest husband to his house. And children are the reason the relationship changes and turns into a real marriage.[79] In these examples, the connection to the "big" house is clear. We see, however, that the folktale as a whole does not recognize marriages in the forest house. For the folktale, a woman in this circumstance is only a sister. It is possible that the features of this character might be transferred in wondertales to another character— namely, to a princess. If so, then the princess in tales of living water can be related to phenomena of this type. There, the hero sins with the princess. She sets out with her two children to look for her husband and finds him, "and they performed a legal marriage."[80] However, this issue can be conclusively resolved only in connection with studying the princess.

10. The Beauty in the Coffin

It is evident from what has been put forth above that women who lived in the men's houses did so only temporarily. After staying a while, they left the house and got married either to one of the brothers or, more often, to someone in their own settlement. In a historical sense there should be one problem at this point. Everything that happened in the men's house was supposed to be concealed from women. The shrines of the tribe were kept there, ritual dances were practiced, and so forth. But there are no secrets from the "little sister." Can they let her leave the house so easily? "She (i.e., the young woman in the house of the bachelors) is permitted to hear and see the songs and dances from which other women are debarred."[81]

The girl in the tale who lives in the house of the warriors in the woods sometimes suddenly dies; after being dead for a while, she comes back to life and after that marries a prince. A temporary death, as we have seen, is one of the most distinctive and constant characteristics of the initiation rite. We can assume that the woman, before she was let out of the house, was subjected to a rite of initiation. We can even speculate about the reasons for this: the initiation guaranteed the secrets of the house. Here the tale has only slightly changed the internal but not the external sequence of events. She unexpectedly dies, just as unexpectedly comes back to life, and gets married. The only detail here that is not present in history is the unexpectedness. It is precisely leaving the house to marry that requires her initiation—that is, her death and resurrection.

Temporary death was noted previously (chap. 3, sec. 20). Here it is important to establish the external forms of this death, which are related to our wondertale.

From what does the girl die in, for example, "The Magic Mirror"? Bolte-Polívka's materials allow us to establish three groups of objects that cause her death. One group contains objects that pierce the skin: needles, thorns, and splinters. Hairpins and combs, which are inserted into the hair, may also be included in this group. The second group includes things that are taken into the body orally: poisoned apples, pears, grapes, or, less frequently, drinks. The third group consists of items that one can wear. It includes clothing—for example, shirts, dresses, stockings, shoes, and belts—or jewelry such as necklaces, rings, and earrings. Finally, there are cases where the girl turns into an animal or a bird and then turns back into a human. The means of reviving her are very simple: take out the needle or pin from under her skin; shake her body so the poison pops out; or remove her shirt, her ring, and so on.

Some of the methods mentioned above are also present among the ways by which a temporary death was achieved in rites of initiation. One of these was to insert sharp objects into the skin. "The main part of the ceremony consisted of killing the initiate who, due to this, acquired great magical powers. The killing was carried out by an imaginary or magic insertion of sacred shells into the bodies of the initiates; then the boy who fell down came back to life again by the songs."[82] These shells were fired into the initiated boy. The killing seems "imaginary" or "magic" to the researcher or to the outside observer but not to the initiate, who saw himself as actually being killed and resurrected. This case is not an exception. It is well known that in most places in the world disease was attributed to the presence of a foreign object in the body, and treatment consists of the shaman removing this object. In our case, the same reasons are considered responsible for death and for coming back to life.

Another way to call forth a temporary death was poisoning. This method was practiced quite widely. Young men fell down as if dead, lost consciousness, then after a while came to their senses and back to life. For example, in the Lower Congo a priest-magician (*Zauberpriester*) took on leadership of the initiation. He took his pupils to the forest and spent some time with them there. Apparently, with the help of a drug, they were put to sleep and declared dead.[83] We do not hear anything about poisoned fruits. The poison apparently is always administrated in the form of a drink, which also exists in tales, though there the effect of the beverage is often transferred to fruits.

Finally, if the brothers in the men's house dress the girl in gowns, belts, beads, and so on, this is in part a more recent phenomenon and in part the custom of adorning the dead. The initiates were dressed in garments of the dead, after which they were considered to be dead.[84] In places where clothing was not known at all, the initiate was daubed with white clay as a symbol of death. The gown that was put on the girl was a gown of death. In a tale from Samara, a girl is sent the "gown of death." The girl "took it into her head to try on the gown. She put it on, lay down, and died."[85]

The coffin is, of course, a later phenomenon. But the emergence and evolution of the coffin in general can be traced. The coffin's predecessors were wooden storage boxes of animal form. Such storage containers have been documented in many places. Schurtz, for example, reports houses with wooden images of sharks where the bodies of leaders were stored. This is the oldest form of the coffin, which in turn reflects still earlier notions that when a human dies he turns into an animal or is eaten by animals. Later, the coffin begins to lose its animal attributes. For example, in the Egyptian *Book of the Dead,* we can see images of coffins or pedestals on which the mummy lies. They have animal legs, an animal head, and an animal tail. Later, the animal attributes completely disappear, and the coffin takes the form known to us now. From this point of view, transformation of the girl into an animal and back to a human, and putting her in the coffin and removing her from it alive, are the same phenomenon; only their forms are of different degrees of antiquity.

Why is the coffin often made of glass? The answer to this question can be given only in relation to study of the "crystal mountain," the "glass mountain," the "glass house," and the role played in religious beliefs by crystal and quartz—and later glass—all the way to the magic crystals of medieval and more recent times. Special magical powers were attributed to crystal. It played a certain role in initiation ceremonies, and the crystal coffin is only a special case of a more general phenomenon (see chap. 8, sec. 8).

Here another question may arise. Why is only the girl put in the coffin? Why have tales not preserved spikes and the like in connection with boys? This, however, is not quite accurate. In some cases, it is a young man lying in the glass coffin.[86] "Sleeping Beauty" can be compared with the "sleeping young men."[87] Finally, the boy hero, when he goes to the Water-King, also "puts on a white shirt and underpants, as if dressing for death."[88] Yet a tendency toward specifically female forms of temporary death is evident. The ethnographic materials do not demonstrate this differentiation. We should regard it as a phenomenon belonging to a tale tradition whose beginning and cause can be traced only through a special study of this plotline.

11. *Cupid and Psyche*

The whole range of phenomena that has been brought up here is very complex, and of course not all the connections are yet revealed; not all has been discovered and detected. On the other hand, it is quite possible that some analogies might prove to be deceiving.

Thus, a question may be raised regarding the connection of some elements in the tale of Cupid and Psyche with the range of phenomena described above.

Where is Psyche located? Where does her married life with Cupid take place? We know the scenes: they take place in the palace and the garden. But the Psyche of Russian folktales lives in the forest house, and she is the wife of one of twelve brothers. In a northern tale the mistress of the house is an old woman. The young woman comes to her house, and the old woman invites her to lie down behind a curtain inside. "Suddenly there was a clatter and the sound of thunder: Twelve young men are coming. They tell the twelfth brother, 'Do not eat your supper now, you have a bride.'" He sleeps with the young woman who has come to them.[89] Of course, it is easy to argue here that this case is not typical, that here assimilation with the motif of the twelve robbers has taken place. It is possible to view the issue in this way. But a different direction is also feasible here: perhaps the marriage of Psyche and Cupid reflects the phenomenon of temporary marriages with the "brothers" whereby the other brothers are omitted, and the polyandrous temporary marriage is represented by the couple's marriage of a later formation. A number of observations confirm this assumption.

It is not only in Russian tales that Cupid's palace is in the forest; it is a feature of all tales of this type. In a tale from Hanover, a girl comes to the palace for seven years—that is, she lives there temporarily and must tidy up the house, just like the "little sister" familiar to us. The servants, the employees, and the coachmen of the house all vie with each other to spend the night with her.[90]

But this is far from being the only feature that leads to such an idea. The girl is usually presold to a monster. Study of this sale shows that the presold person enters an environment associated with the initiation complex. We saw above that a girl was sold by her parents to the men's house. We saw that usually her parents themselves sent her there. In tales of the Cupid and Psyche type, the girl usually resists in a feeble way. Furthermore, if she finds a meal always ready for her in the new place, then it also very closely resembles those materials cited above.

> "Do not worry, Daddy," said the youngest daughter. "God willing, everything will work out well for me there too. Take me to the dragon." Her father took her there, left her at the palace, said goodbye, and went home. So the fair maiden, the merchant's daughter, walks through different rooms—all gold and velvet, but no one can be seen, not a single human soul. And the time goes by. The beauty grows hungry and thinks, "Oh, how I would like to eat now!" Just as she thinks this, a table appears in front of her, and on the table there is everything: food, drinks, and sweets; only bird's milk is missing.[91]

Here too we easily recognize the "big house" already familiar to us, although in this case it is not named and not described. We have seen above how the girl in these houses is supplied with food. She is served in such a way that she sees no one doing the serving—that is, we have some kind of staging of invisible services. Invisible servants are a constant feature of these tales. In Frazer this is presented very rationalistically. Perhaps, however, the matter here is much deeper. We know that those staying in the house were considered to be staying in the realm of death. One of its features is invisibility. Hence, the "blindness" and the white or black color of the neophytes and so on. Hence, also, as we shall see below, the invisibility cap. This somewhat simulated invisibility, however, was understood to be as real as the simulated masked animal appearance of the inhabitants of the house. We have a disguise of invisibility that the tale has preserved as real invisibility.

Finally, the animal nature of the bridegroom and his sudden disappearance do not contradict but on the contrary confirm our conjecture. The fact that the "forest brothers" have an animal guise is not at all an exception.[92] The initiates and the men living in men's or forest houses were often thought of and disguised as animals. Finally, the morning disappearance of the groom is connected with the motif of the house that stands empty during the day.

All these motifs are found in other tales as well. There is nothing specifically new in them. A more specific issue for the cycle of this kind of tale is the motif of visiting relatives. In wondertales about a magic groom, either the girl herself (sometimes even with her husband) goes to visit her family,[93] or the girl receives guests in her home. The kingdom where Psyche stays has long been understood as the realm of the dead. We have seen that those undergoing initiation are thought of as staying in another world. But if the garden of the serpent were *only* an otherworldly kingdom, then the visits of relatives would be inexplicable. If, however, the garden and the kingdom of the serpent living in a marriage with the girl and the kingdom of the relatives and parents left behind are understood in the sense used here, then the family visit becomes clear. In Apuleius the girl is visited by her sisters. In our wondertales often the opposite happens: the girl visits her parents. "She started to think about her native land."[94] "Let me go to see my mother."[95] "Well, let's go see my parents"[96] and so on. As Webster points out, visiting relatives is allowed after a certain period.[97] Bolte thinks that the tale "loses its character of the miraculous, as the wife manages to persuade her husband to visit her father."[98] This may be so, but in a wondertale, the magical and the nonmagical both can be equally related to historical fact.

12. The Wife at Her Husband's Wedding

The situation described above shows that both young men and some young women had in their lives two marriages in a row. One was a free marriage in the "big house," temporary and collective, and the other took place after returning home, a lasting and regulated marriage from which a family was created.

It is noticeable that in tales, a hero sometimes marries twice, or, rather, he intends to marry a second time, having forgotten his first wife. From the point of view of our material, a question might arise: Could it be that the first wife, met outside the house, somewhere else in another kingdom, and so on, is the temporary wife in the men's house? The second wife, whom the hero is going to marry after returning home, may correspond to the second wife of the regulated marriage. In historical reality, the first wife, the wife of the brothers and of each one of them individually, was abandoned and forgotten. Upon returning home, a permanent, lasting marriage took place, and a family was created. And that is precisely how the hero always wants to act. But the deserted wife "from there" reminds him about herself, and the hero marries the first wife.

If this observation is correct, if it is really a historically conditioned analogy, then it means that the tale here reflects a later stage at which this system was decomposing, when a conflict arose with the social structure characteristic of the agricultural order and demanded different forms of marriage.

Let us consider a few relevant examples. In "The Sea King and Vasilisa the Wise," the hero is presold to the Sea King. He goes to him, marries his daughter, and then is going back home with her. Vasilisa says, "Go forward, prince, and report to your father and mother, while I wait for you here on the road. Just remember my words: kiss everybody, but do not kiss your sister. Otherwise you will forget me."[99] This is puzzling: what actually makes Vasilisa stop on the road? There are no obstacles that would prevent her from entering the city along with the prince. This strange act is not motivated by the tale; it is motivated by history. If she does not stop at the gate, then the conflict between the two wives will not take place while this conflict is a not quite forgotten historical phenomenon. Stopping on the road is the obvious way to connect our motif to the tale.

The interdiction "do not kiss your sister" is also clear to us. Here the "little sister" is the same "little sister" as in the forest house. "Do not kiss" is also quite a clear directive. The young woman asks the hero not to be intimate with other women. However, he does kiss his sister—that is, he enters into another marriage and as a result completely forgets about his first wife. "Our king is marrying his son to a rich princess." It is characteristic that the son is made to marry (rather than marrying on his own) a "rich" girl—in other words, a marriage is arranged. These are two different types of marriage. Vasilisa is forgotten. But in the tale, she always finds a way to remind him about herself in the midst of the wedding feast. "At just that moment the prince remembered about his wife, jumped up from the table," and so on. Nobody pays attention anymore to the poor "king's daughter," and the hero marries Vasilisa. "It was, of course, embarrassing for the bride and the guests, but there was nothing to be done."[100]

One might object that such an interpretation of the kiss has been rationalized. A number of authors propose another interpretation. The forgetfulness is regarded as loss of memory when passing from the realm of the living to the realm of the dead and vice versa. This, for example, is how Antti Aarne sees it: "That the girl belongs to the beings of the other world is clearly seen from the fact that the young man forgets about her when kissing a woman of this world."[101] Such an interpretation is possible. We have seen the ways it is possible to interpret the stay of the hero in the "other world." In the *Book of the Dead* there are prayers for preserving memory (chap. XXII), indicating the presence of a notion of memory loss. However, the kiss contradicts this. Why does obliviousness come with the kiss? The answer remains unclear if one accepts Aarne's interpretation, whereas understanding the kiss and the sister as we have proposed clarifies the matter somewhat more.

The means by which the young woman reminds the young man about herself consists of making a pie from which two doves fly out. "He cut the pie, and male and female doves flew out."[102] These doves are kissing. The love loyalty of the birds reminds the hero of his own infidelity. E. G. Kagarov writes in his study of the wedding ceremony, "The image of a pair of doves is pasted on a loaf of bread 'so that our children will be together as a couple,' or on the edges of the wedding bread two birds are placed with their beaks touching 'so that the young couple will live in harmony.' I compare it to the magic figure of two dolls, tenderly embracing each other and aiming to induce love and harmony in certain people (Portugal)." The author classifies this rite together with syndesmotic or connecting rites.[103] This type of rite is also reflected in tales.

The kiss and forgetfulness occur not only in tales of the Vasilisa and the Sea King type but in others as well. A detailed study of these cases reveals the state of affairs with complete transparency. Even the verbal expression of the formed situation becomes particularly clear in light of the above materials. In a Vyatka tale, the hero has been presold to the devil. He marries the devil's daughter and returns home. "Then he thought to get married and completely forgot about the other woman; and these were her last days before giving birth."[104] The role that children play in the conversion of a temporary marriage into a permanent one was discussed previously. The parents tell their returning son, "Go to deacon's wife to find a bride—she has three daughters—because the bride you had found is a stranger from some faraway place."[105] "Prince Ivan remembered about his old bride and said to the king, 'I cannot take your daughter. I have a bride in the Urals'" (wild places, the forest), and so on.[106] This explains why bigamy is so often found in tales. "If only she were my wife. Well, but I already have a wife, why would I need another one?"[107]

"Finist" also belongs to this type.[108] However, the arrangement of the main characters is somewhat different. The first marriage, which is also the free marriage, takes place not in the woods, not in a different kingdom, but at home. After this the lover in animal form goes away to another kingdom. There he is planning to marry (or has already married) another woman when the young woman finds him, and by buying three nights from her rival, she wins her husband back. The motif of purchased nights is undoubtedly historical as well, but in the materials about men's houses there are no data that would explain this motif accurately. One can only assume that here we have a forbidden relationship of the young woman with the boy-bird—that is, with the mask, the young man who is already outside his home in the "other" kingdom where his fiancée goes to look for him.

13. The Never-Wash

The motif of the wife at her husband's wedding echoes the motif of the husband at his wife's wedding. But before turning to this second motif, we must consider some circumstances of the hero's return home after his initiation.

The unrecognized hero is often dirty, smeared with soot, and so on. This is the Never-Wash. He has made an alliance with the devil, who forbids him to wash. For this, the devil gives him untold wealth, and then the hero marries. He "doesn't cut his hair, doesn't shave, doesn't wipe his nose, doesn't change his clothes."[109] This lasts for fourteen years (in the German folktale seven years), at the end of which the hero says, "Well, my service is over." "After that the devil chopped him into small pieces, threw them into the pot, and started cooking. He cooked everything, washed and gathered all the pieces together in the proper way." He sprinkles him with living and dead water.

The motif of the dirty groom is even more developed in German tales. "For the next seven years you may neither wash, comb your beard or hair, cut your nails, nor once say the Lord's Prayer."[110] Similarly, "You may not wash yourself, comb your hair, trim your beard, cut your nails or your hair, or wipe any water from your eyes."[111] An analogous thing is said of a young woman in the forest. She "blackened her hands and face with soot."[112] She wears skins of different animals (*Allerleirauh*). When in a tale the hero is a man, he wears a bear's skin (*Bärenhäuter*). This feature characterizes heroes or heroines during their stay in the forest or service to the devil, and it precedes marriage, but occasionally it occurs in other contexts: "He got drunk and fell down in the dirt, and after that he got himself smeared in resin, and then got covered in feathers, and then looking so strange he went to the ship."[113]

The prohibition against washing is not just common in the initiation rite; it is almost an indispensable part of the ceremony.[114] The term of this prohibition varies. It lasts the whole period of staying in the enclosure—thirty days, a hundred days, five months, and so on. The initiate not only does not wash during this period, but he also smears himself with ashes. This smearing is very significant: not washing is associated with smearing with soot or clay—that is, actually with black or white coloring. "During his first hundred days he does not wash, and gets so dirty that when he comes out he is not recognized; so dirty is he, they say, that he cannot be seen."[115] Thus, not washing oneself is associated with invisibility. And the white coloring is probably related to this. "They are painted white from head to toe and therefore have a repellent appearance, and since they also do not wash they look unappealing, and dirty."[116] We have seen how white coloring is associated with blindness and invisibility. Black coloring is probably related to the same phenomenon. "They come out black with dirt and soot, and are not to be seen till they have washed."[117] ("Are not to be seen" can also mean "invisible." But the ban too is nothing but an expression of a fictitious invisibility.) For us, however, this is not even important; what is important is establishing the fact of the ban. Here another peculiarity may be established. According to Richard Parkinson, the ban on washing oneself lasts the entire time during which yams mature, from planting to harvest. Permission to wash oneself is given along with the harvest. Here we stand at the origins of later agricultural concepts of a deity's departure beneath the earth, thus promoting fertility. We already know that the rite teaches how to achieve an abundance of game. The same idea is transferred to the products of agriculture. Incidentally, a curious echo of this is also preserved in the Russian wondertale. Here, in a large house in the woods, a young woman says to the hero, "Get up, Prince Ivan, peasant's son. The grain has been harvested; I did everything. Go, cover your face with soot, get yourself all dirty, and go to my father."[118] In this tale, the young woman's father has assigned him the task of planting, growing, and harvesting the bread. So why is it that the hero, to prove that he supposedly has solved this problem, should smear himself with soot? This becomes clear if we take into account the examples above. The harvest depends on being in a state of invisibility, on being unwashed and blackened.

Not washing oneself is also somehow connected to preparations for marriage. "His body was then daubed with mud and filth, and in this condition he was required to go through the camp for several days and nights, throwing filth at whomever he met. Finally, he was given over to the women, who washed him, painted his face, and danced before him."[119] After this kind of return the young man could get married. Let us compare a Russian tale with this: "He was brought in. He was all overgrown with moss. She cut his hair and shaved him with her own hands. . . . Well, now I can marry your son."[120]

The ban on washing constitutes an ethnographic problem that we cannot concentrate on here—it lies beyond our task. It is impossible to draw the exact boundaries between the unwashed hero and the hero who looks like an animal. It is possible that smearing with mud is somehow connected to the make-believe animal image, that it is a kind of mask. A young woman, for instance, not only does not wash and smears herself with soot but also smears herself with honey and feathers.[121] In places where initiation is no longer practiced, or where it has lost its connection to the onset of puberty and has acquired a different character, smearing and getting dirty still hold. For example, in the Greek mysteries the initiate was daubed with clay or gypsum, or sprinkled with flour or bran. Some authors (Samter and others) would see in this the desire to make oneself unrecognizable, and indeed, as we shall see, misrecognition is an indispensable feature of and an indispensable condition for the hero's return from the woods. Thus, not washing is a very complex phenomenon associated with invisibility and blindness, with an animal appearance, and with misrecognition. It is also connected to staying in the realm of death. Samter, citing Radloff, points out that the Siberian shaman who goes to the realm of the dead with the soul of the deceased smears his face with soot.[122] In light of these materials, it can be argued that the hero's change of clothing, which is so frequently seen in folklore (exchanging clothes with a beggar and so on), is a particular case of a change of image that is associated with being in a different world. In one tale from Korguev not only do we see a change of clothes, but it is also interpreted precisely in this sense: "And he went on his way. But his outfit was already different, as if on someone from the other world, and 'a native from the other world' was of course written on the back."[123]

14. The Know-Nothing

The motif of the Never-Wash is closely associated with the motif of the Know-Nothing. The essence of this motif is that the hero arrives home (or in the kingdom of his future wife) unrecognized. On the one hand, he pretends that he does not know anything and does not remember anything. "The tsar asks him, 'So, young fellow, who are you by birth, and what's your name?' 'I don't know.' No matter how much the tsar asked, he kept saying, 'I don't know what my name is.'"[124] Or, "'Who are you?' 'I don't know where I'm from and don't remember my kinship.'" Here the hero has a finger cut off.[125] The horse advises the hero, "Go to the king's garden, lie down in a furrow, and cover your face. Don't show it (he was quite handsome). Whatever they ask you or say to you, you say 'I don't know.'"[126] There are a great many such examples: "'Where have you been, and what have you seen?' 'I haven't been anywhere and didn't see anything.' No matter how much they inquired, he didn't remember anything."[127] "'What's your name?' 'Where are you from?' To all these questions he answered, 'I don't know.' And that's the reason he was nicknamed 'Know-Nothing.'"[128] "'Who are you?' 'I don't know.' 'Are you a human being?' 'I don't know.'"[129] On the other hand, his parents do not recognize their returning son either: "His father couldn't recognize him at all."[130] "Nobody can recognize that he is their son. (Because he got lost. He lived there many years, and got all tattered. I suppose, he was all ragged.)"[131] Similarly, in a Vyatka tale, a father does not recognize his own son.[132]

There is no need to prove that one of the elements of return is reflected here. In these cases, a kind of etiquette demands that the returned boy "forget" his name, his parents, and his home. He is new, different, reborn, a person who died and was resurrected, and a person with a different name. On the other hand, parents also pretend that they do not recognize their son, and if his absence lasted for several years, it is possible that they really do not recognize him.

15. The Bald and the Hooded

The motif of unrecognized arrival often has links to that of a covered or, by contrast, a bare or hairless head. In the example above we saw "cover your face and don't show it." The hero often puts on his head a kind of bladder or an intestine or a rag. "Then he chose tripe, took some intestines, washed them well, and put them on his head. And this became his hat, and he wrapped the guts around his hands."[133] Or, "Ivan the merchant's son released his horse into the wild, dressed himself in a bull's skin, put a bladder on his head, and went to the seashore."[134] "She bought three bulls' skins. He made himself a leather outfit so that no person could be seen, and he sewed on a tail about two fathoms long."[135]

We see that in these cases, the hero for some reason conceals his hair, his head. This motif of a covered head is often connected in a strange way to its opposite: an uncovered, partially bald or completely bald head. Often this motif is associated with the Know-Nothing. "He went to the slaughterhouse, where the cattle were slaughtered, took a bladder, and put it on his head. Then he came to the king for alms. The king asks, 'What is your name?' 'Bald-patch!' 'And your patronymic?' 'Baldness!' 'And where are you from?' 'I'm a passer-by, I do not know where from.'"[136] Here the hero, who has covered his head, calls himself bald. Apparently, the intestines or the bladder are supposed to cover his hair and create the impression of baldness. We see exactly the same in a Dungan tale. "Once there lived three brothers. . . . The youngest wore a hat made of sheep's stomach, and that's why everyone called him 'bald.'"[137] "'And why is he covered with a handkerchief?' the tsar asked. 'Because he's bald. It's unpleasant to look at.'"[138]

On the other hand, the heroes of wondertales are often called bald. "Whatever they ask you, you say 'Bald 'n' Bare.'"[139] In light of the given material, this response means, "Don't you see from what is on my head where I'm from and that I am prohibited from speaking?" Sometimes it is specifically the bald one who solves the riddle of the princess.[140] "This bald one solved my three riddles. Even though he's bald, I'll still marry him," says a princess in an Uzbek tale. "Once there lived seven silly bald men and one cunning slob" begins a Mongolian folktale.[141] This slob is reminiscent of the German Grindkopf, a hero with a matted tangle in his hair. What is going on here? Why such a wide distribution? Why such persistence of this feature?[142]

During the initiation rite, there was quite likely not a single part of the human body that was not subjected to some form of manipulation. Even the insides, as we have seen, were regarded as taken out and replaced. The head and the hair too were subjected to special physical manipulation. The manipulations of the hair were twofold: it was either cut off, burned, or, conversely, allowed to grow long, but in this case, it was hidden under special headwear, which could not be removed.

We have evidence of this from every continent, but most of all from the islands of the Pacific. On the Solomon Islands, only those male members of associations who have long hair, and who during adolescence, that is, during puberty, wear a special kind of conical headdress, can marry. The hair grows into this hat so that it cannot be removed. Nevermann says: "He can never be seen by women without his 'hat' even in the beginning, when this hair is still short. If a woman saw him without the hat, she would immediately be put to death, just as if she had entered the place of the association's gatherings."[143] These young men, starting from the time of the rite and until their marriage, are called *matazezen*. Later the hats are removed along with the hair.[144] In this way, the hat is the sign of a future groom. Nevermann believes that the hair growth helps to increase potency. "With the growth of his hair, a boy grows into a man and acquires sexual potency by wearing 'the wedding hat.'"[145] This is one of dozens of possible explanations. Hair is credited with power, something that can only be pointed out here, recalling at least the story of Samson and Delilah. From the materials cited, it is not clear whether the hat was made of animal intestines or bladders, as seen in our tales. But in Africa such a form apparently existed: "In Gambia the newly circumcised wear . . . a strangely shaped hat with a pair of bull horns."[146] We now also understand why in American myths those who are swallowed and regurgitated by a whale come out of the whale's stomach without hair.

All these materials allow us to place this motif, too—the motif of the hairless groom or the groom with covered hair—in a genetic relationship with the rite of initiation.

16. The Husband at His Wife's Wedding

These details provide some extra touches for considering the motif of the husband at his wife's wedding. However, this case is significantly different from the motif of the wife at her husband's wedding. There the hero meets his betrothed away from home; he returns home and is about to enter another marriage and so on. Here things stand differently. The hero is married (or about to be married) from the beginning of the tale; only after that does he leave home, learn that his wife is going to remarry—"she wants to marry someone else"—and then quickly return just in time for his wife's wedding.[147]

In this case, we are dealing with a marriage that took place before the initiation; we have, therefore, a husband who goes away "to the woods," his long absence, and an attempt by the wife who stays at home to remarry.

But does this assumption contradict the order of getting married, in which initiation was one of the preconditions? What we have here is not a contradiction but a later form. As this custom died off, the rite occurred less and less, sometimes with breaks of ten years and more. Several examples of this can be found in both Schurtz and Webster. Meanwhile, the boys were growing up and getting married without waiting for initiation and were subjected to initiation retroactively. Thus, there were times when men at the age of forty were subjected to initiation alongside boys who had barely reached puberty.[148]

The motif of the husband at his wife's wedding has been studied by Ivan Tolstoi.[149] Professor Tolstoi does not aim to investigate the origins of this motif. But the material he collected allows us to answer a very important question: where is the husband while his wife is waiting for him? Tolstoi very convincingly shows that "the hero goes to the abode of death." In a Vyatka tale the sojourn with the forest spirit lasts twelve years, which fly by like twelve days—"a common motif in the tales of transient time in the kingdom of death, where a year passes as one day to the human mind."[150] In an Arkhangelsk tale, "A pike swallowed Ivan, took him towards the shore, and vomited him out. So Ivan the merchant's son started walking," and so on.[151] We are by now familiar with staying inside an animal as a means of initiation. There are other details leading to the same thing. "A husband returns with a changed appearance and is not recognized either by his wife or by his relatives." Tolstoi quite rightly observes, "It is noteworthy that only the husband's appearance changes;

the tale says nothing about any change of his wife's appearance during their separation."[152]

Finally, if he, according to Professor Tolstoi's observations, "comes home with overgrown hair, in a neglected dirty form, as a ragged stranger,"[153] then here too we have a sure sign of the return "from the woods."

17. The Ban against Praise

The wondertale's connection with the "big house" is not limited to the motifs listed above. Here we have chosen only the least hypothetical ones and the clearest cases of connection. In terms of the hypothesis, additional questions can be raised about the connection of some other restrictions with the "house" complex, such as the motifs of the ban against bragging and the forbidden storeroom.

The returning young man must maintain a profound silence regarding everything he has seen and heard. "Jobson saw a boy, who came out of 'the belly' the night before. There was no way he could induce him to open his mouth; the boy held a finger to his lips."[154] We can easily recognize here the muteness so common in tales. As pointed out by Frobenius, this muteness sometimes has a defined time limit: it lasts for as many days as the rite lasted.

In German tales a young woman, returning from the forest house, does not speak or laugh for a certain time.[155] This muteness occurs in Russian materials as well: "When the lad awoke and stood up, he found himself without a tongue: he couldn't say anything."[156]

This ban applies to all that has been seen and learned in the forest. Violating the ban can lead to death. "Now you will understand what all kind of creatures say, but don't tell anyone about it; if you tell, you will die a death."[157]

Possession of a helper or a magic object or talisman obtained in the forest is particularly surrounded by a special, deep secret. This is why the magical helper forbids the hero, before his return home, to brag about him. "See here, do not boast to anyone that you rode on me; if you do brag, I'll crush you!"[158] The formula "that you rode on me" is simply a more artistic expression than "that you possess me." "Don't tell anybody what you know; if you do tell, you won't live two minutes, you'll die!"[159] "Don't brag about me. Don't brag that you and I built a house in one night."[160] "If you brag about me, then I will not spare you. I'll eat you."[161]

The connection of these prohibitions to the secret helper is entirely obvious. Less clear are the prohibitions in tales such as "The Faithful Servant." "And if anyone hears this and tells him, he will turn to stone up to his knees."[162] Examination of prohibitions in the folktale could be the subject of a special study. It is particularly necessary to examine not only the prohibitions but their *violation* as well.

18. The Forbidden Storeroom

Another ban that is related to the motif of the big house is the motif of the forbidden storeroom. In "The Wonderful Shirt" the hero first lives in the forest, eating roots and berries, and then gets to a house with the usual characteristics of the forest houses.[163] We see the rooms, the emptiness, the table settings, and so on. Three brothers live here in the guise of animals: an eagle, a falcon, and a sparrow. They can turn into young men, and they accept the hero as "their very own brother." He is given a duty: to set the table. The eagle "gave him the keys, let him go everywhere and look at everything, except for one key that hung on the wall, which he ordered him not to take." Of course Ivan unlocks the forbidden storeroom with the key and behind the door sees a horse. After this he falls into an oblivious year-long sleep. This is repeated three times. After the third time the brothers give him the horse, and he leaves.

In this tale, everything is perfectly clear, showing us that in this case, the hero's future helper is in the forbidden room. It is also interesting that violation of the ban does not create any conflict. Historically this is exactly the way it should happen. The ban on the helper would operate only up to a certain point, until the "oblivious sleep," and after that things that were forbidden for the initiate become permissible.

The forbidden storeroom has been investigated many times. Edwin Hartland honestly admits that "the study of folk-tales has not yet made sufficient advances to enable us to trace these myths to a common origin, nor to explain satisfactorily their meaning."[164] William Kirby gives a purely mundane explanation based on the fact that sometimes a woman is kept in the forbidden room. He thinks that "the flat roofs of Eastern houses, combined with the seclusion of women, must make it an almost everyday occurrence in the East."[165] This comparison is quite risky.

Meanwhile, the materials listed above lead to the assumption that the forbidden storeroom also goes back to the complex of the big house. In order to decide whether this is so, we must first find out whether such prohibited premises existed in these houses. Next we must ask what was stored in them. Comparing the results with evidence from folktales, we will have to ask ourselves first what the context of these forbidden storerooms was and, second, what was kept in them.

But here we encounter a difficulty: these houses are not described fully enough in ethnography. Nevertheless, there are some details that point to the existence of such prohibited premises. We know, for example, that in Fiji, there was another enclosure within a fence, a smaller one that contained the "holy of holies" (*das Allerheiligste*).[166] What was stored there is not reported. We know, however, that there were such phenomena not only in the Fiji Islands. It is known that the tribe's sacred objects that were forbidden for the uninitiated were kept in the men's houses. Parkinson reports, "At a certain location on the island there was a place where all the uninitiated were strictly forbidden to enter. Inside this forbidden area (District) there were twelve subdivisions, and each of them had a holy house. Two of the houses were so holy that no one entered them or even came close to them. These houses contained carved wooden birds, fish, crocodiles, sharks, as well as images of people, the sun, and the moon."[167]

Thus we have a report that there were special forbidden premises that contained animals carved out of wood. This already traces some links to the animal helpers who stay in the forbidden storeroom in the wondertale. Furthermore, the images of the sun and the moon were stored there. We shall have to linger more on this fact.

Boas mentions the secret rooms of clubhouses. Among the Kwakiutl the initiation took place in special secret premises (a secret room) of men's houses. The neophyte would sit there for a long time; there, it seems, all the required operations were performed on him.[168] "You go close to the secret room, great magician, you have been inside the secret room" is sung about one of the initiated.[169] Apparently, staying in this room made one become a magician. This is supported by another report. A dance was performed in the house during the rite. The initiate was taught to dance. The house had a secret room whose front side depicted a raven. The raven opened its beak, and the initiate was pushed into it. Then after a while (the period is not specified), he was spat out.[170] This report indicates that in some cases, we do not have a hut and a big house, as seen above, but a big house with a special room for initiation. That is what the secret room is. The name *secret room* is not entirely successful. It was a secret only for the neophyte before the rite, but after the rite had been completed, the room ceased to be a secret.

Let us turn now to the wondertale and ask: Where is the forbidden storeroom located? Here we can specify several cases:

1. In the vast majority of cases, it is inside a big house. One example was provided above. Let us examine two or three more. "The brothers walk and walk until they come to a certain place: a huge, enormous house is standing in front of them." The master of this house is a raven. "He immediately killed them both and threw them down into the basement, buried them, and soaked them in alcohol so that they would look as if they were alive." A few years later the third brother arrives. He is not killed. "'Well,' he [Raven] says, 'here are the keys for you; you can go everywhere, but do not go into the first stable or

to the back room on the upper floor.'"[171] "A house stands in the forest, a huge house. He enters the house and sees golden keys, and one of the rooms is locked."[172] It is impossible to write out all the cases here. Suffice it to say that this phenomenon exists in wondertales and that it is quite common. This demonstrates the connection of the forbidden storeroom to the big house.

2. There is a forbidden storeroom in the robbers' house. For example, in a Belozersk tale, the hero comes to a robbers' house. An old woman hides him in a special storage room. He hears that the robbers want to eat him. On the floor of the room, he sees a shield and picks it up. Underneath, he sees an underground cellar full of dead bodies.[173] Although there is no prohibition here, there is a special room with dead bodies. We see one interesting case of this kind of special room in a Tobolsk tale. A girl enters a robbers' house. An old man takes her to a vault. The floor is made of crystal. There are also three storehouses there. One is full of gold, the second of silver, and the third of corpses. "Your death will be here."[174] The robbers there have green faces. And we have already seen above that the robbers' house is a subvariety of the big house. Thus, these cases also confirm the connection between the motifs of a forbidden or special storeroom and the big house.

3. The forbidden storeroom is a typical and indispensable motif in tales such as "Bluebeard." The type seen in Perrault is unknown in Russian folklore. Here the forest fiancé is in animal form. In a Vyatka folktale, he is a bear. The bear says, "You can go in the two upper chambers, but don't go into the third, the one locked with bast fiber."[175] In these cases there is usually (in Russian folktales) tar boiling in the forbidden room. The girl dips her finger in it "and it falls off."[176] The Russian material does not allow us to make reliable conclusions for the Bluebeard type of tale. But materials from Hartland and Kretschmer let us compile a number of details that point to the same connection as the above for this tale as well. In addition to the lost finger, we also find here that the heroine looks like a bird, that her face is smeared with soot, and that there are hacked-up bodies and the revival of the dead. It is also a characteristic feature of this tale that the fiancé's home is located in the depths of the forest. Kretschmer sees Bluebeard as a ruler of death.

4. The motif of the forbidden storeroom is less frequently encountered in tales like "A Tricky Science." In a Permian tale, a father brings his son to be apprenticed in a house where an old man has lived for five hundred years. There are seven rooms in the house. The son is told

not to go into the seventh room. This prohibition is violated.[177] The motif of "tricky science" was discussed in chapter 3, section 22.

5. A forbidden storeroom is often found in the other world.[178] In legend-type German folktales, the other world is straightforwardly called heaven.[179] In Russian tales, a hero finds himself in a church or a big house at his godfather's; it only gradually becomes clear that he has come to God, that his godfather rules the world.[180] His godfather says, "You can go into all the rooms, but don't even look into one of them."

All five given types are clearly related to one another and can, in one way or another, be traced back to the range of phenomena associated with the big house. In heaven, just as in the robbers' house, a finger is lost or, more often, turns golden. A girl who comes back from the other world for violating the ban loses the power of speech for a certain period and so on. However, this does not yet mean that the motif of the forbidden storeroom by itself can be derived with certainty from the complex of forest houses. There are forms that clearly have nothing to do with this complex. These are, for example:

6. The forbidden storeroom is located in the parental home from the time the tale begins. The secret of this room is kept until the hero's father dies. On his deathbed the father hands his son or his faithful servant the keys to all the rooms, instructing him not to open one of them. Inside this room the hero sees the portrait of an extraordinarily beautiful woman.[181]

7. Sometimes the motif of the forbidden storeroom follows the motif of marriage. In this case, a dragon or Koshchei is in this room. He flies away and carries the hero's wife away with him.[182]

Here we have cited only the most important and common groups. A special study (especially one extending beyond the Russian material) would enable us to establish some other groups as well. Nevertheless, the picture is already becoming clearer. The historicity of the last two cases cannot yet be proven, and therefore we must assume that they result from artistic imagination, expressed in the transfer of the motif to another place, to the beginning of the tale, and its use as motivation for the plot: after the hero sees the portrait, he departs on his quest. The opening, and especially the motivation, is a very unstable part of the tale. The same can be said about the room in the wife's palace. A violation of the prohibition releases the dragon, who carries the wife away, and this compels the hero to search for her—that is, a complication is created, a new plot turn, the wife's disappearance and the quest for her. However, this is merely an assumption. Perhaps something else lies here related to marriage bans, similar to the bans in "Cupid and Psyche."

We shall now briefly consider the other aspect of the matter—namely, the contents of these rooms. There is not always a stable connection between this chamber's location and its contents. This aspect should be considered separately. One may make a preliminary list of what is found in the storeroom, drawing on Hartland's materials.

In addition to animal helpers (usually a horse, a dog, an eagle, or a raven), the storeroom may hold a chained dragon, all sorts of horrors, chopped-up bodies, half-dead people (such as a not quite dead robber chieftain), bones, severed limbs, blood, a bloody basin, a scaffold and ax, and so on. In tales of the legend type, these horrors turn into either the torments of sinners (the hero sees his mother on a fiery wheel, etc.) or the suffering of a deity (crucified alive). It is possible that the fire, sun, and heavenly trinity that the hero sometimes sees there also has quite ancient roots. We have seen that images of the sun and moon were kept in banned areas of men's houses. Everything else is already familiar to us. The connection of the initiation rite with the motif of severing body parts or chopping up bodies was discussed above. We note in passing that the chopped-up bodies in these cases are often brought back to life, since there are also ointments found in the storeroom.

Finally, there is a special group of storage rooms in which women are kept (beauties deprived of their wings or dresses, tied up, and asking for a drink, or just beautiful women or a portrait). We cannot yet establish a direct connection between these and men's houses, as there are no relevant ethnographic materials available. However, we should recall that, based on Frazer, women stayed in special rooms in men's homes where the men did not enter. Here it is possible to see a reflection of marriage bans that have not yet been fully studied. Usually the hero who discovers a woman in the forbidden storeroom marries her. A temporary ban on marriage ends with a marriage. Thus, although this case does not confirm the hypothesis that the motif of the forbidden storeroom is connected with the institution of men's houses, it also does not contradict it.

19. Summary

As we can see, there are striking similarities between the rite of passage and residence in the men's house and what goes on in the forest hut and the big house. Here tales can serve as very valuable historical evidence. They preserved part of the internal mechanism of this rite.

It might even seem to readers unfamiliar with rites of this kind that the similarity is too complete, suspiciously complete. Perhaps this similarity is due more to our presentation than to actual similarities. Perhaps some details of initiation rites have been selected here and taken up with the specific purpose of making them look like tale motifs. Such suspicion is quite appropriate when a similarity seems too great. However, the similarities here appear not only in the details but in the very essence of the process of the initiation rite and its external attributes and typical props.

But of course tales and the rite do not overlap entirely. For example, there are tale features that cannot be explained by the rite in question. These features include the motif in which the hero changes places with the daughter of Yaga or an ogre, causing a mortal blow to strike her while he escapes. Another unexplained detail is the motif of a young woman's silence that helps a young man recover his human shape.

On the other hand, the rite is, of course, broader than the tales, and tales do not reflect everything. For example, it seems that tales do not entirely reflect the political role that the men's associations once played. It must be said, however, that wherever the role of a leader was already developing, men's associations played only a supporting role and had no authority as an institution. Here again tales provide a historically accurate picture. Besides the (politically powerless) "brothers" in a tale, there is also the "tsar," the situation that existed historically.

There is no doubt that not all the links have been found here as yet and that not everything has been discovered. But we have identified the right direction in which research should continue, and this quest will possibly yield even more fruitful results in the future.

II. Donors from beyond the Grave

20. *The Dead Father*

We have analyzed the entire complex of phenomena connected with the institution of initiation and of men's houses.

But it would be wrong, of course, to assume that this institution is the only basis for the formation of tales. The institution was dying out, but the development of plots continued. The changed historical environment also introduced changes into the inner lives of the evolving plots.

Yaga is the most archaic donor in tales but far from the only one. Along with the donor, the object and the circumstances of the gift's transmission change as well. Be that as it may, the connection is still not completely lost. It shows up first of all in the fact that the new donors provide the same gift as Yaga: a helper. However, rather than a forest animal it is a horse that is retroactively attributed to Yaga as well. Second, the new donors are also linked to the realm of death and the world of the ancestors.

The donor who is the spirit of the forest now becomes incomprehensible. He is replaced by the male donor and ancestor. We have seen that Yaga is associated with totemic ancestors too. But the totemic ancestor, often still associated, as we have seen, with succession through the female line, is replaced by a father, grandfather, and great-grandfather with the transition to succession through the male line. Thus, Yaga is replaced by the dead father, who gives the hero a horse no longer in the forest or the hut but from his grave. At the same time, the type of gift also changes. The genuine, true Yaga is in charge of forest animals. She is a reflection of the hunting way of life and societal structure. We see this in the folktale: she calls for wolves, bears, and birds; she gives them to the hero as helpers. The animals of the forest are now replaced by other animals, primarily by the one animal beginning to play a large role in everyday life and in the life of a warrior—a horse. Thus, rewarding the hero with a horse is now attributed to Yaga. But the horse is younger than Yaga. It is not the offspring of the forest; it is the offspring of the open field, where enemies are not shot from behind a bush and where heroic warriors meet in open battle with swords in hand.

It can be seen that the son has a deep, mysterious link with his father. The mystery of this link is reflected by the fact that Ivan must have a firm connection not with his living parents but with dead or dying parents. Living parents play a rather feeble role in the folktale. Their weakness is what forces Ivan to leave. This makes the figure of the deceased father all the more powerful.

This figure is most vividly reflected in the tale "Sivko-Burko," which says,

> The father began to die, and he said, "Children! When I die, each of you should go to my grave, taking turns, to sleep there for three nights," and he died. The old man was buried. The night came, and the older brother had to spend the night on the grave. But he felt somewhat lazy and somewhat scared. So he said to the younger brother, "Ivan-the-Fool! Go to father's grave and spend the night there instead of me. You have nothing to do anyway!" Ivan-the-Fool got ready, went to the tomb, and lay down there. Suddenly at midnight the grave opened, the old man came out, and asked, "Who's there? Is it you, my older boy?" "No, dear father! It's me, Ivan-the-Fool." The old man recognized him and asked, "Why didn't the older boy come?" "Dear father, he sent me instead!" "Then you're the lucky one!" The old man gave a cry and whistled a loud whistle: "Sivko-Burko, prophetic black horse!" Sivko came running, and the earth trembled, sparks spilling from his eyes, a pillar of smoke wisping from his nostrils. "Here, my son, is a good horse for you! And you, horse, serve him as you served me!" Upon saying these words, the old man lay back down in the grave.[183]

So what is the virtue of the hero, or the service he performs for the dead man? For what deed does the dead father give him the horse? The tale here is obviously not fully disclosing something; a certain link has fallen away, and it must be restored for a full understanding of the motif.

Two assumptions are possible, which actually do not exclude but complement each other. Both are confirmed by the material. It is, of course, not just a matter of "sitting." This is too colorless an act of a mortuary cult to be considered ancient. The tale here has discarded rites of sacrifice and libations that were practiced long ago. But it has not discarded them entirely. Thus, we read in one tale, "After their mother's death, the brothers each got a cow. Ivan-the-Fool took his cow and led it into the woods to the spot where his mother was buried. He brought it there and said: 'Mother, do you need the cow?' 'Yes, I need it,' said his mother, 'tether it here!'"[184] This case is obviously very archaic. First, the forest still appears, and second, the hero comes to his mother's grave. This archaic case has also preserved for us the purpose of his coming: he brings a cow to the grave of his mother.

In light of these materials and those cited earlier, the request of the father can be deciphered as "Go to my grave, and perform the required sacrifices there."

But the matter is not yet exhausted and not yet explained. Why does a dead person require sacrifices? If the sacrifices are not performed—that is, if the hunger of the deceased is not satisfied—he will have no rest and will come back to our world as a living ghost. This is what the living and the dead fear, and fear of the dead is based on this. We see that the older brothers are indeed afraid to go to the grave: they are afraid of the dead man. Hence, the second assumption—that sitting at the tomb is some form of apotropaic act. This assumption is supported by some folktale material, and it is supported by ethnographic materials that are very closely related to our wondertale. In a Baloch tale we find the following: "Children, if I die, guard my grave for three nights." The father comes out of the grave as a terrible snake. The hero kills him, digs up the grave, and finds a horse, a sword, and a rifle.[185] There are cases in the Russian folktale repertoire where the funeral service vow is not respected, and the dead man returns.[186]

Once upon a time a peasant lived in a barren place. He had two sons, one in a cradle and a one-year old, and a three-year old daughter. He said to his wife "Tomorrow I will die. Lay me under the icons and burn incense for three days and nights." The man died. The wife burnt incense for two days and nights, but on the third she forgot. The three-year-old girl walked around and said, "Mama, maaa-ma, father's come back to life. He sat up!" "Have you gone nuts or what? How could he sit up? He's dead!" The wife took a look and saw that her husband was sitting on a bench, sharpening his teeth with a whetstone. The wife grabbed the two boys and jumped on top of the stove. The girl was left on the floor. The dead man grabbed the diapers out of the cradle and ate them, and he ate the girl too.[187]

This is the basis of the Christian exorcism of the dead. In tales too the dead person, for whom protective prayers are recited, always tries to come back to life (cf. Gogol's "Vii"). In our wondertale, the hero sometimes comes to the grave to pray.

Ethnographic materials demonstrate the same. People go to "sit" at the graveside in order to put the dead man back into the grave if he gets up. This has been observed from the very earliest times. For example, Karl von den Steinen reports that among the Paresi Indians, after someone dies relatives stay at the graveside for six days, during which a very strict fast is observed. "If the dead man has not come back to life again after six days, then they no longer sit there; then he has arrived in the other world."[188] The same is known from the Papuan Gulf in South New Guinea, where the eldest brother-in-law of the deceased guards the tomb for five days and five nights. From time to time, he gets up, waves his arms in the air, and raises a howl to drive the spirit of the deceased away from the corpse. At the end of the fifth day, relatives arrive. If they believe that the spirit is still there, it is chased away by a collective shout.[189]

The apotropaic nature of these "sittings" is clear. On the basis of this, we can assume that the father's suggestion that his sons go to his grave should provide him with peace in the other world.

Finally, if the dead man gives a horse as a present, this also has a historical foundation in the notion that the ancestors are strong due to their being in the other world, from which all beginnings come. The living person no longer tries to find his way there, as happens in the rite of initiation. The role of magic helper is provided by the dead man. We have the beginnings of such a belief in the very early stages. In South New Guinea, mentioned above, after the body had decomposed, the skull was painted and kept in the house. It was addressed with appeals. On the Gilbert Islands the graves were tended, but sometimes bones were taken and made into fishhooks or other tools.[190] To force a dead mother to help in fishing, a Native American man would lie down on her grave, where he slept and fasted for a few days.[191] In these cases, the production base of the ideas is clear. From here, it is only one step for a dead man to give a magic item or become a helper himself. We shall see this again in the motif of grateful dead men. In North America, "at the beginning of the hunting season a hunter will go to the grave of his father or his paternal uncle, clean away the weeds, and pray to the following effect: 'I have cleaned your grave. I am going on the morrow to the bush to hunt. The bush is not the town; it is a place of death. Grant that I may have success in my hunting, or, at least, that I may return in safety.'"[192]

We have examined the father who gives a horse from beyond the grave. But it can be observed that the father is not the only dead donor. We shall examine a few more such cases, first limiting ourselves to the folktale material according to its various types without bringing historical parallels for each type; then we shall try to give some explanation for the entire group of dead donors.

The motif of passing on a magical agent to the son is sometimes painted as a real, everyday situation. The father leaves an inheritance for his children. "It was time for the old man to die, and he began to apportion his money: he gave the eldest a hundred rubles, and the middle one a hundred rubles, but he didn't want to give any to the Fool, as it would all be lost for nothing anyway."[193] But the fool begs for his share and gets it. With this money he buys a cat and a dog, who turn out to be magical helpers. Thus here too the magic helper is obtained, albeit indirectly, with the help of a dying father.

21. *The Dead Mother*

Accordingly, in those tales where the hero is a woman, it is the mother who hands over the helper. "As she was dying, the merchant's wife summoned her daughter, took a doll out from under the blanket, gave it to her, and said, 'Listen, dear Vasilisa! Remember and obey my final words. I'm dying, and along with my parental blessing I leave this doll for you. Keep her always with you and don't show her to anyone; and when any grief befalls you, give her something to eat and ask her for advice. She will eat and will tell you how to help in the misfortune.'"[194]

This little figure is the girl's magical helper. Very often the mother helps from beyond the grave. In "Swine Skin" a father falls in love with his daughter and wants to marry her. "She goes to the cemetery to the grave of her mother and begins to weep touchingly." So her mother tells her, "Ask him to buy you a dress with many stars around it." The girl does it, but her father is even more in love with her. Then the mother advises her to ask for a dress with a sun and a moon. "Dear mother, my father fell in love with me even stronger." Then the mother advises her to request that a swine cover should be made for her. "The father spat on her and chased her out of the house."[195] It is well known that in the tale of Cinderella, the mother helps the girl from beyond the grave.

In the *Ballad of Svipdag* of the *Poetic Edda*, the hero also turns to his mother:

"Wake thee, Groa! / wake, mother good!
At the doors of the dead I call thee;
Thy son, bethink thee, / thou badst to seek
Thy help at the hill of death."[196]
She bestows on her son ten incantations.

Finally, any kind of dead person can perform the same function in return for an act of kindness. For example, in an Abkhazian tale the hero comes to a funeral: "The deceased was already being carried to the cemetery. And he saw that some people were dragging the dead man by a rope tied around his neck, and others who accompanied him and followed behind were beating the dead man with long sticks." The merchant's son learns that the deceased died without paying his debts. The hero pays the creditors.[197] This, however, is undoubtedly a later, rationalized interpretation of the motif. In Russian tales the hero simply buries the dead man and thus wins himself a helper: the dead person. This motif is investigated in the work of Liljeblad. Unfortunately, however, his conclusions in this work are incorrect even if only because there are no "tales of grateful dead men." Liljeblad combines several types of tales and attempts to study the material as a whole. The author works from the false premise that every motif is originally attached to a certain single tale. In actual fact, the vast majority of motifs of equal morphological significance are mutually interchangeable in the same way that all donors are mutually interchangeable. Liljeblad found only eight Russian "tales about grateful dead men." However, a grateful dead person appears significantly more often and in the most varied tales. None of the examples cited below is given by Liljeblad, although I cite here only a small part of the available material. Moreover, Liljeblad confines himself to comparing only the texts and does not address at all the issue of grateful dead people.

In one variant of the tales about the apples of youth, Yaga advises the hero, "Go, Prince Ivan! There is a certain village, and near it there is a mountain. A dead warrior lies on the mountain like a dog. Go ask the priests whether you can bury the warrior. The warrior has a horse kept behind twelve iron doors and behind twelve copper locks." Prince Ivan indeed buries the warrior and arranges a sumptuous funeral feast for him. "And the dead warrior says to him: 'I thank you, young Prince Ivan, for burying me in a decent way, and I give you my horse.'"[198] There are tales where gravediggers argue and quarrel, not wanting to bury the dead. The hero pays them, and they bury the deceased. Later this dead man becomes the hero's helper.[199] In one variant of "Sivko-Burko" there are three warriors instead of the father.[200] These warriors are the ones who came before Ivan. They do not manage to jump up to the princess's window and are beheaded. Ivan buries them and receives from them three horses: one copper, one silver, and one gold.[201]

23. The Dead Head

The case in which the hero buries a dead warrior's head belongs to the same type. "As he was walking, he tripped over the head of a dead warrior. He pushed it with his foot. And it said to him: 'Do not push me, Ivan Turtygin! But better bury me in the sand.'" Ivan buries the head in sand, and the head tells him where to get the magical berries he will need in the course of the action.[202] This example might throw some light on the dead head that Ruslan encounters.[203] In folktales it does not stick out of the ground but lies on top of it. "A head was lying there, so he dismounted to approach it, sat on it, and said: 'What is this head lying here?'" An interesting dialogue unfolds between the head and Ruslan: "'Head, should I bring you back to life?' And it says to him, 'If I am to die again, then do not bring me back to life; but if I am to live forever, then bring me back to life.'"[204] Here the favor of burial is replaced by the favor of revitalization. The same happens in a Vogul tale.[205]

In the tale about Eruslan Lazarevich the head of a dead man is lying on the ground. In "lubok" folk paintings, by contrast, the head is sticking out of the ground. It is hard to say which image is more ancient. As Otto Waser has pointed out, images of bearded heads growing out of the ground are often found engraved on ancient gems. These heads are speaking, since there is usually a bowed listening figure depicted above them, and the mouth of the head is slightly open. The author compares them with a Gorgon, with the winged heads of seraphim and cherubs, and with other materials, coming to the conclusion that they represent the soul of the deceased; this is likely but has not yet been proven. In tales the head is actually an unburied corpse. Perhaps the idea of the head protruding from the ground is actually the idea of a restless dead man, sticking out in order to stand up or find someone to bury him. The buried and grateful dead man becomes at that point a donor who bestows a sword, horse, magic berries, and so on or an adviser who points the way for the hero, or the dead man himself becomes the helper. The head of Mimir in the *Poetic Edda* is of this type as well. The Vanir kills Mimir and sends his head to the gods. But Odin, with his magic, preserves the head from destruction and grants it the ability to speak. Afterward he often consults it.[206] This example draws a link to the custom of preserving a head or skull. The skull would be painted, decorated, and kept in the house. Of course, this skull or head once represented the deceased person. By having power over his head, they also had power over his whole being. This dead person was forced to help the living.

This explains why some peoples, such as the Dayaks, hunted specifically for heads—because, as Friedrich Burger says, "They think that the souls of the men whose heads they possess must protect them in life and be obedient to them in the other world."[207] But such forcible coercion into service soon gives way to other forms of compulsion. The dead man can be made to serve someone by performing for him all the acts that he, as a dead man, needs. There is a curious example in a Melanesian legend in which Yaga, the dead person, and the head merge into a single image. The hero is on the run, sees a small hut, and enters. In the hut he sees two dead bodies. He picks up the skulls, washes them, and performs other actions over them. The skulls advise him to go in a certain direction—that is, they show him the way, similar to Yaga.[208] The human head can play exactly the same role in Russian tales.[209]

24. *Summary*

We have established a presence in the wondertale of a certain category of characters that we have named donors. Among the donors a special group can be distinguished: dead people. These characters include Yaga, dead parents, a dead person, and a head. They are all functionally related to one another. But they are not only morphologically equivalent; they are linked historically. Yaga has already appeared as the ruler of nature and the sovereign of forces that humans need. To obtain these forces, which are materialized as objects, people descend into the realm of darkness. These notions are furnished with rituals, and from them the plot emerges.

Here we have the most ancient layer. Transmission of a magical agent by Yaga, as we have seen, is not motivated by anything external. It comprises the goal of the rite: the entire rite is performed for the sake of it and its acquisition. In later stages, this function is preserved together with some of the accompanying circumstances; however, the character of the donor is changing, and new motivations are introduced corresponding to the changes. We have seen that Yaga is linked to the world of the dead. A male ancestor emerges with the advent of agriculture and patrilinear family structure and with the emergence of property and its inheritance. The cult of ancestors is created. This is how the father-donor and the father-ancestor appear, though their beginnings can be traced to much earlier.

The nature of this figure's help can vary based on the historical development of peoples. The Vedda turn to him when hunting.[210] Among agricultural peoples, the ancestors bestow fertility: they are in the ground, and from there they send up the fruits of the earth.[211] They help in war by intervening in battles.[212] Finally, in places where a funerary cult has developed, they help after death. As Rohde has pointed out, the cult of the dead stays for a particularly long time because these are dear and intimate gods, and it is easier to turn to them than to official omnipotent deities.[213] Their cult is narrow and practical. Now we understand why a Native American who needs to catch fish lies on the grave of his mother, sleeping and fasting there for a few days. This is precisely the way Cinderella goes to her mother's grave when she has troubles; according to some variants she sprinkles it with her tears while according to others she pours water—that is, performs a libation.

We cannot, of course, go into the phenomenon of the cult of ancestors here in depth; we can only point out the link between this cult and the wondertale. Once the ancestor appears in the cult, he goes on to enter the plot, and the action of the cult becomes motivation for the aid. The father who gives his son Sivko-Burko is essentially also a grateful dead man, but the nature of the favor done for him is not clear in the tale; it becomes clear from comparative materials outside the tales. Yaga is a donor and tester, and it would be strange to call her grateful, although cases can be found and pointed out where the hero does her a favor. The father who gives Sivko still appears as a tester, and the reward is given for passing the test, not in exchange for a favor. A favor is already contained here for the historian and for the researcher but not for the listener. In this, the feature demonstrates that the motif is quite ancient, although it is more recent compared to Yaga.

With the demise of the cult of ancestors, the father disappears, and only the dead man as such remains. The test disappears entirely, and the favor advances to the foreground. This creates the image of the "grateful dead man" who gives a horse or other magical means, just like the father and Yaga. This case is the most recent from the entire group.

III. Donor Helpers

25. Grateful Animals

In light of these considerations, another type of donor becomes more comprehensible: grateful animals.

This character is a composite. Grateful animals appear as donors who put themselves at the disposal of the hero or give him a formula to summon them as helpers later. Everyone knows how the hero, lost in the woods and tormented by hunger, sees a crawfish, a hedgehog, or a bird, and, taking aim at it with the intention of killing and eating it, hears a plea for mercy. "Suddenly a hawk is flying. Prince Ivan takes aim: 'Well, hawk, I'll shoot you and eat you as you are, uncooked!' 'Don't eat me, Prince Ivan! At the right time I'll be of use to you.'"[214] The formulas such as "don't eat me" and "whatever you come across, don't eat it" reflect the prohibition against eating an animal that can become a helper.[215] The hero does not always want to eat the animal. Sometimes he does it a favor: fledglings are getting wet in the rain or a whale has washed up on the shore; the hero helps them, and the animals become his invisible helpers. We can assume that this form of compassion for the animal is a more recent form. The wondertale in general does not know compassion. If the hero releases an animal, he does so not out of compassion but on the basis of some agreement. This can be seen especially in cases where an animal is caught in a net or a trap or in the hero's bucket—not when he aims at it but when he has caught it, as in the tale about the golden fish or about Emelia-the-Fool. Emelia hesitates for a long while, and a dialogue unfolds between him and the pike. Emelia does not believe the pike and does not want to set it free. Only after the buckets of water go home on their own is he convinced of the benefits of such a deal, and he releases the pike.[216]

It can be shown that the fish or other animals that Ivan spares and does not eat are animal ancestors; they are animals that cannot be eaten and who help specifically because they are totemic ancestors. Bernhard Ankerman says, "When a person dies, his soul passes into an animal totem that is born at the same moment. And vice versa, when a totem-animal dies, its soul passes to a newborn human in a family that bears that totem's name. This is why the animal should not be killed and cannot be eaten, since otherwise a relative would be killed and eaten."[217]

This belief, typical of totemism, takes a different form with the transition to settled life and agriculture. The *unity* of man and animal is replaced by *friendship* between them; moreover, it is a friendship based on a certain agreement. Here is what Ankerman notes about the decline of totemism:

> An idea prevails in many other tribes that a relationship of friendship exists between man and animal, which is expressed in mutual mercy and help. The origin of this relationship is attributed to the founder of the tribe. It is usually explained by the fact that this founder once in a moment of great need received help from an animal of the sacred kind or was saved by it from danger. Legends that everyone knows tell about this. The tribe's ancestor is lost in the woods and threatened with death by starvation or thirst. An animal leads him to the water spring or shows him the way home. Or he is fleeing from pursuing enemies but is hindered by a wide river. A big fish carries him on its back to the other shore.[218]

If we look attentively at this material, which is very close to our tales but reflects a certain stage in belief, it becomes highly probable that a grateful animal is also an ancestor. Only the moment of taking mercy is absent, because a believer in totemism could not even imagine taking aim at his own totem. Where totemism exists, the prohibition "don't eat this fish" is spoken by people, while later this ban turns into an appeal for mercy attributed to the animal itself. Such an evolution is visible, for example, in a Mexican tale. A lizard begs, "Don't shoot me" and shows the hero the location of his deceased father.[219] We understand why it can do this: it is itself most closely related to the world of the dead ancestors. And if the *lizard* shows the hero his *human* father, not his father according to the line of totemic animal kinship, this happens because totemism among the given people is on the wane, and human ancestors have already become a reality even in the myth, though the relationship with the ancestor animal has not yet been lost. Apparently, this kind of development has the same general traits worldwide. For example, in a Zulu tale the animal caught also knows all the hero's ancestors: "The animal spoke, saying: the child of so and so, of so and so, and of so and so. And he went through the nicknames of his grandfathers until he counted up to ten nicknames that even the man himself did not know."[220]

Actually, this connection of grateful animals to a human ancestor has been retained even in modern European folktales. In "Burenushka" a stepmother orders her stepdaughter's cow to be slaughtered.[221] The cow says, "But you, fair maiden, don't eat my meat." In certain variants, this cow is nothing other than the girl's deceased mother. If she were to eat the cow's meat, she would be taking a piece of her mother's body as food. It could be argued that in this example, the cow is not a grateful animal. But even grateful animals in a narrow sense often turn out to be relatives of the hero. It is true that in contemporaneous Russian tales, an animal cannot say "don't eat me, because I'm your brother." Therefore, this situation is reinterpreted into another: the grateful animal is not the hero's brother or father, but it becomes one. "Don't eat me, and we'll become brothers," says the raven in a Yakut text.[222] It is much more important that the hero and the grateful animal become not brothers (something that is generally common between folktale warriors) but father and son: "Let you be my father, and I'll be your son."[223] "He caught a crane and said to him, 'Be my son.'"[224] The formula "don't eat me, instead let's be brothers" should be understood in a historical perspective as a reinterpretation of "don't eat me because we are brothers." The connection with the totem ancestors is proven by yet another thing: the fact that the grateful animal is actually king of the animals (I am the king of crawfishes, and so on) or, in ethnographic terms, the ruler. This was discussed above in the context of Yaga the ruler. Additionally, it can be proven by yet another fact: sometimes the grateful animal is taken home and nurtured. This case will be examined in the subsequent chapter on helpers.

Zelenin, in his work on Siberian materials, came to exactly the same conclusions as Ankerman did on the basis of African materials. However, the Siberian materials are more difficult than the African, as there is no direct totemism in Siberia, only traces of it, while in Africa the phenomenon of totemism is still alive. The connection of our motif with totemism is so obvious to Zelenin that he does not consider it necessary to prove. "Among those stories where a totemic animal is presented as a creature beneficent to humans, legends about grateful animals must be considered the most archaic," he writes.[225] Zelenin also saw the presence of an agreement-based relationship, which we have traced in the wondertale. "From our perspective, these tales are especially interesting in that they present us with relationships of people with animals based on unions and agreements, which we consider the central place of totemism."[226]

All these analogies show the range of phenomena of the grateful animal to which it should be assigned and that Emmanuel Cosquin was gravely mistaken when he considered this motif to be "a purely Native American idea."[227]

26. *Copper Forehead*

A figure in tales that is sometimes called Copper Forehead or Forest Monster may be considered a variant of the grateful animal. Copper Forehead is a monstrous creature kept in captivity at the court of the king. He asks the prince to release him: "Let me out and I'll be of use to you."[228] "Royal child! Let me out, and I'll be of use to you."[229] "Let me go free, and you'll get anything you want."[230] This character belongs to the category of donors. The formula "I'll be of use to you" matches precisely the words of grateful animals. The hero releases Copper Forehead, and subsequently either the released prisoner himself or his daughters give the hero a magic handkerchief,[231] magic feathers, or a harp[232]; Copper Forehead gives him strength,[233] living water, or a horse; or, like the grateful animals, he puts himself at the hero's disposal and becomes his helper. In order for him to appear, it is enough for the hero to remember him or say his name.

Having established a connection between grateful animals and Copper Forehead, let us now look a bit closer at this figure.

How does he appear in the course of action? We find the most comprehensive example in Afanas'ev. The tale begins with a king who is avaricious and miserly:

> He was always tormented by greed, how to get extra profit and how to collect more quitrent. Once he met an old man with sables, martens, beavers, and foxes. "Stop, old man, where are you from?" "I come from a certain village, and now I work for a man who's a leshii." "And how do you catch the animals?" "Well, the leshii places the nets, and animals are stupid, so they get caught." "All right, listen, old man, I'll fill you with wine and give you some money; show me where you put the nets." The old man was tempted and showed him. The king immediately ordered the leshii captured and chained in an iron pillar, and he placed his own nets in the man's woods.[234]

Next, the story usually develops as follows: the captive asks the prince to let him free; the prince steals the keys and releases the captive. Then the latter becomes the hero's helper or gives him a helper.

Afanas'ev's version shows clearly how this character is introduced in the course of the action. He is found by chance in the forest, brought home, and confined in captivity.

But the same version shows something else as well: they keep leshii in captivity in order to have *power over wild animals*. For us, it is important to establish that in other versions, the leshii himself is zoomorphic. While hunting, "a younger son found a bird, which had rolled out of its nest. He took it home, tied it with twelve chains, and locked it behind twelve locks."[235] This bird is nurtured in exactly the same way as the grateful animal when in some cases it is brought home and nurtured. We already established the connection between grateful animals and totem animals. The affinity of the leshii to grateful animals allows us to assume that the leshii is also an anthropomorphized animal, and power over the leshii makes it possible to control the hunted animals. We know that the totem animal is often "caught and kept in a special room."[236]

This figure in its human form is a feature of many quite varied myths. The tale demonstrates that Bolte was not wrong to suggest that "the reason why the king orders that the demonic creature be chained, initially, was probably the desire to use his prophetic knowledge."[237] Bolte was mistaken in only one thing: it was a matter not only of knowledge but also of power, and initially, this desire reflected purely hunting interests. Citing his sources, Bolte points out that Midas ordered Silenus captured, Numa ordered the forest demon Faunus captured, Solomon—Asmodeus, Rodark—the forest man Merlin, and so on.

This is the oldest hunting nature of this creature. We find that Silenus functionally corresponds to Yaga: he gives the magical agent. Like Yaga, he is a forest creature. Like the grateful animals, he asks for mercy and is kept in captivity and nurtured. All these features clearly point to his origin. He is the master of the forest. In theory he can be related to a sorcerer-teacher, a sage. Contemporary folklore material does not show this. But classical material researched by Ivan Tolstoi shows this clearly.[238] Copper Forehead corresponds to the Silenus of antiquity. "Silenus is captured, in this case, to compel him to do something: to force him to give wealth to somebody, to reveal to people the essence of human life, to familiarize them with the secrets of the universe, and to sing them a marvelous song."[239] The wondertale adds to this something more ancient and indigenous: power over the animal world. The Copper Forehead also provides the magical helper. In this the tale is more archaic than the myth. But in one way the Greek myth has preserved for us something that the tale did not preserve: Silenus reveals to people the secrets of creation and sings for them "marvelous songs." When we look at the wondertale as a whole, as we do below, we shall see that, in American myths, the hero in the forest learns the secrets of the universe as well as dances and songs from a mysterious animal and the master of the animals and brings sacred art designs back with him. Thus, we see that the Silenus of antiquity becomes a sage-teacher. In this way, he also came into the Middle Ages in the image of Asmodeus and other characters corresponding to him. "He possesses a deep secret of knowledge that he learns in the elevated schools of the earth and the firmament."[240]

This purely forest creature lives on into the age of agriculture and confronts agricultural religion. Now a new attitude develops toward him, one that sees him as a forest monster, dangerous, scary, big, and clumsy. He is always caught by *peasants*. The forest is defeated by the field and the garden. Silenus is defeated with wine, but he becomes the enemy and destroyer of fields: he damages and poisons the crops.

Creatures like the leshii or Silenus are often made drunk with wine and taken into captivity. We read in a Russian tale, "The gardener requested three buckets of strong wine and three pails of sweet honey: he took a trough pan, mixed the wine with the honey, put it under the apple tree, and went to sleep. Suddenly a roar went through the garden. . . . A monster came flying. It flew in, saw the trough pan, came down to the ground, drank its fill of wine and fell at once into a deep sleep."[241] We see exactly the same in both antiquity and the Middle Ages. In Maximus of Tyre, "one poor and greedy Phrygian manages to catch the satyr: the sneaky Phrygian mixed wine into the spring from which the satyr came daily to drink."[242] The Phrygian is a peasant. The text mentions "[the Phrygian's] land, and trees, and fields, and meadows, and flowers in the fields." In Ovid he is also caught while drunk. Ivan Tolstoi points to the peasant character of this plot in antiquity. Capturing through intoxication is common in the Middle Ages as well; this can be found in Veselovskii in many examples.

By now this character, albeit hypothetically and in very general terms, is becoming clear. His name, however, is not yet entirely clear. He is called Copper Forehead, "*copper* grandpa," "a man with hands of iron, a head of cast iron, and a body of copper," "an iron thief," and so on. Except for his name, he has no connection with metals. Afanas'ev, in his notes, wants to see in him the guardian of treasures. It would be better to assume that *copper* is synonymous with yellow, and what is meant is not his composition but his color. A copper or yellow color is a variety of golden coloring. And indeed, there are folktales in which this forest creature is depicted as golden. For example, in a tale from Pinega he is "a golden man, a grandpa of huge height."[243] He appears as golden in a manuscript text in the folklore archive of the Academy of Sciences in Leningrad (Kolesnitskaia's collection, in press).[244] But this is not the only interesting thing in the Pinega tale. His touch makes the head of the prince who releases him golden as well. "And he patted him on the head. And because of that Ivan Tsarevich's hair also became golden."[245]

If we consider this case purely from the viewpoint of function, we obtain the following: a forest man turns the object he touches into gold or makes it golden. In Russian folklore this is a rare case, but in antiquity there is something similar to it. Silenus bestows a wicked gift on the man who captured him: everything Midas touches turns to gold. Ivan Tolstoi considers this form more recent. Indeed, gold appears here as a material value whereas initially it meant a different type of value. We have singled out the question of gold and golden color in the tale in a special way for analysis in another chapter, where it becomes clear that gold comes not from metal but from fire. We theoretically postulate a connection between our forest man and fire. In Russian tales this is never directly visible. However, let us point out the striking similarity between this character and the whole environment in the legend of the blacksmith Wieland.

Wieland lives in the deep forest, hunting and forging rings for chain mail. But King Nidgod captures and binds him, severing the tendons on his legs (cf. Hephaestus's lameness), and Wieland works for the king. Just as he gives the king power over hunting in the wondertale, here he is the mythical personification of blacksmith craft. In the tale he is set free by the king's son. In the legend, Wieland kills the princes and forges their skulls and eyes into jewelry (i.e., in light of the comparative materials, he throws them into the fire and throws the corpses under the furnace) and flies away. He makes wings for himself.

In Russian tales the role of Copper Forehead is sometimes taken by a bird, in particular the flaming firebird. This recalls the Greek legend of Talos, the bronze automaton on the island of Crete who would press strangers to his chest and leap into the fire with them. There are myths that portray him as a calf or bull—that is, as an animal. In Russian tales, the bronze (copper) man always has a forest nature. Midway through, he acts in the forest exactly the same way as Yaga. And if we compare the fact that Talos appears in parallel with the Minotaur, who destroys young men and women and not just newcomers, then we see that the fire of bronze Talos is connected to the forest fire, to the stove of Yaga that burns children, and to the furnace of Wieland where he throws the king's sons. But this is only one side of this strange figure.

We have seen that Copper Forehead appears in the wondertale without motivation. Hunters meet him accidentally in the woods. Such casualness and lack of motivation are indicators of great antiquity. In the same way, meeting with Yaga is not motivated by anything external. The missing motivation is felt as a drawback for the modern person and the modern storyteller. This perceived lack is being filled, and, moreover, sometimes the tale uses equally archaic motifs as motivations, linking them together and motivating one motif with another. The forest monster is not always met by chance. The tale begins with *sowing* a field or *planting* an orchard.

Some unusual thief appears every night and spoils the orchard or the crops. The thief is caught and turns out to be a bird or a copper manikin who is taken prisoner and kept at the house. In other words, the motif of Copper Forehead is joined by the motif of *crop destruction*.

Crop destruction is an agricultural motif and therefore of later origin than the motif of Copper Forehead. These motifs intersect. The crop destruction or damage is produced not only by Copper Forehead but by other characters as well—for example, a miraculous mare, a firebird, or a simple thief. On the other hand, Copper Forehead is not always (even if most frequently) introduced into a wondertale via the destruction of crops.

We shall explore the crop destruction motif regardless of who produces the damage, and then we shall examine whether the connection between the motif and the forest creature is accidental or not. Let us cite a few examples. "A man started sowing peas, and some unrecognizable creature got into the habit of coming there." He sends his children to keep watch: "Who is that trampling our peas?"[246] "A man sowed wheat, but every night someone was trampling it all."[247] The same happens with apple trees. Sometimes the apples are not ordinary apples, just as the thief is not a simple thief. We read in Smirnov that the king's son asks to buy an apple tree with golden apples.[248] They buy it, plant it, and admire it, and then suddenly they begin to notice that someone is stealing the apples. In another variant, "The Invisible began to come flying at night and one night broke several trees."[249] In some cases, it is the *forbidden* favorite garden of the king.[250] In one example a peasant and his sons sow wheat, but "instead of greenery everything was lit up with semi-precious stones."[251]

What kind of extraordinary field or extraordinary garden is this, to which a bird or other "Invisible" comes flying at night?

The fact that this reflects an agricultural tradition is beyond doubt. There is one such agricultural rite.[252] On the island of Celebes, before they start planting crops, they inform the earth spirits and spirits of the trees that people are going to begin fieldwork. Then the spirits convey through a priest what sacrifices must be made to them. Any work to be done *must first be done in a small field, which is set up for the dead*. They make two of these gardens: one early in the morning so that the birds of rice (*Reisvögel*), in which the souls of the dead are reincarnated, will not eat the rice and another at sunset in order to protect the plants similarly from mice, in which the dead are also reincarnated.

We can assume that the crop where the birds come flying was once a crop specially designated for dead ancestors. It was supposed to attract the flocks of the dead and thus distract them from the human field. In wondertales it is not an entirely ordinary crop. It is a "secret" garden or field where pearls and other such things grow. At the dawn of the agricultural era there should have been a fear of the dead who reside in the forest, especially in slash farming when the forest is destroyed to plant crops in a field. Frazer writes the following: "Before they plant taro in the ground which has been freshly cleared from the forest they pray to the spirits of the dead, saying, 'Come not so often into the field, remain in the forest. Let the taro of the people who have helped us in clearing the field thrive well. Let the taro of everybody be very great.'"[253] Everything here is illustrative: the fact that they more or less apologize for forest clearing and the fact that we hear only of those who "helped" but not those who actually cleared the field and so on. Whom do they fear in these cases? Who could come flying out of the woods and spoil the crop in revenge for destruction of the forest? We already know who these forest creatures are. They are the very same mysterious, powerful, and wise animal ancestors who have already become anthropomorphic but who still have their bestial form and need to be propitiated; but with luck it is possible to catch them, learn from them, and embrace their power and wisdom.

A sacrifice could also serve as an equivalent method of distraction. Frazer points out that when sowing a field, they put, for example, rice, maize, or sugarcane on it to "induce the spirits not to injure the crops."[254] The sacrifice, of course, has not been preserved in the wondertale. But Greek myth still shows the connection clearly. There the Calydonian boar spoils the crop because no sacrifice was offered. The Calydonian king gives to all the gods the first of the harvest: he gives field fruits to Demeter, grapes to Dionysus, oil to Athena, and so on. But Artemis gets nothing, and she sends an all-devouring wild boar that spoils and destroys the fields and gardens.

But this example contains yet another similarity to the wondertale. Artemis is a forest creature, goddess of forests, and the mistress of animals. Copper Forehead is precisely the same. He lives deep in the forest, and he is the master and patron of hunting. But his authority and power decline with the advent of agriculture. He is drugged with wine and triumphantly put into captivity. Moreover, the form of this captivity is borrowed from forms of imprisoning a totem animal and corresponds to them in both content and meaning: they want to force out of him a successful hunt for sables, martens, and foxes by taking his power over them away from him.

But how is this connected with the motif of crop destruction? If it is correct that the dead come flying to the field, then the leshii of the type in question can also be a creature from the realm of the dead in the forest. Following the leshii he has released, the hero finds himself in an environment that corresponds exactly to Yaga's. He lives in a hut, he gives the hero a horse, and so forth.[255] Thus his appearance in the field and the garden is not accidental and not only creates an artistic motivation: it is also a historically conditioned phenomenon. In the agricultural era, the mysterious forest still maintains its connection to the world of the dead and the ancestors, a connection so vividly reflected in Yaga. With the appearance of sown crops, these beings become dangerous to the fields. They spoil and destroy them, and people attempt to overpower and disarm them. This new agricultural current flows into the wondertale, but it modifies only the tale's beginning. The beginning has a lower resistance in general, and it is the easiest to distort. The middle, on the contrary, is extremely stable. By the middle, this clumsy captive forest monster, whose arms and legs are bound with twelve chains, emerges as a benign protector of the hero, a powerful ruler over life, death, animals, and their mysterious powers, and he acts exactly like Yaga, being her equivalent.

We may confirm the ideas stated above with an antique vase whose image was published by Ivan Tolstoi in his study of Silenus, noted above. The vase was discovered in Eleusis and belongs to the sixth century BCE. One side depicts a farmer leading the captive Silenus to a high-ranking person, who in the wondertale corresponds to the king. The other side has a scene of sowing and plowing. Until now, the two sides of the vase had not been linked. Tolstoi deciphered the side representing the capture of Silenus. We can interpret the other side on the basis of modern tales. The crop is not here by chance. The crop was ruined by Silenus, and this is the reason for capturing him and bringing him before the king. Thus, the internal connection of the two sides of the vase, which archaeologists could not understand, is now understandable.

27. Ransomed Prisoners, Debtors, and So On

We have examined a number of different donors: Yaga, the father, grateful animals, the dead, and the forest spirit. These are the most significant figures of the wondertale canon. Others are of secondary importance by comparison. Most of them are echoes and modifications of the same familiar figures. Any grandmother living close by in the neighborhood can easily be shown to be a faded version of Yaga. Often these are rationalized mundane forms, and only careful study and comparison, or a certain detail, will give away their origin. So, for example, if boys somewhere on the road are beating or torturing a dog or other animal and want to hang it, or a man is going to drown a cat for stealing meat, and the hero pays a ransom and releases them, and in return these animals help him when he is in trouble—then this is the motif of grateful animals in distorted form. As indicated earlier, in these cases the money was received as an inheritance from the deceased father. Thus, the motif of the dead father who provides a helper has been replaced by the motif of a dying father who leaves an inheritance with which the helper is purchased.

The dead donor lies behind other cases as well. A princess has died, and the hero, after bribing the guards, takes a ring from her hand. Thus, even in cases such as these the dead donor quite unexpectedly continues to appear.

Another form of this motif's decomposition is the case where people are whipping an insolvent debtor. He owes ten thousand to a merchant,[256] or he owes one ruble to each person who is beating him,[257] and so forth. Ivan pays the man's debt, and the released man becomes a grateful helper, similar to the dead man or the grateful animals.

Moreover, if the hero feeds a hungry person along his way and the person tells him the secret of how to get a magical ship, then this indirectly reflects the food obtained from Yaga.[258] Yaga gives him both food and a magical agent. Here it is the hero who feeds the old man and gets the magic agent as a reward. This is confirmed, among other things, by the entire dialogue between the old man and the hero, and also by the fact that the meager food the hero has to offer to the old man suddenly turns into buns with various added ingredients and drinks. In other words, we see once again that the donor treats the rewarded person with food.

Finally, numerous cases in which the hero earns the magic agent for himself by working or serving for a very small fee also go back to performing a service for Yaga and completing the tasks that she assigns. This is an internal evolution of the tale under the influence of the reality that has invaded it. Such, for example, is the case where Truth is working for a merchant and earns itself an icon, with which it chases away a dragon or an evil spirit.[259] There are even more realistic cases where the hero works for a master craftsman: "he learned to make expensive items and surpassed the master himself."[260] At the master's house, he finds a magic box. Probably the same kind of deformation lies in the origins of tales in which the hero goes to a hunter or other craftsman to gain proficiency and acquires some magical ability there. Such cases are quite numerous, but they are of secondary importance for us because they are genetically unambiguous as modifications of previously existing tale elements.

5

MAGIC GIFTS

I. The Magical Helper

1. Helpers

The wondertale reaches its high point when the hero receives the magical agent. From this moment on, the end is in sight. There is a huge difference between the hero who left his house and wandered "without knowing where he was going" and the hero departing from Yaga's place. Now the hero walks firmly toward his goal and knows that he will reach it. He is even inclined to boast a bit. For his helper, his wishes "are only a bit of service, not real service." Next, the hero plays a purely passive role. His helper does everything for him, or he acts with the help of a magical agent. His helper delivers him to distant lands, kidnaps the princess, solves her riddles, beats the dragon or the enemy armies, and rescues him from his pursuers. Nevertheless, he is still the hero. The helper is an expression of his strength and ability.

The list of helpers available in the repertoire of Russian wondertales is quite large. Here we can analyze only the most typical. Analysis of the helper is inseparable from analysis of magical items. They function in exactly the same way. For example, the magic carpet, the eagle, the horse, and the wolf transport the hero to another kingdom. Therefore, treatment of magical helpers and magical items is combined in the same chapter.

All the helpers constitute a single type of character. First, we shall consider individual helpers as they are presented in the wondertale. Along the way, we might introduce some materials that explain a given helper.

However, each helper alone cannot explain the whole category. After reviewing each helper individually, we shall consider the whole category and then arrive at a general sense of the helpers as a whole. But this sense too cannot yet be conclusive. We must study all the functions of the helper, and only then will the picture be exhaustive. These functions have been singled out into individual chapters. For example, transportation of the hero to another kingdom, solving the princess's riddles, and the fight with the dragon are studied separately. The issue is broad and complex and cannot be resolved immediately. Its resolution will emerge gradually.

2. The Transformed Hero

We must add to everything said above that in the wondertale the helper may be considered as the hero's personified aptitude. In the forest, the hero obtains either an animal or the ability to transform into an animal. Thus, if the hero in one case mounts a horse and rides, and in the other we read, "As soon as Ivan, the merchant's son, put the ring on his finger, he turned at once into a steed and ran to the courtyard of Elena the Beautiful,"[1] then these events play the same role in the course of the action. For now, we merely register this fact. But it already gives us some explanation of why Ivan, for all his passivity, is still a hero. We have studied the wondertale enough to establish that the hero who has turned into an animal is more archaic than the hero who has received an animal. The hero and his helper are functionally the same thing. The hero-animal has changed to a hero plus an animal.

3. The Eagle

An eagle or some other bird can number among the hero's helpers. The bird's function is always the same: it transports the hero to a different kingdom. This translocation will engage us in a separate chapter. For now, we shall confine ourselves to studying the eagle itself.

In "The Sea King and Vasilisa the Wise," the hero wants to kill an eagle, but the eagle asks him to nurture it. "Take me home and feed me for three years."[2] "Do not spare food on me and nurture me for nine months, and I will repay you for everything. Give me six cows or six bulls each day for food; although it will be hard on you, I will pay it all back to you."[3] The eagle turns out to be extremely demanding and voracious, but the hero patiently gives him everything he demands. "The man obeyed and took the eagle into his house, started feeding it meat: one day he would slaughter a sheep, another day a calf. The man did not live alone in the house; the family was big, and they began to grumble that he was spending everything on the eagle."[4]

We see that the eagle is nourished. What we have before us here is actually a historical phenomenon. Eagles were nurtured among the Siberian peoples, and they were nurtured for a specific purpose. Zelenin writes, "It should be nurtured until it dies, and then it should be buried. One should never complain in these cases about the costs associated with feeding the eagle: it will be paid back a hundredfold. They say that in the old days eagles sometimes came to people's homes for the winter. In such cases it could happen that the house owner fed half of his cattle to the eagle. In the spring, the eagle, before flying away, thanked the hosts by bowing to them, and the hosts in such cases became quickly and unusually rich."[5]

Here the host does the same thing as the hero: he feeds the eagle all his livestock. However, the case reported by Zelenin is of later origin. We know that the eagle was not just released but killed. According to Lev Shternberg, this killing meant sending the eagle away. The Ainu used to kill an eagle, and before killing it they would address the eagle with the following prayer: "O precious deity, O divine bird, I beseech you, hear my words. You do not belong to this world, because your home is where the creator is with his golden eagles. . . . When you come to him [your father], tell him: I have lived for a long time among the Ainu, who raised me like my father and mother."[6] The nurturing and killing of the eagle are intended to appease the spirit, the lord of eagles, and later the creator. The meaning of the prayer is, "They took good care of me—help the people who did this." The act of killing is an act of sending away.

What do we see in the wondertale? It is true that the hero does not kill the eagle. After keeping him for three years, he only *wants* to kill him. "The hunter took a knife and sharpened it on the bar. He said, 'I'll go now and slaughter the eagle; he isn't recuperating anyway but just keeps eating my bread for nothing!'"[7] Yet he still feeds him for another year or two and then *sets him free*. The eagle takes him along to the Thrice-Tenth Kingdom. They fly away together. The moment of flying away in the tale corresponds to sending away via death in the ritual. In the ritual, the eagle is fed and then sent to his fathers. This is reflected in the tale as *setting him free*. The eagle comes not to the father of eagles but to his "elder sister" and tells her the following: "You would have been grieving for me and shedding hot tears forever if I hadn't come upon a benefactor, this hunter. He nursed me and fed me for three years, and thanks to him I am alive";[8] in other words, he behaves exactly as the Ainu demanded from the eagle in their prayer. The reward indeed is not long in coming. "'Thank you, dear man! Here is gold, silver, and semi precious stones for you. Take as much as you would like!' The man does not take anything, just asks for a small copper chest with brass keys."[9]

This case is interesting in that it contains elements of the ritual's decomposition. It shows that the tale reflects its later stage, as we see in other cases as well. Feeding the eagle is expressed as something that is a burden for the hero, as something unnecessary and meaningless. "The eagle ate so much that he ate up all the cattle; the tsar had no more sheep or cows. . . . The tsar borrowed cattle from everywhere and fed the eagle for the whole year."[10] Or the merchant "took the eagle bird and carried it home. He immediately killed a bull and poured a full tub of honey nectar. He thought that this food would be sufficient for the eagle for a long time, but the eagle ate and drank it all at once."[11] Thus, the needlessness and obscurity are expressed quite clearly here. The subsequent enrichment is a *miracle.*

Matching the feeding of an eagle in a tale and the religious reality of Siberia ought to require that we explain that reality as well. But we have already discussed the nurturing of totem animals. Nurturing the eagle is an individual case of the same.

All this entitles us to conclude the following: the motif of feeding an eagle was created on the basis of a custom that once existed. Historically the feeding was preparation for slaughter of a sacrificial animal—that is, for sending it away to the lord with the aim of arousing a favorable disposition in him. In the tale, the killing is resignified into having mercy, setting free, and flying away, while the lord's favorable disposition becomes giving the hero an object that makes him powerful and wealthy.

These conclusions are based mainly on Siberian materials. The Siberian materials on the cult of the eagle are interesting for another reason: they show the relationship between the owners of the eagle and the eagle-helper. There is a very close link between the bird and the shaman. In the Gilyak language,[12] the eagle bears the same name as the shaman: *cham.* For the Trans-Baikal Tungus, the bald eagle is the shaman's guardian and protector. Its image (fashioned of iron) is placed on the shaman's crown on the bars between the horns. The Teleuts call the eagle the "lord-bird of heaven," the shaman's indispensable companion and helper. "It is he who during the shamanistic ritual accompanies him in his journeys to heaven and to the underworld, protecting him from harm on the way; and he also assigns the specific sacrificial animals to the various deities." The shaman's garments are adorned with the eagle's body parts: bones, feathers, and claws. Finally, the shamanic coat, in the view of Siberian peoples, is a representation of the bird. According to this tradition, the Tungus, Yeniseyan Ostiaks,[13] and many others cut out the coat in such a way that it resembles a bird figure, and it is edged with a long fringe, symbolizing this bird's wings and feathers.[14] These materials further demonstrate the common essence of the hero and his helper.

4. *The Winged Horse*

We turn now to another helper of the hero: the horse. It is hardly necessary to prove that the steed or mare enters human culture and human consciousness later than the animals of the forest. The relationship of humans with forest animals is lost in the historical distance, whereas the domestication of the horse is traceable. One more circumstance must be noted with its appearance. The horse did not come to replace forest animals but to fulfill completely new functions in the household economy. One might say that the horse came to replace the deer or perhaps the dog, but one cannot say that the horse came to replace the bird or the bear, that it took over their household roles and their household functions.

So how is this shift reflected in folklore? Once again, we see that a new form of household establishment does not immediately create matching forms of thought. There is a period when these new forms come into conflict with the old way of thinking. The new form of the household introduces new images. These new images create a new religion, but not immediately. The horse is described in language as a bird—that is, an old word is transferred to the new image. The same thing happens in folklore: the horse is clothed in the bird's image. This produces the image of a winged horse. Nikolai Marr notes, "We know now that in prehistoric times a 'horse' also denoted a 'bird,' but a 'bird' is semantically related to the 'sky,' and of course it could not replace the 'horse' on earth in people's everyday life and in the material conditions of pre-history."[15]

Replacing the bird with a horse is apparently a Eurasian phenomenon. Egypt received the horse at a later period, and in America the horse was unknown before the arrival of Europeans.[16] But even there, the same process can be found, although it is found not with the bird but with the bear. In the American myth, the master-bear takes a boy underground and suggests that he choose a bear—that is, a helper. The boy chooses a black bear. "Now the grizzly began to growl and all at once snorted and sprang at the black bear. He got under the black bear and threw it over, and instead of the bear there stood a fine black steed."[17] This example clearly shows how a new animal takes on the religious functions of the old one. The horse replaces the bear as a helper and is acquired "underground" from the master of the bears. But this horse still retains features of its bear origin. It has a bearskin on its neck, exactly the same as the Russian Sivko-Burko, who has bird's wings on his sides. In short, there is an assimilation of one animal to another.

It is curious that the appearance of the horse in America creates exactly the same rites and folk motifs as in Europe. This was already pointed out by Dmitri Anuchin while he was studying Scythian burials that are similar to American ones. According to George Amos Dorsey, if a deceased person had a favorite horse, his relatives would slaughter this horse atop his grave, thinking that it would carry him to the spirit country, or they would cut some horsehair and put it into the grave. The hair gave the same kind of power over the horse as it does in the wondertale.

These cases show a consistent pattern of occurrence of the same ritual and folklore motifs, depending on the effects of domestic and social life. These examples also explain the winged horse.

5. *Nurturing the Horse*

The horse takes on not only the bird's attributes (wings) but also its functions. Similar to the totem animal and the folktale eagle, he is nurtured, although he is not a totem animal. This nurturing, however, takes different forms; it is considerably weaker in comparison to the grand nurturing of the eagle, which devours all the king's cattle. Nurturing gives it magical powers, but externally it is assimilated to reality: "Let me graze on dewy grass during three dawns."[18] This is a weak echo of the same request by the eagle and by the grateful animals, as seen above: "Feed me for three years." "He fed it with the best wheat up to three times, and then they only saw him mount the steed before he galloped away faster than their eyes could follow."[19]

Nurturing the horse is an individual case of nurturing miraculous or magical animals. Thus, grateful animals are nurtured—for example, an eagle, a horse, or even a dragon is nourished by an evil princess or sister. We have already pointed to the totemic origin of this motif. Nurturing the horse demonstrates that this is not just a matter of animal nutrition. The feeding gives the animal magical power. After feeding "on dew-covered grass for twelve mornings" or on "the best type of wheat," it turns from a "mangy foal" into the strong and fiery handsome steed the hero needs. This also supplies it with magical power. "Ivan began to take his horse every morning and evening to the green meadows to graze. And after twelve risings of the sun and twelve settings of the sun, his horse became so strong, so robust and beautiful, that it was impossible to imagine and only possible to tell in a tale; and it was so smart that Ivan only had to think of something, and the horse immediately knew what it was."[20] The magical qualities caused by feeding are expressed even more sharply in another example: "Feed me oats during these days, and I will then hide you under my hoof."[21] This transformation is artistically expressed by means of contrast: before the feeding, it is a mangy foal; after, it is a handsome steed. The image of the mangy foal is a purely folktale formation. The tale loves contrasts: Ivan the Fool becomes a hero, and the lowly peasant girl becomes a princess. We would search in vain for ritual analogies to the motif in which a weak or worn-out animal is nurtured in some religious manner.

6. *The Horse from beyond the Grave*

There are several studies dedicated to the horse in religious beliefs.[22] These studies, which are based on different materials, lead rather uniformly to the conclusion that in religion the horse was once considered a mortuary animal. We need to establish whether the horse of the wondertale (which has not been studied by these researchers) also originates there or whether it arises in a completely different manner.

It would be difficult to conduct a historical study here. Its precursors are other animals. We shall search in vain for any material in ancient times. Our main material is that of civilized peoples.

We have already seen that the horse is given to the hero by his dead father from beyond the grave. There we focused on the giving father; now we shall direct our attention to the horse. What is the historical substrate of this motif? It is known that horses were buried together with warriors. "They killed the horses and slaves with the intention that these beings, buried along with the deceased, would serve him in the grave, as they served him during his life," writes Fustel de Coulanges.[23] This corresponds exactly to the folktale's "serve him as you served me."[24] But how does the horse serve the deceased? The horse is a riding animal. Therefore, Negelein is absolutely correct when he notes, "The custom of giving a horse to the hero at his death follows from its function as one who carries away, a carrier or guide to a better place; we learn this by analogy with the dog, so indispensable for the Eskimo."[25] Eskimos give a dog for the grave; the Greeks give a horse. But there is one contradiction here: in the tale the dead father never leaves the tomb with his horse but resides in that grave with the horse. It is interesting that the Greeks had similar beliefs. Wilhelm Wundt is simply mistaken when he claims, "The soul of the warrior who fell on the battlefield is carried away, according to the beliefs of the Greeks, the Romans, and the Germans, on a swift-footed steed to the spirit kingdom."[26] It is possible that in certain cases this might be true, but as a rule it is incorrect for antiquity.

Originally, as we have seen, the dead person did not go anywhere. With the development of spatial concepts, a long journey and long-range flight began to be ascribed to the dead. After this, when with the transition to sedentary agriculture the focus of interest was concentrated on the ground, when an attachment to one's own land was formed, and when the cult of the ancestors appeared, dead people were imagined not as departing but as living here in the same house, by the hearth, under the threshold, or in the ground, in a grave. The horse remained an attribute of the deceased in general, although in fact it had lost its meaning. For example, as Rohde points out, tomb reliefs have been found in Boeotia in which the deceased is pictured receiving an offering while sitting on a horse or leading a horse.[27] Negelein notes that in general a horse is represented on Greek and even on later Christian gravestones. "It is an indispensable attribute of Heros, i.e., at a later time of a dead man in general."[28] Rohde very cautiously suggests that the horse here is "a symbol of the dead person who enters the spirit world."[29]

Ludolf Malten is more precise in thinking that, in the Hellenic faith, a dead man appears both in the form of a horse and sitting on horseback as its master. Neither one says anything about moving around on a horse. Comparative study of the material shows that the dead person-animal has turned into a dead person plus the animal, and this explains the duality that Rohde did not notice but Malten saw: the dead person is the horse and, at the same time, the master of the horse. There is a contradiction in the wondertale as well, but it is a divergence of a different nature: the father does not fly on the horse; it is the son who does so. Flying on a horse is a more ancient, preagricultural phenomenon that evolved from flying in the form of a bird or riding on a bird. A father who lives with his horse in the grave is a more recent phenomenon that was combined with these later. It reflects worship of ancestors and of the ancestors' graves: the father is no longer flying on the horse.

Here we can also mention that the tale shows more archaic features in some details than Greek religion does. In tales, the horse is given by the dead person; in Greek mythology, the donors of the horse are always gods. For example, Athena gives Bellerophon a bridle, with which he tames Pegasus. The wondertale father sometimes acts in the same way: he either reveals a magic formula or gives a piece of the horse's hair or its bridle.[30]

For now we can limit ourselves to these examples. They show the historical nature of the motif of the horse who abides with the dead man in the grave. These examples respond to the question posed at the start. The horse is presented as a mortuary animal not only in religion but also in the wondertale.

7. The Horse Rejected and Exchanged

In the motif analyzed above, the horse emerged as, in actuality, a mortuary animal, and the wondertale confirms the conclusions reached by researchers of the horse in religion. This observation is confirmed by analysis of the motif of the rejected or false horse. The horse offered by the living father is no good, while the horse given from beyond the grave is a mighty beast. "Every horse he hit on the rump immediately fell to the ground. He did not choose any horse that he liked from among 500 horses and said to his father, 'Father, I haven't chosen any horse among yours; now I'll go into the open field, into the green meadows. Maybe I will find a horse to fit me among the herds there.'"[31]

The horse Ivan rides before his departure is an ordinary horse and is not good enough. Yaga tells him the same thing. Very often, therefore, the hero changes horses at Yaga's house. "She told him to leave his horse at her place and to go to her older sister on her double-winged steed."[32]

At the second sister's, he exchanges this horse for a four winged one, and at the third sister's for a six-winged one.

This is why his father's ordinary horse will not do. It is an earthly creature; it has no wings. At the entrance to the other world, the hero obtains another horse.

8. The Horse in the Basement

What kind of horse is suitable then? Yaga describes it quite precisely: "Why are you saying that your father doesn't have a good horse? He does. It's locked behind three doors and already breaking through the third door with its hoof."[33] A horse from his father's stables is not adequate. Only a horse taken from the crypt is suitable. It is true that the wondertale never calls it a crypt. In tales, it is just a basement or a cellar, sometimes even a "public cellar." But the details leave no doubt that this cellar is actually a grave. "Go into the open field. Twelve oaks grow there; a stone slab is lying under these oaks. Lift this slab, and at once the steed of your great grandfather will jump out."[34] "Under that stone a basement was revealed. Three mighty steeds were standing in this basement, and military harness was hanging on the walls."[35] "The old woman replied, 'Come with me.' She brought him to the mountain and showed him the place: 'Dig this soil up.' Ivan Tsarevich finished digging . . . went under the ground."[36] "On this mountain stood an oak twenty inches thick, and under this oak there was a vault. In this vault, behind the doors, were two stallions."[37] All these are also obvious signs of a grave. The hill, the stone, the slab, and even the tree indicate that the basement is simply a crypt.

When Ivan goes down into the basement, sometimes the horse neighs happily at him. Ivan breaks down the doors, and the horse tears apart the chains. We have seen that magic agents pass through the female line. The initiate receives not some kind of device but the totem symbol of his wife's clan. There is none of this in the tale any longer. The horse passes down through the male line. The hero receives a certain horse "not your grandfather's, but your great-grandfather's." The horse's happy neighing indicates that its genuine, rightful owner, its inheritor, has appeared.

Analysis of this motif confirms the conclusion that the wondertale horse emerges from beyond the grave and completes the picture of the animal's connection to its owner's ancestors.

9. The Color of the Horse's Coat

In light of these materials, the color of the horse is also important to us. It is true that the tale names all kinds of possible colors. It is gray, brown, light chestnut, red, and so on. This diversity reflects reality, but it is additionally due in part to the fact that the image of a horse in a tale often triples, and each of the three horses has a different color. If, however, we look at this diversity a bit more closely, we can note the predominance of two colors: gray and red. The white one is even silver, with "each strand of silver hair"[38]—that is, dazzling white or "bluish white."[39] When the three horses are black, gray, and white, the final one to appear, the most powerful and beautiful, is the white one.[40] On the other hand, when the three horses are gray, black, and red,[41] often the red horse is mentioned last. In Russian icons depicting battles with the dragon, the horse is almost always either entirely white or fiery red. In these cases, the red color clearly represents the color of a flame, corresponding to the horse's fiery nature.

Furthermore, white is the color of otherworldly beings, as Negelein demonstrates clearly in his work dedicated specifically to the meaning of the color white.[42] White is the color of creatures that have lost their corporeality. This is why ghosts are imagined as white. The horse is of this kind too, and it is no accident that he is sometimes called invisible: "In a certain kingdom, in a certain state there are green meadows, and there is an invisible mare, and she has twelve foals."[43] "And the king who was called invisible had been given an invisible steed."[44] In one case, it is called "sky-blue-white."[45] The formula "each strand of silver hair" also points to its white color and to the dazzling character of this color. Hence expressions such as "not only can you not ride it, you can't see it with your eyes."[46]

Wherever the horse plays a religious role, it is always white. "The Buryats portray the lord of the Ule kingdom, Nagad-Sagan-Zorin, as the owner of a white horse with a white hoof."[47] In a Yakut myth, the dragon mockingly invites the hero to mount "a posthumous horse." He mounts a "pure white steed . . . with silver wings that grow in its mid-back, like a bird."[48] Yakuts in general often have a "completely white horse."[49] The Greeks would sacrifice only white horses.[50] In the Apocalypse, death sits atop a "pale horse."[51] In Germanic folk beliefs, death arrives riding a skinny white nag.[52] It is no accident that Horace calls death "pale death" (*pallida mors*). These examples show that the coat color is not an accidental and neutral phenomenon. Even if statistical calculations showed that a gray or white horse does not occupy the first place in frequency of occurrence, that would still prove nothing: the presence of a white or bluish-white horse and its occurrence in beliefs associated with the world beyond the grave make it evident that this is the most archaic form of the horse, while the rest of the coat colors must be recognized as realistic deformations, especially because this form of horse fits the image of the horse in general and its connection with the other world.

10. The Horse's Fiery Nature

Examination of the coat color shows that the horse sometimes appears as reddish, and it is red in icons depicting St. George on horseback fighting the dragon. There is no need here to repeat details regarding the horse's fiery nature: sparks scatter from his nostrils, fire and smoke pour from his ears, and so on. We need to explain this phenomenon.

Why and how does the image of the horse merge with the concept of fire? Is there any material that could show how this connection took place?

We know that the basic function of the horse is mediation between the two realms. It carries the hero to the Thrice-Tenth Kingdom. In religious beliefs, it often carries the deceased to the land of the dead.

Fire was exactly the same kind of mediator. In myths from America, Africa, Oceania, and Siberia, the hero leaves for the sky without any help from animals, exclusively with the help of fire. Here are a few examples. The Yakut have this: "Then he dug a hole of seven fathoms, tore apart seven large trees and made a fire there. He soared to the highest place as a young white hawk."[53] Thus, the hero makes a great fire in order to ascend into the sky. The most interesting thing is that, in doing so, he turns into a bird. This shows that the old zoomorphic images have not yet been forgotten, that here the old tradition of transformation into an animal meets a new factor: fire. But perhaps fire was here first? According to Zelenin, "People . . . at much later times began to view [the] burning of corpses as a way of ascending to heaven."[54] The hero of a Micronesian myth is trying to get to heaven to see his father. He attempts to fly up without success. "But he did not give up his intention. He kindled a large fire, and with the help of the smoke, ascended for the second time into the sky, where he finally reached the embrace of his father."[55] There is no need, however, to dwell on this phenomenon. It is the source of both the cremation of corpses and the burning of sacrifices. Thus, along with animals, fire was once imagined as a mediator between worlds. When the horse appears on the scene, the role of fire is transferred to it. Wondertales are not the only examples of this; religion illustrates it as well. Here we can point to two phenomena as historical background to the tale: the merging of the cult of fire with the cult of the horse, a classic example of which is provided by India, and the role that fire and the horse play in shamanism. The traditional country where horses have long existed, and from which they probably spread throughout the world, is India. And indeed, we see in the Vedic religion the fullest development of the fire-horse in the image of the god Agni. Here is how Oldenberg describes the ceremony of kindling the sacred horse: "The chief priest orders one of his subordinates: 'Bring in the steed.' The horse stands near the spot where the sparking of the fire should occur, so that it observes the friction process. . . . There is no doubt that the horse is nothing other than an incarnation of Agni."[56] Here the horse watches the friction, but in Vedic hymns, it is extracted from the fire striker: "Agni, the infant newborn from the process of rubbing two sticks together."[57] Agni corresponds to the horse not only in numerous details but also in his essence and his primary function. He is the god-mediator ("herald") between two worlds who carries the dead into the sky in fire. In terms of its historical stage, the religion of the Vedas is a very recent phenomenon. The *Rigveda* is a priestly and theological work, though it doubtless indirectly reflects folk beliefs.

Here it is useful to point out that the wondertale horse, just like the Vedic fiery horse Agni, is extracted from flint and steel. But the *Rigveda* has preserved the ancient form of the fire striker: two sticks. The wondertale replaces it with a new formation: flint and steel.

The correspondence between the Vedic Agni and the Russian wondertale horse is so complete that their comparison could constitute the subject of a special study. Ovsianiko-Kulikovskii, in his work on the cult of fire in the era of the Vedas, has collected several hundred epithets for the fire-god Agni.[58] It is true that studying epithets detached from the object with which they are affiliated can lead to false conclusions. However, such epithets as "light backed," "of flaming maw," "fiery headed," "whose sign is smoke," "golden haired," "golden toothed," "of golden beard," and more, when applied to the fire-horse god, correspond too closely to the wondertale to be considered accidental. They and the tale are based on the same ideas.

We shall not elaborate further on this connection, which would lead us too far away from our topic. It is sufficient to point out that the fiery horse, the mediator between two worlds, exists in the religion of a livestock-raising people who created statehood. Study of Agni helps to explain the nature of the horse. It was formed from the merger of beliefs about the horse and fire as mediators between the two worlds. Of the three sources for the steed—the bird, the horse, and fire—fire is the most recent element, and the bird is the most ancient.

We noted above that not only a deity can play the role of mediator between the two worlds (this is a mark of a more recent culture, like the Vedic religion): the shaman can as well. Shamans also operate with the help of fire. Shternberg describes a shamanistic ritual that he himself saw. "If the patient's demon stubbornly refuses to go away, the shaman calls upon a special spirit that turns into a fireball and makes its way into the belly of the shaman and from there into all the most remote parts of his body; so that the shaman during the session emits fire from his mouth, nose, and from any part of his body."[59] This case shows that emitting fire from the mouth, eyes, ears, and so on is not something specific to wondertales.

According to Fridtjof Nansen, Eskimos have similar beliefs. "The mark of shamans is that they breathe out fire."[60] But this is usually done only by a black shaman. Nansen compares him to the fire-breathing devil of the Middle Ages and proposes that the idea of the fire-breathing shaman was formed under European influence; however, quite the opposite is true. The fire-breathing devil is the last reflection of the idea of a fire-breathing mediator between the realms of the living and the dead. The same notion is found among the Yoruba of Africa. Their mythic hero Shango receives a powerful magic device from his father. He eats it. The people assemble in council. They all take turns speaking. When the hero's turn comes, "fire began to burst out of his mouth. Everyone was shocked. Then Shango realized that he, as a god, was not subject to anyone. He stamped his foot and ascended."[61] Here we have the prototype of later fire ascensions, such as the fiery chariots of Elijah.[62] But the horse demonstrates a connection with shamanism not only from this angle, not only as a fire-breathing creature. The shaman often has a horse as an assistant or in general has some connection with one.

Here is how Andrei Popov describes a shamanistic ritual of the Yakuts:[63] "The shaman enters and with the help of his assistant dons his garb. He is given a handful of white horsehair, some of which he throws into the fire: this serves as refreshment for the spirits and wins their good will towards him, because they love smoke from burnt hair very much." It should be added that the shaman is sitting on a white mare's skin. But what kind of strange taste do the spirits have if they "love the smell of burnt hair," and why does it "serve as refreshment for them and win the goodwill of the helper-spirits towards the shaman"? The tale shows quite clearly that burning hair is a magical means of *attracting* a spirit, and whether or not it likes the smell, it has to appear. It is enough to "scorch" three pieces of hair to summon the horse. This is what the shaman is doing.

In this case, it is spirits, not horses, that appear before him, and nothing is said about their shape. But we know that among the shaman's helpers there are horses as well. "In legends of the Buryats certain deceased shamans are considered to own a white, piebald, or black horse, on which they used to ride everywhere during their lifetime, and on which now they visit the neighborhood of their *ulus*."[64] The Minusinsk shaman addresses the *ongon*,[65] called "the patron of the Teleuts," with the following words: "You came here at noon on a blue-gray horse from the Kuznetsk Mountains." In one Yakut myth the devil acts in the following manner: "At that moment the devil turned over his tambourine, sat on it, hit it three times with his stick, and the tambourine turned into a mare with three legs. He climbed onto her and went straight to the east."[66]

11. *The Horse and the Stars*

Here we must point to yet another feature of the horse's appearance. It has "many stars on its flanks, a bright moon on its forehead." It is easy to imagine that the horse, as a mediator between heaven and earth, could be given attributes of the sky. In the *Rigveda* the sky is compared to a horse decorated with pearls: "Like a dark steed adorned with pearl, the Fathers have decorated heaven with stars"[67] Alfred Ludwig notes of this passage that the horse is taken here as a symbol of the sky. We can compare this with the fact that sometimes Agni is also identified with the moon: "As a messenger of heaven thou lightest all night long the families of men."[68]

Nevertheless, it is quite possible that the horse as night sky is a secondary formation from the daytime horse, from the steed-sun. While the image of the steed-moon is somewhat forced and artificial (and occurs rarely), the chariot of the sun god Helios, the chariot of Indra, or the sun boat of the god Ra are filled with jubilance and beauty. And yet they did not enter the wondertale. They died along with the religion. Only disparate weak echoes can be found in images of a purely accessory nature, such as the mare on which Baba Yaga "flies daily around the world" or the three riders in "Vasilisa the Beautiful."[69] The sun is not reflected in the dynamic movement of the tale but rather as a kingdom and a palace, something we will discuss below. In this connection, it is interesting to note that in Egyptian religion the image of breathing fire is attributed preeminently to the sun, and in this respect, the wondertale horse is perhaps also connected to the sun. "O thou who art in thine egg [i.e., Ra], who shinest from thy Disk and risest in thy horizon . . . who giveth blasts of fire from thy mouth."[70]

12. *The Horse and Water*

Another characteristic of the horse is its connection with water. This connection is shared by its European and Asian counterparts: the Indian Agni and the Greek Pegasus. However, this sea horse is somewhat unusual in wondertales; it occurs relatively rarely and is not always the hero's helper. It appears at night and spoils the hayfield, it eats and tramples the hay, and the brothers are sent to catch it. "At the stroke of midnight the weather turned, the sea began to heave, and a wondrous mare emerged from the depths of the sea. It ran up to the first haystack and began to devour the hay."[71] But sometimes the horse-helper is also related to water. An old man the hero encounters says, "Your father has thirty horses, all identical. Go home and order the grooms to give them water from the blue sea. One mare will come forward, enter the water up to its neck, and begin to drink, as the waves begin to rise in the blue sea and sway from coast to coast. This is the one you should take!"[72]

Compared to the chthonic and sepulchral nature of the horse, its water nature is a secondary and later phenomenon. Malten demonstrates this for Greece, Oldenberg for India. Like the wondertale horse, the Greek Pegasus also has a connection to water. With a blow of its hoof, it reveals a new spring on Mt. Helicon, the Hippocrene spring. Here the horse's original chthonic nature is evident. Bellerophon catches it with a bridle given to him by Athena while it is drinking from the well of Pirene on Acrocorinth. This connection with water is seen even more sharply in the divine horses of the sea god Poseidon. Sometimes he gives them to a person who turns to him with a pious prayer. He provides a team of these horses, for example, to Pelops, who with their help captures himself a bride from Oenomaus after beating him in the hippodrome. The Argonauts also encounter a horse with a golden two-sided mane, coming out of the sea.

According to Malten's study, Poseidon was not always the god of the sea; he was once a land god. Initially, he was a chthonic god "who let grace sprout in a seed and in a water spring."[73] At that time he was already associated with the horse. "The ruler of fresh water became the ruler of the sea waters only through coastal inhabitants, or rather through colonization across the sea."[74] With his transformation into the sea god, his horses also became sea horses.[75] And indeed, the image of the horse emerging from the water cannot be primary. It must have evolved historically, and the process can be observed in Greece. Something similar happened in India. The divine horse of Agni is said to be Apam Napat, a child of waters. Oldenberg suggests that Apam Napat was once a special water creature that merged with Agni. He "has a sea water robe."[76] "[Thou] art brought to life from out the waters,"[77] "in the midst of waters beautiful,"[78] and so on.

13. Other Helpers

The horse and the eagle are not the hero's only helpers. Here we cannot possibly provide a full list and system of wondertale helpers; we shall consider only their most essential and important images. Having explored the eagle and the horse as the most typical examples of animal helpers, we shall briefly touch on selected anthropomorphic helpers.

A special category of helpers consists of all sorts of extraordinary experts. Often these are brothers, each of whom possesses some kind of skill. Sometimes they are warriors encountered by chance who have a totally unusual appearance and qualities. There are many different kinds. According to Bolte and Polívka's index, we can estimate about forty names of such experts.

The most prominent figure among them is Frost Snapper or the Cold One. He is depicted variously and sometimes not depicted at all. In one tale he is an old man with his head wrapped in cloth. "Why is your head wrapped?" "My hair is tied up; if I let it loose, there will be a frost."[79] He appears like this in the Brothers Grimm.[80] He is wearing a hat sidewise over one ear. When the hero rebukes him for this, he says, "If I put my hat on straight, a terrible freezing cold will come, and birds will fall dead to the ground."

Russian tales have another more vivid image. "And then there was an old man walking, extremely old and snotty. Snot hung from his nose, as if hanging frozen from the roof."[81] The function of this Frost Snapper is always the same: at the princess's place, a very hot bath is stoked for the heroes in order to destroy them. At that point, the Cold One helps. "He immediately jumped into the bath, blew into one corner, spat into another, and the whole bathhouse cooled down, and there was snow lying in the corners."[82]

The nature of this figure is quite clear. This is the ruler of the weather, the ruler of winter and the frost. Similar figures are found, for example, in the myths of North American Indians.

Many years ago, it was very cold on the earth. A big glacier lay at the upper end of the river, and it emanated an icy cold. All the animals set off to kill the man who made this cold, but they would all freeze. (The coyote also tries, but gets frozen. Then the fox sets off.) The fox continued running, and with each step it took, a fire burst from under its feet. It entered the house (where Frost lived) and stamped its foot once (this repeats four times). Once it had stamped its foot four times, all the ice melted, and it became warm again.[83]

In this case, the ruler of frost and cold is hostile to man. But he submits to the hero, who has already entered another world. It is interesting that in one Russian tale, the old man asks in the same way as the grateful animals, "Ivan Mare's son, feed me with bread, and I'll be of use to you in bad times."[84] As we saw previously, the eagle utters exactly the same request. We can assume that we see here a manifestation of the view that a person can subdue the ruler of nature and force him to serve. And indeed, the hero forces them to serve him. It is true that usually he just meets such figures by chance and takes them along with him. But this incidental event probably overlay other forms of subduing the ruler, one of which could be a propitiatory or other type of sacrifice, expressed here with the words "feed me."

Another similar figure is the Whiskered One. "He walked for a while and came to a river three miles wide. On its shore stood a man who had dammed the river with his mouth; he was catching fish with his whisker, cooking them on his tongue, and eating them."[85] If we try to draw the shape of this Whiskered One, we involuntarily come to the image of a dam and a creel through which water passes. In other words, while Frost Snapper is the personification of natural forces, here we have a personified tool. For now, let us merely take note of this case. The connection of tools to helpers and magical items will be studied below.

Sometimes the storyteller places the Whiskered One not on the shore but in the water. He is the ruler of the river and fish, a deity that bestows an abundance of fish and successful fishing. In fact, he does not play any role in the tale. He is an incidental figure. Sometimes he has the role of a helper who helps the hero to cross the water into a different realm. The hero crosses the water by walking on his mustache: "And on his whiskers, as if on a bridge, pedestrians walk, horsemen gallop, and carts ride."[86] It should be mentioned, however, that even here the fish nature of this creature can be elucidated from comparisons. In some cases, the hero crosses the river on the back of a huge fish. These types of creatures are also found at a certain stage of religious beliefs, for example, in North America. In an American Indian legend, brothers want to test the strength of one of them. They go to the river. "In the evening they settled down for the night and began to tease their brother and pull his hair. But he didn't pay any attention to this. He lay down and put on his beaver hat. Then the river started to rise, and his brothers and sisters had to run from the water to the mountain, while he remained calmly by the fire. Even though everything around was covered with water, he stayed dry near his fire."[87]

It is curious that in this example, exactly as in the Russian and German tales, the movement of the hat arouses the forces of nature. This hat belongs to the category of magical items that will be discussed below. In this example, however, we see only the forces of nature; we do not see the fishing. In another American Indian legend, we read, "'Children, do you know where Azan made a dam on the river?' 'No, where did he do it?' 'At that place over there.' They went there and found Azan, who had dammed the river and nearly emptied the water in order to catch all the fish." They destroy him.[88] Here the creature that puts the dam on the river is again linked to a fish. This creature is not always anthropomorphic. In another American Indian legend, a huge elk stands above the river with his legs spread wide and kills (swallows) everyone who comes down the river.[89]

The Whiskered One's brother is usually the Mountainous One (or Mountain Mover or Mountain Man). "The Mountain warrior strolls about and kicks the mountains with his foot."[90] This is the spirit of the mountains. "They walked and walked and came across a warrior, the Mountain Man. This Mountain Man was shaking the mountain while holding it on his little finger."[91] "You see, I was placed here to turn over the mountains."[92] According to Shternberg, the Gilyaks call a member of the sea master's clan *tol' nivukh*—that is, "a sea man"—and one from the master of the mountains' clan *nal' nivukh*, or "a mountain man." Our folkloric Mountain Man is also this kind of mountain man, one of the "masters of the mountains." His role is not well defined. Sometimes he saves the hero from pursuers,[93] and sometimes he plays the role of a false hero, an older brother who betrays a younger one. But even in cases where he plays the role of the false hero, he obeys the hero. The wondertale hero is a powerful shaman whom the masters of the weather, rivers and fish, and mountains and forests obey. Like all such skillful helpers, the Mountain Mover is met by chance. But we see the motif of his subordination in Afanas'ev's tale No. 93. "He approached the Mountain Mover and began to ask him; and he replied, 'I would be glad to accept you, Prince Ivan, but there is not much time left for me to live. You see, I was put here to turn over the mountains. When I manage the last ones, my death will come.'" Subsequently, the hero obtains a brush that turns into mountains when thrown, and with this he gives the Mountain Mover new food. Here a motif that is commonly found in flight and pursuit (a comb and a brush usually save a hero immediately from pursuit) is used differently—it has shifted. This shift is very interesting and shows that the life of the ruler of natural forces has to be supported by a person. Without this support, he perishes. The Whiskered One also says, "Feed me." For this support, these rulers assist man after his death while they help the shaman during his life.

Antiquity has its Mountain Movers too, but as already subdued gods. They fight among the giants against Zeus, turning the mountains over and piling them on top of one another to attack the sky.

A third brother or warrior is usually called the Oak Man or Oak Mover. "He saw a man pulling up oaks by the roots: 'Hello, Oak Man! What are you doing?' 'Pulling up oaks.' 'Be my sworn brother and come along with me.'"[94] Later this Oak Man defeats the enemy army. In one tale, he is called not Oak Man but Bow Man: "The warrior Bow Man can bend any tree into a bow."[95] One might think that this is a case of false etymology,[96] but in Greek myth, we find the explicit "bender of pines." Theseus meets this "bender of pines," the bandit Sinis, who binds people to pines and tears them apart, and he punishes him.

It is obvious that if the Whiskered One is the "man of the river," and the Mountain Man is the "man of the mountains," then the Oak Man is the "man of the forest." In this, he is similar to Yaga, in precisely the manner that Cold One or Frost Snapper is similar to the donor Jack Frost. The Oak Man sometimes even acts not as a helper but as a donor. The hero meets a man carrying firewood to the forest. "Why are you taking firewood to the forest?" "This is not ordinary firewood." "What kind is it?" "The kind that, when scattered around, turns suddenly into a whole army."[97]

Thus, from among a large number of various experts, four types can be discerned as rulers of natural forces: Frost Snapper, Whiskered One, Mountain Man, and Oak Man. These obey the hero because of his ceremonial or other acts, but this aspect is preserved in wondertales only in its rudiments and replaced by chance meetings with such helpers.

We can turn to another group of experts who have nothing in common with the rulers over natural forces. These include the archer, the outrunner, the blacksmith, the sharpshooter, the sensor, the helmsman, the swimmer, and others.

A comparison of various materials shows that these are personified abilities that reach into the earth's distance, upward above it, and downward below it. We will encounter them again when we explore their functions in connection with the difficult tasks assigned by the princess.

14. Development of the Concept of the Helper

Despite their diversity, helpers in the wondertale constitute a certain group that is connected by its functional unity.

Everything above regarding distinct types of helpers has only partial significance. We must address the question of helpers in general as a phenomenon of the wondertale canon. We have already encountered the transfer of a helper to the hero. Often the helper is given to the hero by Yaga, whose historical roots have been elucidated. She is connected to initiation, or to ceremonies including the transfer of magical or theurgical power over animals to the boy. However, historical parallels to specific types of helpers did not lead us to the rite of initiation. They led us to shamanism, to the cult of ancestors, and to notions of the afterlife. When the rite died, the figure of the helper did not die with it. It began to develop in accord with economic and social evolution until it reached as far as guardian angels and the saints of the Christian Church. Wondertales too serve as one of the stages in this development.

It is possible to identify basically three stages or links in the history of helpers. The first is acquisition of a helper during an initiation rite. The second is the shaman's acquisition of a helper, and the third is acquisition of a helper in the underworld by a dead person. These three do not follow one after another automatically. They are tentative milestones that indicate the direction of development. Let us first consider helpers in the initiation rite.

This question has been studied very little in ethnography, although it is related to the very essence of initiation. Heinrich Schurtz, who studied the issue of initiation specifically, pays no attention to this aspect of the matter. Hutton Webster has much more to say. "A fundamental doctrine was the belief in a personal guardian spirit (*nagual*) into which by various rites of a phallic character the members of the society were supposed to be metamorphosed."[98]

Thus, during the initiation rite a boy would transform into his own helper. Even if we knew no more than this, we would have the right to raise the question of the connection of the wondertale helper and the institution of initiation. This would explain both its acquisition in the realm of death (for the initiate was assumed to be dead) and the helper's connection to the world of the ancestors. This connection was indicated previously, especially during exploration of the horse and grateful animals. It also explains the helper's connection with the world of the ancestors. In some tribes of North America, the spirit-helper was called Manitou. This Manitou was transferred by inheritance. "When the youth prepares to meet the guardian spirit, he does not expect to find any but those of his clan."[99] Thus, there is a preestablished link between the initiate and his helper. The hero looks first of all for a horse, and not just any horse but his father's; and this horse has long been waiting for its master. In all these cases Webster calls the helper the "guardian spirit" without differentiation. But we know that this helper has an animal nature. Part of this ceremony consisted of dances, during which skins of different animals were worn: bulls, bears, swans, wolves, and so on. Their heads were used as masks.[100] This symbolized the transformation into an animal. On the other hand, this ability was passed on by the ancestors and the elders who perform the initiation rite.[101] The initiated men invoked the helper with songs and dances.[102] The wondertale has not retained the songs or dances. It replaces them with spells or formulas. In places where multistage secret brotherhoods evolved, transition from a lower to a higher stage was permitted only to those who possessed such a helper. "Admission to these societies rests upon the acquisition by every boy at puberty of a personal guardian spirit (*manitou*, or 'individual totem') the same as that of the secret society to which he claims entrance."[103] In the Kwakiutl tribe, these helpers and the privileges associated with them, which were obtained by each honorable family, were transmitted to direct descendants through the male line or, through marriage to the daughter of a male child, to a son-in-law and through him to his grandchildren.[104] All these indications are very important. Among other things, they explain the testing of the hero, who had to prove before his marriage that he had a helper. As we shall see, they are the basis of the motif of "difficult tasks." They are what connects acquisition of the helper to entrance into matrimony, as we shall see in our analysis of the princess.

But even Webster, from whom these data were taken, says nothing about the meaning and significance of acquiring the helper. Here we can refer to a legend found in Boas.

Once, a man went into the mountains to hunt mountain goats. There
he met a black bear who took him into its house. It taught him the art
of catching salmon and building a boat. After two years, he returned
to his homeland. When he came back all the people were afraid of him,
because he looked like a bear. . . . He could not speak and did not want
to eat anything cooked. Then they rubbed him with magic herbs and he
became a man again. . . . From that time on, whenever he needed help,
he always went to his friend, the bear, and the bear always helped him.
In the winter he caught fresh salmon for him, when no one else could
catch it. This man built a house and painted a bear on it. His sister
wove a bear in a blanket that is used for dancing. Therefore, the sister's
descendants have the bear as their symbol.[105]

Everything is clear in this story: the two-year stay in the bear's house,
the fact that the hero upon returning has lost his ability to speak, and the
fact that he wants to eat only raw food. This case is important because
it exhibits the results of staying in the home of the bear and thus reveals
the purpose and the meaning of the respective rite: the hero returns as a
great hunter who has power over animals. This example also shows why
animal helpers are so diverse. The point is not to acquire a strong animal
(as some anthropologists suggest). This bear teaches him to build a boat
and to fish—an occupation not typical for bears. This function could be
performed by any other animal. The animal is important not due to its
physical strength but because of its connection to and affiliation with the
animal kingdom in general.

This is the oldest form and the oldest source of the motif of the
magic helper. We can only guess what was there before the advent of the
initiation rite, since there are no materials that could shed light on this
proto-form.

Here there is still no variety of functions specific to the helper; in
particular, there is no mediation between the two worlds. There are also
no anthropomorphic or invisible helpers. In light of these materials, we
must recognize the ability of a man to transform into his totem or into
his helper as the most archaic form of control over the helpers. The wondertale has preserved it, as we saw. We have to recognize hunting goals
as the oldest motivators that gave rise to the concept of the helper, the
Manitou, or, in English terminology, the guardian spirit.[106]

However, the wondertale has retained hardly any hunting functions.
There are some vestiges of them—for example, when the hero, living in
the forest with his evil sister, receives the cubs from a wolf, a bear, and a
lion, these animals in the tale are called the hero's "hunt."

Wherever initiation does not exist (or no longer exists), acquisition of
a helper takes place individually. However, the form of acquiring a helper
strongly resembles what happens in the rite except for the absence of a
person conducting the initiation. A young man departs alone for the forest

or the mountain, remains silent, fasts, and so on. This form is found both in America and Africa. Bernhard Ankermann, referring to work by Henri Trilles,[107] notes the following regarding the Fang tribe: "The forefather of every clan (Sippe) had an animal as its *elanela*. Trilles translates this word as '*animal voué à un homme*,' i.e., an animal that is bound to help a man."[108] However, the phenomenon of the individual acquisition of a helper is in general a more recent phenomenon. In these cases, not everyone can acquire a helper, only chosen ones such as shamans, who are considered to be possessors of powerful spirits, or animal helpers. Webster has shown how secret societies gradually locked themselves into castes. But shamans, for the most part, do not form castes. According to Hermann Haeberlin, "Every American Indian has a spirit-helper, which he finds in his adolescence or later; sometimes he has several: one for hunting, one for fishing, one for crafts, one for war, etc. The helpers against diseases are the spirits of the shamans. Most of these spirits take the form of animals."[109]

This leads us to an examination of the shaman's helpers. The elements that are lacking in the figure of the helper that is acquired at initiation—for example, mediation between the two worlds—are provided to us by the shaman's helper. This stage is of later origin. Shternberg writes, "The supernatural power of the shaman lies not in him specifically, but in the spirit-helpers at his disposal. They are the ones that chase away diseases; they take the shaman to the most remote places, inaccessible to ordinary mortals, in order to find and rescue the soul of the patient; they help to bring the soul of the deceased to the other world, and they suggest the answers to all requests addressed to the shaman. Without these spirits the shaman is powerless. The shaman who has lost his spirits ceases to be a shaman and sometimes even dies."[110] The shaman acquires his helpers in various ways. Alfred Kroeber, who studied the religion of American Indians in California, notes,

> The most common way of acquiring shamanistic power in California . . . is by dreaming. A spirit, be it that of an animal, a place, the sun or another natural object, a deceased relative or an entirely unembodied spirit, visits the future medicine-man in his dreams, and the connection thus established between them is the source and basis of the latter's power. The spirit becomes his guardian spirit or "personal." From it he receives the song or rite or knowledge of the charm and understanding which enable him to cause or remove disease and to do and endure what other men cannot.[111]

In the Shasta tribe of California, it is believed that the earth is full of certain "potencies and pains" that reside mainly in human form in cliffs, lakes, rapids, the sun, the moon, and so on; or they are animals that bring forth sickness, death, and every kind of evil. They are the helpers of shamans.[112] Acquiring helpers there happens in a different way than described by Kroeber. The helper "shoots" at the shaman, who experiences a stab of pain (*ein Zucken des Schmerzes*). Let us recall that in the wondertale the horse *kicks* the hero, and after that he acquires power.

Such an abundance of data about shamans' helpers exists that there is no need to go into this material in detail. Let us dwell on only a few cases that are especially close to the wondertale and help to explain it. Of particular interest to us are materials regarding the Altai people as reported by Andrei Anokhin.

> The help of the Aru Kormos is essential for relations with the spirits of heaven and the underworld, the path to which is barred by obstacles. These obstacles are described in detail in shamanistic rituals. A shaman conquers all the obstacles exclusively with the help of the Aru Kormos. During the trip, they act as a live force and protect the shaman from dangers; they fight the evil spirits encountered on the way. The Aru Kormos invisibly surround the shaman: they sit on his shoulder, on his head, arms, legs; they surround his body on all sides, and because of this they are called the armor or the hoop during invocations (some shamans have more, some less). The head of all the spirits that make up the shaman's armor is always a personal intimate guardian-spirit from which the shaman traces his succession.[113]

Here the helper has already lost its animal nature. It has become invisible. Calling the spirit "armor" is quite indicative. The true element of the folkloric helper is the air. Such, for example, is Shmat-Mind and other invisible helpers of the hero. "Shmat-Mind! Are you here?" "I am here, don't worry, I won't leave you."[114] This "invisible creature" is an intermediary between the two worlds. He carries the hero through the air to the other world. But along with invisible helpers, the Altai people also have zoomorphic creatures. One of these is Suyla. He has horse eyes and sees all around him to a distance that can be reached only by riding for thirty days. Some shamans imagine Suyla in the form of a golden eagle with a horse's eyes.[115] This shift does not occur immediately; the transition passes through a number of hybrid creatures.

It can be observed that the hunting function of the helpers gradually fades into the background and is replaced by the functions of healing and mediation between the two worlds. Animals used for transportation begin to acquire particular importance (hence the horse), and other means of transportation are integrated with them as well, especially the boat. For example, experts in the wondertale appear in the boat and comprise the ship's crew. The Argonauts, who are very similar to our seven Simeons, also sail in a boat. This journey to the other world, both in antiquity and in our wondertale, completely supplants the hunting backdrop. The shaman and his helpers gradually become not hunters but healers and hunters of souls. In Babylonian myth, when Nergal goes to the underworld, he takes with him seven helpers given to him by his father. Their names are lightning, fever, heat, and so on.

The tablets are poorly preserved, but the absence of hunting, the departure for another kingdom, the personification of the forces of nature, and the connection with shamanism/healing are clearly visible. Later Nergal marries Erishkigal, the queen of the underworld. Of course, the seven assistants help him in this. Thus, this most recent stage is the closest to the wondertale.[116]

This leads us to an examination of the posthumous helper. Initially, when the difference between life and death had not yet been perceived that sharply, naturally there could be no specific figure of a posthumous helper. But since the whole complex of initiation is closely associated with the idea of death, some of its elements passed into the cult of the dead, creating posthumous helpers. A later offshoot could be beliefs in angels—that is, half zoomorphic (winged) beings who carry the soul away to heaven. This is a later phenomenon that flourishes in the state cult of the dead, appearing in its most developed form in ancient Egypt. Based on the works of Boris Turaev, Alfred Wiedemann, James Breasted, and others, we know that these kinds of postmortem helpers existed in Egypt as well. Plates have been found in tombs with the images of genies who, as Turaev puts it, "helped the deceased beyond the grave."

A special examination of this issue in Egyptology lies beyond the scope of this work. Our task is to point to the link that exists in this case.

We have outlined the main stages in the development of the helper. The concept of turning into an animal during initiation appears to be its most archaic form. Later the helper is acquired individually and, still later, only by the shaman. Once he is acquired by the shaman, he takes on new functions of mediation between two worlds, and the helper's hunting nature begins to recede into the background. The image of the helper also begins to change. The animal begins to give way to a spirit, and among the animals a new type emerges that is associated with a person's translocation; thus, an eagle merges with a horse. But if the scheme sketched here is correct, then the wondertale reflects all the stages of the helper's development: it contains both the transformations and the helpers—animals, birds, spirits, the group of skilled men whose connection with hunting tools is still clearly seen in Altai, the horse, and so on. How this figure enters into wondertales is a general question about how religious ideas do so. This will be discussed in the final chapter.

II. The Magical Item

15. *The Item and the Helper*

Examination of the magical helper facilitates and prepares us for examination of the magic item. There is a close connection between the two.

It is easy to see that these items represent only a specific instance of the helper. Helpers, both living creatures and magical items, function essentially in the same way. For example, a horse transports the hero to distant lands, but the same thing is achieved by the flying carpet or the self-walking-boots. A horse beats an enemy army, but a club also beats enemies by itself and even takes them prisoner. Of course, there are specific helpers and specific items that cannot be interchangeable. But these individual cases do not violate the principle of their morphological affinity. The number of magical items in wondertales is so great that a descriptive review of them will not lead to any results. It seems that there is no object that could not appear as a magic item. There are all kinds of clothing (hats, shirts, boots, belts) and adornments (rings, hair pins), tools and weapons (swords, cudgels, crutches, bows, guns, whips, sticks, canes), bags, sacks, purses, containers (barrels), animal body parts (hair, feathers, teeth, heads, hearts, eggs), musical instruments (whistles, horns, harp, violin), household items (tinderboxes, flint, towels, brushes, carpets, yarn balls, mirrors, books, cards), drinks (water, potions), and fruits and berries. No matter how much we classify and enumerate them, the list offers no key to understanding them.

It is no better if we approach the items according to their functions. The same functions are assigned to different items and vice versa. For example, the helpful lads who fulfill the hero's orders can appear from a horn,[117] from a bag,[118] from a barrel,[119] from a drawer,[120] out of a cane when it is struck against the ground,[121] from a magic book,[122] and from a ring.[123] We shall study these functions individually. For example, the function of transporting the hero to the Thrice-Tenth Kingdom will be the subject of a special chapter.

Therefore, let us classify the magical items in a different way: we shall not analyze them based on the groups of items as such or according to their function but by their common origin, as far as the materials allow.

16. Claws, Hair, Pelts, and Teeth

Magic items not only are morphologically akin to magical helpers but also have the same origin. For example, many magic items are in fact parts of an animal's body: pelts, pieces of hair, teeth, and so on. We know that during initiation the young man receives power over animals, and this is expressed externally by giving him part of the animal. From then on, the young man carries it with him in a little bag, or he eats it, or these parts are rubbed into him. Therefore, we must also include ointments in this category: they too are of animal origin, as can be easily seen in the wondertale.

More often, however, part of the animal is placed in a person's hands and serves as the means of power over an animal. This happens even when acquisition of the helper occurs individually. The Arapaho go for this purpose to the top of a mountain. "After two, three, or a maximum of seven days, a guardian spirit appears before the man. Usually it is a small animal in a human form; when it leaves, however, it regains its animal form."[124] The pelt of such an animal is worn after that. From these and similar examples, we conclude that animal parts constitute the oldest form of magic items. The significance of such a gift is preserved with utmost clarity in the wondertale: hairs from the tail of a horse give power over the horse. The same applies to birds: "And then the main bird gets up and gives him a little feather from its head: 'Keep this piece of hair and hide it. If any trouble befalls you, just take out this piece of hair, shift it from one hand to another, and we will help you in every-thing.'"[125] The hero gets a pike bone. At a critical moment, the pike hides him in its nest or swallows him; the hero turns into a pike.[126] Finist the Bright Falcon gives the maiden a feather from its wing: "Wave it to the right side, and instantly all that your heart desires will appear in front of you."[127] The formula "all that your heart desires" is, of course, a late replacement of other older and more precise desires. These desires were concentrated around the animal itself, around the animal as game. This comes through quite clearly in the American myths. "He saw a man sit-ting on a high bank. His legs were hanging over the cliff. He had two round rattles. He sang and struck the rattles against the ground. Then the buffalo came in strings on each side of him and fell over the bank and were killed."[128] It is known that rattles were usually made in the form of an animal, most often a bird. Thus, here too we find the phenomenon that it is not necessary to be the master of a strong animal in order to have power over animals. In principle, a raven can bestow a good hunt of buffalo. Such belief exists among many nations, including those that do not have a rite of initiation. Such a belief also exists among the Vogul hunters. Zelenin writes, "According to Vogul belief, if a person carries with him the muzzle of a fox, a sable, or an ermine, then everything will turn out well for him."[129]

If our observation is correct and there is no necessary link between the animal helper (the subject of assistance) and the hunted animals (the object of assistance), then any animal and any item can serve as helper. This means that the discrepancy between the helper and its function and the detachment of functions from individual animals or items that cre-ates the impression of fantasy is not just a technique of poetic art: it is also historically justified in primordial thinking. When Frazer describes the healer's bags that play a role during the initiation rite, he notes, "The bag is made of the skin of an animal (such as the otter, wild cat, snake, bear, raccoon, wolf, owl, weasel), of which it roughly preserves the shape. Each member of the society has one of these bags, in which he keeps the odds and ends that make up his 'medicine' or charms."[130] These talismans and amulets, which are actually linked to animals, are the prototypes of our "magic gifts"; among them, various kinds of sacks, bags, wallets, little boxes, and so on form a special class. From these bags and caskets, the spirit-helpers appear. This brings us to the items (not only of animal origin) from which spirits appear. But before we turn to these items, we must explore items that we can show originated as tools.

17. *Items That Are Tools*

Everything said so far demonstrates a remarkable feature of primitive thought. It seems that the main role in hunting was not occupied by the instrument—not arrows, nets, snares, or traps. The main thing was magical power and the ability to attract animals. If an animal was killed, it was not because the shooter was dexterous or the arrow was good. It was because the hunter knew the spell that brought the animal under his arrow—because he had magical power over it in the form of a bag of hair or the like. The function of tools at that time was experienced as something secondary. Engels notes, "These various false conceptions of nature, of man's own being, of spirits, magic forces, etc., have for the most part only a negative economic basis; but the low economic development of the prehistoric period is supplemented and also partially conditioned and even caused by the false conceptions of nature."[131] Here we have an example of such a misconception about nature. As tools improve, it is possible to observe the following phenomenon: magical power, attributed first to the animal helper through a part of its body, is now transferred to an item. A person starts noticing his own effort less and the work of the tool more. Thus, we arrive at the belief that a tool works not as a result of a person's efforts (the more perfect the tool, the less effort required) but because of its inherent magical properties. The concept emerges of a tool that operates without a person and instead of a person. The tool now becomes sanctified. The sanctified tool, which is used in the same way as magical hair and so on, is a secondary and later layer in the history of magic items. The functions of the tool are the cause of its sanctification. This is stated very naively, but at the same time quite correctly, in the northern Russian manuscript of the sixteenth century "The Garden of Salvation," dedicated to the conversion of the Lapp people to Christianity: "If he sometimes kills the animal with a stone, he honors the stone, and if he strikes the game with a cudgel, he worships the cudgel."[132] This purely hunting belief still holds in primitive agriculture: some American Natives "pray to their sticks, with which they dig roots."[133] The idea that an instrument acts not because of the worker's effort but by virtue of its inherent special abilities alone, as stated above, leads to the idea of tools that operate without humans. Such tools exist in hunting myths, and they have reached us through the wondertale. In a myth of American natives the Taulipang, the hero only thrusts his knife into the bush, and the knife begins to cut trees by itself. He strikes a tree with an ax, and the ax begins to cut the tree by itself.[134] An arrow, shot at random into the air, strikes birds on its own, and so on.[135]

In wondertales, an ax carves a ship by itself[136] or chops wood,[137] and buckets bring water on their own. Interestingly, the ancient connection to an animal is not yet lost in this particular tale:[138] it is performed according to the pike's command. But this connection is not obligatory in tales. A cudgel strikes enemies on its own and takes them captive; with the help of the broom and the cane "it is possible to overcome anything."[139] Here the connection has already been lost.

18. Items That Conjure Spirits

The material introduced here will enable us to understand better those items used in summoning spirits. Such items can be of animal origin (horsehair) as well as tools (a club) and a whole series of other items (a ring).

The above cases show how objects, especially tools, were once perceived. Power dwells within them. But power is an abstract concept. There are no means for expressing the concept of power in language and in the thinking process. Nevertheless, the process of abstraction still goes on, but this abstracted notion is incorporated in—or, more precisely, expressed as—a living being. This is evident in the hair that summons the horse. The power is intrinsic to the animal as a whole and to all its parts. The hair contains the same power as the whole animal—that is, a horse exists in its hair just as it exists in the bridle or as the whole animal exists in a bone. Expressing power as an invisible being is a further step toward creation of the concept of power, toward the loss of an image and its replacement with a concept. This is how a concept of rings and other items that help to summon a spirit are created. Here we see a higher stage than the worship of a tool. Power is detached from the item and reattached, but to any item that externally has no characteristics of this power. This is the very same "magic object."

However, up to this point we have been discussing these objects as if they were the property not of wondertales but of practices. Did such items really exist in everyday practice? Indeed they did exist and were used, and we believe this phenomenon to be fairly well known, such that we need not dwell on it here. These are the so-called fetishes, amulets, talismans, and so on. In comparative ethnography, this topic still awaits its researcher. The forms and methods of use of these items are sometimes exactly the same as in wondertales. Let us at least point to the tribe that knows "rings that have the ability to connect the person who wears them with certain spirits."[140] Here too, then, the wondertale contains echoes of the past.

19. *The Tinderbox*

Among the items that are able to summon a helper, a special place is occupied by the tinderbox, which most often summons a horse. Wondertales usually feature a flint and steel, sometimes in combination with strands of hair. The hair strands are ignited to summon the horse. The fact that the tinderbox is almost unchangingly (though not exclusively) linked to the horse can be explained by its fiery nature.

The intrinsic magical power of items is manifested most vividly and powerfully in the tinderbox. Flint and steel apparently replaced the more ancient form of the tinderbox when fire was obtained through friction. We have already seen the way Agni is summoned by rubbing two sticks together. The tinderbox, therefore, is in general a magic item used to summon spirits and not just the horse. For example, one Belarusian tale shows the hero in a forest hut finding a tobacco pouch in which there is no tobacco but instead a tinderbox. "a small flint and a piece of steel." "Let me try to strike it! This will prove useful for a traveler. He struck the flint with the steel, and twelve young men jumped out. 'What do you need from us?'"[141] In a German folktale, it is necessary to light a pipe to summon the spirit.[142] This explains Aladdin's lamp, and perhaps the fact that a magical ring must also sometimes be rubbed to make the spirit-helper appear.

20. *The Little Stick*

The stick, twig, and rod originate in completely different beliefs. The items we have discussed so far come from animals or tools. The stick was created as a result of human contact with earth and plants. The wonder-tale has failed to preserve only one circumstance: the twig is cut from a *live* tree, and then it can turn out to be magical, conveying the miraculous properties of fertility, abundance, and life to the person it touches. According to Wilhelm Mannhardt, at different times of year people, animals, and plants are struck or lashed with a green branch (i.e., with a little stick) to make them healthy and strong.[143] He cites many such cases, and they clearly show that here the life force of the plant is transferred to the one who is being struck. The same is attributed to roots and herbs.

In "The Sham Illness," the slain prince comes back to life with the help of a root, which was a gift from an old man. "They took the root, found the grave of Prince Ivan, dug it up, got him out, rubbed him with this root, turned him over three times, and Prince Ivan got up."[144] The power of the root is transferred to the person. In another tale a snake brings another snake back to life by placing a green leaf on it.[145] (See more on this in chap. 7.) This also explains why the "lively whip" brings a dead person back to life.[146]

21. Items That Grant Everlasting Abundance

We must add to everything noted above that not just any item or any kind of item can be magical, only those acquired in a certain manner. While the initiation rite existed, this was an item received from the elders. In the wondertale, it is an item given by the dead father, by Yaga, a grateful dead person whom the hero buried, master animals, and so on. In short, an object is magical if it comes "from over there," which for an earlier stage meant "out of the woods" in the broad sense of the word; later it meant an item brought from another world. In the wondertale, it is brought from the Thrice-Tenth Kingdom. Not every type of water revives the dead; only water carried by a bird from the Thrice-Tenth Kingdom brings the dead back to life. This shows that there is a group of items whose magic power is based on the fact that they come from the kingdom of the dead. And this includes water that restores life or sight, apples that give youth, tablecloths that provide everlasting food and abundance, and so on. For now, let us merely take note of this fact. It can be explained only once the Thrice-Tenth Kingdom and its properties have been examined (see chap. 8).

22. Living and Dead Water and Weak and Strong Water

Among these items, special attention must be given to living and dead water and its variant, strong and weak water. Living and dead water are not opposed but rather complement each other. "He sprinkled Prince Ivan with the dead water, and his body grew back together. He sprinkled him with the living water, and Prince Ivan got up."[147] This is the canonical formula for applying this water.

This raises two questions. First, where does the water come from? And second, why is this water twofold? Why not just sprinkle the dead person with the living water, as in some rare cases actually happens?

To answer this question, we shall look at some of the materials relating to the Greeks' belief in the afterlife. The antique concepts that ancient Greeks linked with belief in the afterlife were apparently often connected to the idea of two kinds of water in the underworld, as is demonstrated, for example, by the south Italic tablets. Thus, the Petelia Gold Tablet,[148] which was placed with a body in the coffin, tells the soul of the deceased that in the house of Hades it will see two different water sources: one on the left, the other on the right. A white cypress grows near the first, but it is not the spring that the soul should approach. The tablet tells the soul to turn to the right, where refreshing water is flowing from the pond of Mnemosyne and around which guardians are standing. The soul should address them and say, "I'm suffering from thirst! Let me drink my fill!"

Let us look closely at this text. It too mentions two waters. One is not guarded and does not present any value for the dead person. The other, by contrast, is guarded very carefully, and before the dead man can receive it he is questioned. What kind of water is this? In the text, it is not called either living or dead. But it is of great value for the deceased. It is water for the dead or, in other words, "dead" water. We can assume that this water soothes the deceased, that it brings him final death or the right to stay in the realm of Hades.

But then what is the role of the other water, which is on the left and guarded by no one? This text does not provide a clear answer. We can guess, based on existing parallels, that this is the "water of life." It is for those dead people who do not enter Hades but return from there. This water has no effect before one enters Hades and therefore is not guarded. This is evident from the Babylonian catabasis, the descent into the underworld, of the goddess Ishtar. As Alfred Jeremias writes, "She is released back after the gatekeeper is forced to sprinkle her with the water of life."[149] If the conjectures made here are correct, this explains why the hero is first sprinkled with dead water and then with living water. The dead water "finishes him off," turns him completely into a dead man. It is kind of a funeral ceremony corresponding to sprinkling with soil. Only now is he a genuine dead man as opposed to a creature that hovers between two worlds and can come back as a vampire. And only now, after sprinkling with the dead water, will the living water work.

If these assumptions are correct, then they throw some light onto "strong" and "weak" water. These waters are on the right and left hands of the visitor, respectively. They are found in the cellar of Yaga or of the dragon.

Both Yaga and the dragon act as guardians of the entrance to the other kingdom. The dragon guards the river and bridge that lead to the Thrice-Tenth Kingdom. "The strong water is on the right hand of the bridge, and the weak on the left."[150] The hero switches these waters before the battle. The hero drinks the "strong" water, kills the dragon, and enters the other kingdom.

The analogy with the Greek material above is fairly complete. Yet it is not absolute. It does not provide a precise answer to the question of what type of water the hero drinks, living water (i.e., for the living) or dead water (i.e., for the dead). Here precision and the original meaning have been lost and erased. This question cannot be answered, along with the question of whether the hero is a dead man or a living creature. He is a living creature who trespasses into the realm of the dead as an insolent intruder and thief. Here too we have a violation of established order. The hero does not drink the water that he, as a dead man, is supposed to. And because of that he gains power; he steals it, just as he steals the rejuvenating apples and other marvelous items.

I think, therefore, that "living and dead water" and "weak and strong water" are one and the same. It is this water that the raven, flying away with two vials, brings back. A dead person who wants to get into the other world uses one type of water. A live person who wants to go there also uses only one type of water. A person who has set out on the path of death, but who wants to come back to life, uses both types of water.

These assumptions must remain hypothetical until other more precise materials are found. But in light of these assumptions, we can say that before Ishtar gets into the other world, she drinks one type of water, "dead" water, and that there is an omission here. When she comes back, she drinks the other water. We need only to add that this twofold water must be distinguished from "healing and living" water, which heals blindness and so on, and which is also obtained in the other world. We will discuss this water when we examine the Thrice-Tenth Kingdom.

23. *Little Dolls*

Thus, examining certain magic items leads us again to the same sphere to which the study of many other elements has also led us: the kingdom of the dead.

Examination of another item, which is on the border of magic helpers and magic items, specifically dolls, also leads us to the same sphere.

This type of doll is found in "Vasilisa the Beautiful."[151] There, a mother is dying: "On her deathbed the merchant's wife called her daughter, took a doll from under her blanket, gave it to the girl, and said: 'I am dying, and together with my maternal blessing, I leave you this doll. Keep it always with you and do not show it to anyone; and if trouble befalls you, give the doll food and ask her for advice.'" In their edited collection of Afanas'ev's tales, Mark Azadovskii, Nikolai Andreev, and Iurii Sokolov tend to view this motif as not belonging to folklore, since it has no folklore analogues. But first of all, analogues do exist. In "The Dirty

Girl," there are dolls accessed with the same formula as that in Afanas'ev: "Dear dolls, eat this and listen to my troubles."[152] In one northern tale, a mother on her deathbed tells her daughter, "I have four dolls in the trunk; when you need something, they will help you."[153] We note, incidentally, the fact that this doll must be fed. Second, dolls are extensively present in the beliefs of quite diverse peoples; moreover, their analogue to the wondertale is quite precise.

In order to understand this motif better, we shall cite another example. In "Prince Danila-the-Talker," a girl who is running from a pursuer gradually sinks into the ground (i.e., goes down to the underworld) and in her place leaves four dolls that respond to the pursuer in her voice.[154] In this example a doll serves as a substitute for the person who passed underground.

This is exactly the role the doll played in the beliefs of many peoples. "It is known that Ostiaks, Goldis, Gilyaks, Orochis, Chinese and, in Europe, Mari, Chuvash, and many other nations used to make a 'wooden idol' or a doll in memory of a deceased family member, considering it the repository of the soul of the deceased. They fed this figure with everything that they ate themselves and in general took care of it, as if it were a living being."[155] This belief is not peculiar to Siberia or Europe. In Africa, among the Eime, when a wife dies and the husband marries a second time, he keeps a doll in his hut "that represents the first wife in the other world. She is treated with all sorts of honors, so that the wife in the other world will not be jealous of the wife in this world."[156] In former Dutch New Guinea, after a death a figure is carved, with whose help they make prophesies. Frazer describes in detail how the soul of a sick person is lured into a doll.[157] In the same way that the doll contained the soul of a sick person, it can generally contain or represent the soul of the deceased. Relatives make a little doll and look after it; the deceased is reincarnated in this doll. They feed the doll at the table, put it to bed, and so on.[158]

In Egypt, this idea was reflected in the mortuary cult. Iurii Frantsev noted this phenomenon in his work on ancient Egyptian tales regarding high priests. "The use of figurines for magical purposes was widely known in ancient Egyptian magic practices. Just as in our wondertale the use of figurines is represented by a figurine helper, so this idea became widespread in the mortuary cult in the form of figurine helpers. the 'ushabti' or 'shawabti.'"[159] And although the figurines in question look like animals, the connection here is still undeniable, since the human ancestor replaced the animal ancestor. As Wiedemann points out, the "ushabti" figurines were in the form of little statues. They were put into the grave of the deceased and were called the "answers"; they were supposed to help in the world of the afterlife.[160]

All these materials show the types of beliefs and customs in which the doll originates. It represents the deceased. It needs to be fed, and then the deceased, reincarnated in this doll, will provide help.

24. Conclusion

The materials cited here show that magic items have different origins according to their content.

The main groups of items that emerge are the following: those of animal origins, those of vegetable origins, those that originate from tools, those of diverse structure that are endowed with either independent or personified powers, and those associated with the cult of the dead.

This is only a preliminary outline. A more detailed analysis might reveal other new groups, and items not considered here could be assigned to the outlined groups.

Such is the picture of the items according to their structure. As a historical category, on the whole they go back to the same roots as the helper, being only variants of the helper.

The entire course of the wondertale and the fact that magic items are provided by Yaga (or her equivalents) or the kings of animals, or are found in the forest, demonstrate the harmony and integrity of the wondertale and its historical value and significance.

Yaga and her gifts represent two sides of a single whole, and the wondertale has preserved this connection quite fully.

6

CROSSING OVER

1. Crossing Over as a Compositional Element

Crossing over to another realm is, as it were, the axis of the wondertale and at the same time its midpoint. Motivating crossing over through the search for a bride, a rare item (the firebird, for example), or through a merchant's journey, which will also provide an appropriate ending (when the bride or item is found), is enough to arrive at the most general, albeit colorless and simple, but still tangible compositional framework for plots of all kinds. The crossing is a highlighted, salient, and extremely vivid moment in the hero's spatial translocation.

Russian tales know quite a lot of forms of such crossing. Here we shall discuss only the typical and frequently recurring methods of crossing over. For example, the hero is transformed into an animal or a bird and runs or flies away; he climbs onto a bird, a horse, or a flying carpet; he puts on self-walking boots, is carried by a spirit or by the devil, travels on a ship, or crosses over on a flying boat; he crosses a river, also on a boat, but with the help of a carrier; he descends into an abyss or climbs mountains using ladders, ropes, thongs, chains, or claws; a tree grows up to the sky and the hero climbs it; or, finally, he is escorted by a guide, whom he follows.

There is no need for us to create a precise catalog of these forms, and there is also no need for a precise taxonomy and classification. The forms of crossing over merge, assimilate, and blend one into another. What is significant here is not the taxonomy but something else: all the types of crossing point to a single source of origin. They come from beliefs about the journey of the deceased to the other world, and some forms also fairly accurately reflect funeral rites.

2. Crossing Over in Animal Form

The wondertale hero sometimes *turns into an animal* in order to cross into another realm or while returning from it. Transforming into animals as a representation of death was discussed previously. Sometimes the hero flies away after a stay at Yaga's home. Before that the hero walked on the ground, but afterward he rises into the air. The transformation is associated with the beginning of movement through the air. The hero changes form only at the moment when he learns about the Thrice-Tenth Kingdom.

It is curious to see which specific animals the hero turns into. Here we can observe a certain shift. "Running through the mountains, they turned into ermines, and fleeing through the blue sea, they turned into gray ducks."[1] We see here animals that are not at all suited for swift crossing. A similar example: "Ivan the Russian Warrior mounted a beaver and went across the sea. He crossed it and got off the beaver."[2] The choice of these animals reveals the origin of this image in hunting and trading game. The figure of the bird appears most often in this context and in general more than any other figures. "The Storm Warrior struck the ground, turned into an eagle, and flew into the palace."[3] A multitude of examples like this may be cited. We shall not repeat here what was said previously about the bird and about its replacement by the horse. The concept of the bird is surely one of the most ancient. But with the introduction of riding animals, the crossing function passes to them, though birds also serve as riding animals: people in tales sit astride them. As Nikolai Marr demonstrates on the basis of linguistic materials, the oldest riding animal in Europe was the deer. These materials were subsequently confirmed by archaeological excavations. The wondertale too has preserved the deer. "Moving a mile away, he turned into a swift deer and ran quickly as an arrow released from a bow. He ran and ran, got tired and turned from a deer to a hare, and sprinted, as a hare, at full speed. He ran and ran, wore out his legs, and turned from a hare to a little golden-headed bird. He began flying even faster. He flew and flew, and in one and a half days he made it to the kingdom where Princess Maria was."[4] It is distinctive that the deer occurs in threefold expression along with the more archaic bird and hare in a single whole. With the advent of the horse, the totemic tradition of transformation ends and something new begins: the animal is mounted and ridden. But on the one hand, it is said occasionally of the hero that he "turned into a horse and ran to the yard of Elena the

Beautiful"[5]—that is, the old forms of employing magic are transferred to the new animal; and on the other hand, the new forms of employing animals (horseback riding), as pointed out above, are transferred to the earlier animal: people sit astride a bird.

3. Sewn into an Animal Skin

The materials listed above may not entirely convince one that the hero's crossing to distant lands originated in the idea of a dead person's passing into another realm. Other forms of this motif leave no doubt.

Another form of crossing is quite common in wondertales: rather than turn into an animal, the hero sews himself inside its skin or climbs into its dead body. A bird picks him up and carries him away. Variations on this motif are quite diverse. In order to lift his worker up to the golden mountain, "the merchant took out a knife, killed a puny nag, emptied all its guts, placed the lad in the horse's belly, put a shovel inside, and stitched it up, while he himself hid in the bushes. Suddenly black ravens with iron noses flew in. They grabbed the carrion, took it to the mountain, and started pecking at it. They ate up the horse and were about to get to the merchant's son."[6] "An eagle came flying, rolled him in a raw skin, and lifted him up to a golden mountain."[7] In this example, we see that the hero not only gets into the animal's corpse but is also wrapped in its skin. In another tale, Ivan happens to be in a pit where some carrion is dumped. "How could he get out? He saw a big bird taking cattle out of the pit. There was a dead cow that had been dumped some time ago. So he tied himself to it. The bird swooped down, grabbed the cow, and carried it out of the pit. It settled on a pine tree, and Prince Ivan was hanging there, as he could not untie himself."[8]

If we compare this to the previous form of crossing, we easily reach the conclusion that this form came later, replacing the transformation. The old and most ancient animal that serves to cross, the bird, is still not forgotten; it performs the role of the carrier. But at the same time, we already see a horse, a cow, and a bull appearing in this motif.

This assumption is confirmed by data. Wearing an animal skin is found in initiation rites and symbolizes consubstantiality with the animal. Boys who were to be initiated danced dressed in the skins of wolves, bears, or buffalo, mimicking their movements and acting as if they were the totem animal.[9]

The same idea manifests itself in burial rites and in the myths of hunting peoples. According to Shternberg, "Since after his death a man turns into his totem animal, naturally this is reflected in the funeral ceremonies too: the deceased is wrapped in a skin of the animal that served as his totem."[10] Thus, among the Owyhee, whose totem is a buffalo, corpses were sewn inside buffalo skins.[11] Nansen observes this custom among the Eskimos. "Often the legs [of the corpse] are bent up to the buttocks, and in this position they are sewn inside an animal skin."[12] Nansen explains this custom with the idea that they want the corpse to occupy as little space as possible in the grave. This would explain binding up the legs, but it does not explain sewing someone inside an animal skin. Rasmussen points out that the Eskimos throw the corpses sewn inside animal skins into the sea.[13] Therefore, the sewing inside of a skin is not necessarily linked to a pit, as Nansen believes. Nansen also does not mention what kind of animal is taken. The same custom of sewing someone inside a skin is observed among the Chukchi.

A corresponding motif exists in myths, and it is quite clear there that putting on an animal skin or getting inside it represents a form of consubstantiality. Most often we see a bird in these cases. For example, a hero catches an eagle. "He shook it so hard that all its bones and flesh fell out. . . . Then he put on the skin of the eagle and flew into the sky to the realm of the dead."[14] Such myths are very common in America. Yehl, the god of the Tlingit tribe, kills a magpie, puts on her feathers, and flies into the sky, where he sets the sun back in its place.[15] The shamanic costume, which often represents a bird, can also be interpreted correspondingly.

This custom is much more prevalent among peoples who practice animal husbandry. Corpses are sewn inside the skins of bulls or cows there, as in the wondertale. Many examples can be found in Africa. According to Johannes Raum, among the Wachagga, "if someone dies, then a person who owns cattle slaughters one of the cows and covers the corpse with its skin."[16] Friedrich Fülleborn writes, "In the Wahehe tribe the deceased was sewn inside the animal skin on which he died." He also notes, "Lamentation for the dead was supposed to last eight days. But since in this hot country a corpse very soon begins to give off a strong odor, it would be sewn inside the skin of an ox; when that no longer helped—then inside a second, third, fourth, and fifth."[17] The fallacy of such a mechanical and rationalized explanation becomes clear from comparison with other cases. Frobenius reports that when a great king died, according to the custom of his fathers, he was sewn inside a cow's skin and set afloat in a lake for three days.

The peoples who produce this custom generally do not suggest any motivation for it. Researchers try to find the motivations on their own. It is supposedly done to prevent odor or to save space in the grave. All these attributed motivations are wrong, of course: the explanation must be sought in the history of the custom, not in its forms.

The peoples we have discussed here are those who live by raising cattle. The Hindu of the times of the Vedas were people of this type, and indeed, we find the same custom there, which we shall turn to now.

India has reached a very high stage of culture, but the old custom of sewing corpses inside animal skins has been preserved there. However, since corpses are also burned, sewing them inside animal skins acquires a special motivation. Before burning the corpse, it is surrounded or covered with the equivalent parts of the cow (i.e., they put a head on the corpse's head, etc.), or they burn a male goat along with the corpse. The god of fire, Agni, carries the deceased away in the flames.[18] So how is this custom motivated? It is done so that Agni will burn, which means eat, the animal not the person. The *Rigveda* says, "Shield thee with flesh against the flames of Agni, encompass thee about with fat and marrow."[19] This motivation is obviously a relatively recent one. German scholars have a special term for the cow whose skin is laid on the corpse: *Umlegetier*, or "an animal for overlaying." The corpse is covered with an animal skin with the hairy side outward, and the head, legs, and tail are still attached.

It is curious that this rite or custom can also be found in the agricultural cultures of antiquity but only in the form of relics.

In Egypt, in ancient times, corpses were buried wrapped in animal skins. Traces of such burials have been found in excavations.[20] Budge considers this the first attempt at mummification. Perhaps this is the case, but for us it is at the same time the last stage of previous forms of burial. Later, when mummification has developed, the wrapping in animal skin takes on a different form while still very clearly preserving the original meaning of consubstantiality. It is no longer the deceased who is wrapped in animal skin but the priest conducting the ceremony. According to Budge, "Before he lay down on his bed, he wrapped himself in the skin of a bull or cow, because he intended the deceased to be reborn through that act, and it was believed that 'passing through' the skin of a bull vicariously a man obtained the gift of new birth."[21] It was assumed that the gods did the same. For example, Anubis crawled through the skin of Osiris. We see here that the animal has become a god and that sewing the deceased inside its skin gave the deceased consubstantiality with it and immortality. The same idea is also reflected in sacrifices. "Now, the skin was also typical of the sacrifice, and through passage through it a man with the strength and life of the victim, and made him the representative of the animal slain. As the bull was a symbol of Osiris, who was himself 'Bull of Amenti,' so was the man who had put on his skin a representative of Osiris."[22]

It seems that the concept of movement is absent here. The skin served, as Alexandre Moret puts it, as a "bloody shroud."[23]

This is because the Egyptians imagined the trip of the deceased not as a flight but mainly in the form of a journey by boat, which for Egyptians was the most natural way of traveling. The role of the bull, however, as an escort to the other world is also not alien to Egypt.

Moret notes, "The bull, who is the associate of Seth and the rival of Osiris, is offered as a sacrifice. After he is killed, he accompanies Osiris to the sky, carrying him on his back; he gives his skin so that a sail can be made from it for the divine boat that carries one over to paradise." The skin has transformed into a sail.[24]

In Greece, putting animal skins on corpses gave way to clothing the gods in animal skins. Heracles was mentioned previously. The image of Dionysus in which he wears the skin of a bull with the horned head hanging down is also known. The animals that accompany the deceased to the other world are now often imagined only as food for the deceased; we have seen the initial introduction of that idea in India. The concept of a human-animal is replaced by the person plus the animal as food or, as Paul Stengel believes, as a servant in the other world. "The edible animals are skinned, and a corpse is placed in their fat tissue, while the corpse of the animal is burned along with jars of honey and oil in a spot very close to the deceased."[25] Horses, however, are not skinned; they have to follow the deceased to serve him in Hades.

All these materials clearly indicate that funeral rites are the source of the motif of a hero who gets into the body of an animal or is sewn inside one. These funeral customs passed through the stage of cattle breeding, but prior to that they reflected the idea of consubstantiality with the animal after death.

4. The Bird

Sewing someone into an animal skin is the beginning of the decline of the early belief in consubstantiality. The same decline is reflected in the motif in which the hero neither transforms into an animal nor sews himself in one but instead uses one for riding. Here we can in addition observe that initially characters ride on animals that once represented the deceased— that is, on birds. Riding animals appear later. We read in a wondertale, "'Sit on my wings; I'll carry you to my country. . . .' The merchant sat on the eagle's wings, and the eagle rushed to the blue sea and rose up very high."[26] In a variant of this tale, the eagle asks the hero three times what he sees beneath them. "The man sat down on the eagle; the eagle soared and flew toward the blue sea. He flew away from the shore and asked the man, 'Look and tell me, what is behind us, and what is in front of us; what is above us, and what is below us?'"[27] The man answers, "Behind us there is land, in front of us the sea, above us the sky, and below us water." The picture changes in the course of the flight.

These examples clearly demonstrate the connection between the image of the bird and the concept of distant space, in particular the sea. While sewing the deceased inside an animal skin, as we have seen, reaches its culmination among the nations of shepherds and herdsmen, the bird is characteristic of coastal inhabitants. For example, it is almost not found in Central Africa, but by contrast, it prevails in the Oceanic islands and among coastal inhabitants of America. Besides the bird or along with it, these peoples have boats, as we shall see. The kingdom of the dead is perceived there as not past forests and mountains and not beneath the earth but beyond the horizon. It is simultaneously the kingdom of the sun and the water. In the visual arts of these peoples, we see wooden images of birds in the form of boats. The deceased here is usually riding a bird. This belief, according to Frobenius, arose under the influence of riding in boats.

In the tale mentioned above, the hero travels to the Sea King; the image of the Sea King is often associated with the sun. In another version, Ivan acquires a Sea Lady and then sets off beyond Thrice-Nine Lands to where the sun sleeps; the Sun King yearns for his lost Sea Lady. Tales of this type are very handy for scholars of the Mythological School. They have wanted to see here a reflection of celestial phenomena. It is true that the Thrice-Tenth Kingdom is often (but not always) the kingdom of the sun. We shall see this below when we discuss this motif. But this is important not as a reflection of notions about the sky and its luminaries but as a reflection of the kingdom of the dead: the bird in particular typically delivers the deceased to this place. According to Wundt, "In Oceania and north-western America, the people's dominant view is that the souls of their ancestors or of recently deceased people live in certain birds. This view is directly connected in these places with a myth, according to which the soul of the deceased treats the sun as its future abiding-place."[28] It has long been known that the bird represents the soul of the deceased,[29] but sometimes researchers have quite vague notions of the origin of this belief. Wundt, for example, believes that the concept of the soul-bird came from the idea that when a corpse was burned the soul departed with the smoke. He writes, "The move of the soul into the smoke, which rises from the burned corpse into the sky, approaches another form of embodiment of the soul . . . namely, its transformation into fast-moving animals, especially birds and other flying creatures."[30] We, on the other hand, consider this idea the second stage of ideas about transformation that developed among seafaring peoples or inhabitants of the coasts.

There is no need to cite a great deal of data here. We shall mention only a few instances as illustrations. Frobenius's book about the outlook of primitive peoples dedicates a whole chapter to the bird. In Tahiti and Tonga, the concept of birds who carry away the soul still existed at the end of the nineteenth century. When a person dies, his soul is taken up by a bird. The bird, consequently, carries the soul to the realm of the other world. Birds that carry away the dead are found, for example, in Oceania (the hornbill), in Australia (the crow), and among the Nootka tribe (the raven). In Tahiti and Tonga people also believe that the bird waits for the soul of the deceased and swallows it. The same hornbill is found among the Dayaks. This bird quickly and confidently leads the souls of the deceased to the city of the dead.

This kind of belief is reflected in rituals and myths. Among the Dayaks, a chicken is tied onto the chest of the deceased. In Borneo, a chicken is sacrificed. In Sumatra, the coffin is sprayed with chicken's blood.[31]

The same idea exists in the myths of Oceania. Maui, who wants to acquire fire, flies on the back of a pigeon to the underworld. The Micronesian tale-myth states, "Take some food with you inside a bird, put a few mats in it, fly, and look for your wife."[32]

In the mythology of northwestern America, we have the figure of Yehl. "Yehl, above all things, is the bird of the dead, the carrier of souls. He invites the spirits of the deceased. He calls the others to mourn with him for the dead."[33]

The notion of the soul-bird or the soul carried away by a bird is preserved in Egypt, in Babylon, and in antiquity, and all these forms are close to the wondertale and clarify it. In Egypt crossing over to another realm takes several forms; like Egyptian beliefs in general, they have no unity or consistency. The bodies of dead kings remain in the pyramids, says Moret, "while their souls, after finding the blessed paths that lead to heaven, move toward the gods; on their way they at times climb the stairway that rises at the edge of the sky, while at other times they cross in a barge, which gloomy Charon rows, and at still others they soar or ascend on the wings of Thoth, the sacred ibis."[34] Examination of the stairs and barge is yet to come; here we are interested in the bird. Flying on a bird is found in the *Book of the Dead*: "I have risen, I have risen like the mighty hawk [of gold] that cometh forth from his egg; I fly and I alight like the hawk which hath a back four cubits wide, and the wings of which are like unto the mother-of-emerald of the south."[35]

This concept is also known in Babylonia. In the epic poem *Gilgamesh*, Eabani dreams that he is summoned to the underworld (Irkalla), "where they wear clothes made of feathers, like birds."[36] Thus, in Babylon, the deceased were perceived as birdlike creatures. A similar idea existed in Greece.[37] For example, a story by pseudo-Callisthenes relates that an eagle soared up when Alexander died. Upon the death of the Cynic Peregrinus Proteus, an earthquake supposedly occurred, and an eagle flew up to the sky, exclaiming in a human voice, "I have left the earth and I am ascending to Olympus."[38] This belief is also reflected in such works as Artemidorus's *Oneirocritica* (dream interpretation). There, every bird that appears in a dream is interpreted as a person and every dreamed flight as the desire of one's soul to discard its earthly shell and fly to Elysium in the form of the soul-bird.[39] In Rome, when an emperor died an eagle was released to carry the soul of the ruler to heaven.[40]

Finally, in Christianity we have the last remnants of this belief in the image of winged angels who carry away the soul.

5. On Horseback

There is no doubt that the horse is of more recent origin than the bird. We described previously how the horse is assimilated with the bird and how the winged horse is in fact a bird-horse. By the time humans began to domesticate the horse, evidently, the idea of transforming into an animal must have already receded into the background, although wondertales exhibit isolated cases of transformation into a horse. The horse appears in rites: it is buried along with the deceased as a riding animal. Malten noticed this shift in ancient Greece. The dead person in the Hellenic (as in the Austro-Germanic) faith appears simultaneously in the form (*Erscheinungsform*) of a horse but also in the form of a rider or the horse's owner. We have already discussed the horse. Thus, the hero's flying on a horse represents another phase of the same idea as riding on a bird: crossing over to the kingdom of the dead. This point is so obvious that we can refrain from mentioning more material here, referring to the already cited works of Anuchin, Negelein, Malten, and others.

6. On a Ship

If the horse does not require special analysis in its capacity as a carrier, since its overall figure was discussed above, we still have not touched on the boat, on the other hand, and therefore we shall dwell on it here in greater detail. The boat or ship in which the hero sets off for his journey is also not quite an ordinary ship. It is a flying ship. "You will see in front of you a ready made ship; board it and fly wherever you need to."[41] "Suddenly the boat went up in the air, and in a flash, like an arrow released, brought them to a high rocky mountain."[42] Along with this, we also find ordinary ships or boats, like the boat of the seven Simeons already discussed.

Previously, in studying the bird, we mentioned that the flying ship also evolved from the bird. The horse had wings transferred to it, while the ship took on only the ability to pass through the air. According to Otto Waser, "One can hardly find a large part of the Earth's population where there is no belief in the ship of souls."[43] I think this is incorrect. While the horse dominates in India, in the Asian steppe, and among the Scythians, the Greeks, the Germans, the Slavs, and so on, the boat is prevalent in the island peoples of Oceania; in Europe, the classic region with a cult

of the boat of the dead, or rather of burial in a boat, is represented by
Scandinavia.

Throughout Oceania, boats are featured in burials in the most varied
ways. They were hung on trees,[44] placed on a special high platform,[45]
simply lowered into the water, or burned. In all these cases, especially
in burning and in exposure on high platforms, the idea of the deceased
traveling through the air clearly filters through.

These representations clearly originate in the image of the bird, even
if we did not know this from the carvings that represent boats in bird
form and depict the "ship of souls." Frobenius states that "a boat in the
shape of a bird carries the soul to the other world." And if on Timor a
boat, upon its arrival to other world, is depicted in gold, this means the
dead person has arrived in the kingdom of the sun.

In Egypt, the boat has merged with the sun. There the boat of the
dead travels over the water along with the sun.[46] In Babylon, we also have
crossing over the sea, as known in the myth of Gilgamesh.

In Greece, there is no such ceremony as burying in a boat. The Greeks,
as A. V. Boldyrev believes, "were never natural-born seafarers." The
Greeks were afraid of the sea. "The ship that set out over the waves of this
sea could always gradually penetrate into these fairy-tale places without
noticing it, and an ordinary sailing trip could easily turn into a voyage in
the kingdoms beyond the grave."[47] For the Greeks, the sea was an alien
element, and burial in a boat did not seem tempting. This contrasts with
the Scandinavians' views where, as Anuchin has shown, boat burials assumed solemn forms that are reflected in the *Edda*.

There are, however, representations in Greece of traveling across a
river with the grim ferryman Charon, also reflected in the folktale. Russian wondertales have retained one particular feature: the old man warns
the hero, "On your way there will be three wide rivers, and there are three
ferries on these rivers. On the first ferry they will cut your right hand, on
the second, your left leg, and on the third, they will remove your head."[48]
If we discard the tripling, we have here the concept of cutting off a hand
during transportation over the river.[49] We encountered cutting off a hand
as a typical element during initiation above. By means of this severing,
the ferryman exposes himself as the ferryman of death.

7. Up a Tree

The motif of a tree, by which it is possible to reach the sky, has similar
origins. "He took a bag and started climbing the oak. He climbed and
climbed and finally reached the sky."[50] Here Russian tales reflect a widespread view that two worlds (and sometimes three: the underground, the
terrestrial, and the celestial) are connected through the tree. Chapter VII

of Shternberg's work on the cult of the eagle of the Siberian peoples is dedicated to this view. For us the most interesting thing is that the idea of a tree-mediator is associated with the notion of a bird. Among the Yakuts each shaman has a "shaman tree" or high pole with slats that look like a staircase and with an image of an eagle at the top. This tree is linked to the ceremony that sanctifies the shaman. Shternberg writes,

> It is striking that the central moment of initiation as a shaman among the Buryat is climbing up a specially erected tree, during which his supreme union with the deities takes place through his marriage to a celestial maiden. . . . The same kind of tree, but smaller, is erected in his yurt. On the breastplate of the Oroch shaman three worlds are depicted: the upper, middle, and lower. The world tree, a larch, is pictured on it, and the shaman climbs this tree to the upper world. If the shaman were to fall from this tree, this would entail the destruction of the whole world.[51]

Shternberg studies the name of this tree among different Siberian peoples and concludes that it means "path." All these materials are extremely interesting, but Shternberg reaches a conclusion that must be considered highly questionable. He traces the shamanic tree back to the notion of the sacred tree in India, "where each Buddha, and even earlier, probably every spiritually-inspired person, like every shaman in Siberia, had his own special tree, with which his strength was connected, called *bodhitaru*, the tree of wisdom and witchcraft."[52] Climbing a tree to the sky, a marriage with the daughter of the sun, or the ascension of the first people from the underworld—such plots exist not only in Asia but in America as well.

Thus, it becomes clear that the tree has little connection to the cult of the dead, except for burial in trees or in the trunks of trees. But the tree-mediator is connected, on the one hand, to shamanic initiation and to the image of the bird; on the other hand, as Anuchin's materials show, it is connected to the boat and the woodblock in which they place the corpse. All these connections have not been studied by ethnographers. Specialized works about the tree by J. H. Philpot and Zelenin do not mention the tree as a mediator between the two worlds.[53] But for our purposes even these references are sufficient.

8. By Stairs or on Belts

The tree is closely associated to crossing via a ladder. Shternberg's materials, mentioned above, show that the shamanic tree takes the shape of a ladder. In one Russian wondertale, a pea grows up to the sky. "And a ladder appeared therefore climbing to this place."[54] The ladder serves not only for climbing to the sky but also for climbing a mountain. "And straightway a ladder appeared in the mountain."[55] For descending to the underworld, belts are used. "Then he came up with the idea of slaughtering his horses, skinning them, cutting the skin into belts, tying them together, weaving a basket, and going down there (i.e., to the underworld)."[56] We can easily recognize the basket, woven from rawhide belts from the horse, as a deformation of the animal skin in which the hero wraps himself. Climbing up the mountain can be accomplished in another somewhat unexpected way: the hero enters a cave, and "as soon as he entered, iron claws placed themselves on his hands and on his feet. And he began to climb the mountains."[57] Bird claws reveal the relationship of this motif too with the image of the bird.

Here we see a variety of forms assimilating one into another, related to lifting up and lowering down. All these forms are relatively recent and easily reveal their initial origins from other forms, particularly from animals. And even though gods who descend on a rope from heaven to earth or hell already appear at quite an early stage, the ladder appears in burial customs only in the stage corresponding to ancient Egypt. There, miniature ladders were found next to some mummies, which the souls could use to lower themselves and ascend to heaven.[58] This ladder is, of course, magical. It can be used only if one knows the magic formulas. This ladder is under the authority of Seth. "Seth appears too without any unfavorable reflection upon him in connection with the Sun-god and his group, and in harmony with this an old doctrine represents Seth as in charge of the ladder by which the dead may ascend to the Sun-god—the ladder up which he himself once climbed."[59] In the *Book of the Dead*, we read, "*Greetings, god's ladder! Stand up, Horus's [ladder]; stand up, [Seth's] ladder!*"[60]

These mechanical means of crossing over (ladders, belts, ropes, chains, hooks, etc.) represent a deformation of the earlier forms. This manner of crossing, just like the previous ones, indicates that notions of crossing into another world are reflected herein.

9. With the Assistance of a Guide

The same may be said when the hero is taken to the other world. Here we touch on a wide range of representations of the soul's guide. "The she-wolf ran forward, and the prince set off riding after her."[61] "Go up on the sea. You will meet a silver bird with a golden crest: follow it wherever it flies."[62] Again we see an animal type of guide, as in the other forms. By comparing the three cases—(1) the hero turns into a bird and flies away,[63] (2) the hero mounts a bird and flies away,[64] and (3) the hero sees a bird and follows it[65]—we observe a splitting, a doubling of the hero. Indeed, guiding the hero's journey is a recent form. It is lacking, for example, in American myths. Wherever the practice of individual shamanism has developed, the guide is the shaman. But he too uses means of movement that we already have seen. A Goldi shaman told Shternberg, "Different souls should be led in different ways: if the Goldi is a reindeer herder by origin, his soul should be carried by a reindeer, and if he is a dog breeder, then by dogs; some others must be carried by a boat."[66]

Wherever hunting ceases to play an economic role, the guide of souls is anthropomorphized but does not lose its original connection with the animal. At a later time in Egypt, for example, this guide was Osiris. "The Osiris of the gods goeth as leader through the Tuat (the underworld), he crasheth through the mountains, he bursteth through the rocks, he maketh glad the heart of every *Khu*."[67] But this is undoubtedly a later phenomenon. An earlier representation is the scarab beetle, into which the dead person sometimes transformed but which later became a guide. "I have come into the House of the King by means of the mantis (*ābit*) which led me hither."[68]

10. Conclusion

What conclusions can we draw from the forms that we have studied here? The first and fundamental conclusion is that all the means of crossing have the same origin: they reflect the idea of the deceased traveling to the underworld. The second is that the variation of forms can often be viewed as a layering of later forms atop earlier ones. Their shift is caused by the change in the forms of production. The oldest form is the totemic representation of human transformation into the totem animal. With the decline of totemism, these forms change. With the appearance of riding animals and the improvement of transportation, at first the forms of crossing begin to change (one rides on a bird), and later the animals change: the deer and horse emerge. The horse initially assimilates with the bird, as does the boat among peoples who did not have the horse; hybrid forms are created in both cases. The figure of the deceased splits into the carrier and the carried, or the guide and the guided. With the transition to agriculture, the guide becomes anthropomorphic and is deified, but his animal nature is still clear from certain rudiments and parallels. Even such forms as the ladder, the tree, and the belt reveal their original animal forms through comparison.

7

AT THE RIVER OF FIRE

I. The Dragon in the Wondertale[1]

1. The Form of the Dragon

The focus of this chapter will be on the dragon's image. We shall concentrate on the motif of battling the dragon. Anyone even superficially familiar with materials on the dragon knows that it is one of the most complex and unresolved figures in global folklore and religion. The figure of the dragon and his role in the wondertale are composed of several details, each of which must be accounted for. No detail, however, is clear without reference to the whole, while the whole, in turn, is composed of details. Methods of presentation vary. We shall proceed as follows: First, we present the wondertale material and give the characteristics of the dragon in tales without drawing on any comparative material. Only after this shall we introduce the comparative material but in a different order, first considering the most ancient, archaic correspondences and then the newer and later ones.

How then does the creator of or listener to a wondertale imagine the dragon? It turns out that the dragon is never described—not in an authentic Russian folktale. We know what the dragon looks like, but this knowledge does not come from the tales themselves. If we wish to draw the dragon based only on materials from tales, it would be difficult to do so. However, some external features of the dragon's image may still be sketched.

First, the dragon is always a creature with several heads. The number of heads varies. Most often there are three, six, nine, or twelve, but occasionally there are five or seven. This is the main permanent and indispensable feature. All other features are mentioned only occasionally and sometimes are not mentioned at all; for example, it is not always mentioned that the dragon is a flying creature. He flies through the air: "All of a sudden they see: less than a mile from them, a dragon is flying."[2] "The dragon came flying and began to hover over the princess."[3] Even in such descriptions of the dragon's flight, his wings are almost never mentioned, as if he soars through the air without them. Nor is his body described.

We do not know whether his skin is scaly, smooth, or covered with fur. His clawed feet and long tail with a tip—favorite details of Lubki prints—are, as a rule, absent in folktales.[4] At times the flight of the dragon recalls the flight of Yaga: "A strong storm is rising; thunder growls, the earth trembles, and the dense forest bends down: the three-headed dragon is flying."[5] Wings are mentioned only once in Afanas'ev's entire collection, when the dragon is said to carry away the princess "on his fiery wings."[6]

The absence of descriptive details conceivably indicates that the storyteller does not entirely understand the image of the dragon. Sometimes the dragon is assimilated with the figure of the hero and is represented as a rider. In these cases, the horse usually stumbles beneath the dragon.

The dragon is a fiery creature: "A fierce dragon flies towards him, scorching with its fire and threatening death."[7] Once again, we do not know how this fire erupts. We know in detail, for example, about the horse's fire, that sparks and smoke come out of its nostrils and ears. When it comes to the dragon, however, we have no such information. Nevertheless, we can say that the dragon's connection with fire is a constant element: "The dragon scorches with its flame and reaves with its claws."[8] The dragon carries this fire inside and belches it: "At that moment the dragon emitted fiery flames; it wanted to burn the prince."[9] "I'll burn your kingdom with fire and scatter the ashes."[10] This is a constant threat formula for the dragon. In one case, a fiery king correlates to the dragon: "You feel the blazing fire within thirty miles of his kingdom."[11]

2. The Link to Water in the Wondertale

But there is yet another natural element with which the dragon is associated. This element is water. He is not only a fire king but also a king of water. These two traits are not mutually exclusive; rather, they are often connected. For example, the Water King sends a letter, kept closed with three black seals, and demands the Princess Martha. He threatens to "destroy all the people and burn the whole kingdom by fire."[12] Here the elements of water and fire clearly do not exclude each other. The dragon's water attribute is seen even in his name. He is the "Black Sea dragon." He resides in water. When he rises out of it, the water behind him also rises: "Then the duck quacked, the shore rattled, the sea started shaking, the sea began to heave—the Mosalsk inlet monster was creeping forth."[13] "Suddenly the dragon emerged, and the water gushed for three yards behind him."[14] In one tale the dragon sleeps on a rock in the sea. He snores, "and when he snores, the wave rolls forward seven miles."[15]

3. The Link to Mountains

The dragon has yet another name: he is "the Mountain Dragon" (Zmei-Gorynych).[16] He dwells in the mountains. This dwelling place does not, however, prevent him from also being a sea monster. "Suddenly it grew cloudy, the wind rustled, and the sea roiled: the dragon came out of the sea and went up the mountain."[17] Although the phrase "up the mountain" can mean simply "up to the shore," it is still impossible to posit two types of dragon—a mountain one and a water one. Sometimes he dwells in the mountains, but when the hero approaches him, he emerges from the water. "They ride for one year, they ride for two years and by now have passed three kingdoms on their way. They see high blue mountains, and between the mountains there are sandy steppes: this is the land of the fierce dragon."[18] Residing in the mountains is a common feature of the dragon.

4. The Dragon Abductor

What, then, are the dragon's actions? The dragon is characterized mainly by two functions. First, he abducts women. The abduction typically occurs unexpectedly and lightning fast. In one tale, a king has three daughters who go for a walk in a beautiful garden. "The Black Sea dragon got into the habit of flying there. One day the king's daughters stayed a little late in the garden, looking at the flowers. The Black Sea dragon suddenly appeared and carried them away on his wings of fire."[19]

Still, the dragon is not the only abductor. Indeed, to understand the dragon fully, we must also examine other abductors who operate in exactly the same way. For example, Koshchei[20] the Deathless can appear as the abductor: "In a certain kingdom, in a certain land there once lived a king. This king had three sons, all of whom had come of age. But suddenly Kosh the Deathless carried off their mother."[21]

Occasionally the abductor is a bird: "At that time a firebird came flying. It grabbed their mother and carried her beyond thrice-nine lands, over thrice-nine seas into its own realm."[22]

The wind or whirlwind frequently appears in the function of ethereal abductor. However, a comparison of these cases reveals that behind the whirlwind there is usually a hidden dragon, Koshchei, or a bird. The whirlwind can be considered an abductor who has lost its animal, its dragon, or other form. In some tales the whirlwind abducts the princess, but when the hero searches for her, she turns out to be in the possession of the dragon.[23] This is stated explicitly in the following example: "In fact, it is not a whirlwind but a fierce dragon."[24] Expressions such as "Koshchei flew out the window as a terrible whirlwind" show the paths by which the animal image was lost.[25] "And suddenly there was a strong wind, sand rose up in a cloud, the child was ripped from the nurse's arms and carried away somewhere unknown."[26] Here we do not see an animal figure, but when the princess is found she is found in the eagle's domain.

Instances of devils, evil spirits, and the like appearing as abductors represent a further deformation influenced by modern religious beliefs contemporary to the storyteller.

5. The Dragon's Extortions

The dragon's functions are not limited to devouring or carrying away a maiden or entering her body in the form of an evil spirit and tormenting her—or entering her dead body and forcing her to devour living beings. Sometimes he arrives with threats, besieges the city, and demands a woman as tribute, either for marriage or to devour violently. This motif can be described succinctly as the dragon's extortions. This is a very common motif, and its characteristics are fairly uniform. Basically, the scheme boils down to the following: The hero finds himself in a foreign country. He notices that all the people there are "rather sad." He learns from random people that a dragon demands one maiden every year (or every month, etc.), and now it is the turn of the king's daughter. It must be emphasized that in these cases the dragon always appears as a water creature. The princess has already been taken to the sea. "He was told that the king had only one daughter—the beautiful princess Poliusha—and tomorrow she would be taken to the dragon to be eaten by him; in this kingdom each month they gave one girl to the seven-headed dragon. . . . Now came the turn of the king's daughter," and she is taken to the sea.[27]

6. The Dragon as Guardian of the Border

In these cases, the dragon resides near a river, often a river of fire. There is a bridge over the river, and it has a name: Currant Berry River. The bridge, moreover, is always made of viburnum (*kalina*). The hero lies in wait for the dragon under the bridge: "Just as midnight arrived, they went under the arrow-wood bridge on the fiery river."[28] The river represents a border. It is impossible to get across the bridge because the dragon guards it. One can cross the bridge only by first killing the dragon: "And they went on their way, and when they drove up to the painted bridge, which no one had ever safely crossed, they had to spend the night there."[29] Here Yaga comes to mind, for she is also a gatekeeper. Yaga guards the periphery, while the dragon guards the heart of the Thrice-Tenth Kingdom. Some of the accompanying imagery recalls Yaga in a particularly vivid way: "They came to the fiery river, a bridge lay across the river, and around the river there was a huge forest."[30] There is sometimes a hut near the river, but no one lives in it. The hero is not questioned there or offered any food. Nevertheless, it is sometimes assimilated to the hut of Yaga, and it sometimes stands on chicken legs. There is no fence; the bones are not planted on stakes but scattered all around: "They come to the Currant Berry River; all along the shore bones of men were scattered and piled up knee-high. They saw a hut, entered it, and found it empty. They decided to stop there for a while."[31] Only after the battle is it said that the hero "went by himself over the bridge to the other side."[32]

7. The Dragon-Devourer

This safeguarding role of the dragon is sometimes given special emphasis: "There runs a wide river, over the river there is an arrow-wood bridge, and under this bridge lives a twelve-headed dragon. He doesn't let any horsemen pass, nor anyone on foot, but devours them all."[33] The dragon's intentions are expressed much more sharply than Yaga's: the dragon's goal is to gobble up the hero, to eat him. "Bid farewell now to the wide world and get yourself into my throat; this way it will be easier on you."[34] "I will eat you up, bones and all." The dragon who holds the princess captive also seeks to swallow the hero, and the princess warns him about this: "He will eat you." Expressions such as "he wants to gobble him up" are repeated very often.[35] Even after the battle, this danger does not yet completely dissipate. On the contrary, it becomes especially threatening. After the dragon is killed, the tale introduces the dragon's mother or mother-in-law, whose sole function is to threaten to eat up the hero, and this threat is sometimes carried out. Thus, the figure of the dragon becomes doubled. What we see here is the devouring dragon as female. She pursues the hero and overtakes him; "a third she-dragon pursued him. She opened her jaws wide from the ground to the sky. . . . How could he be saved?" The hero throws three horses into her mouth, then three falcons and three Hortens (greyhounds). She is still gaining on him, so the hero throws two of his comrades into her jaws. Finally, he reaches the blacksmiths, who grab her by the tongue with hot pincers and thus save him.[36]

In another tale the hero throws three poods of salt into the she-dragon's mouth.[37] There is a tale in which a female dragon transforms into a huge sow and gobbles up two brothers along with their horses. The hero is saved once again by blacksmiths. They drag her by her tongue with pincers and whip her with rods. "The sow began imploring him, 'Stormy Warrior, please let my soul go free for repentance'. . . . 'And why did you eat up my brothers?' 'I will give your brothers back to you right now.' He grabbed her by the ears, the pig spat, and the two brothers with their horses leapt out of her mouth."[38]

8. The Danger of Sleep

There is one danger that the hero must be wary of when meeting with the dragon: that of falling asleep. We encountered this danger in his meeting with Yaga: "They walked and walked, and came into the deep and dense forest. As soon as they entered it, a strong sleepiness came upon them. Frolka-Siden' pulled a snuffbox out of his pocket, tapped on it, opened it, and shoved an armful of tobacco into his nose. Then he started to yell: 'Hey, brothers, let's not fall asleep, let's not start dreaming! Move on!'"[39] This sleep is a delusion. "The prince began to walk back and forth on the bridge, tapping his cane. A jug suddenly jumped in front of him and started to dance. He was staring at it, unable to take his eyes away, and fell into a deep sleep." A false hero falls asleep, while the true hero never does. "The Stormy Warrior spat and gagged on the jug, breaking it into small pieces."[40] In a tale recorded at a factory in the Onega region, the dragon's mother, who helps the heroes, tells them, "Now you set off on your journey. . . . Just do not go to sleep by the sea, otherwise my son will be flying there and will see the horses and you. And if you sleep, you will be defeated; but if you do not sleep, then he will not be able to do anything to you. He will not overcome the two of you."[41] During the battle, the hero's brothers are at the hut and always fall asleep, despite the hero's warning. We see a deformation of this motif when the brothers get drunk the previous evening, oversleep, and miss the meeting with the dragon while the hero is fighting him.

9. The Initial Opponent

The battle itself is usually preceded by boastful squabbles. The dragon brags, but the hero is usually not at a loss for words either: "I will put you in the palm of my hand and slam with the other hand, and no one will even be able to find your bones."[42]

During this squabble, however, a very important fact surfaces: the dragon has an opponent, and this opponent is the hero of the tale. The dragon somehow knows of the hero's existence. Moreover, he knows that he will die at the hands of this particular hero. To put it more precisely, the dragon cannot die by any other hand, for he is immortal and invincible. There is a connection of some kind between the hero and the dragon that originates somewhere outside the story. This relationship began before the story begins: "In the whole world I have no other opponent except Prince Ivan . . . but he is still young. Even the raven would not bring his bones over here."[43]

10. The Battle

We expect the battle, as the culminating point of the whole tale, to be described with enthusiasm, with details that emphasize the hero's strength and prowess. This, however, is not characteristic of the tale's style. In contrast to the heroic epos of many peoples, where the battle, the fighting, is the central part of the song and sometimes even described with a certain lengthiness, the wondertale is simple and short. The battle itself is not described in detail: "The Storm-Warrior got all steamed up, swung his battle mace, and knocked down three of its heads."[44] However, there are some details that require special attention. The dragon never tries to kill the hero with a weapon or with his paws or teeth. He tries to destroy him by driving him into the ground: "The monster creature Chudo-Yudo began to overpower him and drove him up to his knees into the damp earth." In the second battle, "he drove him waist-deep into the damp earth." The dragon can be destroyed only by chopping off all of his heads, but these heads have a miraculous property: they grow back again. "He cut down the nine heads of the monster creature Chudo-Yudo. Chudo-Yudo picked them up, touched them with his fiery finger, and the heads grew back again."[45] Only after the fiery finger is cut down does the hero manage to cut off all the heads.

The third battle is the most fearsome. The brothers at this time, as mentioned, are asleep in the hut. A horse is tied up near the hut. At the decisive moment the hero throws a hat or a boot into the hut. This causes the hut to fall apart, and the horse hurries to the aid of its owner. This is another constant feature in the depiction of the battle: only the horse (or other helpers, such as the hero's pack of hunting dogs) can kill the dragon. "Stallions came running and kicked the dragon on horseback out of the saddle."[46] "The mighty horse rushed to the fight and began gnawing the dragon with its teeth and trampling him with its hooves."[47] "The animals rushed at him and tore him to pieces."[48] "One horse reared and fell up on the dragon's shoulders, and another one hit him on his side with its hooves. The dragon fell, and the horses pressed the dragon down with their legs. These are some horses!"[49]

The battle, of course, ends in victory for the hero. Afterward, however, the hero needs to do one more thing: destroy the dragon completely. The dragon or its heads must be burned. "And he rolled the body into the river of fire."[50] "After he picked up all the parts, he burned them and scattered the ashes in the field."[51] "He made a fire, burned the dragon to ashes, and threw them to the wind."[52] Sometimes the dragon's ashes are thrown into the sea, placed under the bridge, or buried with a stone placed on top.

The battle unfolds somewhat differently, with minor deviations, when the dragon holds a woman captive, in which case the hero sees the princess and talks to her before the battle. Often there are three sisters who hide the hero until the dragon appears, but more often the princess lives in an extraordinary palace. For instance, she lives "in the mountains in a diamond palace."[53] In such cases, the hero almost always falls asleep before the fight, especially in tales in which the princess has been given to the dragon to be devoured. The hero is sound asleep, his head resting on the princess's knees, and it is difficult to wake him up. Thus, we see the dual nature of sleep in the tale. On the one hand, false heroes sleep before the battle or during the battle. On the other hand, the real hero sleeps before the battle. The nature of this sleep is not clear from the tales themselves and requires special consideration.

This exhausts the dragon's typical fundamental features. Now we shall move on to a historical exploration of the dragon.

11. *Literature on the Dragon*

There is a vast amount of literature regarding the dragon. Not only is it impossible to discuss it all here; it is impossible even to list it all. We can only mention some of its categories. Nevertheless, the question of the origin of the dragon figure and the motif of battling with the dragon cannot be considered resolved. All these works are distributed among certain categories, and as such these categories already, with their particular principles and techniques, doom these works to failure. For example, in one category of works the figure of the dragon is viewed as reminiscent of once extant prehistoric animals. These works should be considered erroneous, even for the fact that, as definitively established, humankind appeared on Earth long after these animals became extinct. Wilhelm Bölsche, for example, does not deny this, but he thinks that people restored the idea of them on the basis of their bones.[54] Such a statement is absurd in itself, but it also does not conform to reality as the figure of the winged dragon is a later phenomenon. It emerged before our eyes, and the process of its formation can be traced. Yet these works still contain a theory of some kind, some attempt to substantively explain the phenomenon. A similar attempt is evident in works of another category—namely, the works of those who adhere to the mythological theory, in particular the solar theory.[55] It is pointless to polemicize with such a theory. Ernst

Siecke, for example, argues that the dragon is the dark half of the moon and the hero the light half. However, we must add that the authors of these works collect materials and use them in a very conscientious way, without distorting them or forcing them to fit their theory. Therefore, materials from these works can be safely used; they free us to some extent from the tedious work of collecting the material.

These two types of theories exhaust attempts to explain the phenomenon of the dragon. All other types of works do not even address the issue. The dragon is viewed instead within various frameworks and limits, or in only some of its connections. This includes the characteristics of material within certain territorial boundaries. These works are the most valuable for our purposes. Without claiming any general conclusions, these works create a solid foundation for such conclusions. Especially valuable are Wilfrid Hambly's works on the serpent in Africa and certain works about the serpent in Australia.[56] Very close to this is another type of work accounting for the dragon within a particular ethnic group, nationality, or culture. There is a whole body of literature on the serpent in Egypt and Babylon, which is especially linked to the discovery of tablets detailing the creation of the world. This discovery motivated the comparison of biblical and Babylonian materials. Not counting the works on separate types of dragons, two specific works on the ancient serpent have turned out to be important. One is an old but very substantial and cautious work by Jakob Mähly, and the second is a newer work by Erich Küster.[57] We can add to these Grafton Smith's work with the high-sounding title *The Evolution of the Dragon*, which draws, however, almost exclusively on Mediterranean materials and does not measure up to its title.[58]

The next category consists of works within the framework of a single plot. First of all, we must mention here Edwin Hartland's substantial work on Perseus.[59] We can also include Kurt Ranke's work, which is devoted to tales about the hero battling the dragon.[60] A. I. Nikiforov, in his writings on the hero who defeats the dragon in the north, rightly responds to this work as follows: "Ranke's big book cannot be called research by any means. It is a bibliography of variants with a schematic formal classification of them."[61] Especially fortunate is the legend about George the dragon fighter. There are four major works on this: a work by Aleksandr Kirpichnikov; Aleksei Veselovskii's response, which is actually an independent new work; a work by Aleksandr Rystenko; and a German work by Johann Aufhauser.[62] The authors come to completely different conclusions. This was inevitable, since the very formulation of the question of battling the dragon purely in the context of the legend and not in general leads to erroneous conclusions, despite all the thoroughness of the philological work accomplished.

Finally, the dragon has been studied in various specific connections ("The Dragon and the Tree Cult," "The Dragon and the Sun," "The Dragon and Metallurgy," "The Dragon and the Woman," etc.). We will not cite specific works here, as our goal is not bibliographic.

12. The Distribution of Battling the Dragon

Having taken up the task of studying the figure of the dragon in its historical relations in the abovementioned sense, we must first of all ask ourselves where and among which peoples it is found. The literature frequently suggests that the motif of battling the dragon is quite ancient and that it reflects primitive ideas. This is not true. Paul Ehrenreich has observed that battling the dragon in connection with rescuing a maiden is found only *"in der alten Welt,"*[63] or in Europe, in Asia, and partially in Africa.[64] Yet what Ehrenreich considers to be a principle of territorial distribution is in fact a phenomenon of a historical and stadial nature. Battling the dragon in its developed form is found in all the ancient state religions: in Egypt, Babylonia, in antiquity, India, and China. It merged into Christianity and, as Aufhauser has shown, was canonized by the Catholic Church, though not without resistance.[65] The motif of battling the dragon, however, does not exist among peoples who have not yet formed a state.

From this we can immediately draw the conclusion that the motif of battling the dragon arises together with statehood. Yet such a conclusion still does not account for the sources of this motif. Arguing abstractly, one might assume that the motif was first created together with statehood or emerged as a modification of other motifs that existed before it. Comparing materials positioned according to the cultural stages of the peoples among whom they were recorded reveals that the motif of battling the dragon did not emerge at once but developed from preexisting motifs. Let us now proceed to a more in-depth study of this topic.

II. The Dragon as Devourer

13. Ritual Devouring and Spitting Out

The full picture of the battle in the Russian wondertale includes two main points or axes. One is the battle itself. The other is the she-dragon's pursuit of the hero, who has killed either her husband or her son, and her attempt to swallow him. The she-dragon in these cases appears altogether unexpectedly for the listener. Her appearance in the course of the action is not necessary or motivated; she can easily be removed and is often absent without any damage to the plot.

It was suggested above that the motif of battling the dragon arose not as a new motif but from certain other motifs that existed before it. The data illustrate that *the motif of battling the dragon arose from the motif of devouring* and was overlaid on it. This forces us, first of all, to consider the most archaic form of the dragon—namely, the dragon as devourer.

We know that the key to the wondertale does not lie in the tale itself. So where, besides the tale, do we find imagery of swallowing and spitting up a person? As indicated above, such a rite was part of the system of initiation. While previously it was only pointed out, here we shall deal with it in greater detail, since otherwise the motif of battling the dragon will remain incomprehensible. We need to establish how this ritual was actually performed. Here, of course, there can be no question of researching the rite; we can only provide a characterization of it.

The rite varies in form but also possesses some stable elements. We know about it from the stories of those who underwent it and broke its secrecy, from eyewitness accounts, myths, and visual art materials and from what women and the uninitiated were told of it. One part of the rite involved the initiate creeping through a structure that resembled a monstrous animal. In places where edifices were already in use, this monstrous animal was represented by a specific sort of hut or house. During this process, the initiate was allegedly digested and spat out as a new person. Where edifices did not yet exist, another type of construction was made. For example, in Australia, a snake was represented by a meandering furrow in the ground, a dried-up riverbed, or a shed constructed with a piece of broken tree in front of it representing the maw.[66]

This rite is best recorded on the Oceanic islands. In former German New Guinea, a special house was built for circumcision. Schurtz writes, "It must represent the monster Barlum, who swallows boys."[67] From Hans Nevermann's materials, we know that this monster, known in the former colony of German New Guinea as Barlum, has the form of a snake: "The swallowing of a neophyte by Barlum is not just a fable told to women; here the neophytes really do have to enter into its assumed figure. This is the circumcision house, which the Yabim (tribe) shape like a monster."[68]

The upper beam is a palm tree; the roots or leaves depict hair. "The maw or the entrance to the hut is covered with a net made of coconut leaves and is colorfully painted. The hut becomes narrower and lower towards the 'tail.' The swallowing is symbolized by the neophytes being carried into the 'belly,' while Barlum's voice is heard." In other places, the initiates enter by themselves. The animal swallows them and spits them out. The swallowing and spitting can appear in various forms. For example, the neophytes must weave the animal-hut from the inside by themselves. Having finished it, they entwine themselves; they are now in the stomach. Alternatively, a platform is built upon which the master of the ceremony stands. The neophytes then pass under him. As each of them approaches, he pretends to swallow them and start choking. He takes a sip from a bowl made of coconut, then pretends to feel nauseous, and he sprinkles the boys with water.[69] On Seram (Oceania), they throw the initiates at night into a house through a hole shaped like the open mouth of a crocodile or a cassowary's beak. The natives explain this by saying that the boy was swallowed by the devil.[70] "In some places in Queensland, a roar of rattles is allegedly produced by wizards, who swallow the boys and spew them out as young men." "The women of Queensland think that the sound of rattles is produced by lizards, swallowing the boys and returning them back as young men."[71] In Senegambia, young men are swallowed by Nochcheu, who keeps them for some time in his belly and then returns them to real life.[72] In Africa (the Poro), "the uninitiated believe that the grand master swallows the boys and that those who die from the scarification remain in the body of the devil (the grandmaster)."[73]

Many more such examples could be provided, but quantity is not the important thing. The phenomenon as such is clear, as are its manifestations. Another issue, however, remains to be explained—namely, the motivations for said phenomenon. It is not clear what actually led to the performance of the rite, what was expected from its completion, and what its historical foundations are.

14. The Meaning and Foundations of This Rite

Study of the rite itself gives us no key to understanding it. The key is provided by its accompanying myths. The only problem is that wherever the rite existed as a living practice, the myths were told during the dedication and were kept strictly secret. Only the initiated knew them. They were not openly shared or communicated to Europeans. Rather, they were written down only once the stories had become detached from the rite. They were recorded by Europeans at a later stage and among peoples who had by then lost the living connection with the rite: in America, for instance, among peoples who were forcibly resettled on reservations, based on the recollections of old men, often recorded in English, and so on. In other words, we have only fragments of a myth that, with the loss of its sacral character, had already begun to lose its form. Still, analyzing such myths enables us to formulate the following conclusion: a stay in the stomach of the beast gave the boy who returned magical abilities—in particular, power over the beast. The returned boy was transformed into a great hunter. This reveals the production basis of both the rite and the myth. Their rational basis is prehistoric, rooted in the idea that food gives consubstantiality with the thing that is eaten. In order to connect with the totem animal, to transform into it and thereby enter into the totemic clan, one must be eaten by this animal. The eating can be passive or active (compare blindness and invisibility). In the examples above, we have a form of passive eating by swallowing. We know, however, that the connection could also be accomplished through active eating: during the ritual, a totemic animal is eaten. We do not know whether the initiate, upon entering the animal, ate a piece of the animal that "ate" him. In myths, as we shall see, this almost always happens.

Turning to myth, we must bear in mind that it cannot be regarded as a perfectly accurate illustration of the rite. A complete overlap between myth and ritual is hardly possible. A myth, a story, lives longer than a rite. As indicated, sometimes myths were recorded where a rite was no longer practiced. Therefore, the myth contains elements that are more recent, elements of misunderstanding or of some distortion or modification. For example, staying in the *stomach* is replaced by staying in *a nest* or lair or by the serpent or the snake *entwining itself* around the hero or heroine. Additionally, the form of the benefits the dragon bestowed also changes. With the improvement of hunting tools, the magical hunting character of the benefits disappears. What remains are general magical abilities, two of which develop into particularly salient and frequent forms: the ability to heal and the ability to understand the language of animals.

Let us first look at the hunting benefits bestowed by the dragon. In North American myth, the hero Tlomenatso sees a fire floating on the water. He realizes that this is the two-headed Aigos. He follows the dragon to its lair. There Aigos gives him a piece of transparent stone and leads his soul across all lands. The hero returns, and the next day he catches one seal, the following day two, and so on. They are given to him by Aigos.[74]

Such ideas seem to be based on the view that the art of the hunt is not the actual killing of the animal (this is no great feat) but its delivery into the hunter's hands, and this can be accomplished only through magic. Success in hunting is associated very early on with magical success in general—that is, with the acquisition of magical powers. With the beginning of agriculture, the fruits of the earth are found in the dragon's stomach. In the Admiralty Islands, a myth is recorded with the following episode: "The dragon said, 'Slip into my belly.' The dragon opened up and the man slipped in. He went to look at the fire, he went to look at the taro, he went to look at the sugar cane. He went to look at all the things." The hero picks up all these items and leaves. It is clear that, upon his return, the hero introduces all these things to his people. Josef Meier, who recorded this myth and published it in the original and with a literal translation, adds, "This legend is common lore among all the inhabitants of the Admiralty Islands."[75] From the materials of Nevermann and Georg

Thilenius, we know that not only fire and the first fruits of the earth are extracted from the dragon's stomach but also pottery.[76]

These materials reveal the production basis of the devouring ritual that takes place during initiation and a number of other rites and myths that are only indirectly associated with them. For example, in Australia an individual who wishes to become a shaman plunges into a pond where there are allegedly horrible snakes that "kill" him. He falls ill, loses his mind, and thus gets his powers.[77] The same belief exists in America: "a man who wishes to be fierce, strong, and invulnerable swims at night in lakes inhabited by monsters or thunders. From these, if his courage is sufficient to await and endure their presence, he receives the desired powers."[78] In Tlingit tribes, the shaman who wants to acquire a "new spirit" "allows himself to be swallowed up by the sea" and on the fourth day finds himself hanging upside down in a tree.[79]

These examples show how devouring by animals is replaced by devouring by water, by swimming in a snake-infested pond, or even by "devouring by the sea" and subsequent expulsion.

Thus, we can make the following observation: in ritual, the person who comes out of the serpent or some other animal emerges as a hunter, and in myth he emerges as a great hunter, a great shaman. The first fire too is brought from the belly of the beast, and when agriculture appears, the first fruits of the earth; the art of pottery also has its origins there. We shall see later that a great leader will follow and, still later, a god. In Zulu myth, children who have been swallowed return home: "And there was great joy in the country. The children returned to their grandfather . . . and they made the children their leaders."[80] In an African myth of the relatively developed Basuto tribe, the hero is swallowed by a monster. He returns home, but people do not recognize him as a man and force him to leave the earth.[81] Here we find an embryonic form of deification. Perhaps we have echoes of the same idea in the figure of Kronos, who devours his children and spits them out. And does Kronos not devour his children because he is a father-god and thereby affords divinity to his children? The prophet Jonah, who was swallowed up and spat out by a whale, also belongs to this category. Is it not because he stayed inside a whale that he is a prophet? Ludwig Radermacher, who dedicated a special article to this case, admits that the motif remains completely incomprehensible.[82] The roots of this motif become clear in light of the materials brought forth here.

For now we shall trace only one moment: the moment of ritual devouring and its reflection or analog in myth. The dragon or other monster always appears here as a virtuous being. It is not yet clear how a battle will develop out of this, but even at this point we can see how completely mistaken researchers like Frobenius are when they claim that the virtuous dragon is typical of East Asia and the antagonistic dragon of Europe.[83]

The virtuous dragon—the dragon benefactor—is the first stage of the dragon, which later turns into its opposite. Europe and Asia have nothing to do with it.

15. The Language of the Birds

Since we have already touched upon the dragon benefactor, before proceeding to study the battle with the dragon we can linger on one motif that directly goes back to the range of phenomena mentioned here—namely, that of the hero who acquires knowledge of a bird language.

In a modern Greek story, a dragon swallows a prince in order to teach him the bird tongue and spits him out.[84] In the Kalevala (the seventeenth rune), Väinämöinen lets a huge monster swallow him in order to learn three magic words. He makes a fire in the monster's belly and begins to forge. The monster spits him out and not only gives him the knowledge of the three words but also tells him the history of the universe and gives him omniscience.

In a Dolgan myth, a maiden rescued by the hero says, "'How can I repay you for rescuing me? If you do not get scared of me, I will repay you for your good deed by wrapping myself around you three times.' What could the man do? He agreed. The serpent wrapped itself around him three times and blew in his left ear." The language of birds and fish is then revealed to the hero.[85] A comparison of these two cases shows that wrapping around the neck was a later form of devouring, once devouring was no longer considered something good. In a Viatka tale, a snake who has wrapped itself around the hero's neck "does not bite but squeezes."[86] The hero thus receives omniscience. We pointed out above that a piece of the totemic animal could be eaten during the rite. Hence, it becomes clear that knowledge of the bird language is acquired not only by the hero being devoured and spat out but also by the opposite—by the hero himself eating or licking a small part of the snake, for example, or eating a broth or soup made from snake meat.

In a tale from the Samara region, the hero (named there Stenka Razin) meets the monster Volkodir: "The monster lifted its head and saw the young man, puffed a breath at him, and began to move towards him. . . . Volkodir pulled at him and wanted to swallow him at once." Stenka cuts the dragon open and finds a stone in its stomach; he licks it "and he learned everything in the world."[87] In a tale from Khudiakovka, people roast the meat of a snake, cook soup, and eat it. By eating this soup, the hero acquires the language of the birds.[88] The motif of understanding the language of birds, animals, and fish after eating a snake is quite common in global folklore.[89]

That swallowing in these cases is associated with the rite of initiation can be proven by the fact that knowledge of bird language is acquired in other ways that are, without a doubt, connected to initiation. For example, the hero comes across an old man of the forest or a sage, who cooks him in a cauldron,[90] throws him into the oven three times,[91] or simply instructs him.[92]

There is some confusion in the literature regarding the motif of the birds' language. Bolte links it to the idea that birds have a prophetic gift and participate in human destinies, warning people and so on. Such a comparison is incorrect, since the hero learns to understand the language not only of birds but also of other animals. It also does not explain why it is necessary to eat a snake specifically. Georg Weicker explains this by arguing that snakes are animals of the soul.[93] The matter seems different in the light of our materials. We can assume that the motif of prophetic knowledge, in particular the knowledge of bird language, derives from rites in which a young man has been subjected to swallowing and spitting out or has himself swallowed a piece of an animal, thereby acquiring magical abilities. Originally, the abilities acquired were purely those of hunting; then later other abilities related to pottery, agriculture, and so on arose. As humans gained control over nature and production, the magical character of these abilities and skills was lost. However, abilities that people still felt helpless to acquire, if only in myth (e.g., the seer Melampus and others), are still acquired with the help of snakes. This includes the ability to understand the languages of birds and animals, an echo of the full power the hunter had formerly acquired over the will of an animal, who was to become an obedient tool in man's hands by the power of the rite and a servant to his will.

Traces of devouring for the purpose of conveying magical or sorcerous powers occur sporadically not only in wondertales but also in medieval legends. For example, they are found in tales about Solomon. In a Talmudic legend, Solomon builds a temple with the help of Asmodeus: "The wise king wanted to learn something from the demon, but there was neither time nor opportunity." After constructing the temple, Solomon remains alone with Asmodeus and begins to question him: "'Take off my chain,' says Asmodeus, 'and I will show you my power and exalt you above all men.'" Solomon obeys him. "He swallowed Solomon and spat him out four hundred parasangs away."[94] Subsequently, however, it follows that Solomon is punished for polygamy (having spat out Solomon, Asmodeus himself becomes king), but this is a later resignification that contradicts the beginning of the legend. Solomon has been swallowed to acquire the wisdom of Asmodeus.

16. Diamonds

Sometimes the wondertale hero finds diamonds or precious stones in the stomach or head of the dragon, and the dragon gives them to the hero as a gift: "And in its head there were precious stones."[95] "Come on, go to the fiery dragon across the sea to get the precious stones."[96] "He began to vomit and spat a precious stone out of his body."[97]

This detail too is already present at the stage of myth, before the formation of social classes. Boas cites a case wherein the serpent gives a "piece of transparent stone."[98] The connection to devouring and spitting up is preserved in the Russian wondertale, suggesting that here again we have a link to the rite of initiation. We have seen above that crystals are inserted into the body of the initiate. Rock crystal and quartz play an important role in the earliest stages of shamanism known to us. Alfred Radcliffe-Brown writes, "There is a very widespread association of quartz-crystals with the rainbow-serpent, and throughout Australia quartz-crystals are amongst the most important of the magical substances used by the medicine-men."[99]

There is a connection between the motif of precious stones and that of putting a maiden in a glass coffin in the wondertale (see chap. 4, sec. 10), and the crystal mountain where the dragon dwells is connected too, as well as the princess who sits in a glass tower, from which the hero carries her off on his magical horse (see chap. 8, sec. 8).

17. The Devourer-Carrier

In all the cases we have cited, the dragon is a virtuous being, a giver of magical knowledge and power. Such a beneficent dragon in the repertoire of the wondertale co-occurs with an enemy of the human race, a monster that must be destroyed. It has long been observed that the dragon is a creature with a double nature. Shternberg notes more than once such dualism in concepts of the dragon. This dualism arose in the development of ideas about the creature. They are not two different dragons but rather two stages of the same dragon's development. The initially virtuous dragon later turns into its opposite, and only then does the notion of the monstrous dragon appear, the evil dragon that must be killed. Consequently, a plot of battling the dragon emerges. This plot historically develops not by itself, not evolutionarily or immanently, but because of the contradiction of its original conceptual forms with new forms of society and culture.

Let us begin by observing that in many cases, in both ritual and myth, the devourer himself (monster, beast, dragon) remains stationary, while those who are swallowed move. For example, children leave the house, are swallowed by a monster, are subsequently spat up by him, and then return home. But there are myths of a different nature. The hero is devoured, then in the stomach of the devourer he is transferred to another country, and there he is spat out or cuts himself free. This devourer is often killed by the hero, and thus emerges the motif of battling the dragon. These myths, which are widespread among pre-class peoples, should be studied rather more closely.

Where could the notion that the devourer transfers the hero to another kingdom have originated? It can be argued that here we see the development of certain elements that were present in embryo in the rite. A person who spent time in the stomach of the animal was believed to have ventured into the realm of death, into another world, and he himself believed that he had been there. Having climbed through the belly of the dragon, he climbed into another land. Here the mouth of the animal is a portal into another world. For example, in a Tatar tale, the hero saves a maiden who is actually the dragon's daughter. In gratitude for this, she says to him, "Let the terrible sight of my parent [i.e., the dragon] not scare you. In order to get into his kingdom, we must first pass through the womb of my mother and then through the belly of my father. A horrible darkness will surround us on our way, and the view will be unbearable for the faint of heart, but this is the only way to our kingdom. However, the king of dragons will meet you with honor and favors and will reward you for the valorous feat."[100]

Something apparently happened, however, in the minds of those who passed down these rites and stories that no longer corresponded to their original forms. Myth clearly shows the development here of a sense of space and movement. The appearance of spatial representations compels the devourer to move from his place and embark on a long journey. The notion of the kingdom of death as a zoomorphic entity is replaced by the notion of death as a *distant kingdom*. It is quite obvious that such concepts could emerge only among peoples who had moved beyond a philosophical perception of space to practical experience—that is, among peoples who made long-distance trips. Such were the inhabitants of islands and coasts. Indeed, the myth of the devourer-carrier is predominantly a sea myth. The hero is carried through the sea in the stomach of the devourer, who has the form of a huge fish. Furthermore, by moving the devourer from its place, the narrator in essence removes the meaning of the act of devouring. The forest is replaced by the sea. This means that game hunted in the forest has ceased to be the only source of sustenance and that the corresponding rituals have lost their meaning, but at the same time this change does not represent a revolution profound enough to destroy the old rite and plot completely and to cause them to be forgotten. The researcher sees the connection very clearly, but the bearer of the myth, while still in many respects retaining the old forms, has already forgotten it. An immobile thing turns into a mobile one, something terrible becomes something adventurous and even comical, and something necessary turns into something useless and harmful. The hero in these cases no longer acquires any magical qualities. On the contrary, he sees the devourer as an enemy, and after he is swallowed he kills it while he is in its stomach, striking it from the inside. Here lies the beginning of battling the dragon.

Below, we give a few selected examples. There is so much material that it could constitute a book by itself, and such a book even exists. This is Frobenius's *Age of the Sun-God*, a quite thorough collection of myths. Unfortunately, however, the author's work goes to waste since for him, from the very beginning, the whale represents the sea, the hero swallowed by it is the evening sun, and the hero emerging from the whale is the morning sun. The author does not touch upon or perceive the connection with the rite and with the economic and social lives of the people.

18. The Battle with a Fish as the First Step in Battling the Dragon

Undoubtedly, the myth of the hero who is swallowed and carried away to another country is a very complex phenomenon in the causes of its creation and the variety of its associations. We shall not study the whole cycle of this myth here, including the moment when the hero is carried over. We shall focus only on those parts that lead to battling the dragon.

Let us first consider several cases in which the transfer occurs without any elements of struggle. In Micronesia there is a myth about a boy who is the son of an eel. Women tease him because he has no father. He goes to look for his father and jumps into the water. There he sees an eel with a huge gaping maw. He throws two logs into its maw—inserts them so it will not close—and jumps into it. From there, he is snatched up by a shark, which brings him to a certain shore where many turtle shells are scattered. He returns to the mouth of the shark in the same way and from there goes home, where he gets married.[101] In this myth, we see that the swallowed hero has been transferred to another shore. Turtle shells have clearly come to replace the magic-bearing crystal or quartz of other myths.

This example shows clear signs of decline. The devouring here is unnecessarily repeated. The turtle shells are devoid of any magical power. The marriage is not tied to the previous devouring and return, whereas in the rite these events are a condition for the marriage. Let us move on to other more typical and prevalent examples.

A father assigns a task to his son, but the boy is disobedient. He runs to the water and sets out to sea in a boat with his comrades. Suddenly, the boat starts to rock and shake. The disobedient boy falls into the water, and right away a big fish swallows him. After staying inside the fish for a while, the boy starts to feel hungry. He looks around and sees the fish's liver hanging over him. He begins to cut off the liver with a shell. The fish feels pain and spits the boy out.[102]

In the previous example, the swallowing took place without any consequences for the devourer. Here, however, the hero cuts off pieces of the fish's liver and eats them. It is hard to say whether this is an echo of the former practice of eating a piece of the animal during the rite. In any case, the motif is quite common, and the consumption occurs under various pretexts. The fish, as a result, feels pain and spits out the hero. We see that the expulsion requires some kind of motivation. It is already incomprehensible in itself. It is worth noting that the fish remains alive, and there is still no struggle with the devourer.

Sometimes a fire is made inside the fish in order to get out, as a counterstrategy. A certain chief builds a boat with the help of birds. The hero asks to get into the boat. After much debate, they take him along with them. On the way, a whale swallows them along with the boat, but the hero inserts two spears into the whale's mouth to prop it open. In the whale's stomach, he sees his dead parents. To free himself, he lights a large fire. The whale writhes in pain and swims to a sandbank. Everyone comes out through its open mouth together with the boat. They find themselves in the land of the moon, a land of abundance. They then return home in the same boat.

In this example, the hero sees his deceased parents inside the fish. This shows that inside the fish, he has already entered the realm of the dead. In general, the hero sometimes meets many dead and living people, who were swallowed before him, inside the fish, and he leads them out. We will not dwell on this motif here. We shall only note that in Russian wondertales we also see the translocation of the hero inside a fish and the kindling of a fire.[103] In general, building a fire inside the fish is a widespread motif. It is incomprehensible if one does not know that in ritual and myth all first things, including fire, are acquired from inside the devourer. Also, as we know, the initiate is sometimes subjected to burning inside the devourer. A terrible fire burns within this monster. Therefore, boys coming out of the fish in the myth often complain that it is hot inside, or, as in this case, they make a fire inside the fish to save themselves.

All of this shows that the rite has already been forgotten and its component parts are being used for artistic creation. This can be viewed as decay, a distortion, but these cases show creative reworking of the motif—the fading away of old elements and emergence of new ones. Devouring and spitting out no longer correspond to the forms of production, or to the forms of social life or the ideology of the community. These motifs have gradually been lost. We have already seen how the spitting out is motivated in the myth: it is induced by pain. Spitting out completely disappears in the wondertale, and the devouring lasts longer, as it is artistically a more striking moment. The swallowed hero is no longer spat out but instead cuts himself out. Here is an example: "Many years ago, a man named Mutuk was fishing while standing on a rock when his fishing line got tangled, and he jumped into the water to release it." At that moment a shark swam past, and it swallowed him without harming him. The shark swam to the north. Mutuk felt that it was warm and said to himself, "Now we are in warm waters." When the shark again dove into deeper water, Mutuk felt that it was cold and realized that they had gone deep. Finally, the shark swam to Boigu and at low tide was cast up on the shore. Mutuk felt direct sun rays falling on the fish and realized that he was on land. "Then he took a sharp shell that he was carrying behind his ear and began to cut through the body of the shark until he made a hole big enough. Crawling out of his prison, he saw that all his hair had fallen out."[104]

In this example, the loss of hair attracts special attention. This is a very common feature of such myths. For Frobenius the matter is clear: the loss of hair means that the morning sun has no rays. We can explain this by viewing the dedication essentially as a "tonsure," that during the rite the hair was shaved, scorched, or hidden under a special cover (regarding baldness in the wondertale, see chap. 4, sec. 15).

We should also consider the variety of reasons for which the hero is swallowed. The hero jumps into the water because he is being mocked; he goes on a boat, violating his father's prohibition; he goes on a boat to travel; or he jumps into the water because either a fishing line has gotten tangled or a hook has been lost, and so on. In short, the narrator does not know why the hero must necessarily get in the water and be swallowed; therefore, every narrator motivates it in different ways.

The following example demonstrates that the motif of freeing oneself by cutting through the devourer replaces the former spitting out. A boy is fishing and invites the king of fish to bite. The fish swallows him along with the boat. To get free, the boy pricks the fish's heart. The fish tries to spit him out but fails. The boy hears the fish's body rustling through the sand. Seagulls come flying and peck the fish apart, and the boy gets out.[105]

This example is very important for us in many respects. First, we see that spitting out is still anticipated but has by now been removed. Pricking the heart, which in previous cases had a purely utilitarian purpose (the liver is cut to satisfy hunger), is performed here with the aim of killing the devourer; thus, we again have a moment of counteraction—that is, the killing of the devourer. Second, the example is interesting because the devourer's body is opened up from the outside. Most often this is done by animals, in this case by seagulls. It can be shown how the devourer is afflicted from inside and from outside and how the center of gravity is transferred over time to affliction from the outside. Let us consider another analogous example in which the devourer is opened by people. Two brothers are at the seashore. When a whale appears, they let it swallow them. In the belly of the whale, they see the heart and cut it off. The whale dies and is swept to the shore. People appear and begin to cut the whale, freeing the brothers from inside. "When they saw each other, they started laughing: they had lost their hair in the belly of the whale, that's how hot it was inside."[106]

In this example, everything is perfectly clear once the material has been analyzed. One very remarkable detail stands out: when they get out of the whale, the boys laugh. The ritual character of laughter has been analyzed in a separate work.[107]

The above examples may give the impression that this myth is exclusively marine and aquatic. It is true that it is predominantly aquatic. As we shall see below, this characteristic is related to the aquatic nature of the dragon. Peoples living in the depths of forests, cut off from the world and not migrating or engaging in trade, developed more slowly. Nonetheless, similar development occurred there as well, though at a slower pace. Among these peoples we find much less material, and the picture is less clear. Yet it is necessary to bring up the following example. The hero leaves his house; his father warns him that he will meet a wolf that will inhale him or suck the boy into himself. The hero in fact meets the wolf and begins to mock him: "Indeed you are wonderful! You are really pulling me into yourself!" The hero pretends to resist, as if he is involuntarily coming closer to its maw, and then jumps in. "Inside he found people. Some were alive, some nearly dead, some dead, and some only bones. Above him he saw the heart hanging and beating. Then he said, 'Let us dance! You sing and I will dance!'" Then the people begin to sing. He fastens a knife to his head and begins to dance. With this knife he strikes the heart of the wolf, kills him, cuts the wolf open, frees everyone inside, and goes away.[108] If previously the hero was the one who was devoured, now the hero is the one who destroys the devourer. If in previous cases the devourer was opened because he swallowed the hero, here it is already the other way around: the hero enters the devourer in order to kill it. If in the rite the hero was the one who was swallowed and spat out, becoming the hero because of this fact alone, in this myth the hero is the one who kills the devourer. It is obvious that this shift in the myth reflects a shift taking place in the social lives of the people. The hero mocks the wolf and jumps into its mouth. We have seen some cases of mocking above. At the same time, we see here too that the hero meets dead people in the belly of the devourer. The dead people are spread within the monster, the corpses, the bones, and the other attributes of death inside the devourer or in the death hut—this picture is familiar to us from the characteristics of the rite. The only thing missing is for the hero to revive them, and we would have a typical picture of temporary death. Here the revival has been rationalized and has taken the form of rescue by leading people out of the wolf. It is also noteworthy that the hero dances inside the wolf.

The transfer of the heroic center of gravity in the history of this myth is prepared by an extremely important innovation. All the examples considered so far have been characterized by a single feature: the story centers around *one* person. Magical heroism gives way to personal valor and courage. There is no longer anything heroic about being swallowed. Notably, this transfer of the center of gravity is motivated by a new character. The myth is built around two characters: one is swallowed and the other rescues him. The hero becomes not the one who was swallowed but the one who frees the swallowed. The following tale was recorded in America (specifically among the Nootka tribe):

> A huge whale lived in Gelgat by the name of "the devourer of boats tied together." Everyone passed through this place with great vigilance. Once, the hero's mother was passing in a small boat. It was carried away from shore, and a whale appeared and swallowed the boat with the woman in it. When the hero learned what had happened to his mother, he decided to take revenge. He went along with his brothers down the river to the sea. They started singing a song. After they sang it twice, the water parted, and the whale swallowed their boat. The hero shouted to his brothers to steer the boat directly into its belly. In the belly, they sliced the whale's guts and cut off its heart. As a result, the whale died. It was carried to the shore. On the shore, animals (birds, snails, fish, etc.) ripped open the belly of the whale, and everyone got out. It was so hot in the whale's belly that one of the brothers had lost all his hair.[109]

This story contains the motif of battling the dragon at the pre-class stage of society. On the one hand, the plot resembles that of a wondertale. We have the devouring (in wondertales it is a kidnapping) of a woman, a fight with the monster, and a rescue of the woman. At the same time, however, the struggle is still taking place in old forms; in order to kill the devourer, one must jump into its stomach, must be swallowed by him.

It is quite natural that the swallowing, originating from the rite and preserved in the myth, was replaced by other forms of struggle. Indeed, one can observe how swallowing is replaced by other forms of devouring, and the devourer is killed not from inside but from out. It is a later stage in the development of this plot. Let us give examples that clearly illustrate the transition from devouring and killing from inside to an attack from outside.

In one myth from northwest America, the monster Tsekis is said to devour all the people, leaving only an old man and his granddaughter unharmed. A newcomer hero finds out about this. He puts a magical belt made from the snake Sisiutl on the girl and sends her to fetch water. Tsekis swallows the girl with the magic belt. While the girl is in the stomach of the monster, the hero sings a magical song: "Sisiutl, come to life, wake up and kill him!" The monster floats up, convulsing in death cramps. The hero kills him with his arrows and pulls the girl out.[110]

It is not clear from this myth why the girl is sent into the stomach of the dragon. This is clear from the history of the myth, however; here we have a reflection of the tradition stating that in order to kill the devourer, one must spend time inside it. Although the devourer is struck from the outside, there must still be a person inside the dragon as well. It is also significant that a magical device is used inside, while from the outside the most ordinary rational device is used: a bow and arrow.

The attenuation of killing from within and the enhancement of killing from the outside bring this motif closer to its modern folktale forms. The shift from one to the other goes further. In order to defeat the dragon, one must throw something into its maw, but now it does not always have to be a person. Hot stones can be thrown in. For example, a monster lives in a lake and devours all the people who come to fetch water. The hero (a newcomer) heats up stones and throws them into the monster's maw; then he chops it into pieces. These pieces turn into edible fish.[111] Here it is not completely forgotten that good things come from the devourer. The first things come from him: parts of his body turn into fish. In another example, a snake devours all the people, but one pregnant woman remains. She gives birth to twin boys. The boys then offer the snake palm wine. The snake opens its maw, and the boys throw red-hot stones inside.[112]

Finally, when the motif of throwing magical objects or glowing stones into the mouth disappears, the sheer battle with the dragon remains. Two women are swimming when two monsters (Kurrea—alligators, according to Frobenius) swallow them.[113] The serpents crawl into their cave, which feeds the river with its water, then take away (swallow) all the water, and the river dries up. The husband of the swallowed women tracks down the serpents and strikes them with his spears. The water begins to flow again. He rips open the serpents' bellies and releases his wives.[114]

In this case, the victim is still swallowed. The given serpent is a water creature, which will be discussed below. When the swallowing disappears completely we will find the battle with the dragon in the forms familiar to us. However, just as one can trace the replacement of swallowing the hero, one can also trace the substitute forms of swallowing a woman. The following example no longer contains any swallowing but has still not entirely broken away from this motif. Two women are swimming. They are seen by a crampfish, which takes them onto its stinger and floats away. Two heroes fight it with their spears and kill it. They make a fire to revitalize the women. The heroes let ants sting the women, and this brings them back to life.[115] Carrying them away on the creature's back is an obvious substitute for carrying them away inside its stomach. The connection with fire is not forgotten, but it is distorted; the fire serves to revive the deceased—the last echoes of temporary death.

With the disappearance of these details, we come to battling the dragon in its modern form. Let us provide two examples. A hero-wanderer meets a girl who is carrying rice meal and meat. She is bringing it to a serpent that lives in a well. The hero chops off the beast's heads with a sword.[116] In another example, a marsh snake demands a sacrificial victim every year. "This was a law whose right and origin no one knew." A girl is brought out to the snake. At the right moment, the hero appears on horseback and strikes the snake.[117]

At this point, we interrupt our analysis for a moment. We have attempted to outline a pattern for the plot's development in order to reveal how a certain motif (battling the dragon) develops from an earlier motif (swallowing). Yet we have traced only one of the roots of this motif. It is still impossible to provide an exhaustive answer to the question of why the dragon is killed. Still, one thing is clear even now: the dragon is killed because certain changes have taken place in the life of the people. These changes made the old plot incomprehensible and modified it in accordance with the new ideology. It should be noted that archaic forms are not always attested among the most primitive peoples. Thus, even the Russian wondertale contains a change of location to inside a fish, as well as making a bonfire inside, and having the fish spit out the hero in ways that are strikingly similar to American materials. This is the sense in which the most archaic examples might not be recorded among the most primitive peoples. The reverse relation, however, is impossible: innovation is introduced only when there is a corresponding basis for it. In general, evolution corresponds to stages of cultural development. We have already discussed what caused the moment of changing location. What is notable here is the development of another detail: the dragon or the devourer is struck first by arrows, then by spears, then by a sword. It is obvious that the dragon can be struck with a sword only among peoples who practice metallurgy and blacksmithing. The last two examples were recorded among the Kabyle people.[118] Here the Kabyles are of interest not per se but from the point of view of their economic development. They are a settled people who cultivate olive and fruit trees and carefully tend their fields, and they are experienced in pottery and blacksmithing. At the same time, the Kabyles are brave and warlike. It is at this stage of development that the sword and horse appear. The feudal system subsequently dresses the dragon's challenger in knightly armor. With the change in the form of the battle among the Kabyles, the figure of the dragon also changes: it takes on an agricultural character. Every year, a girl is sacrificed to the dragon, a case that will be analyzed below. In this instance, however, rice and meat are featured. Thus, the plot development happens not by itself but as a result of changes in the economic life and social structure of a people.

The main premise that the motif of battling the dragon arose from the devouring motif can be supported by analyzing cases of battle with the dragon among peoples who have reached the stage of social class development. On the one hand, in materials from pre-class peoples it is possible to find precursors of battling the dragon, and on the other, there are clear traces of earlier devouring in more recent materials. It is true that in the Russian repertoire there are no cases of the hero jumping into the dragon's mouth during the battle, but in general such cases are not so rare.

A Babylonian myth about the creation of the world says, "When Tiamat opened her mouth as far as she could, he [Marduk] let Imhullu get in so that she could not close her mouth."[119] With this act, the battle begins. This passage is not entirely comprehensible. Gressmann interprets "Imhullu" as an evil wind. It is unclear why the wind would prevent Tiamat's mouth from closing. Usually the dragon produces the wind to suck in the hero. At the same time, in such cases a spear is inserted into the serpent's maw, which prevents it from closing. Here we also see a spear: "He placed a spear, slashed her body, tore her insides, and cut out her heart." We should imagine the matter as Marduk inserting the spear into Tiamat's mouth and crawling into her belly. There he tears her insides, cuts her heart, cuts her body open, and comes out. Although it is not stated directly anywhere that Marduk enters the belly of the dragon, it can be reasonably deduced. Gressmann also understands the case in a similar way when he writes in a footnote, "He enters her belly together with the other winds." Budge, who published and translated the text for the British Museum, interprets this episode in the same way, writing the following: "In the Seventh Tablet (1. 108) Marduk is said to have 'entered into *the middle of Tiamat*,' and because he did so he is called 'Nibiru,' i.e., 'he who entered in,' and the 'seizer of the middle' (i.e. the internal organs)."[120]

The hero's entry into the dragon's belly is not sufficiently convincing here. It becomes quite clear in materials from antiquity. According to one version of the myth of Heracles, he jumped into the dragon's mouth in order to save Hesione; stayed there three days, during which he lost all the hair on his head from the heat in the beast's belly; and cut open its belly from the inside.[121] The same is true with regard to the myth of Jason, which depicts, through iconographic sources, how in order to obtain the Golden Fleece in Colchis Jason threw himself into the mouth of the serpent-guard and thus killed him. This version can be found depicted on an Attic vase.[122] A very clear picture of the struggle inside the dragon is provided by the Geseriada. A tiger, huge as a mountain, "noticing a person for a day's journey, swallows him for half a day's journey"; the tiger inhales the person into himself, like the abovementioned American wolf. "Geser . . . miraculously penetrates the mouth of the tiger, and having gotten in there, positions himself in the following way: he rests his two legs on the tiger's two lower fangs, his head touching the roof of the mouth, and his elbows touching the jaws." His companion and friend says of him, "My merciful Khan . . . was swallowed by a black-and-motley tiger, huge as a mountain." The knights attack the tiger from the outside while Geser kills him from the inside.[123] Here the motif of devouring is still connected to the battle in an obvious way. The same is true in a Baloch tale: "The dragon inhaled air in Janget's direction to swallow him, but the latter held a sword in front of his forehead. The dragon approached Janget closely, but as soon as he came up and swallowed him, he split into two parts."[124] Recall that Odin also jumps into the mouth of the wolf Fenrir in the *Edda*.

20. *Conclusion*

Together these materials allow us to draw the following conclusion.

The motif of battling the dragon developed from the motif of devouring. Initially, the devouring was a ritual performed during initiation. This ritual gave the young man or the future shaman magical abilities. In the wondertale these views are reflected, on the one hand, as precious stones found in the head or belly of the dragon, and, on the other, as the acquisition of animal language. In the future, this motif disappears and does not develop further. Devouring is no longer perceived as something beneficial; it happens accidentally. The connection to real-life rituals is lost. A new element is introduced in which the hero moves inside the devourer's stomach. At this stage, utilitarian elements begin to emerge: the heart or liver of the devourer is cut off and eaten. At a later stage, myths become more complex with the introduction of a second character. The first is devoured and the second releases him, jumping into the same maw and ripping open the devourer from within. At this stage, the motif of moving inside the dragon disappears. Substitutions appear; instead of jumping in himself, the hero throws hot stones or magical elements into the would-be devourer's maw, thereby destroying the beast from the inside while the hero kills him from the outside. The form this killing takes gradually changes. The devourer is killed by arrows, a spear, or a sword or struck from above by a horse. From here, we have a direct transition to the forms of battling the dragon that exist in the wondertale. The forms of battle essentially do not change with the emergence of class societies. In some cases, it is still possible to identify traces of devouring even in later forms of battling the dragon.

This evolution is caused by changes in economic life and social structure. With the disappearance of the initiation rite, the significance of devouring and spitting out is lost and is replaced by various transitional forms before disappearing completely. The heroic focal point shifts from devouring to killing the devourer. The forms of the tools themselves change depending on the tools people in fact used at a given time. The more highly developed the culture, the closer the forms of the battle are to those available in the modern wondertale. With the advent of a settled way of life, cattle breeding, and agriculture, the process comes to an end.

III. The Hero in a Barrel

21. *The Ferry Boat*

Before we continue our analysis of the dragon, we must stop to incorporate in our study another motif that receives some illumination in light of the materials cited. It is the motif of the hero in a barrel, box, or boat lowered into the water.

This motif is related to that of the hero in a fish and originates from it. Let us give an example from a tale from the Vyatka region. "They caught me, put me in a barrel, fixed iron hoops on it, and set it off on the water. I sat there for a year and a half, neither alive nor dead. Then, to my happiness, the barrel stopped at the shore with its hole upward." A wolf approached. "I quietly tied the barrel to its tail and poked a penknife into its butt. . . . And it pulled out my barrel and began dragging it over the stumps and the roots. Then the entire barrel broke, and I got home barely alive."[125] In the figure of the wolf that comes to sniff the barrel and smash it, we easily recognize the animals that release the hero from the fish from the outside. In the penknife, we recognize the knife with which the fish is cut open from the inside. In a Permian tale, the barrel is broken by a bull.[126] We even see similarities in simpler cases. Envious people put the hero in a boat; "a little later clouds gathered, a storm arose, waves rose and carried the boat to an unknown destination; they carried it far, far away and cast it onto an island."[127] The boat that tosses out the hero reminds us of the fish that spits him up.

Considerations of external similarity, however, are not sufficient to establish an actual affinity. There are considerations of a different order that compel a connection between these two motifs. The hero's placement in a barrel is motivated in various ways, but there is one cycle in which it enters organically. This cycle consists of predicting that the king's death will be caused by a boy; the boy is cast into the water, the boy is reared in secret by a shepherd or gardener, often with other boys, and finally the boy's accession to the throne takes place.

If our conjecture is correct, then staying in the barrel corresponds to a stay in the belly of the fish; the subsequent secret upbringing together with other boys corresponds to the communal life of initiates under the guidance of an elder; the whole episode is the condition for acquiring the abilities required of a leader. Together these constitute conditioning for accession to the throne. Otto Rank previously compared the barrel to the belly, but he explained it in a Freudian manner.[128] True, the barrel is a belly, but it is not the mother's womb; it is the belly of an animal that bestows magical powers.

The above observations are still not completely exhaustive. We know that the initiation rite and the motif of swallowing and disgorging have a totemic origin. However, not only animals can serve as totems; trees can as well. The barrel can also be recognized as connected to a tradition of the tree. It is possible that both of these traditions have merged in the motif of the hero in the barrel. In a Micronesian myth, four men visit the sun. Upon arriving, they see that their boat has floated away. "Then the sun encased them in thick bamboo that was not yet known on the Palau Islands. They were carried away inside it to the shore of their homeland. After that, they became the first four leaders."[129] The same myths exist about the first people. In northwest America, a myth tells of several women making a large basket, getting inside with their husbands and children, tying it up, and asking to be thrown into the water. The waves and wind carry the basket farther, and it finally lands in Piknakotl. Then they open the basket and come out, becoming the ancestors of the Potomac people.

Apparently, the story of Noah also originates here. He too enters a large boat or ark, seals himself inside it, and comes out from it as the progenitor of people. This association has already been made by Hermann Usener.[130] The tradition of the tree is also evidenced in Egypt (Osiris) and found in Russian tales as well. In a tale from the Penza region, a girl escapes from her father's persecution by hiding in a wooden pillar. This pillar is thrown into the water and floats to another kingdom. Here a prince finds the pillar and orders that it be taken to his room (very similar to the wondertale of the magic mirror). The prince then marries the girl he finds inside.[131] Here the tree plays the same role as the glass coffin. Often a mute maiden is found by the prince in a tree in the forest. She is usually naked and covers herself with her hair, resembling a bird; sometimes she is even covered with feathers. All this points to the source of the motif. The girl in a tree or inside a tree is the same as the girl in a coffin or in a temporary state of death. This corresponds to staying inside an animal. Recall that such a stay is a precondition for marriage and often also a precondition for power.

It is interesting to revisit from this point of view the sojourn of Moses (who afterward becomes the leader and savior of his people) in the

floating basket and the famous autobiography of King Sargon (2600 BC).
That tablet, in Gressmann's translation, reads,

> I, Sargon, am a mighty king, the king of Akkad. My mother was poor
> (a vestal), I didn't know my father; my father's brother lives in the
> mountains. My city, Azupiranu, is located on the banks of the Euphra-
> tes. My vestal mother conceived me, secretly gave birth to me, put me
> in a cane box, sealed the doors with earth resin, and handed me over
> to the river. . . . Then the river carried me and brought me to Akki the
> Waterer. Akki the Waterer, retrieved me by . . . (an ewer). Akki the
> Waterer, took me as his son and reared me. Akki the Waterer made me
> his gardener. While I was a gardener, Ishtar fell in love with me, and I
> reigned for four years.[132]

This is followed by a boastful list of the king's great deeds and campaigns.
But if the whole tablet contains boasting, then its beginning is his self-
glorification too, which, however, is not perceived by the modern mind.
Sargon's greatness began with his placement in a box. He boasts of it on a
par with his campaigns because it proves his right to reign. It also proves
that he is a great king, as do his campaigns.

IV. The Dragon as Abductor

22. *The Dragon's Form*

We set off to study the wondertale dragon, but we have not seen it yet, except for later manifestations (Marduk, Heracles, Jason, etc.). This means
that the dragon is a later phenomenon, that its form developed after its
functions. In fact, what have we seen so far in the role of devourer? In
the initiation rite, these may be the most diverse animals. Typically, the
snake prevails, sometimes fantastically embroidered, as in Australia, but
we have also seen both a bird and a wolf. The animals that carry individuals across the sea naturally take the form of fish. All these animals
will later become part of the serpent, the dragon. A dragon does not
appear among any of the pre-class peoples we have mentioned. There
are (e.g., in Australia) huge snakes and a notion of snakes with fantastic
coloring, but there are no hybrid creatures such as dragons. Although in
North America there is a two-headed serpent, it is not a hybrid creature.
The heads are not located next to each other; instead one is on the tail.
The tail in this case is associated with the stinger, hence the notion of a
second head. The dragon is a later phenomenon. These fantastic animals
are a product of later culture, even urban culture, when the human being
begins to lose intimate and organic connection with the animal, although
the rudiments of hybrid animals occur even earlier—for example, in
Mexico or among the Eskimos. The heyday of such creatures comes in

ancient states such as Egypt, Babylon, ancient India, Greece, and China, where the dragon ended up on coats of arms symbolizing statehood. On the other hand, there is no record of these hybrid animals among genuinely primitive peoples.

The dragon is a mechanical compound of several animals and therefore represents the same phenomenon as the Egyptian sphinxes, ancient centaurs, and so on. Artistic representations of the dragon reveal that along with its main image (a reptile plus a bird), it can be composed of very different animals; it can include not only a crocodile or lizard and a bird but also a panther, a lion, a goat, and other animals. The dragon may be comprised of two, three, or four animals.

Here we may observe another phenomenon. The dragon appears at approximately the same time as anthropomorphic gods. This is not an absolutely mandatory rule, merely a tendency. The question of what qualifies as a god in the history of religion is a very complex one, and we will not be able to resolve it here. The totemic ancestor in the shape of an animal is not a god in the sense of the anthropomorphic Zeus or the shapeless Holy Spirit of Christianity. The deity develops from the animal. With the advent of agriculture and urbanization, the motley animal world of totemic origin begins to lose its reality, and a process of anthropomorphization occurs. The animal acquires a human body. Sometimes the animal's face is the last feature to disappear. Thus, gods are created such as Anubis with a wolf's head, Gor with the head of a red-footed falcon, and so on. On the other hand, the souls of the dead acquire human heads on a bird's body. This is how a person gradually emerges from the animal. The process of anthropomorphization is almost complete in the figure of such gods as Hermes, who has small wings on his heels, until finally the animal turns into an attribute accompanying the god: Zeus, for instance, is depicted with an eagle.

This is one facet of the matter. On the other hand, the animal—not the one that the urban person may deal with but a different one, into which the deceased is transformed (a snake, worm, bird); not the everyday animal but the hypostatic and mysterious one—begins to lose its shape along with its meaning. Just as an animal merges with a human, animals begin to merge with one another. These are beings that no one has ever seen, but they are endowed with mysterious power. They are unearthly and extraordinary. This is how hybrid creatures are created, and one of them is the dragon.

If we now peer into the figure of the dragon (which consists basically of a snake plus a bird) and compare it with everything that has been said, we can conclude that the dragon was formed of two animals that represent the soul, namely a bird and a snake. Initially, a person could turn into any animal after death, a detail that can be confirmed by numerous materials. However, when notions of the kingdom of death begin to appear, this kingdom is localized either high above the earth or far beyond the horizon or, conversely, under the ground. We shall see this in greater detail when we discuss the Thrice-Tenth Kingdom. Consequently, the number of animals into which the deceased person can turn becomes limited. For distant kingdoms, birds are created; for the underground kingdom, there are snakes, worms, and reptiles, among which, apparently, there is not much distinction. The bird and the snake are the most common and widespread animals that represent the soul. They merge in the figure of the dragon. This opinion is also shared by Wundt, who writes, "Perhaps in the winged figure (of the serpent) the notion of a bird representing the soul is hidden, though long forgotten, and the snake-like body of the dragon preserves the notion of a worm, representing the soul."[133] This also accounts for the dragon's wings, its claws, its scaliness, its tail with the stinger, and so on. We shall soon see that this also explains one of its main functions: the abduction of women.

But this still does not explain another constant feature of the dragon: its many-headedness. Just as it consists of many animals, it has many heads. How can this many-headedness be explained? The question can be answered by making an analogy to the horse's features of multiple legs and wings. The eight-legged horse is a familiar figure in folklore. For example, Sleipnir, Odin's horse, has eight legs, and this is by no means the only example. The multilegged image represents nothing other than the horse's speed. The same is true of the multiwinged feature of the folk Russian horse. It can have four, six, or eight wings—a reflection of its flying speed. Similarly, the many-headedness of the dragon accentuates the multiplicity of its maw, which is a hypertrophied image of devouring. The intensification here occurs by amplifying the number, expressing quality through quantity. This is a later phenomenon, since the category of multiplicity in general develops later.

The examples provided above did not contain many-headedness. However, this feature is already found among the Kabyle people, where we have seen a horse. Another way to create an image of devouring is not through *quantity* but through *increasing the size of the maw*; in one Russian tale, the mouth extends from the earth to the sky. In this case, though, it is only one mouth, and there are no multiple heads. In the materials cited so far, multiple heads do not appear either. In these tales, a fish is typically an ordinary fish, yet it can contain thousands of people and sometimes even whole countries. There are also many living and dead people in the stomach of the wolf. At this stage, such disproportion does not give anyone pause. The representation of the fish in the image of the whale already contains an attempt to introduce proportion, and the gaping mouth is an artistically exaggerated introduction of proportion into the image of devouring; it is likewise a later phenomenon.

23. Death the Kidnapper

Analysis of the dragon's form and its role as devourer both lead to the same result: the dragon is genetically associated with death. Here it is possible to see two lines that replace each other—namely, a more ancient one that is still connected with the rite of initiation and a later one that is purely conceptual.

This connection with the concept of death and corresponding rituals can account for another aspect of the dragon: its abductor role.

Here we could engage in studying the history of representations of death. However, early forms of this idea are not reflected in the image of the dragon. The dragon reflects a later mode of conceptualizing death—that is, viewing death as an act of kidnapping. Death occurs because someone has abducted the soul, or one of the souls, of the deceased. Treatment and recovery of the deceased are imagined accordingly: the soul must be kidnapped back and restored to its place. There are wondertales built entirely around abduction and counterabduction.

But who is the kidnapper? We shall soon see that the kidnapper is very often also deceased and that the deceased drag the living with them. The process of forming the concept that the soul is kidnapped by a dead person, usually in the shape of an animal, is inseparable from another process, that of objectivizing the soul. Let us give an example. The Dakota people assume the existence of four souls. There is a soul of the body, which dies with it. Then there is a spirit that always remains with the body or resides in its proximity. Next, there is a soul responsible for the actions of the body, and it departs to the south based on some actions and to the west based on others. The fourth soul, finally, always remains in a lock of the dead man's hair. It is preserved by his relatives until they have a chance to throw it into the country of the enemy, where this soul begins to wander as a ghost, bringing death and disease.[134]

In this case, it is curious that the soul, or one of the souls, that emerges from the dead becomes itself the cause of other people's death. In other words, one of the souls is objectivized, becomes a terrible independent entity, and loses the connection with its master, and this is the one that brings about death.

Objectivization is the belief that the soul is an independent being that can live outside a person. One need not always even die for this to happen. A living person can also have a soul, or one of his souls, existing outside of himself. This is the so-called outer soul, or "bush soul." Koschei possesses such a soul.

For instance, in Bantu a person has four souls, one of which exists externally in the image of an animal that is most intimately connected with the person's body. This may be a leopard, a turtle, a fish, or some other animal.

When we learn that animals kidnap the souls of the living, the question can always be raised regarding whether this animal developed from a zoomorphic dead man. For example, among the Indians of the Tlingit tribe, the otter is thought to have a special supernatural power that includes, among other things, the desire to steal people and, after depriving them of consciousness, to turn them into human otters.[135] Fear of the dead is commonly founded on this notion, even long after the dead have lost their animal shape. For example, in the Society Islands it is believed that "the souls of the dead seem to have been credited with the power of stealing the souls of the living."[136] Frazer has a great many examples of this belief. For example, members of the Tarahumara tribe (Mexico) believe that a death that comes despite all the shaman's attempts to save the patient's life occurs because "those who have gone before have called him or carried him off."[137] The dead pull the living behind them. The Papuans of former British New Guinea believe that "ghosts are known to carry away the souls of living people."[138] Special deities are created whose function is to steal souls. Eldson Best, a Maori researcher, writes, "The lizard represents death. This explains the great dread that the Maori folk entertain for the lizard, and why seeing a lizard is deemed a very serious omen. It is the emissary of Whiro (an evil deity) and the harbinger of death. When the gods decide to destroy a man, they do so by introducing a lizard into his body, and that creature devours his vitals and so causes death." Best adds, "We now see why Whiro is styled the Thief, why he is the patron deity of thieves; for ever he lurks in this world to steal the life of man."[139]

The above examples illustrate that the belief once existed that death occurs because the soul is kidnapped by a dead person in the shape of an animal. One such animal is the dragon.

For example, Turaev notes in his work on the history of the ancient East, "There was once also a notion of a special spirit of death, *ekimmu*, who wandered everywhere sowing disease. A representation of these Babylonian devils has been preserved. These are mostly winged beast-like figurines."[140] Similar phenomena exist in Egypt. The twenty-seventh chapter of *The Book of the Dead* is a prayer addressed to the gods who bear away hearts. In Egypt, however, the devourer (not the kidnapper) of the dead has a slightly different form. He dwells beside a lake of fire and the deceased strikes him, as will be discussed below. In this context, it is interesting to mention the life of the Coptic saint Pisentius, dating to the seventh century. Pisentius describes the agony that the mummy experiences. For him the mummy is a person who led a sinful and wicked life. He provides a mummy's speech:

When they had cast me into the outer darkness I saw a great gulf, which
was more than a hundred cubits deep, and it was filled with reptiles, and
each one of these had seven heads, and all their bodies were covered as
it were with scorpions. And there was another mighty serpent in that
place, and it was exceedingly large, and it was a terrible sight to behold;
and it had in its mouth teeth which were like pegs of iron. And one
laid hold of me and cast me into the mouth of that Worm, which never
stopped devouring; all the wild beasts were gathered together about him
at all times, and when he filled his mouth all the wild beasts which were
round about him filled their mouths with him.

And further: "After a little time my eyes were opened, and I saw death
suspended in the air in many forms. And straightway the Angels of cru-
elty snatched my wretched soul from my body, and they bound it under
the form of a black horse, and dragged me to Ement (Amenti)." These
materials contain many folktale elements. We see here the lake of fire, the
many-headed serpent, a man carried away in the air, and even a horse;
and of course this material brings us closer to an understanding of where
the wondertale comes from. The analogy here is quite comprehensive. It
is enough to remove the theme of death in order to obtain a pure fantasy
devoid of any religious core. We find such a "fantasy" in the wondertale.
These examples contain the theme of death in a very clear form. The only
element forgotten here is that the kidnapper himself was formed from
animals that represent the soul. This is still evident in earlier though rare
cases. For example, the Eskimo Torngarsuk, who abducts the souls of
shamans, can be considered a precursor to the dragon. He resembles a
walrus covered with adhesive suckers. Nansen, analyzing the word *torngarsuk*, comes to the conclusion that it means "disgusting soul."[41] The
Greek Erinyes, or Furies, are also connected to the soul. This connection
is obvious to the researcher but is not always obvious to those who believe
in such beings.

We still lack one additional element for a more accurate understanding. So far we have concentrated all our attention on the figure of the kidnapper. The kidnapped person—in the wondertale, princesses or women
in general, typically beauties—has so far remained out of sight. In the
materials cited above, we have not yet encountered the abducted woman.
We must now turn our attention to this specific element.

24. *Introducing the Erotic Element*

Two very strong instincts have been attributed to the deceased, who
existed due to the objectification of the soul as an independent being:
physical hunger and sexual hunger. First comes physical hunger. Death
the devourer is more ancient than other kinds of death. From this point
of view, the Egyptian devourers of the dead must be recognized as very

archaic. Here, as in Babylon, the erotic theme is still completely absent, while in Greece, for example, it is abundantly present.

As social life continues to develop, satisfaction of sexual feelings comes to the fore. These two kinds of hunger are sometimes assimilated, as in a Russian wondertale: "The dragon seized the princess and dragged her to his den; however, he did not eat her. She was beautiful, so he took her as his wife."[142] There is no place in primitive society for manifestation of individual erotic feelings. The erotic appears relatively late and is introduced into already existing and previously formed religious concepts such as the notion of death-the-abductor. The deity chooses a beloved woman or man from among the mortals. Death occurs when the spirit-abductor falls in love with a living person and carries that person away to the realm of the dead for marriage. In places where individual love has not yet developed, the abductor's longing is simply a longing for the opposite sex and, later, for a particular member of this sex. For example, Richard Parkinson reports the following from the island of New Ireland: The spirits of the deceased—that is, those who are buried in the ground—are called *tangou* or *kenit*. They are invisible during the day, but at night they appear before the living in the form of fiery sparks or lights. The spirits of dead men haunt women, and the spirits of the dead women sneak up on men. When spirits approach, all living people quickly flee as these spirits bring illness, suffering, and death.[143] Furthermore, the spirits of unborn children or women who died in childbirth are known as *gesges*. They also walk during the day in the image of men or women, adorning themselves with special strongly scented herbs, which render them recognizable from a distance. They attempt to lure living men and women and seduce them into sexual intercourse. In particular, they pursue those who have had contact with members of the same totem. These gesges live in gorges and stones.

The erotic coloring of the concept of death continued to grow stronger. Shternberg labels this phenomenon "chosenness": a deity or other creature chooses a beloved girl and carries her off to the realm of death. Shternberg writes, "This idea has become so firmly established in the mind of primitive man that even a whole series of tragic events in an individual's life is ascribed to chosenness. For example, death from lightning, accidental death in a fire, on the water, or death caused by a predatory animal, a tiger, bear, crocodile, etc., is attributed to the fact that some spirit, having fallen in love with a certain person, kills him in order to possess him in the spirit world."[144]

The fact that this phenomenon originated later is evident because it is particularly common in ancient Greece, whereas at earlier stages of development it is still very general and undifferentiated. The Greeks were familiar with amorous abduction as a variety of death. Artemidorus's famous dictum is "If a man dreams of conjugal union with a god or goddess, it means death."[145] Tablets found in tombs represent a woman abducted from a circle of wailing relatives by a beautiful winged youth.[146] "Death in the ancient belief was perceived as marriage with the deity of death; the deceased was celebrating his wedding with this deity."[147] This is also manifested through wedding customs. "The wedding is a typical image on the sarcophagi; the gods of marriage are the gods of death. The funeral procession and the wedding procession are the same; the bride is brought at night with torches, the wedding bed is likened to a deathbed, and the procession around the altar is analogous to funeral rites."[148] There is no need here to cite all the materials that have led scholars of antiquity to these conclusions.

25. Abduction in Myths

From these general comments we now move on to myths. As far as myths are concerned, we can cite several narratives of various primitive peoples about an animal kidnapping a human. As religion develops, the animal is replaced by a god, but these gods still retain zoomorphic elements. Pluto, god of the underworld, carries away Kore, the daughter of Demeter. Pelops carries Hippodamia across the sea in a wondrous chariot. The chariot flying through the air is a substitute for the animal that featured here previously. The list of gods who steal mortal women in Greek mythology is quite impressive. Malten, who specifically studied the abduction of Kore, came to the conclusion that this motif developed from the idea of people kidnapped by death. The erotic element was added later.[149] The wondertale is more archaic than these myths. There the kidnapper still lacks a human face; he preserves his animal-devourer characteristics, which have almost been lost here. However, the myth of Boreas abducting Orithyia while she is playing with her friend the nymph Pharmacea on the shore of Ilissos and carrying her off to Sarpedon's Rock in Thrace has a very close parallel in tales where a girl is carried away by a whirlwind while walking in a garden.

Along with this, in Greece there were also concepts of death as a kidnapper but already devoid of imagery. For example, in Euripides's tragedy *Alcestis* the heroine is carried off by Thanatos, a pale, impersonal deity whose very name means "death." Or there is Hades, to whom a passion for devouring people is ascribed, as Albrecht Dieterich explains.[150] In addition, men in particular are pursued by the Harpies.

If the origin of the motif of the abducted beauty is becoming clear here, that does not mean that everything is completely comprehensible. One can object that the princess, abducted by "death" in the shape of a dragon or the like, nonetheless *never* dies. Her fate is twofold. In earlier materials, her bridegroom wins her back from the dragon. Thus, she seems to have two marriages: one is a forced marriage with an animal (her time spent married to the animal is traced in stories like "Cupid and Psyche"); the other is with a man, a prince. There are cases, however, in which there are not two grooms. The dragon is *not replaced* by a groom but *transformed into* a handsome prince. This is what we find in the story of Cupid and Psyche. In later materials, a woman kidnapped by a god remains as the god's wife. It is not by chance that Koschei, birds, bears, and so on also appear in wondertales, along with the dragon. The fate of the abducted princess leads us to the cycle of the forest house. Here the princess receives the consecration of marriage through Koschei and then passes on to a human fiancé. The further development of this element will be traced in analysis of the prince and princess's wedding night.

V. The Water Dragon

26. *The Dragon's Water Nature*

We see that in the cited examples the fish, shark, whale, dragon, and barrel are always connected with water. Thus, we should study the dragon's aquatic side as well. In the wondertale, the dragon is also a water creature.

We must establish whether the dragon's water nature was introduced later or is inherent in him from the beginning. We have already met water creatures in our discussion of skillful characters. These are the masters of natural forces, including the element of water. Let us remember the old man who holds his knees up. While he keeps them up, the water in the lake is high. As soon as he lowers his knees, the water level also drops. The dragon is exactly the same sort of being. The dragon's rise from the water invariably entails the water rising.

None of the functions of the dragon that we have considered so far are strongly associated with its appearance. The fish, lizard, and bird—the animals that compose the dragon—are also able to swallow and spit out. The guardian of waters is more firmly connected, first with the figure of the snake and then with the serpent-dragon. The concept of the snake as guardian of waters can be found among the most primitive peoples, for example, the peoples of Australia. According to Baldwin Spencer and Francis Gillen, "About fifty miles north-north-west of Alice Springs there is a gorge. [In the gorge is a waterfall with a small permanent pool at its base, which is] said to be inhabited by the spirit of a great dead snake and by some living snakes, the descendants of the former."[151] This serpent (or this snake) is widespread in Australia. Among the descriptions of individual examples, three features are common to all. The snake has large dimensions and a fantastical appearance; it lives in water and can swallow water up, hold it, and spit it back out; and it devours people, who either perish as a result or acquire magical powers and health. In southeastern

Australia, people believed in a snake that "lives in deep permanent lagoons and waterholes,"[152] which represents the natural element of water and has vital importance to people in all parts of Australia. A snake named Kurrea is described as a "snake-like monster of enormous proportions." Others are called Karia, and we are told that they "swallow their victims whole."[153] In other places, this monster is called Yero and "is described as being like a huge eel or serpent. . . . It has a large head with red hair, and a big mouth out of which the rapids are said to emerge. Its body is striped with many colors, and it has healing properties for those who belong to the locality and who if sick may swim in the water and regain their health."[154]

These materials demonstrate that the water dragon can be attested at the earliest stages of social development known to us. Of course, this figure also has its own prehistory, but we possess no materials detailing it, and we shall not retreat into a deeper past merely to speculate. The second thing we see is that the dragon-devourer and the water dragon are one and the same figure. This explains why later in myths, once the motif of translocating the devoured person has been created, the translocation usually occurs over the water or through water. After all, during the initiation rite, the same Australians make an image of the snake with its mouth open. Thus, the dragon-devourer is not something special or different from the water dragon; rather, in some cases one aspect of the snake is more developed, while in others it is another.

Such snakes continue to control the waters of the world's peoples even at more advanced stages of development. According to the view of the inhabitants of Niasse (Oceania), "A terrible crawfish covers the mouth of a snake, and that causes the high tide and the low tide."[155] In places where there is no high or low tide, the serpent simply causes the water to move. The Ainu say that "a trout lived in a lake, and it was so strong that, when it struck its pectoral fins against the shore, it aroused the waves on the opposite shore."[156] In a Dolgan tale, the hero meets a mammoth. "Wherever the mammoth goes, rivers are created; wherever it lies down, lakes are created."[157] The Zulu people are afraid to use the water of a certain lake because it is inhabited by the serpent Umugarna.[158] The Native American Muisca make sacrifices to a serpent or dragon who lives in a lake.[159]

Its connection with fertility is especially clearly traced in agricultural and pastoral Africa: "The python is supposed to give success in fishing. He has power over the river and all that is in it."[160] Thus, the beneficent dragon here is also a water dragon. His connection with the rite is also widely attested. In Africa, the serpent cult's phallic aspect is especially developed. (For detailed materials, see Hambly).[161]

Like the dragon-devourer, the water dragon is originally a creature that, though terrible, is still basically good. He is a water giver, and later he is a creator of fertility, both the fertility of the fields and human fertility.

So how does the motif of battling him arise? Extrinsically, from the plot's perspective, the motif of the dragon *abusing* his power appears. As a water creature, he either holds back the water and creates a drought or, conversely, spits so much water that it causes a flood.

Among the Hopi a snake rose from the pond to the sky, and this in turn made the waters rise, causing a flood.[162] For the Incas the flood occurred "because the three sons of the first man or god named Paha, having nobody to fight with, began to fight the big snake. It retaliated by spitting so much water that it flooded the whole earth."[163] In the last example the relationship is reversed: the serpent emits the water because the brothers start fighting him. Examples of this type are rare at the cultural stage of the Native Americans of the period concerned. The serpent is more often killed because he is a devourer, not because he is a water creature.

Things change, however, with the transition to regular farming and cattle breeding and with the formation of early statehood. This stage introduces anthropomorphic gods. It is important for the farmer that his gods control the water. His gods have human form, whereas the divine beings once considered sacred had animal form. Thus, with the transfer of divinity from animal to god, the gods kill the animals. They snatch power from their hands, take away their control over the water, and begin to control it themselves in the way required by the herdsman and the farmer.

This stage is represented in particularly explicit fashion by India, and it is also evident in Greece and China.

Much has been said about battling the dragon in the *Rigveda* in connection with solar and lunar mythology. Among other things, one significant feature of the dragon Vrtra, who is defeated by the powerful god Indra, is quite evident: he dams the river. The rivers flow again only because Indra kills Vrtra and releases them. Here are a few quotations:

> The rivers say: Indra who wields the thunder dug our channels: he smote down Vrtra, him who stayed our currents.[164]
> (Addressing Indra): Thou in thy vigour having slaughtered Vrtra didst free the floods arrested by the Dragon.[165]
> Thou hast let loose to flow the Seven Rivers.[166]
> Indra . . . slaying Vrtra stayer of their flow.[167]

Compare the entire hymn 33 in Book 1 as well as Book 2, Hymn 51, l. 4; Book 1, Hymn 51, l. 5; Book 1, Hymn 52, ll. 2–6, Book 1, Hymn 121, l. 11; Book 2, Hymn 11, l. 5; Book 8, Hymn 12, l. 26; Book 8, Hymn 85, l. 18; and so on.[168]

The dragon is a water creature in China too. He is a sea or lake creature, and he also lives in wells. The sea dragon lives at the bottom of the sea, in a palace of transparent stones with crystal doors. One can see this palace by bending over the water early in the morning when the weather is calm.[169] In other words, the dragon has changed from a ruler of natural forces into a king or emperor of natural forces after the model of the Chinese emperor. In this context, it is interesting to cite a legend about the foundation of Beijing.[170] Beijing is founded by a prince who fell into disfavor. The city flourishes. Merchants come to the city, trade is growing, there are sufficient provisions in the city, and the prince rules in a just manner. But suddenly a drought occurs. A dragon's cave lies outside the city gates. The dragon has not been seen for thousands of years, yet it is well known that it lives there. As unskilled laborers are digging up the ground in the area to build a wall, they touch this cave, thinking little of the consequences that may follow. The dragon is annoyed and decides to move to another place, but his wife says, "We have lived here thousands of years, and shall we suffer the Prince of Yen to drive us forth thus? If we *do* go we will collect all the water, place it in our *yin-yang* baskets [used for drawing water], and at midnight we will appear in a dream to the Prince, requesting permission to retire. If he gives us permission to do so and allows us also to take our baskets of water with us, he will fall into our trap, for we shall take the water with his own consent."[171] Everything happens in just this way. The dragons appear in the prince's dream in the form of an old man and woman and ask permission to leave Beijing. Subsequently, a terrible drought ensues, and all the waters disappear. The dream is deciphered; the prince hurries after the old people and pierces one of the baskets with a spear, which causes a flood. The prayer of a Buddhist monk makes the water recede, and a spring is formed with a temple built next to it. Supposedly water for the imperial court is drawn from this spring.

Such is the folk myth that Buddhist monks use for their own purposes, just as the Christian religion used battling the dragon for its own purposes, having St. George slay it and convert the people he freed from the dragon to Christianity.

All these examples show that the water dragon (in its pure form, with no admixtures of other representations, which will be discussed below) is killed either for an unknown reason or because he is blamed for drought or keeping back the water, and this motivates fighting him.

In ancient Greece, the Hydra, or Lernaean Hydra, is the same sort of being. In fine arts, the Hydra is represented as a multiheaded snake, with the number of heads varying from three to nine. According to Apollodorus, eight heads were mortal, while the middle one was immortal. It was believed that when the animal spread out, it held back the water. In Lerna, this view was apparently expanded and modified in the sense that when drought occurred, it was believed that the serpent had swallowed all the country's waters, and this is why the locality of Lerna (where the serpent dwelled) was so marshy.[172] As we have just seen, in Chinese and other myths the idea that the dragon swallows or carries away all of a country's water and that the abundance of water (the flood, the tide, the river or, rather, the swamp) depends on the dragon is not peculiar only to antiquity or only to Lerna. The Lernaean Hydra is an individual example of the universal image of the water dragon.

Just such an individual example is the folkloric "Black Sea dragon," the "water king," behind which "the water swept up three arshins."[173]

But this is only one side of the dragon, which in general does not lend itself to one explanation alone. Its significance is diverse and versatile. Any attempts to reduce the whole dragon cycle to one thing, as Frobenius, Siecke, and others do, are doomed a priori to failure.

In Russian tales, the dragon is not a water trapper, and this is not the reason for struggling with him. But in the tales of other peoples, this ancient motivation is distinctly preserved. In a Pshavi tale, the hero "got into a city where the Devi held back the water, demanding a tribute for it in the form of girls."[174] In a Baloch tale, the heroine says, "Today it is the king's turn to send me to the dragon so that it will let some water into the canals, as the city is languishing from thirst."[175] In a Mongolian tale, the king of the dragons, propitiated by human sacrifice, gives water.[176] In a Nart epos, a seven-headed dragon turns into a dog and does not allow water to be obtained.[177] These materials demonstrate that the dragon's water nature is intrinsic to it. Initially, this does not create grounds for fighting the dragon. The dragon controls the water for people's benefit. But in the era of agriculture, this function is transferred to gods who kill the dragon and give people the waters and rivers that were trapped by it. This tradition has developed independently of the tradition of battling devourers. In the Russian wondertale, it is not reflected functionally, but it is reflected through the dragon's water attributes.

27. The Dragon's Requisitions

Study of the dragon's water nature has brought us closer to the figure's agricultural conception. We have this conception in a motif too, which was earlier indicated as "the dragon's requisitions."

Everything noted about the dragon at the beginning is closely connected to hunting as the main productive foundation where this motif arises. A kidnapper carries away a woman. Here, on the other hand, she is brought to the dragon. The forms of these acts correspond to the rite of giving girls away to water demons and gods in order to influence the country's fertility.

The idea that this motif has an agricultural origin arises from examination of its occurrence. It is found in the ancient agricultural countries, in ancient Mexico, Egypt, India, China, and, to a lesser extent, Greece. It reflects the rite of forcibly giving a young woman to a god by bringing her as a sacrifice. Its rudiments are also found at earlier stages, for example, in North America. There are still no crops here nor farming. Instead, the rite is intended to provide a rich catch of fish. But, as indicated above, the rite and the corresponding myths reach their full development only in countries at the stage of early agriculture.

Both Frazer and Shternberg demonstrate quite convincingly that sexual intercourse between human and god was supposed to promote the abundance of crops. This is apparent because, first, such sacrificial marriages were performed before sowing; and second, they were especially widespread where agriculture depended on rivers—in the valleys of the Nile, the Ganges, the Euphrates and Tigris, and the Yellow River. Here a young woman was sacrificed to a creature dwelling in the water. Shternberg writes, "Given that the gods of fertility were considered particularly lustful deities, and at the same time such lustfulness was necessary for the well-being of the people, this is the source of the custom of sacrifice, especially of maidens and young people, depending on the sex of one or the other deity."[178] Such sacrifices could take quite diverse forms, but only those related to water are important here. The general characteristics of this ceremony, in Shternberg's description, are that the young woman is dressed as a bride, decorated with flowers, rubbed with incense, and seated ashore on a special rock or sacred stone; "afterwards a crocodile would drag her into the river, and the people were utterly convinced that she really became the crocodile's wife, believing that, if she turned out not to be a virgin, it would bring her back."

Sacrifices of this kind were aimed at influencing the harvest or the growth of vegetation in general. Among fishing peoples, these rites were supposed to increase the number of fish. This rite is always closely connected to a myth that explains why the sacrifice is necessary and how it originated. For example, the Algonquins and Hurons say that one day it happened that there were no more fish, and famine threatened. Then a very handsome young man (the water god) appeared to the chief in a dream and said, "I lost my wife and cannot find a single woman no man has known before me. This is the reason why you have no luck and why you will have none until you satisfy me." To convince him that his bride is chaste, they marry him to a little girl who obviously has known no other man. In the rite, the girl is wedded with the help of a fishing net—that is, she is thrown into the water.[179]

The life of the Maya tribe, writes Erwin Dieseldorf, depends entirely on maize. In the city of Chichen Itza, the bones and skulls of young women were found as well as beads and other ornaments of girls who, according to the chroniclers, were thrown alive into the pond. This, claims the author, implies that the Mayans wanted to propitiate the gods through the voluntary donation of life, blood, and property. Even now Native

Americans believe that a drought will stop only if someone drowns.[180] We find corresponding myths in American collections.

This group of concepts is even more widespread in Africa. It was believed that every year a large prairie lake, called Mruvia, required the sacrifice of a baby—a smooth-skinned child without scars (evidently a substitute for chastity). This tribute of a baby was incurred each year, and the baby was thrown alive into the pond, as directed. Without this sacrifice, the pond would have dried up. The Buganda people, when going on a long journey, attempted to appease Mukasa, the god of Lake Victoria-Nyanza, sacrificing to him virgins summoned to serve as his spouses. The Akikuyu in former British East Africa worship a serpent that supposedly lives in one of the rivers, and every few years they marry women, especially maidens, to this serpent-god. The Arab traveler Ibn Battuta reports that several people assured him that when the population of the island (meaning the Maldives) worshipped idols, every month an evil spirit would appear to the natives, emerging from the sea in the form of a ship covered with lanterns. Every time the inhabitants noticed this ship, they took a young maiden, dressed her as a bride, drove her to a pagan temple that stood high on the coast, and left her there on the terrace overlooking the sea. The girl spent the night there, and in the morning she would be found dead, but having lost her virginity. Each month when the spirit appeared, lots were cast among the inhabitants. The last virgin sacrificed in this way was saved by a pious Berber who managed to chase away the sea monster by reading the Qur'an.[181]

This case is interesting not only because European ships with lanterns and smoke were mistaken for monsters. Such sacrifices undoubtedly soon came into conflict with evolved forms of agriculture and the corresponding forms of social life and family relations, as well as with forms of religion that had already begun to create gods. With the advent of land ownership, a special new form of family relations appears. Parental love that does not allow the sacrifice of a child consolidates and proliferates. The sympathy that originally belonged to the powerful spirit that sent the harvest is now transferred to the poor victim. If the sacrificial victim is chosen from among enemies on whom a tribute is imposed, this is a sign of the beginning of compassion for the victim. Nevertheless, sometimes the rite cannot be abolished for a long period. Suddenly, however, a stranger appears and frees the young woman. In the heyday of this rite, he would be destroyed as an evildoer who was violating the most vital interests of the people. His action would have threatened the harvest. In the wondertale, however, he is a hero who is honored. It is curious that in such tales, the hero also often comes to an explicitly foreign land. This shift of sympathies also explains the substitutions when, for example, instead of a live woman an effigy was thrown in. Zelenin provides a very interesting example that can be interpreted as an incomplete substitution in his *Taboo of Words*. The spirit Seid, a lover of women, lives at the bottom of a lake. Before the start of the fishing season, they throw him a female doll made of rags, after which the wife of the fisherman who offered such a sacrifice dies: Seid takes her to be his wife.[182] In Egypt, every year before sowing crops, they would dress a maiden in wedding clothes and throw her into the Nile to ensure the flood and obtain a good harvest.[183] Characteristically, this custom ceased with the Arab conquest. The same custom existed in China, where every year they married a maiden to the Yellow River by drowning her; moreover, the most beautiful maidens were chosen for this.[184]

28. Myths

In places where this rite no longer exists, we often find stories of a different nature. Sometimes they are about an event that supposedly happened once; sometimes they are artistically embellished with folktale characteristics; they also appear in collections of "indigenous tales." Very often their original connection with crop yield and fertility has not been completely lost. In a Mexican legend, people are suffering from hunger. Their gods demand a young woman in exchange for the maize. "They should bring her to the Pantitlan whirlpool."[185] The connection with the crop here is completely obvious, and there is no resistance. The African Wadjagga people tell that once the spirits of a river bay carried away a maiden when she was walking with a group of women and dragged her to their city, from which muted screams began to be heard, typical of those with which the dead receive a newcomer. The next day, the inhabitants offered sacrifices that had been indicated by a spirit, and afterward, on the third day, the young woman's corpse was found on the beach.[186] In this example, the connection with the ideas of fertility is no longer preserved, but another connection is clear: the spirits here are called the dead. Sometimes the sacrifice is motivated simply by some danger coming from water animals that must be propitiated. Frazer reports that when the inhabitants of one of the islands of eastern India were threatened by a herd of crocodiles, they attributed this disaster to the crocodile king's passion for a maiden. Therefore, they forced the father of this girl to dress her as a bride and throw her into the arms of the crocodile, her admirer.[187] In the latter example, a purely erotic motivation has overshadowed the more ancient cult motivation; the connection with crops has disappeared.

We have a similar substitution of motivations in Greek myths as well—for example, in the myth of Perseus and Andromeda. Here, Perseus winds up in Ethiopia and finds Andromeda chained to a rock near the seashore. Why is she chained? Her mother once boasted of her beauty before the Nereids, and this aroused their jealousy. The sea god sent a terrible flood and an all-devouring shark. The oracle promised deliverance if the king's daughter was given to this terrible fish to be devoured. Similarly, in the myth of Heracles, the hero encounters a girl in his wanderings who is tied to a rock near the sea-shore on the Trojan coast. This is Hesione, the daughter of Laomedon, who once deceived Poseidon. Poseidon built the Trojan walls but did not receive the promised reward. For this he sent a sea monster, which would regularly devastate the Trojan region until the desperate Laomedon gave him his own daughter. Heracles withstands battle with the monster and frees Hesione.

The legend of the Minotaur preserved the tribute of the defeated tribe as human sacrifices; every seven years, nine youths and nine maidens were sent from Greece for the Minotaur, who would devour them in his laby-rinth. However, the cycle about the Minotaur indicates that the country was struck by drought and epidemics sent by gods.

All these examples lead us to the wondertale. It is hardly necessary to develop the thesis that the wondertale originates in the rite described here or to prove it explicitly. The process itself is obvious as well. Myths have lost the names of gods, the motivations have changed (the motivations had already changed, as we saw, even in myths as compared to rituals), the style of the narration has changed, and the myth has been transformed into a wondertale.

If we compare, on the one hand, the motif of abduction with cor-responding myths (the abduction of Europa by Zeus, etc.) and, on the other, the motif of requisition with its corresponding myths, we see that myths about abduction are less archaic than the tale; here the kidnapper-animal has been transformed into a god-animal, and the myth type of Perseus and Andromeda is more ancient than the tale. Hence it is clear that the relationship between myth and tale is not always the same, and this question cannot be answered cumulatively, as Wundt, Panzer, and others attempt to do.

Religious beliefs can produce religious myth. A tale that is already devoid of any religious coloring can then develop from this myth.

I. M. Tronskii expresses this idea very clearly and succinctly in his work "The Ancient Myth and the Modern Tale," which is mainly devoted to the study of Polyphemus: "A myth that has lost its social significance becomes a folktale."[188] And indeed, the myth of Perseus and Andromeda corresponds entirely to Russian tales.

A more detailed discussion of this issue can be omitted here since this is a general question that cannot be solved based on the example of one motif. But as we advance the hypothesis of the wondertale's connec-tion with myth, it should be noted that the existence of a myth is not the source, or *causa efficiens*, of a tale.

A wondertale can also originate directly from religion, bypassing myth.

Thus, in Greek mythology, there is no abduction of a girl by a dragon. This idea could live among the people without being attested in Greek literature, through which we know the myth. It might even not enter into the literature. On the other hand, the girl's being handed over to the sea monster has been preserved, since this is an agrarian legend, and Greece is an agrarian country where corresponding rituals could also have taken place in ancient times without being reflected in the literature.

One thing, however, is clear: a wondertale and a myth with the same plot cannot coexist at the same time. A tale of Perseus and Andromeda could not yet exist in Greece; there could be only a myth. The tale could appear later in antiquity, even as some embryonic elements of it might have existed alongside myths among the so-called lower popular masses.

VI. The Dragon and the Kingdom of the Dead

29. *The Dragon-Guard*

We saw above, in considering rites of initiation, how closely such rites are related to the idea of being in the realm of the dead. The initiate experiences death, and conversely, death itself is a kind of initiation. This explains why later, when initiation has long been forgotten, the descent into the realm of death, the *catabasis*, is a condition for becoming a hero.

This also explains why the devourer plays such an important role in notions of death.

The water dragon was imagined as a dweller in ponds, lakes, rivers, and seas and on the earth. But these water bodies simultaneously served as the entrance to another kingdom. The way to that other kingdom passes through the mouth of the dragon and through the water, moving inside the water and, later, across the water. This brings us to the water dragon's clear role as a guard. Sitting by the water or in it, he guards it. But in fact the mountain dragon too is connected not with heights but with caves because caves, along with bodies of water, are considered to be entrances to another realm. This is why the dragon sometimes lives in a lair.

We can observe how the dragon, which was perceived to be in water and on earth, begins to be transferred to a more or less magical distance. This transfer is associated with the appearance of spatial representations, concepts of the path traversed by the dead. The dragon that initially dwelled in ponds and lakes (so that people were afraid even to pass near them) is transferred now from the beginning of the deceased's path to its end. The transfer can be of two kinds: either the dragon moves down conceptually into the earth—that is, he becomes a chthonic creature—or by contrast he moves to the heavenly heights and becomes a heavenly, solar, and fiery being. The dragon's chthonic nature is more ancient, but both of these transfers occur relatively late. We can give a generalized sketch of the stages of the devourer that remains in the forest (among peoples with an inward-facing and isolated life); the devourer that has crossed vast spaces over water (among peoples who have reached a higher stage of culture, who know travel and do not live exclusively from hunting in the forest); the devourer that dwells under the earth (where primitive agriculture exists); and the devourer that dwells in the sky (where there is developed agriculture and statehood).

First, we shall analyze the chthonic dragon and then the solar dragon. In both cases the same element, outlined earlier, is developing: hostility toward the dragon. What is more, the chthonic dragon is to some extent still needed and useful, as analysis of the chthonic Cerberus will show. The sky dragon, however, is always an enemy. The chthonic dragon is associated with the realm of the dead. In India, the sky dragon is not connected with him but is a water dragon that was raised up into the sky. In Egypt, it is apparently the chthonic dragon that was raised up into the sky, and it is he whom a dead person meets. The wondertale reflects all stages of the dragon's development.

The first condition for becoming part of the other realm was being swallowed. But the thing that once helped to achieve this turned into its opposite, into an obstacle that had to be overcome in order to get into that kingdom. Devouring no longer occurs and is never more than a threat. This is the last stage in the development of this idea, and this stage too is reflected in the wondertale.

30. *Cerberus*

It is not mere chance that evidence of the chthonic dragon is extremely meager among peoples who have not reached statehood: they do not have it yet. They have primarily a water dragon but transferred to some magical distance. Among people like the Wachagga we see a clear form of transition from the water dragon to the chthonic one.[189]

Still, as indicated above, the concept of an underground keeper of the kingdom of the dead acquires its full development only among agricultural peoples. A typical representative of such guardians is Cerberus, and we must dwell on him to some extent because the figure of Cerberus also explains the guardian role of the wondertale dragon.

The idea that a body of water—a river, pond, or lake—is an entrance to the realm of the dead still holds very firmly in Greece. "The ocean is the first and foremost entrance to the other world," writes R. Ganschinietz, and further, "Flowing waters, absorbed, for example, in swamps or emerging from the earth, were considered an entrance to the underworld, similar to mining tunnels."[190] Creatures that dwelled in these waters had the appearance of dragons or bulls. For example, Achelous, who wooed Deianira and was killed by Heracles, was such a creature. Cerberus belongs to the same category.

Cerberus reveals his old water nature by sitting at the mouth of Acheron, where Heracles finds him. Here the transfer of the dragon to another final point of water is particularly clear. The dragon in a pre-class society sits at the water *source*, at the beginning of the river, while Cerberus, sitting at the river's *end*, confirms the idea that the dragon has been moved *from an exit out of the earth to an entrance into the underworld*. He is close to the dragon of our wondertale both outwardly and functionally. He has three dog heads with poisonous saliva dripping from the maw of each, he has a snake's tail, he has a head on his tail, and his tail stings.

The feature of having two heads or having heads on two opposite sides of the body is very archaic. It is typical in the Americas. There, the serpent almost always has a head on both ends of the body. This concept is based on the fact that the tail of a snake is imagined or perceived as a sting, and it is a different phenomenon from multiheadedness. Cerberus combines these two types in one figure.

When Heracles, following Eurystheus's instructions, brings Cerberus up, Cerberus stings him with his tail. The hair on Cerberus's back and head is made of snakes. As Küster establishes, formerly he was simply called a dragon.[191] According to Hesiod, he affably wags his tail for visitors but lets no one escape.[192] Aeneas, however, cannot enter Tartarus, because Cerberus does not let him. To pacify him, Aeneas throws him a magic honey cake, which makes Cerberus fall asleep.[193] Throwing objects into the guardian's maw is a substitute for the hero entering the mouth himself. It seems to me that these examples demonstrate quite clearly that Cerberus allows the dead to pass, amiably wiggling his tail, but attacks the living, as seen in the *Aeneid*. Thus, the dragon's old role as an accessory in the passageway has not been completely forgotten; at the same time, his guarding role has not yet been fully developed. Cerberus differs from the wondertale dragon in his dog heads—a Greek addition associated with his role as a watchdog. Classical philologists would object that throwing cakes to Cerberus is a purely Greek phenomenon and cannot be interpreted as a substitute for devouring. However, in the wondertale, the hero also throws candies, a pood of salt, and so on at a she-dragon that is about to swallow him.

This interpretation of Cerberus, based on comparative materials, differs from what Dieterich gives in his *Nekyia*. Dieterich considers Cerberus the personification of earth, which absorbs corpses at their burial. He refers to Cerberus eating carrion to support this idea. For Dieterich, he is "the earth's depth, whose open maw absorbs and devours the dead, i.e., makes flesh smolder and leaves only the bones." For us, the devouring of carrion is a rationalized stage of death's devouring.

All these materials suffice to explain the dragon as the guardian of the entrance to the Thrice-Tenth Kingdom.

These Greek materials are very interesting. They offer a further step in the water dragon's transformation into a chthonic dragon, both good and evil. The devouring no longer happens; it is only a threat. The battle does not always take place either. Heracles defeats Cerberus but leaves him alive. Even with all his disgusting features, Cerberus is still considered a creature needed by humans. He is the guardian of Hades.

31. *The Dragon's Transfer to the Sky*

As indicated above, the dragon is transferred not only to the earth's depths but also to the sky. It is impossible to establish exactly when and at what stage of social development this transfer of the devourer and the water dragon takes place.

Peoples who know the sun dragon are always more cultured than those who do not. This concept of a sky dragon does not yet exist, for example, on the Australian continent. It is found in an inchoate stage in the islands of Oceania, and in Africa it exists among peoples who know of primitive agriculture. It is found in a very developed form among the Yakuts, people who practice cattle breeding. It is well developed in Vedic India, but its most explicit forms are found in Egypt.

This transfer had a number of consequences. First, the object of devouring changed. The dragon no longer devoured people; he devoured the sun and was killed as the sun-devourer. On the other hand, sometimes he himself was represented as the sun.

The second consequence is that from the master of the earth's waters it becomes the master of the waters of heaven. The dragon is here perceived as a cloud, holding back the water, the rain. Killing him would produce rain.

The third consequence is that, in places where the concept of a sunny land of the dead is particularly well developed and plays an important role in people's lives, the dragon turns into a creature that guards the heavenly abode of the dead. A typical example of this is found in Egypt.

Finally, the fourth consequence of this transfer: everything surrounding the dragon, including the dragon himself, takes on a fiery nature and coloring. A river becomes the boundary of the realm of the living and the dead, and at the same time it becomes a river of fire. Lakes also become fiery, as does the dragon itself.

We can point to a common belief in the islands of Palau as an example of the embryonic state of the myth of the dragon that devours the sun: the house of the sun is located in the west above the sea, and there a *denzhes* tree grows, forming a dense forest on the shores of that country. In the evening, as the sun approaches the tree, it knocks down the fruits that grow on the tree and throws them into the sea. The sharks that guarded the entrance to the sun country rush at this fruit greedily and do not notice the sun sinking down to reach its house.[194] Here we have rudiments of a concept that develops later among agricultural peoples: that the dragon devours the sun. Representatives of the solar Mythological School consider this concept very ancient, primordial. This is not true. The sun plays a minimal role among hunting peoples.

We find the same concept in the myth of Māui. Māui goes to the place where heaven and earth meet. There gapes the horrible maw of the female progenitor Hine-nui-te-pō. Māui wants to kill her. He warns his companions, the birds, not to laugh as he gets into her mouth. If they laugh, he will die; if they do not laugh, she will die. A small bird, Tivakavaka, laughs, the monster wakes up, and Māui dies. If he had managed to kill her, then people would have stopped dying.[195]

We have analyzed the ban on laughter in another work.[196] Here we would like to highlight certain points: the transfer of a gaping maw from the ground to the horizon and its connection with the idea of death. This example is of later formation compared to dragons that live in water bodies and swallow passersby; it is an earlier inchoate formation compared to the Egyptian dragon that threatens to devour the deceased on his way to the sun, to Ra. This transitional character of the myth corresponds to people's transition from hunting to farming.

Representation of the dragon as the sun's devourer is well developed in Vedic India. The dragon plays a dual role there. On the one hand, he is an earthly creature who detains the flow of rivers, as mentioned above, and this is his older form. On the other, as a celestial creature he detains the rain, but he also detains the sunshine by swallowing the sun.

> When, Indra, thou hadst slain the dragon's firstborn, and overcome the charms of the enchanters, / Then, giving life to Sun and Dawn and Heaven, thou foundest not one foe to stand against thee.[197]
>
> When, Indra, thou whose power is linked with thy Bay Steeds hadst smitten Vrtra, causing floods to flow for man,/ Thou heldst in thine arms the metal thunderbolt, and settest in the heaven the Sun for all to see.[198]
>
> Indra, this Mighty One, the Dragon's slayer, sent forth the flood of waters to the ocean. He gave the Sun his life.[199]

These examples speak not so much of the dragon as of Indra, who kills the dragon and thereby frees the sun, which he then shows to mankind. The very nature of the dragon is pushed into the background here, while the god who defeats the dragon is brought to the fore.

It is noteworthy that Indra kills the dragon with the help of a horse. India is a classic country of horse breeding and perhaps the birthplace of the art of taming horses. The dragon's characteristic trait as the devourer of the sun is also quite clear here.

The dragon appears in just the same way in the wondertale, albeit rarely. "In the kingdom where Ivan lived, there was no day, only night: this was the dragon's doing."[200] "They killed the dragon, took his head, came to its hut, broke its head, and light came out, shining, throughout the whole kingdom."[201] The notion that killing a dragon causes rain ("after killing the dragon, he, i.e., Indra, sends down life-giving water from the sky") is not reflected by the wondertale.

The change that happened to the dragon is quite understandable. While the technologically helpless hunter first needed control over the animal's will, this desire was completely alien to the cattle herder, who managed animals according to his will. He needed the sun, rain, and rivers, and the *Rigveda* reflects these needs.

These observations demonstrate how scholars of the Mythological School were mistaken when they considered the Vedic religion the oldest form of religion. Vedic India is a state with classes, and its religion is late, druidic. However, it reflects folk beliefs that evolved from earlier and more ancient concepts.

32. The Guarding Role of the Celestial Dragon; the Yakuts

In India, the dragon's guarding role has been completely lost. There, it is only a water creature.

In order to trace the guarding role of the heavenly dragon, let us turn to a people at an earlier societal stage, a people who has given a very vivid image of the heavenly guardian of borders—namely, the Yakuts. They are historically a livestock-raising people who breed cattle and horses. But, at the time of the myths' genesis, they do not yet have a well-developed priestly class, they have no written language, and priestly wisdom that brings gods forward has not yet overshadowed the dragon.

Among the Yakuts, the figure of the dragon is quite vivid and extremely rich. The representation is not clad in the form of hymns but in the form of stories—of myths, which are very close in their form to folktales. In Yakut myths, two realms are clearly contrasted, and the dragon reigns in a kingdom that is separated from the people's kingdom by a river. "He galloped for a while and suddenly drove up to a high honorable mountain, whipping up the dust. When he reached the place where heaven and earth meet, where there is a border between the holy (i.e. human) land and the demon land, on the other side for one and a half days' travel a mortal fire rumbled, it whirled up with a whistle; fifteen *versts* from there, earth reptiles and various worms creep, having completely taken over the land."[202]

This example is noteworthy because the serpents and reptiles appear not just in the sky but "at the limit of the holy land"; in other words, we have here a transfer of the dragon to the upper kingdom of the dead.

We see neither a heavenly river nor a fiery lake in India. The Yakuts, by contrast, have a lake. We can observe there how the lake where the dragon used to live, which once was perceived as the dragon's dwelling place in such a concrete way that people were afraid to walk near it, is now transferred to the sky and receives the color of the sun. "After flying for quite a long time, [the hero] flew over *a fiery, burning sea*, descended, and lay down in Eksyukyu's nest on an icy hill. After [the hero] lay there for some time, the noisy Eksyukyu suddenly appeared, flying with a clammer from the south, creating a shadow, and carrying something in its claws."[203]

This dragon is connected to the dead.

> In this way, he lived happily, but one morning his dawning sky did not dawn on time, his sun did not rise on time. As he sat deep in thought, frightened and horrified by all this, a fierce whirlwind suddenly struck the ground with an evil spirit the size of black yearling calves. It lifted all the dry soil upwards like hair, twirling it like a wing. Rain and snow began falling, a blizzard arose, red-flame lights began to sparkle—this was the misfortune that happened. Then a big black cloud climbed into the sky, as if it had arms and legs. And then one night at darkest midnight, it seemed the clouds were breaking apart or the sky was cracking. Such a horrible noise arose, as if his three-part ceiling had been ripped asunder in two directions, and something more than a bang seemed to slam against his floor.[204]

(A detailed description of the monster follows, with iron hair, bloated eyes, tambourines, and a stick.) "I've come to destroy you. I'll carry you off whether you like it or not. My aunt and daughter of the sun lord, the shaman Kegyalliq (whirling smoothly) calls you. Quickly mount your dead horse, put on your burial clothes, eat some of your posthumous food. . . . Now it's time to go." The hero berates him as "a small worm of a flying cloud." He strikes him and the sun appears; the dawn is breaking. Simultaneously, a river appears "and broad flowing water took the place of the field."[205]

This example shows with rare fullness how the figure of one dragon may combine the sky dragon, the devourer of the sun, and the earth dragon, the detainer and kidnapper of rivers who carries men to the realm of the dead.

However, here the dragon, as the guardian of the solar kingdom of the dead, is not yet well developed. The dragon in the solar kingdom of the dead reaches full development only when agriculture develops, when people learn to observe the sun, since they depend upon it and its seasonal return for the harvest. These conditions are not present in Vedic India, among the Yakuts, or among African cattle herders. They are present in ancient Egypt, and indeed, ancient Egypt gives us perhaps the most complete figure of the dragon, with the exception of the dragon that bestows rain, since the harvest in Egypt depends not on the rain but on the annual seasonal flooding of the Nile.

In Egyptian religion, moreover, there is no dragon guardian of waters; the lake is already exclusively fiery. There is only a serpent that is the enemy of the sun and guardian of the kingdom of the dead—a typical concept among developed agricultural peoples. By contrast, in the *Rigveda*, the dragon is exclusively a creature of water (earthly and heavenly), and there is no kingdom of the dead—there is no route there, and there is no movement in it. The Vedas are the creation of a cattle-breeding people. According to Ludwig, the word *grain* does not occur anywhere in the *Rigveda*. Therefore, a sun religion and observation of its course with the invariability of its return could not occur there.

Although Egyptian representations are not especially consistent or uniform, one can still say that the Egyptians imagine the sun as descending in a boat into the kingdom of the dead. The deceased himself turns into the sun. Therefore, the devourer of the sun (devouring always only threatens to happen but never actually happens) is simultaneously the devourer of the deceased who has come to the realm of the dead. This devouring also never happens but only threatens to happen because the newcomer, armed with magical power, vanquishes the serpent Apep and destroys him; after this, he enters the promised kingdom.

33. *The Dragon in Egypt*

Of all the varieties of battling the dragon (among primitive peoples, in the *Rigveda*, in classical antiquity, in Egypt, in China), the Russian wondertale bears the closest resemblance to the Egyptian battle with the creature described in the *Book of the Dead*, in its substance and details (except for the figure of the horse). This does not mean that Egypt was the birthplace of the Russian tale or that this motif came to Europe from Egypt. It means something quite different—namely, that the wondertale reflects the late agricultural conception of the myth. This is the stage after which, on the one hand, decomposition into multitude and diversity begins, decomposition into a variety of local cults (which we have, for example, in Greece with its Hydra, the Gorgon, Medusa, Python, Lernaean Hydra, Ladon, Cerberus, and others). Typicality gives way to individualization. On the other hand, fossilization occurs, or rather ossification; a skeletal frame is created, unshakable for centuries, that is overgrown with the living flesh of a totally different formation: the living flesh of the wondertale. In view of this, Egyptian materials must be discussed in greater detail.

In the *Book of the Dead*, the chief dragon fighter is the sun god Ra. He meets Apep every day on his path and vanquishes him. The battle itself is never described, but his victory over the serpent and its destruction are extolled in detail. We read in the thirty-ninth chapter of the *Book of the Dead*, "[He] (Ra) pierceth thy head, [he] cutteth through thy face, [he] divideth [thy] head on the two sides of the ways, and it is crushed in his land; thy bones are smashed in pieces, thy members are hacked off thee."[206]

The victory is described in greater detail in the cosmogenic text, commonly called *The Book of Overthrowing Apep*. After describing the creation of the world and the creation of the gods, it says:

> I sent them [i.e., the gods],
> Arisen from my members,
> To vanquish the evil enemy.
> He, Apop, falls into the fire,
> The knife sticks out of his head,
> His ear is cut off,
> His name is no longer on this earth.
> I ordered wounds inflicted upon him (?)
> I burned his bones,
> I daily destroyed his soul,
> .... (lacuna)
> I cut off his limbs from his bones.
> I . . . . his legs,
> I chopped up his arms,
> I closed his mouth and his lips,
> I crushed his teeth,
> I cut the tongue out of his mouth,
> I took his speech away from him,
> I blinded his eyes,
> I took his hearing away from him,
> I removed his heart from its place,
> His name exists no longer.[207]

This papyrus was placed in the hands of the dead person, since it protected him from Apep and other serpents on his path. In the *Book of the Dead*, the *I* sometimes stands not only for Ra but also for Osiris, who was identified with the deceased.

Then, in chapter XVII, "Oh, Ra . . . deliver thou the scribe Nebseni, (i.e., the deceased—V. Ia. P.) victorious, from the god whose face is like unto that of a greyhound, whose brows are as those of a man, and who feedeth upon the dead, who watcheth at the Bight of the Lake of Fire, and tear the bodies of the dead, and who devoureth the bodies of the dead and swalloweth the hearts, and who shooteth forth filth, but he himself remaineth unseen."[208] Here we have a fiery lake, swallowing, and spitting back up. All this will await the deceased if he is not supplied with magical knowledge by the *Book of the Dead*.

Here too we see the beginning of the materialization of the concept of swallowing. The serpent-dogs here, like Cerberus, feed on carrion. *The Book of Overthrowing Apep* also mentions cutting out the tongue. But it does not serve there as a way of identifying the hero; it is mentioned along with cutting out the eyes and the heart—the organs that were considered the bearers of the soul (in Egypt, especially the eyes). Until his tongue and eyes are cut out, the serpent cannot be considered killed. That is why the wicked stepmother, when she sends her stepdaughter to death, also demands her eyes and tongue as proof that she is dead. From proof of death in the wondertale, the tongue turns into proof of *a deed of valor*.

Let us cite a few more excerpts from the *Book of the Dead*. "Your enemy, the snake, is handed over to the fire—the serpent-enemy Selau has fallen down flat. His hands are bound with chains, Ra has cut off his legs" (*Book of the Dead*, Chapter V).[209] "According to the desire of my heart, I have come from the Pool of Fire, and I have quenched the fire."[210] Chapter CVIII is of particular interest.

> There is a serpent on the brow of that Mountain, and he measureth thirty cubits in length; the first eight cubits of his length are [covered] with flints and with shining metal plates. The Osiris Nu, triumphant, knoweth the name of this serpent, which [dwelleth] on his hill. "Dweller in his fire" is his name. Now after Ra hath stood still he inclineth his eyes towards him and a stoppage of the boat [of Ra] taketh place, and a mighty sleep cometh upon him that is in the boat deep sleep fell upon the one in the boat, and he gulpeth down seven cubits of the great waters. Thereby he maketh Suti to depart, having the harpoon of iron in him, and thereby he is caused to throw up everything which he hath eaten, and thereby is Set put into his place of restraint.[211]

This passage is interesting to the folklorist mainly for its mention of sleep. We have not encountered this detail anywhere in the materials mentioned previously. In wondertales, the sleep that falls upon the hero before battle is a delusion, a temptation to which the hero never succumbs. The hero must not fall asleep when he meets Yaga either. But in the passage just quoted sleep has a completely opposite meaning. It is a condition for victory. As mentioned above, if the hero talks to the princess before the battle, he usually lies down with his head in her lap. He sleeps before the battle; moreover, a special epithet was even developed for this kind of sleep: "heroic slumber." The princess tries to wake him, but it is very difficult to wake him in such cases.

Regarding swallowing and vomiting up, while an Egyptologist might give a more detailed elaboration of this motif in Egypt, for the folklorist it is a remnant of the more ancient and primitive myth's formation.

All these details of the serpent's image and killing (his fiery nature, the fiery lake, his attempt to devour the newcomer, the meticulous destruction of all his body parts, the detail of cutting out his tongues, the detail of falling asleep) make us posit that the wondertale dragon appeared as a refraction of precisely those concepts in which it was found in developed agricultural states—namely, as a guardian of the kingdom of the dead, as a "devourer of the dead." This is the last stage of wandering, after which the deceased reaches eternal bliss.

34. *Psychostasia*

Here devouring has turned into something terrible and disgusting. But that is not all. It has turned into a *punishment*; the whole motif has been given a moral tone. The devouring (when it occured, though usually it was avoided) was preceded by a trial, and this detail has also been preserved by wondertales. Budge notes, "Those who were convicted at the trial were directly given to the Devourer of the Dead to be torn apart, and they ceased to exist."[212] There would seem to be a contradiction between the fight with the monster and the trial that precedes the devouring. But such contradictions do not stop the Egyptian manner of thinking. The judgment and trial are new phenomena. According to Moret they occur from the sixth dynasty on,[213] whereas the battle is more ancient, and these concepts coexist peacefully. The devourer of the dead is sometimes described as a hybrid creature that looks like a crocodile in front, a hippo in back, and a lion in the middle. Often it is portrayed as a dog. The judgment consisted of weighing the heart of the newly departed on scales. The heart of the deceased lay on one pan—his conscience, either light or burdened by sins. On the other pan was put the truth in the form of a statuette of the goddess Mait or of a feather, the goddess's hieroglyph. From this, it is clear that the lowering of the heart pan meant death, whereas if it was lifted or balanced it meant discharge.

We have only one Russian wondertale that has preserved the weighing of souls or psychostasia. This is "The Witch and the Sun's Sister." There, a sister-witch of Ivan is born, and she devours everyone. He runs away from her to "the Sun's sister."

> At that very time Prince Ivan galloped to reach the palaces of the Sun's sister and shouted: "Sun! Oh, sun! Open the window!" The Sun's sister opened the window, and the prince jumped inside with his horse. The witch started asking for her brother to be handed over. The Sun's sister did not listen to her and did not give him up. Then the witch said: "Let Prince Ivan come with me to the scales, and we shall see who will outweigh whom. If I outweigh him, I will eat him, and if he outweighs me, let him kill me." And they went there. Prince Ivan sat down first on the scales, and then the witch came on. She had just set her foot on it, and Prince Ivan was hurled up with such a force that he directly got to

the sky, to the palaces of the Sun's sister; and the witch-snake remained on the ground.[214]

Here, even the idea that a lesser weight furnishes victory has been preserved, while a heavy one leads to being devoured. Also preserved is the notion that the kingdom the hero comes to is that of the sun. The only detail that has disappeared is that all these events occur before the deceased is admitted to the kingdom of the sun.

35. The Dragon's Connection to Birth

When analyzing the wondertale, we have seen that from the beginning the figure of the dragon is somehow connected to the hero, to his birth. It is not directly stated in the Russian tales that there is a connection between the hero and the dragon from birth, but it appears indirectly in the motif of the adversary. The dragon has never seen the hero before, yet somehow not only does he know of the hero's existence, but he also knows he will perish by the hero's hand. The relationship is seen more clearly in an Indian tale: "The king of serpents, Vaisingi, was born in the underworld; in the sky, King Indra was born, and on the earth King Dhobichand."[215] This feature should also be explained, and while this explanation does encounter immense difficulties, it can be provided only implicitly.

That the dragon is related to death follows quite fully from the given materials. But it is also somehow related to birth.

Let us consider some relevant examples. In the myth of Māui, the hero-god speaks of his birth.

> I know that I was born prematurely on the seashore and that I was thrown into the sea after you (turning to his mother) wrapped me in a lock of your hair, which you had cut off for this purpose. Then the sea grass embraced me with its long tresses; it formed and shaped me. The soft eels wrapped themselves about me to protect me. Myriad flies buzzed around me and laid their eggs on me [so that the maggots could eat me]. Flocks of birds collected around me to peck at me, but at this moment my great ancestor appeared, the sky, Tama-nui-ki-te-rangi, and he saw the flies and the birds. The old man rushed toward me as fast as he could, unwound the eels from around me and found me, a living being.[216]

This myth is quite clearly related to those regarding people being swallowed and spat back out. The difference from the cases discussed above is that here the hero is not in the stomach of a fish but is instead wrapped up by fish. In addition, this example differs in that the hero is born when he comes out of the fish. This case shows that being wrapped up by snakes, fish, and so on is a later form of staying inside the fish.

Such a comparison and explanation seem more probable than the explanation of Erich Küster, Nikolai Kharuzin, and others that the serpent here is a totemic animal whose bite does no harm. Serpents would be placed on children: "If they did not touch them, or bit them but not fatally, then this proved that the children were genuine."[217]

The snake here represents the material origin, the womb. Let us not forget that in the rite of initiation, emerging from the serpent's belly was perceived as a second birth—in fact, as the birth of the hero. We have seen how this was later replaced by being placed in a small chest and lowered into the water. Thus, these concepts related to being born from the serpent have the same source, where the whole complex of battling the dragon originates. The developmental stages can be schematically marked as follows: first, the one who was born of the dragon (i.e., passed through it) is the hero; next, the hero killed the dragon. The historical combination gives us: the one who was born of the dragon kills the dragon.

But the snake can also appear as a father, an ancestor, and this concept is, of course, a later formation. In this case, the dragon becomes a symbol for the phallus. It represents the paternal origin and after some time becomes an ancestor. This concept seems to have been especially developed in Africa; at any rate, a large amount of material was collected in Africa. The peoples who speak the Igbo language think that if a snake approaches a woman, it means she has conceived. Childless women entreat serpents for children. If a pregnant woman dreams about a snake or a water spirit, she believes that her child will be the embodiment of the water spirit. "They are supposed to possess the nature of snakes and are regarded as reincarnations of the water spirits."[218] Here the idea that a person born from a snake has a serpent's strength and nature is clearly evident.

Such an ancestor-serpent in antiquity was Cecrops. He was depicted as half human, half snake or dragon, but, as Küster establishes, he had a pure snake appearance in folk belief.

Cadmus, the founder of Thebes, and Harmony, his wife, turned into serpent-dragons at the end of their lives. According to some sources, Harmony was the daughter of the very dragon Cecrops had killed.[219]

But if the one who was born of a snake is a serpent himself or turns into one, and if the person born from the serpent kills the serpent, then perhaps this is the explanation of the "adversary." Perhaps the hero kills the dragon because historically he is the dragon himself or was born of the dragon—that is, he emerged from the dragon. For some reason, in the Egyptian myth-tale, the island where the serpent lives is called the island of the double. Perhaps our wondertale dragon is afraid of his own double.

To answer these questions, we shall analyze cases of a dragon's death by another dragon.

36. *The Dragon's Death by Another Dragon*

Above we witnessed the case of a serpent defeated when a girl wearing a belt made from a serpent enters his mouth. In the serpent's belly, the belt comes to life and kills it. But of course, the clear, obvious cases of a dragon's death from another dragon can be only of late formation, when the dragon-devourer has completely turned into a terrible creature but the dragon that gives strength and power has not yet been forgotten. The evidence for this is provided by Egypt.

The thirty-second chapter of the *Book of the Dead* is called "The Chapter of Beating Back the Crocodile That Cometh to Carry Away the Magical Words from the Khu in the Underworld." I will cite only the passages of greatest interest to a researcher of folktales. "Get thee back, O Crocodile that dwellest in the West, for the serpent-fiend Naau is in my belly, and I will give him unto thee; let not thy flame be against me. . . . My face is open, my heart is upon its seat, and the crown with the serpent is upon me day by day. I am Ra, who is his own protector, and nothing shall ever cast me to the ground."[220] What, then, actually serves as protection against the serpent?

First, the deceased warns the serpent that he has the serpent Waan in his stomach. Second, he has a crown with a snake on it, and this serves as a defense. In other words, the serpent perishes from its own image. This concept was very common in Egypt and, apparently, not only there. Recall that in the Bible, Moses orders a copper serpent put up to protect the Israelites from serpents.[221] Thus, it appears that one serpent serves as protection against another serpent. The image of a snake appeared on the pharoah's crown. "The sacred serpent that guards the sun appears on the forehead of his earthly double, the Pharaoh, and thus burns his enemies with flames."[222] According to Turaev, it is in the archaic epoch of Egypt that "poetic ideas about nature developed, from which all the richness of mythology emerged. The sun is like the eye of a god, and clouds, fogs, thunderstorms, and nocturnal darkness are like his enemies. The sun disappears into a foreign land when the sky is shadowed and comes back when the god of light chases them off. The sun itself turns into a fire-breathing snake on the forehead of the god and chases them off." By "them" Turaev means here the darkness, fog, and thunder as the sun's enemies. But we know by now that the sun's main enemy is Apep, and he is the one who is defeated by another serpent. This might suggest that there must be cases where two serpents fight. And, indeed, such a case can be found. The *Amduat, or Book of What Is in the Underworld*,[223] a rather late-written source but archaic in its content, describes in detail the journey of Ra's boat in the underworld on the other side of the earth from sunset to sunrise. His entire trip, like the book as a whole, is divided into twelve parts, corresponding to the twelve hours of the night.

At midnight the route turns to the east and passes by Osiris's ancient sacred places: Busiris and Mendes, Osiris Islands, the "Fields of Gifts," and the secret hall with the image of Osiris; here are the mummies of the kings and the blessed dead. Ra addresses them with greetings and calls for a joint struggle against the serpent Apep who has already swallowed all the water of the next hour to hinder the traveling for the god Ra and filled 450 cubits with his body-curves. Apparently, Ra does not have enough strength to fight him, so the serpent Mechen comes to his aid, forming with his body-curves a kind of Naos around him. Isis and other goddesses bind and wound Apep with their incantations.[224]

Turaev is close to considering the content of this book, as he says, "a product of the sick imagination of Egyptian priests."[225] Such an interpretation is antihistorical. While the whole *Book of the Dead* is full of curses addressed to Apep, the oldest notions of the good serpent (from which, as we saw above, the entire range of notions about the serpent emerged) could have lived on among the people, continuing to exist independently of the official religion of the court and the priests; and these concepts overlaid the concepts of the evil Apep. Here decrepit priestly wisdom drew on folk beliefs and canonized them. The doctrine of the good serpent later began to spread again, and it survived in the sect of the Ophites, which took the snake as its main and only deity until the sixth century CE.

Here the archaic good serpent-devourer and the more recent horrible serpent-devourer meet face to face as enemies. The chief serpent fighter Ra passes through the serpent. In the *Amduat*, Ra lives in the underworld in his boat. "In order to get the barge out of there, its rope turns into a serpent, and it is carried through the body of a serpent 1300 cubits long— a symbol of renewal." Ra comes out of the serpent's mouth no longer in "flesh" but in the form of a "scarab."[226]

Are all these materials, however, applicable to the wondertale? Is it possible to say that the wondertale Ivan can kill the dragon because he has passed through him, and because the dragon views him as his double? This is not directly or straightforwardly evident anywhere. The Russian tales have not preserved birth from a dragon and devouring by a dragon as blessings. They have preserved another pattern: birth from a fish. And, indeed, we may note that the person born from a fish is most often the dragon fighter. We have seen above how a stay inside the fish is closely related to staying inside a snake. Thus, although there is no direct proof, there are still indirect indications that confirm our observations. We can, in addition, point to one example where the wondertale dragon can perish only through itself. The usual formula comes down to the statement "I can die only through Ivan." Here it reduces to the assertion "I can perish only through myself," thereby confirming our remarks. We have such a case in a Pskov tale.[227] The hero is walking through the forest and meets a twelve-headed dragon; six of its heads are asleep and six are not. "The dragon was rising, and by now there was no escape from its teeth. It was there and could die only from itself; someone else's power would not be sufficient to take it on."

This excerpt, quite strange at first sight, finds its explanation in the materials provided above: the dragon dies through another dragon, in this case, even through himself. This dragon commits suicide. "Plunging his claws into his chest, he lurched so hard that he was torn in half, fell to the ground with a shriek, and dropped dead."[228] Thus, the Russian wondertale also knows a death of a dragon from another dragon and, furthermore, in a very interesting and significant form: the dragon's death from itself. Two dragons, one attacking and one defeated, have merged here into a single creature. This is because the dragon is such an exceptional enemy and antagonist that the contemporary wondertale is no longer able to have the dragon play the heroic role of the dragon's killer, something that still exists in Egypt. But it is clear now why the dragon knows the enemy and its vanquisher: it is born from the dragon itself; it is the dragon and only the dragon that is the "enemy" who strikes the death blow.

37. Conclusion

Our analysis has come to an end. It is not easy to draw a general conclusion. The dragon is a very complex and diverse phenomenon. Any attempt to give it a single explanation is doomed in advance to failure; general conclusions, nevertheless, always boil diversity down to singularity, thereby distorting the essence of the phenomenon.

The best proof or argumentation is that which is backed up by material evidence. In this respect, much work still needs to be done. There are so many materials still hidden in the collections of so-called uncultured or primitive peoples. The study of Mediterranean cultures has continued for generations. The study of earlier cultures has not yet begun, but the clue lies specifically there, and work therein also requires many years of study.

From this, first of all, follows a methodological conclusion: the phenomenon must be studied in its development. Folklore should be studied not as something detached from economics and social systems but as a derivative of them. This study has attempted to work in such a direction, and some results were obtained. Now it is no longer possible to complain along with Frazer that research and results stand on slippery ground. It is true that for us the dragon is not the sun and not a vegetative being. It does not actually "denote" anything; it is a historical phenomenon whose functions and forms have been changing. The methods applied here have allowed us to trace its historical development from the ritual where it is firmly connected to the social institutions of a clan system and that system's economic interests and where he appears before us as the devourer-benefactor.

We have seen how its integration into the economic sphere of the sea, of travel, of the earth and the sun changes both the dragon's external appearance and its functions; how under the influence of these factors it becomes a water creature, an underground and a celestial creature; how in the state religions of India and Egypt it is vanquished by new gods who control natural forces in accordance with the new interests and requirements of people of a new culture.

We also saw how firm its connection is to concepts of death, concepts that assume such spectacular forms in Egypt.

Wondertales reflect all the stages of this development, starting with the more ancient ones, which feature the acquisition of birds' language through the dragon, as well as the transitional ones, which feature being carried away to foreign lands in the stomach of a fish, and later ones, with the well-developed form of heroic battles on horseback with the help of a sword.

Wondertales have also preserved other features of the dragon's development, such as the concept of judgment before the devourer's gaping maw. Some details have been resignified, such as cutting off the dragon's tongues, but on the whole the tale has very accurately preserved the entire process of the good dragon turning into its opposite. The wondertale has once again proved to be a precious source, a precious storehouse of cultural phenomena that long ago disappeared from our consciousness.

8

BEYOND THE THRICE-NINE LANDS

I. The Thrice-Tenth Kingdom in the Wondertale

1. The Locality

The kingdom where the hero arrives is separated from his father's house by an impenetrable forest, a sea, a fiery river with a bridge where a dragon hides, or an abyss into which the hero falls or descends. This is the "Thrice-Tenth" or "other" or "fantastic" country. A proud and powerful princess reigns there; a dragon dwells there. The hero comes to recover the abducted beauty and to obtain marvelous objects, rejuvenating apples, and living and healing waters that give eternal youth and health.

Previously we addressed how one gets to this realm. Now we must look around in it somewhat. First, we shall examine the picture the wondertale provides, and only after that we shall open the frame and exit into a wider space.

As soon as we begin to look closely at this kingdom, however, we immediately notice that the picture of the Thrice-Tenth Kingdom gives us no kind of external consistency. It turns out that it is impossible to trace a single picture. We must draw several separate ones. This first and foremost concerns its *whereabouts*.

Sometimes this kingdom is located underground: "Ivan walked for a long time or a short time and came across an underground passage. He descended through this passage into a deep abyss and came to an underground kingdom where a six-headed dragon lived and reigned. He saw white stone chambers and went inside."[1]

But there is nothing specifically subterranean in this place. Usually it is not dark at all; the land there is the same as here. "They walked for a long time through the underground passage. Suddenly a light began to gleam. It got brighter and brighter, and they came out into a broad field under the clear sky. A magnificent palace was built on that field, and in that palace lived the father of the beautiful maiden, the king of the subterranean country."[2]

On the other hand, this realm can be located atop a mountain: "Suddenly the boat rose through the air and instantly, like an arrow launched from a bow, brought them to a large rocky mountain."[3] Or, "They sat down, and the bear-king brought them to mountains so steep and lofty that they went up to the very sky. The place was all empty; no one lived there."[4] We have a very special and interesting case in the tale "The Crystal Mountain," which recounts "And he flew to the Thrice-Tenth Kingdom, and that kingdom was more than half drawn into a crystal mountain."[5] "They rode for a long time and finally arrived. He looked around and saw a glass mountain."[6] "There is a crystal mountain at this place."[7]

Finally, it can also be located under the water: "And Prince Ivan set out for the underwater kingdom. He saw that the world there was similar to ours: they also had fields, meadows, and green groves, and sun warmed the ground."[8] Sometimes cities are mentioned that have sunk under lakes, as in the legend of the city of Kitezh.[9]

This kingdom, regardless of its location, sometimes has beautiful meadows. "The bird flew out into green meadows, silken grasses, and azure flowers, and fell to the ground. Prince Ivan rose and began walking through the meadow and stretching his legs."[10] Let us note, however, that no matter how beautiful the nature in this kingdom might be, there is never a forest there, and there are never cultivated fields where wheat crops could ripen.

But there is something else: there are *orchards and trees*, and these trees bear fruit. For the most part the gardens are located on islands: "And the fool saw that they were on a very beautiful island where a multitude of various trees grew with all sorts of fruits."[11] "They came to the island. On that island, there were delicious fruits, plants, and flowers."[12] There are almost always gardens in the tale about rejuvenating apples.

So far, we have not seen a single building in the Thrice-Tenth Kingdom. Sometimes this barrenness is emphasized. "They came to such a mountain that it was impossible to ascend either by walking or by riding. There were no buildings, nothing at all, only a bare mountain."[13] Yet there are certain *structures* in the Thrice-Tenth Kingdom, and these are always palaces. We must take a closer look at this palace as well. It is most often golden: "She lives in a large golden palace." Its architecture is absolutely marvelous: "And that palace is golden, and it stands on a single silver pillar, and the canopy over the palace is of gemstones, the stairs are made of mother-of-pearl and they part on both sides like wings. . . . As soon as they entered, the silver pillar started moaning, the stairs began to move, all the roofs began to sparkle, and the whole palace began turning around and changing place."[14] It is often also made of marble or crystal and is inaccessible. "And they saw in the distance a crystal palace surrounded by a crystal wall."[15] This inaccessibility, however, does not constitute an obstacle for the hero. He climbs over the wall. Sometimes the hero, turning into an ant, penetrates through a chink. Sometimes he flies over after turning into an eagle. Very often the palace is guarded by animals, most often lions or dragons. But they do not resemble the dragon Gorynych. They are easy to pacify. "He walked for a long or short time and saw a golden palace before him, gleaming like fire; terrible dragons teemed at the gate, on golden chains; and nearby there was a well with a golden bucket hanging on a golden chain. Prince Ivan drew water with the bucket and gave it to the dragons to drink, and they lay down."[16]

Sometimes the place where the hero has arrived is described as a *city* or a *kingdom*. "Beyond this pillar a golden city stretches for a hundred miles."[17] "A wide and open blue sea spread before her, and golden domes on high white stone palaces gleamed like fire in the distance."[18] The pseudo-Russian style in painting likes to portray this kingdom with churches, which is not in the true style of wondertales. The wondertale does not know the Heavenly Jerusalem. A later rationalization turns the hero into a merchant, the crossing over into a business voyage, and the city into a port town. "The ship came to a big, rich city, stopped at the wharf, and dropped anchor."[19] We do not know any details about this kingdom except that someone reigns there. "The ship ran on dry land, sailed across the sea, and finally came to the country of the tsar-maiden."[20] "They came to an incredible kingdom, an extraordinary land."[21]

All the elements mentioned above are encountered in numerous combinations: the city can be on an island, in the mountains, under the water, or underground. The same can be said of the palaces, the meadows, and the gardens, which freely combine with one another and are placed in a variety of settings.

2. A Connection to the Sun

When we look more closely at this "extraordinary country," we find that it is connected to the sun. For example, we find in one text that the hero is asked to obtain a branch from a golden pine, "which grows beyond Thrice-Nine Lands in the Thrice-Tenth Kingdom, in the under-the-sun country."[22] This kingdom is located in the sky with the sun. "The prince killed the monster and rode to the diamond palace where his mother, Nastasya the Golden Braid, was living in the house of the twelve-headed dragon. The diamond palace was spinning like a millwheel, and the whole universe was visible from that palace: all the kingdoms and lands, as if on the palm of your hand."[23] Whether this rotation of the palace stands for the rotation of the celestial sphere is not an easy question to answer, but it is obvious that here the sky is present. Its sunny character is even clearer in other tales. For example, the hero is trying to escape from a she-dragon: "She was already close to him and ready to overtake him! At that very moment prince Ivan galloped over to the palaces of the Sun's sister and shouted: 'Sun, oh sun, open your window!' The Sun's sister opened the window, and the prince and his horse jumped into it together."[24] Although there are no variants of this tale, this is by no means the only mention of the sun.

This kingdom is connected with the horizon. "They rode for a while between heaven and earth and came to an unknown island."[25] And although this citation refers more to the journey than to the kingdom, there are other texts where the position of this kingdom on the horizon is made quite clear. "The brave archer mounted his mighty horse and rode across the Thrice-Nine Lands. After a short time or a long time, he reached the end of the world where the red sun rises from the blue sea."[26] This connection with the sky is expressed even more clearly in cases where thunder and lightning are mentioned. The fox (or a cat in boots) says to the hero, "King Fire and Queen Thunder and Lightning[27] are there. They have a daughter, a beautiful princess. I'll get her for you as a wife."[28] And although names do not yet prove anything, nevertheless the connection here is not accidental. Thus, in this kingdom a rumble and peal of thunder are audible. Baba Yaga replies to the question of what causes this rumble: "In our mountains a noise bangs and thunder rumbles, for the beautiful beauty with the black braid, the tsar-maiden, is riding."[29]

3. Gold

Everything at all connected with the Thrice-Tenth Kingdom can take on a golden coloring. We noted above that the palace is golden. The items that one needs to obtain from the Thrice-Tenth Kingdom are almost always golden. These can be, for example, a pig with golden bristles, a duck with golden feathers, a deer with golden horns, a golden-tailed deer, or a golden-maned and golden-tailed horse (not of the Sivko-Burko[30] type).[31] In the tale of the firebird, the firebird sits in a golden cage, the horse has a golden bridle, and the garden of Elena the Beautiful is surrounded by a golden fence.[32] In the tale of Finist the Bright Falcon, the girl, when arriving in another kingdom to see her lover, buys herself three nights with her husband for a golden spindle with a silver base, a silver plate with golden eggs, and a golden embroidery hoop with a needle.[33]

The resident of this kingdom, the princess, is always marked with some kind of golden attribute. She sits in a tall tower with a golden roof.[34] "[He] looks and sees that princess Vasilisa is sailing through the blue sea in a silver boat and rowing with a golden oar."[35] She has golden wings, and her maidservant has silver ones.[36] She flies in a golden chariot. "A multitude of doves flew into this place, covering the whole meadow. In the middle stood a golden throne. In a short while the sky and the earth lit up—a golden chariot was flying through the air with six fiery dragons harnessed to it. The princess, Elena the Wise, was sitting in the chariot, and she was such an incredible beauty that it's impossible either to think of, or to imagine, or to describe in a tale."[37] Even in cases where the princess is represented as a warlike maiden, she gallops on her stately horse "with a golden spear." If her hair is mentioned, it is always golden. Hence her name is "Elena of the Golden Braid, the Uncovered Beauty." In Abkhaz tales, even her face radiates light: "And he saw a beautiful maiden glowing without the sun, standing on a balcony. . . . A light radiated from her, as from the sun, even when there was neither sun nor moon."[38]

This list could be continued to fill entire pages. Gold appears so often, so vividly, and in such diverse forms that one can rightfully call this Thrice-Tenth Kingdom a golden kingdom. It is such a typical and fixed feature that the statement "everything connected with the Thrice-Tenth Kingdom can have a golden coloring" could also be correct in the reverse order: "everything gold-colored reveals its belonging to the other kingdom." Golden coloring is the mark of another kingdom. The firebird's feather can be considered an example of this. Prince Ivan has been on the lookout for the bird: "He sat in waiting for an hour, another, and a third. Suddenly the whole garden was illuminated, as by a multitude of lights: the firebird had flown in." It drops a feather: "This feather was so wonderful and bright that if you brought it into a dark room it would shine, as if a great many candles were burning in that room."[39] This bird really does come flying from "another kingdom," and the hero sets out to look for it. In this case, the connection is completely clear. But even in cases when the connection is not visible directly, the question must be examined and researched. For example, the hero has obtained a wonderful duck: "The owner locked his duck in a dark barn, and at night she laid a golden egg. The peasant went in and saw a great light and, thinking that the barn was burning, cried out at the top of his voice: 'Fire! Fire! Wife, grab the buckets and run to put it out!' They opened the barn, but there was neither smoke nor flame, there was just a golden egg shining."[40]

There is obviously a connection between the two examples. The connection with the Thrice-Tenth Kingdom, however, is not explicit but postulated and needs to be investigated.

The example with the golden eggs is interesting for another reason: it shows that golden coloring is a synonym for something fiery. The same is seen with the firebird's glowing feather. Knowing that the Thrice-Tenth Kingdom is very often at the same time a heavenly and solar kingdom, we can easily conclude that the celestial coloring of objects is an expression of their sun-filled quality. In some cases, this is stated quite clearly. For example, in a Permian tale we read, "'Do you see a fire in that area, like the fire of the sun?' 'I see it,' he says. 'It's not like the fire of the sun, it's her house, which is all made of gold,' he says."[41]

4. *Three Kingdoms*

According to the observations of N. P. Andreev, the tale in which the hero gets into the copper, silver, and gold kingdoms during his journey is the most common in the Russian language, and we may consider it widely known. It seems to us that these three kingdoms arose as a tripling of the Thrice-Tenth Kingdom. Taking into account the wonder-tale's tendency to triple everything, this motif has undoubtedly undergone the same process, which brings about the existence of the three kingdoms in general; but since the Thrice-Tenth Kingdom is golden, the previous ones must be made of silver and copper. It would be unproductive to search here for some kind of connection with notions of the iron, silver, and golden ages, or with the cycle of Hesiodic eras in general. It will also be impossible to find here any connections with concepts of metals. One could also raise a question regarding the representation of the three kingdoms as of heaven, earth, and underworld. But this connection too is not supported by the material: the copper, silver, and gold kingdoms are located not under or on top of one another; rather, one is in front of the other, and usually all three are underground. But since the Thrice-Tenth Kingdom in the folklore canon is the last phase of the hero's journey, after which he returns home, and it would be impossible to arrive there three times (which would have to have been preceded by a return home and a new departure), the first two kingdoms become a sort of transitional phase, and one kingdom, the golden one, becomes the phase of the arrival. Yet such a transitional phase already exists in the wondertale canon—in the hut of Yaga. Thus, we face the curious phenomenon of assimilation of the three kingdoms with Yaga's hut. And indeed, looking through the numerous cases of three kingdoms, we see that some elements in them always derive from the Thrice-Tenth Kingdom and the princess, while others derive from Yaga. Besides their names, the three kingdoms have nothing specific in them. Let us take as an example a variant of Afanas'ev 128; H128. Ivan comes to the copper kingdom. He is met there by "a very beautiful maiden." This, surely, is not Yaga. An inquiry follows and after that his reproach: "You didn't feed me yet, didn't give me drink, but began asking questions." This element is clearly derived from Baba Yaga. Then the maiden gives him a ring—that is, she acts as a donor. However, the gift—the ring—is a veiled betrothal. Yet the hero gets engaged only to the third maiden of the golden kingdom, who is therefore functionally the princess. Other variants can also be analyzed similarly to this variant, and this will give us the right to assert that the three kingdoms are a formation internal to the wondertale. We were unable to find any materials indicating this motif's connection with primitive thinking or primitive rites.

5. The Theriomorphism of the Thrice-Tenth Kingdom

But our study of the Thrice-Tenth Kingdom is still far from complete. There is one more feature: this kingdom is sometimes represented as a kingdom not of people but of animals.

It is true that these indications are encountered less frequently, and these conceptions are somewhat overshadowed by the magnificent palaces of gold, marble, and mother-of-pearl, but they are still of particular interest for the researcher. Thus, when the princess is abducted by an animal, it takes her to its kingdom, where there are no people. Since the abductor is most often a dragon, this kingdom is often a kingdom of dragons. "He walked for a long time, following the yarn ball; many years flew by, and he came to a land where there was no human soul, no birds, and no animals, only serpents swarming. It was the dragon kingdom."[42] Tale 233; H233 notes, "Prince Vasily mounted his horse and went beyond Thrice-Nine Lands to the Thrice-Tenth Kingdom. He rode for some time and came to the lion kingdom." A lion king lives there, and we make special note of this reference to the king of beasts, as it will be useful to us in the future. After this, the hero enters the serpent and raven kingdoms. The animal nature of the kingdom does not exclude the presence of cities, palaces, and gardens: "Only snakes and reptiles lived in that kingdom." "A large snake lay round the city, wrapping it in a ring, so that its head touched its tail."[43] In a tale from Tobolsk we find, "In front of him he saw a house with two porches: a silver porch and a golden one. He thought: 'Who lives here?' . . . He opened the door to the first room and saw some hens sitting there: 'Could it be that people who are like our chickens live here?'"[44] In "Maria Morevna,"[45] three young women are betrothed to a falcon, a raven, and an eagle. The young women's brother goes to visit them. "He walks for one day, a second day, and at the dawn of the third he sees a wonderful palace; an oak grows beside it, and a bright falcon is seated on the oak." This is a kingdom of falcons. We can assume that the bear king takes the children to the bear kingdom.[46] Let us also note a case where the heroes come to a kingdom of mice. "They sailed on the sea, crossed to the other side, and came to the Thrice-Tenth Kingdom, the land of mice."[47]

II. The Other World

6. Early Forms of the Other World

In sum, there is no uniformity. There is diversity. Let us say in advance that no peoples have a completely uniform image of the other world. It is always represented in diverse and often contradictory ways.

The wondertale expresses the essence of the matter in a very naive fashion but quite accurately: "And the world there is just like ours." But since the world is changing, and the forms of human community are changing, "the other world" changes along with them. Yet we already know that in folklore an old thing does not die with the advent of a new one. Thus do new forms continuously emerge and coexist with old ones until finally, in Egypt or in classical Greece or in a modern wondertale, we witness the appearance of something like a small encyclopedia of all the forms of "the other world" that once existed. A person transfers not only his own social structure (in this case the tribal one, with a later change of a master to a king) but also the forms of life and geographical features of his homeland to the other kingdom. Islanders imagine the other world as an island. The palaces clearly originate in the men's houses, the best buildings of the village, and so on. In addition, a person transfers his own interests there, particularly the interests of craft or production. So for a hunter this kingdom is inhabited by animals. After death, he passes again through the whole ordeal of initiation and continues to hunt in the same way he hunted here, the only difference being that there will be no setbacks in the hunt.

This projection of the actual world to the other world is perfectly vivid by the time of tribal society. The hunter depends entirely on the animal and populates the other world with animals. He ascribes his tribal structure to animals and believes that, after his death, he will become an animal and meet the "master" or, in the language of wondertales, the "king" of the snakes, wolves, fish, crawfish, and so on.

The masters who can send animals to people live there. Shternberg, who studied the bear festival of the Gilyaks, comes to the conclusion that when they kill a bear they send him to his master. He writes, "The soul of the killed bear goes to its master, the master on whom the well-being of man depended."[48] Thus, we can establish that the wondertale has retained this layer, albeit in very pale reflections. This explains why the realm beyond may be inhabited by animals and why the hero meets the

king or master there. In the palace, these animals remind us very much
of the animal-like inhabitants of the "big house," already familiar to us
from chapter 4. In the other world, the people are snakes, lions, bears,
mice, chickens—that is, animals in the totemic sense of the word.

7. *The Maw and the Moving Mountains*

The idea that one must get inside the animal in order to gain power over it
is already familiar to us. Here we have the key to the phenomenon we observed earlier: that the notion of death and forms of initiation demonstrate
a striking similarity. Yet there is no need to assert that one evolved from the
other. The fairy palace in the other world is not only strikingly similar to
the "big house"—it sometimes simply coincides with it in such a way that
it is impossible to draw a precise boundary between them. The entrance to
the kingdom goes through the maws of animals. These maws constantly
close and open. "His kingdom opens for a while; when the serpent draws
apart, then the gates are opened."[49] In this example it is quite clear that
the mouth is the gate. This, on the one hand, is the origin of the slamming
doors that sometimes snatch the hero's heel as well as doors with teeth and
biting doors, and on the other hand, the moving mountains that threaten to
crush the newcomer also arise from here. Let us quote a text in Afanas'ev's
paraphrase: "In that kingdom there are two high mountains. They stand
together, touching each other. Only once a day, they diverge and move
apart and after two or three minutes converge again. The living and healing
waters are stored between these moving mountains."[50] The analogue here
is too great to be accidental. The same periodicity in closing and opening,
the same function of guarding, the same danger of being crushed, the same
biting off or chopping off the heel or a slice of a ship, as in the legend of
the Argonauts. With the decrease of the animal's role as a hunting object,
as the main or even the only source of survival, its function is transferred
to other objects: to the door and the mountains. It is difficult to say why it
shifts to mountains, although such a replacement is quite natural.

But is it not true that the moving mountains are found not only in epic
tales but also in beliefs? Such cases do exist. For example, in Micronesia
(the Gilbert Islands) it was believed that under adverse conditions the soul of
the deceased could be "crushed between two stones and blotted out of existence."[51] This is also the source of the animals, mainly lions and snakes, who
guard the entrance to the palace. The hero needs to throw them a cake or give
them water so he can pass. We have also encountered above the throwing
of an object into the jaws as a later replacement for jumping into the mouth.
This explains the lions and snakes that guard the entrance to the palace.

We will not cite materials proving that the forms of localization of
the other kingdom correspond to forms that once actually existed. We

can find enough materials showing that the other world is represented, not only in wondertales but also in religious beliefs, depending on natural surroundings and the main occupation of the people, either underwater, in the mountains, or far beyond the horizon and so on. Here the spatial concepts that we examined above play a role. The elaboration of these analogues is not difficult; the question itself does not present a problem. Here we are interested in some other more difficult questions, in particular the question of the crystal mountain.

8. Crystal

To understand the motif of the crystal mountain, we must remember that characters go to this country to gain power over animals, power over life and death, illness, and healing. We recognize here, on the one hand, the functions of the shaman and, on the other hand, the functions of the hero who searches for youth-giving apples, living and dead water, and remedies that heal blindness, old age, disease, and illness. A very early form of such a magical remedy, which is obtained in the other world and used for all kinds of magic acts, and which is widespread in Australia and in America, is rock crystal and also quartz. Previously, in the chapter on battling dragons, we saw that quartz was rubbed into the body of the initiate and that diamonds were found in the beast's head. One American myth tells of a young man who was beaten by his father. He felt insulted and decided to die. "He went up to a steep rock, climbed it, and threw himself down, but remained unharmed. He went on and soon saw a mountain in front of him that shone with light. It was the Rock of Naolakoa. There it constantly rained rock crystal. He took four pieces the length of a finger and put them in a row in his hair. He climbed to the top and was completely covered in rock crystal. Soon he noticed that the rock crystal had given him the ability to fly. After this, he flew all over the world."[52]

In full conformity with this, a Dolgan myth recounts, "He got up and began to pace. And he saw that everywhere the earth and sand were made entirely of glass pellets and beads."[53] This myth explains the crystal mountain of Russian tales, the glass mountain of German tales, and so on. In Russian examples, the crystal mountain is connected to the dragon that inhabits it. We have also seen the connection between crystal and the dragon in the rites: crystal was rubbed into the body at initiation. "There is a very widespread association of quartz-crystals with the rainbow-serpent, and throughout Australia quartz-crystals are amongst the most important of the magical substances used by the medicine-men."[54] Thus, this idea is of very early origin. We can assume that the "magic sand" obtained from the dragon is an echo of the same thing.

9. *The Land of Plenty*

We have examined some aspects of the other kingdom that reflect the earliest stages of its development available to us. Already in the "valleys of hunting" of the early forms of the clan system, we observe that the realms of our world and of the other world are quite similar. But there is also a difference: in the other world the abundance of game never ends. An individual projects to another world not only the forms of his own life. He also transfers there his interests and ideals. He is powerless in his struggle against nature, and the things that do not work for him here might succeed there. It is important to note that the hunter in the other world continues his manner of production. Certain forces are stored there that give him power over nature, and they can be transferred to the world of humans. This can help in producing perfect arrows that never miss. But in later stages people cease producing and working in the other world; they only consume there, and the magical devices brought from there ensure eternal consumption.

The appearance of such concepts shows that the attitude toward work has changed. This happens because labor becomes involuntary. Labor servitude is associated with the appearance of property, and property appears with agriculture.

It is known that the earliest form of agricultural production is the cultivation of orchards. With the advent of gardening, orchards and trees appear in the other world as well, and these trees already allow consumption without requiring labor. This form of the other world is known only to peoples who actually cultivate orchards. The form is absent, for example, in North America and among the Siberian peoples, but it is common in Polynesia and Melanesia. For example, Frazer writes that in the Marquesas Islands, "this celestial region was supposed to be a happy land, abounding in bread-fruit paste (*popoi*), pork, and fish, and offering the companionship of the most beautiful women imaginable. There the bread-fruit trees dropped their ripe fruit at every moment to the ground, and the supply of coconuts and bananas never failed. There the souls reposed on mats much finer than those of Nukahiva; and every day they bathed in rivers of coconut oil."[55] This is extremely valuable material for the folklorist, testifying to the early origin of the motif of the *Schlaraffenland*, the land of milk and honey. Bolte and Polívka also consider it "quite ancient," but the oldest parallels they cite refer to antiquity. Compared with what was noted above, Frazer's materials show that magical power over an abundance of animals has been replaced by simple abundance ready for consumption. Here lies the source of the idea of inexhaustible abundance. There, in the land of the dead, food never runs short. If this kind of food is brought from there, it will never be exhausted on earth either. This is the source of the magic tablecloth.

I must note that such conceptions are fraught with a very serious social danger: they lead to the rejection of labor. Later these ideas of the other world as a land of fulfilled hopes and desires fall under the control of the priestly class, consoling the people with the prospect of a reward for their long suffering in this world. These views become reactionary. But at the same time, we can observe something else: the laboring classes sense the harmfulness of such views quite vividly. Healthy human instinct forces a person to deny and reject such concepts. But all the same, their attractiveness makes them immortal. These two contradictory forces create an equivalent force, a comical treatment of this motif. The motif of shores of junket is often associated in the wondertale with comic exaltation of phenomenally lazy people.[56] This comic interpretation is also found in antiquity. We know how widespread the motif is in Greek comedy.[57] We shall have a few words to say on this topic below, when we consider antiquity.

The thoughts expressed here will help us to understand a bit more closely the motif of the forbidden casket.

Initially, objects brought from a different world in myths are safely delivered to people and bring them blessings. We saw this when we analyzed magic objects. We were able to establish the animal, which is to say the hunting origin of many of them.

The situation is different with objects that provide eternal abundance. On the one hand, such objects are treated comically. The magical tablecloth or table is connected with a cudgel, which punishes the unlucky thief by itself. Millstones that give a pancake and a pie with every turn are also treated in a kindheartedly comic fashion. This is a mild form of the reproach mentioned above. On the other hand, a hero who brings from the other world neither fire nor another object useful to people but instead brings an object that provides unearned eternal abundance himself perishes because of it and fails to deliver it to the people. For example, in a Melanesian myth, the hero receives a casket called "Monuya" from the moon. But the moon forbids opening it before returning home. The hero goes back in a boat and, of course, violates the ban. A huge number of fishes suddenly appear from everywhere. There are more and more of them, and they overturn the boat.[58]

We see the same in a Russian wondertale: the hero receives a casket, and cattle come out of it. The whole island is filled with cattle, and the hero is threatened with death.[59] In the Greek myth of Pandora, the forbidden casket contains evil that spreads across the world. This is a literary symbolic treatment of the very same motif.

10. The Kingdom of the Sun

Before we proceed any further, we must trace one more line, namely, that of concepts related to the kingdom of the sun. It is not entirely easy to establish exactly when this specific concept appears. In contrast to other features that become fossilized or deformed, resignified or treated comically, this concept develops further and reaches its apogee in developed religions, as in Egypt. We can establish, for example, that the Yakuts, a people who live by cattle breeding, have very clear ideas about such a kingdom. "[He] came to the master-sun. The daughter of the master-sun, the shaman Kyuegyam, was sitting on an eight-legged copper platform, with her eight-fathom crimson-silk hair wrapped on a silver stake. She sat there and combed her hair with a golden comb."[60] This daughter of the sun is the fourth heroine the hero encounters. (Sometimes in Siberia, as always in North America, the number four plays the same role as our number three.) The first heroine is connected with the clouds, the second with the stars, the third with the moon, and the fourth with the sun. It seems to us that this example confirms our conjecture that emerges from the study of Russian tales, namely, that gold or copper is the coloration of the sun kingdom.

The golden coloring of objects associated with the Thrice-Tenth Kingdom is the coloring of the sun. Peoples who do not have a religion of the sun also have no golden coloring for magic objects.

In order to understand this motif better, it is necessary to trace how ideas about the Thrice-Tenth Kingdom generally evolved during the transition to agriculture. Egypt, Babylon and Assyria, China, and antiquity can serve as examples.

For all the specific characteristics of separate peoples, here it is still possible to detect with perfect clarity the common features that are present in wondertales too. First, as indicated above, old ideas do not disappear; they continue to exist while new ideas are layered on top of them. So far we have seen that peoples ascribe to the otherworldly kingdom the same manner of life and the same forms of production of material life that they themselves are familiar with. The other world repeats this one. The hunter populates it with animals, the gardener with gardens. But this process stops with the transition to agriculture. There is no plowing in the other world, no sowing, and no reaping. The same is true for the Thrice-Tenth Kingdom; agricultural work is *never* conducted there. The animals, gardens, and islands have been preserved in all religions, but in addition, something new has appeared: gods that bestow fertility. Traces of these deities, as we have seen, have also been preserved in the wondertale. This is our first observation. The second is that the solar conception of another kingdom reaches its full development in Egypt. This conception gradually develops and takes on symbolic forms. The most ancient pyramids "still revolve almost entirely around the religion of Ra and the residence of the deceased in a sunny and heavenly place. Subsequent pyramids move more and more towards Osiris."[61] We shall not dwell in depth on Egyptian concepts. It seems that they mainly contain three layers: an animal layer, a fruit-growing layer, and a solar-agricultural layer, which is distinctively monarchical. It is known that the other kingdom is filled with animals, that Egyptians could not explain to Herodotus the reasons for the animal cult, and that he himself could not explain it either. An essential part of this faith also includes trees and orchards. According to Breasted, "One of the most, if not the most, important of the numerous sources from which the departed Pharaoh hoped to draw his sustenance in the realm of Ra was the tree of life on a mysterious isle amid the Field of Offerings, in search of which he sets out in company with the Morning Star."[62] This morning star, by the way, is also a green falcon. This is what the coconut palm that continuously drops its fruit turned into in the agrarian system. This palm is hypostatized in the tree of life, growing in the kingdom of the dead. A person who reaches this tree attains immortality. The old ideas that by staying in the other kingdom you obtain magical power and that if you are able to return you can become a magician and a wizard do not die. The "magic crystal," which we encounter in America, is not forgotten. But here the "crystal mountain" or "crystal rain" has the form of a "crystal sky," which is already devoid of its magical functions. "And Ptah hath covered his sky with crystal."[63] For the first time in world history, the magical function is transferred to another object, full of mystery and power: the book. Egypt was the first to create a "magic book," which in the wondertale is in the possession of the princess or her father. Such ideas dominate both in the official religion of the priests and the court and among the people who know amazing stories about how this magic book was brought back from the kingdom of the dead. Richard Reitzenstein writes,

> Let us take another look at the idea of an island of the dead, guarded by a huge snake. It is not important to us whether the fantasy places it in the lower reaches of the Nile, for example in the delta, or in the upper reaches . . . or in the Red Sea; whether there is one such island or many of them, as in the famous part of the *Book of the Dead*. What is more important for us is attaching the folktale form to the ideas that repeat in a number of prophetic and wonder novellas. Their basis is the true Egyptian concept that a person who wants to obtain higher knowledge and thereby the highest power must become a god; and he becomes a god by wandering through the world of the dead or through the sky.[64]

This "truly Egyptian" view is already known to us from Australian and American materials, and it also comprises the basis of the wondertale.

The "novellas" Reizenstein refers to are *The Adventure of Satni-Khamoins with the Mummies* and the story of *The Shipwrecked Sailor*.[65]

We still must mention the role that gold plays in the Egyptian burial cult. Funeral texts mention a "house of gold." Budge thinks that this refers to "the sarcophagus, or perhaps, the front room of the crypt, or even the place in front of the crypt," noting that "the chambers of the golden house" are the main area of the crypt. Thus, the crypt is imagined as golden.[66]

We see the same multiple layering in Assyria. Let us consider only those materials that are important for understanding the wondertale. Babylon introduces the new concept of the *city* and specifically the city-fortress. "Having preserved the old, primitive ideas about afterlife, the Assyrians, who had developed a high culture, transferred some of its features to the kingdom of the afterlife. They imagined it as a great city with a huge palace where the ruler of the dead, the goddess Allatu, lives. Seven walls surround this vast prison, where the deceased live, deprived of light."[67] More ancient is the Babylonian concept of the garden. After wandering for twenty-four hours, Gilgamesh comes to the sea, where a divine young woman sits on a throne near a beautiful garden with divine trees. He admires one tree in particular and rushes to it. "Its fruit is samtu-stones; the crown yields crystals as fruit; it brings forth fruit that is beautiful to the eyes."[68] Here the crystals familiar to us grow on trees, but at the same time, the most ancient theriomorphic concepts are not forgotten, though they are not preserved in such variety as in Egypt. It has already been mentioned above that the inhabitants of the kingdom of the dead have bird plumage.

11. Antiquity

To this point, we have been analyzing our material in its details, beginning with what appeared earlier and ending with what appeared later. Let us consider one more example of complex, sophisticated notions without dividing them into their component parts, and let us look to classical antiquity in this regard. It becomes clear that certain aspects of these notions are also present in the wondertale. This will serve as an additional argument for the historicity of wondertale notions. Not only is each separate element historical, but so is their colorfulness as well as their logical incompatibility and inconsistency.

Greek beliefs are diverse to the point of chaos. No rigorous, historically grounded study of these notions yet exists. This chaotic nature often gave the skeptical minds of antiquity food for ridicule. It would be enough here to refer to Aristophanes's *Frogs*, which depicts an absolutely impossible other world with the ferryman Charon. Those who cross the river are rowing in time with the croaking of frogs. Radermacher tries to derive from this comedy the exact topography of that world and all its absurdity.[69] The folklorist will find hardly anything new in Greek representations. There are the mountains (Olympus and the underground kingdom), Hades, the islands of the blessed, the underwater kingdom of Poseidon, and the garden of the Hesperides with its golden apples.

Radermacher, referring to Gruppe,[70] writes that the golden color of the apples proves that the garden of the Hesperides once lay underground. He himself is inclined to think that gold is a marker of fabulous wealth here.[71] Both explanations seem incorrect in light of our comparative materials. We must consider a different opinion as having been confirmed—that of Dieterich: "The garden was always thought of in connection to the sun and the sun-god; it was located where the sun rises or, according to more common beliefs, where it sets, in the extreme west."[72]

Such multiplicity is already the beginning of a decline and decomposition. This decomposition creates fertile ground for the appearance of the wondertale. The whole myth of Heracles fetching the apples of the Hesperides is quite close to the tale of the apples of youth; moreover, the tale is even more archaic, preserving the apples' magic quality, whereas in the myth of Heracles, they are just a kind of "rarity." It is impossible not to note the beauty and lively charm of some of the Greek representations. The Greeks seem to have been the first to bring music to the other world—not the magical music of flutes and drums but ordinary human music, which later is maintained throughout all of Europe, from "The Little Scarlet Flower" to the angels playing violins and trumpeting at Mary's feet. Dieterich writes, "The island of the dead is full of sounds. The majority of the inhabitants of that city are kithara players. . . . Similarly, in Lucian [of Samosata], the music of strings, flute, and laudatory songs are heard on the island of the blessed, and even the leaves of the trees, moved by the wind, rustle with song. . . . The Hesperides, guarding the sun-garden, have been called light-voiced singers since ancient times."[73] Here we can recall the "singing tree" of the wondertale.

We shall single out only one detail from the complex of Greek representations: the color gold. The first thing that comes to mind is the palace of Helios. It is described as standing on beautiful pillars, shining with gold and precious stones. Its apexes are made of ivory, and the doors shine with silver. It is interesting that it also stands on pillars, as in the Russian wondertale. Apparently, these are the pillars that support the heavenly sphere. This reminds us of Heracles holding the heavenly sphere on his shoulders. According to Dieterich's observations, the whole race of Helios "is easily recognized by the glow of their eyes, which, like a golden ray, radiates from their faces." This, of course, is a more recent rationalization. This goldenness is characteristic of gods, of the deceased, and of the initiated. Pythagoras, in order to prove that he has been inducted and to demonstrate his divinity, claimed that he had golden limbs, and on occasion, he used to show his golden hip.[74] This reminds us of our hero whose "legs are covered with gold to his knees, his arms covered with silver to his elbows."[75] A golden face, a golden crown, a halo, radiance—all this originates here. This also explains the use of gold in the funeral cult not only in Greece but in other countries as well. For example, the Taoists assert that swallowing gold or pearls does not merely lengthen one's life, it also ensures the existence of the body after death, protecting it from decomposition. Shternberg noted that in China gold is put in the mouth of a dead person.[76] Returning again to antiquity, we should point out that the Roman emperors powdered their faces with gold dust.[77] This also explains the Mycenaean golden masks of the dead. The fact that in China gold is put into everyone's mouth, while in Rome the emperors powdered their faces with golden dust, points to the evolution occurring in these notions. Already in Greece notions exist of a world of the righteous and one of the unrighteous. Gold becomes the property only of the righteous. For example, in Paul's Apocalypse, the place of the righteous, described in detail, is a golden city.[78]

All this explains to a sufficient extent the origin of the motif of wishing to have golden rarities. These are objects from the other world that have lost their magical function, which was to convey longevity and immortality. Apples retained this function while all sorts of "golden crested ducks" lost it.

Thus do we see that the wondertale has preserved various layers, various deposits in the concepts of the Thrice-Tenth Kingdom: we see in it both the oldest hunting elements, elements of early farming and late farming, and corresponding forms of social order and life.

9

THE BRIDE

I. The Seal of the Princess

1. Two Types of Princess

It is a mistake to imagine the princess of the wondertale primarily as a "sweet pretty maiden" or a "rare beauty" who "can be neither recounted in a tale nor described by a pen."[1] It is true that, on the one hand, she is a faithful bride waiting for her betrothed and refusing all who aspire to her hand in the absence of the groom. But on the other hand, she is also insidious, vengeful, and mean. She is always ready to kill, drown, cripple, and rob her bridegroom, and the main task of the hero, who has come or has almost come to possess her, is *to tame* her. He does this quite simply: he beats her with three kinds of rods until she is half dead, and after this happiness ensues.

Sometimes the princess is depicted as a robust woman and a warrior, skillful in shooting and running. She rides a horse, and her enmity toward the groom can take the form of an open contest with the hero.

The two types of princess are defined not so much by the princess's personal qualities as by the course of action. One type is freed by the hero from a dragon; he is her savior. This type is the meek bride. The other type must be taken by force. She is kidnapped or taken against her will by the shrewd hero who has resolved her tasks and riddles without fearing the fact that the heads of his unfortunate predecessors are stuck on poles around her palace.

This sometimes determines not only her attitude toward the groom but also her attitude toward her father. The princess cannot be studied without her father, and the element of marriage cannot be studied without the element of the hero's accession to the throne.

The princess, her father, and the groom can form various "triangles of power." The conquered or forcibly taken princess acts together with her father against the hero and tries to ruin him.

But another combination is also possible: the princess acts together with the hero against her father and sometimes personally kills the old king.

As a woman, she is never described very precisely. In this, Russian tales are different from those of the *Thousand and One Nights*, where a somewhat general canon of female beauty developed. Only one feature of her appearance is mentioned more often in the Russian materials: her golden hair, discussed previously. From this, it is evident that the princess should be studied based not on her external attributes but mainly according to her actions. Her qualities will gradually unfold through her actions.

2. Branding the Hero

When we examined the battle with the dragon, we ignored the princess's role during the battle. Now we must fill this gap. The hero is sleeping before the fight. The princess is unable to wake him up in any way. "She poked and prodded him, be he did not wake up. She started crying tearfully, and a hot tear dripped on his cheek."[2] The tear wakes him. In this and similar cases, the significance of the tear is only to awaken the hero. Often, however, things happen differently. "The dragon crawled closer, ready to seize prince Ivan! But Ivan was still sleeping. Princess Martha had a penknife, with which she cut prince Ivan's cheek. He woke up, jumped to his feet, and came to grips with the dragon." This wounding of the hero has yet another meaning: later he is recognized by the scar. "Father, this is the one who rescued me from the dragons. I did not know who he was, but now I recognize him from the scar on his cheek."[3] Thus, a mark is placed on the hero, a kind of seal. Moreover, this is a bloody seal, and the hero is recognized by it. A wound that was received in a battle has the same significance. The wound plays the role of a bloody seal. The princess takes a handkerchief and bandages the wound. The hero is recognized because of the wound and the handkerchief.

Branding the hero occurs not only during battle. It is not the situation that is important but the fact that the branding takes place *shortly before the wedding.*

We have such a case in "Sivko-Burko." There is no battle here, but nevertheless the hero's branding is expressed in a much more pronounced way. The hero, riding the horse Sivko-Burko, flies up to the window of the princess and kisses her. "He flew off in the royal court with such force that he broke all twelve window panes and kissed the princess, Rare Beauty, and she branded him with a mark on his forehead."[4] Or, "She struck his forehead with a golden ring."[5] "She flicked her finger on his forehead, and a light started to glow there."[6] This branding is found not only in tales such as Sivko-Burko but in others as well. For example, the princess's betrothed turns out to be a wise young man. "She put a seal on his forehead with her golden ring, received him in her palace, and married him."[7] Sometimes this motif undergoes a kind of deformation, which proves, however, that the motif is firmly entrenched in people's minds and that it is used even where it does not fit. For example, one tale begins with the fact that the hero is unhappy in trade. He does not succeed at anything. The tsar learns of this and feels pity for him: "He called him the Unlucky One and ordered a seal put on his forehead, so that he didn't need to pay any taxes."[8]

In addition to these methods of marking the skin, there are other ways to mark the hero. For example, the hero, in the form of a deer, puts his head on the princess's knees. "She took scissors and cut a piece of fur from the deer's head."[9] Cutting a strand of hair is another form of branding. Usually branding serves as a sign that the princess is somehow taking the hero's side. But the evil princess uses the same method in order to destroy the hero. For example, the hero has solved her riddles. "At night when everyone fell into deep sleep she came to them with her magical book, looked into it, and immediately discovered the guilty one. She took scissors and cut off some hair at his temple. 'I will recognize him tomorrow by this mark and order him to be executed.'"[10]

The above examples are quite sufficient to give an idea of the princess's function in the Russian wondertale, which provides a quite complete, rich, and diverse picture of this motif but nevertheless lacks certain details that can illuminate the motif's history. The branding is always associated with subsequent recognition of the obscured hero, which is to say that it has become a purely poetic device. This association is not mandatory in the materials of other peoples, and such materials offer us some important details. For example, in a Lapp myth, a girl responds to courtship of the sun's son in the following way: "Let us mix our blood. Let us unite our hearts for sorrow and joy, the son of a mother not yet my relation."[11] Thus, blood is mixed before marriage. The only thing that is not said here is that the blood is being drunk at the same time. Later in the myth the girl's father makes cuts in their little fingers and mixes their blood.

Is it possible to compare the Russian wondertale to the Lapp myth? If this association holds, if the same phenomenon is reflected here, this would indicate that, while retaining the act of branding itself, the wondertale has resignified it as a mark for recognition. Moreover, its bloody character has taken the form of a wound received during battle, and the mixing of blood has disappeared altogether.

The Lapp myth has better preserved both the forms and the meaning of the rite. Drawing blood and inflicting marks and scars are signs of admission into the clan's association, into the clan's union. Therefore, it is already present in the initiation rite, the rite of admitting a new member into the union. But it is also widespread outside this rite. This is not the only form. Australians, both older and younger men and boys, drink blood if they are relatives and want to strengthen their kinship or at the conclusion of peace between two tribes.[12] Julius Lippert writes, "The marker of kinship for primitive man was exclusively the identity of blood."[13] Therefore, any artificial mixing of blood should also create kinship. Edwin Hartland, Veselovskii in his *Poetics* and elsewhere, Kharuzin, Shternberg, and others provide a long list of peoples who mixed and drank blood when joining a clan union or in order to strengthen it. Georg Schweinfurth notes it among the Africans of the Zande people, Julius Wellhausen among the Arabs where it is also must be accompanied by a joint meal, and Thomas Achelis among the Lydians.[14] It does not matter which body part is cut to extract the blood. But it is natural that uncovered parts of the body feature among peoples who wear clothes, such as the forehead, cheeks, and hands, as we see also in the wondertale. Kharuzin writes that "the blood of a clan's new member must be mixed with the blood of a native son of the clan." These customs "have both legal and religious significance: they are devices for the legal entry of a stranger into a blood-related group, they also serve as a sacred symbol of unity."[15]

Upon marriage, a wife enters her husband's clan, or a husband enters his wife's clan. In the wondertale, the latter always occurs, reflecting matriarchal relationships. Veselovskii was perhaps the only one who clearly singled out "the transfer of blood association to marital relations," as he puts it.[16] Using Hartland's materials, he writes,

> Among some Bengal aborigines, the bridegroom marks his wife with a red pencil. The marriage ceremony of the Biharis consists of letting blood from the little fingers of the bride and the groom; they then anoint each other with this blood. The Kewat and Rajput peoples add this blood to the food of the newlyweds. Among the Wukas (New Guinea), the marriage begins with the couples running away, they are pursued and caught. The next step is to establish the bride's selling price. When the price is established, the husband and wife make cuts on each other's foreheads until blood appears. The rest of the family members of both sides do the same, and this bonds their union.[17]

Veselovskii subsequently cites certain folktales (Annam, Norwegian, and Finnish).

The widespread occurrence of this custom and the variety of its forms make it impossible to draw a full picture of its development in a short sketch. But this is not necessary for our purposes: the connection to folktales is obvious. A Chukchi tale even retains the smearing with blood. Before the wedding, "the lad first of all ordered some deer killed to treat the guests, with the last deer killed for smearing." One of the girls shouts, "Well, hurry up and smear yourself, the blood is getting cold!"[18] Abundant material on this question can be found in a book by Ernst Samter.[19] Tristan and Isolde may be recalled in this connection as well. For Olga Freidenberg, Isolde's goblet is a "fertility cult drink."[20] According to Boris Kazanskii, this goes back to "a drink of purely magical significance."[21] For us, wine is a substitute for blood. Tristan and Isolde perform a wedding ceremony. The amorous character of the drink is a medieval reinterpretation influenced by the preparation of such drinks that was practiced at those times. Tristan and Isolda do not say all that the lovers say in the Lapp myth: "We mix our blood; we unite our hearts."[22]

The subject, however, is not yet fully exhausted. The princess in the wondertale also marks the bridegroom by cutting his hair.

This is not witnessed very often as a marriage custom. Kharuzin writes, "The fraternal alliance is made not only by mixing blood, but by giving away something that inherently belongs to the person, such as hair, a piece of clothing, etc."[23] Incidentally, the princess in the wondertale cuts off not only the hair of the bridegroom but also the tail of his coat.[24]

However, this motif is often encountered as an indicator of admission to the clan's community. Among Australian Aborigines, when a young man returns to the camp after circumcision, he is met by women, who cut several locks of his hair.[25] The practice of cutting hair can be considered an international phenomenon right up to our own days, and its source, its original meaning, is mostly comprehensible. A strand of hair is cut at baptism, at consecration into holy orders, and at monastic tonsure. All these cases point to admission into a new association. They also point to a kind of "consecration," and its connection with initiation is unquestionable. We have here a specific case of manipulating hair, mentioned previously (chap. 4, sec. 15). And if priests in certain denominations do not cut their hair, this may be considered a connection with letting the hair grow, which grants a special power to the initiate.[26]

We know that initiation is experienced as a symbolic death. This explains why cutting hair and drawing blood are applied in various forms at death. When a young person of the North American Sioux tribe dies, his parents cut a lock of hair from his forehead.[27] This indicates his joining the host of the dead and entering their clan. According to the views of the ancient Greeks, Thanatos, king of the underworld and death, cuts a strand of hair from newcomers. Later, when the meaning and significance of these actions are no longer understood, cutting hair is transferred from the dead to those who remain behind. This is the source of the widespread custom of cutting hair as a symbol of mourning. Our explanation of the custom allows us to disagree with the theories of F. B. Jevons and Robertson Smith, who believe that the cutting of hair signifies giving a valuable gift to the deceased or making a sacrifice to him.[28] In the wondertale it is a sign of transition and of admission into the wife's tribal union. Therefore, she is the one who does the branding, not someone else. Below we shall see why her father cannot do it.

II. Difficult Tasks

A. SETTING

3. Difficult Tasks

We turn now to another function of the princess. Before marrying, she tests the groom, assigning him various difficult tasks. The motif of "difficult tasks" is one of the most common in the wondertale. But I must say that there is no complete clarity in the literature regarding what constitutes a "difficult task." When Baba Yaga asks a girl to pick up poppy seeds from the ground, this too can be considered a difficult task. In order to avoid confusion in terminology, it is necessary to stipulate that here "difficult tasks" will refer only to tasks connected to wooing, not to the transfer of a magical agent. There are some cases in which the assignment of difficult tasks is not connected directly to wooing, but the connection can easily be established from comparisons. Such cases will be considered here as well.

"Difficult tasks" present a varied picture. Let us try to clarify it by comparing the materials.

We shall consider two questions in this analysis. The first is what conditions, what types of situations evoke the assignment of difficult tasks, and why. The second is the content of these tasks: what is being assigned. The two issues do not always overlap; the same task may be assigned under different conditions and vice versa. Afterward, it will be possible to raise the general question of the historical foundations of such tasks. And so, under what conditions are difficult tasks assigned?

4. A Call to All the People

Sometimes a task can be assigned at the very beginning of a tale. The story begins as the tsar wishes to give his daughter in marriage and summons all the people, informing them of the terms under which she will marry. The wooing in such cases is provoked by the task, and here it precedes the wooing, which consists of the attempt to resolve it. A typical example is Sivko-Burko. "At that time, suddenly," a "paper" comes from the king, saying that the king will give his daughter to the person who can kiss her on the fly, riding his horse, while she sits on a balcony or in a tower.[29] This is the most famous but by no means the only task assigned in such conditions. For example, "They heard that a paper had come from the tsar that he would give the princess in marriage to the person who built a ship that could fly."[30] There are several such cases, and the tasks in them vary. Nothing is actually said about the tsar's reason for assigning the task. In other words, the tasks have no motivation. One other thing is also still not clear. The tasks are so difficult that they must be deemed impossible. The hero carries them out because he has a magical helper. For now, it is completely unclear whether these tasks should attract suitors, frighten them off, or help to find the only worthy bridegroom.

For the time being, we simply note the case where the task is assigned at the beginning of the tale and the wooing is caused by it; we shall see what picture emerges from the other forms of assigning tasks.

5. Tasks in Response to Wooing

The previous case is characterized by the fact that the task precedes the wooing and generates it. Wondertales also feature the opposite. When the hero woos the bride, the condition is made that he must solve the bride's riddles first. As we have just seen, the first case has no motivation. In the second, however, a motivation is present. "First we must test the bridegroom's strength."[31] "If the old woman's son does all this, then it is possible to give him the queen in marriage: *it means he is very wise*; and if he doesn't, then his head and the old woman's head should be cut off for their offense."[32]

The task is assigned to test the groom. It is not physical "strength" that is meant here but strength of a different kind. The type of strength tested here proceeds from the whole previous course of the story. Analysis of the tasks entails and clearly demonstrates that what is tested here is the power we conditionally call magical, which is embodied in the helper.

But these tasks are also interesting for another reason. They contain an element of threat: "If he doesn't manage to do this, his head should be cut off for his offense." This threat reveals another motivation. Behind the tasks and threats lies not only a desire to have the best groom for the princess but also a concealed hope that such a groom will never be found. The princess's words—"All right, I agree, but first carry out three tasks for me"—are full of treachery.[33] The bridegroom is sent to *perdition*. This reminds us of how a sister, wishing to please her lover by destroying her brother, sends him for wolf's milk. Assigning tasks in this case amounts to an act of hostility toward the groom. In some cases the hostility is expressed quite openly, manifesting itself when the task has already been completed, but then still more tasks with greater danger are assigned.

On this basis we are able to note a second category of tasks that are assigned in response to wooing. These demonstrate that they are assigned for the purpose of testing the groom, but they also contain an element of hostility toward him and are meant to scare him away.

6. *The Princess Who Ran Away and Was Found Again*

The nature of the hostility, only vaguely expressed in the previous case, shows openly in the following type of situation: the princess flies away from the groom or from her husband on a magic carpet or by cunningly retrieving her wings. Her husband tracks her down, but she does not yield to him. She requires him to carry out certain tasks. For example, she demands that he conceal himself while she is determined to find him. When the hero turns into a tiny pin hiding behind a mirror, she cannot find him, and her magic books give her no answer, so she burns the books in annoyance and smashes the mirror. This demonstrates that the princess does not want to marry the hero.[34] But it shows something else too: the tasks contain an element of a *contest of magic.* The princess is herself a magician, but the hero surpasses her. Actually, cases where the king issues a proclamation or when tasks are assigned in response to wooing contain this element as well. When the princess, for example, builds a temple of twelve pillars and twelve rounds of logs, or when she sits on top of a glass mountain, these are ways for her to exhibit her magical power.

All these cases clearly demonstrate that the princess is reluctant to marry. Sometimes this is expressed in a direct way. She consults her grandfather, the Water King, about what she should do. "Prince Ivan is asking me to marry him. *I really don't want to marry him*, but our whole army is beaten."[35] The difficult tasks follow. These examples do not yet completely clarify the problem. But they reveal the bride's hostility toward the groom and demonstrate that the tasks can have characteristics of a competition. When we ask why the princess is hostile to the groom, we receive no answer.

7. *The Princess Stolen by False Heroes*

The tasks are motivated differently when the princess has been kidnapped from the hero by his elder brothers, who have thrown him into an abyss. He comes home and hides at the home of a shoemaker or tailor. The princess, before agreeing to marry the false hero, requires him to perform various tasks.

Sometimes the returned hero learns about the tasks through rumor: "These princes and their mother brought some tsar's daughter with them. The older one wants to marry her, but first she has either sent him somewhere to get the engagement ring, or she has required that he make exactly the same ring."[36]

Here it is clear that the task is assigned in order to find the real groom. Moreover, in these cases, the element of hostility toward the *false* groom stands in for the hostility toward the groom *in general*. On the other hand, in such cases a service is rendered to the real groom: he is given the opportunity to prove himself.

In all these cases, the bride and her father are unanimously hostile toward the real or the false groom. It makes no difference whether the king himself, the future father-in-law, assigns the task or it is performed by the princess bride. Sometimes the tasks are assigned by the father, sometimes by the princess. But this is not always the case. It is possible to trace some differentiation when only the princess's father, the future father-in-law, is hostile to the groom, and the princess, by contrast, helps the hero by deceiving her father.

8. The Water King

This case is typical of tales where the hero has been sold in advance to the Water King. He goes to him, but on his way he gets engaged to the Water King's daughter before meeting the king himself. As soon as the hero reaches the Water King, the latter immediately begins to assign him tasks, which can be either unmotivated or motivated—for example, in the following way: "Because you didn't come for a long time, here's an assignment for you: build a barn for me in one night."[37] Sometimes the fulfillment of tasks is set as a condition for his release. "Try to recognize my youngest daughter. If you recognize her, I'll let you go, if not, then blame yourself for your misfortune."[38]

The storyteller here does not understand what causes the Water King to assign the tasks, and he comes up with a reason of his own. However, these tasks are always followed by marriage to the Water King's daughter, and this simply reflects the wondertale canon: wooing plus difficult tasks plus marriage. The wooing has disappeared, the difficult tasks must be motivated in some other way, and the marriage does not seem to result from fulfillment of the tasks either. These cases are interesting, however, because the bride's father is obviously hostile to his son-in-law. After the marriage the couple flees, and the Water King attempts to overtake and destroy them. The princess goes with the groom against her father.

There are several examples when the assignment of difficult tasks is not directly related to wooing. We have this, for example, in "The Seven Simeons": the king "orders the seven Simeons to show their skills."[39] However, fulfillment of the tasks is still followed by marriage. The connection of the tasks to marriage has turned from one of causation into a mechanical one.

In "The Frog Princess," after marrying off his sons, the king suddenly declares, for no apparent reason, "I want your wives each to bake me a soft white loaf of bread for tomorrow."[40] However, it becomes clear later that this is how the frog-bride is exalted—namely, assigning the tasks leads to distinguishing the magically equipped person from mere mortals, as in the other cases.

9. *The Teacher-Sorcerer*

Since we mentioned tasks that are not related directly to wooing, we cannot ignore the tale "A Tricky Science."[41] Here too the hero is either sold in advance or falls into the hands of a sorcerer, and the latter teaches him sorcery. But the hero turns out to be his captive. The sorcerer assigns the father who has come to get his son a series of tasks. The father fulfills them because he has conspired in advance with his son, just as Prince Ivan fulfills the challenges of the Water King, having conspired in advance with his daughter. The tasks in these cases also often coincide: a son or a bride must be recognized among twelve identical ones. "The sorcerer says to him, 'Well, old man, I have taught your son all the tricks. But if you do not recognize him, he will remain with me forever and ever.'"[42] This tale is similar to that of the hero at the Water King's abode in that a flight ensues. This flight, as will be seen below, has the nature of a contest in magic with the sorcerer. Here there is no hostile father-in-law and princess. The hostile magician-sorcerer functionally corresponds to the hostile father-in-law.

This case stands somewhat apart from all the others. We proposed above using the term *difficult tasks* only when the tasks are directly or indirectly related to wooing. Such is not the case here. The tasks are assigned not to the hero but to his father. The woman is not even in the picture. From this angle, the case does not fit the phenomenon we have been studying, and we could omit it from our discussion. On the other hand, marriage follows fulfillment of the task here too. Thus, either the bride appears ex machina or she is the sorcerer's daughter, which is to say that we sometimes have the same situation as in the tales of the Water King and his daughter. Therefore, we cannot altogether exclude the case. Moreover, the tasks here constitute their own interest, and their content is discussed below.

This exhausts the situations of Russian wondertales in which difficult tasks are assigned. Comparing their characteristics provides no clue to understanding them. We see a rather motley and even contradictory picture. On the one hand, the groom is attracted and desired; they want the bride to have the best groom. On the other hand, they fear the groom and do not want him; they try to destroy him, threaten him with death, and exhibit an open or hidden hostility toward him. For clarity, we should also note elements of hostility toward the future groom on the part of the father-in-law, regardless of the situation in which the task is assigned. This will subsequently help us understand the circumstances of the hero's accession to the throne. This is all the more necessary because the wondertale often tones down the conflict between the son-in-law and the father-in-law, since it cannot make sense of the reasons for their enmity. This enmity does not follow from the tales themselves and is therefore effaced.

One way to efface this enmity is to ascribe it not to the father-in-law but to various envious people, scandalmongers, and slanderers. For example, the hero becomes a rich merchant. Other merchants envy him: "They got angry and informed the king that he was boasting that he could make carpets for the royal chambers in a single night."[43] This is followed by a series of tasks and the conclusion that "the king had no heirs so he adopted the merchant's son." We see that the one who has accomplished the tasks takes the place of the king, and in this case it happens in a peaceful manner.

Sometimes there is another character behind the princess who sets the riddles, namely, a lover who fears her suitors as his rivals. He incites the princess to assign the hero difficult tasks, thus becoming the bearer of hostility toward the groom. Often, however, the enemy is the king himself. Moreover, as indicated above, the hostility manifests itself after the tasks are completed or even after the wedding. Sometimes this is motivated by the fact that the hero is a soldier or a peasant, unequal to the princess. "The tsar considered it improper to give his daughter to a simple peasant and began to think how to get rid of such a son-in-law. And he came up with an idea. 'I will start assigning him various difficult tasks.'"[44] Marko the Rich also assigns a pernicious task to his unwanted son-in-law. "Marko lived with his son-in-law for a month, then a second and a third. One day Marko summoned him and said to him: 'Here's a letter, take it beyond the Thrice-Nine Lands to the Thrice-Tenth Kingdom to my friend, King Dragon, and get twelve years of tribute from him.'"[45] On the other hand, sometimes the son-in-law shows his claws too. Having heard the task, he says, "All right, I'll do it. But if after this the king continues to make excuses, then I'll fight him and take the princess by force."[46] In cases where the king himself is a great magician, he uses his own skills to destroy the hero. One of the constant typical tasks is to tame a horse. "Now you have been assigned a difficult task; after all, the king himself, Unbaptized Forehead, will be the colt. He will carry you beneath the skies, above the forest, below the walking cloud, and he'll break all your bones in an open field."[47]

11. Tasks Assigned to the Old King

The future son-in-law also exhibits hostility. After all the tasks have been completed, their sharp edge comes against the king, and the wheel turns: whereas the future new king always manages to perform all the tasks, the old king usually perishes. Among these types of tasks, we can mention bathing in boiling milk and walking across a bridge as thin as a hair.

This occurs when the hero is sent after some rare object and returns with a princess, whom the king claims for himself; or when the hero is sent to fetch a bride for the king, but she aligns herself with her captor, the hero; or when the elder brothers, after dropping Ivan into an abyss, bring back three princesses. The princesses of the copper kingdom and silver kingdom marry the hero's brothers, while his betrothed does not want to marry anyone. "And the old father took it into his head to marry her himself." He asks the princess from the golden kingdom, "Will you marry me?" "I'll marry you when you sew me shoes without taking my measurements." The hero, who has returned unrecognized, accomplishes this task for the old man. Other tasks follow, and finally, the last one: "Order this milk boiled and bathe in it."[48] The king is of course cooked in the milk and perishes.

B. THE CONTENT OF THE TASKS

Having considered the conditions under which the tasks are assigned, we now turn to the tasks themselves. Only after this will it be possible to draw some conclusions.

The tasks are not always attached to the situation in which they are assigned, and they should be studied separately from it.

There is a great number of tasks, yet they frequently repeat, and their main outlines can be defined.

12. Tasks of Searching

The vast majority of tasks aim at sending the hero to the Thrice-Tenth Kingdom. The hero must prove that he was there, that he is capable of going there and returning, or perish. He is required to get certain items, rare objects, that can be found only there. These objects are always characterized by their golden color. But we already know that the golden coloring of an object is a sign of its belonging to a different realm. Therefore, when the hero is required to obtain a firebird,[49] a golden-bristled pig, a golden-crested duck, a golden-horned deer, a golden-horned goat,[50] and so on, this is a sure sign that the hero must travel to another realm. Sometimes the task is directly set in this way: "There was also this one tsar, see, and he began to issue proclamations, asking who would go beyond Thrice-Nine Lands to the far end of the earth, to the Thrice-Tenth Kingdom."[51] The task "to obtain the sun, moon, and stars"[52] refers to the same place, as well as the tasks of "obtaining the keys from the sun and the moon"[53] and other tasks associated with the sun. Sometimes the tales even speak directly of descending into hell: "Bring me the keys from hell."[54] The hero is required to spend seven years in the tin kingdom[55] and to get healing and living water.[56] This requirement is expressed even more clearly in non-Russian tales: "I demand that you bring information within two days about seven generations of my deceased ancestors."[57]

Among these tasks, special attention may be drawn to the task of obtaining a golden bough. In essence, this task is no different from the task of getting golden apples, a golden deer, a firebird, and so on. "In a certain kingdom there is a golden oak with silver branches. I want you to dig this oak out and transplant it from that kingdom to this one."[58] In one of the versions of the "golden-bristled pig" in Afanas'ev's paraphrase, we find, "After this, the fool obtained the golden-bristled pig with the twelve piglets and a bough from a golden pine, which grows far away in the Thrice-Tenth Kingdom, in the country under the sun."[59]

The "Golden Bough," as is well known, is the topic of Frazer's magisterial study. A person who snatches the golden bough in Diana's sanctuary of Nemi could become the successor of the king-priest. We find something similar in the wondertale. As we shall see below, obtaining the rare object or completion of a difficult task is in general connected to the hero's accession to the throne and often to killing the old king, as in Nemi. But the wondertale shows that Frazer was wrong to focus on the bough. The point is not in the bough but in its golden color. Frazer explains this coloration in a quite naive manner, as the yellowish color of mistletoe. Frazer's entire study goes astray, heading in the wrong direction. Explaining this rite by the cult of trees and forests is just as misleading as if we began to research the pig and the bird as cult animals in order to explain the task of getting the golden-bristled pig or the firebird. This is certainly not the point. The point is that the pretender to the throne must undergo a test that proves he has stayed in the other world. The connection with the forest does not lie where Frazer seeks it.

Comparison of these tasks provides the answer to the question of what, in fact, they want to learn about the hero when they ask him to perform difficult tasks. The part of the tasks that we have examined furnishes a precise answer: there is an element of testing behind the tasks. They want to know whether the hero has been in the underworld, in the kingdom of the sun, and in the other world. Only those who have been there have a right to the hand of the princess.

For now, we confine ourselves merely to establishing the fact. We examined catabasis as a condition of becoming a hero, and there is no need to repeat the cited materials or to offer new ones. The picture of the difficult tasks and their historical roots will unfold before us gradually.

We have not yet considered all the tasks related to this group. We singled out above a group of tasks assigned by the princess who was stolen from the groom by his older brothers. These brothers seek her hand in marriage, but the princess holds them back by assigning them difficult tasks. What kinds of tasks are assigned in this situation? The tasks have a specific character. In this case, they are required to get something related to the wedding: shoes, a wedding dress, a wedding ring, a carriage, among other things. On closer examination, however, we see that these tasks differ from those considered above merely by item, by object, not in their essence. "First she sends him somewhere to get an engagement ring or orders him to make the identical ring."[60] Thus, here too the hero is sent somewhere. The place to which he is sent becomes apparent in the course of the tale and is sometimes indicated quite clearly: "The princess wants you to sew all sorts of dresses for the wedding, dresses like the ones she had in the other world; and it must be done without taking any measurements."[61] "I will marry the person who sews shoes such as I wore in the golden kingdom."[62] "I need a dress like the ones I used to wear on the glass mountain."[63] Here, sending him to the other kingdom is indicated clearly, and even the nature of the ostensible reason is expressed here vividly. The point, of course, is not to get the shoes or the carriage but to test the hero. The brothers, who have not been there, cannot accomplish the task. The hero accomplishes it because he has spent time there.

In these cases, the hero does not make the trip a second time. The objects usually are not obtained (although there are cases when they are obtained) but rather are made, produced. This reveals another side of the difficult tasks. Who can accomplish them? These tasks, generally speaking, cannot be accomplished. The hero manages them only because he has a helper. This demonstrates that the tasks can show not only whether the hero was in the other realm but also whether he acquired a helper there. Indeed, we can observe that there are several tasks that aim directly at finding out whether the hero has a helper. This can be seen from wording such as, "Who assists him?" or, "Probably, the spirits are doing this for

Prince Ivan." In the chapter on helpers, we observed the role played by the horse and how it is acquired. A number of tasks aim to find out whether the hero has control over the magic horse, whether he knows how to handle it. These include, for example, the tasks of breaking an untamed horse,[64] taming a horse,[65] breaking a stallion,[66] or acquiring seventy-seven mares.[67] We could also include here the task of kissing the princess while on horseback.[68] It is not by chance that this task is expressed specifically in this way: "Elena the Beautiful ordered a temple built on twelve pillars with twelve rounds of logs. . . . She will wait for a groom, a striking young man who will kiss her on the lips in one leap while on his *flying horse*."[69] This is not accidental; it is the usual formulation of the task: "The man who, while riding *a horse*, kisses my daughter, the Princess Beauty, while she sits on the third floor, to this man I will give my daughter in marriage."[70] In these cases, the hero proves that he has the means, which not everyone has: he proves that he is equipped with magic. This also includes the task: "Go I know not whither, bring back I know not what."[71] The country to which the hero is sent is the Thrice-Tenth Kingdom, and "I know not what" turns out to be the helper whose name is taboo and expressed indirectly, allegorically. The allegory is incomprehensible to the hero until the moment he acquires the helper.

13. Palace, Garden, Bridge

We often encounter a group consisting of three tasks in different combinations. It includes planting a wonderful garden; sowing, growing, and threshing wheat in one night; and building a golden palace with a bridge to it in a single night. These tasks are sometimes combined with the already familiar task of breaking or taming a horse and occasionally others.

First let us consider the palace. Sometimes the task is to build not a palace but a church,[72] and moreover from pure wax,[73] or a house,[74] or a barn.[75] All these are deformations of the golden palace, which actually occurs most often. Sometimes the three tasks (palace, bridge, and garden) are tied together in one: "Behold, I want to see tomorrow at dawn a golden kingdom built at the seventh mile out to sea, with a golden bridge made from there to our palace. And this bridge should be covered with expensive velvet, and beautiful trees should grow along the railing on both sides, and singing birds should be singing in different voices. If you don't make all this by tomorrow, I'll order you cut into pieces."[76]

The task of building a palace in one night is completely incomprehensible on its own. This motif cannot be understood in isolation. The motif of the golden palace can be understood through the golden palace that stands in the Thrice-Tenth Kingdom. It is the same palace. We examined this palace in a previous chapter, where we recognized in it the elements of the "big house." Hence we can conclude that the task of building a palace is somehow connected to the "big house." It is not yet clear what this connection consists of. Here there seems to have been some resignification. To resolve the issue let us turn to materials relating to the "big houses" at the stage of their historical existence. In a myth from Oceania, a girl is carried away by a spirit. She lives with him, bears a son from him, and returns home with the boy. His peers tease him about his origin and reproach him for not having a father. The mother sends the boy to his father. (In all this, we easily recognize the young woman staying at the forest house, giving birth to a child there, and returning home.)

> He abode in the house of the spirit, and when he was somewhat older, the spirit said to him, "Now we will go to my mother." They came to a place of great heat, where the boy refused to go any farther. The spirit put him in his hand and puffed. Then they went farther and came to a place of great cold, where the boy again refused to go farther. The spirit laid him under his armpits and warmed him. At last they came to the abode of the spirit's mother. The spirit declared that he was come to give to the boy for his own one of the two houses that were there. The spirit's mother said, "Very well; he shall have yonder the House of Health and Valour." Now the house was built on seven platforms of stone, surrounded by seven fences, and fitted out with all sorts of things. "Go now into the house to sleep," said the spirit. "At midnight I will come to wake you; then you must think where you wish me to transport your house." While the boy slept, the house ascended through the earth and came out on the surface of the ground. Later the boy becomes the leader of the tribe. Whenever he steps on the stairs, thunder is heard.[77]

Let us try to analyze this case. One thing is surely clear: he is staying in the "big house." There the boy learns to control the forces of nature. When he is led through the heat and cold, he not only becomes resistant to them but also becomes the master of these natural forces. Although this is not said directly, it is recounted that, upon returning, he controls the thunder. Thus, before becoming the leader, the boy brings back with him this type of art, and he brings the entire house back with him. We can see the hero as an organizer of the universe. He gives the people thunder, and he gives a "house" to people—that is, a social arrangement, as in the other texts, where he brings the people dances and drawings and teaches them sacred rites. We must consider the text above to be a myth told during the rite to the newly initiated as an explanation of what was done to them.

This interpretation is supported by texts recorded in a completely different part of the world, namely in North America. There a boy travels to heaven nine times, and he brings something back each time: a bird, berries, animals, and so on. That is, he brings these things to the people and installs them on earth. The tenth time he disappears and no longer returns. Everyone mourns him, and his mother has a dream. "His mother thought that in her dream she saw a beautiful house, but on awaking, she recognized that what she believed to have been a dream was real. The house was nearby, and her son Më'iLa was sitting in front of it." She wakes up her husband, and they look at the house and run toward it, but as they approach it, the house moves away from them, "and finally they saw that in reality it was up in heaven. Then they sat down and cried, singing: 'Our son is in heaven playing with Nûsnû'sElis (the moon).'" The niece suggests, "Let us make him appear in our dances." Since that time the people dance the "Më'iLa dance."[78]

Here we see the hero even more clearly as the arranger of the world, of social organization, and of people's customs. The hero also brings a house to the people, but it is "invisible," "in heaven," which is to say that it is concealed, taboo; it is in a "different world." Boas points out this legend's connection with rituals—that is, with the social life of the tribe—and this is also evident at the end of the legend. Let us cite another similar case, recorded in the same tribe. The hero goes upriver to catch salmon but does not find a single fish. He faints and sees a handsome man. This is the thunderbolt man, "thundering from one end of the world to the other." The hero asks him for a magical treasure. The thunderbolt man says to him, "Make a house and invite all the tribes." He shows him the carving of a thunderbird with its legs apart and says, "The bird's legs are the door of the house." Then the thunderbolt man shows him a carved image of the thunderbolt man's father. "The next night, all this will be in your village." In addition, he gives him the water of life and other gifts.

In all these cases, the palace is miraculously transported to the hero's village, along with the carved images and amulets; that is, a cult is being established. In the examples above, the house is transferred by the will of the thunderbolt man or the spirit; in the wondertale it is transported by the power of the helper. In the wondertale, the palace is transferred not only in the context of assigning difficult tasks. It can be taken along in an egg. "And, of course, they left the feast. She took him to a big open area. He broke the egg, and a palace took shape; and everything in this palace was the same as in the old one, the same as on that mountain."[79] The materials above make it possible to assert that, when the king demands that the hero show him the house, he allegorically demands proof of the hero's knowledge of this house. Simultaneously, the wondertale here reflects stories regarding the organizers of the world who gave the people everything they have in life. We shall see such an organizer in the hero many times, especially in the second half of the task, namely, in the demand that he plant a garden or plow and sow a field.

We have seen in the texts above that the mythical hero not only installs a house on earth but also gives people berries and animals. In the wondertale, building a palace is also usually connected to the skill of controlling nature, but the skill has taken on an agricultural character. "In one night you must plow and harrow, sow the wheat, reap it, thresh it, and put it in the barn."[80] "I want him in one night to plow, harrow, and sow a field, for everything to grow and ripen, and for the flour to be ground and bread baked."[81] This task is known in numerous variants. The hero is tested to see whether he is capable of accelerating the harvest. This requirement was demanded from magicians and sorcerers at the dawn of agriculture. "In Yap the priests or magicians of the sacred groves are usually supposed to possess a magical power of fertilizing certain fruits of the earth, and so of contributing directly to the sustenance of people. Thus, for instance, the High priest or Arch-magician of Tomil is believed to be able to quicken the taro fields and bread-fruit plantations of the whole of Yap. The priest or magician of Olog and Pemogoi understands the magic of sweet potatoes; and the priest or magician of Maki is an expert in the magic of coco-nuts and areca palms." These priests can also bring the sun down to the earth.[82] We see what kind of abilities the future leader or king brings back with him. The ability to control the sun and the heavenly elements is also not entirely forgotten by the wondertale. "I'm not going to marry him. . . . First you ask him to bring the golden sun and the white moons and the many stars of the dark midnight." The hero "allows" and "permits" this—that is, he puts them in their proper place.

These materials demonstrate that the motif of the hero building a palace and planting a garden or providing an unusually fast harvest goes back to the notions of magicians and priests who are able to accelerate the harvest because they have gone through initiation.

These instances also help us to understand another type of testing: the test by fire or by a hot bathhouse.

14. The Bathhouse Test

The task of staying for some time in a hot bathhouse is quite common. "That bathhouse was heated for three months, and it was so hot that it was impossible to approach within five miles of it."[83] The hero is at a loss. "Why? Are you crazy? I'll burn up there!" But then he remembers his helpers, and among them is Frost-Snapper, with whom we are familiar. "'I'll do it, my dear friend! This job is nothing for me.' He quickly jumped into the bathhouse, blew into one corner, spat into another, and the whole bathhouse cooled down, with snow lying in the corners." The hero proves in this task that by having his helpers he controls the forces of nature.

We saw above how in an Oceanic myth the future leader is taken through cold and heat. When we see a bathhouse in Russian tales, this is obviously a later, Russian form of testing by fire. In American myths,

a hero who wants to marry the daughter of the sun or a man "who lives
very far away" is tested by fire. "A big bonfire was made in front of the
seat. Tsowatalalis (the bride's father) put more firewood in the fire to fry
Gyli (the hero). Then Gyli threw shells that he had received from his aunt
into the fire, and they tamed the fire."[84] The hero's aunt corresponds to
our Yaga, the donor. The hero is subjected to more tests, after which the
bride's father says, "You are more than a man, and you will have my
daughter."

In other myths that involve wooing and testing the hero, a female
donor heats a stone until it is red hot and puts it in the hero's mouth. By
doing this, she gives him power over the natural element of fire.[85]

It is possible to assemble many examples showing that very early the
hero in myths is subjected to a fire test before marriage. He passes the
test because he has a magic gift brought from the forest. For us it is more
important to establish something else: the tests available in the myths of
North America accurately reflect wedding customs. Just as in myth, the
groom is tested in reality; moreover, this test has the characteristics of a
staged act. Boas describes such a case. The groom along with his father
and friends depart in a boat to visit the bride. On the way the leader
tries to persuade them not to be afraid. They carry with them the bride-
price of four hundred blankets. They arrive and are invited inside. The
bride's father turns to the visitors, saying, "Now take care, Gua'ts'ēnôx,
for here is the Q'ōmōqoa, a sea monster, who swallows everything, and
there in the rear of the house is he who devoured everyone who tried
to marry the daughter of Ya'qaLasamē, and this fire has hurt everyone
who tried to marry H'ēnEdemîs." Then he addresses himself: "Now,
Chief Ya'qaLasamē, light your fire and let the chief get our daughter
here." He actually makes a fire and says to the visitors, "Now take care,
Gua'ts'ēnôx, for I intend to try you. You said you were not afraid of
Ts'ōnōqoa? Now I will try all of you, chiefs of the Gua'ts'ēnôx. On account of this fire nobody can get my daughter." Then they all lie down on
their backs near the fire, wrapped in blankets. The blankets burn down.
Everyone gets up and boasts. The bride's father praises them: "You are the
first ones who have not run away from my fire." Other tests follow. Before
the groom's party arrives, the future father-in-law makes a bear mask
with a jaw that opens and closes. The mask is set on a bear's skin. Skulls
and bones have been brought in advance from the cemetery and put inside
the skin. Turning to the bear, the bride's father says, "Now you, devourer
of all tribes, step forward, so that Mā'Xua [the bridegroom's father] and
Ga'πaxidalaLē [the names of those who've come before are listed] may see
who has eaten the suitors of my daughter." The bear steps forward; the
bride's father takes a stick and pokes its stomach. The bear spits out seven
skulls and some bones. Then the father turns to the visitors: "Now look

at it, Gua'ts'enôx. These are the bones of the suitors who came to marry my daughter and who ran away from my fire. The devourer of tribes ate them. That is what he vomited. Now come, Hē'nEdemis [daughter], and go to your husband!" This concludes the ceremony.[86]

One may ask what gave the father the right to test the groom. What is the essence of this testing? We know from Boas's materials that the initiation of young Kwakiutl men was paid for not by their fathers but by *their brides' fathers*.[87] The groom entered into the clan of his wife. Before marriage, something like a secondary initiation ceremony takes place (burning, devouring and regurgitating in a somewhat deformed way) before the person who was responsible for the knowledge and the abilities of the groom: the bride's father. The groom shows, in schematic, mimetic ways, that he is strong in all aspects of this test; he shows that he has passed through the fire and is resistant to it.

The myth contains the same thing as the rite. We already know that the myths were communicated to a young man during the initiation and were something like the property of the initiate. They were not supposed to be retold but were made into staged acts on solemn occasions. This is how the epic tradition, preserved also in modern wondertales, emerges. The tale quite often preserves burning of the groom, but it has adopted several exaggerated and nationally colored forms (e.g., the bathhouse). The magical power usually embodied in the object is embodied here in the form of the anthropomorphic helper, the master of natural elements. The fact that his helper passed the test means that the groom passes it as well.

15. *The Test by Food*

The test of the hot bathhouse is very often associated with a test by food. "Well, if you are so clever, then show your bravery: you and your friends eat up twelve fried bulls and twelve bags of baked bread at one meal."[88] "The king ordered a big dinner served. A lot of various dishes were placed on the table. The glutton began to eat, and he ate up everything."[89] There are special helpers for this task: the Glutton or the glorious heroes Scarfer and Boozer. There is a special case in "The Rolling Pea."[90] Here, the hero meets on his way some shepherds who consistently offer to let him eat the largest ram from their flock, a boar, and finally twelve oxen, twelve rams, and twelve boars. Later, when the hero comes to the dragon, the latter offers him a colander full of iron beans and some iron bread. The hero eats all this.[91] The iron beans and iron bread remind us of the iron bread and iron staff the maiden takes with her in "Finist the Bright Falcon."[92] This allows us to question the connection between testing with food and staying in another world. It seems to be contradicted by the fact that the hero is usually tested not so much with iron food as with a huge *quantity* of food. However, knowing how constant the hero's connection is to the underground and aboveground world, we can assume this connection here too. It is known that among the heroes of ancient mythology, Heracles is notable for his particular voracity. And it is Heracles too who in many ways particularly resembles our hero. He also performs difficult tasks and descends into the underworld. From the underworld, one brings magical abilities, and one of these is the ability to eat a lot. Why? This question cannot be answered through references; we can only state the mere fact. However, we know the nature of the dead (and the hero gains the power of the dead): one of their specific features is that they do not eat. They are invisible, transparent. We shall see further that heroes acquire, among other things, the ability to become invisible. Food does not stay in them but passes through them. Therefore, the hero does not actually eat in the same way as living people do: this eating can last indefinitely, and in wondertales it takes on fantastic proportions. Recall that Yaga and similar creatures often have no spine. This explanation is only a hypothesis, but the hypothesis seems more probable to me than Olga Freidenberg's proposal that the hero is so gluttonous because "death is gluttonous and insatiable."[93]

It is possible that other ideas are reflected here too—for instance, the notion that partaking of a meal collectively creates unity in the clan. "Only members of the family or clan can participate (in the meal). If a foreign visitor is allowed to take part, then this admits him to the clan or brings him under its protection."[94] Here we have a category of marriage rites that include joint meals. However, this is contradicted by the fact that in the wondertale only the groom eats, not the bride, and it does not explain the hero's gluttony. At any rate, we find in this a representation of the ritual meal, which is associated with marriage and a stay in the other world.

16. Contests

Sometimes the hero is tested through a contest before the wedding. At first glance, these contests have a purely athletic nature. Frazer, studying this topic, sees only athletic rivalry in them; he ascribes an ancient origin to the custom and projects it onto "primitive society." "The personal qualities which recommended a man for a royal alliance and succession to the throne would naturally vary according to the popular ideas of the time and the character of the king or his substitute, but it is reasonable to suppose that among them in early society physical strength and beauty would hold a prominent place."[95] "Sometimes apparently the right to the hand of the princess and to the throne has been determined by a race. The Alitemnian Libyans awarded the kingdom to the fleetest runner. Amongst the old Prussians, candidates for nobility raced on horseback to the king, and the one who reached him first was ennobled."[96]

Frazer offers no reason to support this other than saying "we can assume." The issue was decided not by an athletic build, and certainly not by beauty, but by completely different qualities. M. G. Tikhaia-Tsereteli, who worked on Georgian folktales, senses this though she cannot prove it: "The personal qualities of the hero are also typical: beauty, athletic strength, intelligence, and other qualities that reflect his *mythological nature*. These qualities are what determine his union with the princess, not his origin."[97] The author here sees correctly what Frazer does not see: that athletic strength or dexterity reflects the mythological nature of the hero.

Careful study of the wondertale shows that it is not the hero's strength and dexterity but other qualities that are reflected in the contests. Victory is delivered by the magical helper. The hero cannot do anything without this, and his personal strength is not the point.

Let us consider the running contest. "The king's daughter will run to the well for water, and the man who outruns her will get her in marriage. If someone competes and does not outrun her, his head will be chopped off."[98] It is not only the speed of running that is important here; the goal toward which they run is also important. At first glance, the well does not represent anything special. However, comparison of different variants shows that, when they compete in running, water is the race's goal. An Afanas'ev tale shows that this is not ordinary water. There, one must get "the healing and living water" in the shortest time, "before the king finishes his dinner." The hero is distraught: even a year would not be enough time to get the water. Having heard the task, "his companion untied his foot from his ear, ran, and instantly got the healing and living water." On the way back, he lies down to rest, but the Seer or the Insightful One discovers him. Archer wakes him up with a skillful shot, and Swift-Runner arrives with the water in time.[99]

These examples show that it is not enough to run quickly: the important thing is to run quickly beyond Thrice-Nine Lands and return. Later, however, this object is lost, the "living water" transformed into a well, and running fast becomes the goal in itself. The original idea is seen even more clearly in tales where the king, who is three years removed from his land, sends for his magic-killing sword, forgotten by him in his castle. "Our king forgot his magic killing sword and his treasured knife at home; and the ride to the kingdom takes three months! The king promises to give his daughter in marriage to the person who brings it in time."[100] The hero runs from one kingdom to another, turning into different animals.

The same views are openly expressed in shooting contests. At first glance, the whole issue is about the weight and hugeness of the weapons or the tightness of the bow, as in the *Odyssey*. In Afanas'ev,[101] this bow is carried by forty people. The hero's helper breaks it. In Khudiakov, the bow is carried by six oxen, and the arrow by three pairs of horses.[102] But the point is not only to shoot from such a weapon but to shoot *from one kingdom to another*. For example, a princess sends the hero an iron mace weighing three poods through a courier. The hero is distressed. "How is it possible to throw this beyond Thrice-Nine Lands into the Thrice-Tenth Kingdom?" The problem is resolved by the hero's magical helper, his uncle. "The uncle burst into laughter, grabbed the mace with one hand, swung it three times, tossing it to the Thrice-Tenth Kingdom. It flew with a rumble through the mountains and valleys and fell so heavily on the princess's tower that the entire palace shook."[103] Exactly the same thing that happens here with the mace happens in another tale with an arrow. "And in the Indian kingdom, the princess was a powerful sorceress, and she had made a promise to marry." The promise is made in the following way: "If I send you a bow and arrow that has not yet been shot, you must try it. If you manage to shoot and send me word, then I'll marry you." The bow and arrow are carried by oxen. "Suddenly, Ivan the Dearly Bought braced the bow and aimed the arrow. The arrow *flew to the Indian kingdom* and knocked down the second floor of the royal palace."[104]

The magical nature of the tournament contests is also clearly evident through analysis of the helpers who accomplish the tasks set by a warlike princess. We examined these helpers above; in that analysis they emerged as the intermediaries between the two kingdoms.

The thoughts expressed here are also applicable to the very rich materials of antiquity. There are many cases in antiquity where a hero takes possession of a girl after winning a race. In these cases, the hero almost always wins with the aid of a helper or a god. Consequently, Frazer's theory about the personal qualities of the hero is not confirmed by the material of antiquity either. Pelops, according to one version, defeats Oenomaus in a chariot race, having received horses from Poseidon. And if, according to the legend, the Olympic games were established by Endymion, and moreover, *his tomb* was the starting point of the race, and the prize was the power to rule,[105] then perhaps there is a hint here too that the two kingdoms are connected through the race. Scholars of classical studies should study from this point of view the marriage of Melampus to the daughter of Neleus, the labors of Heracles at Aeneas and Eurytus, the battle of Hippomenes for Atalanta, and so on. And finally, if the funeral feast included contests not only among the Greeks but also among other peoples, then do these contests not have a relationship to the crossing over of the deceased from one kingdom to another? For example, Rohde has noticed that games on the grave of the deceased are related to the cult of souls. "The fact that these contests take place at the conclusion of funeral rituals can be explained as the rudiment of an ancient, more forceful cult of the souls."[106] But he is unable to explain this, believing (like other scholars) that the deceased took part in the games and that it was done for his pleasure, a theory expressed earlier by Varron. And although study of the funeral feast is not at all part of our task, we still have to state that the folklore material leads us to think that the contests, the race, and so on are related to the crossing of the deceased into another world.

17. Hide-and-Seek

The hiding task is of special interest to us. The king sends out a call: "Whoever successfully hides from me, the king, will get half of my living and subsistence, my princess in marriage, and upon my death will sit on the throne of the kingdom."[107] This king is a sorcerer, a magician. The false hero who attempts merely to hide in a bathhouse or in a barn is executed. The real hero turns into, for example, an ermine or a falcon, or he hides in their nests or is swallowed by them. However, these types of tasks are more often assigned not by the king but by the princess, the hero's wife who had earlier flown away from him and now is in the Thrice-Tenth Kingdom. The form of that difficult task is typical for this situation. Usually the princess finds the hero twice; on the third try he hides successfully. The princess finds him by looking in a magic mirror or in a magic book. The hero hides successfully when he hides behind the mirror or, after turning into a pin, in the book.

This phenomenon is not very easy to explain. Undoubtedly, the mirror and the book are later phenomena, and they replaced a different method of discovering the hero that existed before. Tikhaia-Tsereteli concludes that hide-and-seek is "a metaphor for immersion into the underworld, into non-existence, and concealment."[108] Although such an interpretation is quite plausible, it cannot be proved historically based on the materials that we have. Based on the analysis of the word *mirror*, the Georgian *sarke*, performed by N. Y. Marr, Tikhaia writes, "When in the numerous tales of the Caucasus, and specifically in Mingrelian tales, the beautiful heroine looks into the 'mirror' in search of the hiding place of her betrothed or the pretender to her heart, it means paleontologically looking into the 'mirror-sky.' She is in fact fortune telling through the sky and its luminaries."[109] The fact that the mirror has replaced the sky can be traced not only in the linguistic material but in folklore too. It is unclear, however, where the luminaries come from in Tikhaia's interpretation. In the wondertale, the hero most often hides the first time in the *sky*, carried away by an eagle. The princess directs her gaze there in the reflection of the mirror. This corresponds to Tikhaia's interpretation, but it nevertheless does not yet explain the requirement of hiding. It can be explained in the following way: the hero must possess the skill of becoming invisible.

Being invisible is an attribute of dwellers in the underworld. The cap of invisibility is the gift of Hades.

Two questions must be addressed: where is the task to hide assigned, and how is it accomplished? In Afanas'ev's tales, the hero finds his wife, who has run away to a kingdom under the ground.[110] In a tale from Perm, she lives in a golden palace with lions near the gate.[111] In one from Khudiakov, she is "in the sky."[112] In one from Smirnov she is "in a magical house."[113] In other words, the hero finds himself in the environment of the familiar "big house," whose connections to the "other kingdom" we have already established. From this angle, it becomes apparent that the hero must demonstrate his invisibility. We have also examined invisibility as part of the rite (cf. the white or black coloring).

On the other hand, the following manner of accomplishing the task leads to the same cycle: the hero hides either in a nest or in an animal's lair or sits on the animal's back while it takes him away, or he is swallowed by an animal, or he turns into one. The latter two forms must be considered original on the basis of everything we know about the rite. It is true that in wondertales this solution yields a negative outcome, but that outcome can be considered a purely wondertale phenomenon caused by the tripling of tasks. Three devouring incidents have a negative outcome, but their form has a historical past; and the final resolution (the hero hides behind a mirror, under a book, under a bed, etc.) demonstrates folkloric craftiness. It has no analogies in the rite and is peculiar to wondertales alone.

Thus, we see that here too the rite seems to be repeated just before the marriage. But now it is repeated as a test of the groom, not as a way of giving him magical power. In this case, his ability to be invisible is tested. This is related to the ability to turn into an animal, to take on its appearance, and his staying inside the animal form is verified. The hero demonstrates the devouring and his ability to be invisible.

This connection perhaps explains the similarity between the motif of hide-and-seek and the motif of reading prayers for a dead princess. There too everything is built on the hero's invisibility, and it actually clarifies an issue that the motif of hide-and-seek only hints at: that invisibility is related to a series of concepts about death, both factual and ritualistic. Reading prayers also often takes place in the setting of the big house. The hero draws a circle around himself. The dead woman cannot step over it. On the third night, the hero hides behind an icon in exactly the same way as he hides in a book or behind a mirror during hide-and-seek. "The princess searched and searched; she searched all the corners but couldn't find him."[114] These words show that here too the hero is hiding. They also reveal the nature of this game of hide-and-seek: the words are said of the living by the dead. Only a dead person is transparent and invisible; thus, the hero has acquired a property of the dead. Exactly the same thing can be found in another version. There, the hero climbs on the stove and thereby becomes invisible. "Just a minute ago he was reading, and now he's disappeared! I can't find him!" This is what the deceased woman says.[115] Is such a coincidence an accident? It is not. The living do not see the dead. But if we assume that this motif reflects the idea that the dead cannot see the living either, then the rational basis of the motif becomes clear. The princess has died and, in fact, cannot see the hero. But this is exactly how her witchcraft skill works—she can still see the living. After all, she devoured all the hero's predecessors. But here comes a hero who is also a sorcerer and a magician. He responds to the sorcery of the deceased woman with his own sorcery and makes himself invisible to her. In tales where the hero is assigned the task of hiding, the princess is also always a great sorceress: she possesses a magic book. The nature of the test here acquires the character of a contest in magic. Both the tester and the one tested are great magicians, but the hero prevails.

18. Recognizing the Sought-after Person

Note that the task of hiding is usually assigned by the princess who has flown away from the hero. The hero goes to look for her. He finds her in her kingdom, and that is where the task is assigned.

In exactly the same way, the Water King in the other kingdom assigns the task of recognizing the sought-after person among twelve identical ones. He shows the hero his twelve daughters, and the hero must recognize the youngest—that is, the bride.

The same task is given to the father who comes to get his son back from the sorcerer. The son has been sent there to study. The father must recognize him from among twelve utterly identical students.

This task is based on the idea that, in the other realm, the person sought *does not have his own individual appearance*. All those who stay there look the same. This idea is found in its pure form in a Dolgan myth. There, an old man's daughter dies. Three years pass. A seer goes to search for her. He falls asleep and in his dream "reaches the place" where the soul of the deceased resides. But he cannot recognize her. "It turns out that there are three completely identical girls with the same faces and clothes. One of them is the old man's daughter, but he cannot find out which one. He counts the seams of their clothes, but they all have the same even count. He grows exhausted by counting." Finally, he recognizes the girl he is searching for when she mentions an object given to her by her mother. He grabs her and carries her away. He wakes up. It turns out that he was asleep for nine days. "But their girl was not moving, she had either died or fallen asleep. He began to put bones into the girl as if into a sack. And she came back to life, *and, having come back to life, became the old man's daughter."* The last words are very important: when the dead person comes back to life, she regains her personal qualities. And, by contrast, when dying, the person loses her personal qualities and features and becomes unrecognizable.[116]

This myth is primordial compared to the wondertale and far more ancient. Moreover, it demonstrates the connection of the motif of staying in the "other kingdom." We have seen above the connection between "A Tricky Science" and the cycle of the big house. The sorcerer's students are considered to be in a state of death, and all are identical.

It must be also noted that in cases where the hero is not alone but has a retinue, they all look so similar to one another that it is impossible to tell them apart. The consistent wording for expressing this similarity is "voice identical to voice, hair to hair."[117] This similarity leads us to the forest brotherhood where all are identical or invisible since they are in a state of simulated death.

But not everything is clear yet. The task of finding the person hiding among identical others is not only found in shamanic practice; it is also encountered as a wedding ritual and was recorded as late as the nineteenth century throughout Europe. Samter's *Geburt, Hochzeit, Tod* collects especially copious material. Evgenii Kagarov also writes about this in his work on wedding rituals. We shall offer several examples here. In the Vosges region, on the wedding day the bridegroom must choose his betrothed from a large crowd of maidens. In Sardinia, after the groom arrives at the engagement ceremony, he is led to a room where as many girls as possible sit in a row, all in silence and tensely calm. The same is recorded in many other places. For example, in Berry, France, at the end of a wedding all the women stand in a row. The bridegroom walks behind them and must recognize the bride based on her exposed legs.[118]

Kagarov cites five different explanations from the literature for this widespread custom. The author himself is inclined to explain it in a very laconic manner as "a trick for deceiving the spirits."[119] This explanation is shared by eleven other authors as well. Kagarov includes this rite in a series of exaptation or dissimulation rituals (ritual fictions). However, none of these authors includes either folklore materials or material on shamanism. Kagarov's explanation is provided from the point of view of the custom's purpose. But the fact of the matter is that this purpose is never expressed overtly, and one can speculate about it as much as one wishes. What kind of "spirits" are we talking about here? The point is not in the purpose but in the causes: the question that should be raised is not *what the purpose of this rite is* but *how it arose.* Folktale material allows us to establish the motif's origin. Interpretation of the rite, which outlived the foundation on which it was created, is impossible. We can only study the ways it has been resignified. In the case of the wedding ceremony, however, there is not even any resignification; for some un-known reason it is traditionally performed as a game, and no one won-ders about its purpose. This creates grounds for "interpretation" of this rite in the literature, an erroneous path that allows an infinite number of arbitrary solutions.

19. *The Wedding Night*

The wondertale could end with a wedding. But sometimes another im-portant test awaits the hero, that of the first night. Usually the test of the first night is not expressed in the form of a task. In essence, however, it is the same trial as the others, and occasionally it is in fact expressed in the form of a task: "The king sent out a call, saying that he would give his daughter in marriage to the man who would spend the night with her."[120] I have attempted to show in another work that the task of find-ing certain attributes of the princess, such as "I will give my daughter in marriage to the person who can guess the location of her birthmark,"[121] is a euphemism for a test of a different nature.[122]

What is the covert danger of this night? The wondertale provides a rather varied picture. Most often we find that the princess lays her heavy hand upon the hero. The helper knows about this danger and warns the prince. "Be careful, your majesty, don't make a mistake. She will try to test your strength during the first three nights. She will lay her hand on you and start pressing hard. You won't be able to bear it."[123] "The minute they went to bed, she placed her hand on him with supernatural force."[124]

Pressing him with her hands is not a simple test of strength. The princess is striving *to smother her bridegroom.* "The princess laid one hand on him and then the other; then she grabbed a pillow and started smothering him with it."[125]

Sometimes all the princess's bridegrooms mysteriously die on the first night. "In this town the king sent out a proclamation that he had given his daughter for marriage to three grooms. After the wedding ceremony, they would put the couple to bed, and later the young woman would be alive, but the young man dead. And the king sent out a call that he would give his whole kingdom to the man who agreed to marry her."[126] But there is also a danger of another kind: a dragon often flies in to visit the princess.[127] We shall address this issue below. But no matter what the danger might be, whether it is laying her hands on him, strangling him, the sudden and unexplained death of the bridegroom, or the fact that a dragon often flies in to visit her, there is always only one way out. The helper takes the place of the groom. "If you lie down with your wife and try to leave, God help you! It will be better if I lie down with her." Or: "If you want to stay alive, allow me to lie down with the princess instead of you."[128] "Better let me lie down in your place."[129] "Go quickly out of the room, and I'll come there in your place."[130] These examples show with sufficient clarity that here we are dealing with a certain wondertale norm, a canon, according to which the defloration is carried out not by the groom himself but by his magically armed and mighty helper. It is true that the tales do not state this directly. He supposedly only pushes her against the wall, squeezes her hand, and so on. Nevertheless, the picture is clear enough.

This does not exhaust the events of the first night. Usually, after taming her, the helper takes three types of rods and flogs the princess. "Then he grabbed her by her braid, yanked her out of the bed and began to lash her with a whip. When he finished lashing her, he threw her on the bed. He went out and sent in Kuzma Ferapontovich" (i.e., the hero).[131] "Mishka Vodovoz [water carrier] grabbed her by the collar, slammed her against the floor, used up two iron rods and a brass one on her, and threw her down as if she were a dog. . . . 'All right, Prince Ivan, flop on the bed! Now nothing bad will happen to you!'"[132]

This is a brief, general outline of the first night. It is quite obvious that some very ancient cogitative phenomena are reflected here that have certain realistic marital relations as their foundation.

The wondertale itself, when examined in greater detail, shows that the sexual power of the groom is being tested. However, it is not a matter of that alone. The general picture consists of the groom's powerlessness, the woman's demonic power, and the power of the helper, which is superior to her power: it is he who overpowers the princess. A study of the helper reveals his forest origin. From this point of view, the tale of Katoma is particularly interesting to us.[133] The princess, defeated by the helper, seeks to separate her husband from his helper. She succeeds. Katoma's legs are amputated, and he begins to live in the woods with another maimed person. There he leads a life already familiar to us from the chapter on the big house. He restores his legs and comes back home. In this way he gains power over the princess. "And the princess thought, 'Well, if he managed to get his legs back, there is nothing more I can do to him,' and she began asking him and the prince for forgiveness." Once again we see a situation already familiar to us: staying in the forest is a condition for marriage, and the hero must prove that he has done so. In this way, the wondertale itself provides an answer to the question of why the helper replaces the hero in the nuptial bed.

However, not everything is clear yet. First of all, it is not apparent what the danger really consists of and why the grooms have been dying on the first night. We shall be able to answer this question by examining materials that belong to older cultural stages. American and Siberian materials show that the danger comes not at all from laying a strong hand upon the hero. It is of a purely sexual nature. The woman has teeth in her vagina. In North American myth all the bridegrooms of a certain very beautiful woman have been dying. Finally, one of the bridegrooms comes up with the idea of inserting a stone inside her at the right moment. "*Ex illo tempore vagina innocens semper fuit.*"[134] This motif is fairly common. Shternberg cites a very interesting and important case from Gilyak folklore. Six Ainu people go seal hunting and lose their way. They arrive "on the other side." There, six women are sitting on a platform, cleaning fish. The women invite the guests to their yurt and hold a fine feast for them. "They climbed onto bunk beds, lay down, and fell asleep. After a while one of them got up, climbed down, and lay down in the bed of one of the women. They whispered for a while, then he climbed on her, and then: 'ow, ow, ow!' and he was dead." The same happens with the second man. "Their master gets up, goes outside, goes down to the shore, picks up a round stone, carries it inside the yurt, and climbs up onto his bed. After lying down for a while, he gets up and approaches the woman lying on the left bunk bed at the end, adjoining the middle bunk. He climbs up and lies down in her bed. They whisper for a while, then suddenly there is a rasping sound. He climbed on top of her, pushed the stone inside her, and she bit it. It broke all her teeth there, didn't leave a single one."[135] After this everything proceeds without problems; the woman has been rendered harmless. Shternberg, noting similar cases in the materials of Boas and Vladimir Bogoraz-Tan, gives a rationalistic explanation of the motif in the footnotes. In his opinion, it all boils down to a female disease. However, we must reject such an explanation. There are many diseases, but for some reason, other diseases do not generate myths, whereas this disease does. In addition, such an explanation does not account for the inevitable and sudden death of the man in these cases. It would be more correct to say that the motif figuratively reflects the idea of the danger of women's defloration and that this danger has a mythological nature, reflecting the notion of women's power. The myth reported by Shternberg is interesting for another reason. We see in it something like a kingdom of women. Only women live on the mysterious shore the Ainu have reached. The woman's magical power corresponds to a certain social structure, a special organization where society is founded by women, who are also doing all the work and ruling, and who perhaps destroy all men by enticing strangers into a short marriage, something like the Amazons. In the wondertale, the princess to whom the hero aspires is also a girl warrior, a warlike tsar-maiden, and the sovereign ruler of her own kingdom.

In later religions, the female ruler turns into a goddess with mixed features of a goddess of hunting and farming. Such goddesses kill their lovers on the first night. This can be traced in the cults of Asia Minor and of antiquity, but there the killing sometimes turns into castration, serving as an etiological legend for explaining the castration of priests. According to Eduard Hahn, "It is without doubt that in the most ancient myth, Aphrodite herself in the form of a boar killed her lover, or caused his death through castration, as the mother of gods in Asia Minor did with her Attis. . . . We have a significant indication that Ishtar killed all her lovers in the same way as Artemis did with Actaeon, and as Isis killed her beloved Maneros."[136]

These materials demonstrate how long the idea of the danger of the first sexual intercourse has held on. There the mighty woman is already a goddess, but the danger of interacting with her remains the same.

Thus, the first intercourse with a woman is dangerous for men. Certain data suggest that at some point a ritual defloration was performed as a special rite during the initiation of girls. There is very little data about this in ethnographic literature, but nevertheless such an assumption is possible. This idea is expressed by Reitzenstein, according to whom, "It is more or less clear that in many such festivals a certain person playing the main role comes to the fore. We should see in him the echoes of the sorcerer who initially performed these rites. He wore certain masks, which in most cases very clearly show him as the earthly representative of the forest spirit."[137] Reitzenstein claims that the transformation of a girl into a woman occurs specifically during these rites. "The main element of the initiation festivals should be considered the transformation of girls into women not through marriage or sexual intercourse, but through the initiation ceremonies (*Reifezeremonien*), which aim at the woman's fertilization, while intercourse took place long before that." If a child was born before the initiation, the child was killed, "since such a child is not considered to be a human being, i.e., they assume that he was not born from the clan's ancestors."[138]

This theory, although not sufficiently supported by ethnographic data, still allows at least a hypothetical explanation of the wondertale scenario—that is, it answers the question why the helper lies with the bride on the wedding night first and the hero does so after him. The concepts associated with this practice at one time apparently had deep roots and wide distribution. They are reflected not only in wondertales. "In Montenegro, on the first night after the wedding, the groomsman (*Brautführer*) sleeps next to the bride, supposedly 'in a good way.' In Bosnia, every male guest at the wedding has the custom of pressing the bride against the wall, symbolically portraying a conjugal embrace."[139]

If Reitzenstein's theory is correct, we can assume that two events separated in time—a ritual defloration before marriage, carried out by a "deity," and the wedding night with the husband—were later merged into a single event. At this point the defloration does not happen before the wedding but *after* it. Therefore, the person who performs this act must appear immediately after the marriage, on the first night. The human wedding night has merged with the totemic defloration. Defloration is performed by the "forest spirit," or the hero's helper in the wondertale, and the hero receives the bride from his hands.

In light of Reitzenstein's theory the abduction of the princess by the dragon can also be interpreted as abduction for the purpose of totemic defloration. In light of this theory, her cohabitation with the dragon or with Koshchei, the dragon's sojourn in a secret closet, and so forth offer a resolution of sorts. From this point of view, the killing of Koshchei or the dragon must be recognized as a later phenomenon, similar to the burning of Yaga. A new social system and new matrimonial forms compel seeing the masked figure who performs the defloration not as a benefactor but as a rapist, and he is killed. Typically, in cases where the dragon flies to visit the bride, the battle with the dragon takes place in the bedroom on the wedding night. "'Prince, don't sleep with your wife on the first night or something bad will happen! Better let me go in your place!' The prince agreed. . . . It was midnight; suddenly winds began to rustle—here arrived a twelve-headed dragon, flying. Bulat the Fine began to fight him. He chopped off all twelve heads and threw them out the window."[140] Here too, then, we see a double thread. On one hand, defloration by the helper (always expressed indirectly in the wondertale) is perceived as a blessing; on the other hand, there is a battle with the rapist, and he is destroyed.

Reitzenstein's theory allows him to provide a brilliant solution to the problem of the sword between the spouses. This is a rather rare motif in Russian tales,[141] but the motif is quite widespread in world folklore. Reitzenstein shows that a wooden carved image of a totemic character is placed between the couple on their wedding night. The ancestor's spirit supposedly conceives the child while on the first night the groom abstains from intercourse. Later this "fertilizing instrument became a separating instrument"; it turns into the sword between the man and the woman. Perhaps this gives a new interpretation for the abstinence on the first night practiced to the present day. Kagarov interprets it as an apotropaic technique.[142] It is possible that such abstinence comes from the view that on this night the woman is impregnated by a totemic ancestor. The *droit de seigneur* comes from this notion as well. This right is later transferred from the magically stronger person to the socially stronger one and becomes a means of usurping conjugal rights.

But all this does not explain one additional detail in the picture of the wedding night: we have not yet explained the torture of the bride.

It is characteristic that in cases reflecting an earlier stage, when a woman is represented with teeth in her vagina, we do not see the motif of beating her. These teeth are a symbol, a figurative expression of her great power and superiority over the man. Pulling out her teeth and torturing her are the same phenomena, which deprives the woman of her power.

From now on the princess is submissive and *obeys her husband*. This is the whole point. The old power of the woman has long been broken by man's domination. But there is one more area where a man is still afraid of a woman; she has power and authority because of her ability to produce offspring. Historically too, the power of the woman is founded on a sexual basis. She is strong and dangerous as a result of this sexuality. And it is not so essential whether this is expressed by means of teeth or of laying her hand on her groom or smothering him. Fear of the wedding night is fear of the power of the tsar-maiden who has not yet been broken. She is deprived of this power through the power of initiation, which only men undergo. From now on, the woman is subjugated. She has lost all her power to the man, having retreated from the final stronghold where, it was presumed, she could exhibit her mysterious might. From now on, the man reigns supreme.

20. *Preliminary Conclusions*

The tasks mentioned to this point do not exhaust the material. It is impossible here to exhaust all the difficult tasks that occur in the Russian wondertale repertoire. We can only outline the categories of these tasks in order to reveal whether there is a certain unity and system in their variety and diversity and to find directions in which historical investigations might be carried out.

What have we determined to this point? What conclusions can be drawn from the tasks considered above and the conditions in which they are assigned?

First, it turns out that the most diverse tasks do not actually constitute diverse, heterogeneous material. They show a close affinity among themselves. They represent the same phenomenon. The following general principle can be formulated: before receiving the hand of the princess, the hero is subjected to various tests that he can perform only if he has gone through all that is canonical for the hero—that is, if he has a magical helper and possesses magical means and powers. In terms of their content, the tasks, for all their diversity, also reveal a degree of unity. The hero proves in various ways that he has either visited the other world (tasks of looking for something, being sent to hell, etc.) or that he possesses the characteristics of a dead person. He can become invisible (the hide-and-seek test), he can eat endlessly, he has no individualized appearance, and so on. The visit to the other world is important not just as a journey; it is important for its results, which are twofold. They are associated, on one hand, with the religion of the clan system and, on the other, with marital or premarital customs. The hero is no ordinary person. By solving difficult tasks, he demonstrates that he controls the sun, thunder, cold, and heat and that he can produce crops. This is a mythical tradition that reflects the story of totemic ancestors who created or organized the world. An ancestor brought the people the first fruits of the earth, taught them all the arts and skills, taught them their dances, established human customs, and gave them their social structure. This is the line of mythical legends.

In addition, these myths also reflect concrete quotidian or ritualistic reality. Each clan has its own magical helper, its own amulets, dances, and stories. The researcher sees a general pattern in them. For the amulet's owner, for those trained in specific dances, these amulets and dances are something different from the amulets or dances of others. Analysis of the difficult tasks is inseparable from analysis of the helper and of the whole situation in which he is acquired. Above, we saw in the figure of Yaga the mother-in-law of the hero, the mother, the aunt, or the sister of his *wife*. In this connection, Boas's description of the Kwakiutl wedding ceremony, quoted above, becomes especially important. It turns out that the initiation of the young man was paid for not by his father but by the father of the bride. This means that the bridegroom was initiated into the secrets not of his own clan or tribe but into the secrets of his wife's clan. When we examined Yaga, we saw that the helper was passed down by inheritance. The materials indicate that the hero received a helper or an amulet that was specific to his wife's clan and different from all other amulets and helpers. Whereas the wondertale shows that the hero is being tested for owning a helper, the ethnographic materials show that the bridegroom was tested for mastery of the secrets specific to the clan association into which he would be accepted through marriage. The father of the bride, who paid for the initiation, had the right to test the bridegroom preliminarily. Before marriage, a ceremony was performed that mimicked initiation, where the groom demonstrated that he had passed all the requisite tests.

III. The Hero's Accession to the Throne

21. *Frazer on the Succession of Kings*

"Difficult tasks" precede not only the marriage but also the hero's accession to the throne. Below we shall see that accession is accompanied by slaying the old king. There is some connection between the tasks, the slaying of the king, and the hero's accession.

It is difficult to trace the specific historical roots of the tasks in isolation. By contrast, the inheritance of power and its transition from one person to another is a thoroughly historical rather than a wondertale phenomenon. The forms of this transition have changed over the course of history. One form was studied by Frazer; he formulated it as follows:

> Among some Aryan peoples, at a certain stage of their social evolution, it has been customary to regard women and not men as the channels in which royal blood flows, and to bestow the kingdom in each successive generation on a man of another family, and often of another country (who marries one of the princesses and reigns over his wife's people). A common type of popular tale, which relates how an adventurer, coming to a strange land, wins the hand of the king's daughter and with her the half or the whole of the kingdom, may well be a reminiscence of a real custom.[143]

Analysis of the wondertale both confirms Frazer's supposition and shows that this practice was much more widespread than he assumed without undertaking a special study of folktales. As Frazer himself shows, the old king was usually killed by the new one. Wondertales have preserved this specific circumstance, so to this point it is possible to agree with him. Frazer even connects the phenomenon of inheritance through the female line (through the king's daughter) with a stage of social development. But he was a bourgeois scholar, and even where he gropes toward the right path he still cannot go beyond the thinking and beliefs of his class.

The theory of the succession of kings lies at the heart of the *Golden Bough*. But Frazer, probably without noticing it, gives all his attention to the king who is replaced. The hero who overthrows the old king remains out of the author's field of vision, and this circumstance turns out to be fatal for the whole analysis. For Frazer, the replacement is "some rival," "any strong man," and so on.[144] It is possible that the wondertale has better preserved the former situation and that not "any strong man" could become king. Moreover, Frazer says little about the regulation of this succession. Of course, not any person could come at any time, kill the king, and take his place. The only norm he discusses is the periodicity of succession. Kings are replaced after five, ten, and twelve years. (There are other time spans as well.) The king can also be replaced when he falls ill. The reason for forcible replacement of the old king with a new one is that it is believed that the king, who is simultaneously priest and sorcerer, one who ensures the well-being of the fields and herds, begins to lose his magical powers with the coming of old age or not long before that. This threatens the entire people with disaster. He will be replaced, therefore, by a stronger successor.

It seems to us that the folklore material gives enough evidence to claim that this successor is supposed to provide proof of his magical power and that the roots of the "difficult tasks" lie here as well.

22. *Succession to the Throne in the Wondertale*

What kind of kingdom does the prince inherit? He almost never inherits his own father's kingdom. He comes to a foreign land, marries a princess there after solving difficult tasks, and stays there to reign. If this is told in countries where for a long time the power has been passing from father to son, not from father-in-law to son-in-law, it means that the wondertale has preserved an older condition. But of course, we should not be surprised that the situation that existed in European monarchies should also be reflected in wondertales. Having obtained the princess, the hero sometimes returns home and takes over the kingdom from his father. This is a tribute to later forms of succession to the throne.

The story of the hero's accession to the throne sometimes unfolds with the first words of the tale. The king addresses the people with a proclamation that he will give his daughter and half his kingdom to the person who solves this or that task. The tale never explains what makes the king do this. Frazer's materials demonstrate that the succession of kings occurred periodically. We can assume that for the wondertale king too, *the time has come* to be replaced. Thus, the king's proclamation—for instance, "A paper came from the tsar: whoever built a ship that could fly, the tsar would give him the princess in marriage"—represents the moment of abdication from the throne. We see that this moment is associated with assignment of a task. From Frazer's materials, it is clear that one reason for overthrowing the king was the beginning of his magical impotence (sometimes associated with the onset of declining sexual potency). The Russian wondertale does not preserve this. The king there is only the ruler of the people but not the ruler of nature. There is, however, a Dolgan myth in which this circumstance is expressed quite distinctly. The king sits in the dark; "he did not know the sun, he did not know the moon either" (see chap. 2, sec. 3). He generates the well-being of people: "Children did not stop being born; people did not end when they died." But then his daughter is born, and she reaches the age of marriage. "The game stopped flying, the fish started disappearing and decreasing, the grass ceased growing," and so on. What does this mean? Obviously, children reaching marriageable age, the creation of a new generation, shows that it is time for the old generation to leave, to give way to the new one. The king is no longer able to control nature. Later, this king is reproached, for "the sun has disappeared because of his sins." The king assigns a difficult task: to break through the sky and turn the sun around. He promises his daughter and half his kingdom to the person who does this.[145] Here the original reason for the removal of the king, which has been established by Frazer as a historical phenomenon—namely, the loss of magical power—has been preserved very clearly. The difficult task, the marriage, and the acquisition of power constitute an inseparable complex. This example shows with particular clarity that the presence of an adult daughter and the appearance of the groom present a mortal danger for the old king. The father-in-law and the son-in-law here are primordial enemies. If power passes through the *son-in-law*, the king has to have an *adult daughter*. When she reaches marriageable age and has a fiancé, that is the moment to give away the kingdom along with the daughter.

We now understand why the tasks are of a dual nature. They must attract the groom because public opinion demands it, but at the same time, they must scare the bridegroom away because their accomplishment will entail the death of the old king. The princess's position is also twofold. As a daughter, she will hate the bridegroom who brings death to her father. As the transmitter of the throne, she must fulfill her civic duty and go along with the groom against her father. She either seeks to kill the bridegroom or seeks to kill her father. She does both in different tales single-handedly.

The example above from Dolgan folklore is not unique, but it is quite complete and clear. Traces of the young man's magical superiority over the old man are also found in Russian wondertales. "He's so crafty, we'll marry our daughter to him."[146] We shall see the impotence of the king again below in discussing the task of bathing in milk.

23. *Old Age*

This impotence is the result of old age. It was precisely old age, illness, and infirmities that served as an incentive for replacing the king. Frazer cites many such cases: "The town of Gatri is ruled by a king who is elected by the big men of the town as follows. When in the opinion of the big men the king has reigned long enough, *they give out that 'the king is sick'—a formula understood by all to mean that they are going to kill him.*"[147] Old age features both at the beginning and at the end of wondertales. "One tsar got very old and his eyes grew poor." He wants, for example, to be thirty years younger and sends his sons "to find his youth"; he "began to grow old," and so on.[148] This begins the tale, while the end is the hero's accession to the throne. More often, old age appears in the end as the reason for the transfer of power. "Well, Vanya, I've grown old and now I relinquish everything. I'm giving you the whole kingdom. If you want it, live well and reign. I hand everything over to you."[149] "Since the tsar was already of old age, he placed his crown on the head of Ivan, the peasant's son."[150]

Let us note that in all these examples, the power is transferred not to "any strong person" but to the son-in-law who has solved the "difficult task" and thereby proven his strength.

24. Oracles

Along with the expiration of the king's reign, the onset of old age, and the decline of his strength, there is another reason that sometimes causes replacement of the old king by the new. This is the phenomenon of oracles. It is quite obvious that oracles are a secondary phenomenon here. The people's will is expressed through the mouth of the gods, inserted into their mouth. "The Ethiopian kings of Meroe were worshipped as gods; but whenever the priests chose, they sent a messenger to the king, ordering him to die, and alleging an oracle of the gods as their authority for the command."[151] The wording "whenever the priests chose" causes some bewilderment. They obviously were supposed to want it for some reason, probably again because the term was expiring or the king did not satisfy them. Here we cannot go into the essence of the study of oracles and the great role they play in religion and myth. We can address only one aspect of this phenomenon.

The wondertale, like historical reality, knows two ways of transferring the throne. The first is from the king to his son-in-law through his daughter. The princess transmits the throne. This is a conflict situation leading to murdering the keeper of the throne and marrying his daughter, the transmitter of the throne. The second is when the throne is passed from father to son without any conflict. The first form is an early one; the second is later. With the advent of the second form, the conflict disappears *from reality*, but it does not disappear from myth, does not disappear *from the consciousness* of people: ideology does not always immediately register the changes that have occurred. When the old conflict is transferred to a new relationship, we have the case found in Oedipus and also preserved in wondertales. The heir is not the son-in-law but the son. When the conflict is preserved and transferred to the new relationship, then he, the heir, kills the keeper of the throne—the *son* kills his *father*. Furthermore, under the old order the king's daughter is the transmitter of the throne, but under the new, if the king is childless, either a new king is elected or the king's widow serves as transmitter. By preserving marriage to the transmitter of the throne and transferring it to the new conditions, myth creates a plot with marriage to the king's widow—the mother of the heir. The son marries his mother. But since such a case goes against public morality, this act is made unintentional. The old order is also preserved, where the heir is an alien. To keep him as an alien, he must be separated from his father. For this reason the oracle enters the picture. By the way, we must note that the difficult task has also been preserved: Oedipus solves the riddle of the Sphinx. But this task turns from a demonstration of his magical power into liberation of the people from disaster. This determines his right to the throne, not his magical power. With the transfer of power from father-in-law to son-in-law, the death of the old king was a preestablished phenomenon and did not require any oracles. But with the transfer from father to son, the death of the king (the father) from the heir (his son) becomes something unnatural or impious. It is also motivated by the will of the gods and by a horrible destiny. This is also evident in the fact that these oracular pronouncements are more often made regarding nephews and sons than about sons-in-law. Perseus's grandfather was told that he would lose the throne through the hands of his *grandson*; Laius was foretold that he would perish by his *son*; and Pelias was told that he would hand over the kingdom to a hero with one sandal. In this hero, he recognizes his *nephew*, that is, a representative of *his own* family.

These more recent cases are poorly reflected in the wondertale, which retains a more archaic situation: the hero kills his father-in-law, marries, and takes over the kingdom without any oracle's involvement. The oracle exists only in cases where the father is killed or humiliated. If the prophecy does not involve the father and his son, but the son-in-law and his father-in-law, then the tale contains elements of later origin. Such is the tale of Marko the Rich, which resembles not so much a folktale as a legend. One version says, "He will replace the master on this estate,"[152] but for the folklorist this means, "He will replace the king in this kingdom." In German folklore, this tale is told not about a merchant but about a king. "There was once a poor woman who gave birth to a little son; and as he came into the world with a caul on, it was predicted that in his fourteenth year he would have the king's daughter for his wife."[153] The king tries in every way to get rid of the hero. These examples illustrate the observation that the death of the king from his successor is known in advance and that in wondertales, as in historical reality, this circumstance is expressed through the mouths of oracles. Moreover, the oracle emerged when people had already begun to doubt the need for such a form of replacing the king.

25. *The Killing of the King in the Wondertale*

Is the old king really killed in the wondertale while conceding his kingdom to his son-in-law? At first glance it seems that this is not quite so. The conflict is settled peacefully. The king gives his son-in-law half the kingdom, and both continue to reign; there is no murder. Or, after marrying the king's daughter, the hero peacefully awaits the death of his father-in-law and ascends the throne only after the king's death. Or, he continues to reside with the king as a kind of hanger-on. There are other ways of circumventing and mitigating this conflict. But all these cases cannot hide from us the original state of affairs. First, the hero gets *the whole* kingdom, and second, the old king is simultaneously *killed*.

It is very common in wondertales for the hero to receive the whole kingdom, not half of it; there is no need for any proof. Here are a few examples: "And he gave his daughter to Ivan the Fool and gave him his entire kingdom."[154] "And he gave him his entire kingdom."[155] "Whoever gets it, he will give that person the whole kingdom."[156] "He gave him the whole kingdom,"[157] and so on. These cases preserve the original and historically attested form, while the "half-kingdom" is a later wondertale replacement.

The same can be said of killing the king. The wondertale attempts to conceal this circumstance or soften it, but not very successfully. How is the king killed in the wondertale? Sometimes he is killed with the magic items acquired by the hero. The hero's magical weapon is the cause of the king's death. Even the magical self-playing harp can serve this purpose. "The fool stuffed his ears with a flower, came to the tsar and made the self-playing harp play. As soon as the magic harp started playing, the tsar, his boyars, and the court guards all fell asleep. The fool took the steel sword from the wall and killed the king."[158] "'Hey, club, beat and pound!' The club rushed, struck once or twice, and killed the evil king. And the fool became the king and reigned long and kindly."[159] The fact that the king here appears evil does not change the matter. In a variant of this tale, suddenly a self-swallowing wolf appears and devours the tsar. This wolf is the hero's helper, the functional equivalent of a magical object, such as a club or a pipe. "The fool became tsar and lived with his beautiful queen and the wolf happily ever after." A particularly interesting example is in Afanas'ev's tale No. 212 (H212), in which the old king perishes from his adversary's army: "The tsar saw his army running, so he rushed to stop the troops, but alas! Half an hour later, he himself was killed. When the battle ended, the people gathered and began to beg the archer to take upon himself the whole kingdom. He agreed and became king, and his wife became queen." This case is noteworthy in that we indeed encounter delivering the king over to his enemy, one of the forms of killing the king. This form appears late and already represents a transition to all sorts of compromises. This was practiced in Central Angola where the king had the title of Matiamvo. A Portuguese expedition learned the following: "Our Matiamvo . . . have usually either died in war or by forcible death. The current Matiamvo is going to die at the hands of the executioner, for through begging he has already obtained a long life. After we sentence Matiamvo to death, we usually invite him to participate in a war with the enemy and we accompany him and his family to the war. If he survives, we enter another war and fight for three or four days in a row. Then we suddenly leave Matiamvo with his family to the mercy of fate."[160] In these cases, the king kills himself and his family. Although there is no direct relationship between tales and reality, this case shows how a custom (or motif) that has come into conflict with an emerging new phenomenon is modified correspondingly. Both the tale and historical reality make the king die in a war, and this form replaces the former brutal murder by strangulation and the like.

But such softened, compromised forms are not mandatory. It is possible to find cases where the old king is killed directly. "The father says, 'OK, now chop off my head.' The soldier answers: 'I can't cut your head off.' The tsar's daughter takes a saber and says: 'The tsar's word never changes.' And she cuts off his head."[161] "So she took the saber and cut off the tsar's head, and took the shepherd by his ear and kissed him on the mouth. 'May you be my husband, and I your wife,'"[162] and so forth.

26. *The False Hero*

In this manner we see that the death of the old king is not an exception at all. However, this case still contradicts the established inheritance from father to son, which attempts to evade this kind of forced death. On the other hand, wondertales know another way around this situation, which does not correspond to the historically established reality of the storyteller's time. Shortly before the accession of the hero, toward the very end of the story, a new and unexpected character is introduced. This can be an army general or a water carrier who, during the battle with the dragon, sits behind the bush and then claims credit for the whole victory. Neither historical reality nor the sphere of rites, beliefs, and myths contain this figure. We must consider it a purely wondertale figure that arose on the ground of the tales themselves. It seems to us that this figure is a sort of scapegoat, on the whole created in accord with the same principles that generate such substitute characters both in the sphere of ritual and in folklore. His function is to take on himself the death, punishment, or killing that was originally assigned to the king. The cycle of accession, marriage, someone's death, or killing someone is preserved with a shift of killing from one character to another, introduced in an ad hoc fashion.

27. *The Rope Bridge*

Sometimes the death of the old king happens in a different way. He is told to cross a pit, walking on a rope or a narrow plank, and he falls in. This case is usually associated with a situation in which the hero brings back a beauty. The king wants to marry her, but the hero does not agree. He says, "I have prepared a deep pit, and a thin plank lies over this pit. Whoever walks across it will take the queen for himself." "Alright, Vanyusha. You go ahead first!" The hero walks across successfully, while the old king falls in.[163] Now we must examine the specific motif of the thin bridge and its use in this case. The origin of this motif poses no puzzle. A huge amount of material shows that it comes from the notion that the realm of the dead is separated from the realm of the living by such a bridge, sometimes made of a strand of hair, over which the dead or their souls pass. Isidor Schefteloviz collected an especially large quantity of material on this "hellish bridge."[164] Among the Inca, the deceased went to the "land of the mute." They had to cross the river on a bridge made of a hair and were helped by a dog.[165] In North America there is the notion of a bridge resting on the head of a buffalo. As soon as someone steps on this bridge, the buffalo lowers its head.[166] It is interesting that the motif of the bridge almost always includes an animal. The Eskimos also have a bridge that leads through the abyss to the land of the dead, and it is as thin as a blade.[167] These notions are quite common.[168] In Parsism, this image is expressed very vividly.

> On the fourth day after death, the soul comes at sunrise to the place of judgment at the bridge of Tshinwat. Before crossing, the evil spirits make their accusations. The good and evil deeds are weighed on accurate scales. Now the soul must pass over the perilous bridge. . . . A righteous soul can cross joyfully, led by a beautiful girl who embodies the soul's good deeds, and accompanied by kind dogs that guard the bridge. Then the soul comes to paradise, and finally to the golden throne of Ahuramazda. . . . The evil souls, by contrast, find no helpers. They stumble on the hair-thin bridge and fall into the abyss. The evil demon seizes them and carries them away to the place of darkness.[169]

The wondertale bridge reflects the same notions. It is thin, made of hair, and slippery, and there is an abyss beneath it.

But how is this notion connected to the killing of the king? We believe that the materials cited above allow us to make the following conclusion: crossing the thin bridge occurs after death. Second, those who have no helpers fall; at the beginning the helpers had animal form, and later they took the form of embodied good deeds. What in religious representations is the *consequence* of death is shown in the wondertale as the *cause* of death. It can be assumed that the king was killed, and it was apparently believed that because he was devoid of magical power (the reason for his being killed), he could not cross the bridge and fell into the abyss.

The wondertale transfers this moment to the bounds of life and turns the consequence of death into the cause of death. Such a transfer is quite justified artistically, for it contains condemnation of the old king and shows his weakness and awkwardness, which echo his magical weakness.

28. Boiling Milk

Besides testing the old king with a bridge, the wondertale knows another trial for the old king that leads to his death: the test with boiling milk. "'We cannot get married yet: you are old, I'm young. I know a method to make you young: put two cauldrons in the yard, one with goat milk, the other with water. Everything must be ready by evening.' Ivan bathed and became such a fine fellow that it is impossible to describe, but the tsar got cooked in the cauldrons."[170]

This motif seems less clear than that of the hanging bridge. First, there are remote indications that the king who was to be killed was subjected to ceremonial bathing before the killing. For example, in the province of Quilacare (in South India), the priest-king reigns for twelve years. After that, a festival is arranged. "The king has a wooden scaffolding made, spread over with silken hangings: and on that day he goes to bathe at a tank with great ceremonies and sound of music."[171] After this, the king commits suicide on the stage, cutting off his nose, ears, and lips and the soft parts of his body; he throws these into the crowd. It is as though he is making a sacrifice of himself. Then the king cuts his own throat. It is possible, however, that we have a local custom here and that the bathing is more or less incidental. On the other hand, we have materials showing that the soul of the deceased was subjected to bathing (specifically to two baths, as in a wondertale) in the underworld. For example, according to the beliefs of the aborigines of Katio,[172] the god of the underworld has two buckets: one with boiling water, the other with cold water. When a "black soul" (i.e., a sinful soul) becomes white after the two baths, it can enter the heavens. If not, it is doomed to many years of hard labor.[173]

Such materials lead us to the same range of views as the thin bridge. However, there is one difference between the example above and the wondertale: there we have water, and in wondertales it is usually milk. In the example above, it is goat's milk; sometimes it is mare's milk, and sometimes the source of milk is not mentioned. Passing through this milk provides beauty. The hero comes out of it handsome. But he also becomes handsome when he passes through the ears of a horse. Here we have the notion of a rejuvenating or cleansing bath, but at the same time we see a connection of this bath to passing through an animal. While in the Russian wondertale the hero passes through the horse's ears, in a Georgian tale he is required to bathe in the milk of the horses living at the bottom of the sea.[174] In the Georgian tale, the old king is also cooked in a cauldron, and when the hero plunges into the milk, a horse takes some snow from his ear and pours it into the milk, cooling it in this way. We are forced, therefore, to conclude that the basis of this motif is the transfiguration, the apotheosis of the hero. The motif of the old king's death is artificially attached to it. It is known that the one who reached the realm of the dead experienced a transformation, and here too we have a reflection of this notion.

29. *Conclusions*

What conclusions can we draw from all that has been said? We cannot claim that everything has been made completely transparent in the details. But one thing is clear at any rate: the struggle for the throne between the hero and the old king is quite a historical phenomenon. Here the wondertale reflects the transition of power from father-in-law to son-in-law through a woman, the daughter. Wondertales show something else as well: before receiving the hand of the princess and the throne along with her, the son-in-law is subjected to a test to prove that he passed the previous tests. This test has a premarital character and should at the same time demonstrate the hero's ability to control nature. The wondertale has also preserved traces of the transition to a new social order. New social orders influence old forms, and then phenomena such as the accession of Oedipus arise; or tales adapt new social orders to old ones, settling the conflict peacefully by, for example, giving the hero half the kingdom. Such phenomena are not historical with regard to their content, but they can be explained historically only as a result of the change of one social order to another and the resulting inconsistencies and contradictions.

IV. Magical Escape

30. *Escape in the Wondertale*

The wondertale ends with marriage and the hero's accession to the throne. But our study would be incomplete if we did not consider another motif, which does not have a specific place in the tale. This is the motif of magical escape.

Escape has no definite place in relation to the motifs it follows. But it usually occurs at the end, sometimes even after the marriage. The wondertale can end after the hero visits Yaga or another donor, after he obtains the desired object, after the battle with the dragon, after marriage, and so on. Escape and pursuit can follow each of these stages, and there is a tendency (though not a rule) to give certain forms to the flight and pursuit depending on the stage in which the flight occurs. For instance, the hero can escape after his stay with Yaga. In these cases, he often escapes by throwing a comb behind him that turns into a forest, a stone that becomes a mountain, or a towel that becomes a river. Or he escapes onto a tree, or jumps from one tree to another, while Yaga gnaws the trunk. A girl is sometimes rescued by a stove, an apple tree, and a river, all of which conceal her. If a girl is escaping forest robbers, she is concealed by an oncoming cart driver with hay, pots, or skins in his cart. A boy escapes the pursuit of the sorcerer by turning into a perch, a bird, a grain, a ring, and so on consecutively. The sorcerer accordingly turns into a pike, a hawk, a rooster, and the like. The abducted princess too turns into a fish, a swan, or a star; she is caught by a skilled person. After battle with the dragon, the hero is sometimes pursued by the dragon's wife: she and her daughters turn into alluring wells, beds, and apple trees. The dragon's wife chases the hero and wants to swallow him. The hero, after staying with the tsar-maiden and stealing the apples of youth, flees on a horse, and the princess flies after him. But Yaga exchanges his horse for him, and he gets away safely. Riding a horse, Koschei catches with up the hero. After the hero marries the daughter of the Water King, he and his wife escape by turning into, for example, a church and a priest or a well and a dipper. Finally, the hero sometimes escapes on a ship, and the pursuer strikes him with fire from the sky, or vice versa—the hero lights up gunpowder and scorches the pursuer's wings, which causes the latter to fall.

We have listed ten types of chase and rescue. Antti Aarne, who made a special study of escape, takes into account only two of its forms, and Iokhelson's work on escape does not differentiate at all among the forms of flight and chase.[175]

The problem here is twofold: first, the origin of the escape motif as such; second, the diversity of its forms. We cannot study specifically all the types of escape here. We shall examine only those forms that cast some light on the problem of flight in general.

31. *Escape by Throwing a Comb*

In these cases, it is often (but not always) children who run away from Yaga. They throw a flint or a small stone behind, and it turns into a mountain. They throw a comb and a towel. These magical items are stolen by the hero from Yaga, or, if the fleeing characters are escaping on horseback, the items are taken from the horse's ear.[176] In addition, other things can be taken out of the ear: a wooden chip becomes a forest, a small vial becomes a river.

We will not give variants and varieties here. The works of Aarne and Iokhelson provide them in large numbers. Comparing a large number of variants does not solve the problem. We note only that this form is associated not only with Yaga. Heroes flee in the same way from the bear king,[177] and in the tale of Finist,[178] and from Elena the Beautiful.[179] We will be able to understand this form in its relation to the wondertale as a whole and from some historical parallels.

Let us first consider parallels. American analogues demonstrate the following features: rather than stealing the item that can save him from pursuit (as in our tales when a piece of linen cloth is stolen), the hero steals fire. This is a quite significant difference. He brings fire to the people. He is the introducer of fire. But he is not only the fire introducer; he also introduces forests, rivers, and mountains. He establishes them when he throws the items behind him. And this is a significant difference. The items thrown behind the hero also differ from the items thrown in the wondertale. They are animal parts. For example, the forest is formed from hair, a lake from fish oil, and so on. This explains why in Russian tales the hero sometimes gets a wooden chip from the horse's ear, and the chip turns into a forest. We see, therefore, that forests, mountains, and rivers are created by the power of the helper. We already know how the helper is acquired and that the helper is the bearer of the hero's magical abilities. Another difference is that in Russian tales it is enough to toss an object, while in the cases of American myths, the heroes sometimes sing a song and beat time.[180] These materials suggest that the motif of throwing a comb arose as a myth about the organizer of the world.

But does this not contradict the entire course of the wondertale? Does it not contradict all that we know about the hero? There is no contradiction. On the contrary, this situation offers an explanation for a certain awkwardness in the wondertale: the hero steals the very object that saves him from pursuit. Comparison shows that earlier this was a different object. Above, we have seen the hero as the organizer of the world. We saw that he puts the sun in its place, that he speeds up the harvest, and that he brings back these abilities from another world. Here we see faded remnants of the same idea. Power over natural forces is brought from the other world.

In an American myth, a coyote and a fox kidnap fire. They run "from side to side, and the pursuers gallop after them to and fro. That is why the Yoakum River meanders." In this case, the fugitives, who are at the same time the thieves of fire, create a river for people while saving themselves. Similarly, the hero creates the forests, the mountains, and the rivers, and in historical perspective the entire myth is about the creation of nature.

I must note a degree of perplexity in the literature regarding this topic. Iokhelson, who took a purely descriptive path, admits that he cannot find a rationale for this motif. For now, the hypothesis proposed here is only a hypothesis, no more. A different hypothesis is proposed by Bogoraz Tan: "The very construction of this myth corresponds to the theories of the Freudian school regarding the affinity of dreams and myth, for this myth with its triple repetition and the monster's persistent urge to break through a barrier and seize the escaping victim is quite reminiscent of the obsessive image of pursuit in the manner it is constructed in a dream."[181] Thus, we see that even such great scholars as Bogoraz-Tan do not venture beyond Freudianism. As for Aarne's theory, there will be a few words about it below. We must compare this form with others in order to find a general solution.

32. *Escape with Transformations*

This form is typical mainly for tales such as "The Sea King and Vasilisa the Wise."[182] There, the girl stolen from the Sea King possesses magical means. "She turned the horses into a well, herself into a ladle, and the prince into a very old man." The second time, she "turned the prince into an old priest and herself into an ancient church," and the third time, she turns the horses into a river of mead with banks made of pudding, the prince into a drake, and herself into a gray duck. "The Sea King threw himself upon the pudding and the mead, he ate and ate, and drank and drank, until he burst and gave up the ghost."[183]

Aarne, who specifically studied escape, knew only six cases of this form recorded outside of Europe, whereas the forms found in Europe are so numerous that he did not even count them. We convert this geographical principle of Aarne into a historical principle. For us the myths of America, Africa, Polynesia, and Asia are among the sources for the study of the wondertale, as they present it at a more ancient stage of its development. If this form does not exist in America, Africa, and so on, it means that it is a later form and that it was created on the basis of the wondertale itself, not on the basis of any primitive relations. The typical items into which the fugitives transform point to this too: a well and a ladle, a church and a priest. If we had these forms in the myths of peoples who have not yet developed a class society, then we would have to show that the church replaced some other objects that existed earlier. But there are no such data, and it remains for us to assume that this motif arose when there were already churches and priests—that is, when wondertales already existed, which means comparatively very late. Only the lake or the river could occur before, and indeed they also existed earlier as the final element of the escape and pursuit. We have this element in the previous form as well.

While the church, the tree, and so on serve as means of deceiving the pursuer, the water itself serves as an obstacle, as do the forest, mountains, and water in the previous form. Thus, the third element of this form fully corresponds to the third element of the previous form. It was borrowed entirely from the older form. Aarne believes that in general the whole form analyzed here (with the fugitives' transformation) developed from the first form but underwent a modification. Studying both of these varieties according to the methods of the Finnish school and reducing each to its archetype, he writes, "There is no doubt that one version has changed into the other. I believe it is very easy to arrive at this conclusion. There is nothing to be done but compare the prevalence of these versions with each other."[184] Thus, if one form is rare and the other is found often, this means that one originated from the other. This statement sounds naive. To prove that it is correct, the transitional forms must be examined against relevant materials. It is necessary to show the stages of one form's transition into the other. Yet the very extensive material Aarne collected leads to the assertion that all cases belong to either one variety or the other; and he himself also constructs two archetypes, not one. Therefore, it is more correct to say that we still do not know how this variety arose; we can only establish with some degree of probability that one emerged earlier and the other later and that it is recent in general. But we cannot assert that one arose from the other.

33. The Dragon's Transformation into Wells, Apple Trees, and So On

But something else can definitely be asserted. Sometimes it is not the fugitive who is transformed but the pursuer. After the battle with the dragon, the dragon's relatives (his mother-in-law, his sisters) chase the fleeing ones. In order to destroy them, the pursuers turn into the same objects that fugitives turn into in the other tales: an apple tree and a well with a ladle. If the heroes eat the apples or drink the water, they will burst.

In these cases, however, the church is missing, which is understandable, since male and female dragons are akin to the devil and cannot turn into a church. The similarity of these objects to those into which fugitives transform elsewhere makes one think that one form has directly emerged from the other. But it is impossible to say which of them is older. As in the previous case, the third element in this form of pursuit and rescue is quite ancient. After the pursuit of the female dragons (which were not mentioned in the tale before and were introduced ad hoc) turns out to be unsuccessful, the dragon-mother flies in pursuit and tries to devour the fugitives. This case has already been analyzed above.

34. Flight and Pursuit with Successive Transformations

We have three varieties or three forms of this type of pursuit and rescue. In the tale of the Seven Simeons,[185] the role of the fleeing person is performed by the abducted princess, who is chased by the hero, or rather by seven heroes: "The princess turned into a white swan and flew off the ship." The archer shoots her down, the swimmer retrieves her, and the healer cures her. Fuller forms include a series of transformations. "She fell, struck the ship, turned into a duck, and flew away," or, "She struck the ship and turned into a star, then went up to the sky." Archer shoots it, and the star falls onto the ship.[186]

In these cases, flight and pursuit are expressed very clearly. Here both those who escape and those who pursue turn into various objects. The nature of the flight is expressed less vividly in tales where the prince's wife is turned into, for example, a bird or a duck, and later the prince tries to restore her human form, but she turns into different animals. On the other hand, the speed of the transformation from one animal to another is expressed here more vividly. "He seized the princess Marya; she turned into a frog, then into a lizard and all sorts of snakes, and afterwards into a spindle."[187] "As soon as she flies in, you try to catch her by the head; and as you catch her, she will start turning into a frog, a toad, a snake, and other reptiles, and afterwards she'll turn into an arrow. Take this arrow and break it in half."[188]

In both cases, the princess, whether acquired or retrieved, turns into various animals, resisting her return or transportation from the other kingdom to ours.

A third case of this kind of successive transformations is found in tales such as "A Tricky Science."[189] There the student runs away from the sorcerer. The running student turns into a horse, a ruff, a ring, a grain, and a hawk. The pursuing sorcerer turns into a wolf, a pike, a man, and a rooster, respectively. The hawk tears the rooster apart.[190]

All these varieties can be studied together. But where should one look for the sources of the motif? If we follow the descriptive method that is usually practiced in these cases, we will not achieve any results. If, however, we assume that the young woman's transformation into an animal comes from the idea of a person's transformation into an animal at death, then we might find a direction to move forward. Let us note that the princess turns into a duck and the prince restores her human form. A duck is one of the most common animals whose image is associated with death. The reverse transformation into a human being reflects the idea of coming back to life. Let us try to look in this direction for comparative materials and see whether they provide any explanations.

Returning from the land of the dead to the land of the living is accompanied by transformation into animals. "Yoruba and Popo peoples believe that good men after death spend their time between reincarnations in different animals, or, more correctly, the spirits materialize into animals at will."[191] We find similar views in Egypt: "If he (the deceased) did not like it there anymore, he could return to earth and visit places that once were dear to him. He could visit his grave and accept the sacrifices made to him there. Or he could turn into a heron, a swallow, a snake, a crocodile, or a god, and assume the image of anything he wanted."[192]

What do these materials show? They demonstrate that the view according to which the image of the deceased does not have to be associated with only one animal is historical. The deceased can turn into various animals by choice. Moreover, we see that this view accompanies the idea of coming back to the earth. When the deceased comes back, he turns into various animals. Undoubtedly, this notion is comparatively late; we shall see further that it is particularly abundant in antiquity. But it also exists at earlier stages of social development, albeit less often, yet with the original clarity and purity. If a second character is added, a pursuer, then this transformation acquires speed; the transformations follow one after another in sequence. For example, in Oceanic myths, there is a case in which "a man wants to bring his wife back from the world of the dead, but she shies away from him, continuously assuming the images of different birds."[193] Here the idea that is glossed over by the time of the wondertale is expressed openly: such a transformation happens when someone is forced to return from the other world. The deceased resists and tries to avoid it, constantly undergoing new transformations.

Wherever the concept of a soul has evolved, a belief could develop that it is not the whole person but only the person's soul that is incarnated in animals; a doctrine of metempsychosis was able to evolve, the classical form of which is known in India. This is why the Tibetan tale about the tricky science describes the episode of flight and pursuit as it does: "The soul of the king jumped out of the fish into a dove that was flying by."[194] The same phenomenon of chasing after souls is found in Siberian shamanism. The Buryat shaman searches for the soul of a sick man in the woods and steppes and under the water, just as the sorcerer searches for the fleeing boy. If he cannot find it, he must go to the kingdom of the dead. Sometimes the ruler of this kingdom will only agree to let the sought-after person depart in return for another soul. "If the patient consents to the substitution, the shaman turns himself into a hawk, pounces upon the soul of a friend (i.e., the patient's substitute) as it soars from his slumbering body in the form of a lark, and hands over the fluttering, struggling thing to the grim warden of the dead, who thereupon sets the soul of the sick man at liberty."[195]

We see here the same thing that we have seen in the wondertale, when the fleeing character turns into a swan, and the pursuer rushes at him in the form of a predatory bird.[196] Among Siberian peoples, this motif in general is often told as a shamanistic hunt for the soul of the deceased. "The old man looked at the dead man's face. And, indeed, it was [his] son. He grew angry and threw himself at his son. The son fled from him, turned into a loon, and flew away. The old man hurried after him in the form of a hawk."[197] Thus, we again see that consecutive transformation into animals occurs when there is a forced return from the other world into the realm of the living.

If these observations and conclusions are correct, then they explain many things in the materials of antiquity. Versions and forms of this concept in antiquity are often taken as parallels to folktales, but they are as mysterious in themselves as the tale, and they receive illumination through the materials given above. "Into a lion, a serpent, fire, moisture / She transformed in my arms." This is what Peleus says of Thetis in the lost tragedy of Sophocles *The Lovers of Achilles*.[198] Thetis, daughter of Nereus, is a Nereid, an immortal goddess who lives in the underwater kingdom. She "marries a mortal unwillingly on Zeus's command."[199] It was foretold that her son would be greater than her father; as a result, no gods wanted to take her as their wife, and she was forced to marry a mortal. She underwent transformations when she was taken from the underground or the underwater kingdom into the kingdom of humans. The nature of the resistance here is quite clear. In the same way, Nereus protected himself from Heracles with sequential transformations. Achelous, the river god, also undergoes a series of transformations in his struggle with Heracles. He turns into a snake and a bull, and only after Heracles breaks his horn does he admit defeat. In all these cases, it is water creatures who undergo transformation. In the wondertale too, the princess on a ship turns into animals while the gray duck comes from the river.

The last element in the young woman's transformation is a spindle. The spindle must be broken and thrown over one's shoulder. In materials from antiquity, the last element is a broken *horn*. We should consider the transformation from animal into object to be a later formation. A broken horn is the same phenomenon as torn out hair—namely, a deprivation of power. Breaking objects was widely practiced at a person's death and was preserved in the breaking of a sword over the heads of those condemned to death or in breaking a stick when entering into marriage. It accompanied the transition from one condition of being to another.

The world of antiquity thus retains, albeit not invariably, the connection of the two worlds in conjunction with the motif of successive transformation. Malten, referring to Radermacher, cites a case in which "Thanatos assumes different images. Empusa also belongs here."[200] Underground and underwater creatures specifically possess this ability. "The ruler of the underworld, Periclymenus, receives from Poseidon the gift of changing his appearance (*sich in die mannigfachsten Gestalten zu verwandeln*), a gift that the Neo-Hellenic god of death, Haros, also possesses." The same applies to the well-known Proteus. Radermacher has quite a lot of materials on this topic, and he noticed one circumstance in these cases: the somewhat constant correlation of such transformations with the element of water. (The gift is given by Poseidon, etc.) Hence, Radermacher concludes that this motif arose as an observation of the variability of water, the play of the waves, and so on. Water creatures are as changeable as water itself, and the transformations considered here are nothing but different manifestations of the water gods (*Epiphanie der Wassergötter*).[201] In light of the materials presented above, the matter seems completely different, and Radermacher's opinion should be considered erroneous. Such an error is inevitable in an isolated and purely descriptive study of the material.

35. *The Decisive Obstacle*

We will not analyze other types of pursuit here. We have examined its most important "classic" forms and obtained the following picture: we see that the main types of escape and pursuit were historically constructed around return from the realm of the dead to that of the living. Aarne was inclined to such an explanation too, although it does not follow at all from the materials he offered. And he too noticed that the final obstacle is often water, a river, and he incidentally compared this river to the one that separates the realm of the living from the realm of the dead. Indeed, the river as the last obstacle has a special significance. The pursuer digs through the mountains and forests, but the river finally stops him. The first two obstacles are mechanical, while the last is magical. In the wondertale, however, this obstacle is also treated as mechanical: the pursuer tries to drink the water. Nevertheless, it can be seen that this form is secondary from the fact that often there is not a river but a lake, and the pursuer never attempts to go around it. The water stops him like a boundary. On the other hand, very often this river is presented as fiery. "'Broom, turn into a fiery river!' . . . There was nothing they could do, and they went back."[202] "River of fire, melt!"[203] "She waved her handkerchief, and a fiery river formed."[204] "Prince Ivan waved behind him with a handkerchief and suddenly a fiery lake was formed."[205]

We have seen above that the fiery river separates the two kingdoms. But even when there is no river, the sense of a magical boundary is sometimes expressed quite clearly. "But the young man had already made his way to his land and did not fear her: she did not dare to gallop there, she only stared at him."[206] We now understand why the pursuer cannot cross the border: his power does not extend to the realm of the living.

The same thing is expressed in another tale, but here the storyteller has unintentionally added a hint of his incomprehension of this phenomenon: "He chased her for a long time, and failed to catch up with her by only ten yards: she flew on the carpet into *Rus'*,[207] while he somehow could not enter Rus', so he went back."[208] It is evident that the storyteller involuntarily asked himself the question: Why could the pursuer not enter Rus'?

Such a conclusion is fully consistent with the whole picture given by the development of the wondertale's course of action. We know by now that the hero penetrates into the "other kingdom." We have recognized this kingdom as the realm of the dead, expressed as the Thrice-Tenth Kingdom, as well as by other specific forms, such as the forest, in particular the forest where the sorcerer-teacher lives. The hero arrives there as a living person, as a kidnapper and an intruder, causing the masters of this realm to be angry and pursue him.

Everything noted so far sheds light on the meaning of the escape and some of its forms, but it does not explain the fact of the escape itself. Aarne's theory is confirmed by numerous materials, which he himself did not include. The return is a return from the other world. But this does not explain why the return takes the form of an escape. The escape is not reflected in the rite or in the return after initiation. Neither is it reflected in the shaman's return from the other world. Yet it appears in myths, legends, and tales everywhere in the world.

It remains for us to assume that the escape results from the *theft* of an object from the other world. The question of the reason behind escaping is thereby reduced to that of the reason for the theft. The concept of the theft is late. It came about with the advent of private property and was preceded by simply taking. At the earliest stages of economic development, a person hardly produces anything yet; he merely takes from nature, leading a life consistent with a hunting and subsistence economy. Therefore, he does not imagine the first things that lead to a culture as being produced, only as things that can be taken by force. The first fire is stolen. The first arrows, the first seeds, and so on are stolen and brought from the sky.

Hence the huge role that theft plays in folklore. *In the rite*, the magic agent is *given*, and the return occurs peacefully. *In the myth*, it is already often *stolen*, and the return takes the form of an escape. *The myth lives beyond the rite and is reborn in the wondertale.* When rewarding or bestowing is replaced by stealing, it shows that property relations have come into conflict with primitive communism and the absence of ownership. The hero takes a certain property from its owner, an otherworldly creature, subsequently a god, and brings it to people, giving it to them to be their property. It is not by chance that Hermes, the intermediary between the two worlds, is at the same time a thief and, later, also the patron of trade.

Yet alongside this thievery, which is connected to escape, the wondertale preserves the peaceful transmission of the magical agent by Yaga and the return without any sort of flight, which rather accurately reflects the rite.

10

THE WONDERTALE AS A WHOLE

1. The Unity of the Wondertale

We have examined the wondertale in the sequence of its components' composition. These compositional components are the same for different plots. They consistently proceed from one to another and form a whole. We have examined the sources of each such motif. But we have not yet compared these sources in their relation to one another. In other words, we know the sources of individual motifs, but we do not yet know the source of their sequence through the course of action. We do not know the source of the wondertale as a whole.

A cursory retrospective glance at the sources examined here shows that many wondertale motifs date back to various social institutions, among which the initiation rite occupies a special place. We see further that an important role is occupied by ideas of the afterlife and the journey to the other world. These two cycles quantitatively provide a maximum number of motifs. Besides this, some motifs have a different origin.

If we list the results by arranging them according to their sources or historical correspondences, we obtain the following picture. The following motifs can be traced back to the initiation cycle: taking or sending children away to the woods, or their abduction by the forest spirit; the hut; selling children in advance; Yaga beating the heroes; chopping off a finger; showing those who remain behind the putative signs of death; Yaga's stove; hacking into pieces and bringing back to life; devouring and regurgitating; receiving a magic agent or a magic helper; transvestism; the forest teacher;

and a tricky science. The subsequent period up to getting married and the element of return are reflected in the motifs of the big house, the set table inside this house, hunters, robbers, the dear sister, the beauty in the coffin, and the beauty in the magic garden and palace (Psyche) as well as in motifs of the unwashed one, the husband at his wife's wedding, the wife at her husband's wedding, the forbidden store room, and others.

These correspondences allow us to assert that the initiation cycle constitutes the most ancient foundation of the wondertale. These motifs taken as a whole can develop into countless varieties of tales.

Another cycle that reveals complete correspondence with the wondertale is the cycle of ideas about death. It includes the abduction of girls by dragons; various kinds of miraculous birth that represent a return of the deceased; sending out for a journey with iron footwear and so on; the forest as an entrance to the other realm; the hero's scent; sprinkling the doors of the hut; eating at Yaga's house; the figure of the ferryman-guide; the long journey on, for example, an eagle, horse, or boat; the battle with the entrance's guardian, who wants to eat the newcomer; weighing on scales; and arrival in the other kingdom, including all the accessories surrounding such an arrival.

Combining these two cycles gives almost all (though nevertheless not all) the basic components of the wondertale. It is impossible to draw an exact line between these two cycles. We know that the whole initiation rite was imagined as a visit to the realm of death; conversely, the deceased experience all that the initiate experiences: he receives a helper, meets a devourer, and so on.

If we think of everything that happened to the initiated and tell it in sequential order, we obtain the same composition on which the wondertale is structured. If we recount everything that is supposed to happen to the deceased in sequential order, we obtain the same core structure but with the addition of elements that are not found in the line of the specified rites. These two cycles combined together provide almost all the basic building blocks of the wondertale.

What have we found? That the compositional unity of the wondertale lies not in any particular features of the human psyche nor in any specific artistic creativity; it lies in the historical reality of the past. People recount now what they once did and depicted; the things they did not do, they imagined. Of these two cycles, the first (the rite) dies off earlier than the second. The rite is no longer practiced. Ideas about death live longer; they develop and are modified without any remaining connection to the rite. The disappearance of the rite is associated with the disappearance of hunting as the sole or main source of subsistence.

Based on everything that has been said here, further formation of the plot should be conceived such that after the particular core was created it began to absorb new details or tricky situations from new, later aspects of reality. On the one hand, a new way of life creates new genres (the novelistic tale), which develop on a different foundation than the composition and plots of the wondertale. Stated differently, development takes place by accretion, substitution, resignification, and so on. On the other hand, such development takes place by new formations.

Thus, the motif of the royal children shut in a dungeon comes from the custom of isolating kings, priests, magicians, and their children. This is an accretion. The motif of the deceased father or grateful dead man who gives the hero a horse functionally corresponds to Yaga giving a horse. Here, under the influence of the cult of ancestors—that is, of a later phenomenon—we have a resignification and deformation of the donor figure with preservation of the gift function. On this basis, the question of motifs that are not related to the cycles mentioned above should be addressed in each case individually. This applies, for example, to the motif of the hero's marriage and accession to the throne. In the image of the princess, we recognize, on the one hand, an independent woman, maintainer of the family and of totemic magic. She is the "tsar-maiden." On the other hand, she can be compared to the heavenly wife of a shaman and also to the widow or daughter of a king killed and eliminated by his successor.

It is very difficult to analyze the whole range of motifs associated with difficult tasks. It is impossible to prove exactly that here the wondertale has retained the custom of testing the magical power of the successor. However, based on numerous indirect indicators, this can be asserted with some degree of probability.

Furthermore, the law of preserving the composition but replacing the characters remains firm, and this is the direction in which the wondertale's further development unfolds. Everyday life, a changed manner of life—this is where the replacement material is found. For example, it turns out that it is possible to see Baba Yaga behind the beggar woman, the men's house behind the two-story house with a balcony, and so on.

This conclusion does not correspond to current ideas about the wondertale. Usually it is believed that individual prehistoric elements are interspersed in the tales, but the whole is a product of "free" artistic creativity. We see that the wondertale consists of elements that go back to phenomena and ideas that existed in a pre-class society.

2. The Wondertale as a Genre

We have uncovered the sources of individual motifs. We have discovered that the way they are connected, their sequence, is also not an accidental phenomenon. But this does not explain the emergence of the wondertale as such.

What is the most ancient stage of tale-telling? We know from the above that during the initiation something was narrated to younger boys. But what exactly was narrated?

The correspondence of the composition of myths and wondertales to the sequence of events that took place during initiation makes one think that they recount the same thing that happened to the young man. However, this was told not about him but about the ancestor, the founder of the clan and its customs, who, having been born in a miraculous way, and having visited the kingdom of bears, wolves, and so on, brought back fire, magic dances (the very ones the boys are taught), and more. These events were at first not so much narrated as enacted dramatically. They also served as a subject for fine arts. It is impossible to understand the carvings and ornaments of many peoples without knowing their legends and folktales. The meaning of the actions that were performed over the initiate were revealed to him. The stories likened him to the character about which they were told. The stories were part of the cult and were taboo. These bans are a second reason to favor the view that they were narrating something with a direct relation to the rite.

Unfortunately, the vast majority of story collections of so-called primitive peoples consist only of texts. We know nothing about the environment in which they were told, the circumstances accompanying the stories, and so on. There are exceptions, however. Sometimes collectors not only provide the texts but also report some details about the ways the stories occur in society.

A very full account of how such tales are treated is provided by Dorsey in the introduction to his collection *Traditions of the Skidi Pawnee.*[1] He speaks of the numerous ceremonies and dances, including that of transferring sacred little bundles (or pouches or sheaves). These are amulets of some kind. They are kept in the house and considered to be its relics. Everyone's well-being, luck in hunting, and so forth depend on them. Their contents vary: they may contain feathers, grain, tobacco leaves, or other items. In short, we recognize in them the prototype of our "magic gifts." "Each bundle ceremony and each dance was accompanied, not only by its ritual, but by its tale of origin."[2] Dorsey's collection shows that the story of the origin of these amulets should be understood as explanations of how, for example, the first owner of this bundle went into the woods and met a buffalo. It took him to the buffalo kingdom, where he received this amulet, learned the dances, and came back. He taught the people all this and became their leader. "This tale was generally the personal property of the keeper or owner of the bundle or the dance, and, as a rule was related immediately after the recitation of the ritual or at the time of the transmission of the possession of the bundle or ceremony to the next owner."[3] The story is thus part of the ritual and the rite. It is attached to it and to the person who becomes the amulet's owner. The story is a kind of verbal amulet, a means of magic effect on the surrounding world. "Thus, each of these tales was esoteric. . . . Hence it is that only with the greatest difficulty can anything like an origin myth of the Skidi as a whole be obtained."[4]

Two things are important in this account. First, as already indicated, the stories exist along with the ritual and form an integral part of it. Second, we see here the origin of a phenomenon that we can trace up to our own day—namely, the ban against narrating. The ban was made and observed not because of etiquette but because of the magic functions inherent in the story and in the act of telling stories. "As he (the storyteller) tells them he gives out from himself a certain part of his life, levying a direct contribution upon its termination. Thus, as one middle-aged individual exclaimed, 'I cannot tell you all that I know, for I am not yet ready to die.' Or, as an old priest expressed it, 'I know that my days are short. My life is no longer of use. There is no reason why I should not tell you all that I know.'"[5]

We shall return to bans below, but for now let us examine the relationship such stories have with the ritual. One can argue that the phenomenon Dorsey mentions is an idiosyncratic, local phenomenon. Apparently, Dorsey himself understood it this way. He does not adduce any comparative material. However, this is not correct. It is true that the connection between the story and the rite cannot be strictly *proven* here. It should be *demonstrated* on the basis of a large body of material. Here we can refer to Boas's collection of Native American legends and to his research on the social organizations and secret unions of the Kwakiutl. The collection contains only texts. From the point of view of traditional folklore studies, these are "Native American versions" or "variants" of many well-known European tales and motifs. There is an impression that these are merely fictional stories. But things change completely as soon as we become acquainted not with the texts alone but with the social organization of at least one of the tribes. These texts suddenly appear in a completely new light. We see how closely they are connected to the entire structure of this tribe's life. In fact, neither the rites nor the tribal institutions are intelligible without the stories—"the legends," as Boas calls them—and the obverse is also true: the stories become understandable only after study of the social life. They are included in social life not only as components; in the tribe's view, they serve as one of the conditions of life along with tools and amulets and are protected and guarded as the greatest sacred objects. "Myths are, literally speaking, the tribe's most precious treasure. They are at the very core of what the tribe reveres as sacred. The most important myths are known only to old people, who zealously guard their secrecy. . . . The old guardians of this secret knowledge sit in their settlement, mute as sphinxes, and ponder to what extend they can entrust the knowledge of their ancestors to the younger generation without attracting any danger, and at what precise moment this transfer of secrets can be most fruitful."[6] Myths not only are components of life but constitute a part of each individual person. Taking the story away from a person means taking away his life. Here the myth has production and social functions, and that is not an idiosyncratic phenomenon—it is the rule. Disclosing the myth would deprive it of its sacred character and, simultaneously, of its magical or, in Lévi-Bruhl's words, "mystical" power. If its myths were lost, the tribe would not survive.

Unlike the wondertale, which is a relic in its plot content, here we have a living connection to the whole reality of a people and its production, social order, and beliefs. The animals the hero or the ancestor of the initiate encountered were depicted on pillars; the items mentioned in these legends were put on and worn during dances; in the dances, they depict bears, owls, crows, and other animals who have supplied the initiate with magical power.

The materials and views cited here answer the question of how a certain category of myth evolves, but they still do not explain how our wondertale evolves.

In the first chapter we established that the wondertale is not conditioned by the structure of the society in which it exists. Now we can elaborate on this. The plot and composition of the wondertale are conditioned by the stage of development of the tribal system; we have taken the North American tribes studied by Dorsey, Boas, and others as a representative example. We see here a direct correspondence between base and superstructure. The new social function of the plot, its purely *artistic* usage, is associated with the disappearance of the system that created it. The external beginning of this process, the process of transforming the myth into a wondertale, is seen when the plot and the act of reciting are detached from the ritual. The moment of detachment from the rite is the beginning of the wondertale's history, whereas it is syncretic with the rite in its prehistory. This detachment could occur either naturally or as a historical necessity, or it could be artificially accelerated by the appearance of Europeans, the Christianization of Native Americans, and the forcible resettlement of whole tribes to other, worse lands, a change in the way of life, a change in the mode of production, and so on. Dorsey notes this detachment too. Let us not forget that Europeans have been in America for more than five hundred years and that we often find here only an echo of the primordial situation—its disintegration, fragments, and traces that are only more or less clear. "Naturally, these myths of the origins of bundles and dances do not always remain the exclusive property of the priesthood; they find their way among the ordinary people, where, when told, they lose much of their original meaning. Thus, by a gradual process of deterioration, they come to be regarded as of no especial religious significance, and are told as tales are told."[7] Dorsey calls the process of detachment from the rite spoilage. However, the wondertale, already devoid of religious functions, does not in itself represent a thing reduced, compared to the myth from which it originated. On the contrary, released from the bonds of religious conventions, wondertales break free into the open air of artistic creativity, driven by other social factors, and begin to live a full-blooded life.

This explains the origin not only of the plot from the point of view of its content but of the wondertale as an artistic story.

We repeat that this position cannot really be *proven*; it can be demonstrated on the basis of a large amount of material, which is impossible to do here. But there is still one additional reason for doubt. We are talking only about wondertales. We consider it possible to single them out from among other tales and study them independently. Having broken the contact, we must close it again at the end of our work, for studying other genres may introduce a change in our concept of the formation of the wondertale.

We have examined rites and myths of so-called primitive peoples and linked them to modern wondertales, but we have not studied the tales of these peoples; we did not take into account the possibility of an artistic tradition *from the very beginning*.

Although we have not studied plots here that are not connected to the wondertale, we can still assume that not only wondertales but many other tales (e.g., animal tales) have the same origin. This could be verified by a special monograph devoted to these genres; we cannot prove it here. Studying the collections of Native American tales leads to the conclusion that this material is entirely ritualistic—that is, that the tale in our sense of this word is as yet unknown there. Such a point of view will seem unconvincing to the folklorist, but ethnographers, who are familiar with more than just texts, are more likely to accept the possibility of such a position. Richard Neuhauss observed it in former German New Guinea. The local inhabitants "were familiar only with legends: they were not familiar either with folktales or with fables. Stories that appear to us like fairytales are for them legends the same as the others."[8] Lévi-Bruhl also considers this position confirmed and cites the given evidence as proof.[9] This can be confirmed by analysis of animal tales as well. For example, in North America, there is a special category of tales about the coyote. These are funny stories about a coyote's tricks. The Native Americans of Skidi tell the following: "Coyote is a fine fellow. He knows all things, and it's impossible to destroy him. In addition, he is full of wild quirks and is very cunning. He can be bested only with the greatest difficulty, and he is seldom entirely defeated." But these "tales" are told *when a certain venture is about to take place*, and the coyote's dexterity is meant to pass to the narrator. Bogoraz-Tan observes the same in Koryak-Kamchadal folklore that we note with regard to Native American folklore. "Koryak-Kamchadal folklore is remarkable for its cheerful, derisive nature. Many extraordinary and funny stories are told about the raven Kutkh: how he fought with the little mouse-girls, how he set fire to his own house, and so on. Kutkh sometimes appears in the form of a man, and sometimes in the form of a raven. Their folklore treats him with absolute disrespect, yet at the same time Kutkh is also the Raven-creator *who created the heavens and the earth*. Kutkh created man, obtained fire for him, and then gave him animals for hunting."[10] What Bogoraz-Tan considers disrespect, in fact, may be a feeling of admiration for the raven's craftiness, as Dorsey has pointed out. In any case, if the raven about whom such funny things are told is the creator of heaven and earth, and if the stories are told before hunting, then here too the sacred character of the story is undeniable. This supports the idea that not only wondertales have a sacral nature. After all, the initiation rite is far from being the only rite; there were also seasonal hunting and field-crop rites and a variety of other rites, and each of them could have its own origin myth. The connection of these rites to myths and the connection of both to tales are not yet fully explored. To resolve this question, the entire folklore of pre-class peoples must be studied in detail. To do this here would lead us too far afield, and for our purposes there is no immediate need for it.

From all that has been said, it is clear that a "profanation" of the sacred plot begins very early (by "profanation," we mean the transformation of a sacred story into a profane one—i.e., nonspiritual, nonesoteric, artistic). This is the moment of birth of the wondertale as such. But it is impossible to distinguish where the sacred story ends and the wondertale begins. As Zelenin demonstrated in his "Religio-Magical Function of the Wondertale," bans on recounting wondertales and the attribution to them of magical influence on various kinds of work hold to the present even among cultured peoples.[11] We know the same thing about Vogul tales, about Mari tales, and so on. But these are still relics, remnants. The Native American tale, by contrast, is almost entirely a sacred story, a myth, even though it is already beginning to separate from the rite, and it contains the rudiments of a purely artistic story similar to modern folktales.

Thus the wondertale has adopted the social and ideological culture of earlier eras. But it would be a mistake to say that it is the only successor of religion. Religion as such has also changed over time, and it contains extremely ancient relics. All concepts of the afterlife and the fate of the deceased that were developed in Egypt and Greece and later in Christianity arose much earlier. Here we must also mention shamanism, which likewise absorbed many elements from prehistoric eras that were preserved by wondertales.

If we collect shamans' stories about their rituals—how the shaman traveled to another world in search of a soul, who helped him in this, how he was transferred there, and so on—and compare these to the journey or flight of the wondertale hero, we see a correspondence between them. We have tracked this for individual elements, but there will also be a correlation for the whole. This can explain the unity of composition of the myth, the story of afterlife travel, the story of the shaman, the wondertale and, beyond these, the epic poem, the bylina, and the heroic song. With the emergence of feudal culture, folkloric plots become the property of the ruling class. On the basis of this folklore, cycles of heroic tales are created, such as "Tristan and Isolde," "The Song of the Nibelungen," and so on. In other words, the movement is from bottom to top, not from top to bottom as some theoreticians have claimed.

In this work, a historical explanation has been provided for a phenomenon that has always been considered difficult to explain: the universal similarity of folkloric plots. This similarity is much wider and deeper than it appears to the naked eye. Neither the migration theory nor the theory of unity of the human psyche put forward by the anthropological school solves this problem. The problem is solved by the historical study of folklore in its connection to the production of material life.

A problem considered so difficult has nevertheless proven soluble. But any resolved problem immediately raises new ones. The study of folklore can proceed along two lines: toward studying the similarity of phenomena and toward the study of differences. Folklore, and in particular the wondertale, is not simply uniform; with all its uniformity, it is extremely rich and diverse. The study of this diversity, of individual plots, is more difficult than the study of compositional similarity. If the solution offered here does turn out to be correct, then at least it will make it possible to begin the study of individual plots, and the problem of their interpretation and history, in a new way.

AFTERWORD

Vladimir Propp and His *Historical Roots of the Wondertale*
Sergei Nekliudov, Russian State University for the Humanities

1. There is a concept sometimes applied to an individual who has left a particularly noticeable mark on the cultural or social life of an era: *a person of the century*. After the various and sundry summations of the past century, we can say with full confidence that the name of Vladimir Propp, who pioneered the development of the structural method in the humanities, should figure among the greatest humanities scholars of his era, alongside Roman Jakobson and Claude Lévi-Strauss.

Some books constitute events, even revelations. These works radically change the view of scholarship on its own subject and lead it out of a state of methodological stagnation; they impact research for decades into the future. Such books undoubtedly include *Morphology of the Folktale*, and Propp can be considered a *person of the century* first and foremost as the author of this work.

Vladimir Yakovlevich Propp (1895–1970) was born in St. Petersburg in a family of wealthy German peasant-colonists who had moved from the Volga region to the capital of the Russian Empire.[1] He graduated, in 1913, from Anninsky College and, in 1918, from the Faculty of History and Philology of St. Petersburg University, specializing in Slavic and Russian philology.[2] After this he worked as a teacher and a German language instructor in secondary and higher educational institutions in Leningrad. At the start of his engagement in research in the field of folklore, Propp collaborated in the 1920s–30s with various scholarly institutions in Leningrad: The Folktale Commission of the Russian Geographical Society,[3] the Institute for Comparative Study of the Literatures and Languages of the West and East,[4] the Institute of the History of Arts,[5] the Institute of Russian Literature, and the Institute of Ethnography in the USSR Academy of Sciences. Most of his life, however, is connected with the Philological School of Leningrad University, where he worked from 1932 to 1969, becoming a professor in the Department of Folklore in 1938 and defending his doctoral dissertation in 1939.[6]

Propp's research began to appear in print in the second half of the 1920s. Apart from four textbooks of the German language, he published four monographs: *The Morphology of the Folktale* (1928), *Historical Roots of the Wondertale* (1946), *The Russian Heroic Epic* (1955), and *Russian Agrarian Holidays* (1963), plus two more works that appeared after his death: *Problems of the Comic and Laughter* (1976) and *The Russian Folktale* (1984). In addition, Propp wrote some three dozen articles in addition to many reviews of scholarly papers, abstracts, and other publications and prepared several fundamental collections of Russian folk texts for publication.[7]

A number of his works have been translated into foreign languages; this is especially true of the world-famous *Morphology of the Folktale*, which has apparently been translated into all languages that have a scholarly literature on folklore. Reborn in the context of structural-semiotic studies of the mid-twentieth century, this work had an enormous impact on the current state of narratology, the theory of narrative construction, not only in folklore but in a wider range of structural-semiotic studies. Beginning in the 1960s, its presence was increasingly felt in the scholarly world (in works by Claude Lévi-Strauss, Algirdas Greimas, Claude Brémond, Alan Dundes, Pierre Maranda, and others).[8]

It was in the 1960s, as translations of *Morphology of the Folktale* were published one after the other (in English, Italian, Polish, etc.), that the opportunity to republish the famous book in its homeland finally arose. The history of this publication, carried out as part of an "Oriental" series, is remarkable in its own way.[9] In spring 1967, at a meeting of the Academic Council of the Institute of Asian Peoples of the USSR's Academy of Sciences, one of its members recalled *Morphology of the Folktale* and said that it was high time to reprint the book. The proposal, entered in the minutes of the meeting, acquired something of an official status, and the editors of Oriental Studies tried to take advantage of this. However, its practical implementation required a book series in which such a publication would be appropriate. There was, of course, no such series suitable for *Morphology of the Folktale* in the publishing house of Oriental Studies, and this prompted us to think about creating a new series. In the Soviet Union, any initiative required the approval of the authorities, a difficult bureaucratic procedure with no guarantee of success. Fortunately, the series itself was not subject to approval, only its editorial board was, and a suitable board was identified within the publishing house to oversee the series Tales and Myths of the Peoples of the East, to be dedicated to scholarly translations of Eastern narrative folklore. This allowed the establishment of a new series (with the same editorial board) without additional hassle: "Tales and Myths of the Peoples of the East," in which, according to the plan, Eastern folklore was included in a range of broad typological comparisons, based on the achievements of modern theoretical folklore.[10] *Morphology of the Folktale* inaugurated the series.[11]

It remains to be added that this re-edition forty years after the book's first publication was not a mere reprinting. Propp prepared the manuscript anew, making corrections (though these were not substantial).[12] Thus, the text published in 1969 represents the author's last edition of this work.

2. Questions of folktale study occupy a central place in Propp's scholarly work. As mentioned above, his first work was *Morphology*, and three of his six monographs as well as a significant part of his articles are devoted to the folktale. He studied almost exclusively folktales during the first twenty years of his research—that is, before the publication of *Historical Roots of the Wondertale* in 1946. However, Propp repeatedly returned to this genre later—for example, when preparing the 1955 publication of Afanas'ev's famous collection,[13] when analyzing the cumulative tale,[14] and while teaching a specialized course at Leningrad State University, which formed the basis of his posthumously published book *The Russian Folktale*.[15]

The point, however, is not the quantitative predominance of folktale studies in this scholar's legacy but rather that it was he who made one of the major discoveries in twentieth-century philological scholarship precisely in this area of research. The conceptual depth of *Morphology of the Folktale* turned out to be so significant, the book so ahead of its time, that only three decades later did the humanities mature enough to provide the conditions for its adequate understanding as well as new interpretations, including some not previously provided by the author. It is worth recalling that the book's original title was *Morphology of the Wondertale*[16] while Propp's preliminary report on the results of his investigation was called, even more precisely, "Morphology of the Russian Wondertale."[17] However, even then the author probably had the feeling that the work's result far exceeded the original plan, which led to a formulation of the final name—generalized and concise.[18] Furthermore, "Propp's formula," which turned out to be extremely universal and viable (it continues to work to this day), escaped the control of its creator, who repeatedly objected to the far too broad interpretation of his discovery and subsequently was inclined even to completely abandon the term *morphology*, replacing it with the term *composition*.[19] At any rate, in his last book, *The Russian Folktale*, the expression *morphology of the folktale* is barely used at all.

The continuous nature of Propp's folktale research consists of describing the structure of the phenomenon in order to study its genesis ("before answering the question of where the tale comes from, you need to answer the question of what it is").[20] Paradoxically, the result of this preparatory stage of the analysis so much exceeded the result of the main stage that other works by Propp were not comparable to the *Morphology of the Folktale*, no matter how bright and talented they were. Moreover, they were also recursively illuminated by the reflected light of *Morphology*. It must be said that this was completely justified with regard to his works of folktale studies because what they quite realistically represent is a cycle of research—from *Morphology of the Folktale* and *Transformation of Wondertales* through the analysis of individual tales plots, themes, and motifs up to *Historical Roots of the Wondertale*.

Like many discoveries, the idea of *Morphology*, according to Propp, appeared unexpectedly. The author explained its birth as heuristic: the idea arose from a rather casual observation "with a fresh eye" when, after graduating from Petrograd University, he started to read Afanas'ev's collection of Russian folktales to supplement his education.[21] The critical review of earlier works of folktale literature in the book's first chapter may have been done retroactively to place his study in line with the wider context of world folklore scholarship. But, of course, the author did accept certain initial philological concepts. The main value for him was in A. N. Veselovskii's works on poetics,[22] and it was Veselovskii, incidentally, who first used the expression—in 1884!—*morphology of the folktale*.[23] It should be added that the term *morphology* in the sense of *composition* was often used in the 1920s: recall the works of M. A. Petrovskii "The Morphology of Pushkin's 'Shot'" (1925) and "The Morphology of a Short Story" (1927).[24] But mainly it is A. I. Nikiforov, "On the Question of the Morphological Study of the Folktale" (1928),[25] that parallels Propp's research in the full sense of the word.

Viktor Shklovsky's *Theory of Prose*[26] also had a certain impact on Propp, although in itself the idea of *Morphology* was not directly related to the formalists' views on the literary work as a system of devices[27] (which is hardly effective in studying folklore)[28] but rather harkens back to completely different philosophical and methodological premises. Propp emphasized that in his work, the term *morphology* had nothing to do with grammar; it had a broader ontological meaning and corresponded to Goethe's concepts as applied to botany and osteology.[29]

This, among other things, explains Propp's vexation when Goethe's epigraphs[30] were removed in the English translation of *Morphology of the Folktale*. They were by no means ornamental in nature but were supposed to express the main idea of the book, which "dimly appeared" to the author already during its creation:[31] "The study of the folktale in many respects can be compared with the study of organic formations in nature." "The field of nature and the field of human creativity are not separated. There is something that unites them, there are some laws common to them that can be studied by similar methods."[32] On this subject he wrote the following in his article "The Transformation of Wondertales," published almost simultaneously with *Morphology*, in 1928: "The study of the wondertale may be compared to the study of organic formations in nature. . . . Both fields allow two points of view: either the internal similarity of two externally unrelated phenomena cannot be traced to a common genetic root (theory of spontaneous generation) or else this morphological similarity results from a genetic tie (theory of origin by metamorphoses or transformations traceable to certain causes)."[33] Similar considerations dictated the supportive evaluation of the "paleontological" method of Nikolai Yakovlevich Marr[34] as applied to folklore material. Propp saw here the flip side of stadial-historical analysis (which he considered one of the main achievements of Soviet folklore scholarship),[35] and for him, the principle of stadial development was similar to the law of biological evolution: "The question of the origin of species, posed by Darwin, may be posed in our area as well."[36]

Reproaches for reductionism and excessive enthusiasm for "stadial evolutionary" models are hardly appropriate here. The conceptual base of Propp's research developed in an intellectual climate where the historical essence of tradition was an indispensable aspect of its study, and the historical process itself was understood in a significantly different way from today. In addition, at that time scholarly analysis was focused mainly on integral, self-sufficient forms of culture in their structural distinctness rather than fundamentally "open" texts and "intermediate" zones in the semantic field of tradition, which became so much more interesting due to the poststructuralist epistemological turn. In the epoch when *Morphology of the Folktale* was created, scholarship strove for clarity and found it. Propp, who by his own admission loved to classify and systematize everything,[37] was an ideal representative for such clarity of thought. The analytical tools he uses are logical and rigorous, and the results of the analysis are convincing in their transparency and orderliness. This, in combination with great talent, allowed the scholar to play the role that was destined for him in scholarship.

I would like to repeat again that although Propp is an internationally recognized founder of structural folklore studies, to whom we owe one of the first experimental results in the development and application of structural methods in the humanities, all this refers to him only as the author of *The Morphology the Folktale*. For the author himself, this work was part of a wider stadial-typological project, which he had completed by the mid-1940s. This is when his book *The Historical Roots of the Wondertale* was published.

3. The manuscript of *Morphology of the Folktale* submitted to the Academia publishing house on the initiative of Viktor Zhirmunskii, editor of the series *Questions of Poetics*, included another, final chapter. It outlined historical or rather historical-genetic prospects for the analysis the author had accomplished and a further project of stadial-typological study; its results were subsequently embodied in *The Historical Roots of the Wondertale*. However, at the time Zhirmunskii considered this chapter not yet complete and recommended that the author finalize it but for the time being remove it from the book, and this was done.[38] This move gave *Morphology of the Folktale* greater integrity and completeness but separated it from the originally planned continuation. It is worth repeating once again that according to the author's intention, the books were conceived as a duology, with *Morphology* playing more of a preparatory role and *Historical Roots* the principal and conclusive role. However, as we know, time had other plans.

Having published *Morphology*, Propp moved on to the next stage of his project: to establish broad ethnographic correspondences to individual plots and motifs of the wondertale. According to the conception the author adhered to in this case, such comparative analysis would make it possible to establish the ritual-mythological base of the tales' semantics and thus help discover their genesis. His articles published in 1934–41 (and some later ones)[39] had similar trends, and nearly ten years after publishing *Morphology*, Propp finally completed the first edition of the monograph *Historical Roots of the Wondertale*. It was defended as his doctoral dissertation (1939);[40] however, the outbreak of the war prevented its publication. The book that was completed by the author over these years was published only in 1946.[41]

The epistemological basis of the study that Propp carried out is so-called ritual theory,[42] according to which (in a very simplified summary) a mythological narrative arises as a commentary to the rite, gets separated from the ritual after a syncretic mythological ritual system collapses, and turns into a folktale or other folklore genre as a result of the desacralization of its narrative expressions.

In *Historical Roots of the Wondertale* Propp emerges, to a certain extent, as a successor of the ideas of Pierre Saintyves (Émile Nourry), who suggested that the plot of the wondertale dates back to the rite of initiation.[43] A similar idea was generally present in Soviet science of the 1920–30s—one can recall the hypothesis of "initiatory" motifs in the legend of Tristan and Isolde[44] but especially in the comprehensive analysis of the folktale motif of "a house in the forest" undertaken by Solomon Ya. Lur'e.[45] In these articles, unlike *Historical Roots*, Saintyves's book is not mentioned at all (which does not exclude the possibility of its influence). Propp, on the other hand, critically examined all three works, treating most sympathetically Lurie's study, which was conducted in parallel with his own, and referring to it repeatedly in his monograph. Yet there is no doubt that Propp developed this hypothesis incomparably more thoroughly, more deeply, using more extensive material than his predecessors, including Saintyves, and he moved far beyond them in terms of detail, reason, and the technique of his proofs.[46]

Historical Roots of the Wondertale was published in a very unfavorable period for Soviet scholarship. It was a time of monstrous political and ideological campaigns, the devastation of the remaining schools and research trends, the persecution of scholars, including through their expulsion from universities and academic institutions, the deprivation of their rights to professional activities, and even arrests.[47] Propp's monograph[48] did not escape attacks either. Party critics saw "mysticism," in it, "perversion and falsification of the true picture of social relations." He was reproached for referring to the works of the "idealists" Frazer and Lévy-Bruhl and the "bourgeois" Finnish school and for the lack of reliance on the works of Russia's "revolutionary-democratic" publicists of the nineteenth century—namely, Nikolai Dobrolyubov and Nikolai Chernyshevsky as well as the writer Maxim Gorky, canonized in the USSR, who considered fairy tales the embodiment of man's dream for a bright future. Propp was accused of speaking of the "social lower classes" while he should, according to Gorky's definition, have made a clear statement about the "working oppressed masses," the "working people."[49] The "discussions" of Propp's book organized by the leadership of the Institute of Ethnography at the USSR's Academy of Sciences presented total ideological defamation typical of that time.[50]

Because of this, a real scholarly discussion of *Historical Roots* never took place.[51] The only exception was Viktor Zhirmunskii's review, which was an immediate response to the release of the book and had a chance to appear before the devastating ideological criticism of it. Giving highest praise to Propp's research, Zhirmunskii nevertheless considered it an exaggeration to trace all wondertales to the rite of initiation. According to this reviewer, only some of the tales could be genetically associated with this rite, primarily plots of the quest type (AT# 550–551) and those regarding the hero's trial in a forest hut ("children at an ogre's house," AT 311, 312, 314, 327).[52] Many folklorists agree with Zhirmunskii's view,[53] but no broader discussion of the questions that Propp's book raises took place—not even a decade later when it became possible thanks to the de-Stalinizing "thaw" of the ideological climate. It is interesting that the monograph itself was not reprinted until forty years after its first publication.[54]

Historical Roots of the Wondertale was, of course, well known to specialists, and they turned to it according to their scientific interests as to an authoritative work,[55] although there were also critical remarks about some specific interpretations of folklore motifs and images (the "blindness of a demon," Baba Yaga "the forest mistress," the fairy-tale dragon).[56] A favorable attitude toward the book was also facilitated by the fact that it was during this period (the late 1970s to the early 1990s) that comparative historical studies of folklore texts and traditions were especially evolving in the Soviet Union in connection with ethnographic materials.[57] This was a fruitful direction, terminating the interdisciplinary boundaries between folklore studies and ethnology,[58] which ultimately contributed to the process of the anthropologization of folklore observed in our time. Propp's book also played an important role here—almost no other Russian or Soviet works reveal the ethnographic parallels to the wondertale plot with such completeness, depth, or consistency.

However, all the above mainly relates to the state of scholarly tradition in the USSR. Outside the borders of the country, the book remained much less known and, in any case, far less popular.[59] An exception was the Italian translation, which appeared almost immediately after the book's publication in the USSR. It was reprinted at least six times and allowed Carlo Ginzburg, somewhat later, to appreciate *Historical Roots* highly as "a great book, despite its shortcomings," notably as part of the duology conceived by Propp: "The reference to Goethe (to Goethe the morphologist) is given openly by Wittgenstein, as well as in Propp's *Morphology of the Folktale* written in the same years. But, unlike Wittgenstein, Propp considered morphological analysis as a tool that is useful for historical research, not as an alternative to the latter."[60] This translation, however, was not able to help popularize the book outside of Italy. The small acquaintance with *Historical Roots* greatly influenced the reception of *Morphology* in global scholarship. Such a reception, by its nature, did not fully correspond to Propp's original plan for the wondertale study.[61]

A good example in this regard is Claude Lévi-Strauss's review, which is especially significant for its academic impact.[62] Lévi-Strauss overall highly praised the work of the Soviet folklorist but at the same time made a number of comments of principle and some worthwhile suggestions. A rather sharp answer by Propp followed,[63] the tone of which was possibly due to linguistic, ideological, and cultural reasons.[64] First, one suspects that in some places, Propp did not quite adequately interpret his critic's text. Second, he took the definition of *formalist* not as an indication of belonging to a reputable scholarly school but as an accusation (a trace of the Soviet "criticism of formalism"[65]). And third, he had very approximate knowledge of Lévi-Strauss, considering him an armchair philosopher-structuralist and probably not being aware of his widely known cultural-anthropological studies, including his fieldwork.[66]

It must be said that Lévi-Strauss's familiarity with Propp's works was not much greater, which is of considerable importance for the subsequent polemic; a substantial role in this is attributed to the not quite successful translation, which conveyed Propp's ideas with some oversimplifications and even distortion.[67] According to E. M. Meletinsky, "He [Lévi-Strauss] conceives his polemic against Propp as that of a structuralist against a formalist, believing that Propp separates form from content, folktale from myth, ignores ethnographic context, and thus builds a grammar without a lexicon, as it were, disregarding the fact that folklore as a specific phenomenon differs from all other linguistic phenomena, and that it combines dictionary and syntax in one function."[68] The reproach of neglecting the ethnographic context and detaching form from content can be explained only by Lévi-Strauss's complete unfamiliarity with Propp's works of the 1930s through the early 1940s (the 1949 Italian edition of *Historical Roots* was apparently unknown to him) while reckoning him among the "formal school," an idea that became firmly rooted in scholarly circles outside the USSR, is historically and methodologically erroneous,[69] as noted above.

However, the critical comments of Lévi-Strauss are by no means limited to the above misunderstanding. They have a much more serious basis, which involves these two researchers' fundamentally different approaches to the material; they came to the solution of related problems from opposite directions (from the wondertale and from myth).

For Propp the syntagmatic analysis of the wondertale is an introduction, on the one hand, to its history and, on the other hand, to the study of the "special *logical* structure of the tale, which led to the analysis of the tale as a myth."[70] He calls the wondertale "mythical" on the grounds of its mythological genesis. All this is not very different from the attitude of Lévi-Strauss,[71] who sees in the tale a "faded" myth. He proceeds from the fact that myth belongs simultaneously to the two Saussurean categories (*langue* and *parole*): as a narrative of the past, it is diachronic and irreversible in time, and as a tool for explaining the present and future it is synchronous and reversible in time.

We can say that for Lévi-Strauss the genre differences between myth and wondertale are altogether irrelevant, as is the narrative aspect in general.[72] Propp, on the contrary, arrives at the historical paradigm of the wondertale and its ritual-mythological roots through analysis of its syntagmatic structure.

Historical Roots concerns precisely this.

4. As noted above,[73] Propp uses the word *tale* in the singular everywhere ("Morphology of the [folk]tale," "Historical roots of the wondertale," "The Russian [folk]tale"), speaking of this genre type ("wondertale") as a kind of integrated entity. This is understandable, and the author himself explains his approach to the material very clearly: "The comparative study of plots opens wide historical perspectives. What needs historical explanation is not individual plots but the compositional system to which they belong. This approach will bring out the historical connections among them and pave the way for the study of individual plots."[74] Thus, according to E. M. Meletinsky, Propp's reduction of all wondertales to one is not a mistake (as Lévi-Strauss believed[75]) but rather a condition for achieving the set purpose: "to determine the specificity of the tale and to describe and explain its uniform structure."[76]

In this regard, all the methodological criticism of Propp's concept in essence misses its target. From the beginning, he defines with utmost clarity the contours and the basic framework of his project, whose subject of study is neither a single tale nor a single plot but material for further analysis. As if anticipating a qualm that the data corpus is possibly insufficient and that there are as many "exceptions" as "correct" cases,[77] Propp prejustifies the criteria for his selection: one hundred texts from Afanas'ev's collection (in consecutive order, without skipping any), which allows us to draw conclusions not only about the stability of the elements under consideration ("the functions") but also about their finite number. At a certain point, there are no more new "functions" detected, and therefore, after checking the pattern identified against the control material, you can declare the work complete.[78] The exceptions, apparently, should be considered simply as natural oscillations around the established stable structure.

This structure, defined in the epigraph to *Morphology*'s chapter 9 via Goethe's "Archetypal Plant" (*Urpflanze*),[79] is not a product of reconstruction of the "proto-form" or "proto-text" but, on the contrary, the result of constructing a model that cannot have any genuine manifestations in the historical past but is able to explain all the potential diversity of forms of the given tradition generated by the process of evolutionary morphology (Goethe: "The doctrine of forms is the doctrine of transformations").[80] All this also applies to *Historical Roots*, in which, through broad ethnographic commentary on the supporting elements of this model, a ritual-mythological structure is constructed that represents the paradigmatic aspect of the same model.[81]

Strictly speaking, it would seem that the tenets and goals of the research project, clearly defined from the beginning, should have forestalled the doubts of its most attentive reviewers. For example, V. N. Peretts has noted of Propp's goals that grammar is not a substrate but an abstraction of language and that it is hardly possible to deduce the proto-form of the

wondertale from the description of tale functions.[82] A counterargument
to this would be that "Propp's formula" is by no means the "proto-form"
of the wondertale (as he directly specifies in the text of the book). If Lévi-
Strauss saw in *Morphology* an attempt to create a grammar without a
lexicon (although folklore "builds a grammar without a lexicon, as it
were, disregarding the fact that folklore as a specific phenomenon differs
from all other linguistic phenomena, and that it combines dictionary
and syntax in one function"[83]), then, as noted above, Propp turned to the
"dictionary" and the "lexicon" in his *Historical Roots* while his intention
was thoroughly outlined already in the text of *Morphology*.

Perhaps the main thing is that despite all the valid objections (to the arbi-
trariness of individual semantic reconstructions and, most important, to the
exaggerated role of archaic initiation rites in the genesis of narrative structures), Propp's duology very convincingly and clearly establishes a structural
isomorphism of the verbal narrative-folk text on the one hand and, on the
other hand, the ceremonial-action text. In addition, the ritual and narrative
models are understood in a broad sense, and their instrumental application
is highly effective in analyzing completely different traditions that are far
from both the wondertale and the rite of initiation. In this regard, the heuristic potential of Propp's research project cannot be considered exhausted.

In the syntagmatic model (*Morphology of the Folktale*), the structural
elements of the narrative (the functions) are connected "in contiguity" as
an unbroken "horizontal" sequence. In *Historical Roots*, each function
(ideally, of course) acquires an equivalent in the archaic ritual tradition
and thereby acquires a deep mythological semantics ("deep," i.e., existing
only in reconstruction). The relations between the narrative and the ritualistic elements (as well as the two models themselves, the narrative and
the ritual) deserve the name *paradigmatic* (according to Louis Hjelmslev).

These paradigmatic relationships can be used to provide a historical
explanation for the genesis of the wondertale, which Propp does, and to
do so in an extremely categorical manner that provoked tenable objections. However, the real significance of this book today is not in historical
and genetic reconstructions (in some cases, dubious or outdated)[84] but
in establishing a broad equivalence between narrative and ritual models
(which, incidentally, is perfectly demonstrated on completely different
material in the works of Elena Novik).[85]

Finally, there is one additional reason to recommend to the current
reader this book, which first saw the light three-quarters of a century ago:
even if many of the constructions and concepts of the author cannot be
accepted from the standpoint of present knowledge, like Frazer's *Golden
Bough*, it is extremely interesting to read.

Notes

Translators' Introduction

1. Vladimir Propp, *Morfologiia skazki* (Leningrad: "Academia," 1928); Vladimir Propp, *Morphology of the Folktale*, trans. Lawrence Scott with an introduction by Svatava Pirkova-Jakobson (Bloomington: Indiana University Research Center in Anthropology, Folklore, and Linguistics, 1958).

2. Anatoly Liberman, ed., *Theory and History of Folklore*, trans. Ariadna Y. Martin and Richard P. Martin (Minneapolis: University of Minnesota Press, 1984), 71.

3. Ibid., 70, 73.

4. Ibid., 68.

5. Propp, *Morphology of the Folktale* (1958).

6. Vladimir Propp, *Morphology of the Folktale*, trans. Laurence Scott [and] with an intro. Svatava Pirkova-Jakobson, rev. and ed. with a Preface by Louis A. Wagner and a new intro. Alan Dundes (Austin: University of Texas Press, 1968).

7. Liberman, *Theory and History of Folklore*, 67–81.

8. Propp, *Morphology* (1968), 5.

9. "The Structural and Historical Study of the Wondertale," which contains Propp's response to Lévi-Strauss, was first published in Italian. Gian Luigi Bravo, ed., *Vladimir Ja. Propp. Morfologia della fiaba*, Con un intervento di Claude Levi-Strauss e una replica dell'autore (Torino: Giulio Einaudi Editore, 1966).

10. Liberman, *Theory and History of Folklore*, 70–71.

11. Ibid., 71.

12. Ibid., 71–72.

13. See chapter 1, section 13.

14. Michael McCarthy, *The Moth Snowstorm. Nature and Joy* (New York: John Murray, 2015).

15. Propp, *Morphology* (1968), ix, emphasis added.

16. Ibid., xix.

17. F. P. Filin, compiler, *Slovar' russkikh narodnykh govorov* (Leningrad: Nauka, 2021).

18. Some of these were removed by the editors of the second and third editions, as they rightly judged that such references had served only to comply

with Soviet requirements. Since this is a translation of the third edition, we have not attempted to restore cuts made by that edition's Russian editors.

1. Premises

1. Mikhail N. Speranskii, *Russkaia ustnaia slovesnost'* (Moscow: A. M. Mikhailov, 1917), 222. The bylina is a traditional Russian oral epic narrative poem that incorporates elements of history (translators' note).

2. Aleksandr N. Veselovskii, *Stat'i o skazke* (Moscow: Akademii nauk SSSR, 1938), 83–128.

3. Leo Frobenius, *Die Weltanschauung der Naturvölker* (Weimar: E. Felber, 1898), 242.

4. Aleksandr I. Nikiforov, *Izvestiia otdeleniia russkogo iazyka i slovesnosti*, vol. 31 (Leningrad: Izdatel'stvo Akademii Nauk SSSR, 1926), 353–69.

5. On the translation of the title *Morfologiia skazki* into English and the erroneous assumption that the word *skazka* necessarily means "folktale," see our translators' introduction and Sergei Nekliudov's afterword in the present volume (translators' note).

6. Italics in the source. As other premises are not italicized by the author, we assume that he wished to draw special attention here (translators' note).

7. Georg Polívka, "Čichám člověčinu—ruský dech, ruskou 'kost,'" *Národopisný věstník českoslovanský* 17 (1924): 104; Ludwig Radermacher, "Walfischmythen," *Archiv für Religionswissenschaft* 9 (1906): 248–52; Walter Baumgartner, "Jephtas Gelübde Jud. 11, 30–40," *Archiv für Religionswissenschaft* 18 (1915): 240–49.

8. Lutz Mackensen, *Der singende Knochen: Ein Beitrag zur vergleichenden Märchenforschung.* (Helsinki: Suomalainen tiedeakatemia, 1923); Sven S. Liljeblad, *Die Tobiasgeschichte und andere Märchen mit Toten Helfern* (Lund: P. Lindstedts Univ.-Bokhandel, 1927).

9. K. Marx and F. Engels, *Sochinenie*, vol. 13 (Moskva: Izdatel'stvo politicheskoi literatury, 1955–74), 7; Karl Marx, "Preface to *A Contribution to the Critique of Political Economy*," in *The Marx-Engels Reader*, ed. Robert C. Tucker (New York: W. W. Norton, 1978), 4.

10. An incorrect pronunciation of the Russian *Sekund-Maior* (Second Major), reflecting folk etymology, as the Russian секун (*sekun*) could be interpreted as a "flogger," from the verb сечь, секу (*sech', seku*), "to flog, I flog" (translators' note).

11. Marx, "Preface to *A Contribution*," 5.

12. Lewis H. Morgan, *Ancient Society, or Researches in the Lines of Human Progress from Savagery through Barbarism to Civilization* (New York: Henry Holt, 1877), 444.

13. Marx and Engels, *Sochinenie*, vol. 21, 6.

14. Friedrich Engels, *Herr Eugen Dühring's Revolution in Science ("Anti-Dühring")*, trans. Emile Burns, ed. C. P. Dutt (New York: International Publishers, 1966), 344–45.

15. Afanas'ev No. 100; H100.

16. Vladimir Propp, "K voprosu o proiskhozhdenii volshebnoi skazki (Volshebnoe derevo na mogile)," *Sovetskaia. Etnografiia*, nos. 1–2 (1934): 128–51.

17. Vladimir I. Lenin, "On the Question of Dialectics," in *V. I. Lenin: Collected Works*, 4th ed., trans. Clemens Dutt, ed. Stewart Smith, vol. 38 (Moscow: Foreign Languages Publishing House, 1961), 360.

18. Friedrich Engels, *Dialectics of Nature*, trans. and ed. Clemens Dutt (New York: International Publishers, 1940), 482.

19. Dmitrii K. Zelenin, *Kul't ongonov v Sibiri: perezhitki totemizma v ideologii sibirskikh narodov*, Trudy Instituta antropologii i etnografii Akademii nauk SSSR, vol. 14, no. 3 (Moscow: Izdatel'stvo Akademii Nauk SSSR, 1936), 232.

20. I. M. Tronskii, "Antichnyi mif i sovremennaia skazka," in *Sergeiu Fëdorovichu Ol'denburgu* (Leningrad: Gosudarstvennoe uchebno-pedogicheskoe izdatel'stvo Ministersvta Prosveshchenia RSFSR, 1934), 523–34.

21. Alfred L. Kroeber, *Gros Ventre Myths and Tales*, Anthropological Papers of the American Museum of Natural History, vol. 1, pt. 3 (New York: Trustees, 1907).

22. V. N. Chernetsov, *Vogul'skie skazki: Sbornik fol'klora naroda mansi (vogulov)* (Leningrad: Khudozhestvennaia literatura, 1935), 18. Ilya Muromets is a hero of the Russian heroic epic (*bylina*) (translators' note).

23. On the assumptions of Propp's period regarding the relative levels of development of peoples around the world, please see the introduction to this volume.

24. Ulrich von Wilamowitz-Moellendorff, "Die griechische Heldensage I & II," *Sitzungsberichte der Preussischen Akademie der Wissenschaften zu Berlin. Philosophisch-historische Klasse* 7 (1925): 41–62, 214–42.

25. Here Propp refers to the Russian historical school, which attempted to connect Russian heroic poetry and historical reality (translators' note).

26. Aby Warburg, "A Lecture on Serpent Ritual," *Journal of the Warburg Institute* 2, no. 4 (1939): 286.

27. Hermann K. Usener, *Die Sintfluthsagen, Untersucht von Hermann Usener; mit fünf Abbildungen und einer Münztafel* (Bonn: F. Cohen, 1899).

28. Engels, *Dialectics of Nature*, 159.

2. Beginnings

1. Afanas'ev No. 113; H113.

2. Afanas'ev No. 265; H265.

3. Afanas'ev No. 197; H197.

4. Afanas'ev No. 265; H265. The *terem* is the upper floor of a large dwelling intended for the seclusion of women. In the fifteenth to seventeenth centuries, Russian noble and royal women were confined to such separate quarters (translators' note).

5. Smirnov 1917: No. 43.

6. Afanas'ev No. 113; H113.

7. Afanas'ev No. 277; H277.

8. Afanas'ev No. 201; H201.

9. James G. Frazer, *The Golden Bough*, vol. 3, pt. 2, *Taboo and the Perils of the Soul*, 3rd ed. (London: Macmillan, 1911), 1–17, https://archive.org/details/goldenboughstud03fraz.

10. Ibid., 123.

11. Ibid., 124.

12. Afanas'ev No. 202, cf. No. 201; H202, cf. H201.

13. Khudiakov 1862: No. 53.

14. Afanas'ev No. 140; H140.

15. Nikolai E. Onchukov, *Severnye skazki: Arkhangel'skaia i Olenetskaia gg*, Zapiski Russkogo geograficheskogo obshchestva po otdeleniiu etnografii, vol. 33 (St. Petersburg: A. S. Suvorin, 1908), 4.

16. *Zhivaia Starina: Periodicheskoe izdatel'stvo otdeleniia etnografii Imper- atorskogo Russkogo geograficheskogo obshchestva* 21, nos. 2–4 (1912): 367.

17. Khudiakov 1862: No. 110.

18. M. G. Tikhaia-Tsereteli, "Zhenskii obraz mzeθunaqav gruzinskikh skazok," in *Tristan i Isol'da: Ot geroini liubvi feodal'noi Evropy do bogini matriarkhal'noi Afroevrazii*, ed. Nikolai Ia Marr (Leningrad: Akademii nauk, 1932), 138.

19. Grimm, No. 88.

20. Smirnov 1917: No. 12.

21. Ibid., No. 303.

22. Ibid., No. 357.

23. Zelenin 1915: No. 105.

24. Ibid., No. 28.

25. Smirnov 1917: No. 10.

26. Afanas'ev No. 202; H202.

27. Zelenin 1914: No. 18.

28. Khudiakov 1862: No. 21.

29. Arsenii Konstaninovich Khazhba and Victor Iosifovich Kukba, eds. and trans. *Abkhazskie skazki* (Sukhumi: Alashara, 1935), 49.

30. Sadovnikov 1884: No. 11.

31. James G. Frazer, *The Golden Bough*, vol. 10, *Balder the Beautiful, Festi- vals of Europe and the Doctrine of the External Soul*, vol. 1, 3rd ed. (London: Macmillan, 1913), 19, https://archive.org/details/1913goldenboughs10fraz. Frazer here quotes Antonio de Herrera, *General History of the vast Continent and Islands of America*, vol. 88, trans. Capt. John Stevens (London: Jer. Bat- ley, 1725–26) (translators' note).

32. Afanas'ev No. 560; H560.

33. Grimm, No. 12 (Rapunzel).

34. Tikhaia-Tsereteli, "Zhenskii obraz mzeθunaqav gruzinskikh skazok," 151.

35. Frazer, *Golden Bough*, vol. 10, 73–74.

36. Propp does not cite the Von Der Leyen book in question but appears to have in mind his *Das Märchen in den Göttersagen der Edda* (Berlin: Reimer, 1899) (translators' note).

37. Karnaukhova 1934: No. 42.

38. Frazer, *Golden Bough*, vol. 3, pt. 2, 1.

39. Zelenin 1915: No. 105.

40. Martin P. Nilsson, *Primitive Religion*, Religionsgeschichtliche Volks- bücher für die deutsche christliche Gegenwart, series 3, Allgemeine Religion- sgeschichte, nos. 13–14 (Tübingen: Mohr Siebeck, 1911), 7.

41. Daniel G. Brinton, "The Folk-Lore of Yucatan," *Folk-Lore Journal* 1, no. 1 (1883): 251.

42. I. I. Snegirev, trans., *Skazki Zulu* (Moscow: Akademii nauk, 1937), 91.

43. Vladimir M. Vikent'ev, *Drevne-egipetskaia povest' o dvukh brat'iakh*, Kul'turno-istoricheskie pamiatniki Drevnego Vostoka, vol. 4 (Moscow: A. A. Levenson, 1917), 39; Vasilii V. Struve, "Ishtar'—Isol'da v drevnevostochnoi mifologii," in Marr, *Tristan i Isol'da*, 55. Vikent'ev is a Russian translation of the Egyptian text "The Tale of the Two Brothers" (translators' note).

44. Smirnov 1917: No. 323.

45. Frank H. Cushing, *Zuñi Folk Tales* (New York: G. P. Putnam's Sons, 1901), 132.

46. Raphael Karstens, "Die altpemanische Religion," *Archiv für Religions-swissenschaft* 25, no. 1/2 (1927).

47. Grimm, No. 198.

48. Ivan P. Minaev, *Indeiskie skazki i legendy, sobrannye v Kamaone v 1875 g* (St. Petersburg: V. F. Demakov, 1877), 82.

49. M. K. Azadovskii, *Verkhnelenskie skazki* (Irkutsk: Ogiz, 1938), 5.

50. Aleksandr N. Veselovskii, "Skazaniia o krasavitse v tereme i russkaia bylina o podsolnechnom Tsarstve," *Zhurnal Ministerstva Narodnogo Pros-veshcheniia* 196 (1878); *Sobranie sochinenii*, vol. 2 (St. Petersburg: Tipografiia Imperatorskoi akademii nauk, 1913), e.g., 70 and passim.

51. Afanas'ev No. 177; H177.

52. Smirnov 1917: No. 35.

53. Afanas'ev No. 234; H234.

54. Afanas'ev No. 268; H268.

55. *Zhivaia Starina*, 275.

56. Sadovnikov 1884: No. 60.

57. Karnaukhova 1934: No. 14.

58. Smirnov 1917: No. 130.

59. Nikolai N. Kharuzin, *Etnografiia*, vol. 4, *Verovaniia*, ed. Vera and Aleksei Kharuzin (St. Petersburg: Gosudarstvennaia tipografiia, 1905), 260.

60. Franz Boas, *Indianische Sagen von der nord-pazifischen Küste Amerikas* (Berlin: A. Ascher, 1895), 41.

61. Julius von Negelein, "Die Reise der Seele ins Jenseits," *ZVV* 11 (1901), 151.

62. Kharuzin, *Etnografiia*, 260.

63. Negelein, "Die Reise der Seele," 151.

64. Richard Reitzenstein, "Zwei hellenistische Hymnen," *Archiv für Religionswissenschaft* 8 (1905): 178.

65. E. A. Wallis Budge, *The Book of the Dead* (New York: Barnes & Noble, 1951) [CXXV], 377. Unless otherwise noted, for this text we have referenced Budge's translation throughout this book.

66. Struve, "Ishtar,'" 51.

67. Ernst Samter, *Geburt, Hochzeit, Tod: Beiträge zur vergleichenden Volkskunde* (Leipzig: B. G. Teubner, 1911), 206.

68. Negelein, "Das Pferd in der Volksmedizin," 151.

69. Lev Ia. Shternberg, *Pervobytnaia religiia v svete etnografii* (Leningrad: Izdatel'stvo Instituta narodov Severa TSIK SSSR im. P. G. Smidovicha, 1936), 330.

70. Kharuzin, *Etnografiia*, 260.

71. Dmitrii N. Anuchin, *"Sani, lad'ia i koni, kak prinadlezhnosti pokhoronnogo Obrjada," Drevnosti. Trudy Moskovskogo arkheologicheskogo obshchestva* 14 (1890): 179.

3. The Mysterious Forest

1. Propp's Yaga is a frequent abbreviation for the full name Baba Yaga (translators' note).

2. In English in the source (translators' note).

3. Pierre Saintyves was the pen name of Emile Nourry (1870–1935), a French publisher, bookseller, and folklorist often credited with the hypothesis that many common folktales had their origins in pagan ritual (translators' note).

4. Pierre Saintyves, *Les contes de Perrault et les récits parallèles: leurs origines, coutumes primitives et liturgies populaires* (Paris: Emile Nourry, 1923), 235–75.

5. Boris V. Kazanskii, "Antichnye aspekty siuzheta Tristana i Isol'dy," in *Tristan i Isol'da: Ot geroini liubvi feodal'noi Evropy do bogini matriarkhal'noi Afroevrazii,* ed. Nikolai Ia. Marr (Leningrad: Akademii nauk, 1932), 135.

6. Solomon Ia. Lur'e, "Dom v lesu," *Iazyk i literatura* 8 (1932): 159–94.

7. Heinrich Schurtz, *Altersklassen und Männerbünde: Eine Darstellung der Grundformen der Gesellschaft* (Berlin: G. Reimer, 1902); Hutton Webster, *Primitive Secret Societies* (New York: Macmillan, 1908); Edwin M. Loeb, *Tribal Initiations and Secret Societies,* vol. 25, no. 3 (Berkeley: University of California Publications in American Archaeology and Ethnology, 1929); Arnold van Gennep, *Les rites de passage, etudes systematiques des rites* (Paris: Emile Nourry, 1909).

8. Franz Boas, "The Social Organization and the Secret Societies of the Kwakiutl Indians," Report of the U.S. National Museum for 1895 (Washington, DC: United States National Museum, 1897); Frobenius, *Die Weltanschauung der Naturvölker*; Hans Nevermann, *Ergebnisse der Südsee-Expedition, 1908–1910,* vol. 3, *Admirälitats-inseln* (Hamburg: L. Friederichsen, 1934).

9. The leshii and rusalka are spirits or minor deities associated with Slavic mythology. The leshii is a male spirit associated with the forest while the rusalka is a nymph, often malicious toward humans and frequently associated with water (translators' note).

10. Zelenin 1914: No. 16.

11. Ibid., No. 41.

12. George A. Dorsey, *Traditions of the Skidi-Pawnee,* Memoirs of the American Folklore Society, vol. 8 (New York: Houghton, Mifflin, 1904), 74.

13. Frobenius, *Die Weltanschauung der Naturvölker,* 203.

14. William H. Roscher, *Ausführliches Lexikon der griechischen und römischen Mythologie* (Leipzig: B. G. Teubner, 1884).

15. Virgil, *The Aeneid,* trans. James Rhoades (Chicago: William Benton, 1952), 217.

16. Afanas'ev No. 235; H235.

17. Korguev 1939: No. 7.

18. Afanas'ev No. 560; H560.

19. Korguev 1939: No. 7.

20. Ibid., No. 17.

21. Smirnov 1917: No. 1.

22. Kroeber, *Gros Ventre,* 84.

23. Afanas'ev No. 14; Kroeber, *Gros Ventre,* 84.

24. Afanas'ev No. 114; H114.

25. Afanas'ev No. 140; H140.

26. Afanas'ev No. 272; H272.

27. Afanas'ev No. 172; H172.

28. Afanas'ev No. 176; H176.

29. Boas, *Indianische Sagen,* 4.

30. Andrei A. Popov, *Dolganskii fol'klor* (Moscow: Sovetskii pisatel', 1937), 55–56.

31. Afanas'ev No. 103; H103.

32. Khudiakov 1862: No. 59.

33. Boas, *Indianische Sagen*, 166.

34. Boris A. Turaev, *Egipetskaia literatura* (Moscow: Izd. M. i S. Sabash-nikovykh, 1920), 56.

35. Propp erroneously references chapter 127 of the Egyptian *Book of the Dead* here. The "naming of the parts of the door" passage is, in fact, found in chapter 125. Budge, *The Book of the Dead*, [CXXV], 375–76.

36. Loeb, *Tribal Initiations*, 256.

37. Richard Parkinson, *Dreißig Jahre in der Südsee: Land und Leute, Sitten und Gebräuche im Bismarckarchipel und auf den deutschen Salomoinseln* (Stuttgart: Strecker & Schröder, 1907), 72.

38. Loeb, *Tribal Initiations*, 257.

39. Ibid., 261.

40. Parkinson, *Dreißig Jahre in der Südsee*, 606.

41. Afanas'ev No. 104; H104.

42. Afanas'ev No. 104; H104.

43. Boas, *Indianische Sagen*, 239, 253, 118.

44. A Russian expression suggesting the action of sniffing and detecting a certain, usually unpleasant odor (translators' note).

45. Afanas'ev No. 137; H137.

46. Karnaukhova 1934: No. 7.

47. Afanas'ev No. 139; H139.

48. Georg Polívka, "Čichám člověčinu—ruský dech. ruskou 'kost,'" *Národopisný věstník českoslovanský* 17 (1924): 3–19.

49. Boas, *Indianische Sagen*, 4.

50. Anna H. Gayton, "The Orpheus Myth in North America," *Journal of American Folklore* 48, no. 189 (1935): 263–93.

51. Ibid., 267.

52. Friedrich Fülleborn, *Deutsche-Ost-Afrika: Wissenschaftliche Forschungsresultate über Land und Leute unseres ostafrikanischen Schutzgebietes und der angrenzenden Länder*, vol. 9 (Berlin: Dietrich Reimer, 1906).

53. Snegirev 1937: No. 123.

54. James G. Frazer, *The Fear of the Dead in Primitive Religion*, vol. 1 (London: Macmillan, 1933), 143.

55. Popov, *Dolganskii fol'klor*, 169.

56. Boas, *Indianische Sagen*, 96, cf. 41.

57. Dorsey, *Traditions of the Skidi-Pawnee*, 75.

58. Hans Nevermann, *Masken und Geheimbunde in Melanesien* (Berlin: Verlag von Reimar Hobbing, 1933), 66.

59. Boas, "Social Organization," 449.

60. Afanas'ev No. 105; H105.

61. Ibid.

62. Afanas'ev No. 137; H137.

63. Korguev, *Skazki Karel'skogo Belomor'ia*, No. 9.

64. Boas, *Indianische Sagen*, 239.

65. James G. Frazer, *The Belief in Immortality and the Worship of the Dead*, vol. 2 (London: Macmillan, 1922), 28.

66. Wallis E. A. Budge, *The Book of Opening the Mouth*, Books on Egypt and Chaldaea, vols. 26–27 (London: Kegan, Paul Trench, Trübner, 1909), 3.

67. Budge, *Book of the Dead* [CXXII], 350–51.

68. Budge, *Book of the Dead* [CVI], 313.

69. James H. Breasted, *Development of Religion and Thought in Ancient Egypt* (London: Scribner, 1912), 60.

70. Hugo Gressmann, *Altorientalische Texte und Bilder zum Alten Testament* (Tübingen: J. C. B. Mohr, 1909), 42.

71. Wilhelm Bousset, "Die Himmelsreise der Seele," *Archiv für Religionswissenschaft* 4 (1901): 156.

72. Hermann Güntert, *Kalypso: Bedeutungsgeschichtliche untersuchungen auf dem Gebiet der indogermanischen Sprachen* (Halle: Niemeyer, 1919), 79, 80, 151.

73. Erwin Rohde, *Psyche: Seelencult und Unsterblichkeitsglaube der Griechen*, vol. 1, 4th ed. (Tübingen: J. C. B. Mohr, 1907), 241.

74. Afanas'ev No. 102; H102.

75. Afanas'ev No. 137; H137.

76. Güntert, *Kalypso*, 74.

77. Ibid.

78. Zelenin 1915: No. 11.

79. Afanas'ev Nos. 249, 250; H249, 250.

80. Zelenin 1915: No. 11.

81. Güntert, *Kalypso*, 75.

82. A *Drude* is a malevolent nocturnal Bavarian/Tyrolean spirit; its mark is the pentagram (translators' note).

83. Aleksandr A. Potebnia, "O mificheskom znachenii nekotorykh obriadov i poverii. II. Baba-Iaga," *Chteniia v imperatorskom obshchestve istorii i drevnostei rossiiskikh pri Moskovskom universitete*, no. 2 (1865): 85–232. Potebnia connects the Russian word *blindness (slepota)* etymologically to the root *lep*, which in Slavic languages has the meaning "pretty." According to Max Vasmer, however, these words are not in fact related. See Max Vasmer, *Russisches Etymologische Wörterbuch* (Heidelberg: Carl Winter, 1953) (translators' note).

84. The name Zhikhar originally referred to a small, naughty house spirit or house dweller. It comes from the same root as the Russian *zhit'*, "to live." In the tale in question, Zhikhar is a tiny creature (translators' note).

85. Afanas'ev No. 106; H106.

86. Khudiakov 1862: No. 52.

87. "The One-Eyed Evil," Afanas'ev No. 302; H302.

88. Hans Vordemfelde, "Die Hexe im deutschen Volksmärchen," in *Festschrift Eugen Mogk zum 70. Geburtstag* (Halle an der Saale: Verlag von Max Niemeyer, 1924), 558–74.

89. George A. Dorsey and Alfred L. Kroeber, *Traditions of the Arapaho. Collected under the Auspices of the Field Columbian Museum and of the American Museum of Natural History*, Anthropological Series, vol. 5 (Chicago: Field Columbian Museum, 1903), 301.

90. Boas, *Indianische Sagen*, 55.

91. See Afanas'ev No. 137; H137; Zelenin 1915: No. 100.

92. Frobenius, *Die Masken und Geheimbünde Afrikas*, Abhandlungen der Kaiserlichen Leopoldinisch-Carolinischen Deutschen Akademie der Naturforscher, vol. 74, no. 1 (Halle: Druck von E. Karras, 1898), 62.

93. Nevermann, *Masken und Geheimbunde*, 26.

94. Afanas'ev No. 303.

95. Afanas'ev No. 93; H93.

96. Snegirev 1937: No. 21.

97. Onchukov 1908: No. 178. The ridge in a garden or a pole for hanging towels and so on (translators' note).

98. Smirnov 1917: No. 150.

99. Onchukov 1908: No. 8. Elisions in the source (translators' note).

100. Onchukov 1908: No. 3.

101. Afanas'ev No. 157; H157.

102. Afanas'ev No. 212; H212.

103. Afanas'ev No. 272; H385.

104. Afanas'ev No. 565; H565.

105. Smirnov 1917: No. 304.

106. Fridtjof Nansen, *Eskimoleben* (Berlin: Heinrich Meyer, 1903), 220–25.

107. Popov, *Dolganskii fol'klor*, 137.

108. Zelenin 1936: No. 206.

109. Dorsey and Kroeber, *Traditions of the Arapaho*, 287.

110. Boas, *Indianische Sagen*, 111.

111. Onchukov 1908: No. 178.

112. Afanas'ev No. 137; H137.

113. Smirnov 1917: No. 150.

114. Khudiakov 1862: No. 103.

115. Breasted, *Development of Religion and Thought*, 117.

116. Afanas'ev No. 174; H174.

117. Karnaukhova 1934: No. 46. The mare's name, Zolotitsa, derives from the Russian *zoloto*, or gold, suggesting Golden Mare (translators' note).

118. An old Slavic stringed instrument (translators' note).

119. Afanas'ev No. 216; H216.

120. Smirnov 1917: No. 310.

121. Afanas'ev No. 216, notes, var. 3.

122. Afanas'ev No. 216, var. 2.

123. Afanas'ev No. 131; H131.

124. Popov, *Dolganskii fol'klor*, 144–45.

125. Gayton, "Orpheus Myth," 268.

126. Peter Jensen, *Das Gilgamesch-Epos in der Weltliteratur* (Strasbourg: Karl J. Trübner, 1906), 46.

127. Gressmann, *Altorientalische Texte*, 56.

128. Samter, *Geburt, Hochzeit, Tod*, 132.

129. Webster, *Primitive Secret Societies*, 102.

130. Ibid., 21.

131. Afanas'ev No. 112; H112; RFT 389.

132. Afanas'ev No. 280; H280.

133. Smirnov 1917: No. 233.

134. Zelenin 1915: No. 122.

135. *Zhivaia Starina*, 249.

136. Afanas'ev No. 209; H209.

137. Smirnov 1917: No. 85.

138. Afanas'ev No. 193; H193.

139. Korguev 1939. No. 19.

140. Afanas'ev No. 102; H102.

141. Afanas'ev No. 95; H95.

142. Afanas'ev No. 96; H96; RFT 366.

143. Frobenius, *Die Masken*, 119.

144. Webster, *Primitive Secret Societies*, 103.

145. Ibid., 168.

146. Ibid., 187, 178.

147. Rohde, *Psyche*, 410; on intimidation of children, see Albrecht Dieterich, *Mutter Erde: Ein versuch über volksreligion*, 3rd ed. (Leipzig: Teubner, 1925), 48.

148. Parkinson, *Dreißig Jahre in der Südsee*, 599.

149. Schurtz, *Altersklassen und Männerbünde*, 384, 371.

150. *Zhivaia Starina*, 247.

151. Baumgartner, "Jephtas Gelübde Jud. 11, 30–40," 240–49.

152. Sadovnikov 1884: No. 99.

153. Ibid., No. 11.

154. Zelenin 1915: No. 118.

155. Zelenin 1914: No. 24.

156. Smirnov 1917: No. 73.

157. Ibid., No. 221.

158. Afanas'ev No. 249; H249.

159. Paul Kretschmer, "Das Märchen von Blaubart," in *Mitteilungen der Antropologischen Gesellschaft in Wien*, ed. Wilhelm Hein, vol. 31 (Wien: Selestverlag der *gesellschaft*, 1909), 62–112.

160. Zelenin 1915: No. 30.

161. Webster, *Primitive Secret Societies*, 33.

162. Ibid., 26; Schurtz, *Altersklassen und Männerbünde*, 97.

163. Webster, *Primitive Secret Societies*, 185.

164. Schurtz, *Altersklassen und Männerbünde*, 98.

165. The name Usynia derives from the Russian word for mustache and is therefore sometimes rendered in English translations as Mustaches (translators' note).

166. Afanas'ev No. 141; H141.

167. Afanas'ev No. 139; H139.

168. Zelenin 1914: No. 22.

169. Loeb, *Tribal Initiations*, 253.

170. Schurtz, *Altersklassen und Männerbünde*, 385.

171. Frobenius, *Die Masken*, 126.

172. Schurtz, *Alterklassen und Männerbünde*, 107.

173. Zelenin 1936: 314.

174. *Zhivaia Starina*, 380.

175. Onchukov 1908: No. 45.

176. Zelenin 1915: No. (a) 1.

177. Webster, *Primitive Secret Societies*, 185.

178. Zelenin 1915: No. 11.

179. Smirnov 1917: No. 250.

180. Ibid., No. 217.

181. Zelenin 1914: No. 13.

182. Smirnov 1917, No. 344.

183. Ibid., No. 127.

184. Khudiakov 1862: No. 58.

185. Ludwig Radermacher, *Das Jenseits im Mythos der Hellenen* (Bonn. A. Marcus and E. Weber, 1903), 139.

186. Afanas'ev No. 344; H344.

187. Zelenin 1915: No. 72.

188. *Zhivaia Starina*, 446; Lur'e, "Dom v lesu," 179.

189. Khudiakov 1862: No. 41.

190. Smirnov 1917: No. 243.

191. Loeb, *Tribal Initiations*, 262; Boas, *Indianische Sagen*, for instance, 555, 568.

192. Webster, *Primitive Secret Societies*, 38.

193. Schurtz, *Altersklassen und Männerbünde*, 404.

194. Ibid., 434.

195. Webster, *Primitive Secret Societies*, 174.

196. Boas, "Social Organization," 568, 659.

197. Saintyves, *Les contes de Perrault*, 381.

198. Ibid., 380.

199. Schurtz, *Altersklassen und Männerbünde*, 397.

200. Boas, "Social Organization," 491.

201. This quotation is unreferenced in Propp's text (translators' note).

202. N. P. Dyrenkova, "Poluchenie shamanskogo dara po vozreniiam turetskikh plemen," *Sbornik MAE* 9 (1930): 267–91.

203. Ibid., 273.

204. Ibid.

205. Ibid., 274.

206. Salomon Reinach, "La mort d'Orphée," in *Cultes, mythes et religions*, vol. 2 (Paris: Leroux, 1906).

207. A. Jacoby, "Zum Zerstückelungs- und Wiederbelebungswunder der indischen Fakire," *Archiv für Religionswissenschaft* 17 (1914): 465.

208. Grimm 1884, Nos. 178–179.

209. Grimm, No. 46; Grimm 1884, No. 179.

210. Onchukov 1908: No. 45.

211. Ibid.

212. *Zhivaia Starina*, 462.

213. Zelenin 1915: No. 20.

214. Zelenin 1914: No. 2.

215. Smirnov 1917: No. 310.

216. See, for instance, ibid., No. 155.

217. Ibid., No. 270.

218. Ivan I. Tolstoi, "Neudachnoe vrachevanie: antichnaia parallel' k russkoi skazke," *Iazyk i literatura* 8 (1932).

219. Smirnov 1917: No. 142.

220. Baldwin Spencer and Francis Gillen, *The Native Tribes of Central Australia* (London: Macmillan, 1899).

221. Thomas Achelis, *Die Religion der Naturvolker im Umriss* (Berlin: Göschen, 1919), 11.

222. Robert H. Mathews, "Some Initiation Ceremonies of the Aborigines of Victoria," *ZfE* 37, no. 6 (1905): 872–79.

223. Schurtz, *Altersklassen und Männerbünde*, 385.

224. Nevermann, *Masken und Geheimbunde*, 25.

225. Frazer 1922: 315.

226. Smirnov 1917: No. 72.

227. Zelenin 1915: No. 30.

228. Johannes Bolte and Georg Polivka, *Anmerkungen zu den Kinder- und Hausmärchen der Brüder Grimm*, vol. 3 (Leipzig: Dieterich'sche Verlagsbuchhandlung, 1918), 147.

229. Frazer, *Belief in Immortality*, vol. 2, 242.

230. Diane J. Rayor, trans., *The Homeric Hymns: A Translation, with Introduction and Notes* (Berkeley: University of California Press, 2004), 25. Propp references the Russian translation of Vikentii Veresaev in *Gomerovy gimny* (Moscow: Izdatel'stvo 'Nedra,' 1926), 54.

231. Tronskii, "Antichnyi mif i sovremennaia skazka," in *Sergeiu Fedorovichu Ol'denburgu: k piatidesiatiletiiu nauchno-obshchestvennoĭ deiatel'nosti, 1882–1932: sbornik statei* (Leningrad: Izdatel'stvo Akademii Nauk SSSR), 531.

232. In Haney's translation in CFA (v. 2, 319) this tale is called "Clever Learning" (translators' note).

233. Khudiakov 1862: No. 94.

234. Sadovnikov 1884: No. 64.

235. Afanas'ev No. 251; H251.

236. Smirnov 1917: No. 72.

237. Afanas'ev No. 252; H252.

238. Zelenin 1914: No. 57.

239. Afanas'ev No. 253; H253.

240. Khudiakova 1862: No. 19.

241. Ibid.

242. Smirnov 1917: No. 72.

243. Khudiakov 1862: No. 94.

244. Sadovnikov 1884: No. 64.

245. Webster, *Primitive Secret Societies*, 7.

246. Ibid., 50–51.

247. Ibid., 178.

248. Gennep, *Les rites de passage*.

249. Webster, *Primitive Secret Societies*, 183.

250. Schurtz, *Altersklassen und Männerbünde*, 641.

251. Zelenin 1914: No. 43.

252. The Russian phrase used here, "*Sam s lokot'*," is both colorful and mysterious. Literally, "itself elbow-sized," or perhaps "an It the size of an elbow," it suggests something impish and supernatural. Our "goblin" is an approximation (translators' note).

253. Smirnov 1917: No. 4.

254. Afanas'ev No. 199; H199; Jeremiah Curtin, *Myths and Folk-Tales of the Russians, Western Slavs, and Magyars* (London: Sampson Low, Marston, Searle, & Rivington, 1891), 162–63.

255. *Zhivaia Starina*, 269.

256. Zelenin 1915: No. 40.

257. Zelenin 1914: No. 1.

258. Zelenin 1936: No. 237.

259. Webster, *Primitive Secret Societies*, 61.

260. Ibid., 125.

261. Schurtz, *Altersklassen und Männerbünde*, 396.

262. Webster, *Primitive Secret Societies*, 139.
263. Mathews, "Some Initiation Ceremonies."
264. Zelenin 1915: No. 47.
265. Ibid., 32.
266. Sadovnikov 1884: No. 9.
267. Karnaukhova 1934: No. 7.
268. Korguev 1939: No. 7.
269. Ibid., 9.
270. Zelenin 1914: No. 1.
271. Nevermann, *Masken und Geheimbünde*, 74.
272. Dorsey, *Traditions of the Skidi-Pawnee*, 68 (emphasis added).
273. Nevermann, *Masken und Geheimbünde*, 88.
274. Ibid., 88; Parkinson, *Dreißig Jahre in der Südsee*, 578.
275. Nevermann, *Masken und Geheimbunde*, 126, 99.
276. Parkinson, *Dreißig Jahre in der Südsee*, 605.
277. There are many parallels in the system of Johannes Hertel, *Indische Märchen* (Jena: E. Diederichs, 1921), 371, mainly from antiquity. Cf. also Theodor Benfey, *Pantschatantra*, Pt. 1, *Einleitung: Ueber das indische Grundwerk und dessen Ausflüsse, sowie über die Quellen und Verbreitung des Inhalts der Selben* (Leipzig: Braukhaus, 1859) (author's note).
278. Olga M. Freidenberg, *Poetika siuzheta i zhanra: Period antichnoi literatury* (Leningrad: Khudozhestvennaia literatura, 1936), 103.

4. The Big House

1. Khudiakov 1862: No. 12.
2. Sokolov 1915: No. 27.
3. Karnaukhova 1934: No. 47.
4. Zelenin 1914: No. 303.
5. Ibid., No. 1.
6. Afanas'ev No. 211; H211.
7. Afanas'ev No. 199; H199.
8. Afanas'ev No. 185; H185.
9. Schurtz, *Altersklassen und Männerbünde*, 235.
10. On the skulls' details, see Frobenius, *Die Masken*.
11. Afanas'ev No. 222; H222.
12. Nevermann, *Masken und Geheimbünde*, 87.
13. Smirnov 1917: No. 182.
14. Ibid., No. 135.
15. Onchukov 1908: No. 45.
16. Korguev 1939: No. 24.
17. Afanas'ev No. 203; H203.
18. Korguev 1939: No. 12.
19. Afanas'ev No. 214; H214.
20. Sadovnikov 1884: No. 17.
21. *Zhivaia Starina*, 346.
22. Schurtz, *Altersklassen und Männerbünde*, 216.
23. Ibid., 245.
24. Zelenin 1914: No. 2.
25. Onchukov 1908: No. 45.

26. Zelenin 1914: No. 2.

27. Vikent'ev, *Drevneegipetskaia povest' o dvukh brat'iakh*, 38.

28. Parkinson, *Dreißig Jahre in der Südsee*, 576.

29. Smirnov 1917: No. 79.

30. Zelenin 1914: No. 305.

31. Smirnov 1917: No. 229.

32. Afanas'ev No. 203; H203.

33. Sadovnikov 1884: No. 17; on robbers, see below.

34. Afanas'ev No. 211, variant.

35. Ivan Zarubin, ed., *Beludzhskie skazki* (Leningrad: Nauka, 1932), 40.

36. Snegirev 1937: No. 92.

37. Zelenin 1914: No. 305.

38. Webster, *Primitive Secret Societies*, 81.

39. Ibid., 157.

40. Loeb, *Tribal Initiations*, 251.

41. Zelenin 1914: No. 61.

42. Frazer, *Belief in Immortality*, vol. 2, 22.

43. Afanas'ev No. 200; H200.

44. *Zhivaia Starina*, 359.

45. Schurtz, *Altersklassen und Männerbünde*, 321.

46. Afanas'ev No. 212; H212.

47. Schurtz, *Altersklassen und Männerbünde*, 107, 379, 425.

48. Zelenin 1914: No. 17.

49. Ibid., No. 71.

50. Zelenin 1915: No. 45.

51. Khudiakov 1862: No. 80.

52. Schurtz, *Altersklassen und Männerbünde*, 126, 130.

53. Zelenin 1915: No. 52.

54. Schurtz, *Altersklassen und Männerbünde*, 379.

55. Ibid., 169.

56. Lur'e, "Dom v lesu," 188; he also offers other examples, particularly from antiquity.

57. Afanas'ev No. 200; H200.

58. Afanas'ev No. 198; H198.

59. Grimm, No. 9; Lur'e, "Dom v lesu," 168.

60. Schurtz, *Altersklassen und Männerbünde*, 87.

61. Webster, *Primitive Secret Societies*, 169.

62. Schurtz, *Altersklassen und Männerbünde*, 296.

63. Zelenin 1914: No. 20.

64. Sadovnikov 1884: No. 107.

65. James G. Frazer, *The Belief in Immortality*, vol. 3 (London: Macmillan, 1924), 217.

66. Afanas'ev No. 210; H210.

67. Afanas'ev No. 211; H211.

68. Zelenin 1915: No. 116.

69. Afanas'ev No. 344.

70. Boris Iakovlevich Vladimirtsov, trans., intro., commentary, *Volshebnyi mertvets: Mongol'sko-oiratskie skazki* (Petrograd: Vsemirnaia literatura, 1923), 31.

71. Zelenin 1914: No. 23.

72. Webster, *Primitive Secret Societies*, 169.

73. Frazer, *Belief in Immortality*, vol. 3, 218.

74. Khudiakov 1862: No. 34.

75. Lur'e, "Dom v lesu."

76. Schurtz, *Altersklassen und Männerbünde*, 134.

77. Ibid., 91.

78. Zelenin 1914: No. 13.

79. Onchukov 1908: No. 85.

80. Afanas'ev No. 178; H178.

81. Frazer, *Belief in Immortality*, vol. 3, 161.

82. Schurtz, *Altersklassen und Männerbünde*, 404.

83. Ibid., 436; see also Webster, *Primitive Secret Societies*, e.g., 173.

84. Frobenius, *Die Masken*, 50.

85. Sadovnikov 1884: No. 17.

86. *Zhivaia Starina*, 339.

87. Smirnov 1917: No. 56.

88. Zelenin 1914: No. 8.

89. Onchukov 1908: No. 178, the "Cupid and Psyche" type.

90. Bolte and Polivka, *Anmerkungen*, vol. II [1932], 88, 231.

91. Afanas'ev No. 276; H276.

92. Cf., Afanas'ev No. 209; H209.

93. Grimm, No. 88.

94. Zelenin 1915: No. 13.

95. Khudiakov 1862: No. 63.

96. Smirnov 1917: No. 126.

97. Webster, *Primitive Secret Societies*, 78.

98. Bolte and Polivka, *Anmerkungen*, vol. I [1932], 46, 400.

99. Afanas'ev No. 219; H219.

100. Korguev 1939: No. 6.

101. Antti Aarne, *Die magische Flucht: Eine Märchenstudie* (Helsinki: Suomalainen tiede akatemia, Academia scientiarum fennica, 1930), 155.

102. Karnaukhova 1934: No. 1.

103. Evgenii G. Kagarov, "Sostav i proiskhozhdenie svadebnoi obriadnosti," *Sb. MAE* 8, no. 29 (1929): 182–83.

104. Zelenin 1915: No. 118.

105. Smirnov 1917: No. 97.

106. Zelenin 1914: No. 12.

107. Korguev 1939: No. 6.

108. Afanas'ev No. 235; H235.

109. Afanas'ev No. 278; H278.

110. Grimm, No. 101.

111. Grimm, No. 100.

112. Grimm, No. 65.

113. Korguev 1939: No. 10.

114. Schurtz, *Altersklassen und Männerbünde*, 383, 385; Robert H. Codrington, *The Melanesians: Studies in their Anthropology and Folklore* (Oxford: Clarendon, 1891), e.g., 81, 87.

115. Codrington, *Melanesians*, 82.

116. Frobenius, *Die Masken*, 45.

117. Codrington, *Melanesians*, 87.

118. Smirnov 1917: No. 126.

119. Webster, *Primitive Secret Societies*, 79.
120. Khudiakov 1862: No. 83.
121. Grimm No. 46.
122. Samter, *Geburt, Hochzeit, Tod*, 95.
123. Korguev 1939: No. 10.
124. Zelenin 1914: No. 2.
125. Khudiakov 1862: No. 41.
126. *Zhivaia Starina*, 242.
127. Smirnov 1917: No. 5.
128. Ibid., No. 305.
129. Karnaukhova 1934: No. 47.
130. Khudiakov 1862: No. 1.
131. Zelenin 1914: No. 12.
132. Zelenin 1915: No. 85.
133. Zelenin 1914: No. 2.
134. Afanas'ev No. 295; H295.
135. Karnaukhova 1934: No. 47.
136. Khudiakov 1862: No. 4.
137. Aleksandr K. Borovkov, ed., *Skazki narodov Vostoka* (Moscow: Izd. Akademii Nauk, 1938), 27.
138. Karnaukhova 1934: No. 91.
139. *Zhivaia Starina*, 334.
140. Ibid., 481.
141. Borovkov, *Skazki narodov Vostoka*, 33, 40.
142. Compare the baldness of the Prophet Elijah (IV Kings, the Old Testament of the Bible, II, 23).
143. Nevermann, *Masken und Geheimbünde*, 139.
144. Cf. Parkinson, *Dreißig Jahre in der Südsee*, 658; Loeb, *Tribal Initiations*, 256.
145. Nevermann, *Masken und Geheimbünde*, 160.
146. Frobenius, *Die Masken*, 146.
147. Smirnov 1917: No. 135.
148. Wilhelm Schmidt, "Die geheime Jünglingsweihe der Karesau-lnsulaner (Deutsch-Neuguinea)," *Anthropos* 2, no. 5 (1907): 1029–56; Codrington, *Melanesians*, 71; Nevermann, *Masken und Geheimbünde*, e.g., 18.
149. Ivan Tolstoi, "Vozvrashchenie muzha v 'Odissee' i russkoi skazke," in *Sergeiu Fedorovichu Ol'denburgu: K piatidesiatiletiiu nauch-obshchestvennoi deiatel'nosti. 1882–1932* (Leningrad: Izdatel'stvo Akademii Nauk SSSR, 1934).
150. Ibid., 66.
151. Onchukov 1908: No. 35; Tolstoi, "Vozvrashchenie muzha," 66.
152. Tolstoi, "Vozvrashchenie muzha," 66.
153. Ibid., 516.
154. Frobenius, *Die Masken*, 146.
155. Grimm, No. 9.
156. Zelenin 1914: No. 107.
157. Afanas'ev No. 248; H248.
158. Afanas'ev No. 242; H242.
159. Khudiakov 1862: No. 38.
160. Afanas'ev No. 313; H313.

161. Zelenin 1914: No. 13.

162. Afanas'ev No. 158; H158.

163. Afanas'ev No. 209; H209.

164. Edwin S. Hartland, "The Forbidden Chamber," *Folk-Lore Journal* 3, no. 1 (1885): 193–94.

165. William F. Kirby, "The Forbidden Doors of *The Thousand and One Nights*," *Folk-Lore Journal* 5, no. 2 (1887): 113.

166. Schurtz, *Altersklassen und Männerbünde*, 387.

167. Parkinson, *Dreißig Jahre in der Südsee*, 666.

168. Boas, "Social Organization," 613.

169. Ibid., 573.

170. Ibid., 404.

171. Smirnov 1917: No. 11.

172. Ibid., No. 316.

173. Sokolov 1915: No. 15.

174. Smirnov 1917: No. 344.

175. Zelenin 1915: No. 16.

176. Khudiakov 1862: No. 58.

177. Zelenin 1914: No. 1.

178. Grimm, No. 3.

179. A folk narrative with Christian religious content—for example, tales about the lives of saints (translators' note).

180. Smirnov 1917: No. 28.

181. Grimm, No. 6.

182. Afanas'ev No. 159; H159.

183. Afanas'ev No. 179; H179.

184. Smirnov 1917: No. 306.

185. Zarubin, *Beludzhskie skazki*, 198.

186. Onchukov 1908: No. 45.

187. Ibid.

188. Karl von den Steinen, *Unter den Naturvölkern Zentral-Brasiliens: Reiseschilderung und ergebnisse der zweiten Schingú-expedition, 1887 1888* (Berlin: Reimer, 1894), 434.

189. Genrikh Kunov, *Proiskhozhdenie religii i very v boga* (Moscow: Kommunist, 1919), 115.

190. Frazer, *Belief in Immortality*, vol. 3, 47.

191. Hermann Haeberlin and Erna Günther, "Ethnographische Notizen über die Indianerstämme des Puget-Sundes," *ZfE* 56, no. 1/4 (1924): 59.

192. Frazer, *Fear of the Dead*, 80.

193. Afanas'ev No. 216; H216.

194. Afanas'ev No. 104; H104.

195. Afanas'ev No. 290; H290.

196. Henry Adams Bellows, *The Poetic Edda. Translated from the Icelandic with an Introduction and Notes* (Princeton, NJ: Princeton University Press, 1936), 235.

197. Arsenii Konstaninovich Khazhba, ed. and trans., *Abkhazskie skazki* (Sukhumi: Alashara, 1935), 151.

198. Afanas'ev No. 176; H176.

199. Smirnov 1917: No. 86.

200. The Russian "Sivko-Burko," which is sometimes spelled Sivka-Burka, signifies "the gray-brown one" (translators' note).

201. Smirnov 1917: No. 9.

202. Sadovnikov 1884: No. 2.

203. Ruslan is the hero of Alexander Pushkin's 1820 narrative poem *Ruslan and Liudmila* (translators' note).

204. Smirnov 1917: No. 220.

205. Chernetsov, *Vogul'skie skazki*, 87.

206. Bellows, *The Poetic Edda*, vol. I, Lays of the gods, Voluspo, stanzas 46–47 [Sofiia A. Sviridenko, trans., intro., and commentary, *Edda: Skandinavskii epos* (Moscow: M. i S. Sabashnikovy, 1917), 106.]

207. Friedrich Burger, *Unter den Kannibalen der Südsee* (Dresden: Deutsche Buchwerkstätten, 1923), 39.

208. Frobenius, *Die Weltanschauung*, 208.

209. Khudiakov 1862: No. 13.

210. Charles G. Seligman and Brenda Z. Zeligman, *The Veddas* (Cambridge: University Press, 1911), 131.

211. Dieterich, *Mutter Erde*.

212. Rohde, *Psyche*, 195–196.

213. Ibid., 184.

214. Afanas'ev No. 157; H157.

215. Afanas'ev No. 170; H170.

216. Afanas'ev No. 165; H165.

217. Bernhard Ankermann, "Die Verbreitung und Formen des Totemismus in Afrika," *Zeitschrift für Ethnologie* 47, no. 2/3 (1915): 142.

218. Ibid.

219. Walter Krickeberg, *Märchen der Azteken und Inkaperuaner Maya und Muisca* (Jena: Diederichs, 1928), 195.

220. Snegirev 1937: No. 211.

221. Afanas'ev No. 100; H100.

222. *Zhivaia starina*, 475.

223. Onchukov 1908: No. 16.

224. Afanas'ev No. 187; H187.

225. Zelenin 1936: No. 233.

226. Ibid., No. 235.

227. Emmanuel Cosquin, *Études folkloriques, recherches sur les migrations des contes populaires et leur point de départ* (Paris: E. Champion, 1922), 25; Saintyves, *Les contes de Perrault*, 31.

228. Smirnov 1917: 159.

229. Afanas'ev No. 123; H123.

230. Onchukov 1908: No. 150.

231. Khudiakov 1862: No. 44.

232. Ibid., No. 115.

233. Afanas'ev No. 125; H125.

234. Afanas'ev No. 123; H123.

235. Smirnov 1917: No. 303.

236. Kharuzin, *Etnografiia*, 76–77, 151.

237. Bolte and Polivka, *Anmerkungen*, vol. III [1932], 106.

238. Ivan I. Tolstoi, "Sviazannyi i osvobozhdennyi silen," in *Pamiati akademika N. Ia. Marra (1864–1934)* (Moscow: Akademii nauk, 1938).

239. Ivan I. Tolstoi, *Stat'i o fol'klore* (Moscow: Nauka, 1966), 99.

240. Aleksandr N. Veselovskii, *Slavianskie skazaniia o Solomone i Kitovrase*, vol. 8 of *Sobranie sochinenii* (Petrograd: Akademii nauk SSSR, 1921), 143.

241. Afanas'ev No. 124, variant 1.
242. Tolstoi, "Sviazannyi i osvobozhdennyi silen," 441.
243. Karnaukhova 1934: No. 91.
244. We believe the author in question is Irina Mikhailovna Kolesnitskaia. According to the editors of the 1986 edition of *Historical Roots of the Wondertale*, the book in question was never published (translators' note).
245. Karnaukhova 1934: No. 91.
246. Afanas'ev No. 124; H124.
247. Khudiakov 1862: 115.
248. Smirnov 1917: No. 159.
249. Ibid., No. 181.
250. Afanas'ev No. 124, variant 1.
251. Afanas'ev No. 124, variant 2.
252. Jan P. B. Josselin de Jong, "Religionen der Naturvolker Indonesiens," *Archiv für Religionswissenschaft* 30, no. 3/4 (1933): 373.
253. Frazer, *Fear of the Dead*, 83.
254. Ibid., 85.
255. Afanas'ev No. 123; H123.
256. Afanas'ev No. 158; H158.
257. Afanas'ev No. 199; H199.
258. Afanas'ev No. 144; H144.
259. Afanas'ev No. 115; H115.
260. Afanas'ev No. 189; H189.

5. Magic Gifts

1. Afanas'ev No. 209; H209.
2. Afanas'ev No. 219; H219.
3. Korguev 1939: No. 6.
4. Ibid., No. 220.
5. Zelenin 1936: No. 183.
6. Shternberg, *Pervobytnaia religiia*, 119.
7. Afanas'ev No. 221; H221.
8. Afanas'ev No. 221; H221.
9. Afanas'ev No. 220; H220.
10. Afanas'ev No. 219; H219.
11. Afanas'ev No. 224; H224.
12. The Gilyak language and people are now known as Nivkh (translators' note).
13. Ostiak is a name formerly used to refer to the Khanty, Ket, and Selkup indigenous peoples of Siberia (translators' note).
14. Shternberg, *Pervobytnaia religiia*, 121.
15. Nikolai Ia. Marr, "Sredstva peredvizheniia, orudiia samozashchity i proizvodstva v doistorii," in *Izbrannye raboty*, vol. 3 (Moscow: Gosudarstvennoe sotsial'no-ekonomicheskoe izdatel'stvo, 1934), 125; Marr, "'Loshad''/'ptitsa' totem urarto-etrusskogo plemeni, i eshche dva etapa v ego migratsii," in *Iafeticheskii sbornik*, vol. 1 (Petrograd: Kolos, 1922), 133.
16. Gertrud Hermes, "Der Zug des gezähmten Pferdes durch Europa," *Anthropos* 32, no. 1/2 (1937): 105–46.
17. Dorsey, *Traditions of the Skidi-Pawnee*, 139.
18. Afanas'ev No. 160; H160.

19. Sokolov 1915: No. 112.

20. Afanas'ev No. 185; H185.

21. Smirnov 1917: No. 341.

22. Anuchin "Sani, lad'ia i koni"; Julius von Negelein, "Das Pferd im See-lenglauben und Totenkult," *Zeitschrift des Vereins für Volkskunde* (ZVV: Berlin) 11 (1901): 406–20; Negelein, "Das Pferd in der Volksmedizin"; Negelein, *Das Pferd im arischen Altertum*, Teutonia: Arbeiten zur ger-manischen Philologie, vol. 2 (Königsberg: Gräfe & Unzer, 1903); Paul Sten-gel, "Aides klytopolos," *Archiv für Religionswissenschaft* 8 (1905): 203–13; Ludolf Malten, "Das Pferd im Totenglauben," *Jahrbuch des Kaiserlich deutschen archäologischen Instituts*, vol. 29 (Berlin: Deutsches Archäolo-gisches Institut, 1914); Ludwig Radermacher, *Hippolytos und Thekla: Stu-dien zur Geschichte von Legende und Kultus*, Kaiserliche Akademie der Wissenschaften in Wien, Philosophisch-historische Klasse, Sitzungsberichte 182.3 (Vienna: Alfred Hölder, 1916); M. Oldfield Howey, *The Horse in Magic and Myth* (London: W. Rider, 1923); Mikhail G. Khudiakov, "Kul't konia v Prikam'i," in *Iz istorii dokapitalisticheskikh formatsii: sb. statei k 45-letiiu nauch. deiatel'nosti N. Ia. Marra*, ed. S. N. Bykovskii et al. Izvestiia Gosudarstvennoi akademii istorii material'noi kul'tury, no. 100 (Moscow/Leningrad: Akademii nauk, 1933).

23. Fiustel' de-Kulanzh, *Grazhdanskaia obshchina drevnego mira* (St. Pe-tersburg: Tip. B. M. Vol'fa, 1906). The reference is to the Russian translation by "A. M." of the 1864 work *La Cité antique* by Numa Denis Fustel de Cou-langes (translators' note).

24. Afanas'ev No. 179; H179.

25. Negelein, "Das Pferd im Seelenglauben und Totenkult," 373.

26. Wilhelm Wundt, *Mif i religiia* (St. Petersburg: Brokgauz and Efron, 1912), 111.

27. Rohde, *Psyche*, 241.

28. Negelein, "Das Pferd im Seelenglauben und Totenkult," 378.

29. Rohde, *Psyche*, 241.

30. Afanas'ev Nos. 182, 184, 170; H182, 184, 170.

31. Cf., Ibid.

32. Afanas'ev No. 171; H171.

33. Afanas'ev No. 175; H175.

34. Sokolov 1915: No. 112.

35. Afanas'ev No. 137; H137.

36. Afanas'ev No. 156; H156.

37. A. D. Soimonov, ed., *Pesni i skazki na Onezhskom zavode* (Petrodo-vodsk: Karel'skii nauchno-issledovatel'skii institut kul'tury, 1937), 143.

38. Afanas'ev No. 138; H138.

39. Smirnov 1917: No. 298.

40. Iu. A. Iavorskii, *Pamiatniki Galitsko-russkoi narodnoi slovesnosti*, vyp. 1, no. 27 (Kiev: Zapiski IRGO, 1915), 312; black, red, and gray—Afanas'ev No. 184; H184.

41. Afanas'ev No. 139; H139.

42. Julius von Negelein, "Die Seele als Vogel," *Globus* 79 (1901): 357–61, 381–84.

43. Smirnov 1917: No. 184.

44. Smirnov 1917: No. 181.

45. Smirnov 1917: No. 298.

46. Khudiakov 1862: No. 36.

47. Zelenin 1936: No. 218.

48. Khudiakov 1890: No. 142.

49. Ibid., No. 137.

50. Stengel, "Aides klytopolos," 212.

51. Malten, "Das Pferd im Totenglauben," 188.

52. Ibid., 211.

53. Khudiakov 1890: No. 97.

54. Zelenin 1936: No. 257.

55. Frobenius, *Die Weltanschauung*, 116.

56. Hermann Oldenberg, *Die Religion des Veda* (Berlin: W. Hertz, 1894), 77.

57. *Rigveda*, Book VII, Hymn I [07-001], 1 (https://en.wikisource.org/wiki/The_Hymns_of_the_Rigveda/Book_7/Hymn_1). Propp employed Alfred Ludwig's German-language translation of the *Rigveda* published in Prague from 1876 to 1883. Here and throughout we quote the 1896 *Rigveda* translation of Ralph T. H. Griffith available through Wikisource. The entire text is also available at https://sacred-texts.com/hin/rigveda/index.htm (translators' note).

58. Dmitrii N. Ovsianiko-Kulikovskii, *K istorii kul'ta ognia u indusov v epokhu ved* (Odessa: n. p., 1887).

59. Shternberg, *Pervobytnaia religiia*, 46.

60. Nansen, *Eskimoleben*, 252.

61. Frobenius, *Die Weltanschauung*, 235.

62. R. Holland, "Zur Typik der Himmelfahrt," *Archiv für Religionswissenschaft* 23, no. 3/4 (1925): 207–20.

63. Andrei A. Popov, "Materialy po shamanstvu: Kul't bogini Aisyt u iakutov," in *Kul'tura i pis'mennost' Vostoka*, vol. 3 (Baku: Izdanie VTsK NTA, 1928), 130.

64. Zelenin 1936: No. 299. *Ulus* is a district, place, or administrative unit (translators' note).

65. The spirit of the ancestors of a family or clan in the shamanism of Mongolia; a common term in Turkish and Mongol mythologies (translators' note).

66. Khudiakov 1890: No. 142.

67. *Rigveda* Book X, Hymn LXVIII [10-068], 11 (https://en.wikisource.org/wiki/The_Hymns_of_the_Rigveda/Book_10/Hymn_68).

68. *Rigveda* Book II, Hymn II, 2 (https://en.wikisource.org/wiki/The_Hymns_of_the_Rigveda/Book_2/Hymn_2).

69. Afanas'ev No. 159; H159. As she is walking in the woods toward the hut of Baba Yaga, Vasilisa sees three riders in succession: first a white rider on a white horse, then a red rider on a red horse, and finally a black rider on a black horse. Later Baba Yaga explains to her that these are the three parts of the day: morning, midday and evening/night. Baba Yaga in fact calls them "my white day," "my red/beautiful sun," and "my black night." The sun was considered something diffferent from the lightening of the sky, which is understandable at a high latitude, as the summer sun dips below the horizon and is not visible; this is still a "white night." There is only one version of "Vasilisa the Beautfiul" (translators' note).

70. Budge, *Book of the Dead* [XVII], 104.

71. Afanas'ev No. 105; H105.

72. Afanas'ev No. 157; H157.

73. Malten, "Das Pferd im Totenglauben," 179.

74. Ibid.

75. Ibid., 179, 181, 185.

76. Propp's reference here (Book V, Hymn LXV, verse 2) does not appear to correspond to the correct passage of the *Rigveda*. There is, however, a similar passage at I, LXV, 2, which Griffith renders as "The waters feed with praise the growing Babe" (translators' note).

77. *Rigveda*, Book II, Hymn I (02-001), 1 (https://en.wikisource.org/wiki/The_Hymns_of_the_Rigveda/Book_2/Hymn_1).

78. Ibid., 3. The Russian version quoted by Propp differs slightly, reading literally, "He is enabled by the waters in lakes" (translators' note).

79. Khudiakov 1862: No. 33.

80. Grimm 1822: No. 71.

81. Smirnov 1917: No. 183.

82. Afanas'ev No. 137; H137.

83. Boas 1895: No. 5.

84. Smirnov 1917: No. 183.

85. Afanas'ev No. 141; H141.

86. Afanas'ev No. 142; H142.

87. Boas 1895: No. 23.

88. Curt N. Unkel, "Sagen der Tembé-Indianer," *ZfE* 47 (1915): 286.

89. Boas 1895: No. 2.

90. Afanas'ev No. 83; H83.

91. Zelenin 1915: No. 45.

92. Afanas'ev No. 93; H93.

93. Afanas'ev No. 93; H93.

94. Khudiakov 1862: No. 33.

95. Afanas'ev No. 142; H142.

96. The Russian makes Propp's supposition regarding a false etymology clear: in this tale we have Dugynia, or "Bow Man," rather than Dubynia, or "Oak Man" (translators' note).

97. Afanas'ev No. 144; H144.

98. Webster, *Primitive Secret Societies*, 125.

99. Ibid., 151; Boas 1895: No. 393.

100. Webster, *Primitive Secret Societies*, 183.

101. Ibid., 61.

102. Ibid., 151.

103. Ibid., 152.

104. Ibid., 150.

105. Boas 1895: No. 293.

106. In English in the source text (translators' note).

107. The French missionary and ethnographer Henri Trilles (1866–1949) traveled widely in Gabon and French Congo and compiled tales, legends, and ethnographic texts on the Fang (translators' note).

108. Ankermann, "Die Verbreitung und Formen," 139.

109. Haeberlin and Günther, "Ethnographische Notizen."

110. Shternberg, *Pervobytnaia religiia*, 141.

111. Alfred L. Kroeber, *The Religion of the Indians of California*, vol. 4, no. 6 (Berkeley: University of California Publications in American Archaeology and Ethnology, 1907), 327–28.

112. Konrad Preuss, "Religionen der Naturvölker Amerikas, 1906–1909," *Archiv für Religionswissenschaft* 14, nos. 1–2 (1911): 235.

113. Andrei V. Anokhin, *Materialy po shamanstvu u altaitsev. Sbornik muzeia antropologii i etnografii pri Rossiiskoi Akademii Nauk (Sb. MAE)* 4, no. 2. (1924): 29.

114. Afanas'ev No. 212; H212.

115. Anokhin, *Materialy po shamanstvu u altaitsev*, 13.

116. Alfred Jeremias, *Hölle und Paradies bei den Babyloniern* (Leipzig: J. C. Hinrichs, 1903), 22.

117. Afanas'ev No. 186; H186.

118. Afanas'ev No. 187; H187.

119. Afanas'ev No. 197; H197.

120. Afanas'ev No. 189; H189.

121. Afanas'ev No. 193; H193.

122. Afanas'ev No. 212; H212.

123. Afanas'ev Nos. 156, 190, 191; H156, 190, 191.

124. Preuss, "Religionen der Naturvölker Amerikas," 249.

125. Zelenin 1915: No. 129.

126. *Zhivaia Starina*, 265; variants: he receives a crow's bone, a lion's claw, a fish scale, and so on.

127. Afanas'ev No. 235; H235.

128. Kroeber, Alfred L. *Gros Ventre Myths and Tales*. Anthropological Papers of the American Museum of Natural History. Vol. 1, pt. 3, 75. New York: Trustees, 1907.

129. Zelenin 1929: No. 56.

130. James G. Frazer, *The Golden Bough*, vol. 11, *Balder the Beautiful, the Fire Festivals of Europe and the Doctrine of the External Soul*, vol. 2 (London: MacMillan, 1913), 268, https://archive.org/details/goldenboughstudy11fraz.

131. Friedrich Engels, "Letter to Conrad Schmidt," October 27, 1890, quoted by Propp in Marx and Engels, *Sochineniia*, vol. 37, 419. We reference the English translation of Donna Torr, available at https://www.marxists.org/archive/marx/works/1890/letters/90_10_27.htm (translators' note).

132. Nikolai N. Kharuzin, *Russkie lopari: ocherki proshlogo i sovremennogo byta* (Moscow: Tovarishchestvo Skoropechatnii A. A. Levinson, 1890), 137.

133. Shternberg, *Pervobytnaia religiia*, 268.

134. Theodor Koch-Grünberg, *Mythen und Legenden der Taulipang- und Arekuna-Indianer*, Vol. 2 of *Vom Roroima zum Orinoco: Ergebnisse einer Reise in Nordbrasilien und Venezuela in den Jahren 1911–1913* (Berlin: Dietrich Reimer, 1924), 125.

135. Ibid., 92.

136. Afanas'ev No. 212; H212.

137. Afanas'ev No. 165; H165.

138. "Emelia the Simpleton": The Magic pike gives Emelia (the hero) a magic spell ("By the pike's command, by my will") with which he orders buckets of water to go home on their own (translators' note).

139. Afanas'ev No. 185; H185.

140. Frobenius, *Die Weltanschauung*, 326.

141. V. N. Dobrovol'skii, *Smolenskii etnograficheskii sbornik*, Zapiski Imperatorskogo Russkogo geograficheskogo obshchestva po otdeleniiu

etnografii, vol. 20 (St. Petersburg: Russkoe geografixheskoe obshchestvo, 1891), 557.

142. Grimm 1822: No. 116.

143. No explicit reference provided (translators' note).

144. Afanas'ev No. 207; H207.

145. Afanas'ev No. 206.

146. Onchukov 1908: No. 3.

147. Afanas'ev No. 168.

148. Georg Kaibel, ed., *Inscriptiones graecae Siciliae et Italiae: additis graecis Galliae, Hispaniae, Britanniae, Germaniae inscriptionibus* (Berlin: Georg Reimer, 1890), 158; Albrecht Dieterich, *Nekyia: Beiträge zur Erklärung der neuentdeckten Petrusapokalypse* (Leipzig: Teubner, 1893), 86.

149. Jeremias, *Hölle und Paradies*, 32.

150. Afanas'ev No. 137.

151. Afanas'ev No. 104; H104.

152. Smirnov 1917: No. 214.

153. Karnaukhova 1934: No. 151.

154. Afanas'ev No. 114; H114.

155. Zelenin 1936: No. 137.

156. Carl Meinhof, *Die Religionen der Afrikaner in ihrem Zusammenhang mit dem Wirtschaftsleben*, Institutet for sammenlignende kulturforskning, Serie A: Forelesninger, vol. 7 (Oslo: Institutet for sammenlignende kulturforskning, 1926), 63.

157. Frazer, *Golden Bough*, vol. 3, pt. 2, 53–54.

158. Kharuzin, *Etnografiia*, 234.

159. Iurii P. Frantsov, "Drevneegipetskie skazki o verkhovnykh zhretsakh," *Sovetskii fol'klor*, no. 2/3 (1935): 171–72.

160. Alfred Wiedemann, *Die Toten und ihre Reiche im Glauben der alten Ägypter*, 2nd ed. (Leipzig: J. C. Hinrichs, 1902).

6. Crossing Over

1. Smirnov 1917: No. 298.

2. Khudiakov 1862: No. 62.

3. Afanas'ev No. 136; H136.

4. Afanas'ev No. 259; H259.

5. Afanas'ev No. 209; H209.

6. Afanas'ev No. 243; H243.

7. Smirnov 1917: No. 49.

8. Afanas'ev No. 189; H189.

9. Webster, *Primitive Secret Societies*, 183.

10. Shternberg, *Pervobytnaia religiia*, 477.

11. Josef Kohler, *Der Ursprung der Melusinensage: Eine ethnologische Untersuchung* (Leipzig: E. Pfeiffer, 1895), 39.

12. Nansen, *Eskimoleben*, 216.

13. Knud Rasmussen, *Grönlandsagen* (Berlin: Gyldendalscher, 1922), 254.

14. Frobenius, *Die Weltanschauung* , 27, 153; Boas 1895: No. 38.

15. Frobenius, *Die Weltanschauung*, 30.

16. Johannes Raum, "Die Religion der Landschaft Moschi am Kalimandjaro," *Archiv für Religionswissenschaft* 14 (1911): 184.

17. Fülleborn, *Deutsche-Ost-Afrika*, 184, 148.

18. Johannes Hertel, *Die arische Feuerlehre* (Leipzig: Haessel, 1925), 18.

19. *Rigveda*, Book X, Hymn XVI [10–016]: 7 (https://en.wikisource.org/wiki/The_Hymns_of_the_Rigveda/Book_10/Hymn_16). Propp's Russian version, which appears to be his own translation of Alfred Ludwig's 1883 German translation, is more explicit: «Против Агни обложи себя оболочкой из частей коровы», or, "Cover yourself with a coat of cow parts against Agni" (translators' note).

20. E. A. Wallis Budge, *The Book of the Dead*, vol. 1 (London: Trustees of the British Museum, 1922), xxi.

21. Budge, *Book of Opening the Mouth*, 31

22. Ibid., 31–32.

23. Alexandre Moret [Russian transliteration: More Aleksandr], *Tsari i bogi Egipta* [*Kings and Gods of Egypt*], trans. E. Gregorovich (Moscow: M. i S. Sabashnikovy, 1914), 9.

24. Ibid., 110.

25. Stengel, "Aides klytopolos," 208.

26. Afanas'ev No. 224; H224.

27. Afanas'ev No. 220; H220.

28. Wundt, *Mif i religiia*, 109.

29. Von Negelein, "Die Seele als Vogel"; Georg Weicker, *Der Seelenvogel in der alten Litteratur und Kunst: Eine mythologisch-archäologische Untersuchung* (Leipzig: Teubner, 1900).

30. Wundt, *Mif i religiia*, 108.

31. Frobenius, *Die Weltanschauung*.

32. Paul Hambruch, *Südseemärchen aus Australien, Neu-Guinea, Fidji, Karolinen, Samoa, Tonga, Hawaii, Neu-Seeland* (Jena: E. Diederichs, 1912), 168.

33. Frobenius, *Die Weltanschauung*, 26.

34. Moret, *Tsari i bogi Egipta*, 134.

35. Budge, *Book of the Dead* [LXXVII], 249.

36. Jensen, *Das Gilgamesch-Epos in der Weltliteratur*, 10.

37. Weicker, *Der Seelenvogel in der alten Litteratur und Kunst*, 23.

38. Holland, "Zur Typik der Himmelfahrt," 210.

39. Weicker, *Der Seelenvogel in der alten Litteratur und Kunst*, 23.

40. Holland, "Zur Typik der Himmelfahrt," 213.

41. Afanas'ev No. 144; H144.

42. Afanas'ev No. 138; H138.

43. Otto Waser, "Charon," *Archiv für Religionswissenschaft* 1 (1898): 152–82.

44. Frazer, *Belief in Immortality*, vol. 2, 20.

45. Frobenius, *Die Weltanschauung*, 14.

46. Wiedemann, *Die Toten*, 10.

47. A. V. Boldyrev, "Religiia drevnegrecheskikh morekhodov," in *Religiia i obshchestvo: Sbornik statei po izucheniiu sotsial'nikh osnov religioznykh iavlenii drevnego mira* (Leningrad: Leningradskii gosudarstvenii universitet, 1926), 145–46.

48. Afanas'ev No. 173; H173.

49. Cf. Onchukov 1908: No. 3.

50. Afanas'ev No. 188; H188.

51. Shternberg, *Pervobytnaia religiia*, 123.

52. Ibid., 124.

53. Dmitrii K. Zelenin, *Totemy—derev'ia v skazaniiakh i obriadakh evro-peiskikh narodov* (Moscow: Akademii nauk SSSR, 1937); J. H. Philpot, *The Sacred Tree* (London: Macmillan, 1897).

54. Smirnov 1917: No. 43.

55. Afanas'ev No. 156; H156.

56. Khudiakov 1862: No. 2.

57. Afanas'ev No. 129; H129.

58. Shternberg, *Pervobytnaia religiia*, 34.

59. Breasted, *Development of Religion and Thought*, 40.

60. Propp, or perhaps one of his subsequent editors, appears to have mis-identified the source of this line. It is not found in *The Book of the Dead* LIII as indicated but in the pyramid text of Pepi I, l, 544. We have provided the translation from James P. Allen, trans., intro, notes, *The Ancient Egyptian Pyramid Texts* (Atlanta: Society of Biblical Literature, 2005), 191.

61. Afanas'ev No. 161; H161.

62. Afanas'ev No. 130; H130.

63. Afanas'ev No. 136; H136.

64. Afanas'ev No. 128; H128.

65. Afanas'ev No. 130; H130.

66. Shternberg, *Pervobytnaia religiia*, 328.

67. Budge, *Book of the Dead* [XV], 84. *Khu* is a part of the soul that has left the body after death in ancient Egyptian mythology (translators' note).

68. Budge, *Book of the Dead* LXXVI, 247. This reference is misattrib-uted to chapter XV of the *Book of the Dead*. There is variation, moreover, among the extant translations of the Egyptian source for what Propp refers to here as a "beetle" (*zhuk*). P. Le Page Renoult and E. Naville render it as "Bird-Fly"; Stephen Quirke has "*abyt*-insect"; and Budge, whose translation ("mantis") we have quoted above, notes, "i.e., the 'praying μαντις,' i.e., 'di-viner,' or 'soothsayer' (*Mantis religiosa*), an insect of the Mantidae class." See P. Le Page Renoult and E. Naville, *The Egyptian Book of the Dead. Trans-lation and Commentary* (London: Society of Biblical Archaeology, 1904), https://www.gutenberg.org/files/69566/69566-h/69566-h.htm#ch076; Stephen Quirke, *Going Out in Daylight prt m hrw. The Ancient Egyptian Book of the Dead. translation, sources, meanings* (London: Golden House, 2013), 181; and Budge, *Book of the Dead*, 247 (translators' note).

7. At the River of Fire

1. As noted in our introduction, the word most frequently used in the text, *zmei*, is polyvalent and, depending on context, can suggest a large winged fire-breathing beast or an animal that slithers on the ground. Propp, further-more, sometimes uses the more specific word *zmeia*, which we have rendered as snake. Otherwise, where it is clear from context that Propp is referring to a crawling creature, we have used *serpent*, and where the beast in question flies and exhibits other traits associated with the wondertale dragon, we have used *dragon*. (translators' note).

2. Afanas'ev No. 131; H131.

3. Afanas'ev No. 171; H171.

4. The *lubok* (pl. *lubki*) was a popular print with simple graphics and themes drawn from literature, religion, and popular culture (translators' note).

5. Afanas'ev No. 129, variant.

6. Afanas'ev No. 131; H131.

7. Afanas'ev No. 155; H155.

8. Khudiakov 1862: No. 119.

9. Afanas'ev No. 562; H562.

10. Afanas'ev No. 271; H271.

11. Afanas'ev No. 206; H206.

12. Afanas'ev No. 125; H125.

13. Afanas'ev No. 136; H136.

14. Afanas'ev No. 125; H125.

15. Afanas'ev No. 132; H132.

16. The name Gorynych means "son of the mountain" and is constructed in a manner similar to Russian patronymic names such as Aleksandrovich or Borisovich (translators' note).

17. Afanas'ev No. 155; H155.

18. Afanas'ev No. 560; H560.

19. Afanas'ev No. 131; H131.

20. The root of the name Koshchei is the same as in *kost'* (bone) and thus seems to refer to a creature of bones or a skeleton-like creature (translators' note).

21. Afanas'ev No. 156; H156. Kosh is a dialectal variant of Koshchei (translators' note).

22. Smirnov 1917: No. 31.

23. Smirnov 1917: No. 160.

24. Afanas'ev No. 560; H560.

25. Afanas'ev No. 159; H159.

26. Khudiakov 1862: No. 53.

27. Afanas'ev No. 171; H171.

28. Afanas'ev No. 134; H134.

29. Smirnov 1917: No. 150.

30. Afanas'ev No. 138; H138.

31. Afanas'ev No. 137; H137.

32. Afanas'ev No. 562; H562.

33. Afanas'ev No. 562; H562.

34. Afanas'ev No. 155; H155.

35. Afanas'ev No. 562; H562.

36. Afanas'ev No. 134; H134.

37. Afanas'ev No. 135; H135. A pood is an old East Slavic measurement equal to approximately thirty-six pounds (translators' note).

38. Afanas'ev No. 136; H136.

39. Afanas'ev No. 131; H131.

40. Afanas'ev No. 136; H136.

41. Soymonov, *Pesni i skazki*, 144.

42. Afanas'ev No. 560; H560.

43. Afanas'ev No. 129, variant.

44. Afanas'ev No. 136; H136.

45. Afanas'ev No. 137; H137.

46. Afanas'ev No. 136; H136.

47. Afanas'ev No. 129, variant.

48. Afanas'ev No. 201; H201.

49. Soymonov, *Pesni i skazki*, 145.

50. Afanas'ev No. 134; H134.

51. Afanas'ev No. 132; H132.

52. Afanas'ev No. 129, variant.

53. Afanas'ev No. 129, variant.

54. Wilhelm Bölsche, *Drachen: Sage und Naturwissenschaft, eine volkstümliche Darstellung* (Stuttgart: Kosmos, 1921).

55. Ernst Siecke, *Drachenkämpfe: Untersuchungen zur Indogermanischen Sagenkunde* (Leipzig: Hinrichs, 1907); Leo Frobenius, *Das Zeitalter des Sonnengottes* (Berlin: G. Reimer, 1904).

56. Wilfrid D. Hambly, *Serpent Worship in Africa* (Chicago: Field Museum of Natural History, 1931).

57. Jakob Mähly, *Die Schlange im Mythus und Cultus der classischen Völker* (Basel: Buchdruckerei von C. Schultze, 1867); Erich Küster, *Die Schlange in der griechischen Kunst und Religion* (Giessen: Verlag von Alfred Töpelmann, 1913).

58. Grafton Elliot Smith, *The Evolution of the Dragon* (Manchester: The University Press, 1919).

59. Edwin S. Hartland, *The Legend of Perseus*, vols. 1–3 (London: D. Nutt, 1894–96).

60. Kurt Ranke, *Die zwei Brüder: Eine Studie zur vergleichenden Märchenforschung*, FFC, vol. 114 (Helsinki: Suomalainen Tiedeakatemia, 1934).

61. Aleksandr I. Nikiforov, "Pobeditel' zmeia: Iz severnorusskikh skazok," *Sovetskii fol'klor*, no. 4/5 (1936): 144.

62. Aleksandr Kirpichnikov, *Sviatoi Georgii i Egorii khrabryi: Issledovanie literaturnoi istorii khristianskoi legendy* (St. Petersburg: V. S. Balasheva, 1879); Aleksandr N. Veselovskii, "Sviatoi Georgii v legendakh i obriadakh," *Razyskaniia v oblasti russkogo dukhovnogo stikha. Sbornik Otdeleniia russkogo iazyka i slovesnosti AN 21, no. 2 (1880)*; Aleksandr V. Rystenko, *Legenda o sviatom Georgii i drakone* (Odessa: Ekon, 1909); Johann B. Aufhauser, *Das Drachenwunder des heiligen Georg in der griechischen und lateinischen Überlieferung*, Byzantinisches Archiv, vol. 5 (Leipzig: B.G. Teubner, 1911).

63. "In the Old World" (translators' note).

64. Paul Ehrenreich, *Die Mythen und Legenden der südamerikanischen Urvölker und ihre Beziehungen zu denen Noramerikas und der alten Welt* (Berlin: A. Asher, 1905), 72.

65. Aufhauser, *Das Drachenwunder des heiligen Georg*.

66. Alfred R. Radcliffe-Brown, "The Rainbow-Serpent Myth in South-East Australia," *Oceania* 1, no. 3 (1930): 344.

67. Schurtz, *Altersklassen und Männerbünde*, 224.

68. Nevermann, *Masken und Geheimbunde in Melanesien*, 24.

69. Ibid., 24, 40, 56.

70. Frobenius, *Die Weltanschauung*, 198.

71. Webster, *Primitive Secret Societies*, 99.

72. Frobenius, *Die Weltanschauung*, 199.

73. Loeb, *Tribal Initiations*, 264.

74. Boas, *Indianische Sagen*, 81.

75. Josef Meier, "Mythen und Sagen der Admiralitätsinsulaner," *Anthropos* 2, no. 4 (1907): 653.

76. Nevermann, *Ergebnisse der Südsee-Expedition*, 369.

77. Adolphus P. Elkin, "The Rainbow-Serpent Myth in North-West Australia," *Oceania* 1, no. 3 (1930): 349–52.

78. Kroeber, *Gros Ventre*, 328.

79. Frobenius, *Die Weltanschauung*, 198.

80. Frobenius, *Das Zeitalter des Sonnengottes*, 113.

81. Frobenius, *Die Weltanschauung*, 106.

82. Radermacher, "Walfischmythen."

83. Frobenius, *Das Zeitalter des Sonnengottes*, 145.

84. Johann G. Hahn, *Griechische und albanesische Märchen*, vol. 1
(Leipzig: W. Engelmann, 1864), 23.

85. Popov, *Dolganskii fol'klor*, 101.

86. Zelenin 1915: No. 106.

87. Sadovnikov 1884: No. 110. The name Volkodir contains the Russian
root for "wolf" (*volk*) (translators' note).

88. Khudiakov 1862: No. 38.

89. Cf. Grimm 1822: No. 17 and parallels in Bolte and Polívka, *Anmerkungen*.

90. Zelenin 1915: No. 30.

91. Smirnov 1917: No. 72.

92. Afanas'ev No. 252; H252.

93. Weicker, *Der Seelenvogel in der alten Litteratur und Kunst*, 25.

94. Veselovskii, *Slavianskie skazaniia o Solomone i Kitovrase*, 136.

95. Nikiforov, "Pobeditel' zmeia," 205.

96. Smirnov 1917: No. 362.

97. Sadovnikov 1884: No. 6.

98. Boas 1895: No. 81.

99. Radcliffe-Brown, "Rainbow-Serpent Myth," 342.

100. S. D. Kotsiubinskii, ed., *Skazki i legendy tatar Kryma*, recorded by K. U.
Useinov (Simferopol: Gosizdat Krym, 1936), 169.

101. Frazer, *Belief in Immortality*, vol. 2, 195.

102. Frobenius, *Das Zeitalter des Sonnengottes*, 91.

103. See, for example, Afanas'ev Nos. 240 and 242, variant.

104. Frobenius, *Die Weltanschauung*, 189. This reference does not appear in
Propp's text but was added by the editor of the 1986 edition of *Istoricheskie
korni* (translators' note).

105. Frobenius, *Das Zeitalter des Sonnegottes*, 93.

106. Boas, *Indianische Sagen*, 101.

107. Vladimir Ia. Propp, "Ritual'nyi smekh v fol'klore: Po povodu skazki o
Nesmeiane," *Uchenye Zapiski Leningradskogo gosudarstvennogo universiteta imeni A. A. Zhdanova* 3, no. 46, Seriia filologicheskikh nauk, 151–175
(Leningrad: Izd. Leningradskogo gosudarstvennogo universiteta, 1939).

108. Kroeber, *Gros Ventre*, 85.

109. Frobenius, *Das Zeitalter des Sonnegottes*, 82.

110. Frobenius, *Die Weltanschauung*, 97.

111. Frobenius, *Das Zeitalter des Sonnegottes*, 96.

112. Ibid., 70.

113. Kurrea: a serpentlike monster in aboriginal myths (translators' note).

114. Frobenius, *Das Zeitalter des Sonnegottes*, 73.

115. Ibid., 74.

116. Frobenius, *Die Weltanschauung*, 70.

117. Frobenius, *Das Zeitalter des Sonnegottes*, 121.

118. A Berber ethnic group native to Algeria (translators' note).

119. Gressmann, *Altorientalische Texte und Bilder*, 78.

120. E. A. Wallis Budge, *The Babylonian Legends of the Creation and the Fight between Bel and the Dragon: As Told by Assyrian Tablets from Nineven* (London: The British Museum, 1921), 20.

121. Siecke, *Drachenkämpfe*, 15–16.

122. Radermacher, *Das Jenseits im Mythos der Hellenen*, 66.

123. Sergei A. Kozin, trans., intro., commentary, *Geseriada: Skazaniia o milostivom Geser Mergen-khane, iskorenitele desiati zol v desiati stranakh sveta* (Moscow: Izdatel'stvo akademii nauk SSSR, 1935), 91–97.

124. Zarubin, *Beludzhskie skazki,* 125.

125. Zelenin 1915: No. 34.

126. Zelenin 1914: No. 57.

127. Afanas'ev No. 237; H237.

128. Otto Rank, *Der Mythus von der Geburt des Helden* (Leipzig and Vienna: Franz Deuticke, 1909).

129. Frobenius, *Die Weltanschauung*, 204.

130. Usener, *Die Sintfluthsagen* (translators' note).

131. Smirnov 1917: No. 252.

132. Gressmann, *Altorientalische Texte und Bilder zum Alten Testament*, 79.

133. Wundt, *Mif i religiia*, 110.

134. Lucien Lévy-Bruhl, *Das Denken der Naturvölker*, 2nd ed. (Vienna: Wilhelm Braumüller 1929), 65.

135. S. A. Ratner-Shternberg, "Muzeinye materialy po tlingitskomu shamanstvu," *Sb. MAE* 6 (1927): 83.

136. Frazer, *Golden Bough*, vol. 3, pt. 2, 54.

137. Frazer, *Fear of the Dead*, 71.

138. Ibid., 37.

139. Elsdon Best, *The Maori*, vol. 1 (Wellington: H.H. Tombs, 1924), 107.

140. Boris A. Turaev, *Klassicheskii Vostok: Posmertnyi trud* (Leningrad: Brokgauz-Efron, 1924), 223.

141. Nansen, *Eskimoleben*.

142. Afanas'ev No. 148; H148.

143. Parkinson *Dreißig Jahre in der Südsee*, 308.

144. Shternberg, *Pervobytnaia religiia*, 140.

145. Radermacher, *Das Jenseits im Mythos der Hellenen*, 113.

146. Ibid., 112.

147. Güntert, *Kalypso*, 151.

148. Freidenberg, *Poetika siuzheta i zhanra*, 78.

149. Ludolf Malten, "Der Raub der Kore," *Archiv für Religionswissenschaft* 12 (1909).

150. Dieterich, *Nekyia*, 47.

151. Spencer and Gillen, *Native Tribes of Central Australia*, 444.

152. Radcliffe-Brown, "Rainbow-Serpent Myth in South-East Australia," 343–44.

153. Ibid.

154. Ursula McConnel, "The Rainbow-Serpent in North Queensland," *Oceania* 1, no. 3 (1930): 348.

155. Frobenius, *Das Zeitalter des Sonnengottes*, 78.

156. Ibid., 153.

157. Popov, *Dolganskii fol'klor*, 83.

158. Frobenius, *Die Weltanschauung*, 84.

159. Krickeberg, *Märchen der Azteken*, 237.

160. Hambly, *Serpent Worship in Africa*, 19.

161. Ibid.

162. *Mitteilungen der Anthropologischen Gesellschaft in Wien*, vol. 39, 101 (1909). This reference appears to be faulty in the source (translators' note).

163. Krickeberg, *Märchen der Azteken*, 279.

164. *Rigveda* Book 3, Hymn 33 [03-033]: https://en.wikisource.org/wiki/The_Hymns_of_the_Rigveda/Book_3/Hymn_33.

165. *Rigveda* Book 4, Hymn 17 [04-017]: https://en.wikisource.org/wiki/The_Hymns_of_the_Rigveda/Book_4/Hymn_17.

166. *Rigveda* Book 1, Hymn 32 [01-032]: https://en.wikisource.org/wiki/The_Hymns_of_the_Rigveda/Book_1/Hymn_32.

167. *Rigveda* Book I, Hymn 52 [01-052]: https://en.wikisource.org/wiki/The_Hymns_of_the_Rigveda/Book_1/Hymn_52.

168. See the individual books with hymn and indicated line numbers at https://en.wikisource.org/wiki/The_Hymns_of_the_Rigveda (translators' note).

169. Edward T. C. Werner, *Myths and Legends of China*, 2nd ed. (London: George G. Harrap, 1924), 210.

170. Ibid., 232.

171. Ibid.

172. Roscher, *Ausführliches Lexikon*, 2767.

173. The arshin was an Old Russian measurement unit corresponding to a forearm (translators' note).

174. N. M. Driagin, "Liubovnye motivy martovskogo eposa gortsev Severnogo Kabkaza," in *Tristan i Isol'da: Ot geroini liubvi feodal'noi Evrony do bogini matriarkhal'noi Afrevrazii*, ed. Nikolai Ia. Marr (Leningrad: Akademii nauk, 1932), 187.

175. Zarubin, *Beludzhskie skazki*, 185.

176. Boris Iakovlevich Vladimirtsov, trans., intro., commentary, *Volshebnyi mertvets: Mongol'sko-oiratskie skazki* (Petrograd, 1923), 38.

177. Driagin, "Liubovnye motivy," 187.

178. Shternberg, *Pervobytnaia religiia*, 466.

179. Ibid., 358; James Frazer, *Zolotaia vetv'* [*The Golden Bough*] (Moscow: Nauchnoe obshchestvo "Ateist," 1928), 143.

180. Erwin Paul Dieseldorf, "Kunst und Religion der Mayavölker im alten und heutigen Mittelamerika," *ZfE* 57, no. 1/2 (1925): 7.

181. Frazer, *Zolotaia vetv'*, 144.

182. Dmitrii K. Zelenin, "Tabu slov u narodov Vostochoi Evropy i Severnoi Azii," *Sb. MAE* 8 (1929): 65.

183. Frazer, *Zolotaia vetv'*, 3, 35.

184. Shternberg, *Pervobytnaia religiia*, 357.

185. Krickeberg, *Märchen der Azteken*, 73.

186. Bruno Gutmann, "Opferstätten der Wadschagga," *Archiv für Religionswissenschaft* 12 (1909): 94.

187. Frazer, *Zolotaia vetv'*, 144.

188. Tronskii, "Antichnyi mif," 534.

189. Gutmann, "Opferstätten der Wadschagga."

190. See *katabasis* in Roscher, *Ausführliches Lexikon*, 2377, 2379.

191. Küster, *Die Schlange*, 90.

192. Georgii Vlastov, trans., ed., *Gesiod* (St. Petersburg: tip. t-va "Ob-shchestva pol'zy," 1885), 218.

193. Virgil, *The Aeneid*, trans. James Rhoades (Chicago: William Benton, 1952), Book VI, l, 417.

194. Propp does not provide a source for this story, although it appears in his book in quotation marks (translators' note).

195. Frobenius, *Die Weltanschauung*, 183.

196. Propp, "Ritual'nyi smekh."

197. *Rigveda* Book I, Hymn 32 [01-032], l. 4: https://en.wikisource.org/wiki/The_Hymns_of_the_Rigveda/Book_1/Hymn_32.

198. *Rigveda* Book I, Hymn 52 [01-052], l. 8: https://en.wikisource.org/wiki/The_Hymns_of_the_Rigveda/Book_1/Hymn_52.

199. *Rigveda* Book II, Hymn 19 [01-019], l. 3: https://en.wikisource.org/wiki/The_Hymns_of_the_Rigveda/Book_2/Hymn_19.

200. Afanas'ev No. 135; H135.

201. Ibid.

202. Khudiakov 1890: No. 180. A verst is a Russian unit of distance equal to 1.067 kilometers (translators' note).

203. Khudiakov 1890: No. 227.

204. Khudiakov 1890: No. 39.

205. Ibid.

206. Budge, *Book of the Dead*, 169.

207. Gressmann, *Altorientalische Texte und Bilder zum Alten Testament*, 101.

208. Budge, *Book of the Dead*, 106.

209. Quotation from the *Book of the Dead* misattributed in the source.

210. Budge, *Book of the Dead*, Chapter XXII, 132.

211. Budge, *Book of the Dead*, 315.

212. Budge, *Book of the Dead*, 21.

213. Moret, *Tsari i bogi Egipta*, 140.

214. Afanas'ev No. 93; H93.

215. Minaev, *Indeiskie skazki i legendy*, 126: and, similarly, 118.

216. **Frobenius, Das Zeitalter des Sonnengottes, 67.**

217. Ibid., 101.

218. Hambly, *Serpent Worship in Africa*, 24.

219. James G. Frazer, *The Golden Bough*, vol. 4, *The Dying God* (London: Macmillan, 1911), 105, https://archive.org/details/goldenboughstudy-04fraz.

220. Budge, *Book of the Dead*, 155–57.

221. Numbers 21:8–9.

222. Boris A. Turaev, *Egipetskaia literatura* (Moscow: Izd. M. i S. Sabash-nikovykh, 1920), 41.

223. Ibid., 186, and pages immediately following.

224. Ibid., 188.

225. Ibid., 190.

226. Ibid., 188, and pages immediately following.

227. Smirnov 1917: No. 111.

228. Ibid. The quoted sentence has no explicit subject or object, thereby re
inforcing the sense of ambiguous reflexivity the author highlights: "Kogti v
grud' zapustal i rvanul tak sil'no, chto razorvalsia popolam i s vizgom na zem-
liu grianulsia e zdokh" (translators' note).

8. Beyond the Thrice-Nine Lands

1. Afanas'ev No. 237; H237.
2. Afanas'ev No. 191; H191.
3. Afanas'ev No. 138; H138.
4. Afanas'ev No. 201; H201.
5. Afanas'ev No. 162; H162.
6. Zelenin 1914: No. 59.
7. Zelenin 1915: No. 3.
8. Afanas'ev No. 222; H222.
9. Afanas'ev No. 216, variant 3.
10. Afanas'ev No. 157; H157.
11. Afanas'ev No. 165; H165.
12. Khudiakov 1862: No. 41.
13. Ibid., No. 82.
14. Afanas'ev No. 560; H560.
15. Afanas'ev No. 559; H559.
16. Afanas'ev No. 129; H129.
17. Afanas'ev No. 220; H220.
18. Afanas'ev No. 235; H235.
19. Afanas'ev No. 242; H242.
20. Afanas'ev No. 170; H170.
21. Afanas'ev No. 137; H137.
22. Afanas'ev No. 564; H564.
23. Afanas'ev No. 129, variant.
24. Afanas'ev No. 93; H93.
25. Afanas'ev No. 146; H146.
26. Afanas'ev No. 169; H169.
27. The name is a pun on the Russian word for "lightning," *molniia* (translators' note).
28. Afanas'ev No. 164, variant.
29. Afanas'ev No. 178; H178.
30. See note 201 in chap. 4 (translators' note).
31. Afanas'ev No. 182; H182.
32. Afanas'ev No. 168; H168.
33. Afanas'ev No. 234; H234.
34. Afanas'ev No. 158; H158.
35. Afanas'ev No. 169; H169.
36. Afanas'ev No. 237; H237.
37. Afanas'ev No. 236; H236.
38. Khazhba, *Abkhazskie skazki*, 4.
39. Afanas'ev No. 168; H168.
40. Afanas'ev No. 196, variant.
41. Zelenin 1914: No. 1.
42. Afanas'ev, No. 191, variant.

43. Afanas'ev No. 178, variant.

44. Smirnov 1917: No. 335.

45. Afanas'ev No. 159; H159.

46. Afanas'ev No. 201; H201.

47. Afanas'ev No. 191, cf. Nos. 217, 218; H191, cf. H217, H218.

48. Shternberg, *Pervobytnaia religiia*, 43.

49. Zelenin 1914: No. 13.

50. Afanas'ev No. 204, variant 2.

51. Frazer, *Belief in Immortality*, vol. 3, 49.

52. Boas, *Indianische Sagen*, 152.

53. Popov, *Dolganskii fol'klor*, 70.

54. Radcliffe-Brown, "Rainbow-Serpent Myth in South-East Australia," 342.

55. Frazer, *Belief in Immortality*, vol. 2, 363.

56. Grimm 1822: No. 151.

57. Bolte and Polívka, *Anmerkungen*, vol. III [1932], 158.

58. Hambruch, *Südseemärchen*, 96.

59. Afanas'ev No. 219; H219.

60. Khudiakov 1890: No. 78.

61. Turaev, *Egipetskaia literatura*, 38.

62. Breasted, *Development of Religion and Thought*, 133.

63. Budge, *Book of the Dead* [LXIV], 212. This text is misattributed to *Book of the Dead*, XIV in the source (translators' note).

64. Propp here refers to the German classical philologist of ancient Greek religion and gnosticism Richard August Reitzenstein (1861–1931). The quotation is left unattributed in the text (translators' note).

65. Gaston Maspero, *Les Contes populaires de l'Égypte ancienne*, 3rd ed. (Paris: Guilmoto, 1900), https://archive.org/details/lescontespopulaioomasp.

66. Budge, *Book of Opening the Mouth*, 9, 27.

67. Kharuzin, *Etnografiia*, 233.

68. Jeremias, *Hölle und Paradies*, 36.

69. Radermacher, *Das Jenseits im Mythos der Hellenen*, 3 and onward.

70. Propp does not provide a reference, but the author in question is German mythologist Otto Gruppe (1851–1921), best known for his *Griechische Mythologie und Religion-geschichte* (1906) and *Geschichte der Klassischen Mythologie und Religionsgeschichte wahrend des Mittelalteis in Abenland und wahrand Neuzeit*. It is unclear which one of these Radermacher is citing (translators' note).

71. Radermacher, *Das Jenseits im Mythos der Hellenen*, 44.

72. Dieterich, *Nekyia*, 21.

73. Ibid., 36.

74. Ibid., 38.

75. Afanas'ev No. 283; H283.

76. Shternberg, *Pervobytnaia religiia*, 383.

77. Dieterich, *Nekyia*, 41.

78. Holland, "Zur Typik der Himmelfahrt," 217.

9. The Bride

1. A typical formula for introducing the heroine in Russian wondertales (translators' note).

2. Afanas'ev No. 155; H155.

3. Afanas'ev No. 125; H125.

4. Afanas'ev No. 183; H183.

5. Afanas'ev No. 182; H182.

6. Karnaukhova 1934: No. 8.

7. Afanas'ev No. 195; H195.

8. Afanas'ev No. 215; H215.

9. Afanas'ev No. 259; H259.

10. Afanas'ev No. 240; H240.

11. Kharuzin, *Russkie lopari*, 347.

12. Spencer and Gillen, *Native Tribes of Central Australia*, 461.

13. Julius Lippert, *Istoriia kul'tury* (St. Petersburg: F. Pavlenkova, 1902), 187, 213.

14. Georg Schweinfurth, *Im Herzen von Afrika*, 3rd ed. (Leipzig: Salzwasser-Verlag Gmbh, 1918), 274; Julius Wellhausen, *Reste arabischen Heidentums*, 2nd ed. (Berlin: G. Reimer, 1927), 274; Achelis, *Die Religion der Naturvölker im Umriss*, 95.

15. Kharuzin, *Etnografiia*, 350.

16. Aleksandr Veselovskii, *Poetika siuzhetov*, in *Sobranie sochinenii*, series 1, *Poetika*, vol. 2, no. 1. (St. Petersburg: Tipografiia Imperatorskoi akademii nauk, 1913), 121.

17. Kharuzin, *Etnografiia*, 350.

18. *Zhivaia starina*, 501–502.

19. Ernst Samter, *Geburt, Hochzeit, Tod: Beitrage zur vergleichenden Volkskunde* (Leipzig: Teubner, 1911).

20. Olga M. Freidenberg, "Siuzhet Tristana i Isol'dy v mifologemakh Egeiskogo otrezka Sredizemnomor'ia," in Marr, *Tristan i Isol'da*, 96.

21. Kazanskii, "Antichnye aspekty," 126.

22. Evgenii G. Kagarov, "Sostav i proiskhozhdenie svadebnoi obriadnosti," *Sb. MAE* 8, no. 29 (1929): 182.

23. Kharuzin, *Etnografiia*, 351.

24. Smirnov 1917: No. 85 and elsewhere.

25. Spencer and Gillen, *Native Tribes of Central Australia*, 258.

26. Cf. also Veselovskii, *Poetika siuzhetov*, 125.

27. Lévy-Bruhl, *Das Denken der Naturvölker*, 285.

28. Lippert, *Istoriia kul'tury*, 364; Shternberg, *Pervobytnaia religiia*, 204–207.

29. Afanas'ev No. 180; H180.

30. Afanas'ev No. 144; H144.

31. Afanas'ev No. 200; H200.

32. Afanas'ev No. 191; H191.

33. Afanas'ev No. 240; H240.

34. Smirnov 1917: No. 355.

35. Afanas'ev No. 136; H136, emphasis added.

36. Afanas'ev No. 156; H156.

37. Afanas'ev No. 225; H225.

38. Afanas'ev No. 220; H220.

39. Afanas'ev No. 146; H146.

40. Afanas'ev 267–269; H267–269; Afanas'ev No. 269; H269.

41. Afanas'ev 245–250; H245–250.

42. Afanas'ev No. 249; H249.

43. Smirnov 1917: No. 310.

44. Afanas'ev No. 144; H144.

45. Afanas'ev No. 305; H305.

46. Afanas'ev No. 144; H144.

47. Afanas'ev No. 224; H224.

48. Afanas'ev No. 130, 170; H130, H170.

49. Khudiakov 1862: No. 1.

50. Afanas'ev Nos. 182–184; Smirnov 1917: 8.

51. Smirnov 1917: No. 12.

52. Afanas'ev No. 249; H249.

53. Afanas'ev No. 304; H304.

54. Afanas'ev No. 353; H353.

55. Afanas'ev No. 270; H270.

56. Afanas'ev No. 144; H144.

57. Zarubin, *Beludzhskie skazki*, 46, 32, 194.

58. Khudiakov 1862: No. 85.

59. Afanas'ev No. 564; H564.

60. Afanas'ev No. 156; H156.

61. Afanas'ev No. 132; H132.

62. Karnaukhova 1934: No. 41.

63. Zelenin 1914: No. 59.

64. Afanas'ev No. 200; H200.

65. Afanas'ev No. 198; H198.

66. Afanas'ev No. 224; H224.

67. Afanas'ev No. 170; H170.

68. Afanas'ev No. 180; H180.

69. Afanas'ev No. 180; H180, emphasis added.

70. Afanas'ev No. 182; H182, emphasis added.

71. Afanas'ev No. 212; H212.

72. Smirnov 1917: No. 35.

73. Karnaukhova 1934: No. 1.

74. Smirnov 1917: No. 34.

75. Afanas'ev No. 225; H225.

76. Afanas'ev No. 129; H129.

77. Frazer, *Belief in Immortality*, vol. 3, 193.

78. Boas, "Social Organization," 413–14.

79. Korguev 1939: No. 12.

80. Afanas'ev No. 225; H225.

81. Karnaukhova 1934: No. 1.

82. Frazer, *Belief in Immortality*, vol. 3, 185.

83. Afanas'ev No. 137; H137.

84. Boas, *Indianische Sagen*, 136.

85. Ibid., 66.

86. Boas, "Social Organization," 363–64.

87. Ibid., 54.

88. Afanas'ev No. 144; H144.

89. Afanas'ev No. 138; H138.

90. Afanas'ev Nos. 133–134; H133–134.

91. Afanas'ev No. 134; H134.

92. Afanas'ev No. 235; II235.

93. Freidenberg, "Siuzhet Tristana i Isol'dy," 91.

94. Nilsson, *Primitive Religion*, 75.

95. James G. Frazer, *The Golden Bough: A Study in Magic and Religion*, vol. 2, pts. 1–2, *The Magic Art and the Evolution of Kings* (London: Macmillan, 1911), 296, https://archive.org/details/goldenboughstudy02frazuoft.

96. Ibid., 299.

97. Tikhaia-Tsereteli, "Zhenskii obraz," 172, emphasis added.

98. Khudiakov 1862: No. 33.

99. Afanas'ev No. 144; H144.

100. Khudiakov 1862: No. 3.

101. Afanas'ev No. 200; H200.

102. Khudiakov 1862: No. 19.

103. Afanas'ev No. 198, variant.

104. Khudiakov 1862: No. 19, emphasis added.

105. Frazer, *Zolotaia vetv'*, 154. Propp refers to the 1928 Russian translation. The English source, which we have quoted here, can be found in James Frazer, *The Magic Art and the Evolution of Kings*, vol. II (New York: St. Martin's, 1913), 299 (translators' note).

106. Rohde, *Psyche*, 19.

107. Onchukov 1908: No. 2.

108. Tikhaia-Tsereteli, "Zhenskii obraz," 157.

109. Ibid., 138.

110. Afanas'ev No. 237; H237.

111. Zelenin 1914: No. 1.

112. Khudiakov 1862: No. 63.

113. Smirnov 1917: No. 49.

114. Afanas'ev No. 364; H364.

115. Afanas'ev No. 367; H367.

116. Popov, *Dolganskii fol'klor*, 65, emphasis added.

117. Karnaukhova 1934: No. 66.

118. Samter, *Geburt, Hochzeit, Tod*, 98.

119. Kagarov, "Sostav i proiskhozhdenie svadebnoi obriadnosti," 162.

120. Smirnov 1917: No. 142.

121. Zelenin 1915: No. 12.

122. Propp, "Ritual'nyi smekh," 168.

123. Afanas'ev No. 116, variant.

124. Khudiakov 1862: No. 19.

125. Afanas'ev No. 76; H76.

126. Sadovnikov 1884: No. 5.

127. Afanas'ev No. 158, variant 2.

128. Afanas'ev No. 136; H136.

129. Afanas'ev No. 158, variant 2.

130. Afanas'ev No. 198; H198.

131. Sokolov 1915: No. 72.

132. Sokolov 1915: No. 143.

133. Afanas'ev No. 198; H198.

134. Dorsey and Kroeber, *Traditions of the Arapaho*, 260.

135. Lev Ia. Shrernberg, *Materialy po izucheniiu giliatskogo iazyka i fol'klora*, vol. 1. (St. Petersburg: tip. Imperatorskoi Akademii nauk, 1908), 159.

136. Eduard Hahn, *Demeter und Baubo: Versuch einer Theorie der Entstehung unsres Ackerbaus* (Lübeck: Selbstverlag des verfassers, 1896), 52.

137. Richard Reitzenstein, "Der Kausalzusammenhang zwischen Geschlechtsverkehr und Empfängnis in Glaube und Brauch der Natur- and Kulturvölker," *ZfE* 41 (1909): 682.

138. Ibid.

139. Georg Buschan, *Die Sitten der Völker. Liebe, Ehe, Heirat, Geburt, Religion, Aberglaube, Lebensgewohnheiten, Kultureingentümlichkeiten, Tod und Bestattung bei allen Völkern der Erde* (Stuttgart: Union Deutsche Verlagsgesellschaft, 1914), v–vi.

140. Afanas'ev No. 158, variant.

141. Soimonov, *Pesni i skazki*, 162.

142. Kagarov, "Sostav i proiskhozhdenie svadebnoi obriadnosti," 167.

143. Frazer, *Golden Bough*, vol. 2, 280.

144. Frazer, *Zolotaia vetv'*, vol. 2, 111; vol. 1, 22. Here too Propp refers to Russian versions of the Frazer text; unfortunately, we have not been able to identify exactly where they have been drawn from so have limited ourselves to translating the Russian words used in the source (translators' note).

145. Popov, *Dolganskii fol'klor*, e.g., 113.

146. Khudiakov 1862: No. 94.

147. Frazer, *Golden Bough*, vol. 4, 34, emphasis added.

148. Afanas'ev No. 171; H171.

149. Nikiforov, "Pobeditel' zmeia," 209.

150. Afanas'ev No. 571; H571.

151. Frazer, *Golden Bough*, vol. 4, 15, emphasis added.

152. Smirnov 1917: No. 242.

153. Grimm 1822: No. 29; HT, 119.

154. Smirnov 1917: 221.

155. Khudiakov 1862: 1.

156. Zelenin 1915: 114.

157. Afanas'ev 185; H185.

158. Afanas'ev 216, variant.

159. Afanas'ev 216; H216.

160. Frazer, *Golden Bough*, vol. 4, 259.

161. Zelenin 1915: 105.

162. Smirnov 1917: 30.

163. Afanas'ev 137; H137.

164. Isidor Scheftelowitz, "Das Fisch-Symbol in Judentum und Christentum," *Archiv für Religionswissenschaft* 14, no. 3/4 (1911): 1–53, 327–92.

165. Krickeberg, *Märchen der Azteken*, 286.

166. Kroeber, *Religion of the Indians of California*, 85.

167. Nansen, *Eskimoleben*, 221.

168. Shternberg, *Pervobytnaia religiia*, 325.

169. Achelis, *Die Religion der Naturvölker im Umriss*, 17.

170. Smirnov 1917: No. 321.

171. Frazer, *Zolotaia vetv'*, 262. Propp refers to a Russian translation the source for which can be found in Frazer, *Golden Bough*, 2nd ed., vol. 2, 14.

172. The Chocó or Katío are an indigenous people of Panama and Colombia (translators' note).

173. Josef Schilling and Maria Schilling, "Religion und soziale Verhältnisse der Catios-Indianer in Kolumbien," *Archiv für Religionswissenschaft* 23, no. 3/4 (1925): 278–97.

174. Tikhaia-Tsereteli, "Zhenskii obraz," 145.

175. Aarne, *Die magische Flucht*; Vladimir I. Iokhel'son [Vladimir Jochelson], "'Magicheskoe begstvo' kak obshcherasprostranennyi skazochno-mificheskii episod," in *Sbornik v chest' semidesiatiletiia professora D. N. Anuchina* (Moscow: IOLEAE, 1913), 155–66.

176. Afanas'ev No. 201, variant.

177. Afanas'ev No. 201; H201.

178. Zelenin 1914: No. 67.

179. Afanas'ev No. 176; H176.

180. Boas, *Indianische Sagen*, e.g., 72, 99, 187, 240, 267.

181. Vladimir G. Bogoraz-Tan, "Mif ob umiraiushchem i voskresaiushchem zvere," *Khudozhestvennyi fol'klor*, vol. 1 (1926), 68.

182. Afanas'ev Nos. 219–226; H219–226.

183. Afanas'ev No. 219; H219.

184. Aarne, *Die magische Flucht*, 93.

185. Afanas'ev No. 145; H145.

186. Smirnov 1917: No. 304.

187. Afanas'ev No. 101; H101.

188. Afanas'ev No. 570; H570.

189. Afanas'ev No. 249–253; H249–253.

190. Afanas'ev No. 249; H249.

191. Hambly, *Serpent Worship in Africa*, 25.

192. Wiedemann, *Die Toten und ihre Reiche*, 32.

193. Frobenius, *Die Weltanschauung der Naturvölker*, 11.

194. *Zhivaia starina*, 419.

195. Frazer, *Golden Bough*, vol. 2, 57.

196. Afanas'ev No. 251; H251.

197. Chernetsov, *Vogul'skie skazki*, 78.

198. Sofokl [Sophocles], *Dramy*, vol. 3, trans. F. Zelinskii (Moscow: M. i S. Sabashnikovy, 1915), 280.

199. Tronskii, "Antichnyi mif i sovremennaia skazka," 531.

200. Malten, "Das Pferd im Totenglauben," 130.

201. Radermacher, *Das Jenseits im Mythos der Hellenen*, 107.

202. Khudiakov 1862: No. 1.

203. Afanas'ev No. 175; H175.

204. Zelenin 1914: No. 55.

205. Afanas'ev No. 117; H117.

206. Afanas'ev No. 171; H171.

207. Here Rus' appears as an old name for the ancient territory of the Eastern Slavs (translators' note).

208. Afanas'ev No. 267; H267.

10. The Wondertale as a Whole

1. Dorsey, *Traditions of the Skidi-Pawnee*.

2. Ibid., xxi.

3. Ibid., xxi–xxii.

4. Ibid., xxii.

5. Ibid.

6. Lucien Lévy-Bruhl, *Sverkh'estestvennoe v pervobytnom myshlenii* (Moscow: OGIZ, 1937), 262.

7. Dorsey, *Traditions of the Skidi-Pawnee*, xxii.

8. Richard Neuhauss, *Deutsch-Neu-Guinea*, vol. 3, *Beiträge der Missionare Keysser, Stolz, Zahn, Lehner, Bamler* (Berlin: Dietrich Reimer, 1911), 161.

9. Lévy-Bruhl, *Sverkh'estestvennoe*, 267.

10. Vladimir G. Bogoraz-Tan, "Osnovnye tipy fol'klora severnoi Evrazii i severnoi Ameriki," ["The Main Types of Folklore of Northern Eurasia and North America"], *Sovetskii fol'klor*, no. 4/5 (1936): 29.

11. Dmitri K. Zelenin, "Religiozno-magicheskaia funktsiia volshebnykh skazok," in *K piatidesiatiletiiu nauch.-obshchestv. deiatelnosti. 1882–1932*, ed. S. F. Ol'denburg (Leningrad: Izd. Akademii nauk SSSR, 1934), 215–41.

Afterword

1. The name given at birth was Herman Voldemar.

2. Anninsky College was one of the non-Orthodox Lutheran schools in St. Petersburg, formed in the eighteenth century at the church of St. Anne.

3. Its official full name was initially the Folktale Commission of the Department of Ethnography of the Imperial Russian Geographical Society. It operated from 1896 to 1908, then again from 1911 to 1915, then finally from 1921 until it ceased to exist in 1928.

4. The A. N. Veselovskii Institute for the Comparative Study of Literatures and Languages of West and East (a.k.a., the Research Institute of Comparative History of Literatures and Languages of West and East) at Petrograd/Leningrad University was created in 1921, transformed into the State Institute of Speech Culture (Research Institute of Speech Culture) in 1930, and dissolved in 1933.

5. The State Institute of the History of Arts (St. Petersburg/Petrograd/Leningrad) was formed in 1912 and liquidated in 1931. The Department of the History of Verbal Arts at the Institute of the History of Arts (which included a folklore section) was chaired by V. M. Zhirmunsky and included B. M. Eikhenbaum, Yu. N. Tynianov, B. V. Tomashevskii, V. B. Shklovsky, V. M. Alekseev, M. L. Hoffman, and N. S. Gumilev. In 1923, Academia Publishing House was handed over to the Institute, which a few years later published Propp's *Morfologiia skazki* (*The Morphology of the Folktale*).

6. For more on Propp's biography see A. N. Martynov, *Vladimir Yakovlevich Propp: Zhiznennyi put'. Nauchnaia deiatel'nost'* (St. Petersburg: Dmitrii Bulanin, 2006).

7. See Liberman, *Theory and History of Folklore*, ix–xxxi and 225–27. On Propp and his scholarly heritage, see E. E. Warner, *Vladimir Iakovlevich Propp i russkaia fol'kloristika* (St. Petersburg: Filologicheskii fakul'tet Sankt-Peterburgskogo gos. Universiteta, 2005) and Jack V. Haney's "Review of Warner 2005," *Folklorica: Journal of the Slavic and East European Folkore Association* XI (2006): 117–19.

8. Warner, *Vladimir Iakovlevich Propp*, 15–20; B. Nathorst, *Formal or Structural Studies of Traditional Tales: The Usefulness of Some Methodological Proposals Advanced by Vladimir Propp, Alan Dundes, Claude*

Lévi-Strauss and Edmund Leach, trans. Donald Burton (Stockholm, 1969); Alan Dundes, "From Etic to Emic Units in the Structural Study of Folktales," in *The Meaning of Folklore: The Analytical Essays of Alan Dundes,* ed. S. J. Bronner (Logan, UT: Utah State University Press, 2007), 88–106; Elli Köngäs Maranda and Pierre Maranda, *Structural Models in Folklore and Transformational Essays* (The Hague: Mouton, 1971); J. L. Fischer, "The Sociopsychological Analysis of Folklore," *Current Anthropology* 4 (1963): 235–296; William O. Hendricks, *Essays on Semioliguistics and Verbal Art* (Berlin: De Gruyter, 1974), 90–126; and Max Lüthi, "Vladimir Propp, Morphologie des Marchens," *Zeitschrift für Volkskunde* 69 (1973): 290–93.

9. The author of this afterword worked at the time in the main editorial office of *Oriental Literature* (Nauka Publishers) and was a witness to and participant in the described events as well as the editor of the new edition of *Morphology of the Folktale;* see Sergei Nekliudov, "'U istokov serii: rozhdenie "cherepashki,"' 'U vremeni v plenu,'" in *Pamiati Sergeia Sergeevicha Tsel'nik. Sbornik Statei* (Moscow: Rossiiskii gumanitarnyi universitet, 2000), 14–23.

10. This series has existed for more than half a century and includes more than fifty volumes, both original domestic studies and translations of the works of major foreign scholars.

11. Vladimir A. Propp, *Morfologiia skazki,* 2nd ed. (Moscow: Nauka, 1969).

12. Among the noteworthy corrections is a significant change in the preface: "*historical* study of the folktale" (Propp, *Morfologiia skazki,* 8 instead of "studying the folktale as *a myth*" [Ibid., 7]) as well as the replacement of the term *vreditel'* (pest) by the term *antagonist* throughout the book. This, apparently, is associated with changes in Soviet political rhetoric—a shift away from agricultural discourse (mainly regarding harmful insects) through a metaphorical assimilation of such insects, as in "pests of the Soviet rural community" (beginning in approximately 1925), toward the image of the worst form of ideological enemy (beginning in approximately 1928). See G. Orlova, "Rozhdenie vreditelia: otritsatel'naia politicheskaia sakralizatsiya v strane sovetov (1920-e)," in *Zeit-Räume Neue Tendenzen in der historischen Kulturforschung aus der Perspektive der Slavistik,* Hrsg. von Susi K. Frank und Igor' P. Smirnov (*Wiener Slawistischer Almanach,* 2003), vol. 49, 309–13, 325. It seems that the concept of the pest in Propp is at first directly related to this discourse: "Enemies make their way to all our organizations. They take possession of our trust and malevolently deceive us. They pretend to be our loyal friends and therefore are more dangerous than open enemies" (*Pravda,* July 6, 1928); "this person has too many different masks, and he wears each one fairly decently and naturally" (*Pravda,* May 24, 1928) (qtd. in Ibid., 318). In Propp's work we find: "The pest's role is to disturb the peace of a happy family, cause some kind of misfortune, cause harm, damage. . . . He came, sneaked up, flew in, etc., and began to act. . . . The pest tries to deceive his victim in order to take possession of him or his property. First, the pest assumes the appearance of somebody else" (Vladimir Propp, *Morfologiia skazki* [Leningrad: Academia, 1928], 37–38). Just after 1928, the term assumes a particularly broad and threatening character. It is understandable that subsequently the author tried to eliminate this term. For a detailed account, see M. Vaiskopf, "Morfologiia strakha," *Novoe literaturnoe obozrenie,* no. 24 (1997): 53–58.

13. A. N. Afanas'ev, *Narodnye russkie skazki,* vols. 1–3, Text compiled and with introduction and commentary by Vladimir Ia. Propp (Moscow: Goslitizdat, 1957).

14. Vladimir Propp, "Kumuliativnaia skazka," in *Fol'klor i deistvitel'nost'. Izbrannye stat'i* (Moscow: GRVL-Nauka, 1976), 241–57. A somewhat more complete edition (based on preserved archival materials) can be found in Vladimir Propp, *Morfologiia volshebnoi skazki. Istoricheskie korni volshebnoĭ skazki* (Moscow: Labirint, 1998), 251–68.

15. Vladimir Propp, *Russkaia skazka* (Leningrad: Publishing House of Leningrad State University, 1984).

16. Liberman, *Theory and History of Folklore*, 70. Also, see the translators' introduction to this volume.

17. Sergei F. Ol'denburg, ed., *Skazochnaia komissia v 1926 g. Obzor rabot* (Leningrad: Gosudarstvennoe russkoe geograficheskoe obshchestvo, 1927), 48–49.

18. When in 1968 I suggested to Vladimir Yakovlevich that he return to the book its original (and more precise) title, he refused, noting that the work had already entered into scholarly use as *Morphology of the Folktale* and that changing the title could create the erroneous idea that it was some other work. He also refused (in my opinion, unwisely) to republish the 1928 article. See also Vladimir Propp, "Morphology of the Russian Folktale," in *Unknown Pages of Russian Folklore*, ed. A. L. Toporkov (Moscow: Indrik, 2015), 201–15.

19. Liberman, *Theory and History of Folklore*, 73.

20. "Before throwing light upon the question of the tale's origin, one must first answer the question as to what the tale itself represents." Propp, *Morphology* [1968], 5.

21. See "The Structural and Historical Study of the Wondertale," in *Theory and History of Folklore*, ed. Liberman. (Minneapolis: University of Minnesota Press, 1984), 69.

22. Veselovskii, *Poetika siuzhetov.*

23. "It would be interesting to do a *morphology of the folktale* and to trace its development from the simplest folktale elements to their most complex combination. Then we would discover that the older the tale, the simpler its structure; and the more recent, the more complicated"; see Aleksandr N. Veselovskii, "Iz lektsii po istorii eposa" (1884), in Istoricheskaia poetika, ed., intr., and notes by V. M. Zhirmunskii (Leningrad: Khudozhestvennaia literatura, 1940), 455. Emphasis added. We can state that Propp resolved this question.

24. M. A. Petrovskii, "Morfologiia novelly," in *Ars Poetica: Sbornik statei B. I. Yarho, A. M. Peshkovskogo, M. A. Petrovskogo, M. P. Stoliarova, R. O. Shor*, ed. M. A. Petrovskii, vol. 1 (Moscow: Moskovskii gosudarstvennyi akademii khudozhestvennyi nauk, 1927), 69–100; and M. A. Petrovskii, "Morfologiia pushkinskogo 'Vystrela,'" in *Problemy poetiki*, ed. V. Ya. Briusov (Moscow: Zemlia i fabrika, 1925), 171–204.

25. Aleksandr I. Nikiforov, "K voprosu o morfologicheskom izuchenii narodnoi skazki," in *Sbornik statei v chest' akad. A. I. Sobolevskogo*, ed. V. N. Peretts (Leningrad: Akademii nauk SSSR, 1928), 172–178.

26. Viktor Shklovskii, *O teorii prozy* (Moscow: Krug, 1925).

27. Viktor Shklovskii, "Iskusstvo kak priem," in *Sborniki po teorii poeticheskogo iazyka*, ed. O. Brik (Petrograd: Opoyaz, 1917), 3–14.

28. In later years, Propp spoke out rather negatively about formalism, contrasting it in a positive sense with the concept of structuralism: see Liberman,

Theory and History of Folklore, /1–73, "Otkrytaia lektsiia," *Zhivaia Starina* 3, no. 7 (1995): 29–30 (originally presented at a graduate seminar in the Department of Russian Literature, Leningrad State University, March 1, 1966).

29. See I. P. Eckermann, *Gespräche mit Goethe in den letzten Jahren seines Lebens*, 1823–1832, Bd. I–III (Leipzig: Brockhaus, 1836).

30. Liberman, *Theory and History of Folklore*, 68.

31. It is worth recalling here that in his student years, Propp belonged to a circle of young Petersburg philologists and poets united by their interest in the philosophy of artistic creation and the aesthetics and poetics of Romanticism. These were Viktor Zhirmunskii (engaged at that time with German Romanticism), Boris Eikhenbaum (in his pre-OPOYAZ period), Iurii A. Nikolskii, Ekaterina Malkina, and Vsevolod A. Rozhdestvenskii.

32. Propp, *Morphology of the Folktale* [1968], xxv; Liberman, *Theory and History of Folklore*, 68–69.

33. Liberman, *Theory and History of Folklore*, 82.

34. I. Sorlin, "Aux origines de l'étude typologique et historique du folklore: l'Institut de linguistique de N. Ja. Marr et le jeune Propp," *Regards sur l'anthropologie Sovietique, Cahiers du monde Russe et Sovietique* 31, Nos. 2–3 (Avril–Septembre 1990): 275–84. On Nikolai Yakovlevich Marr (1864–1934), see D. I. Petrenko and K. E. Stein, "On the Linguistic Paleontology of Culture," *Culture and Civilization* VII, no. 3A (2017): 552–62.

35. Propp, *Russkaia skazka*, 161–70.

36. Liberman, *Theory and History of Folklore*, 82. The Darwinian problem of "the origin of species" arises in folklore as well.

37. A. N. Martynova, "Iz vospominanii o V. Ya. Proppe," *Zhivaya starina* 3, no. 7 (1995): 22. Cf. a contemporary's recollection of Russian literature lessons conducted by the young teacher Propp "with such logical clarity as perhaps could not be heard even in the lessons of mathematics." T. I. Silman and V. G. Admoni, *My vspominaem: roman* (St. Petersburg: Kompozitor, 1993), 94.

38. Eleazar Meletinsky, "Marriage: Its Function and Position in the Structure of Folktales," in *Soviet Structural Folkloristics*, ed. Pierre Marranda, vol. 1 (Berlin: De Gruyter, 1974), 61–72; K. W. Chistov, "V. Ya. Propp—Legends and Facts," *International Folklore Review: Folklore Studies from Overseas* IV (1986): 11–12. Many years later, Zhirmunskii would say, half-jokingly, that it was he who had made a "formalist" out of Propp. When the new edition of *Morphology* was being prepared in 1968, I suggested to Vladimir Yakovlevich that he add back this once-removed chapter at least as an appendix, but he refused, explaining that the text had not been preserved.

39. Propp, "K voprosu o proiskhozhdenii volshebnoi skazki," 128–15; Vladimir Propp, "Muzhskoi dom v russkoi skazke," *Uch. zap. LGU* 1, no. 20. Ser. filol. nauk. (1939): 174–98; Propp, "Ritual'nyi smekh"; Liberman, *Theory and History of Folklore*, 124–46; Vladimir Propp, "Motiv chudesnogo rozhdeniia," *Uch. zap. LGU* 12, no. 81. Ser. filol. Nauk (1941). 67–97. See also Vladimir Propp, "Edip v svete fol'klora," *Uch. zap. LGU* 9, no. 72. Ser. filol. nauk. (1944). 138–75.

40. Chistov, "V. Ya. Propp," 12.

41. Vladimir Propp, *Istoricheskie korni volshebnoi skazki*, ed. I. M. Tronskii (Leningrad: Leningradskii gosudarstvennyi universitet, 1946).

42. See more on this in S. E. Hyman, "The Ritual View of Myth and the Mythic," *Journal of American Folklore* LXVIII, no. 270 (October–December

1955): 462–72; and W. Bascom, "The Myth-Ritual Theory," *Journal of American Folklore* LXX, no. 276 (April–June 1957): 103–14.

43. Saintyves, *Les contes de Perrault.*

44. Kazanskii, "Antichnye aspekty," 135.

45. Lur'e, "Dom v lesu."

46. Warner, *Vladimir Iakovlevich Propp,* 65–68.

47. See A. Kojevnikov, "Rituals of Stalinist Culture at Work: Science and the Games of Intraparty Democracy circa 1948," *Russian Review* LVII (January 1998): 25–52.; Loren R. Graham, *Science and Philosophy in the Soviet Union* (New York: Knopf, 1972); and Loren R. Graham, *Science in Russia and the Soviet Union: A Short History* (Cambridge: Cambridge University Press, 2004).

48. Chistov, "V. Ya. Propp," 13; B. N. Putilov, "Vladimiru Iakovlevichu Proppu—100 let," *Etnograficheskoe Obozrenie,* no. 6 (1995): 149; and Warner, *Vladimir Iakovlevich Propp,* 70–78.

49. M. Kuznetsov and I. Dmitrakov, "Protiv burzhuaznykh traditsii v fol'kloristike (O knige Prof. V. Ia. Proppa *Istoricheskie korni volshebnoi skazki,*" *Sovetskaia etnografiia,* no. 2 (1948): 230–39.

50. V. K. Sokolova, "Diskussii po voprosam fol'kloristiki na zasedanijakh sektora fol'klora Instituta etnografii," *Sovetskaia etnografija,* no. 3 (1948): 139–46; and V. Chicherov, "Obsuzhdenie na zasedanijakh uchenogo soveta Instituta etnografii osnovnykh nedostatkov i zadach raboty sovetskikh fol'kloristov," *Sovetskaia etnografija,* no. 3 (1948): 146–63.

51. Warner, *Vladimir Iakovlevich Propp,* 70.

52. V. M. Zhirmunskii, "Propp, V. Ya. Istoricheskie korni volshebnoi skazki," *Sovetskaia kniga,* no. 5 (1947): 97–103.; see also Chistov, "V. Ya. Propp," 13.

53. For example, Meletinsky, "Marriage," 64.

54. Vladimir Propp, *Istoricheskie korni volshebnoi skazki,* ed. I. M. Tronskii (Leningrad: Leningradskii gosudarstvennyi universitet, 1984). This took place seventeen years after the reprint of *Morfologija skazki* in 1969 and ten years after the reprint of a separate volume of his selected articles entitled *Fol'klor i deistvitel'nost'.*

55. It is curious that this particular circumstance provokes especially strong protest from B. Kerbelite in her "anti-Propp" article, "Poisk obriada v skazkakh (zametki o knige V. Ya. Proppa)," *Consortium omnis vitae. Collection of articles on the 70th anniversary of Professor F. P. Fedorov* (Daugavpils: Daugavpils universitatis, 2009), 66–82. In any case, the author focuses more on criticizing details than on the book's main concept.

56. For example, N. V. Novikov, *Obrazy vostochnoslaviaynskoi volshebnoi skazki* (Leningrad: Nauka, 1974), 177–79.

57. B. N. Putilov, ed., *Fol'klor i etnografiia: Sviazi fol'klora s drevnimi predstavleniiami i obriadami* (Leningrad: Nauka, 1977); B. N. Putilov, ed., *Fol'klor i etnografiia: U etnograficheskikh istokov fol'klornykh siuzhetov i obrazov. Sbornik nauchnykh trudov* (Leningrad: Nauka, 1984); A. K. Baiburin, ed., *Etnicheskie stereotipy povedeniia* (Leningrad: Nauka, 1985); A. S. Myl'nikov, ed., *Etnograficheskoe izuchenie znakovykh sredstv kul'tury* (Leningrad: Nauka, 1989); B. N. Putilov, ed., *Fol'klor i etnografiia: Problemy rekonstrukcii faktov traditsionnoi kul'tury. Sbornik naychnykh trudov* (Leningrad: Nauka, 1990); B. N. Baiburin and I. S. Kon, eds., *Etnicheskie stereotipy muzhskogo i zhenskogo povedeniia* (St. Petersburg: Nauka, 1991);

B. N. Baiburin, ed. *Fol'klor i etnograficheskaia deistvitel'nost'* (St. Petersburg:
Nauka, 1992); see also Warner, *Vladimir Iakovlevich Propp*, 64–65.

58. Soviet philological folklore studies vigorously opposed this—in the So-
viet/Russian tradition, folklore is part of philological sciences while ethnology
belongs to the historical sciences.

59. There are translations into Italian (as *Le radici storiche dei raconti di
fate*), beginning with Einaudi's 1949 edition, followed by repeated reprints
in 1972, 1976, 1979, 1985, 1989, and 1992; into Romanian (as *Rădăcinile
istorice ale basmului fantastic*) in 1973; into Spanish (as *Las raíces históricas
del cuento*) in 1974; into French (as *Les racines historiques du conte merveilleux*) in 1983; and into Japanese (as *Mahō mukashi-banashi-no kigen*) in
1983. Prior to the present edition, only the introductory and final chapters of
the book had been translated into English, in Liberman, *Theory and History
of Folklore*, 100–23.

60. Carlo Ginzburg, *Miti, emblemi, spie: Morfologia e storia* (Torino: Einaudi, 1986), xv.

61. Warner, *Vladimir Iakovlevich Propp*, 15–20.

62. Claude Lévi-Strauss, "Structure and Form: Reflections on a Work by
Vladimir Propp" (1960), in *Structural Anthropology*, vol. II (New York: Basic
Books, 1976), 115–45; the article was reprinted in Liberman, *Theory and His-
tory of Folklore*, 167–88.

63. See Liberman, *Theory and History of Folklore*, 67–81. This discus-
sion has generated a number of productive reflections in the academic
tradition: Eleazar Meletinsky, "Structural-Typological Study of Folk-
tales," in *Soviet Structural Folkloristics: Texts by Meletinsky, Nekludov,
Novik, and Segal with Tests of the Approach by Jilek and Jilek-Aaal,
Reid, and Layton*, ed. P. Maranda, vol. 1 (The Hague: Mouton, 1974);
Serge Shishkoff, "The Structure of Fairytales: Propp vs. Levi-Straus,"
Dispositio 1, no. 3 (1976): 271–76; Alan Dundes, "Binary Opposition in
Myth: The Propp / Lévi-Strauss Debate in Retrospect," *Western Folk-
lore* 56, no. 1 (Winter 1997): 39–50; Terence Patrick Murphy, "Vladimir
Propp vs. Claude Lévi-Strauss: A Critical Note," https://www.academia.
edu/30710047/Vladimir_Propp_vs_Claude_L%C3%A9vi-Strauss_A_Criti-
cal_Note (accessed April 30, 2025).

64. M. Guister, "Prizrak formalizma: Polemika Proppa i Levi-Staussa kak
kommunikativnaia neudacha," *Fol'klor: struktura, tipologiia, semiotika* II,
no. 4 (2020), 155–69; M. Guister, "Les études sur le conte merveilleux en
Russie: Tradition orale et conte littéraire (XIXe-XXIe siècle)," *Féeries*, no. 6
(2009): 225–40.

65. Victor Erlich, *Russian Formalism: History, Doctrine* ('S Gravenhage:
Mouton, 1955); A. Hansen-Love, *Der russische Formalismus* (Wien: Östereichische Akademie der Wissenschaften, 1978). After the crackdown on
the Formalist school in the 1930s, the term *formalism* became practically a
curse word in the USSR; see, for example, N. M. Gribachev, "Protiv kosmopolitizma i formalizma v poezii," *Pravda*, February 16, 1949.

66. Claude Lévi-Strauss, *Les Structures élémentaires de la parenté* (Paris:
Presses Universitaires de France, 1949); Lévi-Strauss, *Tristes tropiques* (Paris:
Pion, 1955); Lévi-Strauss, "The Structural Study of Myth," *Journal of American Folklore* LXVIII, no. 270 (1955): 428–44; Lévi Strauss, *Anthropologie
structurale* (Paris: Pion, 1958).

67. Warner, *Vladimir Iakovlevich Propp*, 31–42.

68. Meletinsky, "Structural-Typological Study of Folktales," 30.

69. Ibid., 31; Warner, *Vladimir Iakovlevich Propp*, 19–31.

70. Liberman, *Theory and History of Folklore*, xxvi.

71. Meletinsky, "Structural-Typological Study of Folktales," 30–31.

72. Ibid., 25–26, 29.

73. Kerbelite, "Poisk obriada v skazkakh."

74. Liberman, *Theory and History of Folklore*, 72.

75. "The reduction of all folktales to a basic scheme is seen as a consequence of this approach." Meletinsky, "Structural-Typological Study of Folktales," 30.

76. "The reduction of all fairytales to one basic scheme is therefore not a fallacy; it rather follows from a research objective"; "it also directly serves Propp's purpose, namely, to determine the specificity of the folktale, and to describe and explain its uniform structure." Ibid., 31.

77. V. N. Peretz, "Нова метода вивчати казки," *Етнографічний вісник*, no. 9 (1930): 187–95.

78. Propp, *Morfologiia skazki* (1969), 23–24.

79. "The 'Archetypal Plant' (*Urpflanze*) will be the most amazing creature in the world. Nature itself will envy me. With this model and the key to it, it will then be possible to invent plants to infinity, which should be consistent, that is, which, although they do not exist, could exist. They are not some kind of poetic or pictorial shadows or illusions, but they are characterized by inner truth and necessity. The same law can be applied to all living things" (Propp, *Morfologiia skazki* [1969], 83).

80. The epigraph to chapter VIII (Propp, *Morfologiia skazki* [1969], 79).

81. Cf., "the similarity, for example, of a wondertale and an initiation rite permits us to talk only about the description of the ritual by the tale, its recoding, that is: a semantic correlation, and not about genesis. Moreover, it could be the case that a broader typological correlation between texts and rituals of different traditions is realized here." A. K. Baiburin and G. A. Levinton, "О соотношении фольклорных и этнографических фактов," *Acta Ethnographica Academiae Scientiarium Hungaricae* XXXII, nos. 1–4 (1983): 23.

82. Peretz, "Нова метода вивчати казки," 187–95.

83. Meletinsky, "Structural-Typological Study of Folktales," 30.

84. Ginzburg, *Miti, emblemi, spie*, xv.

85. E. S. Novik, "The Archaic Epic and Its Relationship to Ritual," *Soviet Anthropology and Archeology* 28, no. 2 (Fall 1989), 20–100; and Novik, "Ritual and Folklore in Siberian Shamanism. Experiment in a Comparison of Structures [The Archaic Epic and its Relationship to Ritual]," in *Shamanism. Soviet Studies of Traditional Religion in Siberia and Central Asia*, ed. Margorie Mandelstam Balzer (New York: M. E. Sharpe, 1990), 121–85.

Aarne, Antti. *Die magische Flucht: Eine Märchenstudie*. Helsinki: Suomalainen tiede akatemia, Academia scientiarum fennica, 1930.
———. *Verzeichnis der Märchentypen*. Folklore Fellows Communications, No. 3. Helsinki: Suomalaisen Tiedeakatemian Toimituksia, 1910.
Achelis, Thomas. *Die Religion der Naturvölker im Umriss*. Berlin: de Gruyter, 1919.
Afanas'ev, A. N. *Narodnye russkie skazki*. Edited by M. K. Azadovskiĭ, N. P. Andreev, and Iu. M. Sokolov. Leningrad: Goslitizdat, 1936–40.
———. *Narodnye russkie skazki*. Vols. 1–3. Text compiled and with introduction and commentary by Vladimir Ia. Propp. Moscow: Goslitizdat, 1957.
Allen, James P., trans., intro, notes. *The Ancient Egyptian Pyramid Texts*. Atlanta: Society of Biblical Literature, 2005.
Ankermann, Bernhard. "Die Verbreitung und Formen des Totemismus in Afrika." *Zeitschrift für Ethnologie (ZfE)* 47, no. 2/3 (1915): 114–80.
Anokhin, Andrei V. *Materialy po shamanstvu u altaitsev, sobrannye vo vremia puteshestvii po Altaiu v 1910–1912. Po porucheniiu Russkogo komiteta dlia izucheniia Srednei i Vostochnoi Azii. Sbornik Muzeia antropologii i etnografii pri Rossiiskoi Akademii nauk (Sb. MAE)* 4, no. 2 (1924). https://lib.kunstkamera.ru/files/lib/mae_ras_vol_4-2/mae_ras_vol_4-2.pdf.
Anuchin, Dmitrii N. "Sani, lad'ia i koni, kak prinadlezhnosti pokhoronnogo obriada." *Drevnosti. Trudy Moskovskogo arkheologicheskogo obshchestva* 14 (1890): 81–226.
Aufhauser, Johann B. *Das Drachenwunder des heiligen Georg in der griechischen und lateinischen Überlieferung*. Byzantinisches Archiv, vol. 5. Leipzig: B. G. Teubner, 1911.
Azadovskii, M. K. *Verkhnelenskie skazki*. Irkutsk: Ogiz, 1938.
Baiburin, A. K., ed. *Etnicheskie stereotipy povedeniia*. Leningrad: Nauka, 1985.
———. *Fol'klor i etnograficheskaia deistvitel'nost'*. St. Petersburg: Nauka, 1992.
Baiburin, A. K., and G. A. Levinton. "O sootnoshenii fol'klornykh i etnograficheskikh faktov." *Acta Ethnographica Academiae Scientiarium Hungaricae* 32, nos. 1–4 (1983): 3–31.

Baiburin, A. K., and I. S. Kon, eds. *Etnicheskie stereotipy muzhskogo i zhenskogo povedeniia*. St. Petersburg: Nauka, 1991.

Bascom, W. "The Myth-Ritual Theory." *Journal of American Folklore* LXX, no. 276 (April–June 1957): 103–14.

Baumgartner, Walter. "Jephtas Gelübde Jud. 11, 30–40." *Archiv für Religionswissenschaft* 18 (1915): 240–49.

Bédier, Joseph. *Les fabliaux: études de littérature populaire et d'histoire littéraire du Moyen âge*. Paris: Bouillon, 1893.

Bellows, Henry Adams. *The Poetic Edda: Translated from the Icelandic with an Introduction and Notes*. Princeton, NJ: Princeton University Press, 1936.

Benfey, Theodor. *Pantschatantra*. Pt. 1, *Einleitung: Ueber das indische Grundwerk und dessen Ausflüsse, sowie über die Quellen und Verbreitung des Inhalts derselben*. Leipzig: Brockhaus, 1859.

Best, Elsdon. *The Maori*. Vol. 1. Wellington: H. H. Tombs, 1924.

Boas, Franz. *Indianische Sagen von der nord-pazifischen Küste Amerikas*. Berlin: A. Ascher, 1895.

———. "The Social Organization and the Secret Societies of the Kwakiutl Indians." Report of the US National Museum for 1895. Washington, DC: United States National Museum, 1897.

Bogoraz-Tan, Vladimir G. "Mif ob umiraiushchem i voskresaiushchem zvere." In *Khudozhestvennyi fol'klor*, edited by Iurii Matveevich Sokolov, vol. 1, 66–76. Moscow: Tipografiia Gosizdata "Krasnii proletarii," 1926.

———. "Osnovnye tipy fol'klora severnoi Evrazii i severnoi Ameriki." *Sovetskii fol'klor*, no. 4/5 (1936): 29–50.

Boldyrev, A. V. "Religiia drevnegrecheskikh morekhodov." In *Religiia i obshchestvo: Sbornik statei po izucheniiu sotsial'nikh osnov religioznykh iavlenii drevnego mira*, edited by V. V. Vysotskogo, 144–67. Leningrad: Kn-vo "Seiatel'", 1926.

Bölsche, Wilhelm. *Drachen: Sage und Naturwissenschaft, eine volkstümliche Darstellung*. Stuttgart: Kosmos, 1929.

Bolte, Johannes, and Georg Polivka. *Anmerkungen zu den Kinder- und Hausmärchen der Brüder Grimm*. Vols. 1–5. Leipzig: Dieterich'sche Verlagsbuchhandlung, 1913–32.

Borovkov, Aleksandr K., ed. *Skazki narodov Vostoka*. Moscow: Izd. Akademii nauk, 1938.

Bouchal, Leo, ed., *Mitteilungen der Anthropologischen Gesellschaft in Wien*. Vol. 39. Vienna: Alfred Hölder, 1909.

Bousset, Wilhelm. "Die Himmelsreise der Seele." *Archiv für Religionswissenschaft* 4 (1901): 136–69, 229–73.

Bravo, Gian Luigi, ed. *Vladimir Ja. Propp. Morfologia della fiaba*. Con un intervento di Claude Levi-Strauss e una replica dell'autore. Torino: Giulio Einaudi Editore, 1966.

Breasted, James H. *Development of Religion and Thought in Ancient Egypt*. London: Scribner, 1912.

Brinton, Daniel G. "The Folk-Lore of Yucatan." *Folk-Lore Journal* 1, no. 1 (1883): 244–56.

Budge, Wallis E. A. *The Babylonian Legends of the Creation and the Fight between Bel and the Dragon: As Told by Assyrian Tablets from Nineven*. London: The British Museum, 1921.

———. *The Book of Opening the Mouth*. Books on Egypt and Chaldaea, vols. 26–27. London: Kegan, Paul Trench, Trübner, 1909.

———. *The Book of the Dead*. New York: Barnes & Noble, 1951.

———. *Coptic Apocrypha in the Dialect of Upper Egypt*. Oxford: Oxford University Press, 1913.

Burger, Friedrich. *Unter den Kannibalen der Südsee*. Dresden: Deutsche Buchwerkstätten, 1923.

Buschan, Georg. *Die Sitten der Völker. Liebe, Ehe, Heirat, Geburt, Religion, Aberglaube, Lebensgewohnheiten, Kultureingentümlichkeiten, Tod und Bestattung bei allen Völkern der Erde*. Stuttgart: Union Deutsche Verlagsgesellschaft, 1914.

Chernetsov, V. N. *Vogul'skie skazki: Sbornik fol'klora naroda mansi (vogulov)*. Leningrad: Khudozhestvennaia literatura, 1935.

Chicherov, V. "Obsuzhdenie na zasedaniiakh uchenogo soveta Instituta etnografii osnovnykh nedostatkov i zadach raboty sovetskikh fol'kloristov." *Sovetskaia etnografija*, no. 3 (1948): 146–63.

Chistov, K. W. "V. Ya. Propp—Legend and Fact." *International Folklore Review: Folklore Studies from Overseas* 4 (1984): 8–17.

Codrington, Robert H. *The Melanesians: Studies in their Anthropology and Folklore*. Oxford: Clarendon, 1891.

Cosquin, Emmanuel. *Études folkloriques, recherches sur les migrations des contes populaires et leur point de départ*. Paris: E. Champion, 1922.

Curtin, Jeremiah. *Myths and Folk-Tales of the Russians, Western Slavs, and Magyars*. London: Sampson Low, Marston, Searle, & Rivington, 1891.

Cushing, Frank H. *Zuñi Folk Tales*. New York: G. P. Putnam's Sons, 1901.

Dieseldorf, Erwin Paul. "Kunst und Religion der Mayavölker im alten und heutigen Mittelamerika." *ZfE* 57, no. 1/2 (1925): 1–45.

Dieterich, Albrecht. *Mutter Erde: Ein versuch über volksreligion*. 3rd ed. Leipzig: Teubner, 1925.

———. *Nekyia: Beiträge zur Erklärung der neuentdeckten Petrusapokalypse*. Leipzig: Teubner, 1893.

Dobrovol'skii, V. N. *Smolenskii etnograficheskii sbornik*. Zapiski Imperatorskogo Russkogo geograficheskogo obshchestva po otdeleniiu etnografii, vol. 20. St. Petersburg: Russkoe geograficheskoe obshchestvo, 1891.

Dorsey, George A. *Traditions of the Skidi Pawnee*. Memoirs of the American Folklore Society, vol. 8. New York: Houghton, Mifflin, 1904.

Dorsey, George A., and Alfred L. Kroeber. *Traditions of the Arapaho. Collected under the Auspices of the Field Columbian Museum and of the American Museum of Natural History*. Anthropological Series, vol. 5. Chicago: Field Columbian Museum, 1903.

Driagin, N. M. "Liubovnye motivy martovskogo eposa gortsev Severnogo Kabkaza." In *Tristan i Isol'da: Ot geroini liubvi feodal'noi Evrony do bogini matriarkhal'noi Afrevrazii*, edited by Nikolai Ia. Marr. Leningrad: Akademii nauk, 1932.

Dundes, Alan. "Binary Opposition in Myth: The Propp / Lévi-Strauss Debate in Retrospect." *Western Folklore* 56, no. 1 (Winter 1997): 39–50.

———. "From Etic to Emic Units in the Structural Study of Folktales." In *The Meaning of Folklore: The Analytical Essays of Alan Dundes*, edited and introduced by S. J. Bronner, 88–106. Logan, UT: Utah State University Press, 2007.

Dyrenkova, N. P. "Poluchenie shamanskogo dara po vozreniiam turetskikh plemen." *Sb. MAE* 9 (1930): 267–91.

Eckermann, I. P. *Gespräche mit Goethe in den letzten Jahren seines Lebens, 1823–1832.* Vols. 1–3. Leipzig: Brockhaus, 1836.

Ehrenreich, Paul. *Die Mythen und Legenden der südamerikanischen Urvölker und ihre Beziehungen zu denen Nordamerikas und der alten Welt.* Berlin: A. Asher, 1905.

Elkin, Adolphus P. "The Rainbow-Serpent Myth in North-West Australia." *Oceania* 1, no. 3 (1930): 349–52.

Engels, Friedrich. *Dialectics of Nature.* Translated and edited by Clemens Dutt. New York: International Publishers, 1940.

———. *Herr Eugen Dühring's Revolution in Science ("Anti-Dühring").* Translated by Emile Burns, edited by C. P. Dutt. New York: International Publishers, 1966.

———. "Letter 214. Engels to Conrad Schmidt. 27 October 1890." In *Selected Correspondence, 1846–1895,* by Karl Marx and Friedrich Engels, translated by Dona Torr, 477–84. New York: International Publishers, 1942.

———. "The Origin of the Family, Private Property and the State." In *Karl Marx and Friedrich Engels: Selected Works in Two Volumes,* by Karl Marx and Friedrich Engels, vol. 2, 170–327. Moscow: Foreign Languages Publishing House, 1962.

Erlich, Victor. *Russian Formalism: History, Doctrine.* 'S Gravenhage: Mouton, 1955.

Filin, F. P., compiler. *Slovar' russkikh narodnykh govorov.* Leningrad: Nauka, 2021.

Fischer, J. L. "The Sociopsychological Analysis of Folklore." *Current Anthropology* 4 (1963): 235–96.

Fiustel' de-Kulanzh, N. D. [Fustel de Coulanges, Numa Denis]. *Grazhdanskaia obshchina drevnego mira.* Translated by A. M. St. Petersburg: Tip. B. M. Vol'fa, 1906.

Frantsov, Iurii P. "Drevneegipetskie skazki o verkhovnykh zhretsakh." *Sovetskii fol'klor,* no. 2/3 (1935): 159–231.

Frazer, James G. *The Belief in Immortality.* Vol. 3. London: Macmillan, 1924.

———. *The Belief in Immortality and the Worship of the Dead.* Vol. 2. London: Macmillan, 1922.

———. *The Fear of the Dead in Primitive Religion.* Vol. 1. London: Macmillan, 1933.

———. *The Golden Bough: A Study in Magic and Religion.* Vol. 2, pts. 1–2, *The Magic Art and the Evolution of Kings.* London: Macmillan, 1911. https://archive.org/details/goldenboughstudy02frazuoft.

———. *The Golden Bough.* Vol. 3, pt. 2, *Taboo and the Perils of the Soul.* 3rd ed. London: Macmillan, 1911. https://archive.org/details/goldenbough-studo3fraz.

———. *The Golden Bough.* Vol. 4, *The Dying God.* London: Macmillan, 1911. https://archive.org/details/goldenboughstudyo4fraz.

———. *The Golden Bough.* Vol. 10, *Balder the Beautiful, Festivals of Europe and the Doctrine of the External Soul.* Vol. 1. 3rd ed. London: Macmillan, 1913. https://archive.org/details/1913goldenboughs10fraz.

———. *The Golden Bough.* Vol. 11, *Balder the Beautiful, the Fire Festivals of Europe and the Doctrine of the External Soul.* Vol. 2. London: Macmillan, 1913. https://archive.org/details/goldenboughstudy11fraz.

———. *Zolotaia vetv'* [*The Golden Bough*]. Vols. 1–3. Moscow: Nauchnoe obshchestvo "Ateist," 1928.

Freidenberg, Olga M. *Poetika siuzheta i zhanra: Period antichnoi literatury.* Leningrad: Khudozhestvennaia literatura, 1936.

———. "Siuzhet Tristana i Isol'dy v mifologemakh egeiskogo otrezka Sredizemnomor'ia." In Marr, *Tristan i Isol'da,* 91–114. Leningrad: Akademii nauk, 1932.

Frobenius, Leo. *Das Zeitalter des Sonnengottes.* Berlin: G. Reimer, 1904.

———. *Die Masken und Geheimbünde Afrikas.* Abhandlungen der Kaiserlichen Leopoldinisch-Carolinischen Deutschen Akademie der Naturforscher, vol. 74, no. 1. Halle: Druck von E. Karras, 1898.

———. *Die Weltanschauung der Naturvölker.* Weimar: E. Felber, 1898.

Fülleborn, Friedrich. *Deutsche-Ost-Afrika: Wissenschaftliche Forschungsresultate über Land und Leute unseres ostafrikanischen Schutzgebietes und der angrenzenden Länder.* Vol. 9. Berlin: Dietrich Reimer, 1906.

Gayton, Anna H. "The Orpheus Myth in North America." *Journal of American Folklore* 48, no. 189 (1935): 263–93.

Gennep, Arnold van. *Les rites de passage, etudes systematiques des rites.* Paris: Emile Nourry, 1909.

———. *Mythes et legendes d'Australie: études d'ethnographie et de sociologie.* Paris: Emile Nourry, 1906.

Ginzburg, Carlo. *Miti, emblemi, spie: Morfologia e storia.* Torino: Einaudi, 1986.

Graham, Loren R. *Science and Philosophy in the Soviet Union.* New York: Knopf, 1972.

———. *Science in Russia and the Soviet Union: A Short History.* Cambridge: Cambridge University Press, 2004.

Gressmann, Hugo. *Altorientalische Texte und Bilder zum Alten Testament.* Tübingen: J. C. B. Mohr, 1909.

Gribachev, N. M. "Protiv kosmopolitizma i formalizma v poezii." *Pravda,* February 16, 1949.

Griffith, Ralph T. H. *The Hymns of the Rigveda: Translated with a Popular Commentary.* 2nd ed. Benares: J. Lazarus, 1896. https://en.wikisource.org/wiki/The_Rig_Veda and https://sacred-texts.com/hin/rigveda/index.htm.

Grimm, Jacob, and Wilhelm Grimm. *Household Tales.* Vol. 1. Translated by Margaret Hunt. London: Bell and Sons, 1884.

———. *Kinder- und Hausmarchen.* Vols. 1–3. Berlin: G. Reimer, 1822.

Guister, M. "Les études sur le conte merveilleux en Russie: Tradition orale et conte littéraire (XIXe-XXIe siècle)." *Féeries,* no. 6 (2009): 225–40.

———. "Prizrak formalizma: Polemika Proppa i Levi-Staussa kak kommunikativnaia neudacha." *Fol'klor: struktura, tipologiia, semiotika* 2, no. 4 (2019): 155–69

Güntert, Hermann. *Kalypso: Bedeutungsgeschichtliche Untersuchungen auf dem Gebiet der indogermanischen Sprachen.* Halle: Niemeyer, 1919.

Guterman, Norbert, trans. *Russian Fairy Tales.* Collected by Alexander Afanas'ev. New York: Panrheon, 1975.

Gutmann, Bruno. "Opferstätten der Wadschagga." *Archiv für Religionswissenschaft* 12 (1909): 83–100.

Haeberlin, Hermann, and Erna Günther. "Ethnographische Notizen über die Indianerstämme des Puget-Sundes." *ZfE* 56, no. 1/4 (1924): 1–74.

Hahn, Eduard. *Demeter und Baubo: Versuch einer Theorie der Entstehung unsres Ackerbaus.* Lübeck: Selbstverlag des verfassers, 1896.

Hahn, Johann G. *Griechische und albanesische Märchen.* Vol. 1. Leipzig: W. Engelmann, 1864.

Hambly, Wilfrid D. *Serpent Worship in Africa.* Field Museum of Natural History: Anthropological Series, vol. 21, no. 1. Chicago: Field Museum of Natural History, 1931.

Hambruch, Paul. *Südseemärchen aus Australien, Neu-Guinea, Fidji, Karolinen, Samoa, Tonga, Hawaii, Neu-Seeland.* Jena: E. Diederichs, 1912.

Haney, Jack V. *The Complete Folktales of A. N. Afanas'ev.* Vol. 1. Jackson: University Press of Mississippi, 2014.

———, ed. "Review of Warner 2005." *Folklorica: Journal of the Slavic and East European Folkore Association* XI (2006): 117–19.

Hansen-Love, A. *Der russische Formalismus.* Wien: Östereichische Akademie der Wissenschaften, 1978.

Hartland, Edwin S. "The Forbidden Chamber." *Folk-Lore Journal* 3, no. 1 (1885): 193–242.

———. *The Legend of Perseus.* Vols. 1–3. London: D. Nutt, 1894–96.

Hendricks, William O. *Essays on Semioliguistics and Verbal Art.* Berlin: De Gruyter, 1974.

Hermes, Gertrud. "Der Zug des gezähmten Pferdes durch Europa." *Anthropos* 32, no. 1/2 (1937): 105–46.

Herrera, Antonio de. *General History of the Vast Continent and Islands of America,* Translated by Capt. John Stevens. London: Jer. Batley, 1725–26.

Hertel, Johannes. *Die arische Feuerlehre.* Leipzig: Haessel, 1925.

———. *Indische Märchen.* Jena: E. Diederichs, 1921.

Holland, R. "Zur Typik der Himmelfahrt." *Archiv für Religionswissenschaft* 23, no. 3/4 (1925): 207–20.

Howey, M. Oldfield. *The Horse in Magic and Myth.* London: W. Rider, 1923.

Hyman, S. E. "The Ritual View of Myth and the Mythic." *Journal of American Folklore* LXVIII, no. 270 (October–December 1955): 462–72.

Iavorskii, Iu. A. *Pamiatniki Galitsko-russkoi narodnoi slovesnosti.* Vol. 1, no. 27. Kiev: Zapiski IRGO, 1915.

Iokhel'son, Vladimir I. [Jochelson, Vladimir]. "'Magicheskoe begstvo' kak obshcherasprostranennyi skazochno-mificheskii episod." In *Sbornik v chest' semidesiatiletiia professora D. N. Anuchina,* edited by V. V. Bogdanov. Moscow: IOLEAE, 1913.

Jacoby, A. "Zum Zerstückelungs- und Wiederbelebungswunder der indischen Fakire." *Archiv für Religionswissenschaft* 17 (1914): 455–75.

Jensen, Peter. *Das Gilgamesch-Epos in der Weltliteratur.* Strasbourg: Karl J. Trübner, 1906.

Jeremias, Alfred. *Hölle und Paradies bei den Babyloniern.* Leipzig: J. C. Hinrichs, 1903.

Josselin de Jong, Jan P. B. "Religionen der Naturvölker Indonesiens." *Archiv für Religionswissenschaft* 30, no. 3/4 (1933): 174–98, 360–82.

Kagarov, Evgenii G. "Sostav i proiskhozhdenie svadebnoi obriadnosti." *Sb. MAE* 8, no. 29 (1929): 152–95.

Kaibel, Georg, ed. *Inscriptiones Graecae*. Vol. 14, *Inscriptiones Siciliae et Italiae: additis graecis Galliae, Hispaniae, Britanniae, Germaniae inscriptionibus*. Berlin: Georg Reimer, 1890.

Karnaukhova, I. V. *Skazki i predaniia Severnogo kraia*. Polnoe sobranie russkikh skazok: Dovoennye sobraniia, vol. 12. Moscow: Akademii nauk, 1934.

Karskii, E. F., ed., *Izvestiia Otdeleniia russkogo iazyka i slovesnosti Akademii nauk Soiuza Sovetskikh Sotsialisticheskikh Respublik*, vol. 31, 353–69. Leningrad: Izdatel'stvo Akademii nauk SSSR, 1926.

Karsten, Rafael. "Die altperuanische Religion." *Archiv für Religionswissenschaft* 25, no. 1/2 (1927): 36–51.

Kazanskii, Boris V. "Antichnye aspekty siuzheta Tristana i Isol'dy." In Marr, *Tristan i Isol'da*, 115–35. Leningrad: Akademii nauk, 1932.

Kerbelite, B. "Poisk obriada v skazkakh (zametki o knige V. Ya. Proppa)." In *Consortium omnis vitae: sbornik statei k 70-letiiu professora F. P. Fedorova*, edited by Anna Stankeviča and Samuils Švarcbands, 66–82. Daugavpils: Daugavpils Universitātes Akadēmiskais apgāds "Saule," 2009.

Kharuzin, Nikolai N. *Etnografiia*. Vol. 4, *Verovaniia*. Edited by Vera and Aleksei Kharuzin. St. Petersburg: Gosudarstvennaia tipografiia, 1905.

———. *Russkie lopari: ocherki proshlogo i sovremennogo byta*. Moscow: Tovarishchestvo skoropechatnii A. A. Levinson, 1890.

Khazhba, Arsenii Konstaninovich, and Victor Iosifovich Kukba, eds. and trans. *Abkhazskie skazki*. Sukhumi: Alashara, 1935.

Khudiakov, I. A. *Velikorusskie skazki*, issues 1–3. Moscow: Tip. V. Gracheva, 1860–62.

———. *Verkhoianskii sbornik*. Zapiski Vostochno-Sibirskogo otdela Imperatorskogo russkogo geograficheskogo obshchestva po etnografii, vol. 1, no. 3. Irkutsk: Tip. K. I. Vitkovskoi, 1890.

Khudiakov, Mikhail G. "Kul't konia v Prikam'i." In *Iz istorii dokapitalisticheskikh formatsii: sb. statei k 45-letiiu nauch. deiatel'nosti N. Ia. Marra*, edited by S. N. Bykovskii et al. Izvestiia Gosudarstvennoi akademii istorii material'noi kul'tury, no. 100. Moscow: Akademii nauk, 1933.

Kirby, William F. "The Forbidden Doors of *The Thousand and One Nights*." *Folk-Lore Journal* 5, no. 2 (1887): 112–24.

Kirpichnikov, Aleksandr. *Sviatoi Georgii i Egorii khrabryi: Issledovanie literaturnoi istorii khristianskoi legendy*. St. Petersburg: Tip. V. S. Balasheva, 1879.

Koch-Grünberg, Theodor. *Mythen und Legenden der Taulipang- und Arekuna-Indianer*. Vol. 2 of *Vom Roroima zum Orinoco: Ergebnisse einer Reise in Nordbrasilien und Venezuela in den Jahren 1911–1913*. Berlin: Dietrich Reimer, 1924.

Kohler, Josef. *Der Ursprung der Melusinensage: Eine ethnologische Untersuchung*. Leipzig: E. Pfeiffer, 1895.

Kojevnikov, A. "Rituals of Stalinist Culture at Work: Science and the Games of Intraparty Democracy circa 1948." *Russian Review* 57 (January 1998): 25–52.

Köngas Maranda, Elli, and Pierre Maranda. *Structural Models in Folklore and Transformational Essays*. The Hague: Mouton, 1971.

Korguev, Matvei M. *Skazki Karel'skogo Belomor'ia.* Vol. 1. Edited by Mark
　　K. Azadovskii. Introduction and commentaries by Aleksandr N. Nechaev.
　　Petrozavodsk: Karel'skoe gos. izd-vo, 1939.
Kotsiubinskii, S. D., ed. *Skazki i legendy tatar Kryma.* Recorded by K. U.
　　Useinov. Simferopol: Gosizdat Krym, 1936.
Kozin, Sergei A., trans., intro, commentary. *Geseriada: Skazanie o milos-
　　tivom Geser Mergen-khane, iskorenitele desiati zol v desiati stranakh
　　sveta.* Moscow: Izdatel'stvo Akademii nauk SSSR, 1935.
Kretschmer, Paul. "Das Märchen von Blaubart." In *Mitteilungen der Antro-
　　pologischen Gesellschaft in Wien,* edited by Wilhelm Hein, vol. 31, 62–
　　112. Vienna: Selestverlag der gesellschaft, 1901.
Krickeberg, Walter. *Märchen der Azteken und Inkaperuaner Maya und
　　Muisca.* Jena: Diederichs, 1928.
Kroeber, Alfred L. *Gros Ventre Myths and Tales.* Anthropological Papers of
　　the American Museum of Natural History, vol. 1, pt. 3. New York: Trust-
　　ees, 1907.
———. *The Religion of the Indians of California.* University of California
　　Publications in American Archaeology and Ethnology, vol. 4, no. 6.
　　Berkeley: University Press, 1907.
Kunov, Genrikh. *Proiskhozhdenie religii i very v boga.* Moscow: Kommunist,
　　1919.
Küster, Erich. *Die Schlange in der griechischen Kunst und Religion.* Religion-
　　sgeschichtliche Versuche und Vorarbeiten, vol. 13, no. 2. Giessen: Verlag
　　von Alfred Töpelmann, 1913.
Kuznetsov, M., and I. Dmitrakov. "Protiv burzhuaznykh traditsii v
　　fol'kloristike (O knige Prof. V. Ia. Proppa *Istoricheskie korni volshebnoi
　　skazki.*" *Sovetskaia etnografiia,* no. 2 (1948): 230–39.
Lenin, Vladimir I. "On the Question of Dialectics." In *V. I. Lenin: Collected
　　Works,* 4th ed., translated by Clemens Dutt, edited by Stewart Smith, vol.
　　38, 359–63. Moscow: Foreign Languages Publishing House, 1961.
Le Page Renoult, P., and E. Naville. *The Egyptian Book of the Dead. Trans-
　　lation and Commentary.* London: Society of Biblical Archeology, 1904.
　　https://www.gutenberg.org/files/69566/69566-h/69566-h.htm#cho76.
Lévi-Strauss, Claude. *Anthropologie structurale.* Paris: Pion, 1958.
———. *Les Structures élémentaires de la parenté.* Paris: Presses Universitaires
　　de France, 1949.
———. *Structural Anthropology.* Vol. 2. New York: Basic Books, 1976.
———. "The Structural Study of Myth." *Journal of American Folklore* LX-
　　VIII, no. 270 (1955): 428–44.
———. *Tristes tropiques.* Paris: Pion, 1955.
Lévy-Bruhl, Lucien. *Das Denken der Naturvölker.* 2nd ed. Vienna: Wilhelm
　　Braumüller, 1929.
———. *Sverkh'estestvennoe v pervobytnom myshlenii.* Moscow: OGIZ,
　　1937.
Liberman, Anatoly, ed. *Theory and History of Folklore.* Translated by Ari-
　　adna Y. Martin and Richard P. Martin. Minneapolis: University of Min-
　　nesota Press, 1984.
Liljeblad, Sven S. *Die Tobiasgeschichte und andere Märchen mit Toten Helf-
　　ern.* Lund: P. Lindstedts Univ.-Bokhandel, 1927.
Lippert, Julius. *Istoriia kul'tury.* St. Petersburg: F. Pavlenkova, 1902.

Loeb, Edwin M. *Tribal Initiations and Secret Societies*. Vol. 25, no. 3. Berkeley: University of California Publications in American Archaeology and Ethnology, 1929.

Ludwig, Alfred. *Der Rigveda, oder Die heiligen Hymnen der Brahmana*. Vols. 1–5. Prague: F. Tempsky, 1876–83.

Lur'e, Solomon Ia. "Dom v lesu." *Iazyk i literatura* 8 (1932): 159–94.

Lüthi, Max. "Vladimir Propp, Morphologie des Marchens." *Zeitschrift für Volkskunde* 69 (1973): 290–93.

Mackensen, Lutz. *Der singende Knochen: Ein Beitrag zur vergleichenden Märchenforschung*. Helsinki: Suomalainen tiedeakatemia, 1923.

Mähly, Jakob. *Die Schlange im Mythus und Cultus der classischen Völker*. Basel: Buchdruckerei von C. Schultze, 1867.

Malten, Ludolf. "Das Pferd im Totenglauben." *Jahrbuch des Kaiserlich deutschen archäologischen Instituts* 29 (1914): 179–256.

———. "Der Raub der Kore." *Archiv für Religionswissenschaft* 12, nos. 2–3 (1909): 285–312.

Marr, Nikolai Ia. "'Loshad''/'ptitsa' totem urarto-etrusskogo plemeni, i eshche dva etapa v ego migratsii." *Iafeticheskii sbornik* 1 (1922): 133–36.

———. "Sredstva peredvizheniia, orudiia samozashchity i proizvodstva v doistorii." In *Izbrannye raboty*. Vol. 3, edited by V. B. Aptekar', 123–50. Moscow: Gosudarstvennoe sotsial'no-ekonomicheskoe izdatel'stvo, 1934.

———. *Tristan i Isol'da: Ot geroini liubvi feodal'noi Evropy do bogini matriarkhal'noi Afroevrazii*. Leningrad: Akademii nauk, 1932.

Martynova, A. N. "Iz vospominanii o V. Ya. Proppe." *Zhivaia starina* 3, no. 7 (1995): 21–22.

———. *Vladimir Yakovlevich Propp: Zhiznennyi put'. Nauchnaia deiatel'nost'*. St. Petersburg: Dmitrii Bulanin, 2006.

Marx, K., and F. Engels, *Sochineniia*. Vol. 13. Moscow: Izdatel'stvo politicheskoi literatury, 1955–74.

Marx, K., and F. Engels. *Sochineniia*. 2nd ed. Moscow: Izdatel'stvo politicheskoi literatury, 1955–81.

Marx, Karl. "Preface to *A Contribution to the Critique of Political Economy*." In *The Marx-Engels Reader*, edited by Robert C. Tucker, 3–6. New York: W. W. Norton, 1978.

Maspero, Gaston. *Les Contes populaires de l'Égypte ancienne*. 3rd ed. Paris: Guilmoto, 1900. https://archive.org/details/lescontespopulai-oomasp.

Mathews, Robert H. "Some Initiation Ceremonies of the Aborigines of Victoria." *ZfE* 37, no. 6 (1905): 872–79.

McCarthy, Michael. *The Moth Snowstorm: Nature and Joy*. New York: John Murray, 2015.

McConnel, Ursula. "The Rainbow-Serpent in North Queensland." *Oceania* 1, no. 3 (1930): 347–49.

Meier, Josef. "Mythen und Sagen der Admiralitätsinsulaner." *Anthropos* 2, no. 4 (1907): 646–67; no. 5 (1907): 933–41; vol. 3, no. 2 (1908): 193–206; no. 4 (1908): 651–71; vol. 4, no. 2 (1909): 354–74.

Meinhof, Carl. *Die Religionen der Afrikaner in ihrem Zusammenhang mit dem Wirtschaftsleben*. Instituttet for sammenlignende kulturforskning, Serie A: Forelesninger, vol. 7. Oslo: H. Aschehoug, 1926.

Meletinsky, Eleazar. "Marriage: Its Function and Position in the Structure of Folktales." In *Soviet Structural Folkloristics*, edited by Pierre Marranda, vol. 1, 61–72. Berlin: De Gruyter, 1974.

———. "Structural-Typological Study of Folktales." In *Soviet Structural Folkloristics: Texts by Meletinsky, Nekliudov, Novik, and Segal with Tests of the Approach by Jilek and Jilek-Aaal, Reid, and Layton*. Vol. 1, introduction and edited by P. Maranda, 19–52. The Hague: Mouton, 1974.

Minaev, Ivan P. *Indeiskie skazki i legendy, sobrannye v Kamaone v 1875 g.* St. Petersburg: V. F. Demakov, 1877.

Molotov, V. M., and M. A. Savel'ev. *Leninskii sbornik.* Vol. 12. Moscow: Gosizdat, 1930.

Moret, Alexandre [Russian transliteration: More, Aleksandr]. *Tsari i bogi Egipta [Kings and Gods of Egypt].* Translated by E. Gregorovich. Moscow: M. i S. Sabashnikovy, 1914.

Morgan, Lewis H. *Ancient Society, or Researches in the Lines of Human Progress from Savagery through Barbarism to Civilization.* New York: Henry Holt, 1877.

Murphy, Terence Patrick. "Vladimir Propp vs. Claude Lévi-Strauss: A Critical Note." https://www.academia.edu/30710047/Vladimir_Propp_vs_Claude_L%C3%A9vi-Strauss_A_Critical_Note (accessed May 8, 2025)

Myl'nikov, A. S., ed. *Etnograficheskoe izuchenie znakovykh sredstv kul'tury.* Leningrad: Nauka, 1989.

Nansen, Fridtjof. *Eskimoleben.* Berlin: Heinrich Meyer, 1903.

Nathorst, B. *Formal or Structural Studies of Traditional Tales: The Usefulness of Some Methodological Proposals Advanced by Vladimir Propp, Alan Dundes, Claude Lévi-Strauss and Edmund Leach.* Translated by Donald Burton. Stockholm: University of Stockholm, 1969.

Naville, Edouard. *Das Aegyptische Todtenbuch der XIII. bis XX. Dynastie: aus verschiedenen Urkunden.* Vols. 1–3. Berlin: A. Asher, 1886.

Negelein, Julius von. *Das Pferd im arischen Altertum.* Teutonia: Arbeiten zur germanischen Philologie, vol. 2. Königsberg: Gräfe & Unzer, 1903.

———. "Das Pferd im Seelenglauben und Totenkult." *Zeitschrift des Vereins für Volkskunde (ZVV)* 11 (1901): 406–20.

———. "Das Pferd im Seelenglauben und Totenkult." *ZVV* 12 (1902): 14–25.

———. "Das Pferd in der Volksmedizin." *Globus* 80, no. 13 (1901): 201–04.

———. "Die Reise der Seele ins Jenseits." *ZVV* 11 (1901): 16–28, 149–58, 263–71.

———. "Die Seele als Vogel." *Globus* 79, no. 23 (1901): 357–61, 381–84.

———. "Die volksthümliche Bedeutung der weissen Farbe." *ZfE* 33, no. 1 (1901): 53–100.

Nekliudov, Sergei. "U istokov serii: rozhdenie 'cherepashki.'" In *"U vremeni v plenu": Pamiati Sergeia Sergeevicha Tsel'nikera: Sbornik statei,* edited by I. V. Stebleva, 14–23. Moscow: Vostochnaia literatura, 2000.

Neuhauss, Richard. *Deutsch-Neu-Guinea.* Vol. 3, *Beiträge der Missionare Keysser, Stolz, Zahn, Lehner, Bamler.* Berlin: Dietrich Reimer, 1911.

Nevermann, Hans. *Ergebnisse der Südsee-Expedition, 1908–1910.* Vol. 3, *Admirälitats-inseln.* Hamburg: L. Friederichsen, 1934.

———. *Masken und Geheimbünde in Melanesien.* Berlin: Verlag von Reimar Hobbing, 1933.

Nikiforov, Aleksandr I. "K voprosu o morfologicheskom izuchenii narodnoi skazki." In *Sbornik statei v chest' akad. A. I. Sobolevskogo*, edited by V. N. Peretts, 172–78. Leningrad: Izdatel'stvo Akademii nauk SSSR, 1928.

———. "Pobeditel' zmeia: Iz severnorusskikh skazok." *Sovetskii fol'klor*, no. 4/5 (1936): 143–243.

———. "Review of *Kaiser und Abt*, by Walter Anderson; *Die Legende von den zwei Erzündern*, by N. P. Andreev; and *Skazka*, vol. 1, by R. M. Volkov." In *Izvestiia Otdeleniia russkogo iazyka i slovesnosti Akademii nauk Soiuza Sovetskikh Sotsialisticheskikh Respublik*, edited by E. F. Karskii, vol. 31, 353–69. Leningrad: Izdatel'stvo Akademii nauk SSSR, 1926.

———. *Skazochnye materialy Zaonezh'ia, sobrannye v 1926 godu. Skazochnaia Komissiia v 1926 g. Obzor Rabot*. Leningrad: Gosudarstvennoe russkoe geograficheskoe obshchestvo, 1927.

Nilsson, Martin P. *Primitive Religion*. Religionsgeschichtliche Volksbücher für die deutsche christliche Gegenwart, series 3, Allgemeine Religionsgeschichte, nos. 13–14. Tübingen: Mohr Siebeck, 1911.

Novik, E. S. "The Archaic Epic and Its Relationship to Ritual." *Soviet Anthropology and Archeology* 28, no. 2 (1989): 20–100.

———. "Ritual and Folklore in Siberian Shamanism. Experiment in a Comparison of Structures [The Archaic Epic and Its Relationship to Ritual]." In *Shamanism. Soviet Studies of Traditional Religion in Siberia and Central Asia*, edited by Margorie Mandelstam Balzer, 121–85. Armonk, NY: M. E. Sharpe, 1990.

Novikov, N. V. *Obrazy vostochnoslaviaynskoi volshebnoi skazki*. Leningrad: Nauka, 1974.

Oldenberg, Hermann. *Die Religion des Veda*. Berlin: W. Hertz, 1894.

Ol'denburg, Sergei F. "Fablo vostochnogo proiskhozhdeniia." *Zhurnal Ministerstva narodnogo prosveshcheniia* 345, no. 4, pt. 2 (1903): 217–38.

———, ed. *Skazochnaia komissiia v 1926 g. Obzor rabot*. Leningrad: Gosudarstvennoe russkoe geograficheskoe obshchestvo, 1927.

Onchukov, Nikolai E. *Severnye skazki: Arkhangel'skaia i Olenetskaia gg.* Zapiski Russkogo geograficheskogo obshchestva po otdeleniiu etnografii, vol. 33. St. Petersburg: A. S. Suvorin, 1908.

Orlova, G. "Rozhdenie vreditelia: otritsatel'naia politicheskaia sakralizatsiya v strane sovetov (1920-e)." In *Zeit-Räume Neue Tendenzen in der historischen Kulturforschung aus der Perspektive der Slavistik*. Vol. 49, edited by Susi K. Frank und Igor' P. Smirnov, 309–46. Wiener Slawistischer Almanach. Vienna: Gesellschaft zur Förderung slawistischer Studien, 2003.

Ovid. *Metamorfozy*. Translated by Sergei V. Shervinskii. Leningrad: Academia, 1937.

Ovsianiko-Kulikovskii, Dmitrii N. *K istorii kul'ta ognia u indusov v epokhu ved*. Odessa: n.p., 1887.

Parkinson, Richard. *Dreißig Jahre in der Südsee: Land und Leute, Sitten und Gebräuche im Bismarckarchipel und auf den deutschen Salomoinseln*. Stuttgart: Strecker & Schröder, 1907.

Peretts, V. N. "Nova metoda vyvchaty kazky." *Etnografichnyi visnyk*, no. 9 (1930): 187–95.

Peretz, V. N. "Nova metoda vivchati kazki." *Etnografichnii visnik*, no. 9 (Kiev, 1930): 187–95.

Petrenko, D. I., and K. E. Stein. "On the Linguistic Paleontology of Culture." *Culture and Civilization* VII, no. 3A (2017): 552–62.

Petrovskii, M. A. "Morfologiia novelly." In *Ars Poetica: Sbornik statei B. I. Yarho, A. M. Peshkovskogo, M. A. Petrovskogo, M. P. Stoliarova, R. O. Shor.*Vol. 1, edited by M. A. Petrovskii, 69–100. Moscow: Brücken-Verlag, 1927.

———. "Morfologiia pushkinskogo 'Vystrela.'" In *Problemy poetiki*, edited by V. Ya. Briusov, 171–204. Moscow: Zemlia i fabrika, 1925.

Philpot, J. H. *The Sacred Tree.* London: Macmillan, 1897.

Polívka, Georg. "Čichám člověčinu—ruský dech, ruskou 'kost.'" *Národopisný věstník českoslovanský* 17 (1924): 3–19.

Popov, Andrei A. *Dolganskii fol'klor.* Moscow: Sovetskii pisatel', 1937.

———. "Materialy po shamanstvu: Kul't bogini Aisyt u iakutov." In *Kul'tura i pis'mennost' Vostoka*, bk. 3, 125–33. Baku: Izdanie VTsK NTA, 1928.

Potebnia, Aleksandr A. "O mificheskom znachenii nekotorykh obriadov i poverii. II. Baba-Iaga." *Chteniia v imperatorskom obshchestve istorii i drevnostei rossiiskikh pri Moskovskom universitete*, vol. 2 (1865): 85–232.

Preuss, Konrad Th. *Die geistige Kultur der Naturvölker.* Leipzig: B. G. Teubner, 1914.

———. "Religionen der Naturvölker Amerikas, 1906–1909." *Archiv für Religionswissenschaft* 14, nos. 1–2 (1911): 212–301.

Propp, Vladimir. "Edip v svete fol'klora." *Uchenye Zapiski Leningradskogo gosudarstvennogo universiteta imeni A. A. Zhdanova (Uch. zap. LGU)*, no. 72, *Seriia filologicheskikh nauk*, issue 9 (1944): 138–75.

———. *Fol'klor i deistvitel'nost'. Izbrannye stat'i.* Moscow: GRVL-Nauka, 1976.

———. *Istoricheskie korni volshebnoi skazki*, edited by I. M. Tronskii. Leningrad: Izd. Leningradskogo gosudarstvennogo universiteta, 1946.

———. *Istoricheskie korni volshebnoi skazki.* Leningrad: Izd. Leningradskogo universiteta, 1984.

———. "K voprosu o proiskhozhdenii volshebnoi skazki (Volshebnoe derevo na mogile)." *Sovetskaia Etnografiia*, nos. 1–2 (1934): 128–51.

———. *Morfologiia skazki.* Leningrad: Academia, 1928.

———. *Morfologiia skazki.* 2nd ed. Moscow: Nauka, 1969.

———. *Morfologiia volshebnoi skazki. Istoricheskie korni volshebnoĭ skazki.* Moscow: Labirint, 1998.

———. *Morphology of the Folktale.* Translated by Laurence Scott [and] with an introduction by Svatava Pirkova-Jakobson. Revised and edited with a Preface by Louis A. Wagner and a new introduction by Alan Dundes. Austin: University of Texas Press, 1968.

———. *Morphology of the Folktale.* Translated by Laurence Scott with an Introduction by Svatava Pirkova-Jakobson. Bloomington: Indiana University Research Center in Anthropology, Folklore, and Linguistics, 1958.

———. "Morphology of the Russian Folktale." In *Unknown Pages of Russian Folklore*, edited by A. L. Toporkov, 201–15. Moscow: Indrik, 2015.

———. "Motiv chudesnogo rozhdeniia." *Uch. zap. LGU*, no. 81, *Seriia filologicheskikh nauk*, issue 12 (1941): 67–97.

———. "Muzhskoi dom v russkoi skazke." *Uch. zap. LGU*, no. 20, *Seriia filologicheskikh nauk*, issue 1 (1939): 174–98.

———. "Otkrytaia lektsiia." *Zhivaia starina* 3, no. 7 (1995): 11–17.

———. *Poetika fol'klora*. Moscow: Labirint, 1998.

———. "Ritual'nyi smekh v fol'klore: Po povodu skazki o Nesmeiane." *Uch. zap. LGU*, no. 46, *Seriia filologicheskikh nauk*, issue 3 (1939): 151–75.

———. *Russkaia skazka*. Leningrad: Publishing House of Leningrad State University, 1984.

———. "Volshebnoe derevo na mogile." *Sovetskaia etnografiia*, nos. 1–2 (1934): 128–51.

Putilov, B. N., ed. *Fol'klor i etnografiia: Problemy rekonstrukcii faktov traditsionnoi kul'tury. Sbornik naychnykh trudov*. Leningrad: Nauka, 1990.

———. *Fol'klor i etnografiia: Sviazi fol'klora s drevnimi predstavleniiami i obriadami*. Leningrad: Nauka, 1977.

———. *Fol'klor i etnografiia: U etnograficheskikh istokov fol'klornykh siuzhetov i obrazov. Sbornik nauchnykh trudov*. Leningrad: Nauka, 1984.

———. "Vladimiru Iakovlevichu Proppu—100 let." *Etnograficheskoe Obozrenie*, no. 6 (1995): 145–56.

Quirke, Stephen. *Going Out in Daylight prt m hrw. The Ancient Egyptian Book of the Dead Translation, Sources, Meanings*. London: Golden House, 2013.

Radcliffe-Brown, Alfred R. "The Rainbow-Serpent Myth in South-East Australia." *Oceania* 1, no. 3 (1930): 349–52.

Radermacher, Ludwig. *Das Jenseits im Mythos der Hellenen*. Bonn: A. Marcus and E. Weber, 1903.

———. *Hippolytos und Thekla: Studien zur Geschichte von Legende und Kultus*. Kaiserliche Akademie der Wissenschaften in Wien, Philosophisch-historische Klasse, Sitzungsberichte, vol. 182, no. 3. Vienna: Alfred Hölder, 1916.

. "Walfischmythen." *Archiv für Religionswissenschaft* 9 (1906): 248–52.

Rank, Otto. *Der Mythus von der Geburt des Helden*. Leipzig: Franz Deuticke, 1909.

———. *The Myth of the Birth of the Hero. A Psychological Exploration of Myth*. Translated by Gregory Richter and James Lieberman, introduction by Robert A. Segal. Baltimore: Johns Hopkins University Press, 2015.

Ranke, Kurt. *Die zwei Brüder: Eine Studie zur vergleichenden Märchenforschung*. FFC, vol. 114. Helsinki: Suomalainen Tiedeakatemia, 1934.

Rasmussen, Knud. *Grönlandsagen*. Berlin: Gyldendalscher, 1922.

Ratner-Shternberg, S. A. "Muzeinye materialy po tlingitskomu shamanstvu." *Sb. MAE* 6 (1927): 79–114.

Raum, Johannes. "Die Religion der Landschaft Moschi am Kalimandjaro." *Archiv für Religionswissenschaft* 14 (1911): 159–211.

Rayor, Diane J., trans. *The Homeric Hymns: A Translation, with Introduction and Notes*. Berkeley: University of California Press, 2004.

Reinach, Salomon. "La mort d'Orphée." In *Cultes, mythes et religions*, vol. 2, 85–122. Paris: Leroux, 1906.

Reitzenstein, Richard. "Der Kausalzusammenhang zwischen Geschlechtsverkehr und Empfängnis in Glaube und Brauch der Natur- and Kulturvölker." *Zeitschrift für Ethnologie* 41 (1909): 644–83.

. "Zwei hellenistische Hymnen." *Archiv für Religionswissenschaft* 8 (1905): 167–90.

Rohde, Erwin. *Psyche: Seelencult und Unsterblichkeitsglaube der Griechen.* Vol. 1. 4th ed. Tübingen: J. C. B. Mohr, 1907.

Roscher, William H. *Ausführliches Lexikon der griechischen und römischen Mythologie.* Leipzig: B. G. Teubner, 1884.

Rystenko, Aleksandr V. *Legenda o sviatom Georgii i drakone.* Odessa: Ekon, 1909.

Sadovnikov, Dmitrii N. *Skazki i predaniia Severnogo kraia.* Zapiski Russkogo geograficheskogo obshchestva po otdeleniiu etnografii, vol. 12. St. Petersburg: Tip. Ministerstva vnutrennykh del, 1884.

Saintyves, Pierre. *Les contes de Perrault et les récits parallèles: leurs origines (coutumes primitives et liturgies populaires).* Paris: Emile Nourry, 1923.

Samter, Ernst. *Geburt, Hochzeit, Tod: Beiträge zur vergleichenden Volkskunde.* Leipzig: B. G. Teubner, 1911.

Scheftelowitz, Isidor. "Das Fisch-Symbol in Judentum und Christentum." *Archiv für Religionswissenschaft* 14, no. 3/4 (1911): 1–53, 327–92.

Schilling, Josef, and Maria Schilling. "Religion und soziale Verhältnisse der Catios-Indianer in Kolumbien." *Archiv für Religionswissenschaft* 23, no. 3/4 (1925): 278–97.

Schmidt, Wilhelm. "Die geheime Jünglingsweihe der Karesau-Insulaner (Deutsch-Neuguinea)." *Anthropos* 2, no. 5 (1907): 1029–56.

Schurtz, Heinrich. *Altersklassen und Männerbünde: Eine Darstellung der Grundformen der Gesellschaft.* Berlin: G. Reimer, 1902.

Schweinfurth, Georg. *Im Herzen von Afrika.* 3rd ed. Leipzig: Salzwasser-Verlag Gmbh, 1918.

Seligman, Charles G., and Brenda Z. Zeligman. *The Veddas.* Cambridge: University Press, 1911.

Shishkoff, Serge. "The Structure of Fairytales: Propp vs. Levi-Straus." *Dispositio* 1, no. 3 (1976): 271–76.

Shklovskii, Viktor. "Iskusstvo kak priem." O. Brik et al., eds., *Sborniki po teorii poeticheskogo iazyka,* no. 2 (1917): 3–14.

———. *O teorii prozy.* Moscow: "Krug," 1925.

Shternberg, Lev Ia. *Materialy po izucheniiu giliatskogo iazyka i fol'klora.* Vol. 1. St. Petersburg: Tip. Imperatorskoi Akademii nauk, 1908.

———. *Pervobytnaia religiia v svete etnografii.* Leningrad: Izdatel'stvo Instituta narodov Severa TSIK SSSR im. P. G. Smidovicha, 1936.

Siecke, Ernst. *Drachenkämpfe: Untersuchungen zur Indogermanischen Sagenkunde.* Mythologische Bibliothek, vol. 1, no. 1, Gesellschaft für Vergleichende Mythenforschung. Leipzig: Hinrichs, 1907.

Silman, T. I., and V. G. Admoni. *My vspominaem: roman.* St. Petersburg: Kompozitor, 1993.

Smirnov, A. M. *Sbornik velikorusskikh skazok Arkhiva Russkogo geograficheskogo obshchestva.* Zapiski Russkogo geograficheskogo obshchestva po otdeleniiu etnografii, vol. 44, nos. 1–2. Petrograd: Rossiiskoi akademii nauk, 1917.

Smith, Grafton Elliot. *The Evolution of the Dragon.* Manchester: University Press, 1919.

Snegirev, I. I., trans., introduction, commentary. *Skazki Zulu.* Moscow: Akademii nauk, 1937.

Soimonov, A. D., ed. *Pesni i skazki na Onezhskom zavode.* Petrozavodsk: Karel'skii nauchno-issledovatel'skii institut kul'tury, 1937.

Sokolov, Boris M., and Iurii M. Sokolov. *Skazki i pesni Belozerskogo kraia: sbornik B. i IU. Sokolovykh.* Moscow: Pechatnia A. I. Snegirevoi, 1915.

Sokolova, V. K. "Diskussii po voprosam fol'kloristiki na zasedanijakh sektora fol'klora Instituta etnografii." *Sovetskaia etnografija,* no. 3 (1948): 139–46.

Sophocles. *Sofokl: Dramy.* Vol. 3. Translated and with an introduction by Fyodor Zelinskii. Moscow: M. i S. Sabashnikovy, 1915.

Sorlin, I. "Aux origines de l'étude typologique et historique du folklore: l'Institut de linguistique de N. Ja. Marr et le jeune Propp." *Regards sur l'anthropologie Sovietique, Cahiers du monde Russe et Sovietique* 31, nos. 2–3 (April–September 1990): 275–84.

Spencer, Baldwin, and Francis Gillen. *The Native Tribes of Central Australia.* London: Macmillan, 1899.

Speranskii, Mikhail N. *Russkaia ustnaia slovesnost'.* Moscow: A. M. Mikhailov, 1917.

Steinen, Karl von den. *Unter den Naturvölkern Zentral-Brasiliens: Reiseschilderung und ergebnisse der zweiten Schingú-expedition, 1887–1888.* Berlin: Reimer, 1894.

Stengel, Paul. "Aides klytopolos." *Archiv für Religionswissenschaft* 8 (1905): 203–13.

Struve, Vasilii V. "Ishtar'-Isol'da v drevne-vostochnoi mifologii." In Marr, *Tristan I Isol'da,* 49–70. Leningrad: Akademii nauk, 1932.

Sviridenko, Sofiia A., trans., introduction, and commentary. *Edda: Skandinavskii epos.* Moscow: M. i S. Sabashnikovy, 1917.

Tikhaia-Tsereteli, M. G. "Zhenskii obraz mzeθunaqav gruzinskikh skazok." In Marr, *Tristan i Isol'da,* 137–74.

Tolstoi, Ivan I. "Neudachnoe vrachevanie (Antichnaia parallel' k russkoi skazke)." In *Iazyk i literatura.* Vol. 8, edited by N. P. Andreev, 245–63. Leningrad: Akademiia nauk SSSR, 1932.

———. *Stat'i o fol'klore.* Moscow: Nauka, 1966.

———. "Sviazannyi i osvobozhdennyi silen." In *Pamiati akademika N. Ia. Marra (1864–1934),* edited by I. I. Meshchaninov. Moscow: Akademii nauk SSSR, 1938.

———. "Vozvrashchenie muzha v 'Odissee' i russkoi skazke." In *Sergeiu Fëdorovichu Ol'denburgu: K piatidesiatiletiiu nauch-obshchestvennoi deiatel'nosti, 1882–1932,* edited by I. Iu. Krachkovskii, 509–22. Leningrad: Akademiia nauk SSSR, 1934.

Tronskii, I. M. "Antichnyi mif i sovremennaia skazka." In *Sergeiu Fëdorovichu Ol'denburgu: k piatidesiatiletiiu nauchno-obshchestvennoĭ deiatel'nosti, 1882–1932: sbornik statei,* edited by I. Iu. Krachkovskii, 523–34. Leningrad: Izdatel'stvo Akademii nauk SSSR, 1934.

Turaev, Boris A. *Egipetskaia literatura.* Moscow: Izd. M. i S. Sabashnikovykh, 1920.

———. *Klassicheskii Vostok: Posmertnyi trud.* Leningrad: Brokgauz-Efron, 1924.

Unkel, Curt N. "Sagen der Tembé-Indianer." *ZfE* 47 (1915): 281–301.

Usener, Hermann K. *Die Sintfluthsagen. Untersucht von Hermann Usener; mit fünf Abbildungen und einer Munztafel.* Bonn: F. Cohen, 1899.

Vaiskopf, M. "Morfologiia strakha." *Novoe literaturnoe obozrenie,* no. 24 (1997): 53–58.

Vasmer, Max. *Russisches Etymologische Wörterbuch*. Heidelberg: Carl Winter, 1953.

Veresaev, Vikentii V., trans. *Gomerovy gimny*. Moscow: Izdatel'stvo "Nedra," 1926.

Veselovskii, Aleksandr N. *Istoricheskaia poetika*. Edited by V. M. Zhirmunskii. Leningrad: Khudozhestvennaia literatura, 1940.

———. *Poetika siuzhetov*. In *Sobranie sochinenii*, series 1, *Poetika*, vol. 2, no. 1. St. Petersburg: Tipografiia Imperatorskoi akademii nauk, 1913.

———. "Skazaniia o krasavitse v tereme i russkaia bylina o podsolnechnom Tsarstve." *Zhurnal Ministerstva narodnogo prosveshcheniia* 196 (1878): 183–238.

———. *Slavianskie skazaniia o Solomone i Kitovrase i zapadnye legendy o Morol'fe i Merline*. Vol. 8, pt. 1 of *Sobranie sochinenii*. Petrograd: Izdatel'stvo Akademii nauk SSSR, 1921.

———. *Sobranie sochinenii*, vol. 2. St. Petersburg: Tipografiia Imperatorskoi akademii nauk, 1913.

———. "Sravnitel'naia mifologiia i ee metod." In *Sobranie sochinenii*, vol. 16, *Stat'i o skazke*, 83–128. Moscow: Akademii nauk SSSR, 1938.

———. "Sviatoi Georgii v legendakh i obriadakh." *Razyskaniia v oblasti russkogo dukhovnogo stikha. Sbornik Otdeleniia russkogo iazyka i slovesnosti AN* 21, no. 2 (1880).

Vikent'ev, Vladimir M. *Drevne-egipetskaia povest' o dvukh brat'iakh*. Kul'turno-istoricheskie pamiatniki Drevnego Vostoka, vol. 4. Moscow: A. A. Levenson, 1917.

Virgil. *The Aeneid*. Translated by James Rhoades. Chicago: William Benton, 1952.

———. *Eneida*. Translated by Valerii Ia. Briusov and Sergei M. Solov'ev. Moscow: Academia, 1933.

Vladimirtsov, Boris Iakovlevich, trans., intro., commentary. *Volshebnyi mertvets: Mongol'sko-oiratskie skazki*. Petrograd: Vsemirnaia literatura, 1923.

Vlastov, Georgii, trans., ed. *Gesiod*. St. Petersburg: Tip. t-va "Obshchestva pol'zy," 1885.

Volkov, Roman M. *Skazka: Rozyskaniia po siuzhetoslozheniiu narodnoi skazki*. Vol. 1, *Skazka velikorusskaia, ukrainskaia, belorusskaia*. Odessa: Gos. izd-vo Ukrainy, 1924.

Von der Leyen, Friedrich. *Das Märchen in den Göttersagen der Edda*. Berlin: Reimer, 1899.

Vordemfelde, Hans. "Die Hexe im deutschen Volksmärchen." In *Festschrift Eugen Mogk zum 70. Geburtstag*, 558–74. Halle an der Saale: Verlag von Max Niemeyer, 1924.

Warburg, Aby. "A Lecture on Serpent Ritual." *Journal of the Warburg Institute* 2, no. 4 (1939): 277–92.

Warner, E. E. *Vladimir Iakovlevich Propp i russkaia fol'kloristika*. St. Petersburg: Filologicheskii fakul'tet Sankt-Peterburgskogo gos. universiteta, 2005.

Waser, Otto. "Charon." *Archiv für Religionswissenschaft* 1 (1898): 152–82.

Webster, Hutton. *Primitive Secret Societies*. New York: Macmillan, 1908.

Weicker, Georg. *Der Seelenvogel in der alten Litteratur und Kunst: Eine mythologisch-archäologische Untersuchung*. Leipzig: Teubner, 1900.

Wellhausen, Julius. *Reste arabischen Heidentums*. 2nd ed. Berlin: G. Reimer, 1927.

Werner, Edward T. C. *Myths and Legends of China*. 2nd ed. London: George G. Harrap, 1924.

Wiedemann, Alfred. *Die Toten und ihre Reiche im Glauben der alten Ägypter*. 2nd ed. Leipzig: J. C. Hinrichs, 1902.

Wilamowitz-Moellendorff, Ulrich von. "Die griechische Heldensage I & II." *Sitzungsberichte der Preussischen Akademie der Wissenschaften zu Berlin. Philosophisch-historische Klasse* 7 (1925): 41–62, 214–42.

Wundt, Wilhelm. *Mif i religiia*. St. Petersburg: Brokgauz and Efron, 1912.

———. *Völkerpsychologie: eine untersuchung der Entwicklungsgesetze von Sprache, Mythus und Sitte*. Vol. 2, *Die Sprache*, pt. 1. Leipzig: Wilhelm Engelmann, 1904. https://archive.org/details/vlkerpsychologi11wund.

Zarubin, Ivan, ed. *Beludzhskie skazki*. Leningrad: Izdatel'stvo Akademii nauk SSSR, 1932.

Zelenin, Dmitrii K. *Kul't ongonov v Sibiri: perezhitki totemizma v ideologii sibirskikh narodov*. Trudy Instituta antropologii i etnografii Akademii nauk SSSR, vol. 14, no. 3. Moscow: Izdatel'stvo Akademii nauk SSSR, 1936.

———. "Religiozno-magicheskaia funktsiia volshebnykh skazok." In *Sergeiu Fedorovichu Ol'denburgu k piatidesetiletiiu nauchno-obshchestvennoi deiatelnosti, 1882–1932*, edited by I. Iu. Krachkovskii, 215–41. Leningrad: Izdatel'stvo Akademii nauk SSSR, 1934.

———. "Tabu slov u narodov Vostochnoi Evropy i Severnoi Azii." *Sb. MAE* 8 (1929): 1–144.

———. *Totemy—derev'ia v skazaniiakh i obriadakh evropeiskikh narodov*. Moscow: Akademii nauk SSSR, 1937.

———. *Velikorusskie skazki Permskoi gubernii*. Zapiski Russkogo geograficheskogo obshchestva po otdeleniiu etnografii, vol. 41. Petrograd: Rossiskoi akademii nauk, 1914.

———. *Velikorusskie skazki Viatskoi gubernii*. Zapiski Russkogo geograficheskogo obshchestva po otdeleniiu etnografii, vol. 42. Petrograd: Rossiskoi akademii nauk, 1915.

Zhirmunskii, V. M. "Propp, V. Ya. Istoricheskie korni volshebnoi skazki." *Sovetskaia kniga*, no. 5 (1947): 97–103.

Zhivaia starina: Periodicheskoe izdatel'stvo otdeleniia etnografii Imperatorskogo Russkogo geograficheskogo obshchestva 21, nos. 2–4 (1912), edited by V. I. Lamanskii. Petrograd: Imperatorskaia akademiia nauk, 1914.

Aarne, Antti: 113, 316, 318, 324

abduction: 29, 31, 65, 102, 103, 124, 224, 226, 228, 229, 237, 238, 255, 261, 302, 316, 319, 325, 326. *See also:* kidnap

abductor: 37, 92, 194, 195, 221, 223

ability, abilities: 145, 146, 163, 164, 165, 171, 207, 218, 220, 289, 292, 296, 304, 315, 317, 322; ability to speak: 165

Abkhazia(n): 25, 131, 259

aborigines: xiv, xvii, 13, 34, 275, 276, 314, 373n113

absence: 119, 168, 272

abstinence: 57, 303

abundance: 173, 211, 233, 234, 265; everlasting abundance: 174, 266

abyss: 179, 255, 279, 313

accession: 219–220, 273, 282, 305, 307–308, 312, 315, 327

Achelis, Thomas: 275

Achelous: 240, 322

Acheron: 240

Achilles: 84, 91

Acricorinth: 159

Actaeon: 302

Admiralty Islands: 204

admission: 275, 276, 277

adolescence: 118, 166; adolescent(s): 29, 37

Adonis: 78

The Adventure of Satni-Khamoins with the Mummies: 268

adversary: 249, 250, 311

Aeneas: 41, 240, 294

Afanas'ev, Aleksandr N.: xvi, 27, 40, 48, 98, 102, 137–139, 162, 176–177, 193, 336, 343

Africa(n): 13, 14, 23, 48, 64, 78, 99, 118, 136, 155, 157, 166, 177, 182, 200, 201, 203, 205, 235, 236, 241, 245, 250, 260, 261, 263, 275, 284, 293, 296, 311, 318; British East Africa (former): 235; Central Africa: 185; Central Angola: 311

afterlife: 45, 84, 163, 174, 177, 269, 325, 332, 333

Agni: 155–156, 158, 173, 183, 369n19

agony: 72, 225

agrarian: 29, 238, 268

agriculture: 6, 46, 61, 92, 94, 100, 101, 112, 115, 133, 135, 139, 141–143, 151, 171, 183, 191, 204, 205, 207, 216, 219, 222, 230, 233–235, 239, 241, 242, 244, 245, 248, 256, 265, 267, 268, 289, 385n12

Ahuramazda: 313

Aigos: 204

Ainu: 13, 147, 230, 301

air: 28, 167, 180, 188, 193, 218, 226, 228, 256

Akikuyu: 235

Akkad: 221

Aladdin's lamp: 173

Alcestis: 228

Algonquin: 234

"Ali Baba and the Forty Thieves": 45
Alitemnian Libyan(s): 292
alive: 219, 234, 235, 241
Allatu: 269
Allen, James P.: 370n60
Alexander (of Macedonia): 186
Altai: 167, 168
altar: 33, 228
Amazon(s): 301
ambrosia: 52, 84
Amduat: 251, 252
America (Native): 13, 14, 23, 41, 43,
    45, 49, 50, 53, 59, 63, 77, 102, 118,
    129, 133, 137, 138, 149, 155, 160,
    161, 166, 170–172, 182, 185, 186,
    189, 190, 203, 205, 214, 216, 218,
    220, 230, 231, 235, 240, 264, 268,
    289, 300, 317, 318, 329, 331–332
amulet(s): 171, 172, 288, 305, 328–329
analysis: xi–xvii, xix–xx, 16, 19, 28,
    31, 33, 35, 52–53, 55, 57, 92, 140,
    145, 152–153, 164, 178, 187, 216,
    219, 224, 229, 239, 253, 277, 278,
    294–295, 305–306, 331, 337–343
ancestor(s): 35, 60, 127, 129, 133–136,
    141–143, 151–153, 163, 164, 177,
    220, 249, 250, 284, 302, 303, 327,
    330, 365n65
"The Ancient Myth and the Modern
    Tale": 237
Andreev, Nikolai P.: 27, 176, 260
Andromeda: 236, 237, 238
angel(s): 168, 186, 226, 270
Angola: 311
animal(s): 6, 9, 25, 36, 39, 40, 43–47,
    53, 58, 59, 60, 61, 67, 73, 76, 82,
    85, 88, 90, 92, 100, 107–109, 111,
    114, 116, 119, 122, 125–127, 134–
    137, 139, 142, 143, 146, 148–150,
    167, 168–172, 174, 177–181, 183,
    184, 187, 190, 191, 195, 199, 202,
    204–207, 209, 211, 218, 220–229,
    231, 232, 236, 237, 243, 257, 261–
    268, 287, 288, 293, 296, 313, 314,
    317, 320–322, 330, 332; grateful
    animals: 134, 136, 137, 143, 144,
    149, 150, 155, 160, 163–165, 166,
    185; animal husbandry: 182; ani-
    mal tales: 331; predatory animal:
    227; wild animals: 138

Ankerman, Bernhard: 135, 136, 166
Annam: 275
Anoes Island: 96
Anokhin, Andrei: 167
ant(s): 215, 257
antagonist: 385n12
anthropological school: 333; anthro-
    pologists: xvii, 165; anthropologi-
    zation: 341
anthropomorphic: 142, 159, 161, 165,
    191, 222, 231, 291; anthropomor-
    phization: 47, 53, 222
antiquity: 11, 13–15, 17, 52, 62, 68,
    72, 78, 81, 83–84, 109, 138–140,
    151, 162, 167, 183, 186, 201, 217,
    228, 233, 238, 245, 250, 265–267,
    269, 271, 292, 294, 301, 321, 322,
    357n277, 358n56
Anubis: 183, 222
Anuchin, Dmitri: 35, 149, 187, 188,
    189
Apam Napat: 159
Apep: 245, 246, 251
Aphrodite: 302
Apis: 59
Apocalypse: 154, 271
Apollodorus: 232
apotheosis: 314
apotropaic: 128, 129, 303
apple(s): 11, 99, 139, 141, 176, 269,
    270, 271; apples of youth: 131, 174,
    255, 263, 270, 316; apple tree(s):
    316, 319; poisoned apple(s): 107
apprentice: 101, 123
Apuleius: 111
aquatic: 213, 229. *See also* water
Arab(s): 235, 236, 275
Arapaho: 170
archer(s): 6, 100, 163, 258, 293, 311,
    319
archetypes: 2, 319
Argonauts: 159, 167, 263
Aristophanes: 269
ark (Noah's): 220
Arkhangelsk: 119
arm(s): 167, 236, 242, 244, 246, 270,
    322
"The Armless Maiden" (*Koso-
    ruchka*): 40, 74
armor: 167, 216

Baumgartner, Walter: 4, 69
bead(s): 108, 234, 264
bear(s): 34, 36, 59, 60, 86, 87, 114,
    123, 127, 149, 164, 165, 171, 227,
    290, 328, 330; black bear(s): 165,
    181, 229; bear-king: 256, 261, 316
beard(s): 69, 114, 132, 156
bearskin: 34, 149
beast(s): 47, 53, 58, 62, 152, 203, 205,
    208, 216–218, 225, 226, 261, 264,
    303, 325, 370; king of beasts: 261;
    wild beasts: 226
beaten: 279; beating(s): 71, 143, 144,
    159, 213, 251, 264, 272, 325; beat-
    ing time: 317
beauty, beauties: 26, 107, 110, 124,
    125, 226–228, 236, 255, 258–260,
    265, 269, 270, 272, 273, 286, 292,
    293, 301, 312, 313, 326
beaver(s): 137, 161, 180
bed(s): 177, 183, 228, 296, 299, 300,
    301, 316
beggar: 116, 327
beginning: 143, 221, 240, 277, 278,
    308
Beijing: 232
Belarus(ian): 86, 104, 173
belief(s): xiii, xvi, xvii, 11, 24, 27,
    28, 30, 38, 50, 54, 61, 68, 80, 81,
    85, 88, 92, 109, 129, 135, 150, 151,
    154–157, 161, 163, 168, 170, 171,
    173, 174, 177, 178, 180, 184–187,
    195, 205, 224, 225, 228, 237, 241,
    243, 250, 252, 263, 264, 269, 270,
    306, 312, 314, 321, 330
Bellerophon: 152, 159
belly: 181, 202–206, 209, 212, 214,
    215, 217, 218, 220, 250, 251
beloved: 227, 298
belt(s): 71, 169, 189–190, 191, 251
bench: 25, 52, 61, 71, 128
benefactor: 90, 147, 205, 206, 208,
    254, 303
beneficent: 136, 208, 230
benefit: 65, 69, 79, 135, 204, 218, 233
Benfey, Theodor: 357n277
Bengal: 34, 275
Benin: 23
Berber: 235

berries: 22, 66, 121, 132, 169, 287,
    288
Berry (France): 298
besieging: xv, 195
Best, Eldson: 225
betel nuts: 104
betrothal: 261; betrothed: 272, 274,
    283, 295
Bible: 200, 251
"big house": 93, 95, 97–99, 101, 103,
    105, 107, 109–111, 113, 115, 117,
    119–125, 263, 287, 296, 298, 300,
    326
Bihari(s): 275
bird(s): 9, 24, 47, 51, 52, 58, 67, 82,
    85, 90, 91, 100, 107, 114, 122, 123,
    127, 134, 138, 140, 141, 148–150,
    152, 154–156, 160, 168, 170, 172,
    174, 179–182, 184–191, 194, 205,
    207, 211, 220–223, 229, 242, 249,
    254, 256, 259, 261, 269, 286–288,
    320, 321; bird-horse: 187; preda-
    tory bird: 321
birth: 64, 68, 106, 113, 249, 250, 252,
    310, 326, 328, 332
bite: 250; biting: 206, 263
"Black Sea Dragon": 193, 194, 233
blacksmith(s): 33, 73–74, 82, 101, 140,
    163, 196, 197; blacksmithing: 13, 216
bladder: 117, 118
blanket(s): 165, 176, 290
blessed: 252; blessing(s): 130, 176,
    252, 266, 303
blind, blindness: 53–57, 73, 77, 87,
    102, 110, 115, 116, 176, 204, 246,
    264, 341, 352n83; blinding: 246
blood: 18, 77–79, 103, 125, 183, 186,
    234, 273–276, 306
"Bluebeard": 38, 78, 123
boar: 142, 291, 302
Boas, Franz: 12, 34, 49, 60, 81, 86,
    94, 122, 164, 208, 288, 290, 291,
    301, 305, 329, 330
boasting: 145, 197, 236, 282; boast-
    ful: 221. See also bragging
boat(s): 34, 158, 165, 167, 179, 183–
    185, 187–189, 191, 210, 212, 214,
    219, 220, 245, 247, 251, 252, 256,
    259, 266, 290, 326

buffalo: 59, 90, 91, 170, 181, 182, 313, 328
Bugunda: 235
building: 256, 262, 280, 289
Bulat the Fine: 303
bull(s): 73, 117, 118, 140, 146, 148, 164, 181, 183, 184, 219, 240, 291
bundle(s): 328, 330
burden: 148, 248
"Burenushka": 136
Burger, Friedrich: 132
burial(s): 8, 35, 53, 122, 131, 132, 149, 151, 174, 181, 183, 187–190, 199, 240, 244, 268
burning: 57, 81–83, 90, 92, 140, 155, 157, 183, 185, 188, 198, 211, 227, 244, 246, 251, 259, 279, 291, 303. *See also* combustion
bursting: 157, 318, 319
Buryat(s): 72, 154, 157, 189, 321
"bush soul": 224
bush(es): 41, 172, 181
Bushmen: 13
Busiris: 252
butter: 44, 45
bylina, byliny: 1, 18, 333, 346n1

Cadmus: 250
cage: 24, 258
cake: 240, 263
calf: 140, 146
California: 34, 166
Calydonian boar: 142
Calypso: 52, 53
canal(s): 233
candy, candies: 240
cane: 169, 172, 197
cannibal(ism): 16, 77–79, 82; ritual cannibalism: 101
capitalism: 5
captive, captivity: 137, 139, 142, 143, 172, 196, 199, 281
capture, capturing: 139, 140, 143, 159
Carco: 68
cards: 169; playing: 63
carpet(s): 169
carrier: 179, 186, 187, 191, 221, 227, 228, 233, 312, 313

carrion: 181, 240, 247
carrying: 184, 210, 215, 221, 228, 236, 244, 251, 254, 287, 295
cart: 161, 316
carving(s): 177, 188, 328
caskets: 171, 266
cassowary: 203
castration: 301–302
cat: 44, 45, 130, 143; cat in boots: 258
catabasis: 175, 238, 285
Catholic Church: 201
cattle: 62, 117, 147, 148, 150, 181, 182, 184, 219, 231, 241, 243, 245, 266, 267
Caucasus: 295
cauldron: 13, 82, 85, 90, 207, 314
cave(s): 41, 76, 190, 215, 232, 238
Cecrops: 250
Celebes: 141
celestial dragon: 243, 254
cellar: 123, 153, 175
cemetery: 130, 131, 290
centaur(s): 222
Ceram: 46
Cerberus: 44, 239, 240, 245, 247
ceremonial: 10, 344; ceremony, ceremonies: 86, 94, 107, 163, 175, 181, 183, 188, 189, 203, 276, 298, 299, 305, 314, 328
chain(s): 73, 74, 125, 137, 138, 140, 143, 153, 179, 190, 207, 247; chained: 236, 257
challenge: 216, 281
chamber(s): 22, 24, 51, 87, 123, 125, 255, 268, 282
character(s): 5, 24, 36, 44, 50, 53, 57, 61, 62, 66, 68, 84, 89, 106, 113, 133, 134, 137, 138–141, 145, 184, 218, 229, 264, 312, 316, 321, 327, 328
chariot(s): 157, 228, 259, 294
charm(s): 166, 171, 242
Charon: 186, 188, 269
chase: 316, 319; chasing: 321, 322, 323
cheek: 273, 275, 286
Chernyshevsky, Nikolai: 340
chest: 147, 186, 250, 253
Chichen Itzal: 234
chicken(s): 186, 261, 263
chief(s): 23, 211, 234, 246, 252, 290; chieftain(s): 26, 103, 125

child(ren): 8, 18, 21, 22, 23, 24, 26,
    27, 29, 30, 57, 59, 64, 65, 66, 67,
    68, 69, 70, 71, 83, 85, 88, 92, 97,
    99, 106, 107, 113, 127, 128, 136,
    137, 140, 141, 161, 164, 195, 205,
    208, 220, 227, 235, 250, 261, 302,
    307, 316, 325, 327, 340, 354n147
childless: 250, 309
children's tales: 50
China: 14, 23, 201, 222, 231, 233,
    236, 245, 267, 271
Chinese: 13, 177, 232
chivalric romances: 32
choking: 77, 203
chopping: 66, 72–80, 101, 114, 125,
    172, 198, 215, 216, 246, 263, 293,
    303, 312, 325
chosenness: 89, 101, 152, 166, 227,
    235, 236
Christ: 82
Christian: 129, 151, 232, 361n179;
    Christian Church: 163; Christian-
    ity: 68, 81, 171, 186, 222, 232;
    Christianization: 330
chthonic: 159, 238–239, 241
Chudo-Yudo: 198
Chukchi: 182, 276
church(es): 124, 257, 286, 316, 318, 319
Chuvash: 177
Cinderella: 130, 133
circle: 58, 228, 296
circumcision: 47, 56, 64, 70, 73, 89,
    94, 97, 99, 118, 202, 276
city of the dead: 186
city, cities: 195, 221, 232, 233, 234,
    236, 256, 257, 261, 269, 271
"civilized" people: 12
clan: 59, 61, 82, 153, 161, 164, 166,
    253, 275, 276, 291, 292, 302, 304,
    305, 328, 365n65
class (social class): 208, 217, 306;
    class societies: 218, 243, 318
claws: 148, 169, 179, 190, 193, 223,
    244, 253, 282, 367n126
clay: 34, 35, 90, 108, 115, 116
cleansing: 49, 51, 81, 314
cliff(s): 166, 170
climbing: 179, 181, 186, 188, 189,
    190, 209, 256, 264
cloth: 26, 160, 317

clothing: 62, 65, 66, 75, 102, 104,
    107, 108, 114, 116, 169, 184, 186,
    236, 244, 275, 276, 297
cloud(s): 219, 241, 244, 251, 267, 283;
    cloudy: 194, 195
club: 33, 169, 172, 311
coals: 60, 81
coast(s): 185, 209, 235. *See also*
    seashore; shore(s)
coat(s): 148, 153, 154, 276, 369n19;
    coat(s) of arms: 222
coconut(s): 254, 289; coconut palm: 268
coffin(s): 35, 107, 108, 109, 175, 186,
    279, 285, 326; glass coffin: 208, 220
Colchis: 217
cold: 160, 287, 305, 314; Cold One: 159
color(s): 26, 53, 56, 90, 96, 110, 115,
    139, 140, 153–155, 202, 230, 241,
    244, 258, 260, 267, 270, 284, 296
comb(s): 41, 107, 114, 162, 267, 315,
    316, 317
combustion: 57, 84. *See also* burning
comedy: 266, 269
command: 322; commander(s): 26
commune: 102; communism: 324
companion(s): 218, 242, 293
compassion: 67, 134, 235
concealed: 22, 27, 107, 278, 288, 316
conception: 221, 250, 303
confinement: 23, 26–28, 30, 31, 138,
    347
conflict: 282, 309, 310, 313
consecration: 229, 276
consequences: 24, 211, 232, 241, 318
consubstantiality: 181, 182, 183, 184,
    203
consumption: 52, 71, 82, 211, 265
contest(s): 272, 292, 294, 295; contest
    of magic: 279, 281, 297
control: 7, 18, 28, 90, 138, 165, 207,
    230, 231, 233, 243, 254, 286, 287,
    289, 305, 307, 315
conversion (obrashchenie): 9, 171
Cook Islands: 82–83
cook(ing): 25, 37, 77, 78–80, 82, 83,
    85, 92, 101, 102, 114, 160, 206,
    207; cooked: 105, 165, 283, 314
Cook, James: 95
copper: 131, 137, 139, 140, 141, 147,
    251, 260, 267, 283

Copper Forehead: 137, 138, 139, 140, 141, 142
Coptic: 225
corpse(s): 53, 60, 78, 79, 101, 106, 123, 129, 132, 140, 155, 181, 182, 183, 184, 185, 189, 213, 236, 240
corresponding: 5, 6, 8, 30, 37, 47, 50, 53, 57–59, 64, 69, 71, 77, 80, 88, 90, 91, 102, 112, 133, 138, 139, 143, 147, 151, 154, 156, 175, 182, 190, 192, 209, 211, 216, 220, 224, 233–235, 237, 238, 242, 251, 263, 271–281, 290, 295, 301, 312, 317, 318, 325–328, 333, 339, 341, 366
Cosquin, Emmanuel: 137
Cossack: 56
costume: 86, 92, 182
counterabduction: 224
country: 2, 41, 52, 53, 155, 182, 184, 195, 205, 208, 210, 224, 232, 233, 237, 238, 241, 242, 255, 256, 257, 264, 284, 286, 306, 341
courage: 205, 214
court: 14, 137, 232, 252, 268, 273, 311; courtship: 274
courtyard: 85, 95, 146
cow(s): 8, 9, 19, 73, 128, 136, 146, 148, 181, 183, 369n19
coyote(s): 59, 160, 317, 331–332
crack(ing): 27, 106, 244
cradle: 77, 128, 129
craft(s): 140, 166, 262; craftsman: 70, 84, 144
crawfish: 134, 136, 230, 262
crawling: xv, 77, 80, 81, 183, 212, 215, 217, 273, 370n1
creation: 200, 217, 246; creativity: 326, 327, 331, 338, 387n31
creator: 14, 92, 147, 192, 230, 332
crest: 190, 271, 284
Crete: 140
crew: 33, 167
crocodile(s): 46, 122, 203, 222, 227, 234, 236, 248, 251, 321
crone: 90, 91
crop(s): 10, 28, 86, 141, 142, 143, 234, 236, 256, 304, 332; crop destruction: 141

crossing: 179, 180, 181, 186, 187, 188, 190, 191, 239, 257, 262, 294, 295, 312, 313
crow(s): 29, 185, 330, 367n126
crowd: 298, 314
crown(ed): 3, 148, 251, 270, 308
crucifixion: 125
crushing: 120, 246, 263
crutch(es): 33, 169
crypt: 51, 153, 268
crystal(s): 76, 109, 123, 208, 210, 231, 257, 264, 268, 269, 279, 285; crystal mountain: 208, 264
"The Crystal Mountain": 256
cudgel(s): 169, 171, 172, 266
cult: 7, 14, 50, 51, 59, 61, 62, 78, 133, 134, 148, 151, 155, 163, 168, 178, 187, 189, 230, 236, 245, 268, 270, 284, 288, 294–295, 301, 327, 328; fertility cult: 276
culture(s): ix, xiii, xiv, xvii, 4, 12, 13, 17, 78, 148, 158, 182, 183, 200, 208, 216, 219, 221, 239, 241, 253, 254, 269, 324, 332, 333, 338; cultural stage: 59, 201, 231, 300; urban culture: 221
Cupid: 110
"Cupid and Psyche": 104, 109, 110, 125, 229
Currant Berry River: 195
current(s): 143, 231
curse: 57, 91, 252
custom(s): 8, 10, 148, 178, 182, 183, 184, 228, 234, 276, 288, 290, 298
cutting: 172, 188, 206, 208, 211, 212, 213, 217, 218, 219, 246, 247, 248, 254, 274, 302, 305, 306, 311, 312, 314, 327, 328
Cybele: 61
cycle(s): 41, 111, 210, 219, 229, 233, 237, 260, 296, 298, 312, 325–327, 333
Cynic. *See* Proteus, Peregrinus (the Cynic)

Dakota: 224
dam: 161, 231
damage: 3, 78, 139, 141, 385n12
Danaë: 27, 29
dance(s), dancing: 15, 40, 46, 48, 60, 69, 76, 78, 86, 87, 94, 107, 122,

devil(s): 4, 29, 53, 56, 67, 69, 70, 82,
    102, 113, 114, 157, 179, 195, 203,
    225, 319
devourer: 208, 209, 210, 211, 212,
    214, 215, 218, 219, 221, 225, 226,
    228, 230, 231, 233, 238, 239, 243,
    245, 248, 251, 252, 254, 319, 326;
    Devourer of the Dead: 248; de-
    vouring: 39, 158, 195, 196, 199,
    201, 202, 205, 206, 207, 210, 214,
    217, 218, 219, 223, 224, 225, 226,
    229, 237, 239, 240, 241, 242, 246,
    248, 249, 290, 291, 296, 297, 311,
    325
dew: 150, 160
dexterity: 101, 171, 293, 332
diamond(s): 199, 207, 258, 264
Diana: 284
Dictionary of Russian Dialects: xvi
Dieseldorf, Erwin: 234
Dieterich, Albrecht: 228, 240, 270
difficult task(s): 3, 31, 38, 43, 163,
    164, 277, 279, 280, 281, 282, 283,
    284, 285, 288, 292, 295, 304, 305,
    306, 307, 309, 327
digging: 48, 153, 171, 284
Dionysus: 142, 184; Dionysus Za-
    greus: 78
dipper: 316; dipping: 74, 75, 77
"The Dirty Girl": 176–177
disaster: 21, 22, 65, 236, 306, 309
disease(s): 86, 166, 224, 225, 264, 301
distant kingdoms, land(s): 32, 145,
    169, 181, 209, 223, 238
distortion: 204, 211
divinity: 84, 205, 270. *See also* deity
Dobrolyubov, Nikolai: 340
Dobrynia Nikitich: 6
dog(s): 44, 125, 130, 131, 143, 149,
    151, 191, 198, 233, 240, 247, 248,
    300, 313. *See also* Cerberus
Dolgan: 43, 49, 58, 63, 206, 230, 264,
    297, 307, 308
doll(s): 113, 130, 176–178, 236
domestication: 149, 187
Don Quixote: 32
donor: 36, 64, 90, 92, 93, 126, 127,
    131, 132, 133, 134, 137, 143, 162,
    290, 315, 327; dead donor: 130,
    144, 152

door(s): 30, 43, 44, 45, 47, 61, 62, 95,
    153, 221, 231, 263, 270, 288, 326,
    351n9
Dorsey, George Amos: 90, 149,
    328–329; *Traditions of the Skidi
    Pawnee*: 328, 330, 331, 332
double: 7, 152, 196, 208, 250–252,
    303
dove(s): 24, 113, 259, 321
dragging: 219, 226, 227, 236
dragon(s): xv, 3, 18, 22, 27, 29, 31,
    110, 144, 145, 146, 175, 192, 193,
    194, 195, 196, 197, 198, 199, 200,
    201, 202, 206, 207, 208, 209, 210,
    214, 215, 216, 217, 218, 219, 221,
    222, 223, 224, 225, 226, 227, 228,
    229, 230, 231, 232, 233, 237, 238,
    239, 240, 241, 242, 243, 244, 245,
    246, 248, 249, 250, 251, 252, 253,
    254, 255, 257, 258, 259, 261, 264,
    273, 282, 291, 299, 303, 312, 315,
    316, 319, 326, 341, 370n1; chained:
    125 "The Dragon and Metallurgy":
    201; The Dragon and the Sun":
    201; "The Dragon and the Tree
    Cult": 201; "The Dragon and the
    Woman": 200; multi-headed: 192–
    193, 216, 221, 223, 226, 232, 240;
    sea dragon: 231; son dragon: 240;
    winged: 15, 124, 150, 154, 155, 199
drawing: 81, 232, 275, 276, 287
dream(s): 22, 51, 90, 166, 186, 197,
    227, 232, 234, 250, 288, 297, 317–
    318; dreaming: 166, 197
dress(es): 87, 130, 285
drink(s): 49, 51, 61, 69, 72, 79, 107,
    110, 139, 144, 158, 159, 175, 257,
    260, 275, 276, 318, 323
droit de seigneur: 303
dropping: 90, 253, 257, 265, 283
drought: 231, 232, 235, 237
drowning: 143, 236, 237
Drude (Drudenfuß): 54, 352n82
drug: 108; drugged: 142
drum(s): 270, 317
drunk: 197, 291
dualism: 208; duality; 83, 152
duck(s): 22, 180, 194, 258, 259, 318,
    319, 320, 322; "golden crested
    ducks": 271, 284

Erishkigal: 168
ermine(s): 170, 180, 295
erotic: 226–227, 228, 236
Eruslan Lazarevich: 132
escape: 240, 253, 315, 316, 317, 318,
    320, 324
escort: 179, 183
Eskimo(s): 58, 151, 157, 182, 221,
    226, 313
Ethiopia(n): 23, 236, 309
ethnographer(s): 28, 30, 75, 88, 189,
    331
ethnographic: 16, 38, 39, 116, 128,
    136, 341, 342, 343
ethnography: 10, 163, 172; ethnology:
    389n58
euphemism: 69, 299
Euphrates: 221, 234
Eurasian: 149
Euripides: 228
Europa: 237
Europe: 68, 177, 180, 187, 201,
    205, 206, 245, 270, 298, 318;
    European(s): 12, 38, 86, 136, 149,
    157, 158, 203, 235, 307, 329, 330
Eurystheus: 240
Eurytus: 294
evening: 81, 94, 150, 161, 197, 210,
    241, 314
evil: 92, 150, 165, 166, 195, 208, 217,
    225, 240, 246, 252, 313; evil king:
    311; evil princess: 274; evil spirit(s):
    35, 144, 195, 235, 244, 266, 313
evolution: 11, 61, 108, 135, 144, 163,
    200, 216, 219, 271, 338
Evolution of the Dragon, The: 200
exaggeration: 57, 61, 224, 291, 340,
    344
exchange: 152, 321
execution: 65, 295; executioner: 311
exit: 76, 240
exogamy: 6, 88
exorcism: 129
expert(s): 159, 163, 167
exposure: 188
expulsion: 31, 66, 205, 211
extraordinary: 96, 159, 199, 222, 257,
    332
eye(s): 2, 24, 42, 44, 47, 55–57, 70,
    73–75, 77, 95, 96, 114, 127, 140,

154, 156, 167, 197, 199, 226, 244,
    246, 247, 251, 269, 270, 308

face(s): 23, 30, 115, 116, 123, 222,
    251, 259, 270, 271, 297
factory: 5, 197
failed doctoring: 79
fairy: 263; fairy-tale 341
faith: 152, 268
"The Faithful Servant": 120
falcon: 121, 196, 222, 261, 268, 295
falling: 255, 312, 313, 316, 320
falling asleep: 197, 247, 248
false hero(es): 73, 199, 277, 295, 312
family, families: 5, 21, 25, 30, 66,
    67, 89, 90, 97, 99, 106, 111–112,
    135, 146, 158, 164, 177, 235, 275,
    292, 306, 310, 311, 327, 365n65,
    385n12
Fang tribe: 166, 366n107
fangs: 90, 218
fantasy: 170, 226, 268
farmer: 143, 231
farming: 13, 231, 234, 242, 271, 301;
    slash farming: 142
fasting: 29, 129, 133, 166
fat: 183, 184
fate: 228, 229, 311, 332
father(s): 7, 22, 24, 65, 67, 68, 70,
    78, 82, 85, 89, 95, 99, 102, 111,
    112, 115, 117, 123, 124, 127, 129,
    130, 134, 136, 143, 147, 152, 164,
    167, 182, 205, 209, 210, 213, 220,
    221, 236, 250, 254, 255, 264, 268,
    272–273, 274, 277, 280, 281, 283,
    287, 288, 290, 297, 305, 307, 309,
    310, 311, 312, 322; dead father:
    126, 127, 130, 143, 151, 153, 158,
    174, 327
father-in-law: 7, 280, 281, 282, 290,
    307, 308, 310, 315
faun: 53
Faunus: 138
fear: 22, 24, 27, 29, 30, 68, 128, 142,
    225, 272, 282, 304, 323
feast: 131, 288, 294–295, 301
feather(s): 43, 62, 90, 100, 114, 116,
    137, 148, 169, 170, 182, 186, 220,
    248, 258, 259, 260, 328
feeding: 144, 146, 148, 160, 177, 178

genics: 168
geography, geographical: 262, 318
George the dragon killer: 200
George, St.: 155, 232
Georgian: 24, 26, 293, 295, 314
German(s): 14, 24, 26, 54, 55, 58, 73,
    84, 102, 114, 118, 120, 124, 151,
    154, 161, 173, 183, 187, 264, 310,
    334, 369n19
Geser: 218; Geseriada: 217
gesges: 227
ghost(s): 46, 83, 128, 154, 224, 225
giant(s): 53, 162
gift(s): 60, 87–88, 90, 103, 126, 140,
    170, 174, 178, 207, 261, 277, 288,
    296, 322, 327. *See also* present
Gilbert Islands: 129, 263
Gilgamesh: 269; *Gilgamesh*: 186, 188.
    See also epic: *Epic of Gilgamesh*
Gillen, Francis: 81, 229
Gilyak(s): 148, 161, 177, 262, 301,
    363n12
gingerbread house: 50
Ginzburg, Carlo: 341
girl(s): 8, 9, 22, 24, 25, 27, 29, 31,
    44, 48, 55, 74, 75, 78, 87, 103, 113,
    124, 129, 177, 214–216, 220, 227,
    228, 233, 235, 237, 238, 251, 258,
    274, 275, 277, 287, 297, 298, 302,
    313, 315, 318, 326; little girl: 234.
    See also maiden
glass: 109, 208, 220, 256, 264, 279.
    See also coffin: glass coffin
glow: 81, 83, 215, 259, 260, 270, 274
glutton: 291; gluttonous: 292
gnawing: 198, 315
goat(s): 22, 29, 53, 73, 165, 183, 222,
    284, 314
gobbler: 63; gobbling: 196
god(s): 11, 23, 47, 78, 82–84, 91, 133,
    142, 152, 155, 157, 158, 159, 162,
    182–184, 186, 190, 191, 205, 222,
    225, 227–229, 231, 235–237, 242,
    243, 246, 251, 252, 254, 267, 268,
    270, 294, 309, 310, 314, 321, 322,
    324; first god: 231, 233, 234; God:
    25, 102, 124, 299; thunder god: 49;
    water god(s): 234, 323
goddaughter: 70
goddess(es): 34, 61, 62, 83–84, 142,
    175, 228, 248, 252, 269, 301, 322

godfather: 70, 124
Goethe, Johann Wolfgang von: 337–
    338, 341, 343
Gogol', Nikolai: 56; "Viy": 56, 129
gold: 73, 110, 123, 131, 140, 147, 175,
    186, 188, 258–259, 268, 270
golden: 139, 140, 156, 159, 190, 259,
    260, 269–271, 284, 286, 353n117;
    golden apple(s): 141, 269, 284;
    golden bough: 284; golden city:
    271; golden eagle(s): 147, 167;
    golden egg(s): 259–260; golden
    finger: 124; golden fish: 135;
    Golden Fleece: 217; golden
    kingdom: 260–261, 283, 285,
    286; golden mountain: 181;
    golden palace(s): 256–257, 296;
    golden ring: 74, 274; golden
    throne: 313
Goldi(s): 177, 191
good: 22, 24, 31, 43, 74, 88, 104, 105,
    127, 130, 147, 153, 157, 170, 171,
    206, 215, 230, 236, 241, 252, 254,
    302, 313, 320
goose/geese: 43, 54
Gor: 222
gorge(s): 227, 229
Gorgon: 132, 245
Gorky, Maxim: 340
grain: 115, 245, 316, 320, 328
Granada: 26
grandchild(ren): 164
granddaughter: 214
grandfather(s): 82, 136, 153, 205, 279,
    310
grandmother: 143
grandpa: 139
Grandpa of the Woods: 85
grandson: 310
grapes: 107, 142
grass(es): 150, 249, 256, 307
grateful animals. *See under* animal(s)
grateful dead man/men: 129, 131,
    134, 144, 327; person: 174
grave(s): 34, 85, 126–130, 133, 149–153,
    168, 174, 177, 182, 188, 294, 321.
    See also tomb(s)
gravestone(s): 151. *See also* tombstone(s)
grazing: 150
great-grandfather: 153
Greco-Roman: 14, 72

jewelry: 107, 140

Jonah: 205

journey: 21, 32–34, 43, 49, 56, 62–64, 69, 148, 151, 167, 179, 183, 187, 190, 197, 209, 217, 235, 251, 258, 260, 304, 326, 333; to the other world: 34, 35, 151, 179, 180, 325

judgment: xi, 248, 254, 313

jug: 197

jumping: 23, 43, 47, 58, 82, 112, 128, 131, 153, 160, 173, 197, 210, 212–214, 217, 218, 248, 258, 263, 273, 289, 315, 321

Kabyle: 216, 223

Kagarov, Evgenii G.: 113, 298, 303

Kalevala: 206

Katio: 314

Katoma: 300

Kazanskii, Boris V.: 38, 276

keeper: 239, 328

Kewat: 275

key(s): 121, 122, 123, 124, 137, 147, 284

Khan: 218

Kharuzin, Nikolai: 34, 250, 275

Khu: 251, 370n67

Khudiakov, Ivan A.: 101, 105, 294, 296

Khudiakovka: 206

kicking: 161, 167, 198

kidnapper: 3, 27–29, 31, 37, 55, 67, 68, 102, 145, 214, 224–226, 228, 229, 233, 237, 244, 272, 279, 317, 324; kidnap(ping): 28, 29, 31, 67, 68, 102, 145, 214, 225, 226, 228, 229, 233, 272, 279, 317. *See also* abduction

killing: 75, 106, 108, 122, 135, 147, 148, 151, 170, 171, 175, 181, 182, 195, 201, 204, 208, 210, 213–216, 218, 219, 231, 233, 241–243, 247, 248, 250, 252, 253, 258, 272, 273, 284, 293, 301–303, 306, 308, 310–313, 327

kindling: 155, 211

king(s): xv–xvi, 8, 23, 24, 26–31, 100, 104, 112, 113, 117, 136–138, 141–143, 150, 154, 178, 182, 186, 191, 194, 195, 207, 209, 212, 219, 232, 233, 236, 237, 249, 252, 256, 261–263, 273, 276, 278, 279–283, 288, 289, 291–293, 295, 305, 307, 309, 310, 312, 314, 321, 327; King Dragon: 282; King Fire: 258; king-priest: 284, 306, 314; King Sargon: 221

kingdom: 21, 25, 56, 86, 111, 114, 116, 146, 158, 168, 175, 180, 185, 188, 193, 194, 209, 220, 239, 243, 248, 254, 257–261, 263, 266, 268, 269, 292–294, 296, 297, 301, 306, 307, 310, 311; kingdom of death / the dead: 43, 53, 92, 119, 174, 176, 185, 187, 188, 209, 223, 238, 239, 244, 245, 248, 268, 269, 321, 328; kingdom of the sun: 285; other kingdom: 47, 86, 114, 145, 146, 168, 175, 209, 220, 238, 258, 259, 262, 263, 265, 268, 285, 296–298, 320, 324, 326. *See also* realm of the dead

kinship: 275; kinship system: 89

Kirby, William: 121

Kirpichnikov, Aleksandr: 200

kiss: 112, 113, 273, 274, 278, 286, 312

kitchen: 61, 78

Kitezh: 256

kithara: 270

knee(s): 198, 199, 229, 270, 274

knife: 147, 172, 181, 213, 219, 246, 293

knight: 216, 218

knocking: 40, 57, 73, 198, 241, 294

Know-Nothing: 116–117

Kolesnitskaia, Irina M.: 139, 363n244

Kore: 228

Korguev, Matvei M.: 116

Koryak-Kamchadal: 332

Koshchei the Deathless: 15, 29, 38, 58, 124, 194, 195, 224, 229, 303, 316, 371n20, 371n21

Kretschmer, Paul: 70, 123

Kroeber, Alfred: 13, 166; *Gros Ventre Myths and Tales*: 13

Kronos: 205

Kurrea: 229, 373n113

Küster, Erich: 200, 240, 250

Kutkh: 332

Kuzma Ferapontovich: 300

Loeb, Edwin M.: 94, 101
log(s): 96, 210, 279, 286
lord: 148, 244
Lorraine: 35
loss: 71, 73, 113, 172, 197, 203, 212, 289, 307
lotus-eaters: 52
love: 227, 235
lover(s): 103, 105, 114, 236, 258, 276, 278, 282, 301
Lovers of Achilles, The: 322
Lower Congo: 108
lowering: 188, 190, 219, 250
lubok, lubki: 132, 193, 370n4
Lucian (of Samosata): 270
luck: 234, 328
Ludwig, Alfred: 158, 245, 365n57, 369n19
Lur'e, Solomon Y.: 38, 100, 102, 340; *The House in the Forest*: 38
Lydian(s): 275
lying down: 230, 244, 247, 299, 301

Maat: 62
mace: 198, 294
Mackensen, Lutz: 4
madness: 72, 74. *See also* insanity
magic: 15, 26, 29, 45, 57, 61, 62, 64, 69, 76, 83, 85, 86, 101, 108, 111, 132, 144, 152, 163, 165, 171, 177, 181, 190, 203, 204, 207, 209, 214, 218, 240, 245, 265, 268, 270, 279, 285, 293, 295, 296, 315, 322, 326, 327, 328, 329, 332
magical agent/item/object: xiii, 3, 36, 43, 60, 63, 72, 79, 86, 88, 111, 120, 130, 133, 134, 138, 144, 145, 153, 157, 161, 168–169, 172, 174, 177, 178, 190, 208, 215, 218, 264–267, 274, 277, 311, 316, 318, 324, 325
magical animal: 60, 208
magical book(s): 169, 268, 274, 279, 295, 297. *See also* book(s) *and individual books by title*
magic carpet: 145, 279
magic gift(s): 145, 171, 290, 328
magical helper: xiii, 3, 31, 120, 129, 130, 138, 145, 165, 168, 169, 176, 278, 293, 294, 304, 305, 317, 325; magical impotence: 307; magical

knowledge: 247, 330; magical power(s): 23, 26, 29, 50, 57, 62, 64, 76, 85, 101, 108, 109, 150, 171, 173, 204, 210, 220, 229, 245, 253, 265, 268, 279, 281, 289, 291, 296, 301, 303, 306, 307, 309, 313, 322, 323, 327, 330
"The Magic Mirror": 104, 107, 220
magic tablecloth: 265, 266
magic word(s): 46, 206, 251
magician: 35, 75, 92, 108, 122, 268, 279, 282, 289, 295, 297, 327
Mahabharata: 18
Mähly, Jakob: 200
maiden(s): 19, 24, 26, 33, 62, 79, 95, 98, 105, 110, 136, 170, 189, 195, 206, 208, 209, 220, 234–236, 256, 259, 260, 272, 291, 298. *See also* girl(s)
maize: 142, 234, 236
Maldives: 235
male: 24, 58, 60, 61, 65, 68, 91, 92, 94, 96, 103, 113, 118, 127, 133, 153, 164, 183, 236, 302, 319, 350n9
male line: 127, 153, 164
Malten, Ludolf: 152, 159, 187, 228, 322
mammoth: 230
man, men: 24, 26, 29, 36, 39, 45, 57, 61, 81, 88, 90, 91, 102, 103, 106, 109, 114, 158, 160, 165, 171, 181, 196, 204, 205, 206, 226–228, 229, 234, 242, 246, 275, 301, 304, 305, 320, 321, 332; dead man: 129, 227
mane: 159, 258
Maneros: 302
mangy foal: 150
Manitou: 164, 165
Mannhardt, Wilhelm: 68, 173
mantis: 191, 370n68
manuscript: 139, 171
Maori: 50, 225
Maranda, Pierre: 334
marble: 257, 261
Marduk: 217, 221
mare: 141, 148, 154, 157, 158, 286, 314, 353n117
Mari: 177, 332
Maria Morevna: 261
Maria the Beautiful: 80
Marind: 90

mummy, mummies: 50, 109, 190,
    225, 252, 268
murder: 309, 310, 312
music: 86, 270, 314; musical instru-
    ments: 78, 86. *See also* flutes; gusli
mustache: 161, 354n165
mute: 313; muteness: 120, 124, 220
Mycenaean: 271
myth(s): 11–17, 29, 43, 47–49, 57, 58,
    60, 77, 80, 82–85, 91, 118, 138, 140,
    155, 157, 167, 170–172, 181, 182,
    185, 186, 188, 190, 202–205, 207–
    215, 217, 228, 230, 232–237, 241–
    243, 245, 247, 249, 264, 266, 270,
    274, 276, 287, 289, 290, 292, 297,
    298, 301, 307, 309, 312, 317, 321,
    324, 328–329, 330, 332, 339, 342
mythological nature: 293; mythologi-
    cal structure: 343
Mythological School: 2, 185, 199,
    242, 243
mythology: 251; lunar mythology:
    231; solar mythology: 231

Naau: 251
nakedness: 66, 74, 77, 220
name(s): 45, 56, 71, 117, 136, 137,
    189, 228, 246, 258, 286, 251n35
Nansen, Fridtjof: 157, 182, 226
Narodnye russkie skazki: xvi
Nart: 233
Nastasya the Golden Braid: 258
nation(s): 12, 30, 170, 177, 185
native: 13, 59, 71, 86, 91, 129, 133,
    137, 171, 172, 203, 230, 231, 234,
    235, 275, 329–331
Native American. *See* American
natural forces: 161–163, 229, 232,
    254, 287, 317
nature: 7, 10, 23, 28, 133, 155, 156,
    160, 161, 168, 171, 173, 193, 207,
    208, 213, 229, 231, 233, 240, 241,
    242, 248, 250, 251, 254, 263, 265,
    287–289, 291, 307, 315, 324, 338
Navajo: 68
Near East: 78
needle(s): 107, 108, 148, 259
Negelein, Julius von: 151, 154, 187
neighing: 85, 153
Nekyia: 240

Neleus: 294
Nemi: 284
Neo-Hellenic: 322
neophyte(s): 49, 56, 72, 79, 80, 91, 93,
    101, 110, 122, 202, 203. *See also*
    novice
nephew(s): 89, 310
Nereid(s): 236, 322
Nereus: 322
Nergal: 167, 168
nest(s): 138, 170, 204, 244, 295, 296
net(s): 135, 137, 171, 234
Neuhauss, Richard: 331
Nevermann, Hans: 56, 90, 91, 94,
    118, 202, 204–205
Never-Wash: 114, 116
New Britain: 91
New Guinea: 46, 72, 275; British
    New Guinea: 49, 225; Dutch New
    Guinea: 9; German New Guinea:
    202, 331
New Ireland: 227
new king: 283, 309
New South Wales: 86
newborn: 69, 135, 156
newcomer(s): 236, 245, 248, 276,
    326
Niasse: 230
Niebelungen: 14; *Niebelungenlied*: 18
niece: 44, 89
night: 24, 158, 205, 228, 235, 243,
    244, 251, 280, 286, 299, 301, 303
Nikiforov, Aleksandr I.: 200, 337;
    "On the Question of the Morpho-
    logical Study of the Folktale": 337
Nile: 234, 236, 245, 268
Nilsson, Martin: 28
Noah: 220
nobility: 14, 293
noise: 244, 258
Nootka: 186, 214
north: 44, 212
North America(n): 29, 34, 50, 129,
    161, 164, 204, 221, 234, 265, 267,
    276, 287, 290, 301, 313, 330
Norwegian: 275
nose: 22, 48, 52, 58, 114, 156, 160,
    181, 197, 314
nostrils: 193
novella(s): 268

two worlds: 44, 156, 165–168, 175,
    188, 189, 322, 324
Tylor, Edgar Burnett: xiii

Umugarna: 230
Unbaptized Forehead: 283
uncle: 67, 221, 294
underground: 18, 22, 29, 149, 188,
    223, 239, 254, 255, 257, 260, 269,
    270, 292, 296, 322
underwater: 256, 257, 264, 269, 321,
    322; underwater kingdom: 322
underworld: 34, 41, 48, 51, 52, 76,
    83, 148, 163, 167, 168, 175, 177,
    186, 189–191, 228, 239, 240, 249,
    251, 252, 260, 276, 285, 292, 295,
    296, 314, 317, 322
uninitiated: 68, 86, 88, 91, 95, 101,
    103, 122, 202, 203
union(s): 274, 329
United Soviet Socialist Republic
    (USSR): 13, 334, 340, 341
universe: 8, 44, 138, 206, 258, 287
Unlucky One: 274
unwashed: 115, 116, 326
Upper Guinea: 81
Urals: 96, 113
urbanization: 222
urine: 71
Urpflanze: 343, 390n79
useful: 173, 239, 266
Usener, Hermann: 17, 220
USSR. *See* United Soviet Socialist
    Republic (USSR)
Usynia: 354n165
Uzbek: 118

vagina: 301, 303
Väinämöinen: 206
valley(s): 234, 265, 294
valor: 209, 214, 247
vampire: 175
van Gennep, Arnold: 94
Vanya: 79, 308; Vanyusha: 312. *See
    also* Ivan
Varron: 295
vase: 143, 217
Vasilisa and the Sea King: 113
"Vasilisa the Beautiful": 158, 176
Vasilisa the Golden Braid: 26
Vasmer, Max: 352n83

vault: 123, 153
Vedas: 182, 245; Vedic hymns: 156;
    Vedic religion: 155, 156, 243
Vedda: 133
vegetation: 178, 234, 253
Veresaev, Vikentii: 356n230
Veselovskii, Aleksandr: 2, 139, 200,
    275, 337, 386n23
vestal: 221
vial: 176, 316
viburnum: 195
victim(s): 10, 73, 83, 183, 215, 216,
    230, 235, 318, 385
Victoria: 81, 89
victory: 198, 246, 247, 249, 312
village(s): 67, 75, 99, 105, 131, 137,
    262, 288
violin(s): 86, 87, 169, 270
Virgil: 14, 41, 42; *Aeneid*: 41, 240
virgin(s): 234, 235; virginity: 235
virtue(s): 62, 128
visit: 326; visiting: 328
visitor(s): 41, 55, 56, 63, 92, 98, 175,
    240, 290, 292
visual arts: 185, 202
vodka: 101
Vodovoz, Mishka: 300
Vogul: 13, 132, 170, 332
voice(s): 26, 55, 58, 86, 177, 186, 202,
    259, 270, 286, 298
Volga: 85
Volkodir: 206, 373n87
vomiting up: 119, 208, 247, 291
von den Steinen, Karl: 129
Von der Leyen, Friedrich: 27, 347n36
Vosges: 298
voyage: 188, 257
Vrtra: 231
Vyatka: 24, 53, 72, 73, 82, 87, 89,
    104, 113, 117, 119, 123, 219

Wagner, Louis A.: x, xiv
Wagner, Richard: 14
Wahehe: 182
waist: 198
waking: 199, 214; not waking: 273
walking: 194, 197, 228, 236, 244, 256, 283
wall(s): 101, 232, 237, 257, 269, 302
walrus: 226
wandering: 17, 35, 43, 79, 83, 96, 145,
    216, 224, 225, 237, 248, 268, 269

For Indiana University Press

Sabrina Black, Editorial Assistant
Tony Brewer, Artist and Book Designer
Gary Dunham, Acquisitions Editor and Director
Anna Garnai, Production Coordinator
Sophia Hebert, Assistant Acquisitions Editor
Samantha Heffner, Marketing and Publicity Manager
Katie Huggins, Production Manager
Nancy Lightfoot, Project Manager/Editor
Alyssa Nicole Lucas, Marketing and Publicity Manager
Bethany Mowry, Acquisitions Editor
Dan Pyle, Online Publishing Manager
Michael Regoli, Director of Publishing Operations
Jennifer L. Wilder, Book Designer